REFUGEES IN AN AGE OF GENOCIDE

REFUGEES
IN AN AGE OF
GENOCIDE

Global, National and Local Perspectives
during the Twentieth Century

TONY KUSHNER
and
KATHARINE KNOX

FRANK CASS
LONDON • PORTLAND, OR

First published in 1999 in Great Britain by
FRANK CASS
Newbury House, 900 Eastern Avenue
London IG2 7HH

and in the United States of America by
FRANK CASS
c/o ISBS
5804 N.E. Hassalo Street
Portland, Oregon 97213-3644

Website www.frankcass.com

British Library Cataloguing in Publication Data
Kushner, Tony
Refugees in an age of genocide: global, national and
local perspectives during the twentieth century
1. Refugees 2. Refugees – History – 20th century
I. Title II. Knox, Katharine
325.2'1

ISBN 0 7146 4783 7 (cloth)
ISBN 0 7146 4341 6 (paper)

Library of Congress Cataloging-in-Publication Data
Kushner, Tony (Antony Robin Jeremy)
Refugees in an age of genocide: global, national, and
local perspectives during the twentieth century / Tony Kushner
and Katharine Knox.
   p. cm.
Includes bibliographical references and index.
ISBN 0-7146-4783-7 (cloth). – ISBN 0-7146-4341-6 (paper)
1. Refugees – History – 20th century. 2. Political refugees –
History – 20th century. 3. Persecution – History – 20th century.
4. Genocide – History – 20th century. I. Knox, Katharine,
1972– II. Title.
HV640.K58   1999
362.87'09'04 – dc21   99–12037
                                                            CIP

Typeset by Joanne Edwards
Printed in Great Britain by
Creative Print and Design (Wales), Ebbw Vale

This book is dedicated to Joseph, a dear friend and colleague, whose decision to return to his war-torn homeland of Sierra Leone has left those of us who knew him bereft of a very warm and courageous person.

He paid the ultimate price in war, giving up the safety of refuge in Britain for an uncertain future in his former country.

In spite of coming from different worlds, we can learn much from those – like Joseph – to whom we have the courage to extend the hand of friendship. We can help alleviate, at least in part, the suffering endured when people are forced to live in exile.

Contents

List of Illustrations

Cover illustration
Former Yugoslav refugee returning 'home'

Illustrations within text
Jewish refugees from South Africa arriving in Southampton on the *Cheshire*
Victor, a Belgian refugee, drawn by Eleanor Ruth Dent, 1915
Czech passport of Alice Klausova
School book of Edgar Feuchtwanger (aged 7), Germany, May 1933
Home Office entry document (Dover) of Andras-Endre Rumi

Plate section
Two Belgian refugee soldiers outside Blackmoor Convalescent Home
Cover illustration of 'The Chronicle of the Belgians'
Atlantic Hotel, Southampton
Tombstone of Boris Selesnov (1924–1926)
The Shleimowitz sisters
Atlantic Park Hostel dining room, 1924
Children from Atlantic Park Hostel on the playing fields, 1924
Basque refugee camp, Stoneham (near Eastleigh) from the air, 1937
Basque children offering anti-fascist salute, Stoneham Camp, 1937
Basque youngsters washing up, Stoneham Camp, 1937
Senor Sanchez, radio announcer and interpreter at Stoneham Camp
Alice Klausova with baby, Southampton Children's Hospital, 1939
Polish children in post-war England living in Nissen huts
Polish teachers at the camp at Hiltingbury
Polish Catholic religious celebration, Chandler's Ford, c.1950s
Hungarian freedom fighters in front of a government building
Vietnamese refugees in a detention centre, Hong Kong, 1980s
Vietnamese refugees at Sunshine House, 1984
Christmas party at Sunshine House for Vietnamese refugees, 1980s

Foreword by Sir Herman Ouseley, Commission for Racial Equality

As I write these words, perhaps the greatest European tragedy since the end of the Second World War is being played out in the Balkans. Our television screens are filled with horrific images of tens of thousands of fleeing Kosovars who have suffered (in that terrible phrase) 'ethnic cleansing'. There is universal public sympathy for the Kosovan refugees, and even the tabloid press has demanded that Britain should play its part by providing a safe haven for thousands.

Yet in contrast to the compassion displayed by the public towards the expelled Kosovars, in recent years the prevailing attitudes towards asylum seekers arriving in the UK have been suspicion and hostility. Public discourse on immigration has been increasingly dominated by the notion of 'bogus asylum seekers', flooding into Britain to exploit its supposedly generous benefits system or to commit crime. This is exemplified by the reaction to the arrival in Kent in 1997 and 1998 of Roma asylum seekers, which occasioned headlines that the UK was in danger of being swamped with 'Giro Czechs'; attempts (largely unsuccessful) by the National Front to capitalise on the resentment of local people in whose towns the Roma families were being accommodated; and demands for tighter immigration policies to stem the feared flood.

There is, of course, nothing new about such demands. Immigration policy over the last 35 years has been underpinned by a bipartisan consensus that firm immigration control is necessary to preserve race relations. Persistent racist attitudes and overestimates by the public of the size of the ethnic minority population have convinced successive governments that they must reassure public opinion that immigration controls will be firmly enforced. Successive statutes have further reduced the categories, and hence the numbers, of those entitled to enter and remain in the UK, and have created new legal and practical mechanisms to exclude them, discourage them or to control them once admitted. The emphasis in immigration policy on exclusion and control has had a particularly adverse impact upon people from the New Commonwealth and the Third World. That emphasis has been reinforced by the growth of resistance in western Europe to the admittance of new immigrants and asylum seekers, and the recent development of co-ordinated policies by EU states to strengthen their external borders.

Media reports on immigration policy invariably reinforce negative stereotypes of ethnic minorities: that they are alien, 'illegal', dishonest and 'scroungers'; there are too many of them; they are a drain on the nation's resources, etc. The overall effect is to validate racism and xenophobia, and to undermine positive policies intended to encourage the equal treatment of people from minority communities in the UK. Furthermore, rather than attempt to explain to the public the very restricted scope of present day immigration, governments have tended to seek support for more restrictive policies by highlighting alleged abuses of the system. Far from reassuring the public, this approach encourages sensationalist and racist reports in the media, resulting in further pressure for even harsher restrictions.

The present government has explicitly recognised the important contributions which immigrants have made and continue to make to the economic and cultural life of the UK. It has also, commendably, committed itself to anti-racism, equality of opportunity and social inclusion. In the area of immigration and asylum policy, by contrast, it has shown itself cautious and fearful. The Immigration and Asylum Bill currently before Parliament maintains the emphasis placed by its predecessors on exclusion, control and removal; like them, it is predicated upon the perceived need to restore the confidence of a supposedly racist public in a strict immigration control, its harsh proposals justified by dubious assertions that asylum procedures are widely abused. Unfortunately the government has failed in its responsibility to educate and set examples, and rather than rebut popular misconceptions or challenge bigoted statements, ministers have referred to misleading statistics about refugee recognition rates as evidence of abuse. The fact that an asylum application is ultimately unsuccessful does not mean that it was not made in good faith. Such misrepresentations impugn the honesty of all asylum applicants and harm race relations.

The Bill reflects and will perpetuate the culture of suspicion about asylum seekers which pervades the Home Office. Hence, in the new support system proposed by the Bill, asylum seekers will have no choice where they are accommodated, and will subsist in a parallel economy of vouchers and non-cash provision. This, it is claimed, will act as a deterrent to abusive claims. Those dependent on the support system – most of whom will be from racial groups which are minorities in the UK – will form a stigmatised and readily-identifiable underclass in a separate, lesser category than others in need. Undoubtedly these proposals will cause asylum seekers hardship and may place them in physical danger. They may also engender and validate hostility towards ethnic minorities in general.

Research has shown that asylum seekers are often well-qualified and skilled; they have the potential to make a major contribution to the wealth and cultural diversity of this country, as thousands of refugees have done in the past. Race relations would benefit from policies and practices which recognised this potential, actively welcomed and assisted new arrivals and, whilst their claims for asylum are quickly and fairly determined, ensured that they are treated as the future citizens that many will become.

Under the support system proposed by the new Bill, many asylum seekers will be sent to the regions and accommodated in 'clusters' where it is hoped that they will choose to stay if granted leave to remain. This policy poses obvious challenges, to asylum seekers themselves, to local service providers, which may have little experience of the needs of asylum seekers, and to local people who will have to adapt to their new neighbours. The successful settlement of refugee communities in the new cluster areas, and the extent to which their contribution to society can be maximised, will depend on the ability of local policy makers and service providers to understand and meet their needs and to help negotiate their acceptance by the indigenous community. They will find this book, with its emphasis on the experiences of refugees themselves, and of those in the communities where they settled, an invaluable aid. The narratives it contains are also a timely reminder that refugees and asylum seekers, glimpsed on our television screens in an undifferentiated mass of misery, are ordinary individuals like us to whom something extraordinary has happened.

Preface

This book is the first to provide a history of global refugee movements in the twentieth century to Britain. Despite the importance of refugee movements in the past and the growth of the world refugee population in the present (they number now in the *tens* of millions), the study of refugees at an academic level is still very much in its infancy. The historical profession should have been at the forefront of such studies because of the importance of refugee issues in the past. Unfortunately, it has yet to provide a lead in either carrying out research or writing about this vital and escalating problem. This is thus a pioneer study, designed to bring into the mainstream a subject that many governments and international bodies would be happier to forget. It covers in detail 20 groups of refugees ranging from east European Jews escaping Tsarist oppression before the First World War to world asylum seekers in the last years of the twentieth century who have attempted to reach Britain. In the process it charts the growth of restrictionism leading to the drastic change from open door policies in the 1900s to the racist-inspired controls which dominate responses of the western world to refugees as we approach the millennium.

This study was completed in 1997. At the time of final revision (Spring 1999) the British government had produced an important White Paper entitled 'Fairer, Faster and Firmer – A Modern Approach to Immigration and Asylum', largely incorporated into the 138 clause Immigration and Asylum Bill introduced into Parliament on 9 February 1999. Those connected to refugees have given it a mixed welcome. The White Paper recognises many of the problems faced by people awaiting decisions on their status in the UK and it aims to remove some of the problems caused by the asylum legislation during the 1990s. Nevertheless, it fails to recognise generally that Britain has a very poor recent record on granting asylum, even compared to its partners in 'Fortress Europe'. In the White Paper lip service is paid to Britain's 'long-standing tradition of giving shelter to those fleeing persecution'. Recognition is also given to how 'refugees in turn have contributed much to our society and culture'. But its claim that 'The Government is determined to uphold that tradition' is undermined by the measures which seek to deter asylum seekers from reaching Britain. There is also a tendency to separate 'economic migrants' and 'genuine asylum seekers' throughout the document. This study makes clear with almost all groups considered that making this distinction is very difficult to maintain as economic and political motives are often combined in prompting flight from a homeland.

The White Paper accepts one of the important themes of this study – that the impact of refugees is often felt most powerfully at a local level. We show that where given the resources to do so, local authorities have often responded positively to the needs of refugees and eased their integration into society. Attempts throughout this century to move refugees across Britain have ended in (expensive) failures. The White Paper's suggestion that 'where possible placements [of asylum seekers] would take account of the value of linking to existing communities and the support of voluntary and community groups' appears to have acknowledged the failure of past dispersal policies. The powerful statement, however, that 'Asylum seekers would be expected to take what was available, and would not be able to pick and choose where they were accommodated' indicates that lessons have not been learnt. Indeed, in spite of its token gestures recognising the contribution of refugees to British society and culture, the general tone is to see them as a burden and a problem urgently in need of controlling and directing. The misery caused by the detention of refugees is a recurring theme of the twentieth century. It is regrettable, therefore, that the White Paper stresses that 'detention is necessary to ensure the integrity of our immigration control'.

The major theme of *Refugees in an Age of Genocide* is the interplay of international, national and local factors, without an acknowledgement of which, we argue, the complexity of refugee movements in the twentieth century cannot be understood. Its approach is inclusive, incorporating particularly the experiences of the refugees, as well as those responding to them, through the extensive use of contemporary material and later oral and written testimony. The study of refugees in the twentieth century cannot ignore the role of international relations, the policies of national governments, and the detailed workings of the state apparatus. But by providing a social history perspective, we also emphasise the human element which ultimately should be at the forefront of both the study of refugees and responses to them. The importance of the individual, despite the huge numbers of people now affected by persecution and forced displacement, must be paramount. Beyond those most immediately affected, however, this study argues that the problem of refugees is a universal one for which we are all responsible. Responses to asylum issues, as Auschwitz survivor and campaigner on behalf of all victims of persecution, Rabbi Hugo Gryn, stated before his death, 'are an index of our spiritual and moral civilisation'.

Acknowledgements

The authors, because of the pioneer nature of this study, are indebted to those who have provided support, advice and encouragement. In particular, we would like to thank the committees of the University of Southampton's School of Graduate and Research Studies in the Faculty of Arts and the Hartley Institute in the Hartley Library for research grants that enabled this study to be undertaken. Praise is due especially to Dr Chris Woolgar, Director of the Hartley Institute, who provided enormous support for this project from its early stages through to its completion. His belief in the importance of this work, when some cast doubt about the appropriateness of historians studying refugee movements (apart from those in the distant past), provided a source of much needed and greatly appreciated encouragement to us.

In this work we have emphasised throughout the experiences of those subject to persecution in this violent century and effort has been made to incorporate the voices of refugees to describe their lives before, during and after their forced displacement, as well as those responding to them in places of asylum. We are deeply grateful to those refugees, former refugees and helpers of refugees who were willing to be interviewed and also to share with us unpublished family letters, memoirs, photographs and other documents to make this approach possible. We hope that this study helps in the process of restoring their humanity by emphasising the *ordinariness* of those affected.

Public record offices have still some way to go before their collections reflect the ethnic diversity of Britain in the past and present, and material relating to refugees is particularly scarce. The help of those in local and national archives and libraries who made a particular effort to locate relevant material is thus greatly appreciated. Thanks especially to all those in Special Collections at the University of Southampton, particularly Jenny Ruthven at the Parkes Library and Cope Collection, who took an active interest in our work as well as providing a truly professional service. Donald Hyslop and all those at the Southampton City Heritage Oral History Unit were equally encouraging and provided advice and support in carrying out interviews. The help and assistance of the librarians, archivists and secretaries of the Birmingham Jewish History Group, British Library National Sound Archive, Bodleian Library, the Central Zionist Archives (Jerusalem), Eastleigh and District Local Historical Society, Hampshire Record Office, Imperial War Museum, Jews' Temporary Shelter, London Jewish Museum, London Metropolitan Archives, Manchester Central Reference Library, Manchester Jewish Museum, National Archives (Washington, DC), National Labour Museum, Portsmouth City Library, Public Record Office, the Refugee Council, Rothschild Archive, Southampton City Archives, Southampton Hebrew Congregation, University of Liverpool Archive, University of Manchester Archive, University of Sussex Mass-Observation Archive, the Wiener Library (London) and Winchester Library have been much appreciated. We would like to thank those who provided permission to use material under their copyright, including Cassell Publishers, the Eastleigh and District Local History Society, *The Guardian*, the *Hampshire Chronicle*, Ringpress Books, the *Southern Daily Echo* and the *Southampton Advertiser*.

Clare Bowey provided valuable research assistance during the last stages of this volume and her help is much appreciated. We would also like to thank colleagues and friends who were willing to provide advice on and relevant information for the project, including Martin Alexander, David Cesarani, Andy Charlesworth, Graham Heaney, Colin Holmes, Donald Hyslop, Catharine Kotzin, Louise London, Ken Lunn, Helen McGiveron, Joanna Westphal Newman and Mark Stoyle. The efforts of those who took the time, care and energy to pass on their valuable comments on parts of this book in draft form – Alastair Duke, John Oldfield, Colin Richmond, Joanne Reilly, Anne Rimbey, Greg Walker and Bill Williams – have been of tremendous benefit to us and we would like to take this opportunity of acknowledging our gratitude to them. Tim Reuter provided support and expert advice at a critical stage in the evolution of this project.

We would like to thank our publisher, Frank Cass, for his enthusiasm and commitment to this project and to acknowledge the professionalism and good humour of Rachel Joseph and then Hilary Hewitt who acted as editors. Thanks also to Sybil Lunn who provided the index. In terms of the division of labour over this volume, Tony Kushner was responsible for the afterword, introduction, conclusion and Parts 1 and 2 (with the exception of Chapter 4) and overall editing. Katharine Knox was responsible for Parts 3, 4 and 5.

Katharine Knox: I would like to thank my co-author for the chance to work together on this project which has provided the opportunity to meet so many interesting people from a host of countries. They shared not only their time and stories but often also invited me to their homes and to community events, enabling me to become, if briefly, a part of their lives. I would also like to thank my friends (especially fellow Southampton graduates) and family who helped me to keep going with this project over a long period of time, both financially and emotionally. For those who provided information, particular thanks must go to the Refugee Council, firstly for its assistance in providing access to an interesting array of materials (many of which remain unpublished, but are accessible through its Information Centre), and, secondly, to colleagues for their support in the final stages of the project.

Thanks also to those who offered photographs from private collections, especially Gordon Cox of the Eastleigh and District Local History Society, Peter Minns of the Winchester Action Group for Asylum Seekers, and Paul Rushton, formerly involved with the Vietnamese reception programme in Hampshire, as well as Howard Davies whose current photographs of refugees in Britain and abroad are an important monument in the field of representation of refugee experiences. And a special mention too for a friend, Josh Mowll, who was kind enough to offer assistance with designing the maps for the book. Finally, I would like to add a personal tribute to Geza Gazdag, a Hungarian refugee whom I had the pleasure to know long before I had any understanding of refugee issues, and whose generosity, strength of character and achievement in Britain (establishing the Vanderbilt Tennis Club in London) are a monument to all that refugees can achieve in Britain if they are given the opportunity to stay and rebuild their lives in this country. To all those asylum seekers currently entering Britain, many of whom I met while working at the Refugee Council, I hope similar opportunities may be given, and a welcome fitting for the circumstances in which they are forced to arrive in a foreign land.

Tony Kushner: I would like to thank those in the Parkes Centre and the Department of History at the University of Southampton who have provided a happy and supportive atmosphere in which to be an academic. I am indebted to those who have supported the Parkes Centre, especially Ian Karten, a former refugee from Nazism, and Marks & Spencer, a company of refugee origin which has contributed so much to Britain's culture and economy. It is fitting also that the Department has benefited from the presence and contribution of many former refugees and the descendants of refugees on its staff who have helped enrich the experience of their fellow academics and students alike, though it is ironic that we are now located in a building formerly used as an internment camp during the Second World War. On a personal level, I would like to express my debt to Mag and Jack for their support and immense tolerance, especially in the later stages of this book. It goes without saying that the Cavaliers cricket team (for whom I have been described, through sheer jealousy, by Donald Bloxham as a 'buffet bowler') and Stockport County FC continue to provide sporting inspiration. Again, I would like to thank my family as a whole, including my mother, grandmother (whose 90th birthday party coincided with the finishing of this book), brothers Ben (whose belief that Manchester City will become once again a top team in Europe proves that not all accountants lack imagination and a sense of humour) and Mike, sister-in-law Joanna and nephews Toby and

George for their warmth, love and support. For me, this book is dedicated to the memory of my great-grandparents and grandparents who came to this country as refugees and helped shape its future. It is also dedicated to my uncle, Harold, who died aged just 20 in Italy at the start of 1944, fighting the evil of Nazi-Fascism, and to Jack's brother Sam who was born as this book went to press.

MAPS

Main refugee groups entering the United Kingdom 1870–1945

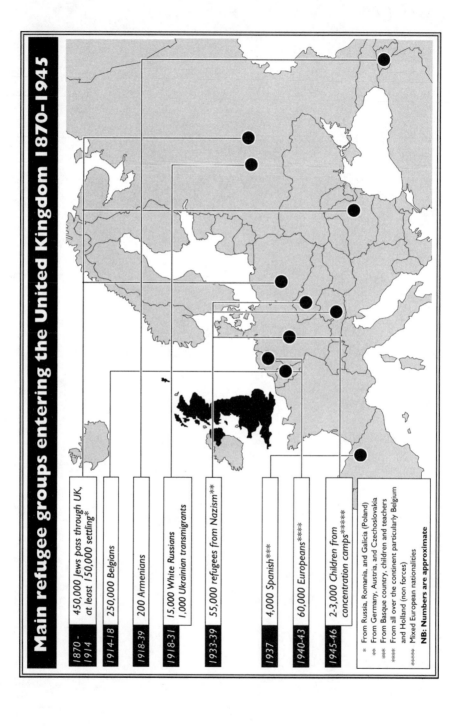

1870–1914	450,000 Jews pass through UK, at least 150,000 settling*
1914–18	250,000 Belgians
1918–39	200 Armenians
1918–31	15,000 White Russians 1,000 Ukrainian transmigrants
1933–39	55,000 refugees from Nazism**
1937	4,000 Spanish***
1940–43	60,000 Europeans****
1945–46	2–3,000 Children from concentration camps*****

* From Russia, Romania, and Galicia (Poland)
** From Germany, Austria, and Czechoslovakia
*** From Basque country, children and teachers
**** From all over the continent particularly Belgium and Holland (non forces)
***** Mixed European nationalities
NB: Numbers are approximate

Main refugee groups entering the United Kingdom 1945-1996

1945	135,000 Poles
1947-9	84,000 EVWs*
1948	2,000 Czechs
1956	22,000 Hungarians**
1972-3	29,000 Ugandan Asians
1973	3,000 Chileans
1975-90	19,000 Vietnamese***
1980s	15,000 Kurds, mainly Turkish
1986-96	15,000 Zaireans
1986-96	12,000 Former Yugoslavs

Additional groups not covered in this book

1967	Poles
1968	Czechs
1968	Iraqis
1974	Greek Cypriots
1980s - 1990s	All over the world in recent years especially from Nigeria, India, Pakistan and Somalia.

* European Volunteer Workers from Latvia, Lithuania and Eastern Europe
** 6,000 on to Canada, 14,500 stay in UK
*** Including small numbers of Laotians and Cambodians - plus additional numbers under family reunion schemes
NB: Numbers are approximate

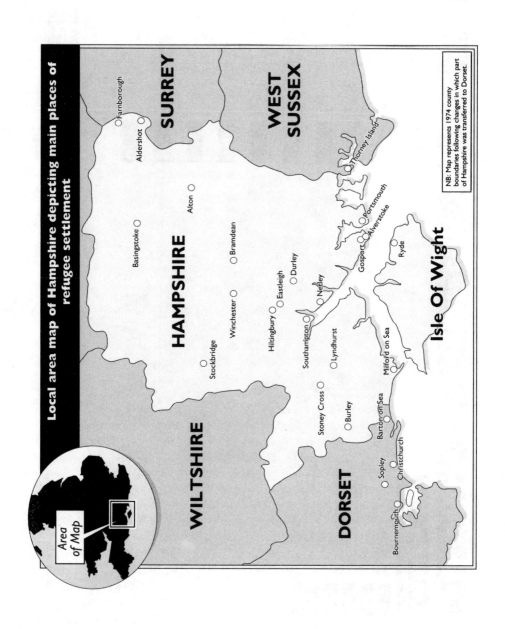

Local area map of Hampshire depicting main places of refugee settlement

NB: Map represents 1974 county boundaries following changes in which part of Hampshire was transferred to Dorset.

Area of Map

SURREY

WEST SUSSEX

HAMPSHIRE

WILTSHIRE

DORSET

Isle Of Wight

Farnborough

Aldershot

Alton

Basingstoke

Bramdean

Winchester

Stockbridge

Hiltingbury

Eastleigh

Durley

Netley

Southampton

Lyndhurst

Stoney Cross

Burley

Barton on Sea

Milford on Sea

Gosport

Alverstoke

Portsmouth

Thorney Island

Ryde

Sopley

Christchurch

Bournemouth

Afterword: Kosovo

It was like a scene from Africa, not from Europe. But this was Europe in early spring and it was raining. More than 20,000 ethnic Albanian refugees from Kosovo were by yesterday massed on the Macedonian border at Blace near the railway line on which they were deported by the Serbs. As you drew closer to the frontier checkpoint across the road, you realise that the vast, dark expanse in the valley below is made up of humanity.[1]

Such comments have not been infrequent in spring 1999 as the western world confronts the appalling tragedy of the victims of the attempt by Slobodan Milosevic, President of the Federal Republic of Yugoslavia, to 'ethnically cleanse' the province of Kosovo. But the reporter's failure to confront the reality that the forced and brutal movement of people has been integral to the *European* experience during the twentieth century is telling. First, it reflects a lack of self-awareness and a tendency to see human brutality and mass misery as 'other' to western, 'civilised' society. Second, it underlines a theme emphasised throughout this study – that many would like to pretend that refugees do not exist and therefore their presence can be ignored and their needs conveniently forgotten. Yet that 'ordinary' Europeans – doctors, teachers, farmers, factory workers and so on – can be dragged out of their homes at gun point, witness the rape, torture and murder of their loved ones and be transformed into people without homes, belongings or legal rights and then dumped into no man's land cold, hungry and frightened *in a matter of hours* should bring home the fact that the experience of becoming a refugee is not at the periphery of the twentieth century but at its everyday heart. In this sense, the transformation of 'day into night', as one Kosovan refugee eloquently put it, is a fitting close to a century that has started and finished with genocide.[2]

For the authors of an overview of refugees in the twentieth century the desperately depressing developments in Kosovo after the failure of the diplomatic initiatives in Paris during February/March 1999 provided a dilemma. The book was in production and it would be impossible to do full justice to the complexity of the Kosovan crisis in the time and space available. Moreover, the situation at the time of writing this afterword, in what was the second week of the Nato attacks, was changing from hour to hour and, in spite of satellite communications, the enormity of the refugee crisis, alongside Serbian censorship, would make any definitive statements at this stage unwise. Nevertheless, some observations in the light of our wider study are in order.

It has been estimated by Nato as of 7 April 1999 that some 1.1 million ethnic Albanians had been internally displaced or forced out of Kosovo since 1991 when the total population of the province was a fraction under 2 million. Since the bombing commenced in late March, some 250,000 were in hiding inside Kosovo (later estimates suggest that this figure may be as high as 400,000, many living perilously in mountainous areas without even the most basic amenities), a further 450,000 having fled its borders. Of the latter, the majority, some 270,000, has crossed into Albania. The next largest number, 130,000, were in Macedonia, but half of these were trapped in no man's land. 36,700 have gone to Montenegro and 7,900 to Bosnia.[3] Previous to the attacks, some 100,000 had sought refuge in European Union countries, less than one tenth of these coming to Britain. The Kosovan exodus has been frequently labelled as the largest refugee movement in Europe since the Second World War but this ignores the massive displacement in Bosnia and Herzegovina earlier in the decade that left up to 2 million uprooted. Put in perspective, the ethnic Albanian refugees represent just two per cent of the current population of the world's forcibly displaced.[4] It is a salutary reminder of the massive scale of the problem on a global level.

Some have taken comfort in attempting to see the Kosovan crisis as specifically Balkan – taking place in a part of Europe which is inherently unstable and liable to break out into ethnic hatred at any point in time. Such an analysis is unfair to the region and it carries with it the assumption that ethnic pluralism was of itself always likely to become divisive. Ethnic hatreds undoubtedly existed in the past and Kosovo was no exception. But instability in the region has often had little to do with ethnicity although unscrupulous politicians, Milosevic among them, have attempted to stir up supposedly ancient hatreds for their own ends. His reversal of the autonomy given to the province by Tito during the 1970s has been at the heart of the current catastrophe. In the years before Milosevic, the many different ethnic groups which made up Kosovo lived in relative harmony. As Noel Malcolm suggests in his magisterial history of the region, whilst it was far from the case that 'Kosovo was always a wonderland of mutual tolerance', the popular view in the west that recent wars in the Balkans were '"ethnic conflicts", created by the bubbling up of obscure but virulent ethnic hatreds among the local populations' was 'essentially false':

> there had never been ethnic wars in the 'ancient' history of Bosnia or Croatia, and the only conflicts with a partly ethnic character to them were modern ones, produced under very special geopolitical conditions (above all, the Second World War). Some

elements of prejudice, linked in some cases to religious issues and in others to memories of the Second World War, did of course exist. But between low-level prejudices on the one hand and military conflict, concentration camps and mass murder on the other, there lies a very long road: it was the political leaders who propelled the people down that road, and not vice-versa.[5]

It will be a tragedy for all groups in the region if the military action or post-war settlement irreparably damaged its sometimes troubled but often fruitful and mutually beneficial pluralism. Through centuries of movement, inter-marriage and cultural exchange, Kosovars have much more in common than they have pulling them apart. It is significant, for example, that the hundreds of thousands of refugees in Albania see 'home' as Kosovo rather than their place of asylum. Although, as Noel Malcolm suggests, 'Most of the families in any part of Kosovo are known to have come from somewhere else', their attachment to Kosovo is no less pronounced.[6]

There is evidence that Milosevic was planning the mass 'ethnic cleansing' of Kosovo before the Nato attacks in late March 1999. The Albanians of Kosovo had been subject to political and economic persecution in the immediate years before, including mass dismissals, assaults on Albanian education and culture, with 'arbitrary and police violence hav[ing] become routine.... In 1994 alone the Council for the Defence of Human Rights and Freedoms in Kosovo recorded 2,157 physical assaults by the police, 3,553 raids on private dwellings and 2,963 arbitrary arrests.' Most chillingly, one major paramilitary nationalist figure in Serbia, now widely linked to some of the most brutal cases of 'ethnic cleansing', described the Albanians as 'tourists'.[7] What is remarkable, however, is how few anticipated that the attacks would lead to a massive refugee crisis. Hindsight, of course, provides perfect vision, and there has been general criticism that the overall forethought of the Nato leadership has been sadly lacking, regardless of the sincerity of its aims (and the introduction of a human rights agenda into international power politics is surely to be welcomed). Nevertheless, the utter absence of planning for a refugee movement, especially given the vulnerability of the Kosovo Albanians, is deeply significant in itself. Only when television pictures after several days of bombing communicated the scale of the desperate exodus did the international authorities make concerted efforts to deal with the specific problems faced by the fresh wave of refugees.[8] Until national and international governments start to recognise that refugee issues need to be placed at the top of their agendas, the forcibly displaced will continue to be treated at best with unprepared and inadequate goodwill and at worst with disbelief, antipathy and outright rejection.

Not untypically, the refugees from Kosovo have been widely perceived as a problem or as a potential burden. Many politicians have urged that the ethnic Albanians be kept together and close to their homes so that the return 'home' can be achieved swiftly when the time arrives. On moral grounds, they argue, dispersal would be wrong as it would, as British Prime Minister Tony Blair suggests, complete Milosevic's policy of 'ethnic cleansing'.[9] Sceptical critics suggest, however, that the opponents of dispersal are happy to suggest that the refugees stay close to their former homes for fear that they will 'flood' their own countries as unwanted asylum seekers. Britain, whose recent record in refugee acceptance, as this study highlights, has been particularly meanspirited, has been very vulnerable to charges of hypocrisy in this respect. There has been a bitter irony that the refugee crisis in Kosovo has coincided with the pushing through of asylum legislation in Britain openly designed to act as a deterrent to entry.[10]

This book has been in production at the same time as a sustained and frightening campaign in certain sections of the press against asylum seekers. The anti-refugee rhetoric has not been without influence, affecting public opinion as well as government policy. It has led to restrictions on the support that can be offered to asylum seekers reaching Britain with the result that, according to a Refugee Council survey, 62 per cent had slept rough at some point since their arrival in the UK; 61 per cent had not enough to eat on a daily basis and 74 per cent were completely penniless 'and did not even have enough money for bus fares and other necessities'. One of the remarkable features of the last few weeks, therefore, has been the launching of refugee appeals by papers such as the *Daily Mail* whose recent attacks on asylum seekers, including Kosovars, has been sustained and ugly.[11]

In the conclusion to this book there is discussion concerning the use of the term 'refugee' by those who have been forcibly displaced. Almost all of the recent arrivals shun the word because it has become one of abuse in British society. It is significant that the one group who have kept to the name – those from Nazism – are now questioning whether they too should abandon the term as its credibility has become so undermined. It is to be hoped that the Kosovan tragedy will restore the legitimacy of the term and reverse the suspicion that has grown and grown against refugees in Britain and elsewhere. It is understandable that some of those displaced from Kosovo prefer to be referred to as 'deportees', fearing that refugee status and therefore exile can easily become permanent.[12] Nevertheless, the position of those languishing in appalling conditions in Macedonian camps has shown the extreme vulnerability of those without any legal rights. As one aid worker at the Bojane refugee camp put it:

> The [Macedonian] government has given a humanitarian status to these people rather than a refugee status. Ask any of them if they have a refugee card. None of them has. It means they have no civil rights, no human rights, no access to health services or legal advice. If you are a tourist – and that is, in effect, what they are – the government of the country you are in has no responsibility for you.[13]

Indeed, 10,000 Kosovo Albanians were forced out of Macedonia. In the words of one of those, Mimoza Pristina, a 21-year old law student: 'They beat us and forced us on to buses. They wouldn't tell us where we were going. I feel as if I am lost in space. I have run out of words for the way I feel. Yes, animals, that is how they made us feel.'[14]

Returning to the *Daily Mail*, a newspaper that has whipped up hatred against refugees across the twentieth century, it is tempting to dismiss its campaign for the displaced from Kosovo as sheer hypocrisy. Yet the success of its appeal, and those of national charities that have followed (a media appeal in Britain realised over £2.5 million on its first day from over 100,000 contributors) suggests something more profound at work.[15] One of the themes of this book is that adherence to the tradition of asylum has waxed and waned across this century, disappearing, for example, almost totally during the 1920s in Britain only to reappear again strongly late in the following decade. In the months before the Kosovo crisis came to a head, opinion polls suggested that commitment to asylum amongst the British population was falling significantly. In February 1997, 75 per cent agreed that 'most refugees arriving in Britain are in need of our help and support' whereas two years later just 49 per cent agreed that people who 'have genuinely suffered political persecution abroad' should be allowed to stay in Britain.[16] One commentator has suggested that

> As the number of refugees languishing in the muddy stinking fields to which they are confined grows with sickening speed, Nato countries have closed their doors. We don't mind images of them on the television screens but the people themselves are not welcome. That would make the story entirely too personal. For us, these people are far away, beyond the firewall that divides the world of misery from the Marks & Spencer. Let them stay in the Balkans, we say. We'll send a cheque.[17]

There is, undoubtedly, evidence of such tendencies, although few have so far publicly voiced them for fear of being labelled grossly insensitive when the pathetic images of orphaned and injured children appear on television screens and front pages on a daily basis. One exception has been the popular tabloid, *The Sun*, which, with perverse honesty, warned its readers 'Would you swap the relative prosperity of life on welfare for a peasant country where there's hardly a house left standing? Once they're here, they're here to stay.'[18] Certainly many of the 10,000 Kosovan asylum seekers reaching Britain before the present crisis have faced antipathy and disbelief. A care worker at a refugee day centre in Barking, East London, reported in October 1998 that

> People aren't making the connection between the pictures of the war on TV and these guys in the streets. They confuse them with Romanians and Slovakians. Even when they're told they're from Kosovo the reaction is still the same – send them back.[19]

Yet the intensity of the media's portrayal of the refugee catastrophe in Kosovo since March 1999, alongside the official recognition of its scale, has, we would argue, encouraged a more humanitarian response. Alongside the cheques, thousands have offered their homes in Britain to the victims of 'ethnic cleansing' and many in local authorities have indicated a strong desire to help once refugees arrive in sizeable numbers. Whether politicians, increasingly conditioned to outdo each other in their appeasement of the alleged anti-refugee sentiment of the British public, can bring themselves to recognise that many feel ashamed by our recent record of dealing with asylum seekers remains to be seen. As has been suggested, 'The victims of Milosevic might meet with a great deal more sympathy in Britain than our pusillanimous politicians fear. We may be nicer, wiser and more determined to do the right thing in Kosovo than they and the right wing press think.'[20] And even sections of the latter seem to have changed their perspective. A leader in *The Express*, in contrast to *The Sun*, argued that 'We must accept some Kosovan refugees in Britain. Those who continue to protest that we cannot afford them and they will never go home again should be ashamed of themselves.' In a remarkable piece of self-awareness, it added 'It is as if, somewhere on the flight from the Balkans to Britain, the displaced Kosovars are transformed from the miserable hungry people in the mud to scrounging, thieving beggars intent on ripping off our welfare state'. The danger remains, however, that once the images from the refugee camps and no man's land fade, so will the revived interest in the needs of refugees and in granting asylum.[21]

So far there have been firm offers by Germany to take 40,000 refugees, the USA and Turkey to take 20,000, Spain to take up to 10,000 with between 4–7,000 places offered by Norway, Denmark, Romania, Sweden, Greece, Canada and Australia.[22] Neither Britain nor France has entered this numbers game although it seems likely, according to the Refugee Council, that Britain may offer places for several thousand people along the lines of the Bosnia Project, giving hope that the Bosnia Programme will not be the last gesture to receive *groups* of refugees in Britain. Whether such dispersal will take place is still unclear. If it is carried out on a mass scale out of necessity then the sensitivities of the refugees themselves must be taken into consideration. Some of the most painful television images from the tragedy have been the forcing of Kosovo Albanians on to planes to Turkey, separated from their families and friends and unaware of their destination. The refugees are powerless but their vulnerability must not be exploited by those who have responsibility for them.[23]

Local initiatives to refugee crises are featured throughout this study. The crisis in Kosovo has been no exception in stimulating localised responses. Women's Aid to former Yugoslavia (WATFY), based in Southampton, has been featured in chapter 13 of this study. In launching a 'Kosova Emergency Appeal' they write that

> Until the NATO bombing WATFY supported two women's groups in Pristina, Kosova, one working with people already displaced by the escalation of Serbian police and military action, and another working on an income generating project for Kosovar women. NATO's bombing campaign, the massive increase in Serbian state violence and the forced expulsions from Kosova meant that our contacts were

severed. We assumed that these groups were no longer operating. Now, women from one group have managed to reach Macedonia. They have contacted us, and asked us to help them start their work again.

As in earlier conflicts in former Yugoslovia, WATFY, through local support, will help 'provide long-term support to refugees once the initial work by the big agencies is over'. Through such important work different worlds can be bridged.[24]

Undoubtedly, unless there is a remarkable change in the military situation, some dispersal, if less systematic, will take place. The British and French reluctance to stipulate a number of refugees may or may not be for the worst of reasons – fear of unleashing xenophobic tendencies at home. Yet the numerical offers of help elsewhere do not necessarily suggest a more liberal response. Indeed, ceilings imply that the refugees are, by nature, a problem which has to be controlled and kept within strict confines. As one commentator has pointed out:

> Under the United Nations' Geneva Convention of 1951, a refugee is a person with genuine fear of persecution. He or she has the right to go to any safe country and ask for asylum. The monarchical pledges from gracious governments ... to take X thousand or Y hundred Kosovars are therefore neither here nor there. The right to sanctuary is not restricted by quotas: it is universal and is being universally ignored.[25]

In this respect Albania, which has taken in by far the greatest number of refugees, acts as a shining humanitarian example. Far from free of its own domestic tensions and, moreover, by far the poorest country in Europe, it has actively welcomed the refugees. Clearly, shared ethnicity has been a critical factor in this positive reception, but Albania shows that refugees do not have to be perceived purely as a problem. If the Albanians are welcoming the refugees 'home' as long as they need it, this too should be the response of the outside world. The long-term objective must, as ever, be to remove the conditions that cause refugee movements. But, realistically, for the foreseeable future the refugee population of the world will continue to grow. The global community has a duty to the dispossessed to make sure that whilst in exile, all places are 'home' for the refugees. The example set by the poorest nations, who house the majority of the world's refugee population, suggest that such a vision is not utopian. Put bluntly, only the selfishness of the prosperous nations stands in the way of its fulfilment.

With grim determination, however, the British government and its state apparatus retain the view that refugees are problem people who should be kept off benefits, refused permission to work and dispersed in the vain attempt to make them invisible. This book stresses the local engagement with refugees across the century. When encouraged and supported by the state, local initiatives have often been extremely successful in helping to restore the humanity and dignity of the refugees and in bringing rewards to the areas in which they settle. Much has been made recently of the hostility on a local

level in areas such as Kent and certain London boroughs to the presence of
sizeable numbers of refugees. In Dover, for example, a local newspaper
editorial referred to the asylum seekers in the town as 'the nation's human
sewage' which it 'want[ed] to ... dross down the drain'. In fact, as few as 800
refugees were housed in the town.[26] Indeed, the example of Atlantic Park
Hostel in the 1920s suggests that even very high numbers of refugees need
not be a problem on a local level. The hostel housed at times almost the same
number of people as its adjacent neighbour, Eastleigh, yet local tensions were
non-existent.[27]

     With care and attention, as well as resources from the state to complement
those of the voluntary sector, refugees can become part of the local scene
enriching life for all. Traumatised and displaced, refugees will always attempt
to congregate together. As this study shows, small to medium reception
centres, where the refugees have a large say in their daily lives and which
prepare them to enter housing in the local community, have been the most
successful in helping the refugees to adapt. These centres must, however,
have a certain decency. The detention centres and prisons used to house
asylum seekers in recent years have been a constant indictment of Britain's
claim to be a humane society committed to human rights. That the
government has been considering using prisons to house an influx of
Kosovan refugees since the Nato actions suggests that its humanitarian
concern towards these victims of 'ethnic cleansing' is deeply flawed. In
addition, the Local Government Association has sent out an 'urgent and
immediate' circular to all local authority chief executives and police forces
appealing for immediate help with accommodation.[28] On the one hand this
reflects that local responses will always be critical in refugee movements. On
the other, the panic which has accompanied the early stages of this refugee
movement is worrying. The long term answer must be to empower local
governments and local people to help integrate refugees rather than to
disperse them to unsatisfactory places where no one else will go in the
misguided hope that they will disappear from the public gaze.

     One final point relating to the Kosovan catastrophe needs to be raised in
relation to *Refugees in an Age of Genocide*. During the Second World War
and immediately after many refused to accept the scale and nature of the
Jewish tragedy. Slowly, from the 1960s, awareness of what became known as
the Holocaust emerged and it has been utilised, as we have shown, in various
campaigns to help refugees (and sometimes to oppose them), often, however,
at the cost of distorting history. The memory of the Holocaust is easily
abused. To see echoes of the Holocaust – that is the attempted systematic
murder of all European Jewry – everywhere is emotionally satisfying but
ultimately unsatisfactory. For those bewildered by the scale of the human
disaster of the 'ethnic cleansing' of Kosovo at first hand, images of the
Holocaust have come, perhaps, too easily to hand. The dangers of the
desperate search to make sense of the horror has been shown by those such

as European Union humanitarian commissioner Emma Bonino who described Kosovo as being 'like Schindler's List'.[29] Unravelling this confusion, the pitiful plight of the refugees is likened to a filmic representation of a novel relating to one specific part of the Holocaust. We have, in short, yet to confront the Holocaust and must be wary of using it too freely as a metaphor. The appalling crowded trains employed by the special units employed by Milosevic to carry out 'ethnic cleansing' on the surface resembled those taking the Jews to the death camps. In this case, however, they were carrying out the cultural but not physical genocide of the Kosovo Albanians.[30] One fears, as with Bosnia, the later discovery of mass graves and there is also increasing disturbing evidence of the occurrence of mass, systematic rape of Kosovo Albanian women. That will be enough to indict Milosevic without labelling him as the new Hitler. The threats offered by his regime, especially in relation to human rights abuses and the overall stability of the region, have to be dealt with on their own terms. Furthermore, the war and the appalling treatment of the Kosovo Albanians should not become yet another excuse for Britain to bask in the nostalgia and moral self-satisfaction that it has endlessly engaged in by evoking the memory of the Second World War.[31]

But there are legimate comparisons to be made between the Nazi era and the present day. Referring, for example, to the limitations of refugee policy during the 1930s to impress upon the need for asylum today is not only reasonable but a moral imperative. In the past we doubted the genuine nature of the refugees just as we do today. Rabbi Hugo Gryn, the Auschwitz survivor, was haunted by the image of the 'St Louis', the ship carrying German Jews which was rejected by country after country in 1939. He argued that, in relation to present day asylum seekers, 'It is a very painful and I have to say this, it is an unacceptable fact, that half a century later, we, and by we I include our political leaders as well, we act as if nothing happened'. His premature death in 1996 was deeply saddening but at least it spared him the pain of watching the images from Kosovo. Hugo Gryn warned against ignoring refugees which he saw as 'part of the process which is the hardening of the caring arteries'.[32] In responding positively to the Kosovan refugees we have the chance to honour his memory by entering the next century pledging to restore, revive and act upon the concept of asylum.

April 1999

NOTES

1. John Hooper, 'In the heart of Europe, a lost tribe fights for a loaf of Bread', *The Guardian*, 3 April 1999. This is not to criticise the excellent quality of Hooper's reporting of the refugee crisis in *The Guardian* and *The Observer*.
2. On the use of the term 'ethnic cleansing', see Tomasz Kamusella, 'Ethnic Cleansing in Silesia 1950–89 and the Ennationalizing Policies of Poland and Germany', *Patterns of Prejudice* Vol.33, No.2 (April 1999), p.52. Its first recent use was by *The Economist* in 1992 to describe the removal

of Muslims from Bosnia; Kosovo Albanian Refugee interviewed on BBC 1, 9 o'clock news, 9 April 1999.

3. Nato figures quoted in *The Guardian*, 7 April 1999.
4. UNHCR figures quoted in John Vidal, 'The endless diaspora', *The Guardian*, 2 April 1999; Nick Hopkins and Alan Travis, 'Britain prepares for refugee influx', *The Guardian*, 6 April 1999. On the Kosova Refugee Support Group which has been set up to deal with the growing number in Britain see 'Voices in exile', *iNexile: The Refugee Council Magazine* (February 1999), pp.14–15.
5. Noel Malcolm, *Kosovo: A Short History* (London: Macmillan, 1998), pp.xxvii–xxix.
6. Ibid, p.179.
7. Ibid, pp.350, 352. The figure is Zeljko Raznatovic, known as Arkan.
8. Alan Travis, 'Refugee aid begins to find a place on the agenda', *The Guardian*, 31 March 1999.
9. Tony Blair in *The Sun*, 6 April 1999. Blair changed his position on refugees several times, possibly under American pressure, in a two-day period. See 'Confusion over plans for refugees', *The Guardian*, 6 April 1999 and Nicholas Watt, 'Hague hits at "disarray"', *The Guardian*, 7 April 1999.
10. Jeremy Hardy, 'The lunatics in charge of asylum', *The Guardian*, 27 February 1999; Nick Cohen, 'A dull and dirty lie', *The Observer*, 4 April 1999; Refugee Council, 'Briefing on the Government's new Immigration & Asylum Bill' (March 1999).
11. Survey quoted in *iNexile: The Refugee Council Magazine* (February 1999), p.3; *Daily Mail*, 2 April 1999. On the *Mail*'s anti-alien record, countered by a Saatchi and Saatchi advertising campaign, see Nick Hardwick, 'Cruel myths', *The Guardian*, 17 February 1999.
12. See *AJR Information* (the journal of the Association of Jewish Refugees) debate from July 1998 onwards; on the change from 'refugee' to 'deportee' see Jonathan Steele in *The Guardian*, 6 April 1999 and Jean Aitchison, 'Language at war', *The Guardian*, 9 April 1999.
13. Daniel Puillet-Breton of Action against Hunger quoted in John Hooper, 'Powerless UN looks on as refugee crisis grows', *The Observer*, 11 April 1999.
14. Quoted in Fergal Keane, 'The familiar diatribe of war zones, from Rwanda to Belfast', *The Independent*, 10 April 1999.
15. Figures from the 'Today' programme, Radio 4, 7 April 1999. See also Amelia Gentleman, 'Charities unite in plea', *The Guardian*, 7 April 1999. After six days of the nationwide appeal the amount donated had exceeded £10 million. See *The Guardian*, 13 April 1999.
16. NOP/IPPR, 'IPPR attitudes to race surveys: Summary of Surveys' (5 February 1997); Guardian/ICM Poll quoted in *The Guardian*, 9 February 1999.
17. Isabel Hilton, 'We imagine war as a Hollywood film', *The Guardian*, 5 April 1999.
18. Leader in *The Sun*, 6 April 1999. See also correspondence in *The Daily Telegraph*, 6 April 1999.
19. Rory Carroll, 'Local people aren't connecting the war with these guys. They want them sent back', *The Guardian*, 10 October 1998 and Alan Travis, 'Refugee pressure on Straw', *The Guardian*, 10 October 1998 on anti-refugee sentiment aimed at the Kosovars.
20. Polly Toynbee, 'People, not pawns', *The Guardian*, 7 April 1999. Information concerning the efforts of local authority workers from informal sources.
21. Leader in *The Express*, 8 April 1999. For fear that the interest in the refugees will start to fade, see Patrick Wintour *et al.*, 'The race against time', *The Observer*, 11 April 1999.
22. UNHCR figures quoted in *The Guardian*, 7 April 1999.
23. Katharine Knox, informal information from the Refugee Council concerning the Bosnia Project model, April 1999. See chapter 13 of this study for an assessment of the Bosnia Programme. The Refugee Council is leading a steering group of organisations including Refugee Action, the Red Cross, Refugee Housing Association, the Scottish Refugee Council and other regional refugee councils to 'support [the] humanitarian evacuation of Kosovar refugees to the UK'. It believes that whilst the reception programme 'could see large numbers of refugees arriving quickly ... it is more likely that the people will come here over a long period of time, similar to the Bosnian crisis a few years ago'. The Refugee Council stresses that the Kosovan refugees in the UK 'should be allowed to work and access benefits, education and healthcare' and that any evacuation programmes 'should take account of the following principles':
    * refugees must only come here if they want to, and they must clearly understand the implications
    * family unity should be preserved
    * NGOs and UNHCR should be allowed a central role
    * any evacuated refugee must be given a secure status after 2 years

From Refugee Council, 'Update of the Kosovo Crisis' (8 April 1999). On this forced transfer, see *The Guardian*, 7 April 1999 and *The Independent*, 7 April 1999.

24. WATFY, 'Kosova Emergency Appeal', Southampton, April 1999.

25. Nick Cohen, 'Refugees? Not in our back yard!', *The Observer*, 11 April 1999.

26. *Dover Express* quoted in 'Don't Believe the hype', *iNexile: The Refugee Council Magazine* (February 1999), pp.12–13. On the alleged hostility of Ealing Council see Alan Travis, 'Fortress Europe's four circles of purgatory', *The Guardian*, 20 October 1998 and response by its Chair of Housing in *The Guardian*, 23 October 1998. Interviews carried out by the 'Today' programme, Radio 4, 6 April 1999 suggested continuing hostility to refugees in Dover, in spite of the war. It must be added that the media has tended to concentrate, as we argue in the introduction and conclusion to this study, on local animosity rather than positive sentiment towards and action on behalf of refugees.

27. See chapter 3 of this study. The only complaint noted by the local council against the Atlantic Park refugees concerned alleged spitting on pavements which, considering the hostel had an existence of nearly ten years, is significant. See the minutes of Eastleigh and Bishopstoke Urban District Council, 4 October 1923 – 23 April 1925, p.236 in Hampshire County Record Office.

28. Local Government circulars quoted by Alan Travis, 'UK Offers shelter', *The Guardian*, 7 April 1999.

29. Bonino quoted by Isabel Hilton, 'We imagine war as a Hollywood film', *The Guardian*, 5 April 1999. The overwhelming nature of the catastrophe has affected even the most experienced of reporters. Fergal Keane, a BBC special correspondent, has written that 'in 15 years of reporting from war zones I have never felt the same degree of strangeness, the feeling of a world turned upside down' in *The Independent*, 10 April 1999.

30. See, for example, Paul Harris, 'The trek of tears towards cataclysm', *Daily Mail*, 2 April 1999 and Martin Samuel, 'Just a step away from the obscenity of Auschwitz', *The Express*, 2 April 1999.

31. Increasing evidence of mass graves has been found as the conflict progressed. The popular press in Britain has been particularly prone to make use of cultural references to the Second World War. See, for example, 'Who do you think you are kidding Mr Milosevic?', *The Mirror*, 7 April 1999 in reference to the much repeated situation comedy, 'Dad's Army'. More generally see Tony Kushner, 'Wrong War, Mate', *Patterns of Prejudice* Vol.29, Nos 2–3 (April–July 1995), pp.3-13.

32. Rabbi Hugo Gryn, 'A Moral and Spiritual Index', from his last speech delivered in summer 1996 and printed by the Refugee Council.

Introduction:
Refugees, Place and Memory

Holocaust survivor Hugo Gryn stated just before his untimely death in 1996 that he believed future historians

> will call the twentieth century not only the century of great wars, but also the century of the refugee. Almost nobody at the end of the century is where they were at the beginning of it. It has been an extraordinary period of movement and upheavals.

Roger Zetter, launching the *Journal of Refugee Studies* in 1988, commented that '"Refugee" constitutes one of the most powerful labels currently in the repertoire of humanitarian concern, national and international public policy and social differentiation'. The writer and critic John Berger adds:

> Displacements of whole populations. Refugees from famine or war. Wave after wave of emigrants, emigrating for either political or economic reasons but emigrating for survival. Ours is the century of enforced travel ... the century of disappearances. The century of people helplessly seeing others, who were close to them, disappear over the horizon.[1]

By employing an inclusive approach this study will attempt to restore the humanity of refugees (defined here as people forced to flee outside their country of origin because of persecution) who are often presented as an undifferentiated mass, analysing their lives before, during and after their displacement. It is the first social history of refugees' movements during the twentieth century and the first comparative one. It explores refugees' experiences and responses to their plight by ordinary people, and by national and international governments and agencies.

WORLD HISTORY, LOCAL STUDIES AND THE REFUGEE

John Berger's century in which people simply disappear seems a long way removed from the specific experience of British localities. But in the twentieth century global, national and local history are interdependent and inseparable. In particular, this study will examine the experiences of refugees who came to, passed through or eventually settled at a local level in Britain, as well as reactions and responses to them at a popular and state level. It will explain why they had to leave their own countries and will set responses to them in an international as well as a British context. Approaching local studies as a form of world history would be anathema to some of its practitioners. Indeed, W. G. Hoskins, who from the 1930s 'helped to raise the standing of English *local* history … to the status of an academic discipline', regarded the subject as an antidote to the ills of modernity:

> It may be that with the growing complexity of life, and the growth in size of every organisation with which we have to deal nowadays … more and more people have been led to take an interest in a particular place and to find out all about it. Some shallow-brained theorists would doubtless call this 'escapism', but the fact is that we are not born internationalists and there comes a time when the complexity and size of modern problems leaves us cold.[2]

The objectives of the sponsors of *The Victoria History of the Counties of England*, conceived in the 1890s, were clear. Local history merely stressed national developments and progress and it would

> trace, county by county, the story of England's growth from its prehistoric condition, through the barbarous age, the settlement of alien peoples, and the gradual welding of many races into a nation which is now the greatest in the globe.[3]

Hoskins, by contrast, like his successors at the department he founded at Leicester in 1948, H. Finberg, Alan Everitt and Charles Phythian-Adams, saw the study of local history as much more than a mere fragment of the national experience. In Finberg's words, 'it deals with a social entity which has a perfectly good claim to be studied for its own sake'. Hoskins argued that:

> It is clear that when we are studying or writing the history of a town or a village, we are dealing with … a true society … gathered together in one place. We can even conceive of certain counties as forming a distinct society, especially those remoter counties on the periphery of England.[4]

Phythian-Adams has developed the approach of defining 'local society' even further. It is identified, he argues, through geographical coherence, societal organisation, shared cultural associations and practices, and 'an appreciable body of indigenous families many of whose representatives over the generations do not stray much from their home territory'. The last factor engenders 'an interlinked core of people who will act as the custodians and the perpetuators of local cultural traditions'. This seems to echo Hoskins' inward-looking, anti-internationalist sentiment, though he had recognised that the idea that 'the majority of our population were rooted to the soil in one place until quite recent times' was false if widespread.[5] Yet though the importance of migration in local history has been recognised, the importance of *immigration* has not. This lacuna was shared with national historiography, but the tendency of immigrants to concentrate in specific areas has made its absence in local studies particularly unfortunate.

Phythian-Adams, however, has insisted

> that the scope of English local history ... transcends any precise notion of England or even the English. The subject simply cannot be regarded as a series of compartmentalised versions of English national history if only because, rather obviously, this island was previously inhabited by Britons of various kinds ... Even for local historians, there is much to be said for an historical view that supersedes the merely national ... Certainly we are not going to derive a very satisfactory notion of the English elements in the British arena without taking account of the presence and influence of 'foreigners' in and on specifically *local* and English cultures ... Besides a general recognition of the influence of London, the outlook of [regional historians] tends to be circumscribed either by a county boundary or by the English coastline.

Phythian-Adams has highlighted the limitations of an English as opposed to a *British* context of local history. In national history, the 'Anglocentric' approach has also been slowly abandoned, but here again *international* connections, apart from diplomatic ones, have been neglected.[6]

The incorporation of immigration and ethnic minority issues into national and local British history is still very much the preserve of specialists. Historical refugee studies are still more marginalised. Michael Marrus has argued that although refugees 'have tramped across the European continent since time immemorial', it is only in the twentieth century that they have 'become an important problem of international politics, seriously affecting relations between states'.[7] Modern refugees' numbers, their hazardous legal status and the length of their exile mark out the modern refugee 'from those of earlier times because their homelessness removed them so dramatically and so uniquely from civil society'. Hannah Arendt argued that refugee movements after the First World War were so large-scale that the solution of naturalising stateless people was no longer valid:

> All discussions about the refugee problems revolved around ... one question: 'How can the refugee be made deportable again?' The Second World War and the D[isplaced] P[ersons] camps were not necessary to show that the only practical substitute for a non-existent homeland was an internment camp. Indeed, as early as the thirties this was the only 'country' the world had to offer the stateless.[8]

Refugees in the twentieth century now have to be counted in the tens of millions and have been increasingly constructed as a 'problem'. Yet their social and spatial marginality has made them invisible: few are willing to face the moral responsibility of caring for them. Academics have been particularly slow to respond to their importance, and the work that has been carried out has 'for the most part ... existed on the periphery [rather than] the mainstream of academic enterprise'. Frequently, what interest has been shown has been in the issues of policy involved. Thus, the only major inter-disciplinary international forum dedicated to the subject lists its interests as 'anthropology, economics, health and education, international relations, law, politics, poverty and sociology'.[9]

The absence of history from this list reflects the general silence on refugee questions in the discipline. Acknowledging immigrant and ethnic minorities has been difficult for British historians because it challenges assumptions of mono-culturalism at both national and regional level. Acknowledging the importance of refugees, however, is even more problematic. In his work on the refugee question in mid-Victorian politics, Bernard Porter indicates the mixed experience of those coming to Britain. The poorer refugees often led a life dominated by poverty and loneliness. In contrast, 'most of the other leading refugees led quite middle-class lives in respectable suburbs; sometimes very English lives ... probably because it was difficult to reproduce continental lives in suburban London.'[10] Yet even the first group, though often made to feel unwelcome, were rarely treated as a specific problem by the state at a local or national level. They were as 'free' as other poor, marginalised sections of the population. In the Victorian era '[t]here were no camps to keep people in a suspended state between full admission and the flight from their original homes'. Refugees as a whole were far less integrated after 1914, becoming part of 'the emergence of a new variety of collective alienation'. But the failure to record their experiences in the historical record adds a further bitter twist to their story. If their presence is 'one of the hallmarks of our time', then modern and contemporary historians have hardly noticed it.[11]

The national and international dimensions are clearly important, but local and regional aspects are also of great significance; those looking at the issues involved at a global level need to pay them more attention. The debate over Czech and Slovak Roma asylum seekers in Dover which broke out in 1997 illustrates the importance of the local. A moral panic followed the arrival and temporary settlement of a few hundred people. Local opposition against (but not local support for) the Roma was magnified by the national press in Britain:

> You might think, from a perusal of the British papers this week, that thousands of illegal 'scrounging gypsies' ... had just swept across the European plains to stage a full-frontal assault on the White Cliffs of Dover.

A local issue became the subject matter of national and international politics.[12]

Local historians need to explore the experiences of refugees and responses to them and to place these in a broader geographical context. Even before the age of instant mass communications it has not been possible to keep the most vile and secret acts of destruction, most notably in the form of genocide, hidden from local populations. 'We think of the concentration camp as an isolated realm' but 'every camp had civilian communities in the immediate vicinity', wrote Gordon Horwitz. Similarly, Robert Jan van Pelt and Deborah

Dwork comment that:

> The crushing number of murders, the overwhelming scale of the crime, as well as the vast, abandoned and deserted site isolate 'Auschwitz' from us. We think of it as a concentration camp enclosed on itself, separated from the rest of the world by 'night' and 'fog'. This almost comfortable demonization relegates the camp and the events that transpired there to the realm of myth, distancing us from an all too concrete historical reality, suppressing the local, regional, and national context of the greatest catastrophe western civilization both permitted and endured, and obscuring the responsibility of the thousands of individuals who enacted the atrocity, step by step.

As Hannah Arendt wrote from a very personal perspective, 'Contemporary history has created a new kind of human being – the kind that are put in concentration camps by their foes and internment camps by their friends.' British internment and refugee camps, however unpleasant, are not to be compared to even the mildest part of the Nazi concentration camp structure. But local studies can demystify and restore to history those sites of mass human confinement which have been a constant, but often hidden feature of the twentieth century.[13]

Small groups of refugees entering Britain after 1918 occasionally experienced a treatment similar to that of the Victorian period. Sir John Hope Simpson said in 1939 of the 4–5,000 White Russian refugees who permanently settled in Britain after the war:

> Many have been naturalized. They do not form an isolated group as in France [where numbers were higher because of the relative absence of immigration control], but mix freely with English people and are well on the way to complete assimilation.[14]

Others were often segregated from the host population, including Jewish refugees from eastern Europe who were the exact contemporaries of the White Russians. Today, thousands of refugees are again kept in obscure and inappropriate places of detention. Yet though segregated, refugee settlements in Britain have never been completely hidden from the local gaze. The failure by historians of twentieth-century Britain and its localities to pay any attention to twentieth-century refugees is only partially explained by problems in locating sources. Far more important is the way that academic-sponsored national and regional history has been and is conceived as a means of exploring perceived ethnic homogeneity of the population and its society and culture. Even researchers concentrating on ethnic minorities in Britain have still tended to marginalise refugees while stressing diversity. This is partly because refugees do not fit easily into general patterns of migration and settlement, local or national. It is often in 'amateur' history that refugees have been best integrated. Such inclusion reflects their genuine importance in local memory and a willingness to incorporate their presence even though they do not fit easily into longer-term narratives.

LOCALITIES AND THE REFUGEES

The local perspective of this study will be particularly (though certainly not exclusively) provided by the county of Hampshire. Students of local studies, particularly within the discipline of history, have often been forced to defend their work by arguing that their chosen area of study is typical of national or even international trends. On this rather superficial level, the county has the necessary blend of national patterns and regional differences to make it an ideal case study. Hampshire was geographically the eighth biggest county at the turn of the century. Population-wise it was the 11th largest in England in the 1901 census with a total of 797,644 residents, continuing to grow since then, reaching over 1.5 million in 1991. There are no reliable breakdowns by county of refugee populations. The 1901 census recorded the number of foreigners; Hampshire had the 11th highest number, matching its place in total population figures. In 1991, the proportion of Hampshire people born outside the United Kingdom, at roughly 4 per cent, corresponds to the country as a whole. Over 70 countries of birth are represented in the county's population today.[15]

Numerically, Hampshire is not particularly unusual for its number of refugees even though it is not readily associated with their presence. Indeed, its external and internal image reflected in histories of the county and in contemporary writings has largely been one of ethnic homogeneity and of an unchanging pastoral image as suggested by Hoskins and many others.[16] But its size, allied to the importance of its coastal ports and proximity to the capital, has led it to experience a wide range of movements. Camps related to its large military presence often were used to accommodate refugees. Certain features of the Hampshire refugee experience were unique – such as Atlantic Park which was the only camp of its type in Britain during the 1920s. The existence of refugee camps and accommodation centres in the county throughout the century mark out Hampshire from the country as a whole. There were hostels for east European refugees before 1914, internment camps in Southampton and prison ships for aliens in Portsmouth at the start of the First World War, camps for Belgian refugees throughout the First World War, Atlantic Park in the 1920s, the Basque camp at North Stoneham in the 1930s, emergency and internment camps for refugees from the European continent in Southampton in spring 1940, homes and hostels for child survivors of the concentration camps, Polish resettlement camps, Barton House, Barton-on-Sea, a home for elderly refugees of many countries, from 1954 until the 1980s; houses and military barracks for Hungarian refugees in 1956, homes for Ugandan Asians during the 1970s, Sopley RAF base and Ockenden Venture's Reception Centre, Alverstoke, for the Vietnamese boat people during the 1970s and the early 1980s, and lastly Haslar Prison and Winchester Prison for world asylum seekers today.

Local studies always provide subtle nuances which add light and shade to our understanding of national and international issues, though in the case of refugees there have been few comparable projects. Studies of immigration have been carried out in Bradford and London. The pathbreaking work of Sylvia Collicot has highlighted the local-national-world links of Haringey before the twentieth century: 'how much more exciting local history becomes when it embraces a wide range of experiences and a world view'.[17] Nevertheless, there are no major studies of refugees in particular localities, though a few local history pamphlets have been published tending to be limited to specific groups and periods. One exception is a short account of the refugee presence in Bournemouth. Although its author, E. G. Bennett, modestly claims that his study does 'not pretend to be a comprehensive account of refugees in the Bournemouth area', it illustrates what can be achieved at the local level, covering a range of groups finishing with the Vietnamese boat people and focusing on life stories. In addition, Steve Cohen's polemic on Britain's 'mistreatment' of refugees in the twentieth century focuses on Manchester and, in contrast to Bennett, provides a more critical perspective.[18]

But none of the existing local literature on refugees provides a comprehensive study, including Leicester, location of the major academic centre for English local history, even though it has been of major importance this century in terms of refugees and responses to them (most infamously in 1972 when the city council advertised in the *Ugandan Argus* to avoid an influx of Asian refugees escaping from President Idi Amin).[19] In spite of these gaps in the literature of localities and refugees, this study will always utilise national and international comparisons.

Until recently in geographical research an informal dualism operated on 'the locality debate': general-specific; abstract-concrete; global-local; important-unimportant. Andrew Sayer concluded that 'some authors would indeed argue that the concerns of locality studies are less important, merely documenting the many ways to skin a cat'. Nevertheless, whereas historical studies of localities have stressed the need to prove typicality, recent work of geographers has moved further, exploring the importance of 'place'. Doreen Massey especially has emphasised that the 'local uniqueness' of places

> is always already a product of wider contacts; the local is always a product in part of 'global' forces, where global in this context refers not necessarily to the planetary scale, but to the geographical beyond, the world beyond the place itself.

Her conclusion has particular relevance:

> The attempt to align 'us' and 'them' with the general concepts of 'local' and 'global' is always deeply problematical. For in the historical and geographical construction of places, the 'other' in general terms is already within. The global is everywhere and already, in one way or another, implicated in the local.

By studying the presence (and absence) of refugees, the relationship between local place and local culture is problematised. The belief that in the past, 'places *were* settled, coherent and bounded, that cultures *were* internally generated and deeply embedded in spatial propinquity' is questioned. Doreen Massey and Pat Jess argue that

> the current era of intensified globalization is characterized not by the complete erasure of place (of whatever dimensions – the local village or the continent), but by a continuing tension between, and process of mutual construction of, the 'global and the local'. 'Places' – their characters and the differences between them – continue to matter: they matter to capital which exploits the different characteristics of place – in other words, uneven development; and they matter to people because of our senses of belonging and identification, and the quality of our geographical imaginations.

This study examines identities; the construction of 'home' by refugees and those receiving them. Whether the county was 'typical' becomes irrelevant when the subject matter is geographically inclusive. The inseparability of the local as against the global is true for the refugees and their descendants who have come from (or moved onto) almost every area of the world. Not surprisingly, their identities and idea of 'home' have been complex and multi-layered. The actor Wolfe Morris (1925–1996), was, according to *The Times'* obituarist

> born in Portsmouth, one of nine children. His grandfather was a Russian Jew who had carried his son (Morris's father) on his shoulders across Europe to start a new life in Britain. His father, after working in Jewish music halls in the East End of London, became a businessman. Wolfe's mother had a glorious mezzo soprano voice, and used to sing at family weddings. Despite his exotic upbringing, and East European features, Morris regarded himself as a Hampshire man.

Global origins and connections are compatible with strong local affinities. But the relationship between local and global is also essential in explaining the responses and reactions to refugees which have to be understood in the context of changing perceptions of Britain's place in the world. In the case of Wolfe Morris, surprise that he could feel a close identification with Hampshire, says more about the obituarist than the late actor. A central theme of this study will be the concept of 'asylum' and its relationship to 'a place called home'.[20]

INTERNATIONAL CHANGE AND THE 'REFUGEE CRISIS'

To understand national and local developments in the history of refugees, the wider context of global changes has to be considered. The movement of refugees has a long history, but it is only this century that the issue has been politicised and internationalised. With the development of technology facilitating travel and communication, the migration of people has increased. As Elizabeth Ferris has shown, the world is moving beyond borders. The combined impact of global economic forces, environmental change and competition for scarce resources has led many to believe that the world is shrinking and international cooperation is required for survival. The mass movement of refugees is a by-product of a world which is becoming more accessible but also more capable of self-destruction as humans have harnessed technology leading to genocide and ecological disaster.[21]

As there are now fewer physical impediments to mobility, refugee movements have increased but, increasingly, states have put up barriers to halt this flow. National identities have become more fluid, throwing old certainties into doubt, but this has been mirrored by more inward-looking tendencies. In consequence, borders are strengthened to control the exclusion of people. Attempts to reassert national identity have manifested themselves in the rise of xenophobia, racist attacks and inter-ethnic conflicts from which Britain has not been immune. In the autumn of 1997 the neo-nazi National Front organised a march in Dover in response to the influx of Czech and Slovak asylum seekers. Individuals experienced considerable verbal abuse and were in fear of physical attacks from extremists.[22] In Britain, as in Europe as a whole, the growth of immigrants and asylum seekers in the 1980s and 1990s has resulted in a rising tide of legislation being used to deter such movements.

The development of the current refugee crisis is rooted in changes that have occurred over the twentieth century. Before this time Europeans migrated in vast numbers to settle in their empires or in the New World, but as the new century dawned, Europe itself was to become the centre of migrations. After the Russian revolution in 1917, the Armenian genocide in 1915 and war in the Balkans, refugees became an international issue. John Hope Simpson, one of the pioneers of refugee studies, wrote in 1938 that, 'The fluidity of population, which before the First World War, both prevented refugee movements and facilitated their solution, has been succeeded by a rigidity of which passport systems, alien registration and restriction rules are symbolic.'[23]

Initially voluntary agencies took the lead in responding to the needs of those displaced in a world where national identity was becoming more exclusive. But the humanitarian response took on a global dimension with a consensus that the scale of the problem required international efforts. In 1921 the League of Nations created a High Commissioner for Refugees, led by Fridtjof Nansen, a Norwegian statesman who had worked for displaced people. His creation, the 'Nansen passport', offered legal documents to refugees, providing them with a recognisable status and enabling them to start afresh. Nansen was succeeded after his death by the American, James McDonald, in 1933. McDonald resigned late in 1935, believing that a large-scale human tragedy was in the making which his organisation was unable to stop because the international community was unwilling to help Jewish refugees fleeing Nazi Germany. In spite of international conferences at Evian in 1938 and Bermuda in 1943, and the creation of an Intergovernmental

Committee on Refugees to deal with the growing problem, only limited numbers of Jews, especially after the outbreak of war, were saved from what later became known as the Holocaust. But realisation of the full scale of Nazi atrocities after 1945 went only a little way towards developing institutions with more backbone when dealing with refugees.

The war left some 30 million people uprooted. As the United Nations was established in the hope of averting another tragedy of this magnitude, agencies were set up to carry out emergency relief programmes for the displaced millions and to organise repatriation schemes. The United Nations Relief and Reconstruction Agency (UNRRA) helped seven million displaced people return to their countries. UNRRA came under criticism as it became embroiled in inter-governmental conflicts with the onset of the Cold War and was replaced by the International Refugee Organisation (IRO) in 1948. Conceived as a temporary agency, the IRO attempted to find permanent solutions for the 1.5 million refugees remaining on the continent. It too was hampered by the Cold War as the IRO was unable to operate in the Soviet occupied zone of Germany. In 1951, the United Nations therefore created another temporary organisation to deal with the remaining refugees in Europe. The United Nations High Commissioner for Refugees (UNHCR) has remained in existence ever since with its mandate renewed repeatedly.

The year 1951 was also when the first attempt was made to provide a universal definition of a refugee. The United Nations Convention on the Status of Refugees, along with the institution of the UNHCR, were to provide the foundations for dealing with international refugee problems. The Convention, still the standard benchmark for establishing refugee status, defined a refugee as:

> Any person who owing to a well founded fear of being persecuted for reasons of race, religion, nationality, membership of a particular social group or political opinion, is outside the country of his nationality and is unable, or owing to such fear, is unwilling to avail himself of the protection of that country; or who, not having a nationality and being outside the country of his former habitual residence, is unable, or owing to such fear, is unwilling to return to it.[24]

The 1951 Convention was modified in 1967 by the Bellagio Protocol which retained the definition of a refugee but removed the time and geographical limitations. Thus an international definition for refugees emerged out of a need to deal with a *European* crisis. Global changes, however, have given it wider ramifications. As decolonisation occurred, and the Cold War struggle for spheres of influence spread, so the migration of peoples to Europe increased. Refugees were no longer simply being displaced within the continent but were fleeing from Asia, Africa and Latin America to Europe. Moreover, the end of the Cold War unleashed political and ethnic conflicts encouraging further mass migration. The implications of such changes were recognised in a report for the Independent Commission on International Humanitarian Issues which suggested that now refugees were coming from geographically and culturally distant areas, this constituted an unprecedented challenge to the legal machinery and conscience of the receiving countries: 'The refugee problem, previously regarded as a factor in east-west relations, now has a north-south dimension to it'.[25]

Refugee issues have come increasingly to be seen in the light of national foreign policy concerns rather than in humanitarian terms. Just as Jewish refugees in the 1930s fell victim to international complacency and other diplomatic priorities, so refugees in the post-war period have suffered (and more rarely, benefited) because of political machinations. The importance of the USA in the United Nations and as a world power has also shaped international responses to refugees. During the Cold War, refugees from communist regimes were welcomed in western Europe in keeping with anti-communist foreign policy and security concerns. In the 1970s, the increasing movement of people from the 'Third World' has activated a less welcoming response from European countries. Environmental, economic and political problems have combined to create instability in much of Asia, Africa and Latin America which, in many countries, still suffer from the after-effects of colonialism. Refugees moving to the wealthier industrialised nations to the north are viewed as a threat to economic and political stability and a force to be excluded.[26] Alleged differences in 'race', culture and traditions have made refugees a focus of suspicion and growing hostility, adding to their marginal status and treatment. Their increasingly diverse backgrounds have made refugees even harder to define.

DEFINING REFUGEES AND COMMON TRENDS IN TWENTIETH-CENTURY MOVEMENTS

The question of what distinguishes a refugee from other immigrants is open to interpretation and has changed over time. In the inter-war period the League of Nations defined refugees according to group affiliation. For instance, the definition of a Russian refugee adopted at the Inter-Governmental Committee in May 1926 included, 'any person of Russian origin who does not enjoy or who no longer enjoys the protection of the government of the Soviet Union and who has not acquired another nationality'.[27] This group definition was also employed at the 1933 Refugee Convention of the League of Nations. Granting refugee status did not depend on individual refugees proving that they had left their home countries because of political persecution. Yet, as Claudena Skran has pointed out, group designation had the disadvantage of causing dissension over which refugee groups should be assisted. German opposition to aid being given to Jews and dissidents fleeing the Third Reich hindered responses to their exodus in the 1930s.[28]

After the Second World War pressure for a universal definition of a refugee gathered momentum, leading to the definition enshrined in the 1951 Convention which emphasised the *causes* of flight. The experience of European Jewry in the Nazi era revealed that membership of one particular national group was not always relevant in explaining who was likely to be persecuted. The definition therefore stressed flight from persecution due to race, politics, religion or social group, in addition to nationality. The Convention remains the clearest conception of the term 'refugee' which is still widely used in designating who is entitled to asylum by receiving societies around the world. To date, 108 countries have now ratified either the Convention or the Protocol.[29]

The Convention has not gone unchallenged since its institution. With growing numbers of people uprooted through economic deprivation as well as political persecution, the 1951 definition has been regarded as irrelevant. The United Nations criterion has also caused controversy as it excludes people displaced en masse by warfare and those who have been uprooted due to violence but who have not left their country of origin. In the 1990s this has left many displaced people from the former Yugoslavia without refugee status in spite of their clear need for help. In 1969 the Organisation of African Unity (OAU) developed its own definition:

> Every person who, owing to external aggression, occupation, foreign domination or events seriously disturbing public order in either part or the whole of his country of origin or nationality, is compelled to leave his place of habitual residence in order to seek refuge in another place outside his country of origin or nationality.[30]

This recognised that masses of people were fleeing from war or violence due to the substantial upheavals on the continent following decolonisation and the establishment of independent nation-states. The Organisation of American States (OAS) also produced its own alternative definition in the Cartagena Declaration of 1984 naming:

> Persons who have fled their country because their lives, safety or freedom have been threatened by generalised violence, foreign aggression, internal conflicts, massive violation of human rights or other circumstances which have seriously disturbed the public order.[31]

As these alternative definitions demonstrate, the emphasis on individual persecution leaves considerable room for manoeuvre in interpretation of who fits the criteria. The right of states to grant asylum rather than the rights of the individual to gain such status are paramount in international practice. This means that refugees are subject to decisions by states with their own political agendas which are not simply acting out of humanitarian concern.

Academics have joined the political debate concerning the distinction between immigrants and refugees. E. F. Kunz has suggested that the main difference between a refugee and an immigrant lies in the push/pull motivation. While immigrants may be lured to migrate to another country by opportunities for a better life, refugees do not have the same element of choice. 'It is the reluctance to uproot oneself, and the absence of positive original motivations to settle elsewhere, which characterises all refugee decisions and distinguishes the refugee from the voluntary migrants.' This is a somewhat subjective interpretation as Kunz accepts that:

> The validity of fear for one's safety which is the creator of all refugees can after all never be tested: it is the individual's interpretation of events and self-perceived danger or revulsion, or role, which motivates the refugee and justifies his stand.[32]

Joly and Cohen argue a further difference between immigrants and refugees is that 'Immigrants cherish the myth of return but in the final analysis the decision to go home remains within their control, however difficult it may prove. For refugees, the possibility of returning home is less feasible.' There are common features that migrants and refugees share:

> The two groups suffer from similar disadvantages in housing, general standards of living, educational opportunities and language learning. Both immigrants and refugees are also the targets of racism, discrimination and hostility on the part of the receiving society.[33]

Another definitional problem is the nature of persecution. Political and economic persecution often go hand-in-hand but the latter is not considered as sufficient criteria for granting refugee status by most governments. Some commentators have argued that refugees are the product of underdevelopment.[34] The World Council of Churches, for example, includes 'victims of systematic economic deprivation' in its working definition of refugees.[35] There is also a growing recognition that environmental disasters cause mass flights of people. Nuclear or chemical explosions, desertification, deforestation and drought-induced famine are a clear threat to people's survival. There have been calls to expand the definition of refugees to include other groups in need. Some argue that broadening the concept will render it meaningless and bring the attendant risk that governments will shut their doors on all groups. Although those fleeing ecological disasters this century have come to Britain (such as the inhabitants of Tristan de Cuna who came to Southampton in the early 1960s and those from Montserrat in the 1990s), 'environmental refugees' will not form part of this study. A specific focus will be kept on the extensive and complex range of groups and individuals who have sought asylum because of political, racial and religious persecution.

While Barry Stein has argued that a refugee is a successful individual temporarily displaced and in need of help to rebuild his/her life, perceptions of refugees as uniform, helpless victims persist. From the first comprehension of a threat and the decision to flee, through the journey to safety, staying in a reception camp, to subsequent repatriation, settlement or resettlement, refugees are often at the mercy of forces beyond their control. Despite the variety of places they have fled and the multitude of reasons for their flight, there are many common features to their experience. Stein has identified various considerations which an individual will weigh up before fleeing home.[36] The imminence of danger affects the timing of flight. For Hungarian revolutionaries in Budapest immediate flight as the Russians advanced was necessary. Fears may be repressed until there is a clear opportunity to leave, as for Vietnamese refugees who needed access to passage on boats to reach safety elsewhere in south-east Asia. A decision taking years to implement does not reduce an individual's claim to asylum as it may be that only when life becomes unbearable can people summon the courage to flee all that is familiar. For many Chileans and German Jews, hope that the situation would improve was one reason why flight was delayed.

Family ties affect departure. Those with no family may find it easier to leave home, although the need to provide a secure future for close relatives may also be a push factor. Young single men have often fled first before trying to bring their families over. Age is important, clearly favouring the young and fit who are more able to embark on a potentially hazardous journey. Resources as well as opportunities may be needed to escape. Many refugees, from the Jews in the 1930s through to the Zaireans in the 1990s, have had to buy their flight to freedom. Geography can also be a factor. Those fleeing Hungary in 1956 had only one non-communist neighbouring country, Austria, to travel to in order to reach the West. Jewish refugees fleeing the expanding German Reich were clearly affected by their location and many initially in the first days of National Socialism sought refuge in neighbouring France. The ability to leave could be affected by the governments of those in danger. Chileans and Ugandan Asians were encouraged to leave under supervised departures by their governments whereas other repressive regimes have made it very difficult to escape.

Gender issues may also have an impact on refugee movements. It is often young single men who have been targeted as potential threats and have thus fled abroad. The Hungarians have been identified primarily as a young male group, as have the Kurds who have come to Britain 30 years later. Persecution of women has often been related to the political activities of family members, while women have themselves become victims of specific forms of persecution, particularly rape as seen in Bosnia and Rwanda. Conceptions of gender roles may also affect migration patterns. The belief that men can cope better with the traumas of flight or that they should undertake this role and find a new safe place for their family may lead to chain migration in which a young man finds sanctuary and establishes himself before applying for asylum for relations. But in recent years as governments have reduced the influx of people, many asylum seekers have only received a temporary status and opportunities for family reunion have diminished. Many Turkish Kurds and Bosnians in Britain have remained separated from close family although they themselves are safe.

The journey to freedom varies considerably. An aeroplane flight from

Chile to Britain does not have the risks of a journey by boat through shark-infested waters which many Vietnamese endured. But the increase in travel mobility has been met with resistance, leading to a new situation of 'refugees in orbit' with its own attendant dangers. Unwelcome asylum seekers are now shuttled from country to country due to restrictive legislation leading to the danger that they will be returned to the country of flight, thereby contravening international law guaranteeing 'non-refoulement'.

For many refugees who have escaped, there is a period of transition in which they are held in reception camps or hostels. The conditions of these may vary according to time, place and resources available. Sometimes refugees will endure the privations of months of communal living in holding centres before they reach a country of resettlement, as has been the notorious case of the Vietnamese, whose accommodation in Hong Kong has been in overcrowded camps surrounded by barbed wire and resembling prisons. Once in the country of resettlement there may be a further transition period in a holding centre.

Several stages in the resettlement process have been identified, which although confined to a study of Chileans, has validity for many refugees.[37] First, there is a feeling of confusion and disorientation on arrival in a new environment with an uncertain future which can be mixed with a sense of elation and relief at having escaped from danger. Exiles may then attempt to reorientate themselves in the new society but disillusion may occur as expectations are not immediately met, especially in the search for a job and learning a new language. Problems may be exacerbated by emotional anxieties stemming from loss and isolation in the new country. Concern about the future and reflection on the past may then lead to feeling a loss of social status, and, in some cases, disappointment at the lack of political participation compared with the level of activity before flight. Finally, there is the need to deal with the future when daily concerns predominate. This process of adaptation and 'acculturation' may take years to achieve and is often incomplete, varying according to age, language, culture, nationality, ethnicity, and gender as well as whether refugees come alone or with friends or family. It may not be achieved at all until the second or third generation when descendants of the original entrants, having grown up in a new county, have greater opportunities to integrate successfully.

The issue of how successfully refugees adapt to life in another country has long been a cause of debate in refugee studies, raising the question of how this can be measured and by whom. Are we to take the word of government agencies, voluntary bodies or listen instead to the views of refugees themselves? As Barry Stein has argued, if the assessments of the government are used, adaptation may be measured in terms of 'solving a problem' and a reduction in the numbers of individuals receiving public assistance.[38] Voluntary bodies may quantify successful resettlement in terms of a fall in the demands they have to deal with from refugees. If housing and work needs are met, a refugee may be seen as having successfully achieved the transition to a new life. Yet from the refugee's own point of view, these measures may be woefully inadequate. A sense of alienation from the host society may persist. Refugees often compare the quality of their new life with the old. While the fear of persecution may have withered away, the initial euphoria is likely to give way to a sense of loss and isolation and a feeling of strangeness living in a foreign country which may never replace a former home. There may also be a sense of guilt at abandoning home and people in an ongoing political struggle. For some people, being a refugee is a burden which they will always carry with them.

'The myth of return' may still be a cherished ideal among refugees for years. Enforced abandonment of their homes may be seen as a temporary but necessary measure and the wish to return only hindered by transient political circumstances. Indeed, for some groups, adaptation can be seen as a betrayal of the country they have left. But even if the political context may change so that return is possible, expectations may, again, be shattered. The euphoria of seeing friends, family, and familiar places may give way to disappointment at changes that have occurred. In the years of exile, homeland and people may have been idealised and depression may set in as values have to be reassessed. Adapting to the new reality, and building a new life yet again can be problematic after years abroad. Children born abroad who have no knowledge of this 'homeland' may find it particularly difficult to adjust. The exile experience requires a total transformation of life.[39]

Refugee movements to Britain reflect global changes and conflicts. Within Britain there has been a shift from freedom of movement at the start of the century to exclusion at its close. The responses of the British state and people have been in flux, but the refugee experience shows signs of continuity. This study will seek throughout to consider the views of those seeking asylum, as well as international and national legal definitions and developments outside their control. The testimony of refugees will be used extensively so that the full complexities of their lives becomes evident, reflecting that every individual has a story and is not simply a 'victim' of the intolerance of others. By focusing on localities in a national and global context, an inclusive approach is employed, beginning with east European Jews leaving Tsarist oppression at the turn of the twentieth century and closing with world asylum seekers at the end of the millennium.[40] Comparisons are essential so that common patterns can be identified, enabling future waves of people to be met with a maturity of approach and understanding. As the anthropologist, Clifford Geertz, suggests, 'We need, in the end, something rather more than local knowledge. We need a way of turning its varieties into commentaries upon another, the one lighting what the other darkens'.[41]

PART 1

The Closing of Asylum, 1900–1932

1

Refugees in the Age of Mass Immigration: From the Late Nineteenth Century to the First World War

THE ORIGINS OF THE JEWISH REFUGEE MOVEMENT

From 1881 (the year of the assassination of Tsar Alexander II) to the outbreak of the First World War, some 2.5 million Jews left the Russian Empire, part of the massive shift of population from eastern and southern Europe. The Jews had lived in Russia for many centuries, developing their own distinctive religious and cultural life, but by the last quarter of the nineteenth century they were largely confined to the 'Pale of Settlement' (15 provinces in the north-west and south-west of Russia – Belorussia, Lithuania, the Ukraine and New Russia), totalling nearly three million people. An additional one million Jews lived in the Kingdom of Poland. Of the Jews of the Pale, it has been estimated that just over 80 per cent lived in towns or *shtetlekh*. The uneven pattern of modernisation in the Russian and Russian Jewish economy and culture, alongside restrictions on freedom and substantial population growth, led to an increasingly impoverished and dislocated Jewish community ripe for emigration. The United States was the biggest recipient of this global movement, with a minimum of 200,000 and a maximum of one million immigrants of all types and from all countries per annum in this period. But if the United States was the dominant place of settlement, other countries, particularly Britain, also experienced an inflow. Statistics in this area are notoriously unreliable, but Lloyd Gartner has estimated that some half a million Jews from the Russian Empire spent at least two years in Britain during the era of mass immigration.[1]

Jews from eastern Europe were no strangers to Britain before 1881; the movement of large numbers of Jews from the Russian Empire began in the 1840s, starting the transformation of British Jewry from its previous domination by those from Germany and Holland. The expansion of Manchester Jewry in the nineteenth century, for example, soon to emerge as the largest provincial community in Britain, was based on this new east European influx.[2] In classic mythology, the Jewish tide of immigration began after the pogroms which affected all Jews following the assassination of the

Tsar in 1881. That the Jewish exodus preceded this event and was actually far more pronounced in the 1890s than in the 1880s indicates that the situation was far more complex than is often assumed. Indeed, many of those leaving the Russian Empire came from areas that were not directly affected by antisemitic violence. Nevertheless, the *fear* as well as the *reality* of violence was of great importance. Although every fresh outbreak of disturbances in the period up to the First World War created a new peak of Jewish refugees, the pressures experienced by the Jews of the Russian Empire were multifarious and extended beyond the experience of extreme collective violence.[3]

None of the factors encouraging Jewish emigration can be seen in isolation. For many, however, economic and other discrimination proved to be intolerable. In short, although the Jewish population of the Russian Empire grew throughout the age of mass immigration – in spite of the millions leaving – the opportunities to make a living and to enjoy a free existence constantly diminished. The drastic limitations on their freedom were illustrated by a five page list of discriminatory legislation gathered in a report by the Russo-Jewish and Jewish Board of Guardians Conjoint Committee (formed in Britain in 1891 to help the victims of Russian persecution) covering the years 1882 to 1908.[4] It highlighted 44 sets of restrictions on the rights of Russian Jews, especially the so-called May Laws of 1882 which prohibited

> attesting leases of real estate, situate outside the Jewish Pale and the prohibition of granting power for the administration thereof by Jews. The prohibition for Jews to settle in the Governments constituting the Jewish Pale outside the towns and villages. The prohibition to make contracts of sale and mortgage in the name of Jews, relating to real estate situate outside the Jewish Pale.[5]

With parallels to the Nazi regime before the Second World War, the Tsarist state encouraged Jewish emigration yet made it difficult and dangerous for Jews to leave. The situation of the Jews worsened at the turn of the century as the Russian economy and political situation deteriorated rapidly. The most infamous massacre of Jews occurred in the city of Kishinev in Bessarabia in 1903. The pogrom left 47 Jews dead and hundreds more seriously injured much to the outrage of international opinion. Although there were other, more murderous pogroms, Kishinev made a particularly deep impact.[6] Its memory was most famously preserved in 'The City of Slaughter' by the Russian Jewish poet Hayyim Nahman Bialik. Its opening lines:

> Arise and go now to the city of slaughter;
> Into its courtyard wind thy way;
> There with thine own hand touch, and with the eyes of thine head,
> Behold on tree, on stone, on fence, on mural clay,
> The spattered blood and dried brains of the dead

were resonant in east European Jewish life throughout the inter-war period and into the Holocaust years.[7]

The misery and suffering of Russian Jews was increased by the disaster of the Russo-Japanese War of 1904 leading to a new wave of pogroms. Medieval accusations of ritual murder combined with other forms of religious prejudice, rampant nationalism and more contemporary antisemitic conspiracy theories, made Jews vulnerable to attack from large sections of the populace. The Tsarist state, while not directly involved in planning the pogroms as was once widely believed, even so proved incapable of dealing adequately with the appalling violence and loss of life.[8]

The Russian revolution of 1905 proved to be the stimulus for a fresh outbreak of violence with close on 50 pogroms in that year alone. Russian right-wingers, most notoriously the Black Hundreds, blamed Jews for spreading socialist and radical politics. Although Jews increasingly mobilised themselves against attack and liberal and radical Russians added their voice of protest, many more took what opportunity there was to leave the land of their oppression. Jack Myers was a British Jew who went to Russia in November 1905 as part of a team allocating relief funding. Some Jewish communal figures in the Western democracies were opposed to the Jews of Russia leaving en masse, believing pessimistically that the receiving societies would be unable to cope and optimistically that Russia might yet be persuaded to treat the Jews as equal citizens with full rights.[9] On witnessing the reality of the Russian Empire Myers recognised how the flow was unstoppable. As he wrote in his diary on 29 November 1905:

> The scene at Kieff station was indescribable [over a hundred people had been killed in the pogrom in the town]. The station is an open one – crowded with people. One sees the haggard care-worn Jews and Jewesses presumably leaving the land of their birth for one where security for life and property will be greater … The confusion is bewildering … We learn something of the character and extent of the damage done in the town during the recent excesses. Eight thousand families numbering at least 40,000 souls were affected and the damage done amounted to some 8 million roubles (nearly one million pounds). Shops and houses were plundered and destroyed, the schools were wrecked, men killed and wounded …. One is not surprised, indeed I wonder greatly that more who can do not express their desire to leave this hapless and cursed land.[10]

Adding to this immense movement were those Jews escaping the intense poverty and discrimination of Galicia, in the eastern province of Austria from where 120,000 Jews out of 900,000 left during the 1890s. An even greater proportion abandoned Romania: some 30 per cent of the country's 270,000 Jews emigrated to the USA alone in the years from 1881 to 1914, having experienced profound antisemitism from state and populace as well as the economic problems affecting east European society as a whole.[11] Cheap steerage tickets on steamships and the growth of mass international communications eased this enormous shift in population, but emigration was not straightforward. The millions attempting to leave faced a Western world that was increasingly hostile to their arrival and settlement. As the nineteenth century came to a close, the prospect of immigration control, formal or informal, and based increasingly on racialised criteria biased against non-'Nordics' (essentially those from eastern and southern Europe as well as Asia), loomed larger. In 1891 the United States Congress passed legislation that enabled immigrants to be rejected on grounds that they were paupers or likely to become public charges.[12] In Britain, the first anti-immigrant organisation was created in the 1880s and attempts were made to pass anti-alien legislation on several occasions in the following decade. Trade improvements in the second half of the 1890s weakened anti-alienism, but it was given fresh impetus by the rampant nationalism, jingoism, xenophobia and antisemitism linked to the Boer War.[13]

The Jewish population of South Africa had increased from roughly 10,000 in 1891 to 24,000 at the start of the Boer War in 1899, largely through the influx of Lithuanian Jews, the so-called 'Peruvians'. The South African census of 1904 recorded over 38,000 Jews but this near-doubling of the Jewish population in five years hides the fact that although many Jewish immigrants were entering South Africa, others were being encouraged or forced to depart.[14] Indeed, the fluidity of Jewish migration patterns was very much part and parcel of the age of mass movement. Transmigrancy, the settling in one country for a limited period before moving on to another, and the return – forced or voluntary – to eastern Europe were integral to the story as a whole. Settled communities made up of east European Jews were formed in this period, or more commonly transformed existing Jewish communities, but alongside such settlements were those still on the move.[15] Britain and its ports played an important role in the complex shifting of populations. The next section will explore the local, national and global aspects of one group of Jewish refugees who arrived in Britain during February 1900 – a vivid case history of the fluidity of Jewish immigrant life at the turn of the century.

THE GROWTH OF ANTI-ALIENISM IN BRITAIN AND BEYOND

Considering the scale of shipping movements between Britain and South Africa throughout the Boer War, it is remarkable how much attention the transport *Cheshire*, carrying just 600 passengers, received before its arrival. It can only be explained by the antisemitism that had intensified in British culture and politics during the Anglo-Boer conflict. Accusations were levelled that the war was being fought for Jewish financial interests and the equally false claim was made that Jews were not supporting or contributing to the British war effort.[16] The first indication of trouble came in a telegram sent by Sir Alfred Milner, British High Commissioner in South Africa. Widely reported in the British press, it warned that 350 foreign Jews on board the *Cheshire* had been allowed to leave South Africa but stressed that they had sufficient funds for further passage once arriving in Britain: 'No help should be given to them on their arrival as anyone asking for it would be an imposter'.[17] In fact, many of the refugees arrived almost penniless and money had to be raised through the Jewish Board of Guardians (via the Lord Mayor of London's fund) to help them on their way. Rather than imposters, the refugees were in an appalling state and took the opportunity of free passage to leave the poverty and increasing hostility of South African society.[18] The responses in Britain to those on board the *Cheshire* ranged from antagonism with barely disguised antisemitism through to sympathy and kindness. Indeed, the terminology used to describe these Jews revealed changing contemporary attitudes with major implications for the century ahead. They were labelled as either unwanted aliens and dangerous foreigners (especially in contrast to the 'honest' Englishmen on board) or refugees deserving pity and support.

The coverage in the *Daily Mail*, a conservative popular newspaper founded in 1896, which had a circulation of over 1.25 million and a theme of anti-alienism throughout its history, was the most hostile. Its sensationalist report, significantly entitled 'So-Called Refugees', was almost totally inaccurate but exposed the mechanisms used at the turn of the century to create a popular Englishness standing in stark contrast to the 'alien Jew':

> There landed yesterday at Southampton from the transport *Cheshire* over 600 so-called refugees, their passages having been paid out of the Lord Mayor's Fund; and, upon the unanimous testimony of the ship's officers, there was scarce a hundred of them that had, by right, deserved such help, and these were the Englishmen of the party. The rest were Jews. The ship seemed alive with them. There were Russian Jews, Polish Jews, German Jews, Peruvian Jews, all kinds of Jews, all manner of Jews. They fought and jostled for the foremost places at the gang-ways; they rushed and pushed and struggled into the troop-shed, where the Mayor of Southampton ... had provided free refreshments .... They fought for places on the train ... the women and children were left to take their chances unaided ... Then, incredible as it may seem, the moment they were in the carriages THEY BEGAN TO GAMBLE ... [t]hese were the penniless refugees and when the Relief Committee passed by they hid their gold and fawned and whined, and, in broken English, asked for money for their train fare.

> There were a few quiet, sad-faced Englishmen – men who had gone to South Africa, who had made a little money, who had lost their all through the war. One man, with scarcely a rag of warm clothing on him, whose only asset was a tin of sandwiches, admitted he was dead broke, but refused to take a half-penny. These men stood by each other in a proud, shame-faced sort of way, and looked on in silence...[19]

The viciousness of this article, and the refusal of the *Daily Mail* to publish a rebuttal, forced the *Jewish Chronicle* into a major defence of those on board and the care that had been provided for them. The Jewish community would have been far happier had no publicity been received at all regarding the *Cheshire*, but the accusations were so powerful that they could not remain unanswered. Moreover, the editor of the *Jewish Chronicle* realised that this specific attack on foreign Jews was part of a much broader antipathy to aliens:

> We are sorry to see that the *Daily Mail* has seen fit to indulge in a very wild tirade against the Jews on the 'Cheshire', to represent them as a set of barbarians, preying upon the charity of the nation .... But the article ... is even more deplorable for what it suggests than what it says. It implies that another ship-load of Jewish 'scum' has arrived here, and is to be dumped down for good on the English shores ... We can only say that we deeply regret that, at a time when the national need demands unity of spirit and aim among all sections of the people, a reputable journal should publish words which, it must know, can have nothing but an exactly contrary effect.[20]

To further contradict the *Daily Mail* report, the *Jewish Chronicle* published a full account of the *Cheshire* based on information provided by those on board:

> ... On Saturday morning, when the Refugees were told of the charges brought against them by the *Daily Mail*, the utmost indignation prevailed. Each and every one of them denied the statements *in toto*, and complained bitterly of the treatment they had received on board the 'Cheshire' ... Mrs Gillies, who had to be detained through ill-health at Southampton, alleges that she was shamefully neglected ... [T]hey were treated on board more like animals than human beings...

In contrast to the image provided by the *Daily Mail*, the refugees were in an utterly marginal and desperate state:

> They view with very little satisfaction and no little misgivings the future that is before them. Fleeing from a country that oppressed them and where they were unable to gain a livelihood, they have now to return to the inhospitable land with no prospects before them.[21]

Away from the national arena, the arrival of the *Cheshire* in Southampton had caused far less fuss. The local minister, Rabbi Holdensky, wrote to the secretary of the Jewish Board of Guardians that he had

> just returned from [an] appointment with the Mayor of this town and have made all arrangements for getting the Refugees of our Faith off as expeditiously as possible ... The Vessel will remain off Netley till Friday morning as lodging 600 people is very difficult besides being mostly undesirable.[22]

With such close planning between the Jewish community and the Mayor of Southampton's office, the arrival of the *Cheshire* passed off without incident as a sympathetic report in the local paper indicated:

> The ship was signalled off at Hurst Castle [several miles from Southampton] at 10.25 yesterday, and she arrived in the Empress Dock shortly after noon. There was a staff of helpers ready to receive the people ... refreshments [were provided and] those who were in need of warm clothing were supplied .... Special trains were provided for [and] the majority of the refugees went direct to London ... Those who had no money to pay their railway fare were provided

with free passes, and everything needful was done to ensure their comfort. There were a few cases of sickness to deal with. Lodgings were found for these doubly unfortunate ones in the town ... The arrangements were carried out most promptly, and by three o'clock the last of the refugees had been provided for.[23]

All concerned with the operation at Southampton docks and beyond were delighted by its smoothness, especially the local Jewish community which was grateful for the help and support provided by the Mayor of the town.[24] Even the Jewish refugees from the *Cheshire* were enlisted to express their gratitude in the *Jewish Chronicle* asking to be allowed

to thank most heartily the Committee of the Poor Jews' Shelter, and also the Committee of the Jewish Board of Guardians, for their kindness towards us Transvaal refugees. Really words cannot be sufficiently expressed for the attention and care they have given on our behalf.[25]

Yet for all the genuine sentiments expressed by the refugees who had experienced only coldness and antipathy from so many for so long, it remained that the Jewish authorities nationally and locally were determined that their stay in Britain was comfortable but essentially short-lived. Indeed, in the period from the early 1880s through to 1905, when the Aliens Act was passed, some 50,000 Jews were moved on by the Jewish Board of Guardians to other countries of emigration or back to their homeland. Not all those repatriated to eastern Europe were unwilling victims. In 1905 the Jewish Board of Guardians reported 'that where applicants press to be returned to parts of Russia and Poland where uninterrupted Railway communications exist, and good cause is shown, the Board may assist them to return'.[26] Others, however, were pressurised to return: the policy in general was designed to keep the number of Jewish 'aliens' in Britain as low as possible. By such management, the Anglo-Jewish establishment hoped to avoid the risk of domestic antisemitism and also the danger of state intervention in the form of immigration control undermining their own authority. Such fears were not misplaced and alien immigration restriction was part of the Conservative Party's programme after the 1900 general election.[27]

A Royal Commission on Alien Immigration was set up following increased pressure for control, most notably in the East End of London. It was there that the anti-alien/antisemitic British Brothers' League was formed in 1901. The League engaged in a mixture of violent street activities and lobbying in Westminster. There was, however, stiff opposition to control from those who deeply valued the liberal tradition of free movements of people. Moreover, the symbolic as well as the practical importance of granting political and religious asylum for those persecuted abroad remained, as Bernard Porter states, 'an inviolate feature of Britain's national life'. To remove it or modify it on a permanent basis was to be no easy task. This was illustrated in 1904 when an Aliens Bill was presented to Parliament and its clauses subject to what one historian has referred to as an 'onslaught'.[28]

Jewish refugees from South Africa arriving in Southampton on the *Cheshire*, February 1900, as sketched by the *Jewish Chronicle*, 9 February 1900.

As part of the campaign against the Bill, the London Committee of Deputies of British Jews (the representative body of British Jewry dealing with the state) organised a meeting in April 1904. One of the major objections raised had resonance for the rest of the century – the problem of refugees proving their status through legal documentation. It is frequently the case that refugees are forced to escape regimes where official corruption is normal. Those seeking asylum have had many or all their rights taken away from them, and therefore their papers are often of a dubious nature or may have been destroyed or withheld. As was stated by the London Committee:

Clause 1 of the Bill empowers the Secretary of State to make regulations providing for the production by the Aliens of such proofs of character and antecedents as may be prescribed, and in default of such proofs the Alien may be refused admission. Should the regulations so made entail the production of an official certificate of character or a passport, they will be certain to constitute a great hardship in the case of Russian, Polish, and Roumanian Jews. At their best, Police Certificates of character in Russia are a farce. In many cases they can be purchased for about 10 roubles... The Passport is granted on the production of the certificate of character and the total cost averages (with moderate bribes) about £3 10s. The likelihood of the Jews getting a certificate of character and a passport in Russia is entirely problematical... Once make these documents essential, and their chance of escape merely depends on the mood of the series of functionaries through whom their application passes, and at best will simply depend on the extent of the rapacity of such officials.[29]

Surprised at the opposition to the Aliens Bill, the Conservatives withdrew it in July 1904 only to announce in the next session of Parliament in February 1905 that legislation in this area was intended. The Marquess of Winchester, outlining the Conservative Party programme, attempted to justify the move historically:

It may strike some noble Lords who can trace their lineage back to the Landing of William the Conqueror as somewhat strange to find that they have been regarded by that Commission as interloping aliens, for I find on the first page – 'The alien immigrant is no newcomer to this country. Following the Norman Conquest many foreigners sought a home here'.

Nevertheless ..., those of us who are satisfied that our lineage carries us back to that far-off day, will derive some comfort from finding that we are not described as either criminal or undesirable. Those who represent constituencies in this country which are pressed in the fields of the lower forms of industry, find that the competition of alien immigrants does affect them very seriously. In districts in the East End of London, and in some of our larger cities, the alien immigrant is found in large and ever-increasing numbers. I know that this is a question which raises the issue ... as to who are desirable immigrants and who are not. The proposals of the Government will be limited to that class of aliens who are refused admission into the United States because they are paupers, and are landed on the first piece of land at which the ship touches, and that is in all probability this country. We have the evidence of police magistrates that the criminal alien is a thoroughly undesirable person ...[30]

But the problem in deciding who was and who was not deserving of entry, even in the much watered-down version of the 1904 Bill, would not go away. Many Liberals feared that the minor nuisance caused by a few criminal aliens and aliens involved in prostitution was not enough to warrant ending unconditional asylum.[31] Major Seely represented the same party as the Marquess of Winchester. Nevertheless, Seely, MP for the Isle of Wight, disliked the Aliens Bill because of his firm commitment to free trade which he 'believed ... to be the ark of the covenant and the foundation of English prosperity and power'.[32] His objections were articulated in the House of Commons in May 1905:

This Bill proposes to keep out a Jew when he is poor, and to admit a Jew when he is rich ... The undesirable is to be excluded if he cannot show that he is in possession of, or is in a position to obtain, a decent way of supporting himself. I do not wish to keep out Jews or anybody, provided they are neither criminal nor diseased. But if you are going to keep out the one or the other, I am not sure that it would not be wiser to keep out the rich Jew and admit the poor Jew ... If hon. Members will look at the part in regard to aliens relieved they will see that the number is so trivial as to make it obvious that we should not sacrifice the great principle of asylum for so small a matter ... It will do no real good for the purpose for which it is intended, but it will gravely injure the shipping interest... If once we admit the principle of the Bill, we abandon one of the highest principles on which the State has been built up. I will never abandon it... [T]he evils which exist are not concerned alone with alien immigration. The evils are particularly concerned with sweating, long hours, and crowded houses in the East End. These cannot be dealt with by the present measure.[33]

Opponents of the Bill like Seely argued that it was not only misguided but also designed to hide the lack of an alternative strategy to appeal to the mass electorate. Rather than a genuine attempt to deal with the real problems of areas such as the East End, they saw it as a political ploy with a General Election looming. In Liberal-dominated Southampton, the importance of the shipping trade meant that 'Everyone who desires that Southampton should flourish should remain steadfast and true to the principles of Free Trade. Protection means ruin'.[34] It followed that there would also be opposition to the Aliens Bill. In April 1905 a local Liberal Association discussed the implications of the proposed legislation:

They must be careful how they went to the country, and with what battle cries. Already 'red herrings' were being drawn across the track by the Tories ... Why, they were getting battle cries ready. There was the Aliens Bill.

One councillor provided a local angle to discredit further the need for control:

They had aliens there in Southampton. He did not know what they had charged them in the way of rates and taxes, but he had known some who had paid these for thirty years, and would they still be called aliens? Let them look around that town and see some of them: they were very desirable citizens.

Providing a more universal perspective he added to applause that 'As Liberals they had always prided themselves upon the fact that they loved those who loved their fellow citizens, and God forbid that they should refuse help to such a man as that in distress'.[35]

The Conservative Party was, however, grimly determined to pass an Aliens Act, even if its clauses were less draconian than was originally intended. On 11 August 1905 it received Royal assent. Compared to the UK legislation that is in place as the twentieth century draws to a close, the Aliens Act of 1905 was a weak measure with only a limited state apparatus to implement it. Moreover, the Liberals who were to administer the Act from January 1906 did so in a generally sympathetic way.[36] Nevertheless, the 1905 Aliens Act in its early years made a great impact on those aliens who were either refused entry or expelled through the order of the Home Secretary. Of equal importance was its symbolic value. A clause was added stating that

> in the case of an immigrant who proves that he is seeking admission to this country solely to avoid persecution or punishment on religious or political grounds or for an offence of a political character, or persecution, involving danger of imprisonment or danger to life or limb, on account of religious belief, leave to land shall not be refused on the ground merely of want of means or the probability of his becoming a charge on the rates.

This was achieved partly through the campaigning of the London Board of Deputies of British Jews, but the unquestioning adherence to the concept of free entry for refugees had been undermined. The clause was also vague and almost meaningless in legal terms. Much more explicit was the definition of an 'undesirable immigrant' who could be excluded:

> (a) if he cannot show that he has in his possession or is in a position to obtain the means to decently supporting himself and his dependants (if any); or
> (b) if he is a lunatic or an idiot, or owing to any disease or infirmity appears likely to become a charge upon the rates or otherwise a detriment to the public; or
> (c) if he has been sentenced in a foreign country with which there is an extradition treaty for a crime.[37]

The 1905 Aliens Act was designed to limit the number of poorer immigrants coming to Britain – in effect, east European Jews and a smaller number of Italians, Chinese and other 'undesirable' foreigners. Britain, however, was far from alone in instituting control. In January 1904 the *Jewish Chronicle* reported on similar moves and movements in the United States:

> As predicted ... the movement for further restriction of immigration ... has been inaugurated... The Anti-Immigration League ... did not wait for the regular session to introduce their measures but the two Senate bills referred to the Committee on immigration were offered during the special session called to ratify the American-Cuban treaty... [T]he first is to introduce the educational test eliminated from the bill approved last March. 'All persons over fifteen years of age and physically capable of reading, who cannot read the English language', are to be excluded to be deported to the country from which they came, at the expense of the steamship or railroad company which brought them...

The *Jewish Chronicle* commented that 'The test and the manner of applying it is to be criticised for want of elasticity, and of not allowing that larger discretion to the immigration officers, which is the feature of the anti-alien restrictions imposed in the British South African Colonies'. Internationally, immigration control was intensifying and cross-fertilising, with its first step to separate 'desirable' immigrants from all others.[38]

Yet in spite of these early attempts at legislation, the flow of immigrants from east to west and from south to north continued relentlessly. In 1907, a peak year, over one million immigrants passed through the Ellis Island immigration station in New York.[39] Britain was one of the main centres of transmigrancy for those seeking to reach the United States. Indeed, some opposed the aliens legislation on pure economic grounds – the London Board of Deputies of British Jews suggested that the transmigrants spent £1 million a year when passing through the country.[40] Southampton was a particular beneficiary of such trade, the scale of which was indicated by a report of the United States Consul in the city on those departing from the port. Apart from the local implications of such movements, however, the report showed the pressure on American officials to ensure that the potential emigrants were of a desirable nature:

> Very special attention is given to the overlooking and embarkation of the emigrants. The medical examination is attended, and such observation made as may be warranted by existing authority ... As the emigrants arrive at the dock station they are shown into an enclosed compartment in a dock shed 100 by 400 feet, well lighted and ventilated. Here the baggage is inspected, and labelled... One by one the emigrants are shown into the passage where the medical examination takes place, under the care and charge of the surgeon of the ship, with assistants. His examination is followed by that of the surgeon representing the English Board of Trade. This double examination is most thorough and complete... In the examination for trachoma the surgeon in charge makes a most painstaking study ... and in all cases where a doubt exists the emigrant is either rejected at once or made to stand aside for a second examination, and in nearly every case, ending with his rejection, on the ground of the actual presence of the disease, or a suspicion of it, they not knowingly take any chances ... With the present low fare the irruption of crowded sections of East London have contributed very heavily – note the number reported as 'Russians' – which were almost wholly of the Jewish type – eye troubles have been found in a largely increased ratio – one inspection taking forty cases out of the line and rejection following chiefly on suspicion.

The Consul, Colonel Swalm, provided emigration statistics from Southampton from 4 June to 6 August 1904. His list showed the global nature of population movements at the turn of the century, including Germans, Austrians (including Hungarians and Galicians), Danes, Russians, Swedes, Norwegians, Syrians as well as the 'English'. Of the total of 7,791 leaving for the USA (4,808 men, 1,638 women and 1,080 children), over half were Russians, most of whom were Jewish.[41] Swalm, as a local account related, was no great friend of the aliens:

> ...his tenure of the office at Southampton dates back only to April 1903 ... [He] holds decidedly strong views on the 'Alien' question, and his remarks on the subject would, probably, startle some of our politicians. In American parlance, he 'has no use for' the pauper immigrant.

Indicating the growing sympathy towards the move to control in Britain, the report put Swalm's views in a sympathetic light, adding that 'He has, no doubt, seen too much of the latter individual on the other side of the Atlantic, for it is certainly no lack of kindness or humanity which prompts the dislike – the qualities in question are the very keynote of the Colonel's character.'[42]

REFUGEES AND LOCAL SOCIETY

At the start of the twentieth century, roughly 4,000 European immigrants, mainly refugees, left Southampton every month to make a new life in the United States. Many others emigrated elsewhere. Such inflows and outflows from the town were bound to make an impact on local society. Indeed, the American and British health authorities were particularly concerned about the state of local lodging houses which dealt with the immigrants.[43] Albert Gibbs, who later became a shipbuilder in Southampton, recalled his childhood during the 1900s and the memories of one such establishment:

> There were ... brothers, Willie and Reggie Doling [and] their father kept the Immigrants' Home. Now the Immigrants' Home was a home that was used to accommodate the people that were coming from Middle Europe as immigrants to go to find a new life in America. Accommodation was very poor, they used to go to sleep on concrete floors with just the coats they came in. They always looked grubby and poor and normally the men had huge beards, I think there was a very big proportion of Jews among them, because they were mostly the people that were being exported from Europe, even in those days. And I used to go down below with the Doling brothers and stand looking at them and ... of course ... as a boy I didn't know what to think about it.[44]

Sam Smith (1908–1983), who was also born and brought up in Southampton, later became an internationally respected artist. He wrote of his childhood:

> Ours was a seaport town. Funnels of great ships dominated the town; and the first drawings I remember were of liners, with rows of wavy decks ... and bulbous funnels blowing out great clouds of scribble ... The sight of Cunarders and their sisters filled me with great pride, which must have spawned from the rather heady patriotism rampant at the time.

In later life Smith returned to the imagery of the big ships in Southampton, but employed a more critical perspective on their nature. He was particularly curious about the immigrants on board: the 'huddled masses yearning to breathe free' as he wrote on one of his most important works 'Bathers in Southampton Water' (1979). Here local bathers are disturbed by the wash of a passing steamer, 'bound for America, with First Class, Second Class, Third Class and STEERAGE PEOPLE'. In his notes, Smith added 'Down in the steerage are the real people'. It has been suggested, 'childhood experiences of the City were to have a lasting influence on his work'. The extensive but disguised presence in Southampton of those refugees travelling steerage en route for the *goldene medineh* (golden land) was a very important part of Sam

Smith's earliest memories, which, like Albert Gibbs, he mused over in later life.

For other local people, who depended on the shipping trade for their livelihood, the impact of the transmigrants was even more pronounced. Although it relates to the 1920s, the testimony of a Southampton man, 'John', who worked on board the Royal Mail ship *Arlanza*, indicates the appalling conditions endured by the many millions who travelled 'steerage' class before the First World War. The *Arlanza* was used to bring refrigerated meat and butter from Argentina back to Southampton. On its return, bunks were installed in the hold of the ship and seaweed-filled palliasses were provided for the immigrants unable to afford anything other than steerage class. Born in 1909, 'John' recalls his journey to Buenos Aires aged 18:

> I had the worst experience of my life ... They gave me a job in third class. God, you never seen anything like it in your life. It was terrible, terrible ... There were Poles, Russians, Germans and Czechs ... a lot of Jews... When they were sea sick ... we had to go down [the hold] with hoses and hose it down [there were no port holes for the immigrants] ... I thought what had I let myself in for here?... Some only had paper parcels ... They had nothing really... I've never seen anything like it and never smelt anything like it.

Such was the impact that he refused to do such work again.[45]

There was thus a remarkably fluid but significant presence in Southampton of Jewish refugees, some arriving in the port looking to settle in Britain and many more leaving Britain as transmigrants. The Farber family had a particular link to such movements. Jack Farber was born in Kovno in Lithuania and came to Manchester in 1887. Multi-lingual, Farber was ideally suited to run a travel business which he did in the heart of Manchester's Jewish immigrant quarter, Cheetham Hill. His daughter Sadie remembers the customers, mainly Jewish immigrants with no English, buying tickets to emigrate to South Africa, Canada, Australia and the United States. American fares were particularly cheap: 'steerage from about £5/£6, about £10 second class and £20 first class'. Much of their business was concentrated in ships leaving from Liverpool, but they also did trade in Southampton where the big liners such as the *Mauritania* and the *Lusitania* operated. The most infamous was the *Titanic*, which sailed from Southampton in 1912. Hidden from memory by the death of the rich and famous on board were the crew of the ship, mainly from Southampton, and also poorer immigrants travelling third class. Far fewer of the crew and the steerage passengers survived the disaster. Farber's dealt with many of these immigrants, Sadie having the painful task of finding out who had survived. The link of the *Titanic* to transmigrancy trade in Jewish refugees is further emphasised in the testimony of Albert Gibbs who recalls that 'Mrs Doling went away on the Titanic to carry out business on behalf of the [Immigrants'] Home and when the Titanic was sunk she was one of the fortunate ones to get into the lifeboat and come home again'. Most of those immigrants leaving for the new world would only stay a matter of nights in Southampton hotels and hostels before recommencing their journey. Nevertheless, they still managed to become part of local memory and identity. This constant flux, however, should not disguise the existence of settled if dynamic Jewish communities in the major urban settlements of Hampshire.[46]

The formal readmission of the Jews in England in the mid-seventeenth century led to settlements in London and then in the provinces. One of the first to be established outside London was in Portsmouth where the synagogue was founded in the 1740s. Jews came to the town because of the attractions of work linked to the port and particularly the town's growing naval presence. An established middle class emerged from its ranks during the nineteenth century, producing the first Anglo-Jewish women writers, the Moss sisters, and later the prominent historian and novelist, Katie Magnus. Although less significant with regards to British Jewry as a whole by the start of the twentieth century, the Portsmouth Jewish community was numerically at its largest, expanding rapidly from the 1880s with the east European influx. In 1902 'it was reported that the number of Jewish families had doubled since 1873, establishing a pattern of some 200 families that became the norm for the present century'.[47] At roughly 500 individuals, Portsmouth was the 12th largest out of 97 Jewish provisional communities in the United Kingdom. In 1850, with a population of 300 people, Portsmouth had the fourth largest provisional Jewish community when there were approximately 35,000 Jews in the country as a whole. By the eve of the First World War, however, and largely as a result of the refugees from the Russian Empire and Romania, the Jewish population of Britain had expanded to 300,000. The East End of London, with over 100,000 Jews, was the largest and most concentrated settlement area. Next came the large industrial cities of Manchester (25–35,000) and Leeds (15–20,000). Alongside these fast-developing centres were settlements in Glasgow, Birmingham, Liverpool, Dublin, Hull and Sunderland, each with more than 1,000 Jews and which, taken together, by 1900 dominated the demographic make-up of British Jewry.[48]

In the 1900s Portsmouth Jewry had a range of formal organisations, secular and religious, including a synagogue, Hebrew classes for children and benevolent societies (including one run by the Jewish ladies of Portsmouth). The benevolent societies reflected the existence of an established and wealthier Jewish elite as well as the presence of poorer brethren. That problems of poverty were increasing at the turn of the century was reflected in the establishment of the *Chevra Bikur Cholum* in 1897 to 'visit the sick and relieve the poor'. It was a dynamic community in terms of the numbers coming in but also with regard to the internal politics of those who had settled longer. Ethnic/religious minorities, even of refugee origin, are rarely homogeneous and Portsmouth Jewry was no exception in having schisms that led to the creation of rival synagogues in the 1760s, 1850s and 1890s. Class and wealth could at times further divide the community although a shared

Jewish identity at times provided cohesion. Secular Jewish matters also added to the complexity and diversity of the community.[49] The Portsmouth Zionist Society attempted to convince local people – Jewish and non-Jewish – that the solution to the persecution of the Jews abroad was to 'find a safe resting-place [Palestine] which they could call their own'. Such international Jewish solidarity was supplemented by a local and national sense of belonging in England. In 1904, Leopold Greenberg of the Jewish Colonial Trust was supported locally when he 'strongly advised every Jew in Portsmouth to vote against any Party candidate who was in favour of placing upon the Statute Book such legislation as had been prognosticated upon alien immigration'.[50]

The elasticity of Jewish population movements and the global nature of Jewish settlement was further illustrated by the family of Ian Mikardo, a prominent Labour Party politician whose parents settled in Portsmouth before the First World War. Mikardo's father, Morris, came from Kutno, near Lodz and settled in Britain during the Boer War. Morris's mother and sister also came to Britain whereas two other sisters settled in New York. Cousins and other family members stayed behind, later to perish in the Holocaust. A similar pattern was evident with Ian Mikardo's mother, Bluma, who came from a village in western Ukraine. She came to London to join an older brother whose wife had died. Ian Mikardo wrote of his father and his early days facing 'the perils of an unknown world' in the East End of London that:

> He didn't know a word of English, or indeed of any language other than Yiddish. The only schooling he had was in synagogue classes, where he was taught to read the Hebrew prayers and recite them by rote ... He couldn't read or write a word of even his own language, nor sign his name. The only skill he had was operating a sewing-machine.[51]

Unhappy with the poverty-induced misery of the East End, Morris saved up to travel steerage to New York, 'but he found the sweatshops were worse there than in London, and so he came back'. As Michael Gold put it in his brutal novel of Jewish tenement life in New York, *Jews Without Money*, 'America is so rich and fat, because it has eaten the tragedy of millions of immigrants'.[52] By now married, Morris hoped for economic security, and in 1907 an opportunity emerged to become a tailor in Portsmouth, then expanding as the naval race between Britain and Germany escalated.

Their son, Ian, was born a year later in the poorer Jewish area of Portsmouth, Portsea, adjacent to the harbour and dockyard:

> The spine running through Portsea is Queen Street, and it was there, and in the smaller streets on the south side of it, that the Jewish quarter developed, with its synagogue, its community centre and its kosher butcher and poulterer and fishmonger. The ghetto-like huddling-together of the immigrants in Queen Street and its environs was almost a carbon copy of that same phenomenon in the Commercial St. area of Spitalfields in East London, though in much smaller numbers and more thinly spread... Like the dockside areas of other great ports

it wasn't a very salubrious place for kids to be brought up in. The houses along that stretch all had cellar-kitchens which were invaded every night, and sometimes even visited in the day, by rats which were presumed to have come to us by some subterranean route under the dockyard wall.

Mikardo's testimony highlighted the economic marginality of east European Jewish life in Britain:

By the time I was old enough to know what was going on around me, my parents had got on a bit out of two wage-packets and had launched out for themselves in a little shop doing alterations and repairs to uniforms and other clothing, and selling outfitting requirements of sailors and marines; but at the beginning of their new life together they were very hard up. A couple of months after the marriage there wasn't enough money in the house to buy what was needed to celebrate the Jewish New Year properly, and Bluma, my mother, pawned her wedding-ring ... to buy a chicken and a bottle of kosher wine and the ingredients for baking a honey-cake and other delicacies...

Like many immigrants and refugees, the Mikardos were divided by language, with only the younger generation fluent in the adopted tongue. At first the family spoke Yiddish:

My grandmother, who did most of the running of the house because mother and father were both working, never acquired, to the day of her death, a single word of English... She had a special soft spot for me because I was her official interpreter in her dealings, such as shopping, with the world outside our front door. Gradually my parents began to learn English from contacts with their customers and their neighbours, but their vocabulary was limited, and sometimes the English and Yiddish were mingled in the same sentence...

Ian Mikardo throughout his political life identified with later refugee and immigrant groups attempting to make a life for themselves in Britain. In particular, he was a strong opponent of racism, drawing upon his own experiences to counteract prejudice:

When I went to school at the age of three I had only a few words of English, and that put me instantly at a disadvantage in relation to my classmates. Fifty-three years later, when I became a Member of Parliament for a constituency containing many Bangladeshi families whose young children had only a few words of English, and saw them harassed by having to study the usual range of school subjects whilst they were unfamiliar with the language of their teachers and their textbooks, I well understood what they were up against...

My memory still recalls that my first teacher was Mr Thomas ... a remote Jehovah-like object of fear, between his blackboard and his desk. He was a racist bully if ever there was one. He delighted in picking on, and ridiculing, the boys who 'couldn't speak properly'. Some of the kids followed his lead, in the way that children can be very cruel and hurtful to other children. Years later, after many other experiences of discrimination, the still painful memories of those childhood days helped me to think about and understand and hate antisemitism and all other forms of racism...

Mikardo, in spite of the poverty of his home and the hostility of some teachers, still managed to do well in his early education. The response to his success showed that even within a few years of settlement, there were times when Jews and non-Jews could join together in celebration of local achievement:

> [At the end of primary school] I was top of the pass-list [for Portsmouth Southern Secondary School for Boys]. In Omega Street School that created an all-time sensation: for the Head and the staff, if not for the boys, that was a bigger success than winning the Junior Schools Football Cup. In the local Jewish community, too, and especially among the new immigrants, I was hailed as something of a hero: they looked on me as carrying their banner, as lifting them up a step from their lowly place in the social scale.[53]

Outside Portsmouth, four other Jewish communities existed in Hampshire. Basingstoke was the smallest where individuals met for religious services in a local college. The Hebrew Congregation in Bournemouth was founded in 1905, forming the basis of what is now a large south coast Jewish settlement. Before the First World War, however, it was a small fledgling community with just 30 members. Although it was to fade away in the inter-war period, the small Jewish community in the garrison town of Aldershot had a population of 54 (excluding soldiers) in 1896. The growth of the town after the Crimean War provided openings for Jewish immigrants and others in much the same way as Portsmouth had done a century earlier. As the historian of the community puts it:

> It became apparent that the village of Aldershot could not supply the needs of the military population and there were soon attracted a few Jewish families of the humbler class ready and able to take advantage of the opportunity offered. Like most Jews living outside London at that time these were small retailers and artisans such as silversmiths and working jewellers.[54]

Southampton had an estimated Jewish population of 75 in 1850. The synagogue was founded in 1864 but unlike Portsmouth did not expand rapidly at the turn of the century. There was an absence of a large-scale east European settlement. In contrast to its south coast rival, Southampton did not offer the right economic opportunities for poorer Jews trying to scratch out a living through the classic Jewish immigrant trades of tailoring, the boot and shoe industry and furniture making. Nevertheless, the role of the settled community in removing poorer Jews was also responsible for its limited growth. Most members of the synagogue were petty traders, especially shopkeepers, without great wealth. In addition, there was a much smaller number of elite seatholders possessing large houses in the area such as Lady Eliot Yorke, Samuel Montagu (later Lord Swaythling) and Claude Montefiore. The relationship between the small shopkeepers and these wealthy individuals was not always congenial. The minister of the community in 1895 commented on the absence of the latter from the local synagogue and remarked that they could 'hardly be called

Southamptonians'. But an even greater gulf existed between these members of the Jewish aristocracy (the so-called 'Cousinhood') and the humble recent refugees from eastern Europe.[55]

The second Lord Swaythling was responsible for developing Townhill Park near Southampton, desiring a country estate to complement his father's hall at South Stoneham nearer the city centre. The memoirs of his son, Ivor Montagu, present a vivid picture of growing up in Townhill Park before the First World War. Montagu, who became a prominent member of the Communist Party of Great Britain, described the estate in Marxist terms, providing an evocative account of its social life:

> The class structure was clearly reflected in the geography: On the ground floor and the first floor U ['us', or the elite] to the north, less U to the south; the basement and the extra top floor at the extreme south end were definitely non-U... In autumn came the shooting parties. Lists of guests to stay would be made out, day-visitors arrived ready in cloth caps and tweed knee-breeches... At this time shoots for me meant going out at lunchtime with the ladies, traversing muddy ruts and helping the house-servants to cover trestle tables with linen, spread our waterproof sheets and unpack the hampers.[56]

Samuel Montagu, the prominent Liberal politician and Jewish philanthropist, had first settled in Hampshire in 1888, a year after founding the Federation of Minor Synagogues; an attempt to organise the small immigrant places of worship that had sprung up with the mass movement of Jewish refugees. Montagu wanted to help his poorer co-religionists but also insisted that they conform to a more 'acceptable' form of behaviour. His was a subtle form of anglicisation, meeting the newcomers half way. It was not in reality a relationship built on equality, but Samuel Montagu showed much more respect for the deep religiousity of the east European Jews than many of his fellow members of the Anglo-Jewish aristocracy. Although his interest was concentrated in national politics – Jewish and non-Jewish – his daughter, Lily Montagu, later wrote that at a local level:

> Through his interest in Hampshire, Samuel Montagu was persuaded to help in every form of local philanthropic effort ... [H]e supported schools, hospitals, and clubs of every description, and gave a small parish hall to his own village of Swaythling, leaving the residents to make what use of it as they desired.[57]

Samuel Montagu died in 1911 but his eldest son and his wife continued this local philanthropic tradition. In Netley, on the Hampshire coast, where the refugees on board the *Cheshire* were left to wait the night before arriving in Southampton, another member of the Jewish 'Cousinhood', Annie Rothschild, by marriage the Honourable Mrs Eliot Yorke, owned 'the charming property of Hamble Cliff, on Southampton Water ... a very original, picturesque domain ... revealing glimpses of the distant shore and the busy water-way'. Along with her sister, Lady Battersea, in 1885 she formed the Jewish Ladies' Society for Preventive and Rescue Work (later the

Jewish Association for the Protection of Women and Children). Mrs Eliot
Yorke was also concerned with general charitable work, especially in the
locality. As Lady Battersea put it:

> Amongst other things she has become a great authority on primary education,
> having had much experience as manager of elementary schools. She is a
> member of the Education Committee of the County Council for Hampshire, and
> for some time the only lady on the Council of the University College of
> Southampton ... She is a well-known personality in her neighbourhood, trotting
> about from morning until evening ... regardless of the toll of years, alert,
> unwearied, helpful, bright and humorous.[58]

The sisters' cousin, and fellow prominent member of the Jewish Association,
Claude Montefiore, shared her strong Hampshire connections. Montefiore
came from one of the longest established and prominent Jewish families in
Britain and was partly brought up in the family's country estate at Coldeast,
near Southampton. It was at a party there that Montefiore was introduced by
Mrs Eliot Yorke to a staff member of University College, Southampton, later
the University of Southampton. Subsequently, Claude Montefiore was its
president from 1913 to 1934, rescuing it after a very difficult period. As the
principal of the college wrote after Montefiore's death in 1938: 'Officially he
was President of the College, but he was far more than this ... his gift to the
College was something which cannot be estimated in monetary figures. His
very existence amongst us gave something to this academic community
which cannot be expressed in words.'[59]

Claude Montefiore held a deeply rooted pride in both his Jewishness and
Englishness. He spent the First World War 'in every way stimulating Jewish
patriotism and emphasizing the debt which the Jews owed to England'. His
son, Leonard, who was later to play a major role in Hampshire in helping
Jewish child survivors of the Holocaust, typified this local and national sense
of loyalty, becoming an officer in the 9th (Territorial) Battalion of his County
Regiment, the Hampshires. Leonard Montefiore's death in 1961 was deeply
mourned by his fellow soldiers:

> During the whole of the 1914–18 war we knew him as a kindly and generous
> 'Companion in Arms' and in the subsequent years as one of the most – if not
> *the* most – faithful adherent and supporter of the 9th Hants Old Comrades'
> Association.[60]

When the second Lord Swaythling died in 1927, it was noted that: 'During
the tennis and cricket weeks at Southampton his house was the headquarters
of the local teams. Nothing connected with Southampton and its
neighbourhood was outside his interest.' It must be stressed, however, that the
world of the majority of Hampshire's Jews was far removed from that of the
Montagus, Montefiores and Rothschilds. Yet their less prominent co-
religionists also managed to shape and to be shaped by the local environment,

such as Lewis Ehrenberg and his wife, east European immigrant-origin entrepreneurs from Portsea, who built a cinema in the Southampton suburb of St Denys. The *Southampton Times* reported its opening in 1914:

> The new picture palace, the 'Scala' ... is commodious and comfortable; an uninterrupted view of the screen being obtainable from all parts ... The star film for the first part of the week was an adaptation of Thomas Hardy's novel 'Tess of the D'Urbevilles', which, with its absorbing interest and variety of incident, proved much to the liking of the large number of picture-goers who visited the Scala upon the opening days ... Altogether the newest picture theatre in Southampton seems to have a prosperous future ahead of it.[61]

With a capacity of 550, the history of the 'Scala' was slightly less glamorous than the one predicted for it. Nevertheless, its role as a cheap and rather basic place of entertainment in the inter-war years is remembered affectionately, though with more than an air of realism:

> It was a very, very small place, [we] used to call it the flea pit or the big hutch ... The sort of films they used to show there were a lot of the H category films, you know, the Frankenstein, Dracula films ... the Mummy, that sort of thing.

The cinema closed down in 1940 as a result of general decline and then war disruption, but for its 26 years it had provided inexpensive if not always wholesome entertainment for thousands of local people. Unlike their upper-class co-religionists, little or nothing is known about the Ehrenbergs, but their obscurity should not undermine their significance as entrepreneurs of what was becoming a global industry and culture.[62]

Taken together, the overall size of the settled Jewish community in Southampton was probably between 50 and 100 although it is probably the case that thousands of refugees passed through or were present in the city at any one time. In spite of the local Jewish aristocracy's presence, it was not a wealthy community and in 1900 the Jewish minister, Reverend Holdinsky, was employed at £100 per annum. Money proved to be an ongoing problem in obtaining a suitable minister and in 1908 Holdinsky resigned and settled in San Antonio, Texas – yet another example of the global nature of Jewish settlement patterns in this period.[63] Indeed, there were a further five ministers in Southampton before the First World War; hardly surprising when consideration is given to their pay and responsibilities:

> To carry out all duties connected with the offices of Reader [in synagogue] and Shochet [responsible for the religious slaughter of animals to obtain kosher meat for the congregation] and to teach at the Sabbath School on Saturday. To attend at the butchers from 9 to 10 am the slaughter house when poultry have to be killed: to be ready to kill cattle whenever required by the butcher and to see that there is always a supply of kosher meat. To collect weekly the subscriptions of the small seat-holders and others monthly. To give in writing to the Secretary each month particulars of each birth, marriage and death.[64]

The Southampton Hebrew Congregation prided itself on its place in the local community but its emphatic desire to show rootedness betrayed an underlying insecurity. The Congregation's sense of loyalty, patriotism and gratitude to Britain was revealed in a letter sent to the Monarchy at the time of Queen Victoria's death:

> The members of the Jewish Community, in the County Borough of Southampton, most respectfully and sincerely offer their condolence in the severe loss, which, not only your Majesty, but the whole British Empire have sustained in the death of Her Late Majesty Queen Victoria. We cannot but remember with gratitude that it was ... in her reign that civil and religious liberty was granted the Jewish people, enabling them to fill high positions in the Ministry, on the Bench, and in the Municipalities.[65]

The Hebrew Congregation was a rather elite institution the membership laws and cost of seat-holding of which left it very difficult, as the President acknowledged in 1911, 'to make it possible [to attract] more members to a religious worship which he considered to be grandest in the world'. In the period before the First World War, the Congregation's relationship with poorer Jewish refugees passing through or settling in Southampton was at best ambivalent. A Jewish Poor Relief Fund was founded in 1876 and periodic appeals were launched for distressed Jews in foreign lands such as the £25 raised for the Jewish Russian Relief Fund in December 1905. In addition, smaller funds were often raised for needy Jewish strangers in Southampton but there were fears that such generosity might lead to an increased presence of poor Jews in the town. In 1895 the minister of the community complained that much of its resources were spent on 'the relief of casual poor, which being a seaport, we get comers from the four corners of the earth'. One particular group of immigrants with a Hampshire connection who posed a particular threat to the reputation of the wider Jewish community were young, unaccompanied Jewish women.[66]

The Jewish Association for the Protection of Women and Children was the first body in the world to concern itself with Jewish involvement in prostitution. By the 1890s concern was growing in the Jewish Association about organised prostitution and particularly the international trade in women known as 'white slavery'.[67] Such fears were confirmed at a special session of the Gentlemen's Committee of the Jewish Association in June 1896:

> The meeting was called to confer with Col. Golsmid [a prominent Jewish communal worker] who, at the request of the Committee, came to kindly give information regarding the traffic in girls to Buenos Aryes [*sic*] and to discuss with them as to the measures which might best be taken to stop the traffic at English ports. Col. Goldsmid ... confirmed the worst fears of the Committee as to the traffic to, and the houses of ill-fame at, Buenos Aryes being in the hands of Jews...[68]

In fact, most of those who got involved in prostitution were not hoodwinked by traffickers but instead regarded it as a way to survive in what was a very difficult world for single women. Put bluntly, prostitution offered more reward than the drudgery of domestic service or the sweatshops. Fears of the Jewish community that innocent young girls travelling alone from eastern Europe would be tricked into the trade and kidnapped to far away places such as South America were largely exaggerated. Nevertheless, a war was waged between Jewish campaigners such as the Reverend I. Singer and the traffickers. Southampton and Portsea were some of the key battlegrounds in the tragi-comedy as the forces of good literally chased the forces of evil, illustrated by the Gentlemen's Committee in October 1899:

> The Secretary reported upon several expeditions made to Southampton in pursuit of traffickers and laid stress upon the indispensability of establishing in that important port an active committee consisting of more than one member. He said that it had also come to his knowledge that girls were being drafted to Portsmouth, Portsea, Cardiff etc. and he pointed out the need of local Committees in these places. The Secretary further informed the Committee that ... he had found the Police of Southampton – as was evidently the case in Liverpool – most keen and anxious to assist him ... The Reverend I. Singer promised to confer with Sir Samuel Montagu regarding the possibility of forming a Committee at Southampton.[69]

The different social worlds of British Jewry and the immigrants from eastern Europe were exposed in other references to Southampton in the Jewish Association's discussions. The two social groups – one reserved and 'English' and the other from the vibrant culture of Yiddishkeit – were often quite simply unable to communicate with one another:

> The Hon. Secretary reported that he had lately attended at Southampton a meeting of the local branch of the Jewish Association ... Its Committee there had come to the conclusion that they could not undertake work similar to ours owing to the difficulty of language, but they would gladly render to this Association any assistance in their power. The Hon. Secretary had informed them that it was the intention of this Committee to employ their own agent at Southampton in that case the 2 agents would become mutually useful in meeting a number of boats arriving or departing at the same time.[70]

Close monitoring of women deemed to be at risk was undertaken. On 4 October 1900, the Jewish Association reported on three girls who

> arrived at the Great Central Station en route for Southampton. Sternheim [the Jewish Association's agent] had difficulty in obtaining their address in Southampton. Upon inquiries being made at the address given, in Southampton, it was found to be satisfactory.

Whether the girls involved welcomed such attention is unclear, but as far as the British Jewish establishment was concerned, such undesirable behaviour, which brought with it the possibility of besmirching the good name of all Jews, had to be quashed at all costs.[71]

Soon the role as agent for the Jewish Association in Southampton was filled exclusively by ministers of the Hebrew Congregation in what was a separate paid activity. Indeed, in 1912, the Congregation refused to increase the pay of the minister, Mr Brown, because 'he earned a considerable fee from the "White Slave Traffic" clerkship'.[72] Looking after vulnerable Jewish refugees using the port of Southampton was to be very much part of the minister's duties until the outbreak of the Second World War. Otherwise, for the large part, the settled, respectable members of the Southampton Hebrew Congregation led very separate lives from those desperate Jewish refugees using the port to start afresh. The Jews of the region identified strongly with their locality even if there was enough evidence of local antipathy to undermine a feeling of being fully 'at home'. They were therefore uneasy about poorer Jews settling in the region although, ironically, some of its communal income, as with the Southampton anti-white slavery work, came from looking after those who arrived at their door. Within the community, more recent settlers were marginal, as was illustrated in 1914 when one of its many ministers was sacked for financial misappropriation. One member tried, unsuccessfully, to defend the minister by appealing to those who were 'foreigners of the same blood'. Insecurity was perhaps less pronounced for the Jewish aristocracy, comfortable in their income and to a large extent at ease with their place in the local world. Ivor Montagu, writing 50 years after leaving the county, could state that:

> I suppose I am, strictly, a Londoner, being Kensington-born and brought up in the Gardens, like Peter Pan. But from that time on so much of my growing up was centred on Townhill, first holidays but then weekends as well, that all my local patriotism is coloured by Hampshire and Southampton.

It remains, however, that a sense of local belonging, including for the elite, was muted by the articulation of antisemitism. As a young child, Montagu was aware of those, like Hilaire Belloc, who attacked his father on grounds of race, refusing to accept that it was possible to be English and Jewish:

> Lord Swaythling, whom the people knew,
> And loved, as Samuel Montagu,
> Is known unto the fiends of hell
> As Mr. Moses Samuel.

Yet even for those whose stay in Hampshire was more transient – as with those on board the *Cheshire* or the transmigrants in the port of Southampton awaiting their steerage passage to a new life in the USA – the county had deep significance. It acted as a point of departure for refugees desperately looking to find a new home and permanent security. In turn, these refugees and their families, whether temporary or permanent settlers, shaped local identities, memories and ideas about 'place'. The war, however, was to change the pattern and scale of the refugee problem for the rest of the century, making the free movement of the persecuted to Britain and its localities a thing of the past. The undermining of asylum in the years before 1914 proved momentous.[73]

2
Refugees and the First World War

The First World War was a watershed in the age of modernity, marking not only the power of new technology to facilitate mass death and destruction – over ten million people were killed – but also a new balance of power within and outside Europe. The war itself and its immediate aftermath created millions of refugees and displaced people – 9.5 million in Europe alone in the mid-1920s, according to one estimate. Refugees, already a growing problem before the conflict, became a permanent and ever-increasing feature of the twentieth-century world. In addition, groups previously marginalised and discriminated against such as Jews in eastern Europe and Armenians in the Turkish Empire were subject to even more murderous attacks (genocidal in the latter case) during and after the conflict.[1]

The problem of refugees had grown so much that it could no longer be adequately dealt with by private agencies or even by individual nation-states. Although rarely at the forefront of policy and more often than not treated as an irritant or a nuisance, refugees were now part of international politics and diplomacy. The problem of refugees was aggravated by the coincident implementation and intensification of stringent immigration controls. Countries such as the United States which before the war had only started to dabble in restrictionism became grimly determined to keep out unwanted foreigners. Refugees, even if deemed worthy of sympathy, were classified and treated as aliens and therefore as fundamentally undesirable. Traditions of asylum, even if adhered to in state rhetoric, became next to meaningless in practice. It is thus no coincidence that France, the European country with the most generous policy towards refugees in the 1920s, was unusual in its positive welcoming of foreign workers (although there was a clear preference for the right 'racial' type of immigrant). The French state saw such policies as a way to make good shortages in the labour supply and to reverse its general decline in population and shortage of suitable (particularly male) workers.[2]

In contrast, Britain, a country ironically with high self-esteem in its treatment of refugees, had a policy of almost total alien exclusion after 1918.[3]

Nevertheless, during the First World War British responses to refugees and aliens still retained an element of flexibility – even if state and public revealed themselves capable of intense intolerance and sometimes violence. The variation in responses was revealed clearly with the contrasting fortunes of Belgians and Germans whose treatment, at least initially, was in inverse proportion.

ANTI-ALIENISM IN THE FIRST WORLD WAR

On 5 August 1914, just 24 hours after Britain declared war on Germany, an Aliens Restrictions Bill was rushed through Parliament and became law the same day, unlike the agonising and hesitant movement toward control in the 1900s. It is true one Member of Parliament, Sir William Byles, warned 'that by this measure we are putting a very dangerous power into the hands of the Home Secretary'. Byles also prophetically wondered how long these powers would remain in force. His, however, was an isolated voice in the House of Commons and there were no amendments to qualify and humanise the proposed legislation: the Home Secretary was given total control over all aliens, including those that might be expected to be wholly sympathetic to the British cause. McKenna, the Liberal Home Secretary, stated that it was the object of the Bill 'to draw a distinction between alien friends and alien enemies', but, as Byles pointed out, 'we may not always have the present Minister dealing with it'.[4] Indeed, the new Act, although an emergency measure, was the foundation of more permanent legislation after the war and was therefore influential in refugee policy for many decades to come. The Aliens Restriction Act, 1914, gave the right to restrict the entry of aliens; required them 'to reside and remain within certain places'; imposed registration provisions; enabled deportation of aliens; and, revealing the absolute control on alien freedom that could now be exercised by the British state, allowed for measures 'for any other matters which appear necessary or expedient with a view to the safety of the realm'.[5]

As Hampshire was a 'protected' area under this Act, those of German origin were particularly vulnerable to the impact of the new legislation. The ports of Southampton and Portsmouth, with their consular and military connections, were closely involved in the issue of alien registration in the first days of the war. US Consular officials in Britain, as in Southampton, assumed the protection of German subjects,[6] but such aliens were still immensely vulnerable. In Portsmouth three-quarters of the local German community had been displaced as early as mid-August 1914.[7] Settled family and communal structures had overnight been destroyed by a state measure. In the House of Commons, one Member pointed out the unease felt by those with a German background:

> As one acquainted with many German subjects, some of whom have been resident in this country for many years, and are much more British in sentiment

than German, I should like some assuring words from the Home Secretary that some regard will be had for those persons. There is a very great deal of apprehension amongst such persons at the present time...

McKenna replied that:

Alien enemies against whom there is no reason whatever to suppose that they are secretly engaged in operations against this country will be subjected to nothing further than registration and the provision that they may not live in the prohibited areas.[8]

The Home Secretary's soothing comments did little to diminish the heartache caused even by this 'mild' introductory state measure to those whose identity was now tied to the locality. The distress caused was graphically illustrated in a court case involving an individual long-based in Portsmouth of German origin turned into an internal menace by the Aliens Restriction Act. Frederick William Herman Lampe, a commission agent of Southsea with German nationality, was charged with contravening the Order by residing in a prohibited area without having a permit to do so. Aged 47, he had been born in Hanover but had lived in England almost all his life, serving in the Berkshire Volunteers. In his defence it was stated that:

Having lived in the country for so many years he had regarded himself as an Englishman, and did not think the order applied to him. The accused could not speak a word of German, and he had never been in Germany since being brought over to England when three years old. He had no German tendencies, and considered himself an Englishman.

In spite of this information, it was reported that 'The Magistrates considered the charge a serious one' and he was given a prison sentence.[9]

That the defence of Lampe was based on his absence of 'German tendencies' indicated the Germanophobia engulfing state and society in Britain during the first months of the conflict. Indeed, popular and official hatred proved to be mutually reinforcing, especially when sections of the public turned violent. The most intensive anti-German riots occurred in 1915 in many towns across Britain. There was an indication of what was to come as early as August 1914 in Portsmouth.[10] The shop of a naturalised Russian was attacked by a crowd who believed its owner to be a German spy, showing how xenophobia knew no bounds.[11]

The measures taken by Home Secretary McKenna at the start of the war, which he hoped would avoid the implementation of more drastic legislation, were used to expel and intern the majority of Germans in Britain by the end of it. Of the 70–75,000 classified as enemy aliens, roughly 32,000 men were interned (including 1,000 in the hastily-transformed Southampton Ice Rink) with a further 20,000 'repatriated'. By November 1914, over 12,000 aliens had been interned, but the pressure for stronger measures within the government, and perhaps even more strongly outside it, continued to grow.

The historian of enemy alien internment during the First World War, J. C. Bird, has commented that 'the militant hardliners in parliament remained a relatively small minority'.[12] In this respect, Hampshire was unusual and disproportionate in containing two of the most virulent anti-German MPs, Brigadier-General Henry Page Croft (Christchurch) and Lord Charles Beresford (Portsmouth). Both men had strong military backgrounds (Beresford was a former admiral) reflecting that of the county as a whole and injecting into the national and local debate a fierce anti-German xenophobia current in large sections of the armed forces.

In 1917 Croft formed the National Party, made up initially of seven right-wing Conservative MPs who demanded protectionism, strong empire, ultra-patriotism, national unity and anti-socialism. All of these were laced with a heavy dose of anti-alienism informed particularly with an animus against German Jews. Hampshire MPs and Lords were over-represented in the National Party, almost all with military backgrounds. One of the other seven MPs was Douglas Carnegie, a former Lieutenant-Colonel and Member for Winchester which contained a large army garrison.[13] Beresford, in particular, was obsessed with the possibility of German enemy aliens becoming military spies. He believed that naval losses of ships coming out of Portsmouth could be explained by the presence of Germans interned on a ship outside the port. Beresford spent the war informing the House of Commons of any Germans resident or even passing through the Hampshire region. His position was clear from the early months of the war: all aliens, even lowly German hairdressers and waiters, 'should be arrested and interned'. This extended even to naturalised Germans: 'The best way is to remove them all, and have them secured .... I do not think that naturalisation can change a man's nature.'[14]

Beresford's language was far more restrained than the hysterical, but influential, journalist and politician Horatio Bottomley, who proclaimed in 1915 that 'You cannot naturalise an unnatural abortion, a hellish freak. But you can exterminate him.' Beresford, although calling for the removal of liberty for all Germans, believed himself to be following the most liberal of motives: 'My earnest and honest belief is this: that you should lock up your alien enemies during this war and not persecute them in any way, and not in any way be ungenerous to them'. He also warned that firm action by the government was necessary to avoid 'people taking these things into their own hands'. Nevertheless, Beresford, like Bottomley, had no room for any possible ambiguity: 'The good German or the good Englishman always remains a German or an Englishman, whether naturalised or not'. The additional problem for Germans in Britain was that once war had been declared, the very possibility of a 'good German' began to disappear. When stories of German atrocities committed against the Belgian people grew in intensity during the autumn months of 1914, the process of demonisation intensified. In turn, this became a justification for further measures against enemy aliens, a process that Beresford was happy to be part of:

I have no personal enmity against them, but I do think that they are the most dangerous people you have got and no hon. Member can deny that after what we have seen taking place in Belgium, and particularly in Antwerp...[15]

By the end of the war, the once prospering German communities of Britain had all but been destroyed. This was reflected in Hampshire as much as any other British county. The 1911 census recorded 877 Hampshire residents born in Germany. The 1921 census showed that their number had 'now reduced to 228'. It commented on the noticeable decline but gave no indication that it was the result of a concerted effort by state and public to erase the German presence.[16] The census also recorded the growth of the Belgian born population from 113 in 1911 to 193 in 1921. Colin Holmes, the foremost historian of immigration in British history, has commented that by studying the history of Belgians 'and incorporating existing studies of other minorities in Britain during the Great War, an interesting comparative study of immigrants and refugees in a wartime context could begin to emerge'. Such an approach is essential with the Belgians, some quarter of a million of whom came to Britain as refugees.[17]

THE ARRIVAL OF BELGIAN REFUGEES

The Belgian refugees 'were all things to all men, not so much flesh-and-blood individuals as multi-faceted symbols of Britain's cause'. To understand why at least initially the Belgians received such a warm and enthusiastic welcome throughout British society is also to fathom the sheer hatred generated against the Germans. The construction of 'Brave Little Belgium' could only be achieved with the parallel belief in the 'evil Hun'. The arbitrary construction of aliens/refugees in Britain as either devils or angels was illustrated at the local level with the case of a 45-year-old caterer in Portsmouth, Charles Hessel. He was charged on remand under the Aliens Restriction Act in September 1914 of residing in Portsmouth without a permit. Hessel had registered as a Belgian but it emerged that he was born in Germany when his Belgian parents had been touring the country. He was brought up in Belgium and his three brothers were serving in the Belgian army. In spite of this ephemeral and accidental connection to Germany, the unfortunate Hessel was imprisoned in Portsmouth. The anxiety in local reporting of this case – 'Belgian or German?' – highlights the manicheism that typified the mood at the start of the war. Alleged German atrocities in Belgium, including some stories later totally discredited, were used as justification by politicians such as Beresford for harsh measures on Germans in Britain. Equally, public and state sympathy for the Belgian refugees were employed as part of the moral war against Germany. The language and emotional 'appeal to the heart' was unrestrained. In Manchester, a local Belgian Relief Fund was established requesting '"new and cast-off clothes" to the whole country which has innocently had to suffer more than words can describe'. It appealed on behalf of 'women who have had ears and other parts of their bodies horribly MUTILATED' and 'babies who have had hands and arms slashed off'.[18]

At a local level, the ten-year-old Ivor Montagu, in his family's estate in Townhill Park, Southampton, recalled the impact of such propaganda:

> I am sure that, at the outset, I did not doubt the current myths about the war ... We had come to the aid of 'brave little Belgium'. That much was clear. Had not [Prime Minister] Mr Asquith said right at the beginning at the Guildhall: 'We shall not sheathe the sword until Belgium has recovered all, and more than all, that she has sacrificed'? I knew all about the deeds of the Hun. My father had passed me the Parliamentary papers on German atrocities in Belgium ...

Yet underneath some of the excesses in the rhetorical reporting of German atrocities was a real basis of terror from which the Belgians had fled. John Horne and Alan Kramer estimate that 'Overall, about 5,500 civilians were deliberately killed by the German army in Belgium in 1914'. In addition to these cold-blooded executions was 'the destruction of towns and buildings of great historic and emotional significance'. These actions led to a mass influx of refugees into cities such as Antwerp and Ostend. Over a million people left Belgium, nearly one-sixth of the population. Initially, half went to Holland and others to Britain and France. In January 1915, Herbert Samuel, the President of the Local Government Board, announced that some 4,000 to 5,000 Belgian refugees a week from Holland were being allowed to come to Britain to remove the strain on Dutch resources. This led to a peak of over 250,000 Belgian refugees in Britain. By the end of 1916 the number had fallen to 160,000 as many refugees returned to the continent or enlisted in the allied forces.

In spite of the huge numbers involved, the Belgian refugees in Britain were not typical of the pre-war population of the country. The four predominantly Flemish, non-French speaking provinces of Antwerp, East Flanders, West Flanders and Limberg accounted for two-thirds of the refugees but only 43.5 per cent of the total Belgian population. The Walloon provinces, according to a contemporary statistician, 'were even more strikingly under-represented'. Moreover, 'among the refugees the urban element was much greater than in Belgium as a whole. Two towns, Antwerp and Ostend, with less than one-sixteenth of the total population of Belgium, furnished one-third of the refugees'. Agricultural workers were under-represented whereas professionals came to Britain in much higher proportions.

The Belgian refugee movement was supported, if somewhat hesitantly, by the British government, in the guilt-ridden atmosphere after the guarantee of Belgian neutrality. In an unprecedented move, Herbert Samuel announced to the House of Commons in September 1914 a general policy of 'state hospitality' to the Belgian refugees:

> In answer to inquiries from the Belgian Government, His Majesty's Government have offered to the victims of the War the hospitality of the British

nation. Arrangements have been made for their transport and for their temporary accommodation at hostels in London.[19]

Samuel added that 'The War Refugees Committee, who have rendered very valuable service hitherto, have consented to co-operate with my Department in [the refugees'] reception and distribution'. He concluded by stressing that 'The Government trust that many individuals throughout the country will be ready to join in offering asylum here until conditions in Belgium enable the refugees to return'.

In reality, the relations between the War Refugees Board, which was formed on 24 August 1914 by leading (mainly female) upper class philanthropists to help the Belgians, and the Local Government Board were often strained. Much of the money for the support of the Belgian refugees came from the state, including the income of the War Refugees Committee, which helped maintain many of the local committees. The government hoped that the War Refugees Board would appear to be privately sponsored to forestall allegations that the state was supporting aliens ahead of its own citizens. As it stated in an official report published at the end of 1914, 'It is characteristic of our national ways that the duty of attending to the refugees should [be] undertaken by voluntary organisations'. It also did not want to discourage charitable donations and so created a screen of state funding for the War Refugee Board which was increasingly under the supervision and direction of civil servants. For the first time, the British state had both encouraged and sponsored a refugee movement and settlement.

For those involved in later refugee work, this was an important precedent. Given the size of the Belgian refugee influx, and the important and innovative role of both British state and populace in its welfare, it is surprising that there has been only one major study of the movement and even that largely limited to the relationship between state and private philanthropy. Its author, Peter Cahalan, argues that the neglect of one of the largest population movements in twentieth-century Britain has a range of explanations, including the marginalisation of Belgian history in general. But he also highlights how 'the refugees were an ephemeral part of the English scene: they disappeared as quickly as they had come'. His comment reinforces one of the major themes of this study: that the process of neglecting refugee presence is often due to their transitional nature. In this respect an unfortunate trend was set by John Hope Simpson in his pathbreaking and magisterial study, *The Refugee Problem* (1939) which excluded from consideration 'purely temporary movements, such as the exile of Belgians and Serbians during the Great War'. In the British case, many of those involved in refugee work in the inter-war period and beyond had their first experiences working with or on behalf of the Belgians. Moreover, the scale of help given to them by state and public was referred to by later campaigners attempting to revive more generous British traditions of hospitality towards refugees. More generally, the Belgians were an important part of life on the Home Front during the First World War and in subsequent memory. As Cahalan suggests, although historians have forgotten the Belgian refugees, it remains

> that in 1914 they were the objects of vast interest in England... The Belgians indeed crystallised many English responses to the war. They were an outward and visible sign of the complex chain of cause and effect which had led Britain into the struggle.[20]

The public concern about the Belgians was matched by practical aid. The numbers of refugees were so great, and their distribution around Britain so widespread, that few would have had no contact with them during the war. At a peak of involvement, for example, 'the existence of over 2,500 [refugee committees] in England, Wales and the Channel Islands was officially known, and it is believed that there were many more'. In the county of Northamptonshire alone, there were at least 303 committees. Their number declined as the war progressed, mainly as a result of the refugees' growing concentration in large cities and away from the countryside where the chances of employment were limited. By 1916, of roughly 160,000 refugees for whom statistics existed, some 65,000 were concentrated in the London area. In Warwickshire, of the 6,000 in the county, 3,800 were in Birmingham and a further 900 in Coventry. The decreasing number of committees also reflected the difficulty in maintaining enthusiasm for such work when the popularity of the Belgians decreased. Nevertheless, Ivor Montagu's memoirs indicate how the coming of the Belgian refugees in autumn 1914 for many in his Hampshire neighbourhood was their initial direct contact to the reality of the conflict:

> Very soon [after the start of the war] changes came into the pattern of our lives at Townhill. First arrived a family of refugees from Belgium. The mother was plump. There was a plump daughter too, 'Boucky', and her two soldier brothers, Pierre and Albert, who came and went as their service alternated with leave. The father, Monsieur le Commandant Cartuyvels du Collaert, was wounded and sat in a wheel-chair ... [Other] big houses in the neighbourhood became adapted for the wounded; Belgian to start with, then our own.

Thereafter, the prominence of the Belgians in the national imagination declined. But by examining the responses at a local level the more complex nature of individual memory and the First World War can be explored within which the place of the Belgians was prominent well beyond 1914. Colin Holmes has suggested that 'A good deal of local activity has been passed over by Cahalan, the recovery of which would constitute a valuable addition to the history of their exile'. The example of Hampshire is an important case study in this respect, not just in terms of rescuing a strand of Belgian history, but also in showing the place of refugees in British localities rarely associated with such movements.[21]

The coastal zones of Hampshire, including the major urban concentrations of Southampton and Portsmouth, were not totally free to allow the settlement of Belgian refugees as they were partially prohibited areas. It is not surprising, therefore, that the numbers present in the county in 1916 were as little as 1,500, or roughly one per cent of the Belgian refugee population in Britain. Excluding London, Scotland and Wales, this was only the 17th largest county concentration in Britain. Even so, many inland Hampshire towns and villages were prominent in the support and welcome they offered to those fleeing German military aggression.

The symbolic importance of the Belgian refugees was clear in contemporary reports relating to their initial welcome. The positive reception given to the Belgians as part of a wider, guilt-ridden moral battle against the Germans was revealed in a public meeting in Winchester during October 1914. The Archdeacon of the town stated to applause that

> within his memory, there was no question that had touched the hearts of the people, not only of England and Europe, but people all over the world, as had the question of Belgium... We had pledged our word to defend Belgium – we swore ... to restore Belgium, to reinstate the unhappy people in their beautiful country once more. It never had been the tradition of the British race ... to regard debts of honour as mere 'scraps of paper' ... Every motive of honour was called out, and every motive of chivalry, too.

Having outlined the emotional case for support, the Archdeacon moved onto practical ways in which local people could become involved in helping the refugees, 'In the first place, they intended, did they not, to give a home to these homeless people'. His comments were reinforced by the contribution at the meeting by another leading person within the Winchester community, Mr M. Rendall, the Headmaster of Winchester College, who argued that:

> We were bound to do all we could for these poor, desolate and homeless refugees, who threw themselves on our mercy ... It was not London only, it was not only Leeds which had taken six thousand of these refugees, but it was for every town to do its part, and especially in the ancient capital of England [Winchester], where they found a beauty much their own.[22]

In the small town of Alresford the same message was repeated in a public meeting, even if the scale of refugee settlement there was much smaller though more typical of the county as a whole. A rather desperate attempt was made to construct a history of Belgium as the bravest of nations even if in reality there had been little military resistance to the German invasion. The Chairman quoted Julius Caesar:

> 'that of all the tribes of Gaul, the Belgians were the bravest' was true today. Had it not been for them now the Germans would have marched on Paris and our country might have suffered such horrors as had been committed in Belgium. Were the people of Alresford going to stand by now and say nothing? No. Other towns in Hampshire were doing something. Winchester had one hundred refugees and were expecting an additional 56 while Alton was sheltering 40. Indeed almost every town and village was doing something ... Alresford could ... take two families.[23]

In these early months, both the Belgian refugees and the British were eager to contribute to a mutually-reinforcing mythology which avoided mention of difficulties or tensions between host and newcomer or, indeed, any reference to past difficulties between the two nations which, as with the issue of Belgian atrocities in the Congo, had caused diplomatic friction and general unease. The Belgian refugees themselves were capable of constructing the British people in the most extravagant of language as the source of all good. A wounded Belgian soldier, Professor Edmund de Somville, recuperating in a Winchester hospital, penned a poem to express his gratitude:

O dear and kindful British land
You stretch to us your heart and hand
Your daughters cover us with crowns
Thus welcomed are we in your towns.

Each nurse and sister is a mother
A mother – as there is no other
Who heals our wounds with love and smile
The pains we feel are not worth while.

Each ward to us a palace is
Whose walls respectfully we kiss.
Where Majors, Colonels, Generals too –
As high nobilities also do –

Congratulate us every day
'You fought as heroes! We dare say:
Brave Belgians, you have saved us all',
'You bravest Gauls! as we you call.'[24]

In Gosport, a crowd of about 3,000 turned up late in the evening to welcome the 60 Belgian refugees invited by the quickly assembled local refugee committee:

> Most of the people assembled appeared at a loss to know whether to cheer or sympathise with the outcasts. But the feelings of all were expressed by one on-looker, who shouted 'We are proud of you'. A hot supper ... and ... comfortable quarters [were] some little mark of the recognition of the duty owing to brave little Belgium.[25]

But as Cahalan has suggested, 'Mythology had to face certain grainy realities', the most blatant of which was that 'the heroic exiles of the speechmakers' fancy often shrank alarmingly in stature when encountered in real life'. Although sentimental sympathy was the most frequent public articulation with regard to the plight of the Belgians, in practice, ambivalence marked both state responses and everyday relations to this massive refugee movement. Revealing a not untypical patronising racism, Lady Battersea wrote in her journal concerning refugees in Aston Clinton, Buckinghamshire, 'the Belgians are simple and pleasant like children, rather vain and conceited about their appearance'.

On an official level, Home Secretary McKenna had stated that as far as the Aliens Restriction Act of 1914 was concerned, Belgian refugees were to be 'treated as friends, and no difficulty w[ould] be put in the way of their landing at any approved port, if they c[ould] satisfy the Aliens Officer that they [were] in fact Belgians and not Germans or Austrians'.[26] But the growth of official and popular anti-alienism in the first months of the war led to the extension of prohibited areas for aliens extensively if not always with sufficient precision. For example, the Home Office initially made Southampton a free port of entry only to be rebuked in October 1914 by the War Office. Another place in dispute where it was unclear whether Belgian refugees were allowed entry was the Isle of Wight. Much correspondence took place on this matter between the Home Office and the civil and military authorities on the island. It was reported to the Home Office that

> some ladies in Ryde [on the Island] were anxious to equip two or three large houses for the reception of the refugees and had had a request to take in one hundred as soon as possible: they wanted to start work ... but before buying material were anxious to know that there would be no difficulty.

The Home Office reply was generally negative; Sir John Pedder, writing to the secretary of the Local Government Board in the Isle of Wight in October 1914:

> I am directed by the Secretary of State to say ... that it is in his opinion undesirable that Belgian refugees should be established in the island. [I]n addition to the general objection to Belgian refugees being established in prohibited areas, there is in the case of the Isle of Wight the further difficulty that aliens, even if they are alien friends, cannot embark for, or land in the island, under the provisions of the Aliens Restriction Order ... [He] is not disposed to give permission for parties of Belgians to embark for or land in the Island.

Pedder also stated with regard to the ports of Southampton and Dover that 'all the Belgian refugees brought there have been cleared out'. It was for this reason presumably that the refugees who had settled in Gosport were transferred to Grayshott, also in Hampshire, later in 1914. By October 1914 the Home Office urged refugee committees in restricted or partly restricted counties such as Hampshire that they should not arrange for further arrival of Belgians. It added, however, that 'The refugees already established within prohibited areas need not, generally speaking, be disturbed'.[27]

The category alien, even when connected to the Belgians, was thus always problematic. This ambivalent official treatment was clear in the thinking of the Home Secretary as early as August 1914 in discussion between the Foreign and Home Office:

> Mr McKenna can only say that, with every wish to show the utmost friendliness to Belgians, he feels some doubt whether it will in many cases be to the advantage even of the refugees themselves, to come to this country; while, if

their numbers should be large, they might after a time become a considerable source of embarrassment.

In such light, it is not surprising that as the war progressed the Belgian refugees were regarded more as an administrative problem rather than a focus of positive sentiment.[28]

THE LOCAL IMPACT OF BELGIAN REFUGEES

Away from the official mind, the ambivalence towards the Belgians in everyday life was apparent in the diary of Eleanor Ruth Dent. Dent was a 15-year-old schoolgirl in Burley, a village in the heart of the New Forest. Rather than continue her studies, she, along with her mother, were involved with a neighbour, Mrs Clough, and other Burley people in the welfare of a group of 'respectable' Belgian refugees:

> The Cloughs possess at Burley Street a large empty house called Blackmoor. It was decided to turn this into a home for superior Belgian Refugees; everybody round kindly lent their superfluous furniture and in a few days the house was ready.

They were told by a Belgian army captain 'that a convalescent home for soldiers was the very thing that was needed'. More beds and furniture were obtained, 'Mrs Hawkins was installed as cook with her husband as general man and old Madame Verheyen as housemaid, and Mummy undertook to do the housekeeping'. By late November 1914, Blackmoor was fully operational as a convalescent home for the Belgians:

> It's a fairly large house, white roughcast with a red roof with a lovely view... Downstairs the men had a large living room furnished with a round table, a piano, several armchairs, a writing table for industries, a gramaphone, ... a war map ... and a portrait of King Albert [of Belgium] ... On the second floor were the large bedrooms which had two of these men each. They were furnished very plainly, beds, wash and stand and chairs, but they were always very clean and very nice... Pinned up in the sitting room were the rules of Blackmoor written in French and signed by Mr and Mrs Clough. I regret to say they were not invariably kept though on the whole we had wonderfully little trouble with the soldiers.... With the good food, fresh air, as much rest and sleep as they desired and in quiet, clean and comfortable surroundings the convalescents had every chance to recover their strength. Many who came to us looking very ill and wretched went away strong and well, and they nearly all wrote to us afterwards saying how happy they had been... The cost of running the convalescent home was at first alone by subscription, the Cloughs contributing the house and paying all the taxes and the Hawkins' wages. Later we received a government grant of 12 shillings per man.[29]

For a bright young person (who later became a prominent illustrator of children's books) looking after the Belgians proved to be a mixed, sometimes frustrating if important life experience.[30] Her diary was written 'as a "souvenir" of the BELGIANS who were the cause of much laughter during the sad years 1914 and 1915'. This laughter was generated by and directed at the Belgians. Her account contains fascinating and often waspish descriptions of ordinary people uprooted by the traumas of a global and bloody conflict. Although a sense of loyalty and high regard for the Belgian refugees remains throughout the account, the individuals described are very human both in their eccentricities and their failings, none more so than Victor, who along with Henri, was one of the first soldiers to arrive at Blackmoor:

> Victor was a fair-haired cheerful looking person, the picture of health. We were told there was nothing the matter with him but he was liable to sudden hysterical seizures, the result I regret to say of cowardice! ... Victor's costumes by reason of their diversity and weirdness deserve a chapter to themselves ... The first warm days of summer brought Victor out like the butterfly arrayed in immaculate white flannels, with a cream silk shirt and white canvas shoes. Where these garments came from I cannot imagine...

> A rumour has reached the ears of Victor and Henri that they are to be medically examined and may eventually be sent to the front. It is said that 2000 Belgian soldiers are lost in England and of that number we can account for two: Victor and Henri. Henri instantly takes to his bed and weeps, but Victor chooses subtler means of evasion. No longer glowing with health with his chest thrown out does he stride along. With a piteous face and shrunken figure and knock knees you now behold him. At that time he was working in our garden and we had told him to do some pumping. After a short time he went to the kitchen and made Bertha feel his heart ... I was so greatly concerned [but was] assured it was only malingering, and so it turned out, for as soon as he was threatened with ... hospital he miraculously recovered.[31]

Although Victor proved to be increasingly difficult to deal with, Ruth Dent retained an affection for him. He was 'very tiresome sometimes', but she concluded her account by suggesting that 'one could not help feeling that there is something nice in Victor, though he is an old goose'. Through the work connected to Blackmoor House and characters such as Victor, Belgian refugees became part of everyday life in the New Forest. The local responses to them were undoubtedly mixed. On 6 August 1915, Ruth Dent wrote how she met a local prominent woman, Mrs Prothero, who

> had many tales about the Belgian soldiers, about their being drunk, ill-treating the donkey and so on. Mrs Clough also told us that someone had written anonymously to commandant Schmidt in Bournemouth that the Belgian soldiers in Burley behaved disgracefully. Really it is odious of people to delight in telling us of the shortcomings of our men. People like Mrs Kennedy, who just sent them a beautiful cake with 'good luck' in pink icing, are much nicer.

Yet even Mrs Prothero thought it was her social duty to invite the Belgians for afternoon tea and there is little indication of any major local hostility to

Victor, a Belgian refugee, drawn by Eleanor Ruth Dent, 1915. From the private collection of Dionis Macnair and with her kind permission.

their presence. Ruth Dent herself had been responsible for arranging occupational therapy for the Belgians who made a variety of toys, clothes and other items. She organised an 'exhibition and sale of articles made by Belgian refugee ladies and Belgian wounded soldiers' which was a huge success: 'everybody was most awfully appreciative and nice'.[32]

Colin Holmes has pointed out that 'At all times public sympathy can be a fickle jade, and, in the event, the enthusiastic popular responses of 1914 toward the Belgians were not always maintained'. Yet it is hardly surprising that the hyperbolic sentiments expressed in the first weeks of war were not sustained. The evidence from Hampshire, where many thousands of wounded soldiers and other Belgian refugees temporarily settled, suggests that most local people continued to accept the newcomers, even as workmates, after the initial welcome had calmed down and they moved out of their original hostels and family homes. A minority, perhaps several thousand in numbers, such as the Dents and the Cloughs, spent much time, energy and care providing for the Belgians' needs. Local resentment was occasional and essentially minor. Elsewhere, particularly in parts of London, hostility was stronger, even approaching the level of violence as was the case in Fulham during May 1916 when anti-Belgian riots erupted. The issue of compulsory conscription and belief that the refugees were receiving higher relief than the families of British soldiers contributed in 1915 to rising tension across the country as a whole. The government responded by insisting on compulsory conscription of the Belgians early in 1916. In Fulham, an additional problem of a dire housing shortage in a poverty-stricken area caused greater friction, although the Belgian refugees themselves were living in appalling conditions. In contrast, in Hampshire many of the refugees, especially those linked to the military, were relatively well-to-do (those offering accommodation had insisted that they be 'respectable'), probably French-speaking and they settled in what were generally more prosperous locations. Much greater hostility was felt by those of Flemish and/or poorer and peasant origin. The government itself contributed to this differentiated treatment, helping to support organisations for the 'better class' Belgians. To a very large extent, increasingly so as the war progressed, responses to and treatment of the Belgian refugees were complicated by class, ethnicity and location.[33]

THE MEMORY AND SIGNIFICANCE OF THE BELGIAN REFUGEES

The Belgian refugees were certainly never the focus of such national interest as they were in the autumn of 1914, but for the individuals themselves and those helping them, it was a critical part of their lives. A former refugee, Lodewijk de Jonghe, who was a child in the war, recalls that when 'we went back home ... everything seemed poor and miserable. But we had many pleasant memories of Alton [in north Hampshire]'. The sleepy and sometimes humorous experiences of the refugees in places such as Burley should not hide the horrors of war from which they came and the devastation that they returned to. Indeed, Ruth Dent's diary was strikingly casual when referring to her work in finding activities for many men who had suffered loss of limbs, recalling 'how one day Mrs Clough took the three poor legless men to have their artificial legs fitted'. Refuge in Britain enabled the process of rebuilding shattered lives and shattered bodies to begin.[34] One of the longest standing refugees at Blackmoor, Burley, returned to the continent in the autumn of 1915. Mr Stroobants wrote in October 1915 expressing gratitude to his host but also giving a glimpse of the scale of human losses in western Europe after just one year of fighting:

> We've had to leave Burley without the pleasure of seeing you again [but] we deeply wanted to say goodbye to you and thank you for all you have done for us since our arrival in Burley; and for all the trouble you've taken to arrange work for my wife which allowed us to make a living. I assure you that we will always be sincerely grateful to you, the day when we will be able to receive you with Mademoiselle Ruth in Belgium ... will be for us a happy day ... We were eventually able to board ... one of the ships that makes the Folkstone-Dieppe crossing... Arrived in Dieppe ... everywhere women in mourning, with long floating black veils, everywhere orphans, everywhere the colour black, attesting to the fact that France gave the allies the best of her blood. You only see soldiers with missing legs or arms, with each step you're confronted with horrible images of the war. It's the same all over France...[35]

Many Belgian refugee soldiers in Britain did not survive their wounds. Their sacrifice was marked by a series of war memorials across the country. In Hampshire this was most prominent in Southampton Cemetery where a monument 'Erected to the Memory of Belgian Patriots By the People of Southampton' was unveiled in May 1916:

> Some of the Belgian soldiers who helped to stem the onrush of the mighty military machine in the early days of the European war found their last resting place in a corner of Southampton Cemetery, near the main gates. They were picked up on the field of battle by British ambulances, and brought to our town, where in spite of careful nursing, they succumbed to their wounds...

> [The Belgian Minister acknowledged the gift and stated] 'This monument, erected on British soil by the citizens of Southampton, in honour of officers and men of the Belgian Army, is a touching symbol of solidarity. These simple and obscure heroes, wounded in Belgium on the field of battle, received their last cares in England where they passed their final and supreme moments. They rest in a friendly land.'[36]

Although such war memorials to the soldiers provided a permanent reminder of their presence, the Belgian refugee experience as a whole has been largely forgotten with regard to 'official' memory. This is an unfortunate lacuna relating to refugee movements, for an example is provided illustrating the potential *flexibility* of state and public responses to even large-scale movements, as well as the bonds of friendship and respect that developed between very different people in difficult circumstances. The reception given at Gosport where

> out of the windows of the [reception] house a Union Jack and the Belgian flag protruded, and they indeed signified a centre of voluntary help ungrudgingly given out of sympathy and pity for whom the colours waved a welcome,

was not untypical of the country as a whole in the first months of the war.[37] On a local level, the memory of the Belgian refugees became deeply ingrained. In Thorverton in Devon, for example, a small rural settlement where many Belgian refugees had been received, 'they were certainly still being talked about quite widely around the village [as late as] the 1970s'. Within family histories, bonds between the former refugees and their British hosts also outlasted the war. Ivor Montagu recalled that his

> first trip abroad was to Belgium when I was still 14, soon after the ending of the 1914 war. I went on the invitation of the refugee family who had been our guests, and especially their paterfamilia, my old écarte partner, then Commandant, now Baron, Cartuyvels du Collaert...[38]

Nor was the impact of the Belgian refugees simply one operating at the level of individual memory. The refugees made a large contribution to the economy and culture of Britain at war. In May 1916, the *Hampshire Telegraph* reflected on their stay in the county, giving a romanticised narrative of their sojourn in Britain (perhaps in defence of the Belgians when they were becoming subject to attack and growing criticism nationally). Nevertheless, it showed their local integration and the efforts refugees themselves had made on behalf of the country that had given them asylum:

> About eighteen months ago there arrived in Portsmouth and Gosport a number of families and portions of families who, it could be seen at a glance, were innocent victims of the war... Mothers, carrying their latest born and with sturdy little sons and daughters, clinging to their skirts, grandparents whose years and grey hairs should have spared them such a cruel fate, came trudging through the station on their way to the hostels that had been prepared for them.

It went on to illustrate how contact with local British culture had 'improved' the refugees, hinting that the refugees were of peasant (and thus probably Flemish) origin:

> One felt sorry for these innocent victims, many of them insufficiently clad, and most of them wearing the native clogs, with their wisps of straw to give them a little ease... Go now to Winchester, where the Belgians have been working hard ... to 'turn the corner' once again, and see how well they have done it. Men who have been earning their 6½d. to 1s. per hour at various occupations, but mostly in building hutments for the military, having been doing their share of war work, and at the same time founding comfortable homes for themselves and families. Girls and young women have found situations as domestic servants or

shop assistants, some at the biggest establishments in the ancient capital of
England, which in certain features of its old architecture may have reminded
them once of their Ypres as it was before the German guns began to make a
target of its buildings. Bright and happy girls they look now that a better day
has dawned for them; and be it said, the clogs have disappeared in favour of the
neatest footwear possible…

The Belgians in Winchester now can scarcely be classed as a community. They
have little residences of their own – flats or tenements in various parts of the
city, furnished partly through the distribution of furniture which was formerly
used in the communal homes, and partly through their own energies and thrift;
while thoughtful visitors have in many cases supplied an article of household
use which had been noticed to be deficient.[39]

The removal of clogs and assimilation of the Belgians was seen patronisingly
as progress. At the end of 1914, the Official Committee of Belgians had
circulated a handbook of 'suggestions and advice' to the refugees in Britain,
worried that too much assimilation might take place. Whilst warning the
refugees 'not [to] accentuate the difference between their customs and those
of the British', it stressed that

every Belgian must be a *good patriot* … Social and family life in Belgium is
marked by friendliness, a good-natured want of ceremony, and a strict
adherence to old-established habits. No one need depart from these; indeed,
nothing is more delightful than to find the characteristic life of Belgium
reproduced in Great Britain.

In contrast to Winchester, especially where the proportion of Belgian workers
was far more concentrated, in Britain as a whole their culture, true to this
appeal, was less watered-down, nowhere more so than in Birtley, County
Durham, where 4,000 refugees were employed in munitions factories. A. J. P.
Taylor referred to the workers, alongside 'Belgian policemen, Belgian law
and even Belgian beer creat[ing] the illusion of a Belgian town'. Similarly, a
post-war British government report referring to the Earl's Court Camp in
London for Belgian refugees, which 100,000 people passed through,
commented that it 'became a Belgian village in miniature, reflecting the daily
life of an industrious people'. Yet as Colin Holmes suggests, evidence of
disturbances in Birtley at the end of 1916 provides 'a qualification to [such]
cosy image[s]'. He adds that although by 1919, the episode

had passed into history … reminders of it existed long afterwards whether in the
shape of the National Projectile Factory at Birtley … what are still called 'the
Belgian houses' in Derby, the painting by Franzoni on the 'Landing of the
Belgian Refugees August 1914', which is in Folkestone Library, and in the
existence of women, now growing old in Belgium, whose name of Angèle
commemorates their birth in England.[40]

In the case of 'enemy aliens', the British state employed draconian measures to satisfy public opinion that this 'menace' was being dealt with. But with the Belgian refugees, public pressure worked in the opposite direction. Initially the government intended restricting entry to a matter of thousands and even then only to Belgians of 'good character'. The refugees, however, were greeted with a spontaneous welcome and, as Cahalan puts it, 'Belgian relief in those early months was a *universally* popular cause'. Moreover, the desperate need to restore Britain's moral pride led to rediscovery of Britain's tradition of refugee asylum: 'They delved into the past to place the Belgian refugees in context, and their search for a usable past took some as far back as the French Huguenots and other Protestant exiles'.[41]

Nevertheless, from the start of their arrival, the Belgian refugees faced problems of being defined as aliens, even if they were generally treated as 'friendly' ones. There were restrictions on their freedom of movement, which was particularly important in certain coastal areas, and many other alien regulations which affected their daily lives. At the start of the war, the extraordinary mythology associated with 'brave little Belgium' protected the refugees from the rising anti-alienism of wartime Britain. Even then, at times, such xenophobia was undifferentiated – all foreigners were linked to the evil 'Hun'. In Alton where another Belgian Refugee Committee existed, Lodewijk de Jonghe recalled how 'one night my uncle and some other Belgians were out walking ... when they were arrested by a Scottish [army] officer who thought they were speaking German'. Flemish-speaking Belgian refugees, who might be mistaken for Germans, were particularly vulnerable to attack and abuse.[42]

As the war progressed and the frustrations, miseries and anxieties of the Home Front intensified, public anti-Belgian sentiment was more marked, although never resembling the ugly anti-Germanism. Such hostility as there was, however, enabled the British state as early as 1916 to press for the quick removal of the Belgian refugees after the conflict. This was largely achieved with less than 10,000 Belgians recorded in the 1921 census. For Hampshire the census commented that the Belgians had 'number[ed] only 113 in 1911', and yet it failed to mention that the figure recorded in 1921 (193) was a tiny fraction of the number present in Hampshire during the war.[43]

In instructions issued to the refugees at the start of the war, the Official Committee of Belgians asked the question: 'Where shall the refugees fix their hopes?' It was accompanied with the most strident of answers:

> On their country. Their country still lives. She has never lived so truly as since she has been invaded. Every exile carries her with him. The tributes to her which he hears – and which strike home to the heart – are her treasures. Hospitality may cheer and comfort him; it can never make him forget the grief of exile, nor distract him from his burning desire to return to his own country, and that country will stand in need of her children, and of their united efforts to restore her beauty, her fertility, and her riches. The time of refuge in Great

> Britain must prepare the Belgians for the heavy task which awaits them on their
> return. No one should think of avoiding this task, or should dream of settling
> abroad, unless for exceptional and various reasons.

The sting in the tail suggests that such fears of non-return were very real to
the Belgian authorities in Britain. Most Belgians were more than happy to
return home, although the crude bureaucratic manner in which this was
executed was a sad ending to their stay in Britain. Indeed, their favourable
treatment in Britain was partly based on the assumption that they would leave
the country as soon as hostilities ceased. This provides the explanation of why,
almost alone of all refugee groups in twentieth-century Britain, the Belgians
were encouraged by the British authorities to maintain their language and
culture. It is revealing to return to the positive report in the *Hampshire
Telegraph* on their successful integration in the region. The article stressed
that the Belgian refugees had 'found a home in England, and fortunately funds
were not wanting to make the future brighter for these outcasts and to set them
on their feet again'. Much was made of their responsible settlement in
Winchester. Nevertheless, it concluded by stating that:

> The refugees have put away with their clogs and shawls many unhappy
> memories. When the cruel blows that their heroic little nation has so bravely
> borne have been avenged, they will probably return to their native land,
> carrying with them, we may be sure, recollections of the helping hand which
> Britannia extended to her sister Belgium.

The easy assumption for both the British and Belgian authorities was that all
the Belgians, whatever local roots they had established, would want to return
immediately. For example, in a history of the University of Southampton's
role as a war hospital, Belgian refugees are shown recuperating. Its author
comments that one of the University buildings 'was the home of a number of
Belgium [*sic*] Refugees, one of whom became a Southampton tram driver
until he was eventually repatriated'. Whether he would have wanted to have
been sent back is open to conjecture. In this respect, a report from the
Liverpool Belgian Refugee Committee written after the war has relevance. It
commented that 'when the time came for the refugees to return to their own
country, the chief difficulty which arose was their unwillingness to leave
England, where they had been so extremely well looked after'. Marriages
between local people and the refugees were just one indication of the close
bonds that developed. Those who were more marginal in Belgian society,
particularly the Flemish-speaking, appear to have been particularly reluctant
to return. Yet although the Belgian refugees were offered immense initial
hospitality and then subsequently became very much part of local landscapes,
Britain, ultimately, was not allowed to be their 'home'. In November 1918
parliamentary questions demanded to know when the Belgians would be
repatriated and at whose expense. Even though by December 1919 the
number remaining was very tiny, the Home Secretary was asked to take

further action so that 'those Belgians who came over during the War [could] now return'. Fearful of local opposition, especially with regard to jobs and housing, an enormous effort was made to repatriate the refugees as speedily as was possible.[44]

Such exclusion and removal was even more drastic for those from Germany and Austria whose numbers were literally decimated during the First World War. Prime Minister Lloyd George, in a letter of May 1919 to those who had been active in the relief of Belgian refugees, wrote of it as a 'great act of humanity'. Ironically, it was the different British traditions of xenophobia, anti-alien restrictionism and racism which were to inform state responses immediately after the war. Lloyd George added in his letter that

> It will ... be a lasting pleasure to those who have been engaged ... to feel that at a time when so much of the energies of mankind has been devoted to destruction, it has been their privilege to take part in alleviating distress and in creating a new bond of fellowship between nations which will continue long after the tragic circumstances that have brought it into being have passed into history.[45]

It was, however, the same Prime Minister in the same year who introduced legislation making it far less possible that British people would again be able to enjoy the same 'privilege' of helping refugees at home. In response to a paper presented to the Royal Statistical Society in January 1916 on 'The Register of Belgian Refugees', Sir Edward Brabrook thanked the author, Mr de Jastrzebski, for a document 'which would stand in history'. Replying, Jastrzebski 'thought the way in which, as a whole, the people of this country received, looked after and gave personal service to the unfortunate sufferers who came from Belgium, would be one of the proudest records in the history of this country'. But the legacy of the First World War, which could have been interpreted in a positive, generous spirit relating to refugees in Britain, was remembered in state policy immediately after 1918 only with reference to the hostility shown to aliens. If nothing else, however, the reception of the Belgians at least indicated that the tradition of refugee asylum in Britain had not been destroyed by the brutality of the First World War. The state, if largely for reasons of guilt (a forerunner to its active assistance of Czech refugees in 1938–39 and Hungarians in 1956), in the first stages of the conflict at least showed itself able to commit resources and moral energy into helping refugees. On a public level, if some were active, especially as the war progressed, in objecting to the Belgian presence, others were to cut their teeth on what would become lives devoted to the needs of refugees. To them, the preciousness of granting asylum was not to be dismissed lightly.[46]

Triumphant Anti-Alienism: The Absence of Asylum, 1919–1932

In 1927, the Board of Deputies of British Jews' President wrote to Sir Robert Gower, MP, objecting to proposals to make the Aliens Act of 1919 permanent rather than subject to annual renewal:

> The right to asylum to victims of religious persecution ... has been one of the great features of this country and it would be deplorable if any legislation permanently deprived people of that right.[1]

Although the threat of permanent legislation was not realised, a policy of almost total restrictionism continued throughout the 1920s. At the end of the decade a Jewish delegation went to the Labour Home Secretary, J. R. Clynes, to ask what place the right of asylum, as outlined in the 1905 Aliens Act, had in the implementation of everyday policy. Clynes was anxious to set the record straight:

> I must correct what is, I find, a widespread misapprehension. The 'right of asylum' in so far as it exists or ever existed is not a right attaching to an alien, but is a right of the Sovereign State to admit a refugee if it thinks fit to do so. The Act of 1905 which you cite in support of your suggestion did no more than provide that an immigrant who proved that he was seeking admission to avoid *inter alia* religious persecution, should not be excluded on the ground merely that he was or was likely to become destitute. The most therefore that you can ask me to do is to restore the position created by the Act of 1905, and this, in view of the changed and changing conditions both here and abroad, is more than I can promise.

Clynes went on that individual applications for those seeking refuge would 'continue to receive sympathetic consideration both [in the Home Office] and at the ports'. Nevertheless, it had been decided by his predecessors since 1918

> to keep within fairly rigid limitations permanent increases to the alien population. After a most careful examination of the position today I cannot say either that that decision was wrong or that the time has yet come when we can, without damage to this country, depart from it. Urgent problems of housing and unemployment are engaging, and I fear will engage for some time to come, the earnest attention of the Government ... In other words, the question of alien

immigration is now indissolubly bound up with other broad questions of national domestic policy.[2]

Five years earlier, Arthur Henderson, the first Labour Home Secretary, had told the Board of Deputies that

one must remember that the alien immigration itself has practically ceased in the way that took place 20 or 30 years ago. Aliens are coming, of course, in certain numbers to the country; but we do not now get immigrant ships coming full of alien immigrants as in the old days.

Henderson, by not referring to *why* this flow to Britain had stopped, implied that it was a natural development rather than resulting from restrictionism in a country which had so recently been an important destination of immigrants/refugees. His Conservative successor, William Joynson-Hicks, was more forthcoming in this respect, informing a Board of Deputies delegation in 1925 that 'The entry of aliens to this country was not a right, it was a privilege, and they were entitled to make what conditions they liked for the exercise of that privilege'.[3]

The situation in the 20 years since the passing of the 1905 Aliens Act had changed remarkably. First, ministers from both the Conservative and the Labour governments had no embarrassment in declaring that Britain was not or was no longer a country of immigration. Second, considerations of refugee asylum were of little concern – policy was, in essence, directed toward aliens. Yet as a contemporary wrote at the end of the inter-war period:

A refugee is an alien with a difference... If he is treated as 'simple foreigner', he, having no status as a national, suffers because a 'foreigner' derives most of his being from his character as a national of his own state; if a state is to grant him favours only on the basis of reciprocity, he suffers for there is none to reciprocate.[4]

Third, alien restriction was almost absolute. The comments of the legal experts, Norman Sibley and Alfred Elias, in 1905 that 'The Right of Asylum is writ in characters of fire on the tablets of our Constitution', belonged to a different age. In 1927 the liberal *Manchester Guardian* commented that the existing temporary and proposed permanent control of aliens would 'once [have] been regarded as utterly "unEnglish"'.[5] Although internationalists campaigned for a return to a more open and generous policy, by the late 1920s they were isolated voices. Indeed, rather than diminish anti-alien sentiment, state measures served to give restrictionists greater legitimacy. Throughout the 1920s more aliens left Britain (with hundreds forcibly removed through deportation) than were allowed permanent entry, but the rhetoric of anti-alien campaigners continued regardless: Britain was still being swamped with undesirable foreigners, many of whom they alleged were illegal immigrants.[6]

Hampshire had a special place in aliens policy during the 1920s. The Atlantic Park Hostel, Eastleigh, more than anywhere else in Britain, represented the changes that had taken place in immigration and refugee policy. This chapter will concentrate first on the Armenian genocide and then on the history of Atlantic Park as illustrations of the absence, in a global perspective, of British asylum policy during the 1920s and early 1930s. But as an indication of the depths to which British xenophobia and racism had plummeted in the years after the war, the hostel will initially be viewed through the mental landscape of Lieutenant-Colonel A. H. Lane. Lane articulated his views in a widely read polemic, *The Alien Menace*, which was published and republished during the late 1920s and early 1930s:

> It [now] appears that Continental nationals *en route* to the United States enter British ports as 'transmigrants', and they are carried onward in British ships. On arrival in America the United States' monthly quota may have become exhausted, and on this account, or by reason of their unfit, diseased, or otherwise unwelcome condition, these passengers are rejected. The transmigrants then become, perforce, the guests of the steamship companies ... and in the meantime they have been lodged in England, at Eastleigh, near Southampton ... As to the Alien camp in Eastleigh, one is tempted to ask what sinister influence is working to ensure that people rejected by America may return to Britain, to settle, instead of sending them back to their respective countries? ... The real question, of course, is: why should England receive those whom the rest of the civilised world have rejected? It is difficult to control the transmigrants in the teeming foreign elements of London. They will commence work, displace British labour, become eligible for the dole, increasing our housing difficulties, spread disease, and permeate our land with anti-patriotic propaganda.[7]

At many other times Lane would have been a marginal figure. He had strong links to antisemitic and quasi-Fascist circles and believed in a worldwide Jewish conspiracy (hence his references to a 'sinister influence'). Nevertheless, Lane acted as a bridge between those obsessed with the 'Jewish peril' and mainstream politics and state practices during the 1920s. That he invented an aliens problem from an example which owed its existence to British and American *anti-alienism* is an indication of the cross-fertilisation/fluidity that existed between politicians such as Home Secretary Joynson-Hicks and the pathologically prejudiced. Before examining the specific context in which Lane's racism operated, however, we will examine the case of the Armenians who have slipped even further into obscurity than the unfortunate refugees in Eastleigh.[8]

THE ABSENCE OF ARMENIAN REFUGEES IN POST-1918 BRITAIN

Those campaigning after 1918 on behalf of the persecuted and oppressed abroad had the problem of invoking what now seemed out of place in the depressed and anxious post-war British mood – the spirit of past generosity towards refugees. It was a problem that was evident in the war itself when disclosures were made about the mass murder of Armenians in the Ottoman Empire. The history of the Armenian people who originated in the Near East is long and complex. The Armenians converted to Christianity in the third century of the Common Era. Their rich culture, language and religion intertwined to produce a rising ethnic/national consciousness. From the fourteenth century onwards they became a minority within the Ottoman Empire sometimes maintaining a semblance of self-rule within it and a growing diaspora beyond Turkish rule.

Relations between the Turks and the Armenians were not always negative. The Armenians retained their distinctive culture, but in many areas of everyday interaction, including business, Turks and Armenians interacted harmoniously. Even so, problems were caused by the Armenians being monotheistic non-Muslims (*dhammis*), and therefore of second class status in the Ottoman Empire. Moreover, as the nineteenth century progressed, the treatment of the Armenian and other minority groups within the empire deteriorated. Growing Turkish nationalism, military conflict with Russia over lands where many Armenians were concentrated and the tensions between traditionalists and modernisers within a crumbling Empire, led to the marginalisation and increasing persecution of Armenians.[9]

The years between 1894 and 1896 were particularly murderous: 100,000 to 200,000 Armenians were massacred and tens of thousands more fled as refugees (including a small number who settled in Britain). The violence was concentrated on the Turkish/Russian borders where sections of the Ottoman Kurdish population victimised and exploited the Armenians. An influx of Armenians into Russian lands resulted – one million by the First World War. In 1908, in a revolutionary mood, the Young Turks came to power which at first appeared to usher in a new mood of optimism amongst the Armenians who thought that the new government's modernising tendencies would create a stable and tolerant environment. Yet as Richard Hovannisian writes:

> One of the most unexpected and, for the Armenians, most tragic metamorphoses in modern history was the process, from 1908 to 1914, that transformed the seemingly liberal, egalitarian Young Turks into extreme chauvinists, bent on creating a new order and eliminating the Armenian Question by eliminating the Armenian people.[10]

Conservative reactions to the Young Turks and general political instability increased tensions, leading to further massacres of Armenians with a peak of violence in 1909. In 1913 in a new political development, ultra-nationalistic Young Turks took control which, with the outbreak of war, heralded disaster for the Armenians. These new leaders hoped to aid the process of modernisation by homogenising the Ottoman Empire away from its multinational, multi-religious reality. At the start of the war the Ottoman Empire endured the further trauma of military defeats. In response, the government sought a suitable scapegoat; the Armenians were accused of disloyalty and of supporting the Russian Empire. It soon became apparent that the campaign of mass violence and deportation was part of an organised policy of state-sponsored genocide. The year 1915 marked the heart of the destruction process, but the murder process continued into the post-war era, leaving up to 1.5 million Armenians dead by the early 1920s. Through the use of mass shootings, concentration camps, starvation, deportation to desert regions and even gassing, the Armenian presence in the Turkish Empire was largely destroyed. Some women and children were spared from murder but were forced to convert to Islam. Cultural as well as physical genocide combined in this unprecedented act of modern mass murder.[11]

In the summer of 1915 news of the massacres came to Britain and the USA. Those in the West who had been campaigning on behalf of the Armenians since the late nineteenth century escalated their work, particularly in publicising and authenticating details of the horrors. Of particular importance in Britain and elsewhere was the collection of documents edited by the historian Arnold Toynbee which were presented to the Foreign Secretary, Viscount Grey, and published as an official paper in 1916. One of the key items was an eye-witness report from an Armenian woman in Cilicia who had escaped the mass killings. She managed to pass on her experiences in a letter hidden in the sole of her shoe:

> In haste and in secret I seize this opportunity of bringing to your ears the cry of agony which goes out from the survivors of the terrible crisis through which we are passing at this moment. They are exterminating our nation… Perhaps this will be the last cry from Armenia that you will hear… These lines cannot describe our misery; it would need volumes of reports to do justice to that… At the present moment there are at [her former province] more than 10,000 deported widows and children… They have been plundered several times over, and have marched along naked and starving…
>
> The massacres have been most violent in the eastern provinces, and the population has been deported wholesale towards the Hauran Desert … where the victims are doomed to a death from natural causes more infallible than massacre. When one remembers that these people were leading a comfortable European life, one is forced to conclude that they will never be able to survive in an alien and inhospitable climate … My friends, I have not time to tell you more; one may say with truth that not a single Armenian is left in Armenia; soon there will be none left in Cilicia either. The Armenian, robbed of his life, his goods, his honour, conveys to you his last cry for help – help to save the lives of the survivors! Money to buy them bread!…. I sign this letter with my blood![12]

Debates inside and outside Parliament indicated that few doubted such stories. The Under-Secretary of State for Foreign Affairs, Lord Robert Cecil, told the House of Commons that

> it may be said, without the least fear of exaggeration, that no more horrible crime has been committed in the history of the world … It is enough to say that no element of horror, outrage, torture, or slaughter was absent from this crime.[13]

In the House of Lords, Viscount Bryce, who had presented the documents to Viscount Grey, added further details and concluded that he did 'not think there [was] any case in history ... in which any crime so hideous and upon so large a scale has been recorded'.[14] Evidence that German officials had encouraged the massacres provided another reason for empathising with the victims. Yet if 'the country ha[d] been shocked by renewed accounts of Armenian massacres' in autumn 1915, it still proved difficult to mobilise British action on behalf of the victims: 'this almost universal and unanimous sympathy, cutting across party lines, ironically remained only a general, vague and diffused humanitarian feeling'.[15]

One of the campaigners in the House of Commons, Aneurin Williams (Liberal), who was also chairman of the British Armenia Committee and the Lord Mayor's Armenian Refugees Fund, was anxious that as well as expressing sympathy, the British government should take action on behalf of the persecuted. Both he and his fellow campaigning MP, T. P. O'Connor (Nationalist), invoked the Belgian example to get their case taken seriously. O'Connor connected the Turkish atrocities committed against the Armenians to those perpetrated by the Germans against the Belgians. He stressed that 'these massacres [against the Armenians] could not have taken place without the connivance, or the sanction, or at least the reticence of the German Government'. O'Connor called for the British government to follow the lead given by American, French and Swiss humanitarians in providing rescue and relief to the Armenians. In turn, Williams stressed the practical work being done to relieve the survivors, especially by their compatriots in the Russian Caucasus. He made reference to the parallel work in Britain where 'we received ... about ... 200,000 Belgian refugees'. Williams called for a reassurance

> that everything that is in the power of the Government – the Army, the Fleet, the Consular service – will be used to help these two classes of people – those who are defending themselves for their lives within Turkish territory, and those who have sought refuge in Russia and elsewhere... [W]e must not forget that we are in the presence of the greatest massacre probably that the world has ever known. Therefore, it behoves us ... to make every sacrifice and put forward every effort to relieve ... suffering, and to save some thousands from death that must still occur unless all our help is forthcoming.[16]

The response of the Under-Secretary of State for Foreign Affairs was clear:

> The hon. Gentleman ... asked me to say, on behalf of the Government, that we would use every resource of the Army and Navy and the Consular services to assist and save the Armenians. I am sure my Hon. Friend will not misunderstand me if I do not give a pledge of that kind quite in those terms. After all, the greatest possible protection for the Armenians is our victory in this War. To that all our main efforts must be bent. Our Army and our Navy, and all our resources must be devoted to destroying the enemy, wherever we can find him, until he accepts terms of peace which will be acceptable to the Allies.

Others in support of the government line went further and suggested that it was 'not very much use at the present moment discussing the Armenian question, because for the moment we have lost all real control in dealing with it'. Such sentiments resemble those expressed by British government officials when confronted with the news of European Jewry's extermination during the Second World War: the best way of helping the victims of persecution was to defeat the enemy; nothing should be done that would deflect the Allies in their military efforts.[17]

Indeed, the parallel problems faced by British campaigners on behalf of the Armenians in the First World War and the Jews in the Second is striking. First, both cases were marked by public horror and concern, but it proved difficult translating this into national and international action. British government policy towards the victims of genocide in both world wars in essence followed the path of expressing sympathy, denying the possibility of help and arguing that nothing should stand in the way of winning the war – however great the humanitarian cause. Second, the campaigners were men and women (more women by the Second World War) of great integrity, but of little power and influence: academics, church figures and members of the minority groups themselves. With regard to the last mentioned, the Armenians in Manchester subscribed £5,000 during the war 'to propagate the Armenian cause by special literature and articles in the newspapers'. In addition, they donated £1,200 to the Armenian General Benevolent Union in 1917 'for the care of the Armenian Refugees in the Caucasus, and for the liberation of women and orphans from the hands of the Kurds'; sums which were bound to pale in insignificance in light of the enormity of the Armenian disaster.[18]

Yet even with this generosity from the Armenian diaspora in Britain, and the support of others, it remains that 'Most of the protagonists of the Armenian cause were idealists, intellectuals and clergymen, and not hard-headed politicians'.[19] This was true also of the Second World War with an additional factor that many of the campaigners on behalf of European Jewry were marginal within their own spheres of influence. Third, the pro-Armenian and pro-Jewish organisations in the First and Second World Wars respectively were essentially voluntary with limited funds and weak organisational structures. There was no national network of local committees in marked contrast to those for the Belgian refugees in the First World War.[20] Fourth, the fate of the Armenians and the Jews was lost amidst other war issues which were of more direct concern to the British war effort. Fifth, the campaigners in Britain were promised action at the end of each war, but in 1918 and 1945 the survivors of the genocides were largely forgotten amidst 'more important' issues of international relations. After 1918 no effort was given to support the paper guarantees of the newly independent but insecure Armenian state. The revival of Turkey and massive dislocation and civil war in the former Russian Empire had a devastating impact on the Armenians.

Starvation and further deportation added thousands more to the number of those murdered. Western relief funding for the starving Armenians and the maintenance of the enormous number of orphans was inadequate. Britain lagged well behind the USA in this respect. Although an independent Armenian state existed from 1918 to 1923, from 1920 under Bolshevik protection, Armenian hopes of self-determination were essentially quashed in the inter-war period, lacking any significant support in Western diplomatic power politics. Moreover, only a tiny fragment of the two million Armenians present in the Ottoman Empire before the war survived. Over two thousand years of Armenian presence and settlement had, in essence, been destroyed.[21] In Europe after 1945, the Jewish survivors languished in Displaced Persons camps, some for years after their liberation by Allied forces. Sixth and lastly, although British governments remained hard-headed in both world wars, the impact of the activists must not be dismissed. The Lord Mayor's Armenian Fund raised some £300,000 between 1915 and 1937 to provide relief to the survivors; the campaigners in the Second World War forced the British government to take more seriously the possibility of helping European Jewry. Without the efforts of such remarkable individuals and the many more ordinary people who gave them support, British responses to the victims of genocide in both world wars would have been even more shaming.[22]

In one specific area, the acceptance of Armenian refugees, the British response after the First World War was, both in comparative and absolute terms, parsimonious. Although there were small established Armenian communities in the major cities of London and Manchester, only 200 survivors of the genocide were allowed entry into Britain during the inter-war period. This was in contrast to France where 63,000 were allowed to settle and a miniscule fraction of the total of the 300,000 to 400,000 Armenian refugees who fled abroad after the war. One area of significant refugee settlement was in Cyprus, the island closest to Cilicia, known as 'Little Armenia'. By 1937 some 2,700 Armenians lived in Cyprus where they 'successfully established themselves in shops, small trades, as artisans or in the professions'. Cyprus became part of the British Empire in 1914. In the inter-war period emigration to Britain grew as Cypriots took advantage of becoming subjects of the British crown. This right was not available for Turkish subjects who were excluded under the post-war aliens legislation. Classified as Turks and often unable to obtain citizenship because of a language test and a £10 fee, Cypriot Armenians found it very difficult to gain entry to Britain.[23]

One such example relating to citizenship comes from the family history of Larry Day whose mother was born in Cyprus in 1925, the daughter of Armenian refugees from the village of Tilbiz, Cilicia. Her father owned a large farm with a small Armenian community of some 80 or 90 people working on it. It was largely an agricultural community with a limited amount of trading and its own church and school. Day's grandfather was in the Ottoman army as an accountant/pay-role type officer... Their relative rural isolation had meant that they didn't [experience] the early executions and massacres. Returning to the farm from a trade mission he was told on the way back not to continue on the way down the road because everyone in the farm, including his parents, had been massacred. This was in 1920/1921. He went to Adana where he met my grandmother and they got married. They then came over on the boat with a number of other Armenians and some Greeks as well from Izmir to Cyprus in 1922/1923...

So they went from relative wealth to being refugees ... in a community of two thousand Armenians on an island which then had a population of just under half a million... Cyprus was regarded as one of the ways out; regarded as a place that would receive them even though initially they had to stay ... in detention camps briefly... They came to Cyprus because there were boats going that way and they also knew that there were lots of countries, including Britain, that were not going to let them in directly ... I saw copies of the documents that were issued to my grandparents ... and it said 'alien' of course, as everyone was ..., but 'presumed Ottoman'. It was at that level ... of lack of receptivity or friendliness that they became 'presumed'. They were just stateless ... they didn't have passports... So Cyprus was the least unsafe, and there were boats going... [Because of the failure to help during and after the war] there was enormous anti-British feeling which was expressed by my mother and other Armenians [on Cyprus].[24]

In inter-war Britain, the memory of the Armenian genocide and the activities of those who had campaigned on their behalf quickly faded. As Hitler, with frightening coldness, is alleged to have said before the invasion of Poland: 'Who, after all, speaks today of the Armenians?' Many of the campaigners in Britain were old and died after the war and the tiny Armenian population, totalling roughly 1,000, had little influence and, unlike in the USA, was not significantly supplemented by refugees from the genocide.[25] The 1921 census for Hampshire suggests that there was only one Armenian-born resident – a woman who lived in Southampton. Whether she had come after the war is unclear, but the very absence of Armenian refugee settlement follows the pattern for the country as a whole. Indeed, John Hope Simpson in 1939 commented that the 200 allowed entry 'were not refugees in the strict sense as none were allowed to enter this country unless they had some means'. Half settled in London and a quarter in Manchester with the rest scattered across the country with families in Southport, Liverpool and Bristol. Simpson suggested that 'The great majority of them [were] Oriental carpet merchants, though some [were] engaged in the fur export trade'.[26]

Since the Second World War, the Armenian presence in Britain has increased more notably, and attempts have been made to memorialise on a public level the destruction that took place during the First World War. On 24 April 1995 a service was held in St Paul's Cathedral to mark the 80th anniversary of the Armenian genocide but this event received no national coverage.[27] Unlike the Holocaust, the Armenian genocide still remains largely forgotten, yet Britain at a political and social level had an intimate knowledge of the tragedy during the First World War. British immigration control and the absence of an asylum policy in the years after the war helped to ease this process of amnesia, leading to the near total absence of survivors who could have communicated their tragic individual and collective stories. But post-war European dislocation was to affect other vulnerable minority groups, especially east European Jews. They too were to find British alien restrictionism an insurmountable obstacle in finding refuge.[28]

POST-WAR ANTI-ALIENISM

The aliens' debate in Parliament in 1904 and 1905 revealed great hesitancy in the move toward control, especially unease about abandoning the right to asylum. Those in favour of restrictionism were careful in their language. In contrast, the 1914 Aliens Restriction Act was passed at immense speed and with very little comment or criticism. In 1919 the House of Commons was again faced with calls for new legislation. Debate, whilst not matching the length of the pre-war years, was far more protracted than in 1914. Nevertheless, the tone and balance had changed fundamentally since the early 1900s. Those calling for continued commitment to asylum were in a distinct minority, and the vocabulary and arguments of the anti-alienists were unrestrained and prejudiced. Ironically, the memory of Britain's past involvement with refugees *was* recalled, but largely to emphasise further the need for drastic controls.

One politician who consistently drew upon the image of Britain as a haven for those who had been persecuted abroad was Sir Donald Maclean, Liberal MP for Peebles and South Midlothian. He emphasised that:

> Certainly one of the greatest claims for moral leadership which this country has made and sustained is the fact that ... we have never refused asylum to all those poor and distressed subjects of oppressed races who have sought asylum here... I do hope that this House will not, owing to panic and popular prejudice which is being exercised today ... allow this great tradition to be lowered and degraded... There are a great many industries in this country which have been founded by political refugees. Art, science, literature, have all been enriched by men and women who have sought sanctuary in these islands. Are we, as one of the results of the War to wreck that noble tradition?[29]

More outraged was the independently-minded Labour MP, Colonel Wedgwood who, whilst also stressing the 'old British traditions of fair play, justice and liberty', was scathing about his fellow MPs 'coming together to persecute the weak'.[30]

Yet the attempt by Maclean and Wedgwood to evoke a noble British tradition failed because past refugees were spoken of in the most derogatory manner in Parliament. In all the major debates MPs lined up to vent their vicious anti-alienism. Not surprisingly, Horatio Bottomley, the Independent MP for South Hackney, who had campaigned against the Germans in Britain with his own peculiar brand of paranoid racism during the war, was at the forefront of the assault on refugee asylum. Arguing that the Germans and Austrian colony 'was one of the contributory causes of the War', he warned Maclean not 'to indulge in copy-book maxims about the rights of refugees. We have been the dumping ground for the refugees of the world for too long.' Elaborating further, Bottomley argued that there was no need for differentiation with regard to restriction of entry: 'every alien at this moment is *prima facie* an undesirable alien'.[31]

Bottomley was concerned to keep every alien out of the country whilst Sir Ernest Wild, making his maiden speech in the Commons as Conservative MP for West Ham, was equally anxious to villify those who had come before the war. Until the 1905 Act, he argued, 'the policy then was for these parasites to come to prey upon the body politic'. Wild accused Jewish aliens of being behind the white slave trade, gambling and generally 'at the bottom of one half, at least, of the vice of this Metropolis and of this country'. Other MPs referred to the pre-war period and how Britain had been flooded by the 'ne'er-do-wells and parasites of the world'; 'the muck, the rubbish, and the refuse of the Continent'; and 'the Asiatic'.[32] It was left, along with Wedgwood, to Captain Ormsby-Gore (MP for Stafford and the only Conservative to speak out against the proposed legislation) to attack the 'cowardly antisemitism' of some anti-alien Members when referring to pre-war refugees whom he, in contrast, recalled had 'been driven out of the ghettoes in Russia and Poland as the result of religious persecution'.[33]

In one of the final debates on the Aliens Restriction Bill, Wedgwood acknowledged that he spoke for only a small section of the Labour Party in highlighting the importance of 'the brotherhood of man and the international spirit of the worker'. A fellow Labour MP outlined his vision of 'a new world for democracy, and all the nations of the world linked together, without any differentiation of the people of different nationalities'. Another, more realistically, suggested that the mood of the aliens debate had been such that Britain should not be linked to the League of Nations 'but … the League of Haters'.[34]

In December 1919 the Aliens Restrictions Act was passed, continuing and extending the provisions of the 1914 legislation. It contained no mention of refugees and asylum, but included many new clauses restricting the entry of aliens into Britain and the freedom of those resident in the country,[35] adding a heavy dose of post-war xenophobia and anti-Bolshevism to what were already extreme measures. The paranoia provided by the October 1917 revolution in Russia enabled another hook on which to hang anti-alienism. Aliens were not only seen as diseased and a danger to the workers and culture of England; they were also now widely perceived as the infectious carriers of communism. Antisemitism permeated such accusations. In 1919 a senior

Home Office official stated boldly to a Jewish immigrant welfare body that clauses of the new Aliens Restrictions Act 'were very largely made to keep out Russians', adding that the British government 'were making enquiries with regard to Bolshevism, and they found that so many Jews were mixed up with it, that they had decided to keep them out'.[36] In the parliamentary debate itself, the anti-alien Hampshire Conservative, Brigadier-General Henry Croft, argued that 'an amazing proportion of the leaders of industrial unrest' were aliens. In case his reference was not explicit enough, Croft launched a diatribe against Litvinoff, the Russian ambassador, whose real name he reminded the Commons 'was Finkelstein'.[37] In 1917 Croft formed the National Party whose Members of Parliament and journals promoted a hatred of Jews and Germans (and especially German Jews). Croft and his followers accused these 'aliens' of promoting Bolshevism and of generally planning to undermine British society. In May 1919, when the aliens debate was developing nationally, Croft wrote in the *Morning Post* that

> Russia is governed by an oligarchy of some 32 persons, not more than 4 of whom are Russians. This oligarchy consists almost entirely of Jews, and many of them are in fact German Jews who have come to Russia with German passports, established themselves as a government.[38]

The label 'undesirable' immigrants thus extended well beyond the category of former enemy aliens and included east European Jews, also embracing Afro-Caribbeans and Asians who, though often subjects of the British Empire, were debarred from entry by legislative means.[39] The most important of these measures was the 1920 Aliens Order which, with a few minor amendments, was annually renewed until it was replaced by the Immigration Act of 1971. For over half a century refugees were subject to its clauses which often proved to be formidable and inpenetrable obstacles to entry enforced by immigration officers armed with a range of exclusionary clauses. Indeed, the only exemption was if the alien was 'in a position to support himself and his dependants' or 'desirous of entering the services of an employer in the United Kingdom [and with] a permit in writing for his engagement issued to the employer by the Minister of Labour'. Even then these exemptions were subject to the individual being of sound mind, body and character. The Aliens Order also provided a wealth of detail relating to the supervision of aliens resident in Britain, including the power of the Home Secretary to make a deportation order against an alien if it was deemed 'to be conducive to the public good'.[40]

The Aliens Restrictions Act and the Aliens Order gave almost unlimited power to the Home Secretary. In practice, much would be determined by the responses of individual immigration officers interpreting the legal measures and the mood of the Home Secretary. Those who had campaigned to maintain Britain's role as a place of refugee asylum feared, with good reason, that the control of aliens would bring with it the removal of the normal checks of the democratic process. As Colin Holmes concludes, 'The liberal procedures of the Victorian age and indeed of the years between 1905 and 1914 belonged to a different and vanished world.' The potential was created for individual Home Secretaries and government officials to put their prejudices into operation. Many British Jews believed it was realised during the 1920s in the form of William Joynson-Hicks (Conservative Home Secretary for much of the decade), who was accused of discriminating against Jewish aliens in terms of entry, naturalisation and deportation. Joynson-Hicks' influence with regard to Jewish aliens was highlighted in the sad and neglected story of the Atlantic Park Hostel from 1922 to 1931.[41]

THE BACKGROUND TO ATLANTIC PARK HOSTEL

There were close to ten million refugees in post-1918 Europe. Factors included the changes in boundaries brought about by the conflict and the extreme nationalism created by the new states brought into existence or revived; the turmoil of revolution and political upheaval (especially the civil war in Russia); genocide, and the sheer economic misery and profound poverty in the aftermath of the slaughter and destruction: all created massive risk for vulnerable minority groups. Violent antisemitism was one of the many unpleasant features of the new Europe as the Jews were rejected in a mood of ugly exclusivity and racism. In the Ukraine alone, over 1,000 pogroms against Jews occurred in the civil war period, leaving 30,000 dead and a further 70,000 injured. As Sylvain Levy, President of the Alliance Israelite of France emphasised in December 1920: 'The tragedy of Eastern Europe, which has already claimed so many victims, and which is a terrible and perpetual menace to many millions of human beings, especially affects the Jewish population.'[42]

Lucien Wolf, a prominent British Jewish international diplomat, also highlighted such problems at a League of Nations conference on Russian refugees, held in Geneva in the late summer of 1921:

> The problem of the Russo-Jewish refugees in Eastern and Central Europe is a sequel to the problem of the Jewish war victims in those regions, which it has vastly aggravated. It was hoped during the war that, immediately after the restoration of peace, the work of hand-to-mouth relief which was then being conducted by various Jewish Funds on a large scale might be transformed into a work of local Reconstruction; but this hope was frustrated by the Bolshevist Revolution and the Civil War in South Russia, which ended in a long series of anti-Jewish pogroms, involving immense loss of life and the destruction of many hundreds of flourishing centres of Jewish activity throughout the Ukraine. The consequence was a panic-stricken flight of Jewish refugees westward and their concentration in the States bordering on the Russian frontier. On the conclusion of peace between Poland and Soviet Russia the frontier between those two countries was opened, whereupon a fresh stream of Jewish refugees, flying from the hardships of the Communist regime, directed itself towards the Border States.

The number of Jewish refugees doubled to 200,000 from 1918 to 1919.[43]

Sylvain Levy stressed that owing to the size of the problem, and 'also to its effects elsewhere, the problem is an international one'. In a letter to its President, Levy argued that:

> Only the League of Nations can undertake this formidable task and all the problems involved. Only the League, which rises above religious and racial interests, and is inspired by generous humanitarian motives, can undertake the task of studying and preparing common remedies applicable to all the various cases.[44]

Taking the inter-war period as a whole, however, the tragedy of refugees was so enormous that the League of Nations proved to have neither the resources nor the influence to make a significant impact on this tide of human misery. Immediately after the war, private relief attempted to deal with the immense problem but, in 1921, in a hesitant recognition that an international agency was required, the League of Nations High Commission for Refugees was created. It initially concentrated its energies on the 800,000 Russians 'scattered throughout Europe, bereft of legal representation' and was headed and dominated by the Norwegian, Fridtjof Nansen, who had been involved with refugee and relief work after 1918. Nansen's problems in getting support for the Commission were immense, as Michael Marrus highlights:

> The Americans ... had rejected the League [of Nations] entirely by the time Nansen's agency was born; the Italians became openly hostile in the following year, when the advent of Fascism prompted an emigration of bitter opponents of Mussolini's new order. Great Britain and the Dominions felt unwilling to receive refugees and feared the High Commissioner might pressure member states to do so. Only the French and Scandinavian countries offered warm support.[45]

Apart from keeping the issue alive and helping to coordinate relief, Nansen's greatest achievement was to create certificates which helped refugees without documentation to receive recognition and status in receiving countries where alien control procedures had tightened since the war. Although it was incomplete and limited largely to Russians and Armenians, the 'Nansen passports' began the process of international legal recognition of the refugee problem. More generally, however, as John Hope Simpson commented 18 years after the creation of the High Commission, its function was limited. First, 'at no time [was] official encouragement ... given to suggestions for the extension of League protection to all classes of refugees'. Second, 'League protection [was] on a temporary basis'. Third, League funds were to be used for administrative purposes only, and whilst 'League organizations [were] expected to co-ordinate efforts made for relief and settlement ... [they could] not spend League funds for those purposes'.[46]

The most effective aid given to refugees was thus left to the nation-states themselves and to private relief agencies. The greatest problem was to convince former immigrant receiving societies that they could benefit economically from the post-war refugees at a time of high unemployment. It was for this reason that in 1924 Nansen suggested that problems of refugee employment, migration and settlement should be transferred from the League to the International Labor Organisation (ILO). Progress was slow, but in the four years from 1925 to 1929 the ILO Refugee Service claimed to have found work for some 60,000 individuals. In the latter year the Service was closed, partly in recognition of the impossibility of carrying out its mission in the context of a global economic crisis. By the end of the decade, emigration from Europe had effectively ceased.[47]

The combination of desperate refugees and the difficulty of finding a place of asylum created a new problem in Europe: that of transmigrants with nowhere to go. The number of transmigrants was a half or a third of that before the war but with the power of American restrictionism, there was much greater likelihood that journeys would not be completed. Before the war, transmigrant centres such as that in Hamburg had been brutal – partly to encourage immigrants to complete their journey as quickly as possible. Paul Weindling describes the process in such centres:

> Having escaped Czarist repression and terrifying pogroms, migrants could expect prison-like regimentation by German medical personnel, border guards and officials... After disembarking from the packed trains, disinfection involved the separation of male and female passengers and consequent breaking up of families, the confiscation of all clothing and possessions, rubbing down with strange, slippery substances, and a shower... For those unfamiliar with modern medical routines, medical inspections could be terrifying, arousing fears of robbery and murder.[48]

In pre-1914 Europe there was great fluidity of movement as refugees moved from one place to another and sometimes back to their homeland. In such population shifts, personal choice played an important role. In contrast, after the First World War refugees, carrying a pariah status, were dumped from one country to another with no state, with the partial exception of France, taking ultimate responsibility for their future welfare. After 1918 the shipping companies returned to what they viewed as the lucrative passenger trade and encouraged individuals to consider emigration. There was, however, a grave danger to those embarking on a new life away from persecution of facing lengthy stays in unsuitable and unsavoury transmigrancy hostels and camps.

A report of the Jews' Temporary Shelter in London covering the period from 1918 to 1921 indicated the misery and horror from which individuals were fleeing:

> [The Ukrainians fleeing civil war and famine] narrated harrowing stories of the massacres that were perpetrated before their eyes, and there was scarcely one who had not sustained some personal loss in those horrible butcheries. Amongst these refugees was a little boy whose parents, brothers and sisters were foully murdered, and he miraculously escaped a similar fate by hiding under a hay-

stack. He was [the] charge of a relative who took him over to his uncle in America...

Pre-1914 such refugees would have faced few bureaucratic obstacles in finding a place of refuge. Another case reported by the Jews' Temporary Shelter, that of an old man 'whose wife the murderers slaughtered before his eyes', indicated the changes that had taken place:

> On arrival in this country on his way to Canada, the Shipping Company discovered that his papers were not in order, and he had to go back to Danzig, in order to get the documentation to enable him to go to Canada. We gave him letters of introduction to the Emigration Committee and the Chief Rabbi in Danzig, urging them to do everything possible for him...

The report went on to describe the uncertainty of finding safety as well as the failure of the local, national and international authorities to anticipate the dilemma of stranded refugees:

> In consequence of the sudden and abnormal transmigration traffic through this country in the year 1920–21, when thousands of transmigrants of all denominations ... arrived here in quick succession from Eastern Europe, the Shipping Companies and the Aliens Authorities found themselves quite unprepared to grapple with the serious situation that had arisen owing to the lack of accommodation. Scores of so-called hostels sprang up in various localities for the reception of these unfortunate wanderers, and complaints were almost daily made to the authorities by the London County Council and Local Sanitary Inspectors, as to the scandalous manner in which the transmigrants were being herded together in small rooms and hovels, quite unfit for human habitation.[49]

Before the war, Liverpool dominated the trade in transmigrancy but Southampton played an increasing role as a port which immigrants passed through. It was marked by the development of John Doling's 'Emigrants' Home Lodging House' which opened in 1895 and extended into a massive four storey building, renamed 'Atlantic Hotel' in 1908. The war, however, destroyed the business.[50] After 1918, the uncertain nature of emigration/immigration made such private business ventures more risky, revealed in the losses made on transmigrants by the Atlantic Park Hostel Company.[51] For those concerned with the welfare of Jewish immigrants, including the dangers faced by unaccompanied women and children, Southampton remained important after 1918, especially when it soon emerged as the most important transatlantic port in Britain during the inter-war period. Ironically, although the small Jewish community of the town would have little direct interaction with those immigrants passing through it, for the synagogue and the payment of its rabbi, the Reverend Gordon, the transmigrants would be crucial. Gordon was employed to check the racket in 'trafficking girls' for prostitution abroad. Much of his income came through the Jewish Association for the Protection of Women and Children (Jewish Association) for such work.[52]

A sum of £50 was given to create a Trans-Emigration Aid Committee within the Southampton Hebrew Committee for those passing through the port. The award coincided, however, with the 1921 immigration quota law in the USA which created a problem of transmigrancy well beyond the scope of a small underfunded local committee. Building on post-war xenophobia and isolationism, a movement for a 'genuine 100 per cent American immigration law' grew in strength with bias against aliens from eastern and southern Europe. Immigration was limited to three per cent of those who had come from each country as measured in the 1910 census, aiming for a maximum of 350,000 per annum. Immigrants from north-western Europe were favoured; the specific quota from Russia was only 25,000.[53] Worse was to follow for those trying to escape from eastern Europe, but the impact of the 1921 Act was itself drastic for transmigrants. The number of stranded people rose rapidly and government agencies worried about disease spreading through the use of 'undesirable and insanitary lodging-houses and so-called hostels'.[54]

Organisations such as the Jewish Association despaired at the problem's unmanageable proportions and placed the blame firmly on shipping companies desperate for trade in the depressed post-war world 'who recruit Emigrants and hold out enducements which often do not materialise'. Reporting to the League of Nations in 1924, the Jewish Association outlined how the dire situation of the transmigrants could easily be exploited by those involved in the international trade in prostitution. It emphasised, however, that although they were reluctant to accept it

> the companies are really responsible for the maintenance of such Emigrants or Deportees, as they accepted them as passengers in the city of origin and agreed to take them to their destination.

By the time this report was submitted to the League of Nations, the international reputation of Atlantic Park Hostel had already become established:

> [It] in the main should serve as a model for all stations where large numbers of migrants have to be housed. Ample accommodation is provided for sleeping, meals, for medical attention and for recreation, and the Hostel is under the management of a capable officer, speaking the languages understood by the majority of the migrants…

Even so, it highlighted 'certain difficulties which arise from the concentration of large numbers in such camps or Hostels and it is, therefore, advisable that the stay of the migrant should be as short as possible'.[55]

It is a reflection of the appalling conditions in the transmigrancy camps in general that Atlantic Park should have been viewed as the most successful attempt to deal with this global problem. It should be remembered, however, that the American authorities, including the Consul in Southampton, John Savage, were anxious to extoll its virtues, attempting to minimise growing criticism aimed at their immigration controls and deteriorating conditions at

Ellis Island. Condemnation was particularly vocal in countries such as Britain which feared that they would suffer the results of American restrictionism. Given Britain's own stance on alien immigration, the moral outrage expressed about American controls contained more than a touch of hypocrisy.[56]

THE ESTABLISHMENT OF ATLANTIC PARK HOSTEL IN THE CONTEXT OF INTERNATIONAL POLITICS

Savage produced two detailed accounts of the hostel of what became one of the biggest transmigrancy camps in the world and certainly the largest in British history. His first report written for the US State Department was written in January 1922, giving a history of the Atlantic Park Hostel up to the point at which it was due to open:

> In order to secure as large a proportion as possible of the second and third class passenger traffic originating on the Continent which is destined for either the United States or Canada, the Canadian Pacific, Cunard and White Star Lines have jointly established an emigrant's hostel at Eastleigh to which they have given the name of 'Atlantic Park'. This hostel, with a present capacity of 5000 passengers, is designed to compare favorably with similar establishments used by competing lines at continental ports, and the facilities provided include modern appliances to ensure the cleanliness of both passengers and baggage before embarkation, as well as a comfortable place in which passengers can be housed while in transit...
>
> [A]ll continental passengers who arrive at east coast ports will be brought to Eastleigh by train and thence conveyed to the park by motorbus, and on the days of embarkation at Southampton they will be transported from the park to the Southampton docks in the same manner. The park consists of thirty acres, fifteen acres of which are covered by the buildings, the balance being used for recreation purposes. The buildings which have been converted to their prospective use were mostly built, and all of them used during the war, as airdromes and barracks by the American Air Force in England... The cost of the land and the buildings and the adaptation of the buildings to their present uses, represents an outlay of approximately six hundred and fifty thousand dollars, which will give some idea of the vastness of the enterprise. Transmigrant passengers will be housed and treated at Atlantic Park without cost. The fare which the continental passenger pays to the steamship company at the point of departure includes all the expenses of the journey until arrival at the port of entry in the United States or Canada as the case may be.

Part of Savage's report dealt with the question of quarantine. Before the war, American immigration officials had carried out medical checks on transmigrants in Britain but after 1918 these were far more extensive and humiliating. 'Disinfecting' transmigrants at Atlantic Park was never as brutal as in the pre-1914 centres described by Weindling, but it was still frightening and disturbing to those at the receiving end. Liza Shleimowitz came to Atlantic Park as a 13-year-old orphan with her four sisters and young brother.

One bitter memory she retained was that of her hair being shaved and of being sprayed with disinfecting water: '[the] four sisters forming a circle to protect their baby brother, Izzy, while they were being hosed down'.[57] Efficiency, rather than humanity, was to be the watchword of the hostel.

The report also described the facilities available in the hostel, including a women's recreation room and a men's smoking room. Yet even to these 'softer' features were added large spaces to enable the control of the immigrants, including:

> a general marshalling room in which the United States Public Health Surgeon will make his inspection. In this room also the usual examination of passports and visas by the consular staff will take place and embarkation tickets will be issued to passengers who are ready to embark.

Before the war, wealthier aliens were generally exempt from the 1905 Aliens Act but after 1918 controls were less differentiated though life was still easier for transmigrants with money. At Atlantic Park, 'better class dormitories' were provided:

> Three separate buildings with 75 double rooms have been set aside as dormitories for second and the better type of third class passengers. The facilities provided in these rooms will be equal to the second class accommodation of any ship and will provide suitable quarters for married people with families, as well as men with their wives. Ample lavatory and bathing accommodation are provided for the persons using these dormitories.

Atlantic Park Hostel was an enormous business venture, but by completion its future was already in jeopardy as the final section of Savage's report candidly admitted:

> Although the park is equipped for opening ... the exact date when it will be utilized as an emigrants' hostel has not yet been fully determined. The present immigration law of the United States, and the uncertainty as to future legislation, have no doubt more or less to do with the indecision of the companies involved to take advantage of the facilities they have provided.[58]

The hostel did open in the spring of 1922. Nevertheless, the shipping companies were not misguided in their fears that further American immigration control would put at risk the whole purpose of the hostel. Intellectual proponents of 'Nordic' superiority combined with the American Federation of Labor and other 'patriotic' organisations to demand a new Quota Act inspired by restrictionism with an even stronger racial bias against east and southern Europeans. In 1924 the quota was cut to two per cent of the 1890 census – a year in which the number of east Europeans and southern Europeans was both relatively and absolutely low. The annual Russian quota, for example, was now only 1,800.[59]

The chances of transmigrants getting caught in the tangle of new quota regulations were high. From early 1923, the history of Atlantic Park Hostel was no longer one of a continuous movement of sojourners. Instead, it was the increasingly pathetic story of 1,200 Ukrainian refugees, largely Jewish, who could not move on, settle in Britain, or return to the land of their persecution. In March 1923 the Chairman of the Jews' Temporary Shelter told his committee how their problem had emerged:

> [O]wing to the 3% Quota Restriction Act ... no more than 3% of each nationality can be admitted each year into the United States. The quota for Russia was, however, open until the last few days when it became suddenly exhausted owing to large numbers of Russians from Vladivostock having landed recently in California, with the result that about 750 transmigrants ... who were supposed to have sailed last week [on] the 'Aquitania' were stopped at the last moment from sailing until the opening of the new quota in July next ... to save them from being returned to Russia, it was found necessary by the heads of the Community ... to pay for their maintenance [at Atlantic Park] until the date they would be able to sail, and that Shelter was asked to look after them on behalf of the Community.[60]

The hopes that the Ukrainians might be allowed to enter the United States the following year were dashed by the new quota law. By early 1924, the fate of the transmigrants in Atlantic Park Hostel became the focus of criticism locally, nationally and internationally. Jewish bodies in particular were concerned about the well-being of individuals for whom no country would take responsibility. That such a small number of refugees could be perceived so problematically across the world indicated the new post-war mood. In February 1925, Joynson-Hicks was asked what he intended doing about the stranded Atlantic Park refugees by a Labour MP sympathetic to their plight. Joynson-Hicks was adamant in his response:

> I have replied quite definitely that under no circumstances will I permit these unfortunate people to be absorbed into our population. It is quite impossible. They are the class of people who come from the east of Europe that we do not want, and America does not want them either.[61]

Organisations such as the Hebrew Sheltering and Immigration Society of America were forced to outline the bleak possibilities to those at Atlantic Park. The local merged and became inseparable from the global as a visit to the refugees by an international delegation in June 1924 revealed. Their position under the new regulations was explained and it was reported that 'Many who realised how serious was their position broke down, while others expressed their indignation at the effect of the laws ...', especially when it was 'pointed out that the 1,800 [Russians] who are to be admitted [to the USA] will be drawn from all over the world, and, further, that there are 840 waiting at Atlantic Park alone'. When it was argued by the delegation that the stranded refugees might consider other countries to which they might emigrate, the local newspaper reported that the suggestion

> was not too kindly received, for many of the women have husbands in the States

and children to maintain, yet owing to the restrictions they are prevented from settling down together.

A former seafarer, describing the appalling conditions for those east Europeans travelling steerage from Southampton to South America during the 1920s, recalled that those on board embarked at Montevideo and Buenos Aires with little idea of how to survive in an alien environment: 'Some of them just went ashore ... and never knew where to go'. It is possible that amongst these desperate steerage passengers were refugees from Atlantic Park. It was hardly surprising, therefore, that few in the hostel were willing to take the following advice from the delegation

> that in view of the improbability of gaining access to the States, emigrants would answer the question [of their plans for the future] in something like the following manner: 'I should prefer to take up farming in South America'.[62]

Details of the delegation's visit in the local newspaper caused deep anxiety to the American Consul in Southampton who wrote to his Secretary of State in Washington that:

> Since the passage of the new Immigration Act the press has contained various references to the plight of these people and the uncertainty as to their future... I have also received numerous letters and telegrams from Members of both branches of Congress and friends and relatives of detained passengers dealing with individual cases and requesting me to use my good offices to allow the persons mentioned to depart for the United States at the earliest opportunity.[63]

One such case was Polikarp Kachura of New York whose wife and two children arrived in Atlantic Park during October 1923. The Kachuras had emigrated to the United States before the First World War and their first son, Michael, was born there in 1914. A year later, Mrs Kachura returned to Russia to see her mother and receive an inheritance left by her father. Shortly after her arrival she had a second son, Ivan, and was taken ill. In her husband's words, 'after that delay, the United States entered the war, and then the Russian Revolution broke out, cutting her off from funds and diplomatic conveniences'. After the war contact between the family was re-established and every effort was made by the Kachuras to reunite. In July 1922 the Department of State gave approval for the American Consulate in Riga to give Mrs Kachura and her children a visa to proceed to the United States. This was issued in October 1923 and the three progressed as far as London and were then transferred to Atlantic Park. By their time of arrival in Eastleigh, however, the Russian quota was filled and although Michael, as an American citizen, could proceed, there was no guarantee that Mrs Kachura and her younger son would be allowed entry.

The key question was whether the authorities would accept that her 1915 visit to Russia was intended to be temporary. Under the 1921 Immigration Act 'an alien who remains abroad in excess of six months shall be presumed to have abandoned his domicile in the United States' unless 'evidence [was produced] to the contrary satisfactory to the appropriate immigration officers'. Yet again, the discretion of local officials was of vital importance regarding the freedom of refugees to move across frontiers. The shipping companies, however, refused to move on transmigrants at Atlantic Park if there was any chance of them being rejected at Ellis Island. The American Consul was told by the White Star Line concerning the Kachuras that

> they will be only too glad to send these people forward if they can receive assurances from any authoritative source that they will be allowed to land on arrival, but the steamship company are not willing to let them go forward without these assurances considering the risk of the penalties involved.[64]

It was through similar stories of bureaucratic inflexibility that many refugees were detained in Atlantic Park awaiting a decision for first months and then years. Meanwhile, the possibilities of moving on to desirable or even undesirable destinations diminished. In 1924 the American Consul in Southampton felt pressurised to produce his second report on the hostel to help quell the criticisms he received on an almost daily basis. His report concluded by pointing out that:

> At the suggestion of the superintendent in charge of the Park, a committee composed of present residents and chosen by them, has been appointed. This committee brings to the manager's attention any suggestions or complaints arising on the part of the passengers, and these reports are received by him in a sympathetic manner. Passengers questioned at random expressed themselves as highly satisfied with the treatment they are receiving...[65]

Some reports were less favourable about the conditions; but good, bad or indifferent, the most important factor affecting the morale of those in Atlantic Park concerned their freedom to find a permanent place of refuge. After the flurry of interest in the dire plight of the stranded refugees in 1924, their situation was soon forgotten. They were simply 1,000 out of 25,000 to 30,000 east Europeans stuck in transmigrancy camps resulting from the new American quota laws. Some, such as the Kachuras, were allowed into the USA, especially if some of the family party could prove that they had American citizenship – but others never made it to their favoured destination. By the end of October 1925, 700 out of roughly 1,000 had left Eastleigh: 630 had gone to the United States as quota and preference (family) passengers, 19 to Argentina, 27 to Palestine and, to quote the Jews' Temporary Shelter, '24 returned to Russia of their own free will'. The Shelter gave those returning clothes and £10 in cash but was most anxious to avoid the impression that it was bribing individuals to go back to their troubled homeland. Under pressure from the Union of Jewish Women, and also the Jewish Association for the Protection of Women and Children, it was decided not to return 'unprotected women and orphans' to Russia.[66]

The choices for those unable to get visas for the United States were limited. The mother of Cyril Orolowitz, Liza Shleimowitz, was typical of those unable to proceed to the United States but fortunate, through family connections, to have other options. Born in the Ukraine, Liza was 13 when she arrived with three of her sisters and a brother at Atlantic Park. Their father, a well-travelled, cultured and educated man, owned a factory in Pavlograd manufacturing buttons and providing lead seals for the Russian postal administration. Liza's sister, Rachel, later described the events after the war which had left her orphaned:

> Her father's worldly possessions, the result of 41 years of strenuous, energetic effort, were confiscated by the Bolshevik. Her mother and father were tied hand and foot, the latter placed face to face with the wall, and with a pistol held to his neck his money demanded. After being subjected to considerable abuse... they were thrown from their home on to the snow-clad earth. Within six days of this treatment her mother, father and two of the children died from hunger, shock and exposure.[67]

The children travelled with their American uncle, Jacob Solomon, from Riga to England late in 1923. Staying briefly at Atlantic Park, they took a ship from Southampton to New York. Solomon assumed that once in the USA he would be allowed to adopt his relatives. In the process of travel, however, one of the daughters, Sema, was lost. It is not clear what happened to her, but she later turned up in Rotterdam, possibly pregnant. Her case illustrates how the fears of middle-class Jewish women's organisations – that stranded transmigrant women and children were at great risk – were not without foundation. Nevertheless, the four other children arrived, temporarily as it turned out, at Ellis Island. Liza later told her son that they were allowed

> to plead the case before a judge to allow them to convince the authorities that they had to be allowed into the States to be adopted. They were told in Russian before the judge's appearance that they had to cry.

This strategy failed and the children were sent back to Southampton and Atlantic Park. Liza recalled the desperation of those days and how 'they were shunted from pillar to post, it went on for ever... They didn't know whether they were coming or going'.[68]

Meanwhile, their uncle made every effort on their behalf. He sent a telegram to the President of the United States, Calvin Coolidge, when the children were detained in Ellis Island, prompting correspondence with the Secretary of Labor, James Davis. Although Davis has been described as having 'an especially lively interest in restriction and ... an ardent attachment to Nordic nationalism', he seems to have expressed genuine regret in refusing entry to these particular Jewish children. He wrote to Coolidge in January 1924 that once the quota had been filled

> there is no discretion vested by Congress in the Secretary of Labor or any one else to admit any more people... It is a source of profound regret to me, Mr President, that the situation is as I find it, but I am utterly powerless to do anything whatever to admit the children referred to by Mr Solomon.[69]

With the children sent back to Southampton, Jacob Solomon made one last desperate attempt to plea for his nephew and nieces to be allowed entry into the United States. The failure of his letter to Coolidge, which ended with an appeal evoking the very essence of American idealism, was ample testimony to the victory of inward-looking, racially exclusive nationalism in the inter-war period:

> Mr President, I appreciate that Congress has passed a law which restricts immigration, and I also appreciate that the quota for Russia is full. But Mr President, when Congress enacted this law, it never intended that these unfortunate orphans should be excluded from this country... I appeal to you, Mr President, as a citizen of good standing, as a beloved father of my children, three of whom have been in the Military Service of the U.S. during the recent war, I appeal to you in the name of God and Humanity to use the power vested in you and lift the load of unhappiness and misfortune from these children and permit them to enter the United States, 'THE LAND OF THE FREE AND THE HOME OF THE BRAVE', so that I may be a father to them.[70]

Unfortunately for Jacob Solomon, the pre-war faith that the United States could transform, as Emma Lazarus's poem on the Statue of Liberty expressed it, the 'huddled masses yearning to be free, the wretched refuse [of Europe's shores]', into 'upright American citizens', had disappeared in the war and its aftermath. Nevertheless, for the Shleimowitz children, family in other parts of the Jewish diaspora provided other possibilities. After ten months at Atlantic Park, Jacob arranged for the children to stay with his brother Isaac, who had emigrated from Russia to Cape Town, South Africa, before the war. Isaac had married but had no children. Along with a further ten orphaned children from other family members left behind in the Ukraine, the four children were adopted by Isaac Solomon and his wife, Liza. The remarkable story was published in the local newspaper during 1929 which commented that the Solomons'

> devotion to human interests in the absence of any children of their own is one of the admirable, practical humanitarian demonstrations by the Jewish community in South Africa to emancipate their relatives from terrible social conditions.[71]

Yet by the time of this article, South African antisemitism had itself grown rapidly. Racial nationalists, stressing 'Nordic' supremacy, claimed that Jews were of inferior stock and should be excluded from the country. Such racist influence at governmental level increased throughout the second half of the 1920s and achieved success in 1930 with the passing of an immigration Quota Act. Similar to the American legislation of 1924, the 1930 Quota Act was designed to control the entry of Jewish and other 'undesirable' immigrants from Europe. Thereafter, it has been commented, 'a camel could have gone through the eye of a needle more easily than a poor Lithuanian immigrant could have entered South Africa for the first time'.[72] The life of the orphaned children, who had escaped these controls by a matter of months, was not easy in South Africa, especially in the depressed economy of the 1930s. Nevertheless, it was in stark contrast to the youngest of the Schlomowitz children, Tuba, who remained behind in eastern Europe. She wrote to her sisters in South Africa throughout the 1930s. Her letters and those from her daughter, Tanya, from the Bolshevik-controlled Ukraine gave a picture of terrible deprivation. Tuba needed constant financial support and medical supplies. After the war she was never heard of again. Such correspondence managed to help maintain global family bonds which were destroyed, one amongst the millions, during the Holocaust. They act as reminders of the Jews who were left behind in Europe, excluded by the worldwide move toward racialised immigration controls in the inter-war period.[73]

Even with financial inducements from a range of Jewish organisations and the help of family networks, by the end of 1924 some 300 people remained at Atlantic Park and there was little prospect of their internment coming to an end. The hope of the British government and the shipping companies remained that the American authorities would relax their immigration laws to solve the embarrassing and increasingly expensive problem once and for all. Yet the failure of this to happen, as well as the equal inflexibility of Joynson-Hicks to accept those remaining as permanent residents, led to what the Jewish Association regarded in March 1925 as a total deadlock.[74] There was pressure from the British government and the shipping companies, in the indelicate words of the Assistant Secretary of State in the State Department, Wilbur Carr,

> to make arrangements to dispose in the most humane way possible of such of these aliens as are not likely to obtain visas to proceed to the United States within a reasonable time.[75]

These refugees, however, were unwanted by the outside world.

ATLANTIC PARK AND BRITISH JEWISH POLITICS

The plight of the stranded Atlantic Park refugees caused internal fighting and much heartache within various Jewish organisations in Britain. The body which assumed greatest responsibility in terms of liaison with the British state was the Jews' Temporary Shelter (JTS). Although it was one of the more generous organisations set up to help the east European Jewish immigrants before the First World War, the Shelter after the war was less flexible and humanitarian in its approach.[76] In 1924, Otto Schiff, the President of the Shelter, 'referred to the implicit confidence placed in the [JTS] by the Home Office and other Government Departments'. It meant, concerning the refugees at Eastleigh, that the oppressive restrictionism of the government remained unchallenged.[77]

Resistance to this policy came from only one member of the Shelter's Executive Committee, Dr Jochelman, a leading figure in the Federation of Ukrainian Jews. The Federation had been set up after the war by pre-1914 east European immigrants to raise funds for victims of the pogroms and famine. Those in the Federation challenged the hegemony of the elite British Jews who claimed to speak for the whole Jewish community. In this specific case, Jochelman asked of his fellow Jewish leaders that '[we] listen first to the cry of the transmigrants, and leave details of procedure for adjustment later on' – a strategy not suited to the authoritarian approaches of many older British Jewish institutions.[78] The Federation wrote to the American government that 'In the name of humanity we beg you to allow the entry of these victims of the war pogroms and famine at the first possible opportunity'. In addition, Jochelman 'urged that representations be made to the Home Office with a view to a proportion of these poor people being allowed to remain in this country'.[79]

This was anathema to the Shelter and, in 1924, when the Federation was refused access to a delegation to meet the Jews at Atlantic Park, Jochelman demanded that Jewish negotiations with the government should be transferred to the Aliens Committee of the Board of Deputies of British Jews. Jochelman hoped that the Board would deal with the matter in a more enlightened and democratic manner. Failing to get his demands, Jochelman resigned and the Shelter continued to act on behalf of British Jewry in matters relating to Atlantic Park. In July 1924 he warned that:

> It is possible that a number of the men may, in desperation, return to Russia, a step which … will be fatal to them, in view of the present economic state of Russia and the sufferings of the Jewish population there.[80]

Although single women and children were exempted, the Federation of Ukrainian Jews failed to stop the repatriation of men from Atlantic Park. Their fate is unknown, though of the 870,000 Jews in the Ukraine at the start of the Nazi invasion in 1941, only roughly 17,000 survived the war.[81]

More generally, Jochelman's campaign to persuade the British government to offer permanent hospitality to some of the refugees failed. In 1926 agreement was made between the Jewish authorities, the shipping companies and the Home Office to clear the camp. The only concession was to grant work permits to some women enabling them to become domestic servants before they left Britain. The Union of Jewish Women, although excluded from the official negotiations with the British government, was given authority over the care of the Atlantic Park women, including finding work and housing for those allowed to leave the camp.[82]

In an atmosphere of ever-intensifying anti-alienism, it is understandable that many British Jewish leaders refused to confront the government's restrictionism. This was particularly the case when from 1924 until 1929 the Home Secretary was Joynson-Hicks. In 1926 he wrote to an anti-alien MP, A.

Hudson, that the recent decision to let some of the women be employed as domestics was taken with full assurances that they would not 'take work which would otherwise be available for our own countrymen'. Yet even with the tiny numbers of people involved, Joynson-Hicks stated that 'the case has given me a great deal of personal anxiety'.[83] Bodies such as the Board of Deputies of British Jews concentrated their energies in securing naturalisation (and sometimes fighting deportation orders) for those aliens who had emigrated before the war rather than pushing for post-war refugees to be allowed asylum.[84]

Many Jews in Britain believed that this strategy was too defensive, especially when it related to the stranded Eastleigh refugees. Criticism was articulated by the leading Jewish newspaper in Britain, the *Jewish Chronicle*, which normally avoided taking sides in communal institutional disputes. In an editorial of February 1925 it emphasised that

> no greater wrong has ever been done to helpless men and women than that inflicted upon these poor people who are stranded at Eastleigh. There seems to be no feasible proposition for the amelioration of their hapless condition... We should have thought that there must be somewhere ... that a comparatively few people could be settled and redeemed from the virtual imprisonment to which they are now subjected.

It added caustically that 'the addition of a few hundred stranded men and women to the general population would not mean the downfall of England or the ruin of the British Empire'.[85]

Some of those exercising authority in British Jewry had a sense of shame that no more was done and that too much power had fallen into the hands of the JTS. Joseph Prag, himself a pre-war immigrant, and a long-standing communal activist, wrote of his concerns to the President of the Board of Deputies of British Jews in June 1927:

> I have long felt that the Aliens Committee [of the Board] was not carrying out the objects for which it was elected... We have done nothing since 1914 and since the war we have handed ourselves over to the Shelter and the Shelter policy, which deals with those here while our duty lies to those both here and who cannot get here. I feel that even the Eastleigh case if properly ventilated would have secured admission for those, comparatively few, unfortunate people. We helped the Home Office to cover it up. Does anybody think British public opinion would have tolerated the keeping of over 200 people in enforced confinement with all its attended evils if we had had the pluck to call its attention to it? Does anybody think that it would have been felt that these 200 would harmfully affect the 48 million of inhabitants? No, the Shelter has a certain policy in these matters, but it is not ours.[86]

LIFE IN ATLANTIC PARK HOSTEL AND THE LOCAL IMPACT

By the late 1920s Prag was one of the few who could recall the more generous mood relating to aliens and refugees in the pre-1914 world.[87] Was he right to

Two Belgian refugee soldiers outside Blackmoor Convalescent Home in the New Forest during the First World War. Photograph from the private collection of Dionis Macnair and with her kind permission.

The Chronicles of the Belgians.

More especially those relating to Blackmoor Convalescent Home

November 1914 –

Eleanor Ruth Dent.

Cover illustration of 'The Chronicle of the Belgians', by Eleanor Ruth Dent. From the private collection of Dionis Macnair and with her kind permission.

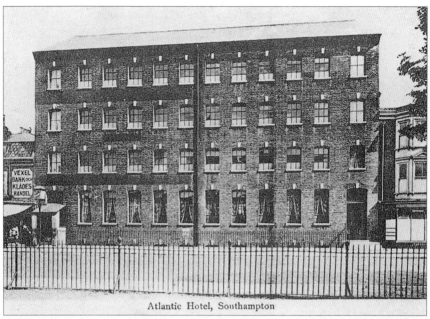

Atlantic Hotel, Southampton, which catered for steerage passengers – immigrants and refugees – transmigrating through England to the 'New World' before the First World War.

Tombstone of Boris Selesnov (1924–1926) who was born and died at Atlantic Park Hostel. Photograph by kind permission of Melissa Dice.

The Shleimowitz sisters photographed at a studio in Eastleigh, 1925, but resident at Atlantic Park Hostel. From the private collection of Cyril Orolowitz and with his kind permission.

Atlantic Park Hostel dining room, 1924. From the records of the American Consul at Southampton.

Children from Atlantic Park Hostel on the playing fields, 1924. From the records of the American Consul at Southampton.

The Basque Refugee Camp at Stoneham (near Eastleigh) from the air, 1937. By kind permission of Gordon Cox, Eastleigh and District Local History Society.

Basque children offering an anti-fascist salute at the Stoneham Camp, 1937. By kind permission of Gordon Cox, Eastleigh and District Local History Society.

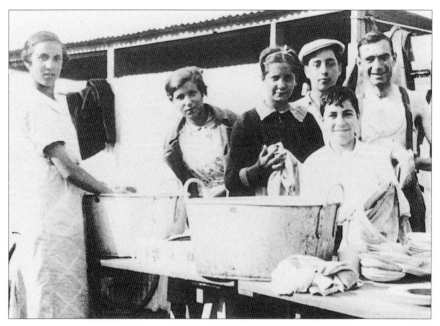

Basque youngsters washing up, Stoneham Camp, 1937. By kind permission of Gordon Cox, Eastleigh and District Local History Society.

Senor Sanchez, the radio announcer and interpreter at Stoneham Camp. By kind permission of Gordon Cox, Eastleigh and District Local History Society.

Alice Klausova with baby at Southampton Children's Hospital, 1939. From the private collection of Alice Sluckin and with her kind permission.

Polish children in post-war England living in Nissen huts. By kind permission of Jan K.

Polish teachers at the camp at Hiltingbury. By kind permission of Stephanie P.

A Polish Catholic religious celebration at Chandler's Ford, c.1950s. By kind permission of Stephanie P.

Hungarian freedom fighters in front of a government building. The Communist emblem has been cut out of their flag. By kind permission of Andy Rumi who is pictured on the far left of the group.

Vietnamese refugees in a detention centre, Hong Kong, during the 1980s. By kind permission of Paul Rushton.

Vietnamese refugees at Sunshine House, 1984 – the last to stay at the centre before it closed. Joyce White of the Women's Royal Voluntary Service, an activist in the local reception centre in Gosport, is shown on the left. By kind permission of Joyce White.

Christmas party at Sunshine House for the Vietnamese refugees, 1980s. By kind permission of Paul Rushton.

Vietnamese family resettled by Ockenden Venture in Hampshire. By kind permission of Paul Rushton.

Kurdish family parting in Turkey. By kind permission of Peter Minns.

Demonstration in Whitehall involving Hampshire activists protesting against the detention of Kurdish asylum seekers in Winchester, August 1989. By kind permission of Peter Minns.

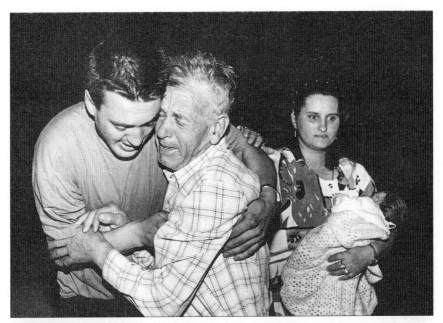

A Bosnian Muslim refugee reunited with his father who had believed him to be killed in the ethnic cleansing of 1992. He had, in fact, fled to the UK where he married another Bosnian refugee. Kljuc, north-west Bosnia. By kind permission of Howard Davies.

Demonstration against the detention of Zairean and other asylum seekers in Haslar, 24 June 1995 – part of a national day of action against detentions and deportations. Photograph by Tony Kushner.

Zairean refugees fleeing to Tanzania, crossing Lake Tanganyika, 1996. By kind permission of L. Taylor (United Nations High Commissioner for Refugees).

suggest that public sympathy could have been elicited for the Eastleigh refugees? There is evidence that the sheer pathos of the stranded refugees at Atlantic Park might have ensured a more generous popular response in Britain had ordinary people been allowed to articulate it. Certainly, national press reports on Atlantic Park, even from generally anti-alien newspapers, were remarkable for their sympathetic reactions to those who had, by the late 1920s, spent the better half of a decade in the camp.

An account of the hostel in the *Daily Express* as late as November 1929 described the depressing reality for those who were unable to join family in the United States or elsewhere in the world. It stressed that 'How these people came to be marooned at Southampton six years ago is one of the world's worst "hard luck" stories'. Slowly, the numbers in Atlantic Park declined as other non-American options were taken up and some died waiting for visas to be granted. By the time of the *Daily Express* report, 28 refugees remained who had been in the hostel for six years. It included the sad story of Mrs Schultz, aged 60 and formerly a headmistress of a girls' school:

> Yes, we are despondent. Our hopes are dead. The children write to me from New York and say, 'You must come to us soon', and I write back saying, 'I think I shall never come before I am dead.' They cannot understand that six years of waiting here has broken my spirit. I do not hope, I have not the courage. I do not complain of the officials here; they are as kind as they can be. Whose fault it is that we have been waiting for six years I do not know. I am now number fifteen on the quota list, but that does not mean that I go soon to New York. It may mean more years of waiting yet... We are trying to smile, but how can we? There are aching hearts here.

The report concluded, however, by providing evidence of local sympathy which suggests that Prag was right to raise the possibility of a more enlightened response:

> The attempts of the parents to feed the children are pathetic. Some of the children who go to school at Eastleigh are fed by the parents of pupils who live in Eastleigh. I saw two of the Russian children returning today from school to the giant hangar at Atlantic Park, which is all they know of home...[88]

By 1929 the misery of those detained at Eastleigh was coming to an end. In 1930 the JTS had 'pleasure in reporting that the last batch of the 1,000 transmigrants ... received their Quota numbers during the year, and are now settled in the United States'. In contrast to the impression given by Colonel Lane in his anti-alien polemic, only one of the refugees was allowed to stay in Britain. Indeed, the refusal of the United States to let this individual emigrate indicated the power internationally of eugenics and racism to determine state policy in the first half of the twentieth century. The 1930 report of the Jews' Temporary Shelter concluded by giving details of the last transmigrant of Atlantic Park who was a

> deaf and dumb boy – who could not proceed to the United States as he was

unable to comply with the Education Clause of the American Immigration Laws, and it is to be feared that he will never be able to emigrate to the United States and will thus remain a permanent charge on the Shelter.[89]

There were even sadder stories from Atlantic Park, particularly those who died waiting for a country to take them, including Boris Selesnov who was born in the camp and died there aged two and a half. Boris and others from the camp are buried in the Southampton Jewish cemetery. Their memories fade along with the photograph in their tombstones. They include Ita Furman, a widow aged 61, formerly of Usman, who died of septicaemia following a whitlow on her right thumb in December 1926 (and whose death from a minor ailment suggests that those at Atlantic Park did not receive good medical treatment). Their stories alone cast doubt on the comfortable reflection of the JTS that the treatment of the transmigrants had 'been carried out in a manner to reflect enduring credit to the name of Anglo-Jewry'.[90] Yet it would be wrong to leave the refugees of Eastleigh as passive and hopeless victims. There was also an important internal history to Atlantic Park including active resistance and local support to improve the quality of the refugees' restricted lives.

An international delegation visiting Atlantic Park in June 1924 was met by Colonel R. D. Barbor, superintendent of the hostel, who

> conducted the party around the little township... The American delegate had to submit to some good-humoured but pointed comparisons with the U.S. facilities at Ellis Island. Even on the sports ground he could not escape the insinuations for two humorously-garbed transmigrants paraded the course with placards on their backs announcing themselves as 'Lord and Lady Ellis Island'.[91]

The reference to the 'little township' is a reminder of the scale of the operation. To some extent, the local population of Eastleigh, which was only two or three times the size of that at the hostel, had little idea of what went on inside the borders of Atlantic Park. The *Eastleigh Weekly News* in October 1926 commented how local 'people are continually seeing large and small contingents of emigrants arrive, but though living so near are unacquainted with the workings of the institution'.[92]

But the constant movement in and out of the transmigrants should not disguise the vibrant inner life of Atlantic Park. One of the most important features of this world was the refugees' continuous protest against the regulations that led to their stateless condition. 'Lord and Lady Ellis Island' were in themselves an indication that the greatest animus was aimed at the American government. By early 1925, however, the protests of those in Atlantic Park moved from the humorous to the serious. Frustrations grew throughout 1924 as it became apparent that the American government would not be flexible for those caught in its new restrictions.

Many of the refugees at Atlantic Park lobbied for the right to proceed to the United States and on 6 January 1925 such protests moved from the individual to the collective level. In what must have been one of the shortest, but most publicised, hunger strikes in modern British history, the refugees managed to receive national and international attention. With headlines in the British press such as 'Hunger Strike By 700 Jews: Complaints at British Ellis Island', and the 'Plight of Russian Refugees Awaiting Visas', the problems of those at Atlantic Park were brought home to an international audience. Ostensibly, the hunger strike concerned the quality of the food in the hostel. But as Colonel Barbor suggested, it was not really

> a question of fish and eggs. To my mind it is much more a matter of psychology. These unfortunate people, for whom I have very real sympathy, have been here over a year, and are naturally despairing of ever reaching their goal – the United States.[93]

The refugees missed only breakfast and lunch before ending their hunger strike in time to have dinner in the evening. One of the protesters' major complaints was that some of the emigrants, who had obtained the necessary visas and passports in order to proceed to the United States, were being kept at Atlantic Park by the shipping companies until they had paid for their maintenance at the hostel. Sums of between £10 and £50 were demanded – well out of the reach of most of those affected. In essence, Canadian Pacific, Cunard and White Star, having initially viewed Atlantic Park as a lucrative financial venture in the hope that the international movement of people would revive after the war, were trying to cut their losses by claiming money from the transmigrants which, under the provisions of the aliens legislation, they had no right to.[94]

There is no doubt, as the *Jewish Chronicle* put it, that Colonel Barbor was 'doing his best for the emigrants in very trying circumstances'. He was described by Morris Myer, a leading British Jewish figure, as a 'very pleasant and courteous gentleman, who takes great interest in the people under his care, and who well understands their peculiar and unenviable position'.[95] Barbor, who had retired from the army after 22 years, had served in South Russia after the armistice and was thus acutely aware of the appalling circumstances from which many of the transmigrants had escaped. An Irishman who had been educated at Dublin University, Barbor was an excellent linguist being fluent in French, Spanish, Italian and, most significantly for the purposes of Atlantic Park, Russian. The fortunate nature of his appointment as manager of the hostel in September 1923 was in marked contrast to his predecessor, Frank Johnson, who was convicted of financial conspiracy in May 1923.[96] The refugees told the *Jewish Guardian* that they held Colonel Barbor in 'high esteem; they speak gratefully of all he does to alleviate their lot by arranging concerts, games, etc., and they have the fullest confidence in, and appreciation of, his good intentions towards them'. Atlantic Park, as Barbor stated,

> was originally intended as a lodging house for a few days. It has become a

bonded warehouse for human goods, and in using the term I do not wish to imply that everything possible is not done to lighten the lot of those forced to remain here.[97]

Colonel Barbor was keen that the refugees had democratic channels through which they could have an input into the daily running of the camp whereas the Atlantic Park Hostel company was exclusively interested in matters of profit and loss. In June 1930 the secretary of the company wrote that 'owing to the serious curtailment of traffic' he was 'directed to give [Barbor] one month's notice'.[98] Under the seven years of Barbor's control, however, an effort was made to conquer the sheer boredom that faced its inhabitants and to move beyond an approach dictated by balance sheets. In terms of their cultural and religious needs, a synagogue was fitted up in the hostel and services were held daily. Rabbi Weitzman, formerly of Manchester, looked after the religious requirements of the Jews at Atlantic Park and was also involved in their general welfare.[99] The refugees themselves put on cultural events including musical evenings, lectures and theatre performances in the large entertainment hall which was provided with a stage, piano and gramophone. Sport was particularly encouraged by Barbor who had been a great athlete in his day. One of the unused dormitories was used as a gymnasium with a tennis and three badminton courts. The large expanse of green space around the buildings became sports fields, particularly utilised for football. Several pitches were laid out and 12 football sides were created, playing in their own Atlantic Park league as well as against neighbouring teams. It was reported that 'the verdict of the locals [was] that the Russians made very good soccer players'.[100]

In 1926, the right-wing *Morning Post* gave a romanticised version of life at Atlantic Park:

> It is the burden and the privilege of the Jew to be the world's greatest wanderer from the days when he sat by the waters of Babylon to the Twentieth Century. But I have been spending the afternoon in a settlement which includes many of the wandering children of Judea who have no need to weep… It was a glimpse of Middle Europe in England. Women with Russian shawls over their heads were sitting in the sun with their babies; small boys in loose blouses were playing happily about, and one tall Russian stood at the canteen wearing an Abraham cap.[101]

This picture of Atlantic Park in Eastleigh as essentially 'other' to life in what, with an equal fantasy, the *Jewish Chronicle* called a 'little Hampshire hamlet' (rather than an expanding railway town on the edge of Southampton), was highly misleading.[102] Out of choice as well as persuasion, the refugees quickly became anglicised, even playing cricket. Their temporary integration into local culture and society was aided by the provision of primary and secondary education for 200 of the Atlantic Park children by Hampshire County Council from 1923 onwards. After just one year the Director of Education reported that the children were 'now fairly proficient in both speaking and writing English'.[103] In addition, there were adult education classes in English and other languages. The 1924 Consular Report on Atlantic Park written, it was claimed, 'from the immigrants' standpoint', commented that such facilities for study were 'eagerly availed of and a larger proportion of the passengers take advantage of the opportunity to learn the language of the country to which they are destined'. Its conclusion that 'to this extent their detention here is an advantage rather than a hardship' distorted reality but reinforced the point that in spite of the frustrations and limitations imposed, a constructive and active cultural, religious, social and educational world was created within Atlantic Park.[104]

There is no doubt also that the involvement of the Union of Jewish Women in providing a social organiser to reside at Atlantic Park from March 1925 onwards improved the range and quality of activities available. However, one area of resentment felt by the refugees was the low quality clothing given to them by their richer co-religionists. The Union of Jewish Women was acutely aware of this feeling but its attempts to address this and other related issues of poverty in Atlantic Park were stamped upon by the men of the JTS. Aside from its importance in national and international politics, Atlantic Park provided a battleground in internal British Jewish power struggles. The old-style leadership of the Jewish elite was under pressure from the new bourgeois emerging from the east European immigration of the pre-1914 period. In terms of gender, middle-class Jewish women attempted to assert themselves more forcefully. Although the JTS was generally victorious in matters relating to the British government, organisations such as the Federation of the Ukrainian Jews and the Union of Jewish Women acted as humanitarian influences in Atlantic Park. Their efforts enabled the political and cultural resistance of the refugees to their plight to be expressed with greater liberty and success.[105]

Of importance to all those at Atlantic Park was the creation of a library which provides evidence of their complex cultural identities. Not surprisingly, given their rich cultural east European Jewish background, there was much demand for Yiddish literature and newspapers. But other newspapers requested indicate that those in Atlantic Park were very much open to and aware of their new British background. The library subscribed to the trade union-sponsored *Daily Herald*, which had highlighted their plight, as well as the *Daily News* and *Daily Chronicle*. Adding a further layer of cross-fertilisation was the regular presence of the *Jewish Guardian*, the organ of the most assimilated Jews in British society, which stressed the rootedness and deep history of the Jews in Britain but also campaigned on behalf of the stranded refugees. In addition, frequent complaints were made that so few Russian books were available. It suggests that the transmigrants had developed a degree of integration in the countries of their birth. Yet further intricacy in the make-up of the residents' sense of place is suggested by the regular supply of American newspapers at the hostel which were especially important for those still hoping to reach their favoured destination. Thus far from being a museum curiosity of 'old world' Jewish life dumped in deepest rural England, the identities of those at Atlantic Park were dynamic and multi-layered. American and British politicians were convinced that these few hundred Jewish refugees would remain an unassimilable alien wedge if allowed permanent residence into their respective countries. These were the same refugees who in 1925 made use of multiple copies of *Oliver Twist* and *Robin Hood and His Merry Men*. Even within the confines of Atlantic Park, the children and adults imbued large quantities of British, or more specifically, English, culture.[106]

The not infrequent deaths in the hostel added another depressing element to the lives of the transmigrants. In contrast, however, were marriages and births in the camp which brightened up daily routines. Unfortunately, one of the most tragic events at Atlantic Park followed a wedding – the suicide of a 22-year-old Russian non-Jew, Raphael Renner – a marriage which provides further evidence of the complex ethnic and religious make-up of the hostel. Renner had married a Jewish fellow resident of Atlantic Park and intended converting to Judaism, receiving a fair amount of teasing. Three weeks after the marriage he hung himself in a wood a mile from Atlantic Park. It would seem that the mixture of religious barriers alongside the cultural fluidity of the camp, as well as the strains and misery of constant waiting, proved too much. Believing that their marriage would never be accepted, he carved on the tree 'This is a very hard day, but love is greater than everything'. This desperately sad story clearly made a deep impression on those in the camp – hundreds went to visit the gruesome scene. That it occurred so far outside the confines of Atlantic Park itself is also significant. Although in principle the refugees were confined to the hostel, in practice they were free to walk around the district. Occasional trips for the children to the New Forest also helped counter isolation, but ultimately the reality for the stranded transmigrants was that they were reliant on the hostel for their accommodation and food. Atlantic Park can thus be best described as an open internment camp. It is for this reason that although Atlantic Park was soon largely forgotten on a collective level, it remained important in memory for those who had daily contact with the refugees or were involved in trying to get their position improved.[107]

Forty years after the camp's closure, an article appeared on Atlantic Park by a local teacher. It evoked a strong response from one of those intimately involved with the education of the refugee children, Winifred Dominy:

> I began my teaching career with the emigrant children who spoke very little English. The school was held in the American built theatre with little equipment beyond stationery and desks. The children were lively and intelligent and very quickly learnt to express themselves in English... I believe that the children who ... were absorbed into the Eastleigh schools made very good scholars and enjoyed the English way of life.[108]

Another local person, Allen Robinson, was less intimately connected to those in the camp, but he remembers its occupants with equal vividness. Moreover, his local contact with the refugees helped to shape an international awareness:

> How I got to know so much about Atlantic Park and the refugees was because, while waiting for my sixteenth birthday to start an apprenticeship at the Railway Works, I took a job at Peacock's, Eastleigh's greengrocer. My duties were to deliver on a trade cycle Colonel Barbor's fruit and vegetable orders twice a week ... I seemed to get on well with the refugee children and they followed me around. I even taught them to ride the trade cycle... All the refugees were very well behaved considering that they were with strange people in a strange land, our England. We tried to teach our own language to each other. I still remember a few phrases such as 'How do you do?' (Zorahstvootyee), 'How are you?' (Kahrahsoho) and 'Very well, thank you' (oohyeen, spahsseebah).[109]

When the first manager of Atlantic Park was arrested for fraud, the local paper reported that 'The case has aroused the greatest interest in the town and district surrounding, by reason of the close proximity of the hostel to Eastleigh'. Eastleigh and Atlantic Park may have been in some respects separate even if they were geographically adjacent towns. Yet on many levels they were intimately linked. When it finally closed its doors in 1931, the *Eastleigh Weekly News* commented on how rather than being an alien presence, it had been part of the local scene for many years: 'Children were born at Atlantic Park and educated in Eastleigh schools'. The local schooling of the children was of particular significance. The Director of Education for the County of Hampshire, David Cowan, was singled out for praise by the JTS for providing a 'secular educational experiment [which] has been eminently successful'. The response of the children themselves when writing to Cowan, even when allowance is made for the niceties of diplomacy, expressed genuine sentiment:

> We ... would like to express our appreciation and gratitude for all you have done for us. We feel that a great start has been given us, and we shall always carry the memory of your great kindness with us. We are [also] thankful to you ... for the wise choice of teachers, who have set us on the right way in English.

With the talent, care and enthusiasm of Hampshire teachers, the life chances of these young victims of international dislocation were greatly enhanced. The presence of refugees is often objected to because of the strain they cause on local resources. Yet the successful education of the children at Atlantic Park by the Hampshire education authorities is just one of many examples of how, in practice, such concerns are misplaced.[110]

There were also those locally who protested against the continued detention of those at Atlantic Park. Most prominent in this respect was Lady Swaythling of the adjacent Townhill Park. Although the different worlds of the rooted Anglo-Jewish aristocracy and the stateless and poverty-stricken refugees of Atlantic Park are hard to exaggerate, Lady Swaythling expressed deep concern at the plight of her neighbours. The Swaythling family's local liberal tradition of helping refugees, which had begun in the late nineteenth century and continued during the First World War, developed further during the 1920s. Apart from material support, Lady Swaythling wrote a strong, open protest letter to President Coolidge, calling upon him to end the misery of those in the hostel. In spite of the international connections of the Swaythlings, her appeal to Coolidge was swiftly rebuked. Nevertheless, her attempts were deeply appreciated by those in Atlantic Park.

The global outlook of the Swaythlings was also apparent when they hosted the second International Conference of the YMCA on Migration in June 1924. Delegates from 12 nations attended the conference at Townhill Park which featured an extensive visit to Atlantic Park. The Mayor of Southampton, welcoming the delegates, stressed that the work they were discussing 'was of worldwide importance, and needed their best thoughts and earnest deliberations'. He added that he was pleased about the location of the conference 'because Southampton, both as a town and a port, was deeply interested in their work. Thousands and thousands of people left the port to seek their future in far off lands.'[111] Indeed, Atlantic Park, and the Southampton region's involvement in international migration and refugee movement more generally, were very much part of the local world. Many were involved in alleviating the plight of those at the hostel through protest, education or friendship. Furthermore, the hostel and the emigration trade were important in the regional economy. The hostel is therefore a classic example of the inseparability of local, national and global history. It was fitting that its memory would be maintained 3,000 miles beyond its buildings and fields: 'After reaching the States, the immigrants formed the Atlantic Park Club of New York, where they held periodical reunions'.[112]

There is no doubt, especially under the benevolent management of Colonel Barbor, that, in the words of an international refugee worker, 'conditions at Eastleigh were incomparably superior to those at any other [transmigrant] camps'.[113] To the JTS, and its chairman, Otto Schiff, Atlantic Park was a success story. This was especially so as concessions had been gained from the Home Office to allow some female transmigrants to stay temporarily in Britain (obtained through a guarantee of British Jewry that these women would not be a charge on the public purse). It proved to be a successful model used during the first years of Nazism to break through the alien restrictionism that negated a meaningful refugee policy in post-war Britain. It would be misleading, however, to leave the 1920s on a note solely of optimism in relation to British refugee policy. Dr Jochelman, the ceaseless campaigner for those at Atlantic Park, provided the comparative framework in which the response of Britain could be judged:

> What was happening ... in other cultured countries? To take France as an example, here too, were some six hundred transmigrants stranded in the ports... The greater part of these emigrants have been admitted to work, to business in several towns; in a word they are no longer desperate prisoners.[114]

More than anything, however, it highlights how refugee matters had become by the 1920s an international issue. At the time it was easy to blame the problems of those at Atlantic Park on the Americans alone. For example, at the YMCA conference in Southampton in June 1924 one delegate commented that:

> There had been growing in America a great spirit of nationalism – selfish, exclusionist nationalism which he considered was the greatest curse of the present day. A slogan that ran through America, 'One hundred per cent American', was largely responsible for this.

Yet the USA was not exceptional in its isolationism. British politicians, with the exception of a few internationalists, were determined that Britain also should no longer be seen as a country of permanent asylum, especially for those who were now perceived as a 'racial' menace. It is easy to forget that the people termed at best at the time as 'aliens', 'immigrants' or 'transmigrants' and at worst as 'horrible types', 'undesirables' or 'parasites' were refugees from persecution who had escaped abject misery. Liza Schlomovitz, for example, was a frightened 13-year-old who had witnessed the most appalling acts of violence against her family. She had been close to starvation for several years living off melted snow and the garbage left behind by soldiers, with only the occasional food parcels from abroad to keep her and her siblings in any semblance of health. Detained after lengthy journeys by both the British and American governments as an unwanted immigrant, it is hardly surprising that she was so insecure about the future as to hide bread under her bed in the dormitory at Atlantic Park. It remained one of the few details Liza recalled in later life about the months she was interned at the hostel. Politicians and bureaucrats were determined that for Liza and the others at Atlantic Park, Britain should not become 'home'. But with the help and support of people locally and nationally, as well as their own resilience and resistance, it was still possible for the refugees to feel some sense of local belonging:

> To some extent, they adopted a British way of life, visiting the shops, going to the pictures ... and sending their children to the Eastleigh schools when the fall in numbers at the hostel meant the closing of the school there.

Atlantic Park became part of their multi-layered and complex identities.[115]

In comparison to the insensitive and mean-spirited official British response, France emerged as the leading and most generous centre of refugee settlement in Europe, best illustrated by the Armenians who were welcomed in tens of thousands. None technically entered Britain as refugees. In the case of Russians, the history of Atlantic Park illustrates the determination of the British state to keep out east European Jews. Yet even with the example of non-Jewish, anti-Bolshevik Russians, 15,000 of whom were allowed entry to Britain after the October 1917 revolution, the vast majority were encouraged, with success, by the British government to move on to France to join a much bigger and more welcomed exile community. But by focusing on the local level, British humanitarianism toward refugees can still be detected. The benevolent sentiment and action expressed at Atlantic Park calls into question the representative nature of the anti-alienism of politicians such as William Joynson-Hicks. It also, on a practical level, provided an indirect link to the more positive responses to refugees in Britain during the first six years of Nazism in Germany. Some of the small concessions ultimately won at Atlantic Park provided a glimmer of hope that Britain might return to becoming a temporary if not a permanent place of refugee asylum.[116]

PART 2

The Fascist Era, 1933–1945

4
Refugees from the Spanish Civil War

THE RISE OF FASCISM AND THE SPANISH CIVIL WAR

The First World War created one of the most volatile political landscapes in the history of Europe, heralding what Eric Hobsbawm describes as 'The Age of Extremes'. The devastation of the war, revolution and counter-revolution, extreme nationalism and economic dislocation created an atmosphere ripe for political extremism to flourish. By the end of the 1930s it appeared that liberal democratic government in Europe was the exception rather than the rule with Britain and Holland unusual in having small 'native' fascist movements. The Bolsheviks in eastern Europe consolidated their control after the October 1917 revolution in Russia and, at the other political extreme, fascist or extreme right-wing dictatorships were in power in Italy, Germany, Spain and Portugal. Romania, Hungary and Poland all experienced intolerant right-wing regimes in which the legal rights of minorities such as Jews were under threat.

Ironically, Italy, the first fascist state, set up by Mussolini after his successful march on Rome in 1922, was one of the last in the inter-war period to discriminate against Jews and, until its racial laws in 1938, was a country of refuge for those escaping the antisemitism of the Third Reich. Initially, the new Italian government created only a few refugees, mainly leading Italian anti-fascists who settled largely in France hoping that their exile would be brief. Eventually, some 10,000 political refugees left Italy. Few settled in Britain, but in the late 1930s, Britain became an important place of temporary refuge for Jews escaping the Third Reich and victims of the Spanish Civil War. It was expected that the majority of Jews would be transmigrants using Britain as a staging post to the United States or Palestine, while it was hoped that the Spanish children would stay only a matter of months until the civil war quietened in the Basque region. In both cases, however, significant numbers stayed in Britain.

Europe during the 1930s was characterised by economic depression and political instability, paving the way for the Second World War. The ideological battleground between the forces of democracy and totalitarianism was most blatantly expressed in the Spanish Civil War, 1936–39. The Republican government, the Frente Popular, a coalition of left-wing parties, elected in 1931, unleashed these conflicts when it challenged the Church and landed aristocracy with its commitment to social reform. Mass strikes, agrarian revolt and anti-Church violence ensued, undermining the fragile Popular Front coalition and polarising politics. On 17 July 1936 the right-wing insurgent, General Franco, led a revolt in Spanish Morocco against the popularly elected government. The attempt to oust the Republican government engendered widespread disapproval in Britain and France but also fear that involvement would result in confrontation between the Axis and the Western powers. Britain and France followed an official policy of non-intervention, entailing an arms embargo with both sides in Spain. It was intended that all nations should act similarly, but Germany and Italy sent considerable arms and equipment to the fascist rebels. Russia and Mexico gave aid to the Republican side but it did not match the armaments provided by the fascists.

The civil war divided Spain, with Madrid, Barcelona and Alicante initially loyal to the government, while Malaga and Burgos joined the insurgents. The rebels occupied the Spanish interior, moving up to the north of the country. Here they met fierce resistance in the area known as Euzkadi, homeland to the Basque people. The Basques were fiercely independent, distinct from either their French or Spanish neighbours, with their own nationalist political party committed to autonomy for the region, the Partido Nacionalista Vasco (PNV). The Basque Nationalist leadership believed that the civil war was a '"struggle between civil rights and Fascism; Republic or monarchy" and that the history of the Basques as a democratic and free people precluded any choice but that of remaining loyal to the elected government'.[1] Battles began in eastern Guipuzcoa by mid-August 1936 and by the end of the month evacuation had begun, with 5,000 women, children and elderly men crossing to France in three days. By October strict rationing was necessary. One refugee recalled, 'Looking back on that time I think the hunger was worse than the bombs. It was always with you. At least, in the refuges, you felt safe from the bombardments. All we talked about was food there, too.'[2]

The situation deteriorated further for the Basques when Franco announced a blockade of the northern coast, preventing the delivery of food. Some Basques moved to Bilbao and as the daily bombardments continued, even rural farms were evacuated. The horror of the war was recounted by one of the children sent to Britain:

> We had just gone through the first three months of the year 1937. There was nothing but misery, hunger and dread for the constant bombing of the 'frankista raids' (German planes)... The noise they produced was something you cannot forget in a lifetime ... Our school in the borough of Abachalo [became] barracks for the soldiers of the Republic and its cellars [were used] as anti-air

raid shelters for the civilians. People were rushing to [the] shelter horror stricken every time the factory horn started blowing. It resulted [in] a mouse trap because those damned junkers knew the location of the barracks and they insisted many times [on] trying to wipe out that military post... Every time war planes were coming to bomb the village, we preferred to hide amongst the bushes up in the hill...[3]

Reports of the situation were publicised abroad and support groups in France were established as early as November 1936. The Comité d'Accueil aux enfants d'Espagne was sponsored by the trade union organisation, CGT, to bring as many orphaned refugee children to France as possible. France was an obvious destination due to its proximity and because President Leon Blum, leader of the Popular Front government, was sympathetic to the Spanish Republicans. After the bombing of Guernica on 26 April 1937, Basque President Aguirre sent out an urgent request across Europe for further asylum for women, children and the elderly, bringing a swift, sympathetic response with the formation of committees to aid the Republic in many countries, including France, Belgium, Denmark, Switzerland and Sweden. 'These committees were, in each country, spearheaded by the Left, through the Popular Front organisations and labour unions, and aided by humanitarian groups such as the Quakers.'[4] Distant countries such as Egypt, Mexico, Russia, Canada and Czechoslovakia sponsored refugee 'colonies' in France and Spain. In all, nearly 120,000 Spaniards were evacuated, 26,000 from Bilbao, 30,974 from Santander and 62,199 from Asturias – all but 13,631 were citizens of Euzkadi. About a quarter of the evacuees were children.[5]

In the British press, when Guernica was bombed, eyewitness accounts had an immediate effect on the public: 'popular feeling for the Basques rose, so that funds for the humanitarian National Joint Committee for Spanish Relief were collected in quantity'.[6] Although most popular sentiment was with the Republic, the state and British business, financial and diplomatic interests conversely favoured the rebels. The governing Conservative Party had little sympathy for the social revolutionary principles of the Republicans.[7] Typical of such hostility was the anti-alien Hampshire MP, Sir Henry Page Croft, who stated at the time of the food blockade, 'We are not going to support the feeding of Red children'.[8] In May 1937, pressed in the Commons over British help for refugees, the new Prime Minister, Neville Chamberlain, responded, 'I am not sure who they are or how many or how we could help', though later agreeing that Britain would protect ships carrying women and children to safety.[9]

SUPPORT FOR THE REPUBLICANS AND ASSISTANCE TO THE REFUGEES

While the official line was ambivalent, popular sympathies for the Republicans found various outlets, particularly Britain's Aid Spain Movement, which was 'the most widespread and representative mass movement in Britain since the mid-nineteenth century days of Chartism ... and the most outstanding example of international solidarity in British history'.[10] Tens of thousands of people were involved in marches, demonstrations, collections, concerts and other social events in support of the Republicans. An estimated £2 million was raised, used to send medical personnel and supplies and foodships to Spain. And in spite of the prevailing pacifism in the country, over 2,000 British volunteers joined the International Brigade to fight alongside the Republicans because of their ideological support for the cause.

Assistance was further augmented with the creation of the National Joint Committee for Spanish Relief (NJCSR), established at the House of Commons on 6 January 1937, with the aim of coordinating fundraising for Spain with the help of interested MPs. By 1938 it acted as an umbrella organisation for at least 150 different fundraising groups. An interim report of the committee in 1939 mentioned some 850 local, regional and national bodies involved with it.[11] The idea of providing temporary shelter for a number of Basque children in Britain was first mooted by the NJCSR in February 1937. It did not go unopposed. Lord Listowel, a Labour member of the committee, in response to the proposal by the Conservative member Captain Macnamara, argued that it was inadvisable to bring children to 'cold and Protestant England'. The political impact of taking Spanish refugees was feared, as it might imply favouring the Republicans, contrary to the policy of non-intervention.[12] But the bombing of Guernica prompted a change of heart. 'The correspondent's eyewitness accounts of wounded and bleeding children fleeing the burning town that Vizcayans venerate galvanised British public opinion. This sense of outrage prompted the British cabinet to agree at last to help Euzkadi's young refugees.'[13] The acceptance of children also diluted the political nature of the gesture. Hampshire was to play a crucial role in the resettlement of the refugees, with Southampton chosen as the port to receive the ships bringing the children to Britain. Local opinion supported the movement:

> Whatever one's views may be concerning the rights and wrongs of the war in Spain, we are all of us without an exception united in pity for these poor children ... they are the innocent victims of a tragedy which they have done nothing to cause and in the perpetuation of which they have taken no hand.[14]

As the *Eastleigh Weekly News* stated, 'Obviously Bilbao was no place for children, where the horrors of air-raids and food shortage were having their terrible effect upon young minds and bodies.'[15]

At the end of April 1937, the Home Office, apparently propelled into action by news reports and the upsurge of popular feeling in Britain, agreed to requests by the National Joint Committee to take in a group of Basque children. This was on condition that the Treasury should not bear any of the cost of the children's maintenance, that the group would eventually be repatriated to Spain, and a tacit agreement that the incomers include non-combatants of all political parties. The British gesture was considered 'niggardly' when compared with France which had already accepted some 10,000 refugees and given them a daily allowance of ten francs.[16] The British government, by contrast, still had misgivings over how many evacuees to take. Stanley Baldwin wrote in May 1937 that he had 'grave doubts as to the desirability on practical grounds of bringing them to this country in large numbers'.[17]

The dilemma inspired by the Basque children was illustrated by the comments of a senior Home Office official, E. N. Cooper, in May 1937. Cooper was approached by the Secretary of the Save the Children Fund, Mr Golden. Golden emphasised that

> his Society which has upwards of twenty years of experience in succouring refugee children in all parts of the world was absolutely opposed in principle to the removal of young children from their native country. Where this had been done the later results were too often deplorable and for his part he would sooner see them die in their own land than rot slowly in exile where they deteriorate physically, morally and mentally.

He added that the move to bring them to Britain 'was actuated largely by political motives' by some on the Joint Committee for Spanish Relief. Cooper shared his concerns, adding that

> some of the Committee may act precipitately and send a large number of children to this country in a ship chartered for the purpose without waiting for Home Office approval to be given to the scheme. It would be manifestly impossible for the Home Office to refuse them leave to land because no other country would take them and they could not be sent back to Spain. His Majesty's Government would then be faced with the problems of having to make financial provision for their maintenance as the charge could scarcely be saddled upon the local Public Assistance Committee. If this attempt to gate-crash were made the Foreign Office and Treasury would be concerned and in view of the Foreign Office policy not to give financial assistance to either party in Spain the Government might find itself seriously embarrassed by the suggested action of the Joint Committee, who are obviously not aware of this possible consequence of their policy, a consequence which some of its left wing members such as Miss Ellen Wilkinson would no doubt welcome ...

Cooper concluded that 'in no circumstances should Basque children be brought to this country unless the Committee is able to satisfy the requirements laid down in the Home Secretary's letter'.[18]

The Home Office was worried about being upstaged by the activities of the National Joint Committee, which was already thinking about bringing the refugees over from Bilbao. Recollecting the evacuation, Leah Manning, one of the activists in support of taking the children, highlighted the lack of official enthusiasm for the campaign:

The Basques had no sympathy either from the Home Office or the Foreign Office. Both regarded the whole thing as a nuisance and myself as an officious busybody. They changed the ages; they changed the policy of receiving family groups; and they demanded that the London Committee should guarantee ten shillings per week per head for each child – this at a time when they expected the children of their own unemployed to survive on five bob a week.[19]

The Home Office, after attempting to limit the intake to 2,000, finally accepted the arrival of 4,000 refugee children. Sir John Simon, the Home Secretary, also stipulated that there should be more girls than boys, that they should be aged five to fifteen and not include family groups. Tom Buchanan argues that 'the basis for their acceptance was a grand humanitarian gesture, as well as, politically, an affront to Franco's side in the Civil War ... the children were merely being kept in safekeeping until the danger had receded – and the Basque government insisted that the evacuees should continue to be taught in Basque and not be subjected to undue religious or political influences.'[20]

It was not only the British who were concerned about the young refugees. The Spanish authorities were worried about the care of the evacuee children. The Spanish Minister of Labour and Social Welfare, Jaime Ayguade, stated in February 1938 that:

> The number of refugees is already over three million.... Of primary importance to us is the problem of refugee children and their future... It is our opinion that the ideal method to raise children is the family regime. They should be surrounded by the human and intimate atmosphere of family life.... [T]housands of Spanish children have been sent abroad; there are children from Republican Spain in France, Mexico, Great Britain, Switzerland...

He added, however, that there were advantages to Spain by this movement which went beyond the immediate safety of the children:

> In all these countries, the Spanish children ... are far away from the dangers and hardships of war and play, eat and study. They learn the language of the country which has taken them in. The children of the Soviet Union, Great Britain, and France, will also learn the Spanish language from contact with our little ones. We [must make sure] that the stay of Spanish citizens abroad – whether long or short – is advantageous to all. We want all refugee children abroad, who are able to do so, to attend trade schools. Each nation is outstanding in a particular branch of industry. The metallurgical industries of Belgium and Czechoslovakia are highly developed. Refugee children from the Spanish regions in which the metallurgical industries thrive will be sent there. When they return they will be of great help in organising Spanish industry on a large scale and will, therefore, more than repay the expenses of the Government in supporting them while abroad ... [We] are trying by all means to prepare ... the Spain of tomorrow...[21]

By May 1937 the NJCSR formed the Basque Children's Committee (BCC) to plan for the care and housing of the arrivals. Local branches were established to raise funds and to provide housing, food and medical care for the children after the initial period in a reception camp. In spite of the concerns of the

Spanish authorities, wherever possible the children were kept together in 'colonies' and offers of accommodation in private houses were generally refused. The membership of the BCC indicated that, contrary to the view expressed by E. N. Cooper, there was cross-party support for the refugees. It was chaired by the Conservative MP Katharine, Duchess of Atholl, assisted by three members of the NJCSR: the Conservative Captain Macnamara, Labour MP Dai Grenfell and Liberal MP Wilfred Roberts. Additionally it included two Quakers, the Independent MP Eleanor Rathbone and Vincent Tewson of the TUC, as well as representatives of the Salvation Army and the Catholic Church who would not join the National Joint Committee. An appeal by Leah Manning in *The Times*, signed by politicians of all parties, confirmed the broad spectrum of support for the cause. It quickly raised £17,000, showing the campaign's popularity.

Tom Buchanan argues that the labour movement in particular played a crucial role in the movement for the refugees, sponsoring a 'Save the Basque Children Fund' bringing a large income from trade union executives and reflecting the internationalist approach of organised labour during the Spanish Civil War. The TUC and the Labour Party created a Spanish Workers' Fund to aid trade unionists and socialists in Spain in July 1936. Nevertheless, he suggests that:

> The Labour movement's support for the Basque children represented a further step in the depoliticisation of its relief work, marking a swing away from a commitment to affiliated political organisations and towards a more personal commitment towards individuals. Moreover, the children were presented as the apolitical victims of the events in Spain, a policy that was somewhat misleading.[22]

The Basque children were popular with ordinary trade unionists as 'they seemed to symbolise the contrast between political innocence and the most brutal forms of fascism, and they felt privileged to be entrusted with them until the danger had passed'.[23] TUC records reveal that it was relatively easy to raise funds at regular shop-floor collections. Complaints in the labour movement that the children were being given privileges over and above those children from areas stricken by unemployment in Britain, Buchanan argues, were marginal and isolated. Local involvement in the labour movement was evident in the Southampton district. The Eastleigh Labour Party set up a Spanish Medical Aid Committee and, in conjunction with the Clarion Cycling Club, made clothes for the Basque refugees.[24] The Southampton City Trades Council fundraised for the Medical Aid for Spain movement and the Hampshire Foodship Committee. Trade union workers were also prominent in setting up facilities in the local reception camp at Eastleigh where the children were housed on arrival in Britain. The welcome accorded to the Basque children was clearly linked to labour support for Spain's Republican government. Locally the Southampton City Trades Council regarded the

British government's non-intervention policy as a 'farce' which brought 'tragic results for Spanish democracy'.[25]

Support for the Basque refugees also came from the Communist Party but such concern on the left was not always trouble free; in Dundee the Spanish Medical Aid Committee and the Trades and Labour Council failed to cooperate in fundraising activities. In contrast to the British labour movement, the Catholic Church's support for the Basques was ambivalent. The Church was instrumental in providing homes for the children but some Catholic workers refused to express solidarity with the Republic because of the massacres of priests and nuns early in the war. Aid for the Basques was qualified by emphasising that it was only for the Catholics amongst them. The *Catholic Times* justified publishing an article about an incident of unruly behaviour by a group of Basque children housed at Brechfa, contrasting the 'Red terrorists' there with the 'passive behaviour and happiness of the Catholic Basque children in Catholic homes'.[26]

THE ARRIVAL OF THE CHILDREN AND LIFE IN THE CAMPS

In Spain there was competition for places aboard the ships to Britain. It was reported that within two weeks between 10,000 and 20,000 children were signed up for the 4,000 places offered by the Assistencia Social.[27] Children were dispersed all over the world by parents who did not know if they would ever see them again, but Britain had a particular appeal because of its historical connection with the Basque region. For years trips had been made by English seamen to Euzkadi, while Basques sometimes sent their children to be educated in England.[28] The children selected for Britain were chosen from political backgrounds in numbers proportionate to the party representation in the Basque parliament. Leah Manning made arrangements in Euzkadi and doctors Richard Ellis and Audrey Russell inspected the children before their departure.

The ships *Habaña* and *Goizeka Izarra* left Spain on 21 May 1937 with 3,889 children, 219 women teachers and aides, including some mothers of the children, and 15 priests aboard.[29] Their arrival in Southampton was greeted with interest both at a local and national level; the BBC broadcast the event[30] and local people gathered to welcome them. Reporters from local papers covered the issue extensively in the months to follow. The child refugees and their parents anticipated that the evacuation would be brief and thus for many of the children the trip was accompanied by a sense of adventure. Jose Maria Villegas recalled, 'I'm quite sure that if [our families] felt that we were going to be abroad, never mind where, for years, no one would have come out. To us it was like going on holiday.'[31] This excitement was temporarily dampened by the journey: with so many crowded on board the ships, rough seas resulting in seasickness, and sad family partings fresh in mind, there was little to enjoy; but much of this depression was forgotten in the excitement of arriving in Southampton where the children were welcomed in a festive mood.

Organising the accommodation for the Basque children tapped the interest of the British public. Members of the local community in Southampton helped set up a reception camp in nearby Eastleigh, which was improvised in under three weeks. Henry Brinton, a leading figure in Anglican affairs and Mr H. W. H. Sams, who had worked abroad with refugees and became the camp commandant, met Jack Pavey of the Southampton Co-operative Society's Development Committee to organise the reception arrangements. The campsite was found through the offer of three fields at North Stoneham, Eastleigh, by a farmer, Mr G. H. Brown. Members of the Labour Party Trades Council and Co-operative Society formed a committee calling for volunteers, and as Jim Fyrth recounts, local union workers were involved in setting up plumbing, digging latrines and laying on gas and water services. Three hundred people, including scouts, guides, members of the YMCA, university students and rotarians, worked over the coronation weekend of King George to set up 200 tents and three marquees. Over 20 depots collected food, toys and clothes across Hampshire for the children.

The local activity was part of a national campaign with fundraising organised by the Lord Mayor of London and the National Joint Committee. At the head of this movement was the Duchess of Atholl, an active supporter of the Spanish Republicans. The Duchess visited Spain in 1937 and on her return established a relief fund, for which she gave speeches in London, Paris and America, making her an apt choice as Chair of both the National Joint Committee for Spanish Relief and the Basque Children's Committee. Her activity on behalf of the Basques, which led her to cooperate with other political factions, including Communists, was so significant that she became known as the 'Red Duchess', losing favour with her party. She later resigned as the government failed to counter fascist aggression but her work for refugees continued and in the 1940s she was involved in a committee welcoming Polish forces to Britain. She spoke at Southampton in May 1937 before the arrival of the children, revealing the commitment of the locality for the 'very big family' it was taking responsibility for:

> We've had most generous offers from many well-known institutions to take a large number of these children but we shall also have to establish homes ourselves in which to receive them... It's been ... really inspiring to find how many voluntary workers here in Southampton and Eastleigh have been ready to come along and give a hand in putting up the camp. I've found no end of boys' brigades and boy scouts and rangers busy just making the final arrangements in the camp [and] dozens of women grappling with what's a very difficult task, the sorting out of a large heterogeneous amount of garments in a very small space...
>
> And then we've had wonderful gifts of food and clothing also. We've had a whole lot of shoes for instance given us by the Boot and Shoes Trades

Operatives Union ... We've had two tons of onions given to us and 40,000 oranges, and perhaps what the children will appreciate most of all ... we've been given enough chocolate to enable each child to have a bit of chocolate daily for the fortnight it will spend in the camp. So I can't help hoping that the children are not going to have too bad a time of it in the camp... [I]t's really wonderful to see the interest that's being taken far and near in these children and to know how many people are helping us to give them a warm welcome.[32]

When the children arrived, the camp became a 'small city in its own right', complete with cinema, concert stage, telephones, showers and toilets.[33] Numerous visitors came to see the children including prominent figures such as Arthur Koestler, the Hungarian war correspondent who had been imprisoned by Franco's regime, who met the children at the docks. Black American actor and political radical, Paul Robeson, and Joe Beckett, the heavyweight boxing champion, were involved in fundraising. Beckett, who came from Southampton, was, despite his fascist connections, a regular attender at the camp, encouraging the children to enjoy sporting activities. Clement Attlee and his wife came, along with other MPs involved in the campaign, such as Wilfred Roberts. The constant stream of visitors even included the King and Queen. In addition to the curiosity and political interest which the children generated, there was a genuine desire among British people to do something. Dorothy Legaretta, in her account of the Basque refugees' life abroad, states that at the Eastleigh camp, 'Everyone seemed willing to help. Even the mayor was seen serving spaghetti in his shirt sleeves to a line of Basque children'.[34]

Both the local and the national press took a considerable interest in the 'Basque babies'. The *Southern Daily Echo* reported their arrival with a mixture of affection and wry amusement when the *Habaña* arrived in Southampton from Bilbao, suggesting that the children were already 'taking cheerfully to camp life at Stoneham' even if military aeroplanes flying over the site had alarmed some of the younger refugees:

Officials have been pleasantly surprised at the conditions of the children. 'They are in a much better state than we imagined, and after plenty of food and as much rest as they can get, I do not think it will be long before they are quite strong again', one said today... 'Already many of the children are picking up English phrases. As we looked in the tents to see if everything was all right they would chorus in a sing song way "O Kay, good night, O Kay good night". Many of them seem to be picking up English much more easily than we can Spanish. They are high-spirited children, and once their hunger is satisfied they become as mischievous as children anywhere. It will be a big job to get them disciplined as most of them have not been to school for ten months.'... The first bus-load arrived at the camp just before eleven o'clock... After the new arrivals were under control and the camp atmosphere became more settled, many of the elder children began to amuse themselves in different ways. Some played with toys which had been thrown over the hedge to them by some of the hundreds of sightseers who crowded to the camp yesterday...[35]

The children anticipated being in Britain for a matter of a few months but for some the sojourn lasted almost two years. For others it even outlasted the Second World War. The children soon became acquainted with national customs and pastimes: 'When we came to England, England was a very peaceful beautiful place [where] the important thing was that you were winning at cricket and tennis'.[36] Their initial life in the camp at North Stoneham is evocatively portrayed by Amador Diaz, reflecting on his experiences as a refugee 50 years later. His first impressions were not favourable:

> The buildings [in Southampton] were small ... not many people in the streets... We left the town and went along a country road [and] saw a thatched cottage... In the bus there were cries of surprise that an advanced country like England should still have cottages with 'straw' roofs! In the industrial area of the Basque Country the roofs of even the poorest of farm cottages were covered in tiles or slates!

They soon discovered the tented 'city' which was to be their temporary home. It was a shock as it is unlikely that any of the children 'had been under canvas before'. The biggest problem, however, was that of language:

> The young man that saw us off the bus, the men and women in the canteen, the two scouts who showed us how to prepare the bedding, could not communicate with us, they knew no Spanish, we knew no English. Even the interpreter's Spanish was difficult to understand... We were to find that many of those wearing the interpreter's badge were not fluent in Spanish. The fact that we used some Basque words in our everyday speech did not help. There were also children, usually young ones, who knew little Spanish having spoken Basque in their homes...

Other early problems were caused by the division of the camp into two, allegedly one section for those who had been cleaned and given new clothes and the other for the children yet to be 'decontaminated': 'In some cases brothers and/or sisters had been separated which created a resentment and mistrust of the Camp authorities that was to last during the whole of our stay at North Stoneham.'

More positively, Amador remembers that on the first day

> the Camp fence by the road ... was full of English people looking at us and offering us sweets, chocolate and even apples... A policeman also walked along the fence on the road side ... he seemed a friendly man and had no pistol, which to us was very different from the solemn Spanish policemen we knew! The fence was going to be a thorn in the flesh of the Camp authorities who would be ... devising ways of keeping us away from it, while we tried to find new means of maintaining contact with the public who provided us with sweets, toys, coins and cigarette cards ... The English spectators also offered us cigarettes and it amused them to see youngsters coughing at the first puffs and soon many began to beg for cigarettes. In retrospective, I can see the spectacle had a resemblance to the monkeys' enclosure at the zoo![37]

A contemporary account of the North Stoneham Camp by Yvonne Cloud and Richard Ellis revealed that those in control of the camp had, at their best, a clear understanding of the needs of these young refugees who had seen so much suffering and were finding life away from home in many ways stressful. Although the children broke many of the items provided for them 'the spirit was one of interest rather than destructiveness, and a very small proportion of four thousand children, showing a lot of interest, can wreck anything at all'. Bartering of goods was prevalent but this was again seen as representing adaptation rather than maliciousness. Such enterprise went beyond food:

> One distinguished visitor from London lost his hat at the Camp and found it at last on the head of a young Basque who refused to part with it on the grounds that he had paid two pesetas for it. He agreed, however, to find the salesman who, in his turn, protested that he had bought it for one peseta ...

Their lack of alienation was apparent, according to Cloud and Ellis, when gangs of helpers were required and volunteers were invited:

> No one in the spineless hope of pleasing steps forward, but instead a judicious voice enquires what is the work and how necessary. Given this information, a willing band is recruited and stipulates its terms and conditions in a business-like way ...

Ultimately they concluded that the children, whatever their grumbles about camp life, accepted the conditions offered to them with reasonable grace:

> One group of older boys set out from the Camp one day for London. They were found many miles away and brought back. They reasoned that it had been their intention on coming to England to see London; they had not travelled so far merely to live in a field and ... they had taken matters into their own hands. It was explained to them that no one in the Camp had the smallest objection to their being placed in a home in or near London when their turn came to be evacuated from the Camp and that they would then reach there by comfortable means and with the assurance that beds and food would be awaiting them. They considered this unromantic view and then agreed with it completely. Their dissatisfaction with life in a field may have remained, but they accepted without hesitation the practical aspect once it had been shown them, and they made no further efforts to leave the Camp...[38]

The feat of organising almost 4,000 children had its problems, including the sheer logistics of handing out food and dealing with the mass of interested visitors. To create some sort of order, eight children were allocated to each tent and given duties on a rota basis, with a daily inspection by the boy scouts. A loudspeaker woke them at eight in the morning and breakfast was provided in large mess tents. There were occasional classes, but most of the time was spent reading, writing letters back home, playing games or doing chores. Inevitably, boredom surfaced, but the camp organisers did their best to keep the children occupied, setting up a cinema at the camp and allowing groups out on excursions, or to visit local people.

Hygiene was also a serious concern. The children were not always prone to use the toilet areas provided for them, which were not particularly pleasant:

> mere trenches dug into the ground surrounded by canvas where the smell of bleach was so strong that it was impossible to remain in them for too long. We could tell who had been to the toilet because their eyes would be watering.[39]

Although the children were given a medical inspection on arrival, it did not rule out possibilities of contagious diseases which, in the confines of the camp, could soon spread and start an epidemic. A particular fear for the camp organisers was an outbreak of typhoid. When a case was discovered at the end of May, the camp was quarantined and all the children were inoculated to prevent the disease spreading. The issue was widely reported in the papers and even led to questions in Parliament as the Minister of Health came under scrutiny for the actions he was taking to prevent an epidemic. Marjorie White, a volunteer telephonist at the camp, noted her reaction to the potential crisis in her log book:

> When my father heard the news he forbade me to go out to the camp ... I defied him and went to the camp the next day and asked to see Major Irwin – I told him I wanted to continue my services and could I have some wages – he said, 'Yes, how much do you want?' and I replied 'Two pounds a week.' So I stayed until the end of the Camp days and did not catch typhoid. My position then was to be in charge of the telephone switchboard and enquiries – no one was allowed into the Camp without first being announced to the officials. The typhoid scare did a lot of good as regards to volunteer helpers. It sorted out the genuine ones from the spongers.[40]

The scare proved to be exaggerated and the five full-time doctors, accompanying nurses and other medical staff contained this and other illnesses including two cases of diphtheria, five cases of scarlet fever, and 22 cases of measles.

That the refugees were children, mostly aged five to 15, inevitably shaped their experiences. On one level their youth made them more vulnerable and in particular the youngest children showed some timidity. Mrs Freda Sibley recalled how as a 20-year-old she volunteered with a friend to help at the camp:

> We were assigned to the hospital wing, in the big house, cleaning the wards. I remember going round the floors, when suddenly a plane flew low over the house. All the children were screaming, and those that could, dived under the beds, yelling, 'bomba, bomba!' We comforted them as best we could, till they calmed down.[41]

In contrast, some of the group of refugees were already verging on adulthood, mature for their age having seen considerable suffering in Spain and then being forced to take on adult responsibilities looking after their siblings in exile. As a result their behaviour was often surprising to adults. Another problem was the existence of distrust between the children and the authorities, compounded by the language barrier. The extent of their political awareness was also unexpected by visitors to the camp.[42] Many of the children disliked what they perceived to be double talk and the ambivalent response of the European powers to the Spanish government as Franco's forces attacked their homes. Their outburst of emotion at the fall of Bilbao, the former home of many of the children, was an indication of their strong responses to events:

> It was an extraordinary experience. There was complete hysteria. The PNV kids from middle class families were completely prostrated ... some of the older boys reacted differently too – they didn't lie down and weep about it – they marched down to Southampton with the intention of getting a boat back to help their parents.

A rather less extreme account of their reactions to this disastrous news was provided by one of the former children:

> [It] was received in silence but soon some of the young ones began to cry while the older ones marched to the administration block asking for more news... Afterwards I learned that [the authorities had] been alerted to calm the hysteria expected from us, but the feeling was rather of repressed tragedy and anger. We were at the height of the solstice so there were more than two hours left of daylight after the news had been read. During these hours we had time to discuss whether our parents would have had time to escape towards Santander or not and also whether we would now be returned to Bilbao at Franco's request. We had little faith in the British Government helping the Republican cause and thoughts that we would be tricked and sent to Franco's Bilbao began to appear in our minds. It was this fear that prompted some to leave the Camp by the copse towards Eastleigh. They were all returned before darkness fell. The following morning the loudspeakers did not play the usual wakey-wakey music.[43]

This particular moment merited national press coverage. The *Daily Dispatch*, generally hostile to the children, still highlighted the anguish caused by the devastating news of Franco's forces taking Bilbao. The response of the authorities at the camp, to provide 'extra delicacies including chocolate and ice cream' so as 'to help the children recover their normal high spirits', was indicative of the gulf between the worlds of the refugees and those helping them. Some children broke camp but most returned voluntarily or were found by local search parties. Captain Macnamara, MP, of the National Committee for Spanish Relief, defended the decision to pass on the news to stop rumours circulating. He admitted that the unsubtle way it was handled led many of the children to believe that 'their parents had been destroyed', adding that some left the camp to grieve in the woods to gain privacy. A camp official commented that:

After the announcement many of the boys felt they must go back to Spain to assist their parents and relatives. It was with this idea that, with tears streaming down their faces, they announced they were packing and going. 'It seemed that the whole camp had burst out crying – and the noise of it froze me from head to toe.'

A letter signed by five girls and four boys, aged from from seven to 15, was sent to the Prime Minister after the news was received:

We have heard with great sorrow that our mothers, sisters, and dear grandparents so full of years have been criminally bombarded by Franco's aeroplanes while they were escaping along the road from Bilbao to Santander. We have also heard that when the Habaña transports those people who cannot escape by road, our mothers and sisters, our grandparents, and those who are sick and very old, the English ships do not escort them as they once escorted us.

We are very grateful for all the tenderness English people have shown us, for the presents they give us, and for all their kindness, but we never forget those who are left at home. It makes us very unhappy that they suffer so much, that they cannot escape the horrors of the siege of Bilbao without being exposed to the bombs and machine-guns of the aviators, or the dangers of being sunk in ships by the enemy. Because of this, the 4,000 children who have been so much the pets of the kind English beg the Prime Minister or whoever commands most in England to send a great big ship – one of those which we saw when we came to England – to protect our mothers and sisters and grandparents, the sick and the aged so that all non-combatants can leave Bilbao whether by sea or by land without danger to their lives. We promise him that we shall be very docile and we shall obey our English friends in everything they tell us.[44]

The fall of Bilbao led to a strong response among the adult Basques at the camp too. But that the majority of the refugees were children was critical: they tended to view things with a strength of feeling which left no room for doubt and required unwavering support from those around them. Yvonne Cloud noted that:

In the tragic circumstances of their dispossession, the children demand more insistently, openly and consciously than other children happily placed, that the external world should be 'for' them – and if not found to be 'for', then rejected as being 'against'.[45]

Discipline was a particular problem in dealing with such a large group of children with divergent political backgrounds. On arrival, they were separated according to the political affiliation of their parents into two camps, one for the Basque Nationalists (of the PNV) and the other for the Socialists, Communists and Anarchists of the Left. The Nationalist camp had a strong Catholic contingent and 15 priests set up a special Catholic Chapel here. The elder children were politicised according to their families' and their own experiences in Spain. In general, the Socialists, as firm supporters of the Republican government, felt no particular allegiance to the local Basque President. They felt that the Basque Nationalists had only come in on the government side at the final hour during the civil war, when Basque independence was threatened, while the Socialists had borne the burden earlier. The Basque Nationalists had much greater loyalty to their own region. While political disagreement was noted among some of the elder children from these backgrounds, the few fascist children in the contingent of refugees offered even greater potential for confrontation. The authorities decided to disperse these children in the camp, keeping their whereabouts secret.

Some have subsequently questioned this policy. In a Spanish account of 'Los Ninos' it was argued that the division of the children, including the separation of those from Catholic and non-Catholic backgrounds, was a great mistake:

> It was like labelling some as Basque children and the others as Spanish children. According to the protagonists themselves, the children went one step further, designating the two groups as the red zone and the fascist camp. The consequences of this division were apparently made manifest in verbal confrontations of a political nature and, also into the occasional tussle, with nocturnal incursions into the opposite side's tents.[46]

Although this political rivalry was considered remarkable among a group so young,[47] it resulted from the circumstances which the children had lived through where the war left no room for equivocation:

> Never since the Basque children came to this country has the matter become so entirely merged with politics; and those psychologists, professional or amateur, who wish the children well and seek at the same time, and in conformity with the children's official status here, to preserve an absolute neutrality, are in a very helpless position.[48]

In addition to concerns over political differences, behaviour differed between boys and girls. In a Spanish study, it was noted 'The girls washed their own clothes and that of their brothers, while the boys roamed around the place'.[49] Such differences were exaggerated in the media, as newspapers commented on the pretty features of the little Spanish girls and took photographs showing them doing their hair while the boys played football.[50] When discipline broke down, older boys were identified as troublemakers. Their propensity to explore and their aggression required special understanding, partly stemming from the freedom they had known in Spain: some had done the work of men in the conflict, such as digging trenches to combat the enemy. There was no room for such activities in their exiled state, though some of the older boys were given the responsibility of policing the camp to dampen unruliness.

The typhoid scare and the difficulties after the fall of Bilbao encouraged the authorities to disperse the children to 'colonies', or homes prepared for them around the country. It was a policy that raised new problems. Friendships with other camp-mates were often all that the children were able to rely on to feel some sense of security in their exile:

The splitting up of these tenuous, newly formed friendships – which must replace parents, relatives and lifelong playmates – is not a grateful task. The need to conform to certain strict divisions of the children militates against the natural desire to preserve the 'gangs', which are often composed of elements officially incompatible.[51]

Brothers and sisters were sometimes separated, particularly those from a Nationalist background who tended to be sent to Catholic homes where boys and girls were kept apart. The camp administrators had a difficult task with some 500 of the children falling into this category. It was largely overcome by keeping Basque Nationalist brothers and sisters together unless it was explicitly stated by the parents or guardians that the children were devout Catholics.[52]

RESPONSES TO THE REFUGEES

The response to the appeal for homes for the refugees was a reflection of the goodwill received by the Basques in Britain. In 1937 90 'colonies' were in existence to house groups of the children,[53] although their quality and nature varied. The Salvation Army and the Catholic Church spearheaded the movement to house the children, while other colonies were run by local Basque Children's Committees. The Archbishop of Westminster, Arthur Hinsley, agreed to accept responsibility for 1,200 Basque children who were Catholics. All parishes were asked to assist, though the request revealed ambivalence towards the refugees: 'We did not bring them and many of us think they ought never to have been brought. However, they are here now. Not one of us, surely, can dare to turn them away'.[54] The children were housed in diocesan orphanages and Catholic boarding schools – the latter among the luckier children able to receive consistent education. The Nazareth House, run by an order of nuns, was one of three centres in Southampton providing homes for the Basques who had to follow a strict daily routine, including attending mass, but they were well cared for and given lessons as well as food and clothes.[55] Another Southampton house at Moorhill, which supported 21 boys and 20 girls aged from six to 13, was maintained through regular contributions from local workers and members of organisations. In addition to teaching conducted in Spanish and English language instruction, the children were taken for regular excursions and became part of the local scene, visiting homes and playing football against school teams.[56]

The Salvation Army hostels, providing homes for 400, tended to be run more severely. Rumours spread that organisers of one centre in Clapton, where several hundred children were staying, used flogging to discipline their charges.[57] The 'colony' attracted attention because the children went on hunger strike in protest at the food they were given and the limits placed on their freedom. One boy escaped but was caught and whipped. Hostile press referred to the boys as 'savages, rebels, beasts'. Boys sent to Brixton and

Hadleigh had to work with alcoholics. Some worked in the laundry and others fed the chickens. One refugee declared, 'We were simply unpaid labour of the most menial kind'.[58] The most rebellious boys were sent to Scarborough which was described as a penal colony. The care of such unsettled cases soon became onerous and by 28 July, Colonel Gordon, who was in charge of the boys, requested that Clapton be returned to ordinary Salvation Army use. The farm colonies closed early the next year. The Ministry of Labour was forced to take on the care of the most unruly boys, some of whom were sent to reformatories and 23 repatriated. The trouble the authorities had with these older boys, some of whom had participated in fighting in Spain, was such that it was joked: 'Why has your child become so unruly? Oh, he's been playing with some Basque children'.[59] Negative incidents began to gain momentum in press coverage of the Basques.[60] Trivial misdemeanours received widespread publicity: a case of children stealing apples and plums from an old man led to a letter of complaint in the local paper.[61]

Dorothy Legarreta has argued that press coverage reflected political bias: right-wing pro-Franco papers tended to view the refugees unfavourably, while left-wing papers were more sympathetic. The Basques, however, at least initially, had been welcomed, characterised as good and moderate Catholics and 'the very opposite of the church-burning anarchism sometimes associated with the Republic in the British press'.[62] The attempt of some of the older children to leave the camp after the fall of Bilbao encouraged the pro-Franco press: 'From that moment, they had a handle on destroying sympathy … donations began to drop off … That was when the Basque Children's Committee got cold feet and brought in thirteen army officers to run the camp, playing right up to the publicity'.[63] The public was clearly affected by this smear campaign. Donations to the BCC fell further when the press reported an alleged riot at the Brechfa colony for the Basques in Wales. A group of older boys had broken windows in the village and threatened villagers with knives. They claimed a villager had knocked one of them down and pointed a gun at them. The *Sunday Dispatch* wrote of a 'night of terror' by hooligans who 'must go'[64] and the *Daily Mail* also called for the 'Basque "Terrors" to be transferred'.[65] Another headline used humour to mask its intolerance: 'Put all these Basques in one exit'.[66] The violence at Brechfa enabled opponents of the campaign for the Basques to brand the children as 'red terrors', alleging that their Communist background was the problem and that they should be repatriated immediately. Yet the press was not uniformly hostile. Criticisms from Lord Ruthven over the indiscipline of the 'Red children' were countered by letters of support,[67] and the *Daily Herald* quoted the National Joint Committee that 'Reports concerning bad behaviour of the Basque boys [were] greatly exaggerated.'[68]

The controversy over the children's behaviour led the journal *John Bull* to examine the evidence. Its report was sympathetic to the pressures on the young refugees, emphasising from the start, if a little melodramatically, 'that many of the children need to be regarded as invalids. Though they have been here nearly three months, their eyes are still wide with terror'. With much pathos it described how:

> Twenty of them, aged from six to fourteen are tucked up in bed each night in a large house at Percy Park, Tynemouth. Directly their guardians leave they get up and dress; then clutching the bundles in which are tied their pathetic possessions, they huddle together to wait for the air raids which no longer threaten them. Infants still cry to be allowed to send sand from Tynemouth beach to make sandbags for their parents.

John Bull criticised the lack of empathy towards the refugees, perhaps exaggerating the force of local antipathy:

> Certain local residents were unwilling for this little colony to find a shelter in their midst. Because of this less than twelve hours after the refugees' arrival, notice to quit was served! In other districts, despite the sympathy of the great mass of the public, unmannerly demonstrations have increased the youngsters' strain...

Its tone was highly defensive, suggesting that much explaining was needed to convince the public that the children were deserving of support and consideration. It also highlighted the respectability of those involved with their welfare: it was hard 'to believe that such members of the Committee as the Duchess of Atholl, Canon Craven (the Roman Catholic representative), and Mr Wilfred Roberts, the Liberal MP, are likely to agree to children being detained here in order to stir up feeling against General Franco'. It related most of the difficulties to the refusal of the Home Office to allow additional Spanish adults to be brought to act as interpreters. The language bar, it argued, was behind most of the disturbances, including the mini-riot at Brechfa, which it believed were due to failures of communication:

> Actually the total damage caused at Brechfa and another disturbance at Scarborough was less than £10. The total number of boys sent in disgrace to France is seventeen... But seventeen out of 4,000 does not seem to us a high proportion, nor does the fact that there has been trouble at only three out of seventy camps... Nor are any of the children being sent to private families, though many hundreds of people have made adoption offers. Some of them are paying instead, the cost of a child's keep, which is about ten shillings a week. Schoolchildren, the Duchess of Atholl tells us, are going without sweets to send a few pence to the funds; one man has sent his old age pension.

John Bull's conclusion revealed the changing attitudes in Britain towards refugees. It was vocal in criticising the lack of official support, stressing that 'while the French Government has contributed more than a million francs towards the cost of its child guests, the British government grants not a farthing to ours'. But the account also emphasised popular desire to help: 'so long as their need remains, we may presume the British public will not be found wanting in generosity'.[69] It was not alone in denouncing hostile press commentary about the refugees. A contributor to the left-wing *New Statesman and Nation* expressed amazement and disgust at the unfavourable reports of the children's behaviour after the fall of Bilbao, trying to bring the problem closer to home by suggesting that

> if 4,000 English children were taken from Brighton to Madrid in time of civil war in England, and then were told that Brighton had fallen to the enemy, and they knew not whether their parents were alive or dead, I am quite sure that the same 'mass hysteria' and 'rioting' would occur even in the absence of a Spanish temperament.

He also believed that reports of 'terrorising of the countryside' at Brechfa were totally distorted.[70]

Jim Fyrth argues that the political right and the Catholic hierarchy began a campaign to send the children home as soon as Bilbao had fallen. In March 1938, when Hitler marched into Austria, staffing and morale problems developed in the 'colonies'. Both the Salvation Army and the Catholic Church reduced their help. The right-wing Conservative backbencher, Sir Thomas Moore, asked the Home Secretary:

> Whether in view of the repeated attacks made on British citizens by refugee Basque children, he will consider in the interests of the refugees themselves, and the safety of our own people, making early arrangements for their return to their own country?[71]

After the troublemakers were deported, questions were raised about returning the rest of the children. By the end of October 1937 the war was over in the north of Spain. But the success of the fascists led the British government to set up an enquiry as to when the children should be sent back. The Basque Children's Legal Commission recommended the return of 500 children at once and the rest to follow soon after. The BCC was less certain and it was seen in some quarters as deliberately obstructing return on political grounds. Consequently a Repatriation Committee, instigated by the Catholic Church leader Arthur Hinsley, and including leading Conservatives such as Douglas Jerrold and Lady Londonderry, began lobbying for the children to be returned.[72] A resolution on the issue in February 1938 in the BCC produced a tied vote. The Duchess of Atholl, as Chair, had the casting vote which she used in favour of 'sending back children to those parents known to be in Insurgent Spain and at liberty ... with the assurance someone accompany the children to bring back any not reunited with their parents'.[73]

In March 1939, the Spanish Civil War ended with victory for Franco but refugees continued to enter France. The British government gave no official help. Moreover, the children in Britain were not a priority: 'Though the BCC still was given office space in the NJCSR central office, all funds were now needed for more pressing humanitarian work in France'.[74] Some 1,600 children remained in 'colonies', hostels for older children or with adoptive parents. Nevertheless, those aged over 14 were given the option of remaining in Britain indefinitely. Official policy changed, allowing the older children to enrol in British state schools. The BCC estimated that 577 Basques would stay in Britain because their parents were dead, in prison, abroad, or missing. The eruption of the Second World War meant many were prevented from returning home. At the end of 1943, Home Office records showed that 411 of the evacuees still lived in Britain. Most of the girls were aged 14–16 and the boys 18–20. Of these, 228 were employed, 18 in armed service, 8 married, 15 living with parents or guardians, and 82 enjoying private hospitality.[75] Dorothy Legarreta argues that those who stayed were mainly on the political left and saw their emigration as political exile. Most came from the industrial belt around Bilbao. One recalled that:

> For a long time, we felt we would be part of the liberation of Spain. We were a very united group, all of us with strong anti-fascist convictions. We kept our aims clear, and engaged in a great deal of political work. We had nothing in common with later Spanish immigrants, who came for economic reasons; ours was a political immigration. We had foresight of what we wanted in our lives.[76]

THE LEGACY OF THE BASQUE REFUGEES

After the Second World War, for those remaining in Britain, years of education had been lost. Relatively few of those who stayed went on to secondary schools or technical colleges, though about 30 did go to university.[77] Some dropped out of education to work in the munitions factories. In May 1939 a Basque Boys' Training Committee was formed which arranged apprenticeships and night school classes in agriculture or technical subjects for boys of working age, renting hostels in London for their accommodation. Wartime regulations meant that the Basques had alien status, but some boys who were old enough enlisted in the British army. Others got jobs in engineering, clothing or industrial factories for war production and the girls went to work in shops, restaurants and clothing factories. There was some hostility towards them as a result. One newspaper commented that 'sweated Basques' were 'conniving through the BCC, with "Red" Trade Unions to give them preferential hiring'. This occurred several years after the arrival of the children, reflecting the undertone of antipathy that they faced during their exile in Britain.[78]

Even though the Basques were widely dispersed, they attempted to keep in touch with each other and were encouraged to do so. The BCC founded a journal for the exiles, *Amistad*, which acted as a linking force, providing notes on alien regulations, details of events for the Basques and a forum for reminiscences. The refugees frequently reunited to perform their traditional dances, which had earlier served as a method of fundraising. Many of them went on to be successful but it is important that some of the problems faced by the Basques in Britain are not forgotten. The lasting effects of exile were not always positive, as the wife of one refugee, Rodolfo, who was born in San Sebastian in 1927, testified:

> [He was] the youngest of three brothers and lived with his father. When the Spanish civil war started and conditions became very bad, his father took the three boys to Bilbao to live in a refuge. In 1937, conditions in Bilbao became worse. Different countries offered to take the children for a few months until the war was over. So Rodolfo didn't decide to come to Britain, he was sent. His father decided to send Rodolfo, and his brother Virgilio to England... They came by ship and had a dreadful journey. The ship was made for 400 passengers and there were 4,091 people on board plus crew! Stormy seas made everyone sick.
>
> When he arrived, Rodolfo knew nothing of Britain being only nine years old... On arrival, they had no plans. Everyone thought they would only be in Great Britain for three months and then return to their parents. Rodolfo found life very difficult with schooling interrupted for long periods in Spain, then coming to a country where they didn't speak the language, the children had to learn as best they could. He attended school for short periods but found it very hard. Regarding local reactions, he found some hostility – remember it was 1937 and the British were suspicious of foreigners! He made friends with some people and lived in lodgings with English people. In the late 1940s, his brother had come to Leamington Spa, where several Basques were living, so he decided to settle there and found work. We married in 1961.

Reflecting on his 'very hard life', the comments of Rodolfo's wife show the complex identities refugees are forced to create in coming to terms with the loss of home and family which can never fully be replaced. In this particular case, return was eventually possible, but local roots established in the place of exile proved hard to break:

> Wars [forced] him to leave his homeland as a boy and then due to politics, [Rodolfo was] not allowed back... He was allowed to return in 1955 and I went with him. It was a very emotional time as you can imagine. Unfortunately his father died, aged 57, before he could see him again. Of course, after the Spanish Civil War ended, many of the children returned to the Basque country, but many didn't due to various factors, and made their lives here. They then had to endure our war from 1939–45 and it was not easy living in Southampton, with the Germans bombing the port... Wars ruined his life ... and he often feels bitter about the fact. We visit San Sebastian most years, a beautiful seaside city. I love it and the Basques are a wonderful friendly race who love life, always singing and dancing, and the food is superb. We are retired now but will continue to live in England, but visit Spain more often.[79]

Those children returning to Spain often found the move difficult after they had learned English and become established in Britain. For some, a return to poor living conditions was shocking and gave rise to feelings of guilt for not having shared the problems of their friends and relatives during the period of exile.[80] The wrench could be so unsettling that some returned to Britain, as happened with the Cabillo brothers who stowed away on a ship to come back.

Their British foster parents agreed to take them in after they were imprisoned.[81] Others, such as Seraphim Martinez, felt they had better opportunities in the place where they had spent their formative years, deciding to settle permanently in Britain.[82]

The friendships established at such a young age among the refugee children often lasted a lifetime. As the Basques got older, reunions became increasingly important. Fifty years after their first arrival, 40 Basques came back to Eastleigh, the number reflecting that strong links with the area remained:

> It was too much for the elderly Basque, with his suit, rolled umbrella and beret. He stood in front of Nazareth House and wept. He cried as he remembered the kindness of Southampton people 50 years ago. They remembered the shop in Hill Lane, now a dairy, they remembered The Dell and the Classic Cinema in Above Bar and the paper boy shouting 'Southern Daily Echo'. Inaki Barinaga told how his 16-year old brother Sabino was such a good footballer that he was spotted playing on a local field and signed up for the Saints. He turned out for the second team, but on his return to Spain made his name with the mighty Real Madrid.

> When the 4,000 young people fled their homeland, where their families were living in air raid shelters and railway tunnels, British people took them to their hearts... But those who lived at Nazareth House never forgot the love shown to them. Back in Bilbao, they kept in touch with each other and called themselves The Children of Nazareth House. 'The people were so kind to us ... fantastic', said Señor Barinaga. 'And we have never forgotten it. It is very emotional for us to come back after fifty years.'[83]

The presence of the Basques in Britain continues to be recalled with fondness both by the former refugees and those that helped them.[84] No other refugee group has received so much attention locally either at the time or in subsequent popular and official memory, including the town of Eastleigh which hosted a play 'Strange Cargo' commemorating the refugees' experiences half a century later. A group of 100 Basques returned to attend its launch. A process of selective memory has operated enabling the Basques to be remembered partly at the expense of other refugee groups. But the privileged status of this story runs the risk of romanticism and nostalgia distorting the reality of the Basque experience in Britain which, for all its successes, had many difficulties. Even for those several hundred Basques who settled in Britain, adaptation was difficult. Some of the Spaniards intermarried with British people but according to one Basque, 'well over half married within the group. Despite the forty years that have passed since their landing at Southampton, the sense of family and blood bond that united them in those early days in a foreign country still remains.'[85] The Basque refugees were treated nationally and locally with sympathy, ambivalence and hostility. It was a complexity of responses which made it difficult for these often traumatised youngsters to re-establish a sense of home. Those fleeing persecution from the Third Reich faced similar dilemmas.

5
Refugees from Nazism, 1933–1939

INTRODUCTION: THE MEANING OF ASYLUM DURING THE 1930s

In contrast to the Basques from the Spanish Civil War, the refugee movement from the Third Reich was less systematic until 1938. By the outbreak of war some 350,000 refugees had escaped Germany, Austria and Czechoslovakia,[1] but this disguises the important year-to-year variations in numbers seeking and finding asylum. The foremost factor affecting the pattern of flight was the level and intensity of Nazi persecution (and the growing proximity of war) so that for the Jews especially, the 18 months after the *Anschluss* in March 1938 were crucial. Nevertheless, other considerations, particularly the availability and suitability of places of asylum, were paramount in individual decisions that were made to escape persecution. Britain became in the months before September 1939 the most important haven for those fleeing Nazi oppression. Its alien entry procedures were gently eased and rescue schemes were created at a point when other countries intensified their restrictionism. As with the 1920s, no country can be viewed in isolation: the problem was so great that an international response was required.[2]

The responses of nation-states and international bodies, particularly the League of Nations, were critical in determining the refugees' fate during the 1930s. Other factors aside from national and global high politics and diplomacy must, however, be considered. From the 1970s, much has been written on liberal democratic reactions and responses to victims of Nazi oppression.[3] But in this rapidly expanding historiography, little work documents and analyses local and individual responses to the refugee crisis.[4] Yet returning to the Spanish Civil War, it was only the efforts and energy of ordinary people such as those at Eastleigh that made humanitarian gestures toward the Basques possible in Britain. Recognition of the inter-dependence of global, national and local initiatives toward the victims of Nazism was given by James McDonald, the League of Nations High Commissioner for Refugees, in July 1935:

The work of the High Commission – the negotiation and direction of international collaboration on behalf of German refugees – is now two-thirds done. For this measure of accomplishment nearly the whole credit is due to private organizations and individuals, Jewish and non-Jewish, whose devoted and ceaseless activities in many parts of the world have helped to make possible the settlement overseas of about 36,000 refugees, the repatriation in Central and Eastern Europe of 18,000 and the establishment elsewhere of from 5,000 to 10,000 more.[5]

But ultimately it was the nation-state which had the power to grant entry to refugees. In autumn 1935, Jews and other racial 'undesirables' were outlawed through the Nazis' Nuremberg Laws. The number of potential refugees expanded and shortly afterwards McDonald resigned:

> The private organizations, Jewish and Christian, may be expected to do their part if the Governments, acting through the League, make possible a solution. But in the new circumstances it will not be enough to continue the activities on behalf of those who flee from the Reich. Efforts must be made to remove or mitigate the causes which create German refugees.[6]

By examining responses to this refugee crisis from a popular as well as a governmental perspective, however, belief in granting asylum can be shown to have survived and even flourished. The restrictionism of the 1920s and the intolerance of the following decade did not counter more positive forces.

Of all modern refugee movements, greatest attention has been given to those escaping the Third Reich. Before the twentieth century, Huguenots were the 'classic' refugee group (the term itself coined to describe their status). It is not surprising that those campaigning in the 1930s made direct comparisons with these earlier refugees. Typical was Viscount Cecil of Chelwood, Chairman of the High Commission for Refugees, who wrote in 1935 that he wished

> it were possible for us in England to renew our experience of the French Huguenots and welcome unreservedly non-Aryan Germans to our shores. I believe it would be not only a fine action in itself, but in the end would increase our national prosperity.[7]

Such an analysis took a long time to be accepted. During the 1930s, even the term 'refugee' was deemed problematic. In January 1938 the chairman of the Jewish Refugees Committee reported a change of name to the 'German Jewish Aid Committee': 'it was unfair to label a German over here as a refugee for the rest of his life'.[8] For contemporaries, the question was whether those fleeing the Third Reich were unwanted aliens – suspect foreigners who might steal British jobs and undermine national unity – or refugees deserving pity and respect? As the name change indicated, referring to those escaping the Third Reich as 'refugees' was not enough to evoke sympathy and understanding.

British official policy and bureaucratic procedures were straightforward: 'In 1933 Britain did not have a refugee policy: any such matter fell under the heading of alien immigration'. Humbert Wolfe, of the Ministry of Labour, stated that government practice was 'not to vary the aliens administration in favour of or against the refugees'. At least Wolfe recognised that those coming from Nazi Germany deserved the title 'refugee'; many simply described them as aliens which was not, as the *Daily Herald* argued in 1938, 'a very nice word'. Along with it came associations such as 'coming to Britain "in hordes" ... taking the "bread from our mouths" [and] not understand[ing] "our British ways"'.[9]

The first success of pro-refugee campaigners came in April 1933. Otto Schiff, President of the Jews' Temporary Shelter, approached the government, along with other leaders of British Jewry, promising, as they had with the transmigrants of Atlantic Park, that 'all expense, whether in respect of temporary or permanent accommodation or maintenance, will be borne by the Jewish community without ultimate charge to the state'. The numbers involved in the 1920s had been small, and though the offer of April 1933 envisaged an equally manageable scheme, it ultimately enabled tens of thousands to find refuge from Nazism: 'The guarantee became the cornerstone of British refugee policy and the Jewish community was held to its promise until after the outbreak of World War II'.[10]

In return for the guarantee, the government was asked to grant temporary asylum to all refugees coming from Germany. There was little or no intention on behalf of British Jewish leaders or the government that Britain should add permanently to its alien population; the refugees allowed entry would be transmigrants awaiting entry into 'proper' immigrant receiving societies such as the USA or, in the particular case of the Jews, Palestine. A few distinguished individuals might be encouraged to emigrate on a permanent basis, such as talented scientists, engineers and industrialists, but for most refugees their stay would be limited to the time it took to retrain and await their visas to other countries. In the first two years of the Nazi regime, such expectations were met. By May 1934 roughly 3,500 refugees had entered Britain but over 1,000 had left. This pattern continued the following year: 'although the stream of immigration was larger in 1935, the figures of those remaining in the country did not appreciably rise'.[11]

Following the pattern of the 1920s, France was the European country in which the largest number of refugees initially settled. At the end of 1933, it had offered refuge to 25,000 out of a total of 59,300 German refugees. This figure declined – by June 1935 only 10,000 German refugees were left in France – but as Norman Bentwich, Director of the High Commission for Refugees, wrote, if somewhat romantically:

> responding to its traditions of liberty, [France] opened its frontiers, and for a considerable time did not require fugitives from Germany to have a visa for admission ... Committees sprang up in France like mushrooms for the assistance of the refugees, some Jewish, some political, some general.[12]

Life as a refugee in France was never easy and early hospitality gave way to the rising xenophobia and antisemitism of the late 1930s, but the mobilisation of French traditions of asylum in the early years of Nazism contrast with the USA which was then only a minor place of refuge.[13]

In May 1934 James McDonald called on the governments of the world to play their part 'to consider the moral claim of the refugees of the right to enter, and to remember that the refugees are not liabilities', singling out the Americans, for specific comment:

> the United States [has been] ... built up, generation after generation, by refugees of all sorts from all parts of the world. I myself am a descendant only of a generation or two removed from refugees.

By April 1934, only 2,500 refugees from Germany had entered the USA. Earlier American restrictionism still operated, intensified by the Great Depression and the growth of domestic antisemitism and xenophobia. With few alternatives, by the mid-1930s the most important place of German Jewish settlement was Palestine.[14]

Britain had been given the Mandate to Palestine in 1920 by the League of Nations and thereafter attempted to balance Zionist demands for a Jewish state and Arab protests about Jewish immigration. Arab unrest and violence grew throughout the 1930s, but in the early years of the Third Reich few obstacles were put in the way of refugees by the British authorities. By June 1935 some 25,000 Jewish refugees from Germany had settled in Palestine. Through Palestine the British government had a key role in the settlement of refugees from the Third Reich,[15] but until 1938 Britain itself was not a major place of refugee settlement. Its importance rested as a centre of temporary asylum. This function increased as the Jewish position in Germany continued to deteriorate. Britain became a victim of others' restrictionism; the difficulty of moving people on left the British government at the outbreak of war with a refugee population of up to 65,000 people. This was at least ten times the scale of settlement intended at the time of the Jewish guarantee and an increase of roughly 50,000 from the number present as late as November 1938.[16]

For many refugees, the 1930s were years of constant flux. Within Europe, bureaucratic obstacles ensured that their stay in any one country would be brief. Their experiences in Britain were part of an insecure, suitcase-dominated world, with permanent status a distant prospect.[17] Saul Friedlander comments that 'It is too often forgotten that Nazi attitudes and policies cannot be fully assessed without knowledge of the lives and indeed of the feelings of the Jewish men, women, and children themselves'. Previous failure to do so has 'turned [them] into a static and abstract element of the historical background'.[18] His inclusive approach will be incorporated here, employing, where possible, a life history approach and illustrating the variations amongst those who experienced persecution and those responding to them.

PATTERNS OF REFUGEE MOVEMENT, 1933–1937

Apart from ease of entry, France was attractive to early refugees from Nazism because of its geographical proximity. Fred Uhlman came from an assimilated German Jewish family from Stuttgart. He left the Third Reich in March 1933 for Paris. His first few weeks were inactive, partly because 'getting paid employment was out of the question' but also due to 'the insistent hope that I might be saved from having to take any decision by the collapse of the Hitler regime'.[19] Other early exiles were less sanguine, though many inside and outside Germany believed that the Nazi government would not last long.[20]

The programme of the National Socialist German Workers' Party in 1920 outlined that no Jew could 'be a German National'. The violent antisemitism of the pre-1933 Nazi Party proved that this was no mere rhetoric. Yet how the Nazis in power were going to deal with their imagined 'Jewish problem' of over half a million people was far from clear. The early months of the Nazi regime did not necessarily provide clarification.[21] On 1 April 1933 a national day of economic boycott against the Jews was launched to satisfy more militant Nazi supporters that antisemitism was being carried out tangibly. Shortly afterwards 'A Law for the Restoration of the Professional Civil Service' was passed, decreeing that 'Civil Servants who are not of Aryan descent are to be retired'. A person was non-Aryan

> if he is descended from non-Aryan, and especially from Jewish parents or grandparents. It is sufficient if one parent or grandparent is non-Aryan. This is to be assumed in particular where one parent or grandparent was of the Jewish religion.[22]

The impact of such antisemitism was uneven, varying according to locality, class/wealth, nationality, sex, and age. In 1933 and 1934, the beginning of 'the economic war against the Jew' was felt more harshly by those whose livelihood was threatened by the first discriminatory measures. The Gerrard family in Berlin show how age and occupation were often crucial factors in the decision to leave or stay.[23] Hilde Gerrard and her husband, Gerhard, came to Britain late in 1938 on domestic servant permits. Hilde grew up in the German town of Kreuzenort. She remembered childhood as

> a large garden in my parents' home, in which I was mostly alone ... It was wonderful. Years later, when I visited my home, I was surprised how much that garden has shrunk – it was so big in my mind.[24]

Her parents ran 'a traditional Jewish home', owning a shop. Hilde moved to Berlin and married in 1929:

> Gerhard accepted a job as [a] bookseller in Berlin ... and I became the secretary of a private hospital. We worked for 4 years in our jobs until Gerhard got a letter ... in January 1933 that his employment was going to be terminated for cultural and racial reasons... Our greatest pleasure was visits to concerts and the theatre

and it seemed that life was going to be a smooth running stream. However, we now [were told] that Jews were not wanted and that made us feel that the ground was giving way under our feet... We wanted to go to America. In 1933 our parents did not want to emigrate, as they had their homes and livelihood in Germany... We did not want to leave them alone and stayed nearer... Therefore Italy [was] considered... Aliens [in Italy] were not allowed to accept a job but could work on their own account. We got an offer as a partner in a firm and we decided to invest our money. In April 1934 we packed up our home and moved to Milan.[25]

For those staying in Nazi Germany, the contrasting testimonies of two Jewish youngsters who eventually settled as refugees in Winchester reveal varying experiences. Edgar Feuchtwanger was from a culturally distinguished and highly integrated German Jewish background. His father was a publisher and his uncle the famous German novelist, Lion Feuchtwanger. Brought up in Munich, a city with a small and largely integrated Jewish population of about 10,000, his relatively 'privileged' position did not remove tension and the close proximity of violence. Edgar's home was very close to Hitler's apartment:

It was ironical that my Jewish family and I could go on living so close to the centre of the new dictatorship for as long as we did, because our name – Feuchtwanger – was hated by the Nazis ... Yet, such was the confusion and anarchy of the early years of the Third Reich that my father, who ran a prestigious academic publishing house, thought he could survive there. I led a normal life ... but there was a sense of menace in the air, which even as a child I could feel. In the days before 30 June 1934, later dubbed the Night of the Long Knives, the atmosphere was particularly oppressive ... I was woken up by the slamming of car doors, boots clattering on the pavement, and raised voices... Despite these menacing events, my family tried to live as normal. That summer we went to our usual holiday resort on Lake Starnberg, close to Munich... Hoping this evil and crazy regime would end, we stayed in Munich for another four years.[26]

Jack Habel's family contrasted greatly to that of the Feuchtwangers. His father and mother were pre-war immigrants from Poland and Romania respectively. His father ran a furniture business, living in what was the Jewish immigrant quarter of Berlin where Jack was born in 1916. Berlin itself had over 170,000 Jews, or roughly one-third of those in Germany before the Nazis came to power. His parents belonged to a small orthodox synagogue. Violent antisemitism was a feature of family and collective experience in this area as early as the 1920s.[27]

The Nazi takeover saw a continuation and intensification of such violence in Berlin, and the extended Habel family and their friends suffered also through the persecution of those with Communist sympathies who became early victims of terror in the concentration camps.[28] Whereas Edgar Feuchtwanger could continue with his education, Jack Habel, who was eight years older, left school in 1933 and for the next few years trained as an upholsterer and later at a farm college. He learned trades including bricklaying and carpentry – 'anything that would help if [it] could get [you] out of the country'. Yet even though the day-to-day experiences of the Habels in the first years of Nazism were more traumatic than those of the Feuchtwangers, there was still resistance to leaving. Although a relatively recent immigrant, Jack's father already identified with his German home. Coming to Berlin in 1911, he

> felt far better under the Germans than under the Poles ... He felt that Berlin, or Germany, was a cultured place, where people [were] reasonable, and not so antisemitic, and he was one of the people who said, 'I'm not in a hurry to leave, because this cannot last' ... I was told ... we were German first, and only by religion were we Jews.[29]

Antisemitism was not so prominent nationally in 1934 and early 1935 but the position of the Jews continued to deteriorate economically, socially and legally. The summer of 1935 witnessed increased violence from young activists on the local level, which, alongside the increasing bureaucratic and legalistic problems in defining 'Jewishness', prompted the Nuremberg Laws announced by Hitler in the autumn. The Reich Citizenship Law of September 1935 defined German nationality. Its first decree, announced two months later, stated that 'A Jew cannot be a Reich citizen'. The disenfranchisement of the Jews was accompanied by the Law for the Protection of German Blood and German Honour, of September 1935, highlighting the social and cultural removal of Jews from everyday life, including the banning of marriages and extramarital intercourse between Jews and 'Germans'.[30]

Although the more blatant aspects of Nazi antisemitism were disguised in 1936 at the time of the Olympic Games in Berlin, the marginalisation of German Jewry continued. It was intensified in 1937 when new measures were taken to 'Aryanise' Jewish businesses and liquidate others. Even in the 'quiet' year of 1936 some 25,000 Jews emigrated, and those remaining examined options available abroad with increasing urgency. Yet most German Jews were still unwilling to consider seriously unattractive or dubious possibilities of life outside Nazi Germany. The events of 1938, however, were to transform a steady movement into a panic exodus. The first, the annexation of Austria with its 180,000 Jews, on 13 March 1938 (the *Anschluss*), was to provide a future model for the Jews of Europe: brutal treatment, expropriation, expulsion and murder. Measures which had taken five years to inflict on German Jewry were enacted in a matter of days and weeks and went alongside antisemitic violence, intimidation and humiliation which were unprecedented, even by Nazi standards. It was also the first time that the concentration camp system was used specifically against Jews *en masse*.[31]

THE *ANSCHLUSS* AND AUSTRIAN JEWRY

By the outbreak of the Second World War, the majority of Austrian Jews had been forced out of their country and those left behind were in a desperate and poverty-stricken state. Liese Richards was born in 1917, growing up in a comfortable middle-class Viennese home. Her parents were very assimilated and had converted to Lutheran Protestantism to avoid antisemitism: 'When my mother was expecting her first baby – my brother – they decided that it would be better for the future of the children'. Liese herself did not experience any personal antisemitism: 'Obviously the fact that I was a member of the Protestant religion didn't put me in with the Jewish people'. To the Nazis, however, her parents' conversion to Christianity made no difference: racially, Liese, her brother, and her parents were unambiguously Jewish. Before March 1938, tension mounted and Liese experienced greater hostility, but it was hardly preparation for the shock of the *Anschluss*. Coming out of a cinema in the Jewish area with a friend, they found:

> the whole town ... seething with emotion and excitement... We were frightened. We said, 'We must go home. Something is happening.'... And the whole night long we heard 'Sieg Heil'... It was a terrible experience ... After that, life became anxious... The Austrians were ... much worse than the Germans had ever been. They started getting the Jewish people out of their shops and putting 'Sau Jude' on the pavement, and making them scrub it, and worse things... [My father] came home one day, and he was sitting there with tears streaming down his face. He'd been in this job ... thirty years or more [and] knew he was going to lose [it]... All the Jewish shops had 'Jew' written on them. Quite a lot of them were destroyed [or] taken over. The first victim in my family was my cousin... They had a little shop, and they were taken out of the shop, and were never seen again ... [amongst] the first ones at that time ... taken to concentration camps ... You weren't allowed to go to any public places ... in the theatres, in the cinemas, in the swimming pools.[32]

Lilian Furst was, at six years old, considerably younger than Liese Richards when the *Anschluss* occurred. Nevertheless, as she writes: 'My first distinct independent memory is of the day the Nazis marched into Vienna'. Like many Austrian Jews, Lilian's parents were from eastern Europe, her father coming from a small Hungarian village.[33] Hungary, like many east European countries, was deeply affected by a wave of post-war antisemitism, including measures in universities limiting the number of Jewish students to a specific quota forcing Desider Furst to come to Vienna to study medicine. Even after qualifying, the depressed economy of Austrian society and antisemitism meant that he had little chance of obtaining work as a doctor, switching instead to dentistry. Established in Austria, he was granted naturalisation in 1928. His wife, Sarah, was born in Potok-Zloty, a village in Galicia near the Russian border. Her orthodox, Yiddish speaking family, like many others, became refugees at the start of the First World War, fearing the antisemitism of the Russian troops, and fleeing westwards to Vienna. Intelligent and determined, Sarah overcame sexual and racial discrimination to gain her medical qualifications. She too after the war was barred from medicine as a 'foreign national' and went into dentistry. Yet, in spite of the problems and discrimination, the first ten years of their marriage, from 1928 to 1938 were very happy:

> Besides medicine, what my mother loved best was the Viennese coffee house. Almost every evening my parents would snatch a bite of supper, change, and bid me goodnight to go off to the coffeehouse where they met friends and family… 'We were driven out of paradise', she would later ruefully comment… [She] loved Vienna, our home, her professional work, and was extremely reluctant to undergo another radical upheaval if it could possibly be avoided.[34]

Lilian's life until the events of 13 March 1938 had been settled and content: 'By all accounts it was an enchanted, almost fairy-tale childhood as long as I remained unaware of the world beyond my family and friends'. But Lilian's ordered and sheltered world changed beyond recognition within months. Her maid was forced to leave and Lilian was transferred to a school solely for Jews. Even as a six-year-old she soon understood that

> we had to make the best of a bad situation. The class grew smaller and smaller as children disappeared mysteriously: into emigration or concentration camps? 'Concentration camp' was one of the terms in a whole new vocabulary I acquired. Exit permit, visa, arrest, disappearances, half-Jew, quarter-Jew, foreign currency…[35]

Desider Furst was under no illusions about the nature of life under the Nazis but they 'decided to wait and see … We loved living in Vienna, we loved our home, and we would not give up everything in a fit of panic'. After dismissal from his job and with conditions deteriorating from day to day, all doubt was removed.[36] Fritz Engel, a fellow dentist, was born in the Innere Stadt district of Vienna in 1897 to an Austrian Jewish mother and Czech Jewish father. Fritz had fought in the Austrian army on the Russian front during the First World War and afterwards struggled to set up a dental practice in Austria, again originally having hoped to become a doctor. His reaction to the *Anschluss* was far more decisive than that of Desider Furst. When news of it was announced '[we] decided at [that] very moment to leave the country immediately, together with our [two young] children, leaving the parents and everything'.[37]

Several days after the *Anschluss*, Adolf Eichmann arrived in Vienna and took control of Jewish affairs in Austria: all Jewish organisations were forced to report to him. Eichmann was keen to systematise and speed up processes to make Austria free of Jews. By August 1938 the Central Office for Jewish Emigration was established in Vienna though 'Paradoxically … [they] invented innumerable obstacles to emigration'. The Jews desperately attempting to leave were pawns in Eichmann's hands. To understand the appalling wave of Jewish suicides in Austria after March 1938, the endless demands for documentation has to be considered alongside the more blatant physical aspects of Nazi antisemitism:

> You had to have not only a current passport, but also certificates that your rent, gas, electricity, telephone, and taxes were fully paid, that you were not abandoning any property, and that you didn't have a relative in an insane asylum as a burden on the state. Each of these certificates was valid for only one month, so that it was virtually impossible to get them all together at the same time.[38]

But 'hardest of all to obtain was a visa to another country; no one wanted us'. Nazi policies of expropriation and refusal to let capital be taken out made the Jewish refugees unattractive to countries of refuge. Abhorrence expressed against Nazi antisemitic methods rarely translated into a desire to help rescue the Jewish victims.[39] In July 1938 an international conference was convened by President Roosevelt in Evian to address the growing refugee problem. Thirty-two countries were represented but, although progress was made, including the setting up of an Inter-Governmental Committee, the rising tide of restrictionism was not stemmed. Moreover, there was reluctance to embarrass Hitler by addressing the causes of the crisis – though it was the increase in Jewish refugees resulting from the *Anschluss* that had prompted Roosevelt to call the conference.[40]

James McDonald resigned as High Commissioner for Refugees in December 1935 because he believed that 'The problem must be tackled at its source if disaster is to be avoided'. McDonald argued that it should be addressed in global diplomacy because 'the protection of the individual from racial and religious intolerance is a vital condition of international peace and security'. The discussions at Evian failed to take on board McDonald's earlier warnings. The policy of appeasement, which came to a head two months later in the Munich conference, meant that embarrassing questions were ignored for the 'good' of international peace. Furthermore, the invitation to Evian stated that 'no country would be expected to receive a greater number of emigrants than is permitted by its existing legislation'.[41]

The Evian conference hardly addressed the pressing problems faced by Austrian Jewry. As a result, increasingly desperate or unlikely places of refuge were considered. Fritz Engel was extremely fortunate, convincing British consular officials that a patent of his could be of great benefit to dentists. He was able to take his young family with him to Britain but had to leave his parents behind to an uncertain fate.[42] The path to freedom for Desider Furst's family proved to be far more complicated and traumatic. As with most refugees leaving Greater Germany in 1938 and 1939, luck also eventually played its part. Having got their passports cleared the next step was to 'get a visa. TO ANYWHERE. Chasing a visa was our most urgent priority in order to get out of this gigantic prison'. All possibilities were considered as, 'By the end of summer our anxiety was turning into despair'. Rumours of ways out abounded. Some proved to be the schemes of confidence tricksters; others, although 'illegal', were successful routes out.[43] As the desperation grew, appalling dilemmas were faced in deciding which highly unlikely scheme to pursue:

> I registered to be put on a list of dentists ... to be admitted to England... It struck me as a fantastic fairy tale... I was offered a passport to a South American country. Its consul had died recently, so I was told, and somebody had got hold of the passports and the official stamps. It would be made out in our name, and we could fly to Lisbon immediately... I heard too late about the possibility of getting a visa to Shanghai; when I went to the Chinese consulate, they had stopped issuing visas. With a certificate of baptism one could enter Yugoslavia... I applied for a landing permit to Australia... We had no prospects of going to Palestine. The legal immigration quota was very small... We never contemplated illegal entry into any country where we wanted to stay permanently. Forged documents were out of the question for us... Our immediate, temporary aim was to get into Holland or Belgium ... we decided to try to escape illegally.[44]

They were successful, but as Lilian Furst writes of their time in Brussels in early 1939: 'If the Belgian police spotted us, we were liable, as illegal immigrants, to be sent back to Germany and into a concentration camp'. They were 'dogged by this fear' but had good news: Desider Furst was 'among the forty Austrian dentists admitted to Great Britain with the prospect of practising there... It was a miracle'. With legal status restored through a six-month visa and a requirement that Desider Furst should re-train at a British dental school and pass examinations before being allowed to practise, a new if uncertain future was possible for the Fursts.[45]

The Fursts and the Engels were somewhat untypical of refugees from Austria who found asylum in Britain before the war: both families travelled together and avoided the heartache of separation. Before leaving Vienna, the Fursts had the option of moving Lilian separately to a couple in Britain. They regarded this as a last resort but thousands of other families were forced to send their children away on their own. On their train journey through Germany, the Fursts saw

> a children's transport, a compartment full of small children with cardboard labels round their necks. Their names and the names and addresses of their recipients were clearly written on them. It was a heart-rending sight. The children, reduced to human parcels, already looked like orphans.[46]

Liese Richards had turned 21 years old during the *Anschluss* and was too old to be eligible for the children's schemes. She too, however, was forced to leave Austria on her own, leaving parents and her brother behind. Liese regarded herself as extremely fortunate in getting a visa enabling her to continue work as a language teacher: most of those offered were 'in the domestic area for the women'. Liese's mother later got a domestic permit but for men it was extremely difficult: 'My brother, for instance, I tried very, very hard to get him out as a doctor, and that was quite impossible, they wouldn't let any doctors into England … my father and brother couldn't come'. Departing from Vienna, the train was

> absolutely packed with refugees, all going to England, and all going on domestic permits… My father came into my compartment on his own, and put his arms round me. It was very, very sad. I didn't need it with my mother because we were so close, but he wanted to really let me know that he cared.[47]

By September 1939, roughly two-thirds of Austrian Jews had escaped though it is important to remember the experiences of those left behind. Norman Bentwich visited Austria as a leading member of the British refugee organisation, the Council for German Jewry, in 1938. He returned to Vienna just weeks before the Second World War:

> The destruction of the Jewish community during that year has been carried through with inconceivable thoroughness… The aim which has been remorselessly pursued is to make life literally unendurable, and so force the people out – anyhow… [D]uring the year 3,000 have died. The death rate is four times what it was in 1937; and of the death rate one eight[h] part is due to suicide. The livelihood of almost all the Jews has been taken away. Every single Jewish shop or business has been 'aryanized', destroyed or shut… All the Jews who live outside what was the Jewish quarter in the Leopoldstadt are being expelled from their houses or apartments – even when they are the owners… The poverty and destitution of the remnant of the Jewish community are heartrending. Well over half … are fed daily through communal soup-kitchens… Some thousands more of the old, infirm and children are maintained by the community in such charitable buildings as remain to it… The one hope for all, young and older, is emigration.[48]

Such possibilities came almost to a close a few weeks later. Only 7,000 Jews survived in Austria during the war and roughly 65,000 were murdered in the Holocaust. Amongst them was the family of Desider Furst's sister who had arrived in Vienna in 1938 with her husband and three children. Another sister and her family perished in Auschwitz and other relatives died in 'unknown places in Hungary'. The brother and father of Liese Richards survived the war; her father reached the Shanghai refugee camp via Marseilles and her brother ended up also in the Far East in a Japanese prisoner of war camp. The family was never reunited. Most relatives of the Engels perished in the 'Final Solution'.[49]

'KRISTALLNACHT' AND AFTER

The family of Edgar Feuchtwanger remained in Munich, hoping that 'this evil and crazy regime would end'. But the experience gained by the Nazis in Austria proved to be a model for the treatment of German Jewry. Aryanisation was intensified, violence increased and more Jews were sent to concentration camps. In October 1938, following the notorious Munich

Conference, the Nazis incorporated the Sudentenland into the Reich, prompting the expulsion of Jews into what was left of Czechoslovakia.[50] The growing momentum to expel Jews was also stimulated by the decision of the increasingly antisemitic Polish state to remove citizenship for those living abroad without special authorisation. The Nazis regarded this as an excuse in October 1938 to expel some 16,000 Polish Jews from Germany, most of whom were left for weeks on the border in a desperate camp near Zbaszyn.[51]

The fear and insecurity caused to all Jews in Germany by the Polish expulsions emerges from the testimony of Anne Mayer who came to Britain just before the war. Anne had left Berlin in 1937 to work as a nanny for a two-year-old boy in a Jewish family in the small town of Plauen im Vogtland near the Czech border:

> By then Jews were not allowed entry or participation in public places … Life continued reasonably normal[ly] for a while, except that people vanished now and then and we heard of secret arrests overnight. In the summer of 1938 tension on the Czech and Polish borders increased. Jews with Polish antecedents were rounded up on trumped-up charges and pushed across into Poland. The remaining Community huddled closer together, redoubling their efforts to get out.

In Paris, the son of one of the families in the Zbaszyn camp took matters into his own hands, assassinating Ernst vom Rath, a minor diplomat, in the German Embassy. Yet again, the Nazis regarded this as an excuse to claim Jewish provocation, leading to the 'Kristallnacht' pogrom of 9 and 10 November 1938 which launched a further stage in European Jewry's destruction.[52]

During 'Kristallnacht', over 100 Jews were killed, thousands of Jewish homes, shops and communal buildings were destroyed and tens of thousands of Jews were sent to concentration camps. The pogrom and its aftermath were experienced in every part of Greater Germany.[53] For some German Jews, particularly the older generation, 'Kristallnacht' was devastating because they could not imagine any other place as 'home'. Ernst Guter came to Britain in 1939 as an agricultural trainee at a Rothschild estate in Hampshire. His memories of 'Kristallnacht' show how its damage extended beyond violence:

> I grew up in a small city not far from Danzig… In 1938, life for Jews in such small provincial cities was already economically and demographically impossible and many of us had migrated to large cities, foremost… Berlin. In Stolp, we had two prominent Jewish doctors. One of them was Dr Berlowitz, our family doctor, a majestic father figure sporting a magnificent beard… The last time I saw him, he was sitting forlornly on a park bench near the Berlin zoo. This was in November. He was in shirtsleeves, without jacket, coat or hat. He did not see me, he did not see anybody. I shall never forget the look of despair on his face.

Dr Sigmund Heilbronn was another Jewish doctor whose family was deeply rooted in German society. A veteran of the First World War who had been awarded an Iron Cross, he started his medical career as the village doctor of Gailingen in the south of Germany near the Swiss border. On 10 November 1938 he was taken by the police to witness the blowing up of the town's synagogue. The SS then

> took me to the cellar of the city hall, the same building where my grandfather was mayor from the year 1870... There I was beaten with whips and ... taken to Dachau. These are my last recollections of the country I was born in, where for hundreds of years my ancestors lived a peace loving and honourable life.[54]

The Jews were fined one thousand million marks to pay for the damage to property. No ambiguity now remained in the position of German Jewry. There was clearly no place for the Jews in the Third Reich and all energy was spent trying to leave. Even the relative peace of the Feuchtwanger family was destroyed by the night of violence and the following days of intense persecution:

> Following the Kristallnacht pogrom, my father spent six weeks in Dachau concentration camp ... I remember seeing him in bed after his release, his shaven head covered with bruises and the marks of frostbite. It was terrifying. We could no longer hope to stay in Germany. My uncle obtained an entry visa to Britain for us and my father put me on a train for England in February 1939 – he and my mother followed later. I grasped as I left that my world, like Europe itself, had changed beyond recognition.[55]

Jack Habel was arrested after the pogrom and kept in a police compound in Berlin for over a week along with 60 other Jews:

> I was the lucky one who was interviewed. And they said 'What have you done about leaving this country?'. And I had on me a piece of paper which said I was given permission to land in England as [an agricultural trainee], but only for one year ... And with that they let me go.

Jack Habel left for London in January 1939 leaving his father and sister behind. He was then sent to a farm outside Portsmouth with his girlfriend who had come to Britain shortly before.[56] But for the majority of those left behind in Greater Germany, escape was harder. Anne Mayer's employer, who was eventually to die in a camp in southern France, was released after 'Kristallnacht'

> with an undertaking to leave Germany by a certain deadline. That unfortunately was not so easy ... Jews were now besieging and milling around every Embassy and Agency for the slim chance of obtaining a visa or permit.[57]

At this critical moment in Jewish history, much depended on the flexibility of the outside world in halting the tendency towards restrictionism. The British government's representative at the Evian conference, Lord Winterton, was reassured that Roosevelt did not expect any significant change in policy from those attending. Winterton, attempting to preserve the image of Britain as a tolerant and decent country, explained that its 'traditional policy of granting asylum [could now] only be applied within narrow limits':

> The United Kingdom has never yet had cause to regret this policy, and refugees have often enriched the life and contributed to the prosperity of the British people. But the United Kingdom is not a country of immigration. It is highly industrialised, fully populated and is still faced with the problem of unemployment.[58]

Winterton believed that the most important role Britain could play would be absorbing some refugees previously allowed temporary entry. A few gestures were made after the conference easing restrictions on entry but these were rather tokenistic compared to the scale of the refugee problem. Winterton also alluded to 'social reasons' stopping greater generosity – the fear of domestic antisemitism if numbers increased.[59]

Nevertheless, in the House of Commons' debate on refugees at the end of November 1938, concern about growing antisemitism, whilst articulated, was not dominant. After Evian, the Chancellor of the Duchy of Lancaster had stated on the government's behalf that 'It is largely public opinion which must be the determining factor' in deciding how many refugees could enter. It was remarked in the Commons that 'Since then recent events have caused public opinion to move forward [positively] with a leap'.[60] The pogrom was an opportunity for many MPs to call for more generous refugee policy. The Home Secretary, Sir Samuel Hoare, warned the Chamber that Britain could not afford such humanitarianism because 'there is the making of a definite anti-Jewish movement' but after 'Kristallnacht' immigration procedures were relaxed, especially in granting domestic permits, and a new scheme came into operation – the Refugee Children's Movement.[61] In the Commons, granting asylum was portrayed as a matter of British pride. Mr Noel Baker, MP for Derby, opened the discussion by raising the spectre of Britain's future reputation:

> Dr. Goebbels said the other day that he hoped that the outside world would soon forget the German Jews. He hopes in vain. His campaign against them will go down in history with St. Bartholomew's Eve as a lasting memory of human shame. Let there go with it another memory, the memory of what the other nations did to wipe the shame away.

Others referred back in history when: 'We in this country have always offered asylum to the afflicted and the distressed'. The Home Secretary reported that senior Jewish refugee workers had come to him with a proposal concerning children:

> They pointed back to the experience during the war, in which we gave homes here to many thousands of Belgian children, in which they were educated, and in which we played an invaluable part in maintaining the life of the Belgian nation. So also with these Jewish and non-Aryan children, I believe that we could find homes in this country without any harm to our own population.

Reference was also made to more recent help given to the Spanish refugees and many MPs referred to the successful relocation of Russians and Armenians after 1918, though Britain's meagre role in the latter was not mentioned. In contrast to the parliamentary debates of 1919, it was suggested that the aliens legislation had never been intended to keep out those being persecuted abroad.[62]

The strength and limitations of British schemes of rescue, most of which gave the refugees only temporary status, splitting families up in the process and often leaving vulnerable members behind, will be explored later. Unfortunately, the scale of the European refugee crisis intensified further in March 1939 when German troops took over the Czechoslovakian provinces of Bohemia and Moravia, including the city of Prague and its large Jewish community with roots in the medieval period. After the Munich agreement, in what was an ill-disguised attempt to hide its guilt, the British government provided £10 million to the Czech government for humanitarian aid, largely but not exclusively to help refugees. At a local level the crudity of this conscience-salving operation was stated explicitly. In Hampshire the Mayor of the army garrison town of Aldershot launched an appeal in aid of the Czech refugees immediately after Munich. It was published with the support of the local newspaper's editor 'because I know that after the events of last week everybody has been offering up their thanks for the very great relief which they felt'. The Council chairman of neighbouring Farnborough was even more explicit in supporting the appeal, revealing the unsavoury human trait of self-deception in defending the indefensible: 'We are all very thankful that war has been averted, and fully appreciate the wonderful and unselfish contribution the Czech nation has made for the preservation of peace'. The government's financial support, as well as that from the public, helped set up the British Committee for Refugees from Czechoslovakia, later the Czech Refugee Trust Fund. The Trust was to help some 8,000 people inside and outside of Czechoslovakia. Sections of the labour movement were particularly involved in helping political Sudetanland victims. Pressure from the left pushed the British government to agree to allocate 350 block visas for those who could be identified as particularly vulnerable to persecution. By the outbreak of war, roughly 5,000 Czech refugees had found asylum in Britain; the only example during the 1930s of a British government-sponsored refugee organisation, even if its funds proved to be inadequate, especially after 15 March 1939 when the Germans entered Prague. Although Eichmann quickly established himself in Prague to 'encourage' emigration, only approximately 25,000 of the 120,000 Jews in Czechoslovakia managed to leave before the Second World War, far lower a proportion than Austria or Germany. The work of the Trust was crucial not only in rescuing refugees but also in settling them in Britain. It was their financial support, for example, which enabled the nine-year-old Vera Schaufeld to come to Britain, maintain her upkeep and continue her education in a Suffolk school.[63]

Vera came from an assimilated and prosperous Jewish family. Her father was a prominent and 'very patriotic' lawyer working for the Czech government. Her mother, who was German, was a doctor. They married in Westphalia in 1929 and their daughter was born a year later. 'My parents did have a very nice life, and I grew up in a very privileged family.' Vera grew up in the town of Klatovy where her father was leader of the Jewish community. Her parents mixed freely on a social level with Jews and non-Jews: 'I grew up very secure in mainstream, Czech life'. Her memories of pre-Nazi life are idealistic, such as visiting 'a nice ice-cream parlour and having ice-cream with my grandmother, in Klatovy'. Once again, the Nazi invasion was to destroy irretrievably this sense of place and home, leading to the splitting up of a close family:

> I remember my parents coming to tell me that I was going to go to England. Now what happened was that my mother came to school to meet me ... which was very unusual, and she took me across the road to a little park... I can remember sitting there, and her telling me that I was going to go to England, and that they were going to follow me very shortly, and it was just for a short time, to go there before them. And that I had to be very grown up and so on, and go. I can remember ... feeling that it was quite an adventure to go away... And going to say goodbye to various school friends ... it made me feel very grown up. Then I can remember the station in Prague, and standing by the window of the train, and my parents were at the station... And seeing my parents waving their handkerchiefs. And that was the last thing, I could see the handkerchiefs waving as the train drew out of Prague station.[64]

Vera's parents, particularly her mother, tried to explain why she had to leave Czechoslovakia, but to such a young child exiled to an unfamiliar place and with little support offered to her, the essential evilness of Nazism made little sense. Vera had been part of a little group of Jewish children who used to visit the shop of one of their member's aunties:

> We used to used to say 'Could we have a drink of water?' and [when she went] away to the kitchen ... we would take money out of the till. I can remember this because when I was in England and I used to lay in bed in boarding school, and think what wicked things that I'd done to deserve being sent away from home, this was one of the things that I was being punished for by being sent to England.

Her parents' attempt to reach Britain was unsuccessful. Other options, including a lecturing job in Shanghai for her father, never materialised. They continued living in Klatovy and were deported, along with Vera's grandmother, to the 'model' concentration camp of Theresienstadt. Her grandmother was reunited with her sister in the camp where both died. Vera's parents were transported to Auschwitz and never returned.[65]

The parents of Alice Sluckin (née Klausova) were also offered help by the Czech Refugee Trust. Her father was born in Prague and her mother came from an assimilated Polish Jewish background. Alice was born in Prague in 1919 and 'as far as Jewishness is concerned, it was a very fringe issue'. By the 1930s her parents had settled in a Sudentenland town and were thus victims of the Nazi annexation in 1938. Both were leading Social Democrats, eligible for support after Munich from the British government:

> My parents could have [left] but they just didn't want to... They felt that they were alright and my father would say '[the Czechs] have always been decent and who would do any harm to me?'

Her father was a medical officer of health whose job was transferred after the Munich agreement, moving from Sudentenland to Prague, giving him a false sense of security. He was well integrated in non-Jewish society in what has been viewed as one of the least antisemitic countries in Europe. Tragically, by the time Prague had been overtaken by the Nazis, the possibilities of her parents leaving Czechoslovakia had seriously diminished. Their daughter, however, was less rooted to the place of her birth. Alice desired to leave because she 'wanted to be independent... It wasn't ... personal fear. It was much more a kind of spirit of adventure'. Finding that there was a shortage of nurses, she applied to various hospitals in Britain:

> It was the only thing that my parents would have agreed I could do. Because other possibilities were ... domestic [service] and my parents were just absolutely against this ... there must be some sort of [prospects for the] future.

Ten years older, Alice's departure was far less traumatic at the time, if not subsequently, than that of Vera Schaufeld:

> It was all kind of overshadowed with being nineteen, when you're really much more concerned with yourself than with other people's feelings or your family's feelings. I remember seeing [my parents] and I remember all my life, right through, the ... scene when ... they took me to the station.

Alice arrived in Dover in March 1939 with a two-year visa. Two weeks later the Germans invaded Prague. Just before the outbreak of war her parents rejected the chance to use false papers to leave along with their 14-year-old son. Instead, remaining in Prague until 1942, they were deported to Theresienstadt and subsequently murdered by the Nazis.[66]

The subtle but important liberalisation of British immigration procedures was not enough to offset counter tendencies elsewhere: the numbers seeking to escape had increased significantly since the Evian Conference. The journey of the *St Louis* illustrated the failure to deal with the refugee crisis in a coordinated manner. The luxury liner left Hamburg in May 1939 with 907 German Jewish refugees on board possessing landing permits issued by Cuba. These were not honoured by the Cuban government and the refugees were left on the ship as other Latin American countries and then the United States refused them entry. In June, after six weeks of fruitless negotiations, the *St Louis* returned to Europe and arrived in Antwerp on 17 June 1939. Yet gestures by four European

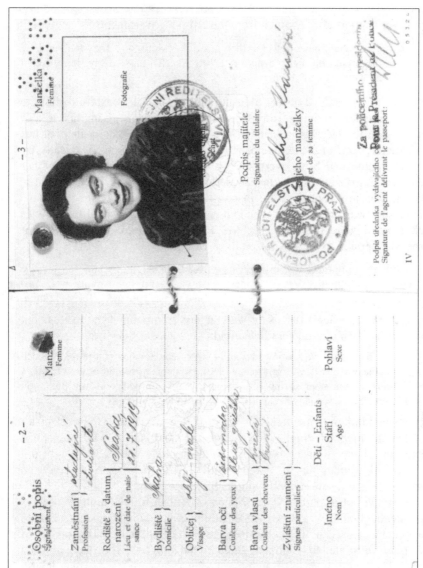

The Czech passport of Alice Klausova. From the private collection of Alice Sluckin and with her kind permission.

governments, including the British, stopped the 907 passengers being returned to Germany. The international attention given to the *St Louis* enabled it to be treated as a special case. The House of Commons was told that there were 'exceptional circumstances which would justify the admission to this country of a proportion of these refugees pending arrangements for their ultimate emigration'. Fears that Britain's liberal reputation might be tarnished after the example provided by Holland to take 200 of the *St Louis* refugees, who arrived in Southampton on 21 June 1939, partly explained Britain's 'positive' response, as did the guarantee offered by Jewish organisations that they would not be a charge on the state. No country wanted a mass influx of Jews and even Britain, as the most important centre of refuge in 1939, pursued policies that, as one stalwart campaigner stated, discriminated against 'the poor, the friendless and the male Jews'. Roughly half those in the borders of the Reich before the war, and particularly the elderly, were left behind.[67]

After the war, Desider Furst remembered that:

> There were quite a number of Austrians who were preparing themselves ... to return 'Home'... They either could not or did not want to try to make a new start in a new country... [In contrast] we were settled in England; Lilian was happy at school and University and we had many friends. We became allergic to Austria and never visited Vienna – England became our home despite our accents!

Lilian Fursts' parents were not born in Austria but became firmly rooted to the country. Both after their flight to Britain developed a deep antipathy to what it had become. In many of the testimonies represented, home, before the Nazi onslaught, was idealised: childhood in particular portrayed in a romantic and cosy manner. It is perhaps unsurprising in the light of the subsequent persecution and rejection, that normal nostalgic tendencies toward childhood, or, in the case of the Fursts, early marriage, were intensified. Nevertheless, such accounts point to a sense of belonging, however complex, that represented the European Jewish experience before the Nazi era. Even by the start of the Second World War, the Nazis had destroyed Jewish communities in Germany, Austria and Czechoslovakia which had existed for hundreds of years. As one British MP put it: '[they are] not condemning the Jews to death; [they are] making it impossible for them to live'.[68]

LOCAL RESPONSES IN BRITAIN TO THE JEWISH PLIGHT

In April 1933, the Rev. M. L. Perlzweig, honorary secretary of the Zionist Federation of Great Britain, addressed the Southampton Brotherhood on the 'Persecution of the Jews'. Although highlighting the role of antisemitism in the Nazi movement, Perlzweig warned his largely Christian audience 'that these things will not stop at Jews... Europe is confronted with a danger of great magnitude'.[69] His address acted as a model for many campaigners during the Nazi era. The measures against the Jews had to be proved so that they did not appear as mere atrocity propaganda and it was crucial to establish that 'the matter of affairs in Germany was of the gravest import not only for the Jews, but for all humanity'. His defensive approach was not necessarily misguided. Until 1938 at least, many in Britain partly blamed German Jews for their own misfortune.[70]

Perlzweig stressed much could be done at a local level to help the Jews abroad: British officials and politicians could 'do more if you stimulate them'. Perlzweig was also keen to provide a specific significance to the locality: 'he hoped if any refugees landed at Southampton, or other ports, they would not be turned back'. Perlzweig proved to be an accurate prophet. Southampton was to play an important role in Jewish refugee movements during the 1930s, reaching a peak in 1939 when over 1,200 refugees arrived there each month on ships coming from Hamburg and Bremerhaven. More generally, the region was a significant place of temporary or permanent settlement and of localised schemes of rescue for those displaced by the Nazis. Responses to Nazism as a whole and Jewish refugees in particular can first be explored by looking at the articulation of sympathy towards the victims at a local level.[71]

The violence of the Nazi movement, its intimidation and destruction of political opponents, as well as its persecution of minorities, caused widespread alarm in Britain during the early months of the regime. But many on the left-liberal side of politics feared that the world would soon start finding ways to accommodate Hitler, leading to the forgetting of his victims. In 1933, the hastily assembled World Committee for the Victims of German Fascism warned that whilst 'manifestations of Fascism are appalling ... the memory of the public is short'.[72] In calling for support, its chairman, Lord Morley, outlined the 'immense suffering that needed help' and painted 'a picture of National Committees [22 were created] all over the world cooperating in the common task of giving that help'. At a public meeting in Portsmouth in November 1933 appealing for help for refugees in Britain, elsewhere, and those suffering in Germany, Lord Morley provided an indication of how, for those involved, international, national and local responses were inseparable, suggesting

> that some people in Portsmouth might provide homes for one or two children whose parents had either been killed, beaten, or put into prison or concentration camps. Perhaps Portsmouth would provide one more bed in the home for the child refugees near Paris [?].

A donation was made for this French refugee home. Morley suggested it would fund a place to 'be called the Portsmouth bed'. By such naming, geographical barriers were overcome to help ease what they saw as a problem for all humanity.[73]

In the local Jewish world, attempts to publicise the fate of the Jews in Nazi

Germany met with mixed responses. In 1933 the President of the Southampton Hebrew Congregation and its rabbi approached the Mayor of the town 'with view to holding a mass meeting of protest'. The Mayor stressed that he was not antisemitic but argued that 'organised mass meetings by Jews would do more harm than good'. The Executive Committee of the Congregation agreed and, instead, a resolution was sent to the city's two Members of Parliament, Sir James Barrie and W. Craven Ellis, 'asking them to raise their disapproval in Parliament against the persecution of Jewish citizens by the Hitler government'. Neither MP spoke in the House of Commons on this issue throughout the Nazi era.[74]

There was dissent from the quiet approach recommended by the leaders of Southampton's Jewish community. One member argued passionately that the Jewish community in Southampton was 'not doing sufficient in comparison to London. In London they were holding mass meetings, boycotting German goods and various other things'. The President responded that 'In Southampton there is only a handful of Jews, most of them business people, therefore we must not do anything rash'.[75] Portsmouth was a larger and more self-confident Jewish community than its south coast neighbour. A press statement in March 1933 on behalf of the town's 150 Jewish families, roughly 700 individuals, deplored 'the tyrannical treatment being meted out to the Jews in Germany'. Yet even this statement revealed defensive tendencies, pointing out the achievements and patriotism of German Jews.[76] One of the key issues dividing British Jewry in 1933 concerned the appropriateness of a boycott of German goods. Those in Portsmouth, after an initial hesitation, were keen to proclaim publicly how they would 'carry on with the boycott until the German Government showed its determination to treat their co-religionists with humanity and justice'.[77]

Though the Jewish community of Southampton wished to avoid public controversy, several of its members were deeply involved with helping the refugees who passed through the port. Reverend Gordon played a key role in dock work, meeting ships and continuing the preventative work he had been engaged in since the war. Others played a similar role and were active in helping refugees settling in the region and defending their cause.[78] The work on behalf of the Basque children in the Southampton region was well publicised. In contrast, local help given to the refugees from Nazism was diffuse, subsequently receiving less attention. It was the isolation of both those involved in rescue work and the refugees themselves that led in 1938 to the formation of a local refugee club whose members came from as far away as Swanwick, ten miles to the east of Southampton, and Lymington, ten miles to the west. The club, alongside the Southampton Committee for Refugees, of which the Mayor was chairman, revealed the ongoing local tradition of welcome towards the displaced:

> Refugees from other lands, driven out by the stress of events, are still coming into this country in considerable numbers. Many of them have found temporary

> homes and working opportunities in this neighbourhood, and the attempt is
> being made by the friends of these unhappy folk to provide them with a
> background of friendliness and help, especially in the matter of languages...
> Southampton people are doing a great deal of useful, quiet work in these
> matters.

A visitor to the club found 'that many of these people are suffering unpleasant
conditions and uncongenial situations out of gratitude for permission to land'.
Nevertheless, they were still 'loyal and appreciative' – even as domestic
servants involved in 'the single-handed preparation of dinners of so many
courses that the worker has often not finished until 10 or 11 pm'. Presenting
the refugees in the most sympathetic manner, she highlighted how local
people were involved and could become involved in helping them.[79] There
were, however, alternative voices locally more sympathetic to the Nazi
regime and hostile to its victims' presence.

As we have seen, during the First World War and the early post-war
period, the Christchurch and then Bournemouth MP, Henry Page Croft, was
a leading figure in a national organised movement with strong local roots
hostile to the 'alien' presence in Britain. Croft's peak of influence, as a
prominent member of Churchill's wartime coalition government, came in the
summer of 1940 when he played a significant role in the internment of aliens,
including his own refugee son-in-law, Fred Uhlman.[80] But it was his
Hampshire friend, Viscount Lymington, who was the first to contribute in the
Nazi era to this unsavoury local xenophobic tradition, injecting into it a heavy
dose of volkisch romanticism and frequent pro-Hitlerism. As early as May
1933, Lymington, as MP for the largely rural Hampshire seat of Basingstoke,
asked the Minister of Health in a parliamentary question 'to state the number
of aliens in receipt of poor relief in England and Wales'. It soon became clear
against whom Lymington's animus was directed. Follow-up questions to the
Home Secretary demanded to know 'the number of Jewish aliens who have
entered the country since 30th January, 1933'. Such contributions from
Lymington and other antisemitic MPs helped ensure that the number of
refugees allowed to enter in the early years of Nazism would be limited and
there was little publicity to any help given for fear of an anti-alien backlash.[81]

Fortunately for those trying to escape, Lymington's career as an MP was
a short one. Developing contacts with leading Nazis, Lymington took over an
organisation concentrated largely in the Wessex region called 'English
Mistery' seeking a return to the soil and believing 'that outside influences
were corrupting our standards and national purpose'.[82] Refugees from fascist
oppression were not welcomed by Lymington and his supporters. Although
most of their xenophobia was directed toward foreign Jews, other refugees
were attacked such as the Basques who were described as 'alien venom'.
Alleged British generosity to these 'undesirable aliens' was contrasted to the
neglect of the truly needy – especially those struggling to make a living off
Hampshire's soil:

'No Room for Refugees': This is the most urgent issue we must face... The first reason for this is that there simply is not room at home for new immigrants.... But there is a deeper reason to revolt against such an immigration. Cross breeding between utterly alien types is physically wrong and psychologically dangerous... The time has come to call a halt.[83]

By the first months of war, Lymington argued that the 'enemy at home' – the refugees – were 'as real as the enemy abroad'. Other members of the English Mistery were so sympathetic to the 'enemy abroad' that they were imprisoned by the government under its emergency defence regulation, 18B. Although its influence should not be exaggerated, his organisation contributed to the atmosphere of suspicion aimed at the refugees throughout the 1930s and beyond.[84] More infamous, in respect of their antisemitism, anti-refugee sentiment and, by the war, their alleged treachery, were Oswald Mosley's British Union of Fascists (BUF) and 'The Link' (a pro-Nazi friendship group).

The BUF was vocal and consistent in its attack on 'the refujews' until it was banned by the government in May 1940. Like Lymington's organisation, the BUF was hostile to all refugees, launching a vicious campaign late in 1938 against an appeal on behalf of refugee children:

Why support a fund to give relief to aliens when poverty and unemployment are rife in Britain? We have been asked in the past four years to support Abyssinians, Basques, Chinese, Czechs, Austrians, Spaniards, and now Jews. MOSLEY SAYS ...*CHARITY BEGINS AT HOME.*

The strength of the BUF was very localised. The East End of London was the only area of mass support. Some success was made in attracting workers in the depressed Lancashire cotton towns and exploiting the tithe issue in rural East Anglia.[85] In Hampshire, the BUF attempted to raise interest from poverty-stricken farmers but with very little success, failing also to attract support in Southampton and Portsmouth in the civil and military dockyards, though several members were active in the Portsmouth region campaigning . against refugees.[86]

More successful on the local scene were those in Hampshire connected to Anglo-German friendship groups. Wilfred Ashley was MP for the New Forest and Christchurch division of Hampshire from 1922 until 1932 when he was created Lord Mount Temple. He was the first President of the Anglo-German Fellowship which began life in 1935 to promote friendship and understanding between the two countries. Like many involved with such organisations, Mount Temple came from a strong military background. He was impressed by large elements of Nazi ideology, especially its anti-socialism. Most of its local membership came from those with links to the armed forces.[87] For those with greater sympathy towards Nazism, 'The Link' was formed in 1937 by the increasingly paranoid Admiral Barry Domville who was Director of Naval Intelligence until 1930. His connections to the

Royal Navy largely explains its strength in Portsmouth. With 100 activists, it was one of the largest branches in Britain which in total had 4,300 members.[88] In matters relating to the persecution of the Jews, many in these organisations believed them to have been exaggerated, arguing that the antisemitism which existed was a natural reaction to malevolent Jewish influence in Germany. Mount Temple acted as an apologist for Nazi Germany in this respect, but the pogrom of November 1938 was for him a turning point. He publicly resigned his chairmanship of the Anglo-German Fellowship as 'a protest against the treatment of the Jews by the German Government'.[89] Locally there were those still willing to defend Nazi actions. Just three days after the pogrom, a letter was published in the *Portsmouth Evening News* asking if the Jews 'have not themselves to blame. If their trading methods ... are like those being employed in the City at the present, is it any wonder they are turned out?'[90]

The activities of such organised extremists made the task of pro-refugee campaigners harder – doubt was cast in the minds of ordinary people about who the newcomers were and if they deserved support. The drift of Anglo-German friendship groups towards undiluted apologetics for Hitler in the last months of peace, and the subsequent charges of disloyalty to Britain, should not disguise the earlier respectability and influence of those who saw much good in the Nazi regime. A good example was provided by W. J. Lucas, Professor of German at University College, Southampton. Speaking to the Portsmouth Post-War Brotherhood in January 1936, Lucas emphasised Hitler's 'great positive achievement' in unifying the German people. Lucas, a frequent visitor to Germany, provided what was a typically confused and contradictory British response to the embarrassing question of Nazi antisemitism: 'One cause was the dissemblance in the German character from the traits of internationalism, individualism, and analyticalism to be found in the Jew'. Having provided what was an explanation close to that of the persecutors, Lucas then argued to the contrary that he 'did not consider the Nazi attitude to the Jews to be justified in view of the service they had rendered to Germany in the past, and the fact that they constituted only about one percent of the total German population'.[91] The major problem was explaining the intensity of Nazi hatred towards the Jews. As the *Southern Daily Echo* argued in an editorial in March 1933: 'If the Nazis have a real grievance against the Jews of Germany they possess legitimate means of obtaining redress. What alienates sympathy is the ready resort to violence; the return to methods of torture'.[92]

At two points during the pre-war period – March/April 1933 and especially November 1938 – the sheer violence of the attacks on the Jews and the sweeping nature of the legislation forced some reconsideration of the nature of Nazi antisemitism. Yet even at these key moments the extensive coverage in national and local newspapers left the reader with conflicting messages. The detail provided was rarely accompanied by editorial comment.[93] Moreover, the absence, or, at best, ambiguity of analysis was accompanied by a tendency to open up the possibility, in the name of 'objective' reporting, that the Nazis might be justified in claiming that anti-Jewish atrocities were exaggerated.[94] Even after the brutality of 'Kristallnacht', the *Portsmouth Evening News* published letters doubting the scale of the atrocities. An editorial, 'The Barbarians', whilst denouncing the pogrom, and the evil of antisemitism, still added, for the sake of 'balance', that 'Nobody will pretend that the social and financial structure of post-War Germany did not suffer at the hands of a minority of Jewish – and Aryan – adventurers'.[95] Other letters, some influenced by extremist organisations, blamed sinister 'international forces' for spreading 'propaganda' against Germany. Although these were countered by other local sympathetic correspondents, Nazi antisemitism in the 1930s was framed within a discourse of 'atrocities' which might or might not be true.[96]

Refugees coming to Britain from Nazism frequently needed to explain at a very basic level the reasons why they had to escape. Major Frank Foley was British Passport Control Officer in Berlin before the war who did perhaps more than anyone within the British civil service to help the Jews escape. In April 1945, when Belsen and Buchenwald were liberated, he wrote: 'We are now reading about and seeing photographs of those places, the names of which were so well known to us in the years before the war. Now the people here finally believe that the stories of 1938–39 were not exaggerated'.[97]

Local responses to the refugees were thus complex consisting of generosity, sympathy, understanding, fear, meanness of spirit and a failure of imagination. The ambivalence and ambiguity towards the refugees, as well as the mixture of knowledge and ignorance, was shown in a school exercise on 'The Jews' carried out by a group of 11 to 14-year-old children mainly within the Southampton suburb of Bitterne.[98] Many of the responses revealed genuine sympathy towards the Jewish plight and a sophisticated understanding of what was happening. They identified with the victims, especially children who 'have been sent over the border with only one mark [and] may never see their parents again but they will have a hate for the people who took their parents away from them and sent them away'.[99]

The illogical nature of Nazi antisemitism was grasped by one 11-year-old boy who commented simply that 'I think Jews are being treated cruelly by the Germans. The Jews are being punished for doing nothing in Germany'. More typical, however, was the ambiguity illustrated by the statement that 'I think the Jews have a lot of money and Hitler is trying to get it off them'. Others followed the easy logic of blaming the victim: 'Most countries are persecuting them because they always own important places such as theatres and hotels'. The contrast with the treatment of the Jews of Britain was also made: in London the Jews 'are not treated like [those] in Germany because they have not done wrong'. Outright hostility was rarer, but the influence of 'adult' anti-alien sources occasionally surfaced as with this 14-year-old girl:

> To my mind Jews are weeds. Wherever they situate themselves, they grow and flourish ... why we should have the Jewish children over here[?]... Why cannot people plead for money for the English poor people and conquer unemployment in England, Ireland and Wales instead of bringing in the dogs over here... If we cleared the Jews from this country, there would not be one single unemployed, and if I could gain power ... I would clear the Jews out.[100]

Although others were suspicious of the Jews as a whole, the majority of the schoolchildren expressed some sympathy and an awareness that help was needed in finding the refugees a place to live: 'I think the Jews should be pitied for the persecution they are receiving from the German Nazis and the Italian Fascists as after all they are human beings and must live somewhere'.[101] In the adult world, the events of 1938 were to shift public opinion, not without resistance, in a similar direction. Yet the fundamental ambivalence towards Jews and the Jewish plight meant that many believed that the refugee plight, as publicised at the Evian conference, would have to be solved away from 'home'.

In July 1938, the *Portsmouth Evening News* published proposals by the philosopher Bertrand Russell to help the persecuted Jews. He argued that the main requirement was to 'bring pressure to bear upon our own Government to be hospitable to refugees, and not too niggardly in granting them permission to earn a living among us'.[102] It brought a full response from the newspaper's main commentator, Raymond Burns, revealing much of the concern and ambivalence in Britain relating to foreign Jews. Burns wanted a political solution to the refugee 'problem' free of 'helpless emotionalism' which would 'evoke a real anti-Semitic problem in Great Britain':

> Three governments, those of Britain, France, and the United States, have the biggest contribution to make to refugee settlement. All three countries, but particularly Britain, are reaching saturation point in the number of refugees and Jews who can be admitted without the development of latent hostility to the newcomers... We have in Britain about one and three-quarters million people out of work... Refugees entering Britain today are undeniably adding to a sense of grievance, which can be understood, among men in Labour Exchange queues... It is perhaps more significant that feeling is spreading among professional men; only recently an organization of doctors protested strongly against the number of Home Office permits for Austrians, some of whom are busy with the cut-price racket...

Acknowledging that these people had to go somewhere, Burns argued that 'some extensive territory will have to be marked out for mass settlement'. Palestine was too problematic but he was excited by the idea of settling refugee Jews in East Africa. He realised that this might be difficult but, he concluded with false altruism, wherever they went, 'for the sake of the refugees, it must not mean Great Britain'.[103] Burns' views were shared by many at the time of the Evian conference. Locally, the *Bournemouth Daily Echo* warned that there was a 'growing feeling of unrest regarding the present practically unrestricted entry into this country of refugees', concluding that 'Just as we don't want too many Jews we don't want too many Chinese or Frenchmen for that matter'. Such comments about a 'saturation point' being reached need to be contextualised: Britain was host to less than 10,000 refugees in July 1938. Commentators such as Burns argued that a large refugee influx would lead to a growth of fascism and antisemitism. Such 'mainstream' restrictionists, however, borrowed heavily from the language of those whose rise they warned about, especially sharing assumptions that foreign Jews would naturally attract hostility.[104]

The determination of the British government to restrict the flow of Jewish refugees led to an immense amount of effort exploring possibilities of movement to far-flung parts of its empire, particularly settlement in East Africa. Eventually, just 650 Jewish refugees went to Kenya. 'All the pressures within and outside Whitehall had resulted by March 1939 in the admission to colonial territories other than Palestine of only about 2,000 refugees from the Reich.' One of those allowed into Kenya was the German Jewish doctor, Sigmund Heilbronn along with his wife and daughter. He was allowed to practise medicine by the British authorities but only on black people. He wrote from Kenya in the 1950s towards the end of his life that he was 'tired of Europe and I will never go back there again. Here I was welcomed by strangers and found my shattered belief in people re-established'.[105] But the narrow vision that saw almost no place internationally, nationally or locally for the refugees did not go unchallenged. Returning to the local level, one Portsmouth correspondent pointed out that:

> No one who has the slightest interest in books or pictures, the theatre or the films, can support Mr Raymond Burns's plea for the relegation of refugees to the wide open spaces of the Empire. Hitler's loss has been our gain in all three fields…[106]

Yet the reality was, in the weeks following the Evian conference, that campaigners fought a defensive battle where the potential merits of the refugees were outweighed by fears of problems they would bring with them. Immediately after 'Kristallnacht', the minister of the Bournemouth Synagogue, Reverend Heilpern, addressed his congregation in despair, asking:

> Am I living in the 20th century or in the Dark Middle Ages?… What is the world doing to stop all this? We are told that history will condemn the inhuman savagery of the Nazis. When history gives its final verdict, it will not only condemn the brutalities of the Nazi regime, but it will also stand aghast at the seeming indifference with which the great Powers looked on at this brutal spectacle.

But the pogrom of November 1938 was to tip the balance of the argument. Lord Mount Temple, having acted as a spokesperson for all that was good in

German and, to an extent, Nazi culture, was forced to capture the new mood, declaring that 'England has the old tradition of interceding for all persecuted and oppressed peoples'. If Jews wanted to seek refuge, he added, 'it is a sacred duty of humanity to offer these persecuted people a shelter'. Campaigners locally and nationally were empowered by the more sympathetic response of the British government and public after 'Kristallnacht', becoming directly involved in the rescue and support of refugees at the time of their greatest crisis. Yet even after the events of 1938, responses to the plight of European Jewry and to the refugees from Nazism were complex. The mixture of antipathy, ambivalence and sympathy affected both the number and type of refugees admitted into Britain. Even for those lucky enough to be allowed entry, their freedom and security were far from complete.[107]

THE REFUGEE CHILDREN'S MOVEMENT

The 'Movement for the Care of Children from Germany', which became known as the Refugee Children's Movement (RCM), was founded in November 1938. Its predecessor was the smaller scale Inter-Aid Committee for Children from Germany, formed in 1936 which had brought 471 children to Britain under its auspices and provided a model of Jewish–Christian cooperation in refugee matters. In December 1938, the former Prime Minister, Lord Baldwin, made a radio broadcast on behalf of refugees. The response was immense, realising £500,000:

> Offers of hospitality poured in from people all over [the] country, at last aware [after the pogrom] of what Nazi persecution really meant and anxious to help the most helpless and innocent of its victims.

They came from 'all areas and classes … from all kinds of homes; from well-known figures of everyday life and from artisans; from the wealthiest homes and from the unemployed'.[108]

Soon 166 local committees were set up in Britain, most formed spontaneously. Immediate attempts were made to pull them together: 'a nation-wide effort to rescue the Jewish and Christian youth of Jewish extraction of Germany was doomed to failure unless there was an organisation which could co-ordinate the work in this country'.[109] Only Belgian refugees and Ugandan Asians matched this scale of response. The local groups were put into 12 regional committees reporting to the central organisation. Though there were local committees in England, Scotland and Wales, the children were unevenly distributed across Britain with bias towards the south of England and to the urban centres. The regional committee in Oxford, covering Oxfordshire, Buckinghamshire, Berkshire, Surrey, Hampshire and the Isle of Wight, was the third biggest with 20 local refugee committees under its control. Hampshire was one of six counties providing between 100 and 250 refugee children with homes with committees in Bournemouth, Portsmouth and Southampton, but whether pro-refugee groups existed in smaller localities is unknown – many local initiatives have been lost to posterity. Seven counties had between 250 and 1,000 children and two had over 1,000. Most counties accommodated less than 100 children. The geographical bias can partly be explained by the children arriving in southern ports, the RCM's central organisation base around London, and possibly regional disparities in wealth distribution.[110]

For the national organisers, two key problems emerged: choosing from the 60,000 plus 'children in Austria and Germany all anxious to seek safety and refuge in this country' and checking the suitability of those offering homes in Britain. Given the lack of resources and immensity of task, arbitrary decisions granting permits to entry were made. Initially, only the 'most urgent' cases were dealt with which was increasingly meaningless as the Jews of Greater Germany became utterly destitute and marginalised. The scheme was opened up further by a system of guarantees. Children could be brought to Britain if a sufficient cash deposit was made and 'provided that the financial situation of the would-be guarantor was sufficiently stable and that the proposed home was found to be suitable'. Roughly two-thirds, or 6,000 children, came to Britain through such guarantees. The RCM acknowledged that the scheme was not necessarily equitable as it tended to favour the wealthier.[111]

It has taken many years to recognise that a significant minority of those who took in the children were highly inappropriate to do so. Treatment of the children varied immensely. On one extreme were those providing unconditional love and support alongside sensitivity to the specific practical, psychological and spiritual needs of the children. On the other were cases of physical, sexual and economic exploitation. The priority in 1938 and 1939 was to get as many children out as possible. As early as 1944, it was acknowledged that the work of the RCM was 'imperfect in many aspects' but without it 'these children must have suffered death … if they had been left within the frontiers of the Greater Reich'. Compromises were made 'in order to expedite the arrival of as many children as possible before the outbreak of hostilities … In this way 9,354 refugee children were brought into this country'.[112]

The children were brought to Britain in groups, or transports, and on arrival 'at Harwich or Southampton the representatives of the Movement would go aboard and proceed to place labels around the necks of the children, bearing the name and number of each one.'[113] In contrast to the ports of Lowestoft and Harwich, where hostels were established, most of the children passed through Southampton very speedily usually en route to London. A random sample of 90 Kindertransport identity cards provides the following breakdown of arrival places: Harwich 75; Southampton 7; Croydon (through the airport) 6; and Dover 2.[114] Most passing through Southampton have few memories of the port but for Lotte Bray, who travelled alone on the *SS Deutschland* from Bremerhaven 'on a cold January day in 1939', it had a special place in her new life as a refugee:

> Germany saw me off in typical fashion, a thorough search by a woman who
> stole my watch and a small signet ring ... The journey was uneventful and as
> we landed at Southampton we saw our first British bobby and – wonder of
> wonders – he smiled at us. I think it was then I made up my mind that I would
> never leave England if it was at all possible – a country where a policeman
> actually smiled must be a good place to settle.[115]

For others, arrival confirmed their sense of loss and loneliness.

Aside from placing children in the county, local committees in Hampshire
sponsored youngsters to live elsewhere. John Grenville was born in Berlin in
1928. He remembers

> very vividly the moment of parting, which must have been terrible for my
> mother who simultaneously saw her three boys leave and was extremely
> uncertain whether she would ever see them again. And that made a very deep
> impression, I am certain, on all the children who left ... to some degree
> overshadow[ing] the rest of their childhood and, I believe, their lives...

Supported at a private school in Essex by the Portsmouth Refugee Committee
and treated with kindness and consideration, it could not compensate for his
immense homesickness which created an intense feeling of insecurity,
manifesting 'itself by wanting to adapt as rapidly as possible to England,
wanting to be accepted as totally English and losing one's German identity
totally'.

Successful at school, Grenville wished to further his academic studies but
the Portsmouth committee insisted that he learn a practical trade through a
technical school in Cambridge. 'The committee took the view that if I did not
do as we were told, they would cease to look after me.' Similar conflict
emerged with the Cambridge Refugee Committee who blocked his entry into
a grammar school. Aged 16, John Grenville became a gardener at Cambridge
University's Peterhouse College. In spite of his professional family
background and classical education in England, Grenville had been redefined
as belonging to the 'lower classes'. When announcing his departure to take a
degree at the London School of Economics, Peterhouse's bursar asked if he
was sure 'because ... we have you in mind for our headporter'.[116]

Grenville's later career, culminating as Professor of History at
Birmingham University, puts into perspective the patronising responses many
refugees faced in Britain but also the resistance to attempts to control their
lives and futures. Vera Schaufeld coming from Czechoslovakia faced similar
problems, but her marginalisation was greater as she was on her own. Vera
was sent to a school in East Anglia where she was 'really very unhappy for a
lot of the time'. Her fellow classmates' lack of understanding was shown
when 'part of their games was pretending that I was a German spy'. Vera was
15 when the war ended, and under great pressure from her sponsors to leave
school and become independent. Realising that her parents were murdered, 'I
wanted to conform to what other people were' and converted to Christianity.

After an incident when her host, after listening to news of attacks on British soldiers in Palestine by Zionist extremists, exclaimed 'Maybe Hitler knew what he was doing after all with the Jews', Vera returned to Judaism and was determined 'that I would be self-supporting until I went to college because I knew that [my host family] didn't want to spend any more money on me'. Signing up to a teaching agency her first position was in a boarding school in the Hampshire village of Alton. In spite of her age (17), lack of experience, and antisemitism from a fellow teacher, Vera coped, using her salary to pay her way through teaching college. She embarked on an educational career which gave her a semblance of security in British society.[117]

The success of former child refugees such as John Grenville and Vera Schaufeld in establishing careers for themselves in Britain has to be contextualised. Grenville recalls that in his Cambridge refugee hostel, 'the majority of the children went to the USA – there were not the opportunities here. One felt it impossible to have equal [chances] in England'. One of his brothers never returned to school – his education ended aged 13 and he was sent to work in a Sheffield foundry. The remarkable resilience and tenacity of the refugee children has to be set alongside the barriers to their progress, including the determination of some refugee committees to keep their charges under control, the rigid class and ethnic stratification of British society and the financial and psychological burdens which many refugees carried with them. Little or no help was offered with regard to the trauma and loss they had experienced which would remain part of their subsequent lives in Britain. A significant minority never recovered from the difficulties of those years. The national refugee bodies wanted to rescue as many people as possible as long as the people under their control could remain largely invisible in British society. Their obsessiveness, in John Grenville's words, in 'exercising their power' was reflected in choosing groups of refugees who they believed would be easier to control – especially children but also women.[118]

DOMESTIC SERVICE AND NURSING

For adults without substantial resources to take out of Greater Germany the only major way into Britain was obtaining a work permit. In the summer of 1939, advertisement columns of the 'quality' British newspapers were full of heart-rending pleas for domestic positions from those trying to escape or from relatives attempting to bring over mothers, fathers and even grandparents through such employment. John Grenville's mother was one of many thousands of Jewish women in the days before the war whose desperate attempt to find such work was unsuccessful. The 20,000 who did find refuge by this route, however, faced not only the problems associated with this demanding occupation, but also the desire of the refugee organisations to keep them in service.[119]

The major attraction of placing refugee women in domestic service for the

British government and the refugee organisations was that it was one of the
few occupations with a shortage of labour, minimising the risk of claims that
'aliens' were stealing 'British' jobs. But other advantages were perceived –
domestic service kept those employed outside the public gaze. Moreover, the
huge demand for servants was nationwide. The refugee organisations relished
the prospect of dispersing the women across Britain and below stairs. The
problem was that few of the refugees, many of whom came from middle-class
backgrounds, relished the prospect of long working days with few days off in
remote parts of the British countryside. But during 1938 and 1939, the
refugee organisations were grimly determined to keep the women scattered
and in service.[120]

A pamphlet produced by the Domestic Bureau of the Refugee
Coordinating Committee gave advice to the refugees and their employers.
Describing the women as 'foreign maids', 'German cooks', 'immigrants', but
never 'refugees', it highlighted how these women were brought over as alien
workers rather than as victims of persecution:

> Immigrants who come into domestic service should remember that, in the first
> instance, they are received into English households through friendliness and
> good will and it behoves them to be a credit to these people and to their religion,
> as the public are apt to judge all from one. Many maids try and stipulate that
> they shall have posts in London, but this is not possible for everyone as the
> Home Office is anxious that immigrants should be distributed over the country.
> The English countryside is very beautiful and country towns are very attractive,
> also the country is cleaner and healthier than London. *It is important that it
> should be realised that immigrants who are here on a domestic permit cannot
> change their occupation...*[121]

These objectives were hardly met. In November 1938 the German Jewish Aid
Committee noted 'that there was a large number of [domestics] in London
who were unwilling to work in the provinces'. The solution advocated was
another example of the financial power the refugee bodies exercised: 'It was
agreed to request [the Central Refugee Coordinating Committee] not to
support such refugees'.[122] Unable to apply to the state for relief, the refugee
women were frequently forced back into service. The issue of refugees
congregating in London was seen as so grave that a conference was called of
all local refugee committees late in 1938 to deal with the 'problem'. It was
announced that hostels for refugee domestics would be created in Manchester
and Bournemouth:

> Girls will be sent on request [there] to be placed by the local committee [which]
> will also be allowed to apply for girls direct from Germany to fill vacant places
> in these hostels if the supply from London does not keep them full.[123]

The desire of the women to leave service or to live in London did not come
from laziness or wilfulness. Although domestic work provided a passport to
escape, it created many problems for the refugees once they had arrived in

Britain. For single women with no family ties, domestic service provided a low paid and exhausting existence which could be tolerated short term. But many of the refugee women had children in Britain or were constantly anxious about those left under Nazi control. Isolation in the countryside often meant separation from sons, daughters and husbands as well as the lack of access to positions of power in the major cities (and especially London) necessary to help relatives abroad. The long hours and subsistence wages were a further hindrance in this respect.

The testimony of Hilde Gerrard, who came to Britain from Italy with her young twins and husband, illustrates such pressures. Working together as a cook and parlourmaid in a house on the Surrey/Hampshire border, she and her husband were separated from their children who were 20 miles away: 'Once a month we were allowed to visit the children and I did not only count the days but also the hours'. News from her parents still in Germany created extra pressure: 'They were desperately trying to leave, but had no entry visas anywhere. If they could not produce one soon, they would be deported. They were too old to be allowed in as domestics and I could not produce a guarantee for them. I was not able to help and nearing a nervous breakdown.' War created further disruption and separation, especially after Gerhard was interned in May 1940. Hilde was left coping with her children in another domestic position in Yorkshire and was faced with the increasingly depressing news about the twins' grandparents. In the middle of the war Hilde suffered a breakdown. Domestic service in Britain, with its frequent move from position to position, alongside government restrictive measures, was not an ideal way to rebuild a life of freedom.[124]

For adults, the next most populous route into Britain was through nursing, again almost exclusively limited to women of working age. Though having a higher status than domestic service as a career, it suffered from similar conditions: poor wages, long, demanding hours and little trade union representation to improve matters. Not surprisingly, there was a supply shortage which several thousand Jewish refugees filled if on a smaller scale than domestic service, partly because of the difficulty of finding out if positions were available as well as the greater skills and aptitude required.[125] In Prague, Alice Sluckin took the initiative and wrote to various hospitals in England: 'one day I got a letter from Southampton's Children's Hospital from the matron ... to say that she would be willing to engage me. The next step was to get a permit and I managed to get [it] through the Quakers ... I think I really owe them my life'. She was put to work immediately on the ward:

> I remember I had a child [with] worms... And I was told to clean him up... I didn't know one end of a child from another and by the time I cleaned the child, I was much dirtier than [him]... It was a small hospital ... [with] about fifty beds and it had two wards... They had another refugee girl who was a trained nurse from the Berlin Jewish hospital and ... she thought the place was just absolutely the lowest of the low, in terms of hygiene and everything. An awful

lot of children died of diarrhoea and vomitting. It was very, very hard work and very long hours, from quarter past seven in the morning until nine o'clock at night.[126]

As a young adult, Alice Sluckin faced the additional worry common to many refugees – trying to help her family back home. A few days after she arrived in Southampton she heard that Prague had been overtaken:

After that I tried very hard to do my best to help my family, to help my brother particularly to get out. He was then a boy of fourteen and I almost succeeded... I met one or two people in the hospital. There was one nurse whose father was a big business man here and they ... guaranteed my brother... And if the war hadn't started, he would have come on 7 September.

By spring 1940, when Alice was settling into her life as a nurse, government measures to combat the 'alien menace' intervened, forcing her to leave the south coast. Encouraged to become a domestic, she resisted and continued nursing in Cambridge dealing with chronic cases of polio. The Czech Refugee Trust supported her even though they still had 'the idea that I was going to be trained as a domestic'. Like John Grenville, however, Alice 'had other ideas', managing to gain a place on a social work course at Leeds University, the basis for a distinguished career as a child psychiatrist.[127] For other refugees, nursing was a satisfying profession in itself, especially when starting life in Britain as domestics.[128] Most refugee domestics would leave or be forced out of their positions at the start of the war, finding more lucrative and less restrictive work. Nevertheless, the power of patriarchy in the job market, alongside xenophobia, stopped the full integration of refugee women. But the employment opportunities in Britain for adult male refugees before the war were even more limited. The British government believed that the most likely source of opposition to refugees would come from men of working age. The emphasis of the refugee bodies, therefore, was to bring men to Britain on temporary permits so that they could be retrained, especially in agriculture, to lead 'productive' lives elsewhere.[129]

SMALLER WORK SCHEMES

The emphasis in Britain on refugees engaging in land work coincided with the ambitions of Zionist bodies which were particularly keen to prepare people for life in Palestine. In January 1939, the German Jewish Aid Committee obtained the agreement of the British government and the National Union of Agricultural Workers to grant 1,000 permits to 'fully qualified Jewish farm workers [to] be employed in those districts where there were no qualified English agricultural workers registered as unemployed'. An additional 500 places were found for unqualified youngsters where the employer would pay board and lodging. Such retraining and relocation was expensive – the refugee organisations spent £200,000 on helping 1,350

German and Austrian Jews come to Britain – but it was a vital scheme, especially for men, whose release from the concentration camps after 'Kristallnacht' depended on receiving visas.[130]

Viscount Lymington had been totally dismissive of the possibility of 'urban' Jews working on the land. Jack Habel conformed to Lymington's worst nightmare – a Jewish refugee of east European origin with left-wing sympathies. Jack's training sponsored by German Zionist organisations led to a 'diploma in farming'. It provided both Jack and his girlfriend with a route to Palestine via Britain.[131] They were sent to a farm near Portsmouth:

> We were given a nice little cottage and I milked cows. I had a herd of ... about 18 cows [which] I had to milk by hand... From a dairyman I became a carter... I [tried to] volunteer in Portsmouth twice, [but] they said 'You go back to the farm, because you're more help ... to the war effort ... than four sailors on the high seas'.[132]

Outside the refugee schemes for children, domestic servants, nurses, and agricultural workers, the chances of finding entry into Britain were limited. The Jewish communities of Germany, Czechoslovakia, and Austria contained many professionals. For them, the opportunities to resettle and practise in Britain were limited largely through opposition from professional bodies. The academic world provided the greatest number of openings. The Academic Assistance Council, later the Society for the Protection of Science and Learning (SPSL), was founded in 1933 to aid 'university teachers ... of whatever country, who, on grounds of religion, political opinion or "race" are unable to carry on their work in their own country'.[133] By the end of 1938 approximately 1,400 academics had been displaced from German universities with an additional 400 forced out of Austrian higher education institutes. Excluding the Austrians, by 'Kristallnacht' the SPSL managed to place permanently 524 academics in 37 countries and 306 temporarily in 25 countries. The USA dominated the permanent places offered (161) followed by Britain (128), Palestine (46) and Turkey (45). In temporary placements, Britain was even more important, with 123 positions created compared to 86 in the USA. The general secretary of the SPSL wrote in 1939 that 'Great Britain ... is one of the several clearing-house countries: the United States is the main terminal country'. Nevertheless, nearly a quarter of the permanent positions created for refugee scholars were in Britain. Although there was some opposition, substantial income for the SPSL came through donations and subscriptions from within the academic community.[134]

The initiative to help a refugee scholar at University College, Southampton, came from Professor A. C. Menzies who was sent a list of displaced refugee physicists by the SPSL in 1933. He chose Professor Karl Weissenberg who worked on related fields and had been removed from the University of Berlin and the Kaiser Wilhelm Institut fur Physik because of his Jewish origins. Weissenberg was appointed Guest Professor, enabling him to continue research.[135] As early as the outbreak of war, the refugee organisations proclaimed the contributions made by these scholars. Weissenberg was highlighted as one of the five outstanding refugee physicists, along with Max Born (Edinburgh University), Peter Ewald (Queen's Belfast), Rudolf Peierls (Birmingham University) and Franz Simon (Clarendon Institute) by the SPSL for his work on theoretical physics, structure of matter, X-Rays, crystalography and the mechanics of colloids. Unfortunately many, including Weissenberg, had their careers interrupted by internment, some subsequently leaving and enriching the contribution made by refugees to the worlds of science and learning in the USA: losses that Britain could ill afford.[136]

At the other extreme of professional generosity, the British Medical Association and particularly its virulently anti-alien trade union wing, the Medical Practioners' Union (MPU), ensured that almost no refugee doctors would be allowed to practise in Britain before the Second World War. After the *Anschluss*, a scheme to bring 500 Austrian Jewish doctors to Britain suggested by the Home Secretary was rejected by the BMA and cut down to a maximum of 50. This was still opposed by the MPU which warned that the refugees would 'dilute our industry'. The world of British dentistry was equally hostile to the refugees. It opposed the entry of foreign, especially Austrian, dentists though they were better trained than their British counterparts. After the *Anschluss*, however, the government granted permits to 40 Austrian dentists, including Desider Furst and Fritz Engel.[137]

Engel had many advantages in re-establishing himself – his dental equipment came to Britain unharmed and he had financial support from relatives. But adjustment was still difficult, especially retraining in the Royal Dental Hospital in London: 'Having ... to study once more at the age of 42 and to pass the rigorous exams I had already passed before, 20 years ago, was rather hard'. He then received permission to practise in Bournemouth from the Home Office and the British Dental Board.[138] Some patients initially regarded him only as a provider of temporary or emergency work, later visiting their 'own' dentist in Harley Street. It took time to convince patients that the policy of regarding teeth 'as potential trouble makers', which should be extracted at the least provocation, was not necessary. In May 1940, however, Fritz was interned. He was fortunate in obtaining an early release and in being granted permission to return to his dental work in Bournemouth: 'It did not take long for me to get successful again'. The affection that Fritz Engel was to develop for Bournemouth was not, however, matched by his fellow refugee dentist, Desider Furst.[139]

As he later wrote, 'Even a well-planned move to a foreign country is a big upheaval.' Desider had the problem of improving his English and resigned himself to the six months retraining, having been allocated to Manchester which meant separation from his family. Desider Furst qualified in March 1940 and bought the practice of a deceased dentist in Bournemouth: 'We saw that the equipment was outdated, but the location was favourable and we were

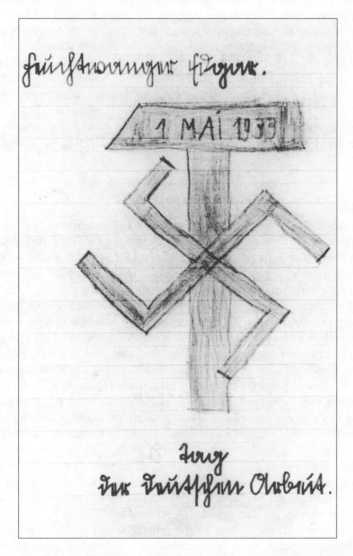

School book of Edgar Feuchtwanger (aged 7), Germany, May 1933. From the private collection of Edgar Feuchtwanger and with his kind permission.

confident that we could revitalise the practice'. All their savings and an additional loan were invested in the practice, but just when the family was to be reunited, Desider was interned. 'It was a bitter blow for us. Financially, we were ruined, and our hopes and expectations were wiped out. Our family was more separated than ever before.' In contrast to Fritz Engel, Desider was not allowed to return to his practice. He had, after internment, to start again the energy-sapping struggle to establish himself in Britain. That he and other refugee dentists and doctors eventually succeeded in their profession is a tribute to the tenacity of these individuals, all of whom were middle-aged when they came to Britain. Retraining, government restrictions and the antipathy of fellow professionals were not minor obstacles. Outside these national schemes, other refugees owed their freedom and ultimately their lives to the vision and generosity of individuals devising their own local projects.[140]

LOCAL INITIATIVES

Winchester College, the oldest public school in Britain, and several of its rivals, developed schemes to take in Jewish refugees. Edgar Feuchtwanger's parents heard that Winchester was making places available and he started there at age 15. No special efforts were made to help integration. Coming to terms with a very traditional public school was not easy: 'When I first went there I found it all a bit strange and forbidding',[141] but after a while he 'began positively to enjoy the life of the school so that I was able to look back with some nostalgia when I left'. After Winchester, Edgar worked chopping trees for the Ministry of Supply in Scotland but was able to enter Magdalene College, Cambridge, in 1944. It was the start of his academic career as a widely recognised historian of modern Britain and Germany at the University of Southampton.[142] George Grun, one of Edgar's fellow refugee students, was interned in 1940 and deported to Canada where he worked 'his way over as a steward in a tramp steamer and [came back] to Winchester by the same transport in which he had left: a Black Maria'. Grun also became an academic, working at the London School of Economics, 'instrumental in building up International History as a separate field for undergraduates and graduates alike, as the first specialist in the history of international relations in the 20th century'.[143] The scheme at Winchester College was designed to provide opportunities for bright young refugees from suitable backgrounds. Its 'generosity' meant no compromise over standards or procedures. The desire to help in no way undermined 'the sink or swim' ethos of this and other public schools.[144]

In another part of the elite world of Hampshire, a unique refugee project was being created by Lionel de Rothschild at Exbury in the New Forest. He had bought the estate after the First World War. A team of 150 men were employed, transforming the 250 acres of woodland around the house into an extensive global collection of temperate trees and shrubs, especially rhododendron. By 1935 the garden was complete, utilising a staff of 75.[145] The British Rothschilds were extensively involved in the funding and organisation of refugee work during the 1930s.[146] After 'Kristallnacht', Lionel de Rothschild combined his philanthropic work with his labour of love, offering four gardening traineeships at Exbury to German refugees. Ernst Guter was one of the four, having heard about the offer when working in Berlin in the *Reichvertretung* (the central Jewish representative body in Nazi Germany). As a 21-year-old, with no specific skills or family influence, this unusual opportunity was a godsend when other avenues of escape failed to materialise. His permit to Britain was temporary with his visa stamped 'Leave to land granted at Harwich … on condition that the holder will emigrate from the United Kingdom on completion of his training'. But with Lionel's encouragement, Ernst continued his education: after a hard day in the gardens, he spent three evenings a week cycling the ten miles to the University College, Southampton, taking evening courses in economics. By spring 1940, Ernst Guter was enrolled at the London School of Economics but internment in May 1940 intervened. He was deported to Canada, along with the other three Exbury refugees and many others.[147]

Ernst later wrote of Lionel de Rothschild that he was:

> devoted to his memory as well as indebted to him for saving my life and starting [a]fresh what has turned out to be a somewhat rewarding career and the founding of a new family in Canada.

Just two miles away at Beaulieu, Lady Forster, a member of a rather older English aristocratic family, the Montagus, was also involved in helping European Jews.[148] Lady Forster owned a cottage in Milford-on-Sea which she provided for the use of refugees in 1938. Anni Engel, who, with her husband, Fritz, had just fled Vienna, was employed to run 'Rose Cottage' as a small hostel for refugee children and adults requiring a holiday or a temporary base whilst obtaining employment in the region. The success of the hostel shows how refugees were not passive recipients of aid but were often active in helping fellow victims of Nazism:

> [Anni] became the centre of great activity. Not only within the area of the cottage, but in helping many relatives and friends from Austria to get working permits and visas to enter England; [obtaining] posts as cooks, parlour maids [etc].[149]

With four rooms at her disposal, several used as mini-dormitories, Anni accommodated up to 15 children and five adult refugees at any one time. To her, Milford-on-Sea and Rose Cottage after the traumas of Vienna under Nazi occupation was 'paradise … I thought I was transferred into heaven'. Looking back with great fondness, she comments that 'It's not easy for youngsters, it's not easy for anybody to become a refugee. But we made it as happy as we could'.[150] Other memories of Rose Cottage were not so happy, including the suicide of a doctor from Vienna in the hostel. He had been given permission to enter Britain as one of the 50 Austrian doctors selected by the Home Office on condition that he retrained in Britain. His wife, however, was left in France and he came to Rose Cottage in a very depressed state.[151]

To Anni Engel, whose life had been settled and full of promise in Vienna and then so cruelly and quickly destroyed, the kindness and generosity of Lady Forster 'was an absolute revelation ... She was a great, great help. [A] wonderful person [who] really wanted to help the Jews'.[152] There were many others in Hampshire of more humble background who were equally determined to support the refugees. The family of Peggy Turner had a smallholding in West End on the outskirts of Southampton.[153] Her father was an independently minded socialist who took every opportunity to pass on his belief in the 'brotherhood of man' to anyone who would listen. Reflecting on her adolescence, Peggy stressed how her teenage years from 1933 were dominated by the presence of refugees staying in the family home for weeks, months and sometimes years. Asked by a local 'do-gooder' to take in three refugees, a decision was made 'to offer them shelter in our home in return for work on the smallholding. The period that followed was an odd mixture, we felt sympathy for their plight, my parents did their best to help them become established in a new country, but I personally found it disturbing for the family unit':

> Over the next few years before the onset of war, there were many ... who used our place as a breathing space before taking off to another part of the world. At the time I was only a child, too young to understand the full extent of the upheaval in their lives, but I still remember the fear on their faces as they described their escape from the Gestapo, their sudden unaccountable bouts of hysteria, their acute apprehension... Our home life became oddly excited as the flow of refugees came to our door. I realise now that many of them were prominent people in their homeland; we enjoyed this influx of cultivated minds.[154]

For the Turner family, taking in the refugees was not especially remarkable. Although theirs was 'only a modest home':

> People gravitated to us so our house was always full of nationalities before the refugees... It all seemed to be part of the way we lived anyway. It was second nature to make people welcome and to be helpful... It was toleration. Not toleration – we didn't put up with them, they were right in the heart of the family.

It was also natural for them to help the victims of Nazism: 'We were aware of forces which we opposed'. A mixture of refugees was given support by the Turners – socialists and other opponents of the Nazi regime as well as Jews. Some stayed long enough to gain expertise in farming by working on the family's land before obtaining their own smallholdings in Hampshire.[155] Albrecht Hammerschlag, one of the first they helped, came from a prominent

Jewish banking family in Berlin.[156] From Southampton he emigrated to Bolivia, revealing the limited opportunities available to refugees.

Comparatively little research has been carried out on refugee movements to Latin America during the 1930s though more went there than to Palestine, the largest place of settlement. The responses of most Latin American countries were confused and contradictory, further complicated by the political instability of their governments. Many Jews entered Latin American countries through visas bought from consular officials abroad which were of dubious status. Thousands of refugees were refused entry when they arrived on the borders of Latin American countries, most notoriously with the Cuban government's refusal to allow those on the *St Louis* to land in 1939. The complexity of refugee movements during the 1930s is neatly encapsulated by the role of Southampton as a port from which some refugees such as Albrecht left for Latin America, and others, including some from the *St Louis*, returned having been rejected across the world.[157]

Initially, the most desirable Latin American countries corresponded to where Jews were established in significant numbers such as Argentina, Brazil, Chile and Mexico. Bolivia and other Latin American countries were less favoured but became, especially after 'Kristallnacht', important options for those desperately wishing to escape. Bolivia in many ways typified Latin American responses to the refugees. First, there was political instability which made life unpredictable. Nazi-influenced groups, especially linked to German immigrants, struggled for power alongside domestically rooted authoritarian regimes. Second, immigration policy was highly racialised, restricting the entry of Mongols, Muslims, Arabs, Russians, Poles, Jews and others. Third, in practice, such policies might be overlooked, especially if entrants provided additional money to gain the 'proper' paperwork (though humanitarian sympathy towards the persecuted was also important in overlooking quotas and other restrictions). Fourth, the Bolivian authorities desired that immigrants should settle on the land, however adverse the conditions. $1 million was invested by an immigrant tin magnate to set up an agricultural colony in Coroico, Bolivia, but this ultimately collapsed. Most Jewish refugees gravitated back to La Paz, the major Bolivian city, and partly as a result of this 'failure', Jewish immigration was officially stopped in May 1940. In the two years previously, Bolivian visas were sold in travel agencies in Europe, with up to 8,000 refugees allowed entry, adding to the 2,000 who had come into the country before 1938, nearing the total of 12–15,000 who went to Brazil. Twice the number settled in Argentina.[158]

Albrecht wrote to the Turners in 1938 describing his life in La Paz, his ironic style perhaps disguising the real problems of settlement – he coped better than most refugees in Bolivia. By the war, thousands relied on relief provided by the American Jewish Joint Distribution Committee to survive in an increasingly hostile climate:

Bolivia is not a bad country to live in. Foreigners are highly respected, and if one has a decent job one is allright. There are no restrictions of any kind, you can piss on the main street, you can beat a policeman up if you feel like it ... only you cannot move from one town to [an]other – not even for a week-end – without having obtained a passport before. Personally I am doing quite well. I am [a] manager and salesman of the most modern shop for imported sweets, wines, frocks and parfums in La Paz ... and if I should not find something really super somewhere else I shall settle down in this business... Of course, there are countries much more beautiful and civilised than Bolivia, but it is difficult to get the permission to stay in those countries, and ... there is much more competition... Naturally, relationships with the Germans have their draw backs... Last night I had to chuck a Nazi out of the shop because he made insulting remarks about my prices... I fear I have lost him for a customer but he has lost one of his front teeth, which he left in the shop.[159]

Reflecting on the 1930s, Peggy Turner believes that whilst she 'didn't go to university, I didn't need to. What I was receiving was a rich, vital background [which] stayed with me all my life'.[160] Many other ordinary people in Britain, especially after 'Kristallnacht' were willing to put themselves out to help the refugees. In big cities, small towns, villages and countryside, either through organised schemes or individual initiatives, the lives of thousands of Jews and non-Jews were saved.

CONCLUSION: PLACE AND IDENTITY

The contribution made by refugees from Nazism has been enormous. At a local level examples include Jack Habel who established a series of furnishing stores across the Wessex region and the many refugee academics who transformed the University of Southampton from a small college into an internationally renowned centre of higher education. Others provided the region with a less spectacular but equally important legacy of talent and commitment. Yet many years on some still struggle to see Britain as 'home'. Fred Uhlman, who arrived in England in 1936 ignorant of its culture, history and language, had no such problems. In spite of the hostility of his father-in-law (who could never bring himself to believe that this 'suspect' foreigner truly belonged in England) and the government's policy of internment, Uhlman believed that he had 'found not only a refuge but a real home in England, which I love more than any other country in the world'.[161] More ironically, Desider Furst, who spent the final years of his life in the USA, when coming into contact with ex-American President Gerald Ford, proclaimed: '"I am British. Once British, always British" – in his strongest Hungarian accent.' Edgar Feuchtwanger, whilst recognising that 'there's a difference in my background ... yet it doesn't obviously now feel I'm a refugee'. He is very settled in Hampshire: 'in a way I've been here nearly all my life except for the first fourteen years'.[162]

But many of the refugees from the 1930s feel greater ambivalence towards Britain. Lilian Furst, who came as a youngster, views home as

where my things are. Home is nowhere ... I float on the periphery, at home yet
not truly so in Europe, Great Britain, or the United States. My geographical
roots are shallow; only those created by the brand mark of the red 'J' run deep
into my being.

A similar uncertainty runs through the testimony of Hilde Gerrard. Having
struggled so hard to establish roots in Britain with her husband and children,
in the middle of the war they received permission from the American
Consulate to enter the United States: 'how much heartache, distress,
homelessness would have been avoided if that permission would have come
earlier'. They decided to stay in Britain, developing an affinity with the
people of the small Lancashire town of Colne where they ran a bookshop for
40 years. Ultimately, however, the damage inflicted by the Nazis could not
simply be disregarded: 'We were uprooted in 1933. Are we really at "home"–
are we cosmopolitans and able to live anywhere? Or are we strangers
everywhere?'

A more profound absence of belonging is articulated by Anni Engel, even
though she has lived in Bournemouth for over 50 years. 'I still am an enemy
alien. What am I? I'm a Jew ... I was brought up in an enemy district all my
life. I was the Jew.' For all the subsequent successes of the refugees, the
damage inflicted in their forced movement remains. As Liese Richards, who
also settled in Bournemouth reflects: 'That I could never go home after I left
was a terrible thing. You had nowhere to go back to. That's a great loss in a
youngster's – in anybody's life.'[163] Most extreme were cases of refugees who
could not adapt at any level such as the suicide at Rose Cottage. The sense of
belonging varies in every refugee life story, changing over time. External
reactions have been critical. As John Grenville highlights, in his early days in
Britain, he tried

> to identify with the English and so one overdid it ... chang[ing] one's name
> from the German name to wipe out all traces of German and taking up sports
> like playing cricket – going to pubs and so on. And that took many years ... till
> gain[ing] a feeling of security – one did play a sort of role and felt a little bit
> false and artificial... It's only really now with the feeling of security that one
> can say – yes, I came from Germany and maybe I am a bit different.[164]

The pressure to assimilate went alongside attempts to exclude, most crudely
by extremists such as Viscount Lymington and Oswald Mosley though theirs
were minority views in Britain as a whole. Nevertheless, removal of the
refugee presence was put into action, as we shall see, by the British state in
1940 and discrimination at work (beyond the occupations from which they
were restricted) and in the social sphere were not uncommon in the refugees'
lives – certainly in their first years in Britain. At the other extreme, the
Turners in Southampton welcomed a whole series of refugees fleeing Nazi
persecution into their home simply because they believed that was the true
nature of hospitality.[165] But ambivalence was the most common response to

the refugees, typified at the start of the war by the Bournemouth Hebrew Congregation. Their president and treasurer wrote to the Chief Rabbi requesting that a group of 40 to 50 young German refugee Yeshivah students *not* be transferred to the town. It was highly inadvisable because 'Since the influx of Jewish people to Bournemouth from different parts, owing to the War, anti-Jewish feeling locally has, unfortunately, been intensified'. Realising that such a request might seem 'unjust', they pointed out that there were already two local refugee hostels for boys and girls catering for 50 children. Sympathy and coldness towards the victims of Nazism often came from the same source, adding further to refugee uncertainty.[166]

At a local level contact with the refugees for many could be short-lived but deeply stirring. At a public meeting in Bournemouth held after the November 1938 pogrom, Mr Elkington of the local Society of Friends

> spoke from an intimate knowledge of the sufferings of some of the victims of the Nazi terror. Not long ago ... he saw a boatload of Hebrew brethren leave Southampton for America: 'It was a veritable boatload of human misery'.

Such sights moved him and others to act: 'When you come into contact with this appalling suffering, you feel you must do something to alleviate it. It is not enough to say we are sorry; we must be practical and help.' But it took some effort and imagination for local people to understand that around them was a story of 'human misery' which was camouflaged by the rigours of everyday life. Just as the refugee story on the *St Louis* was largely lost in Southampton because of the Royal Family's arrival in the port the following day, so the role of the ocean liners of the 1930s in the refugee crisis was equally obscured. These liners symbolised, both nationally and locally, patriotic pride after the grim years of depression. This was particularly true of the *Queen Mary*: 'Right from her maiden voyage the people of Southampton took the ship to their hearts ... the city skyline was not really complete without her mighty funnels'. Subsequently, the ship has become an integral part of official and popular memory in Southampton. It is, however, the rich and famous, royalty and the film stars, who are remembered as its passengers. As with one of Southampton's other famous ships, the *Titanic*, the obscure refugees fleeing persecution and misery have been forgotten. It was these people, however, who made a deep impression on the Anglo-American poet, Louise Macneice, when travelling on the *Queen Mary* from Southampton in Easter 1939:

> The *Queen Mary* going west was packed with refugees, mainly Jews from Central Europe who covered their basic sorrow with volubility; fuss; only for a moment or two when they stopped troubling the water could you see the wreckage on the floor of their mind.[167]

Hampshire was to be home to other refugees until the invasion panic of spring 1940. Just before the war, a whole range of refugees from Europe were present in the county. In July 1939 a garden party took place in Southampton to raise funds for refugee work. The *Southampton Times* reported on the 'cosmopolitan turns' provided at the event by local refugees:

> Basque children from the Moorhill Home performed national songs and dances, and ... a Sudeten German, gave a remarkable demonstration on a gymnastic wheel. Miss Wilensky, a professional dancer from Austria, gave four dances – including two ballet dances specially composed for the occasion.

Local people in costume attempted Spanish and German folk dances and refugees repaid the compliment by performing English routines.[168] Until the government's measures destroyed such fledgling refugee communities, the concept of 'home' had been complicated but enriched by their presence at a local level. Peggy Turner gained, in her own words, a 'lot of pleasure' by living with people who were 'true European[s]]' with global outlooks. The garden party, whilst on one level representing a superficial cosmopolitanism, revealed the often hidden refugee heritage in Britain's localities.

In 1933, Lord Morley called for an international network of committees 'co-operating in the common task of giving help' to refugees. The organisations set up in Hampshire and elsewhere in Britain were very much part of that global response during the 1930s. Although unable to solve the immense problems of human misery created by the Nazis' escalation of terror, local activists' efforts in opening up their homes to the refugees and in identifying with their cause deserved better recognition at the time. Such work is also entitled to an honourable place in the memory of the region. By including the experiences of the refugees and those who acted on their behalf, iconic symbols of the 1930s, such as the *Queen Mary*, can be remembered in more complex ways: ones which allow the concept of 'home' to incorporate the global, national and local.[169]

6

Refugees, the Second World War and the Holocaust

During the Second World War, 'Europe had never seen so many refugees ... the total number of displaced Europeans ... was thirty million or more'. Total war accompanied by genocide, 'ethnic cleansing', and the attempt of the Nazis to 'reorder' the 'racial' map of Europe, led to forced population movements on a new scale.[1] Britain was geographically and culturally remote from the killing fields but could not altogether escape contact with the victims of Nazism. A new wave of refugees arrived after the military disasters of spring 1940 and smaller numbers, survivors of mass murder, managed to flee the continent for the remainder of the war. Few of these arrivals were welcomed and anti-alienism dominated responses. The first victims of such antipathy were, ironically, those who had fled Nazism before September 1939. In spite of the renewed commitment to the concept of asylum and the humanitarian sentiment and activity towards refugees in the late 1930s, hostility and ambivalence had not disappeared; the war provided the opportunity for those in government and populace who had never welcomed the newcomers' presence to put their prejudices into operation.

WAR, INTERNMENT AND AFTER

Most opposition to refugees in the 1930s was linked to economic insecurities, mainly fears that 'British' jobs would be threatened by 'alien' competition. But underneath such concerns were suspicions about the nature of the refugees. Animosity against east European Jewish immigrants from the turn of the century reached a peak during the 1920s. Such blatant hatred was less frequently articulated, except by extremists, against refugees from Nazism, yet general unease remained about their reliability.[2]

At the start of the war, however, it was not clear that the less sympathetically minded would decide the refugees' fate. The Home Office was anxious that the indiscriminatory, devastating and expensive measures taken against 'enemy aliens' in the First World War would not be repeated. The 'Independent National' Home Secretary, Sir John Anderson, stressed in the House of Commons on 4 September 1939 that a liberal policy would be pursued, attempting 'to avoid treating as enemies those who are friendly to the country which has offered them asylum'. A few hundred 'enemy aliens' were interned. They proved to be mainly refugees from Nazism. Why they were seen as posing a particular menace remains a mystery. But the prejudice inherent in these early decisions was given almost free reign nine months later as mass internment was implemented. Contradicting pre-war government plans, hundreds of makeshift internment camps were created to accommodate 'enemy aliens'.[3]

Taunton's School, founded in 1760, was an independent educational establishment in Southampton. In the second week of the war its buildings were taken over by the War Department and

> converted into a prisoner-of-war and internment camp ... The perimeter was
> given a barbed wire fence, windows were barricaded, another fence bisected the
> Field ... The first occupants were internees and merchant seamen, one sad
> figure among the former being Paul Brann [a local performer of German origin]
> whose marionettes had enchanted a School audience in March, 1939.[4]

For those affected, these measures were shattering. Most refugees, however, continued their lives without significant change. Extremists intensified their anti-alien campaign, but until spring 1940 there was little public pressure to remove the refugees' freedom. When, in early March 1940, Sir Henry Page Croft posed the Home Secretary a barely-veiled antisemitic question: 'How many alien Jews have found asylum in Great Britain since 1932?', his was still an isolated voice. Three months later, through his promotion to Under-Secretary at the War Office, and elevation to the House of Lords, Croft was a major government spokesman defending mass internment and deporting of refugees: 27,000 refugees, or roughly half those who had been given asylum, were interned.[5]

The internment measures of 1940 have been explained as panic measures linked to the military crisis confronting the British government after the fall of Norway, Denmark, Belgium, Holland and France. Nevertheless, the *direction* of the measures – who was, and was not interned – has been less satisfactorily accounted for. Analysis of those responsible in the War Office, the military/security world and the secret, unaccountable committees established by the new Prime Minister, suggests that widespread prejudice against the refugees (and particularly their Jewishness) was a major factor. The crisis atmosphere, fuelled by a press anti-alien campaign, empowered previously marginalised figures such as Croft to influence state policy directly. Amongst the first victims were refugees who had settled in Hampshire.[6]

An amendment to the Aliens Order, 1920, enabled the Home Secretary to declare 'protected areas' in which aliens should not remain without the permission of a registration officer. The Aliens (Protected Areas) Order was published on 29 March 1940 and came into force on 15 April 1940. Areas 'protected' included those around the Humber, Harwich, Medway, Thames and Dover, Portsmouth, Plymouth, north of Scotland, Orkney and Zetland, and the Firth of Forth. The Portsmouth area included the major ports and other large Hampshire conurbations.[7] Alice Sluckin at Southampton's Children's Hospital was one of those affected by restrictions introduced on possessions. On 26 May 1940, the Chief Constable of Southampton wrote to all aliens in his district and some 80 individuals of different nationalities surrendered their cameras, field glasses, motor vehicles and firearms. By then, however, most male adult refugees in Hampshire and other protected counties were interned.[8]

Winston Churchill became Prime Minister on 10 May 1940. The following day his new Cabinet met to discuss the invasion threat. Sir John Anderson wished to avoid mass internment, even though he had set in motion the aliens order at the end of March which, if only an enabling measure, was based on the premise that refugees *might* pose a security threat. In the pessimistic atmosphere at the start of May the military and security forces demanded further action. Sir John Dill, Vice-Chief of the Imperial General Staff, outlined that 'In the light of the possibility of invasion, it was very desirable that all enemy aliens in counties on the South-East and East should be interned'. Anderson was by now in a weak position but managed to limit internment to male enemy aliens between 16 and 60.[9] Nevertheless, his earlier aliens order provided a geographical template; rather than the southern coastal strip envisaged by the Home Secretary, 31 counties were affected ranging from Hampshire in the south to Nairn in the north. Roughly 2,000 men were arrested and placed in temporary internment camps – including Lingfield Race Course, Belle Vue Zoo in Manchester, and, most notoriously, Warth Mills, a massive rat-infested ex-factory in Bury.[10]

The use of Taunton's School as an internment camp was revived, acting as a temporary clearing house for male 'enemy aliens' in the locality including the Austrian Jewish refugee dentists in Bournemouth, Fritz Engel and Desider Furst. Both were totally surprised and bewildered by measures that took them away from their families and work for an unknown time and to an unknown destination. Fritz Engel was told by telephone to come to Bournemouth Police Station but granted the 'privilege' of going home to pick up some possessions:

> I was consoled that the internment may only be for a short period and could be over within a few days… I was first taken to Southampton into a building belonging to Taunton's School, already surrounded by electrically loaded barbed wire [joining] about 20 other refugees with whom I was locked up in a large room… A soldier, armed with rifle and bayonet, guarded the only door… Outside stood a bucket to receive our excrement.

Desider Furst was even more demoralised. At Bournemouth Police Station he joined about 30, mainly elderly, Austrian and German men, people he had seen as potential patients and not 'fellow prisoners'. For the young internees at Taunton's

> it was fun [but for] me and some others in a similar position it looked like a catastrophe... After two days we were given a paperbag with food and put on a train under military escort. The episode turned serious – we were regarded as potential enemies. We realised it on the long journey which ended in Liverpool. We marched through the streets in a loose undisciplined column. Some youngsters shouted 'Look at the Jerries!' We were not in the mood to laugh.[11]

Though they played a significant role in transforming the refugees from victims of oppression into suspect enemy aliens, temporary internment centres such as Taunton's have received little attention in contrast to the major camps in the Isle of Man and later Canada and Australia.[12]

The importance of this local input extended beyond buildings and personnel. In announcing the measures of 11 May 1940, the Foreign Office stressed that 'His Majesty's Government are committed by Cabinet decision not to undertake mass internment and there is, of course, no guarantee that by such mass internment we should eliminate dangerous enemy agents'. Three days later, a hysterical and inaccurate report from the Minister at The Hague, Sir Nevile Bland, about the role of so-called 'Fifth Columnists' in the fall of Holland, demolished the liberal line as did popular pressure. Much of the British press followed Bland's line, demanding that 'all Germans and Austrians, at least, ought to be interned at once'.[13] The anti-alien campaign included local government. The Borough of Lytham St Annes sent resolutions to all councils in Britain demanding 'the internment of all enemy aliens, without exception' and asking them to forward such requests to 'the Prime Minister, the Minister of Labour, the Minister of Home Security, the local member of Parliament and to all Local Authorities in the Country'. Rather than delegating policy nationally, some local authorities wanted to be involved in its implementation though there were exceptions, such as Southampton City Council, which refused to become involved in the campaign.[14]

Alleged popular antipathy enabled Churchill to argue that internment 'would probably be much safer for all German-speaking persons themselves'. On 22 May 1940, internment was extended further – all male and female enemy aliens between 16 and 60 classified as 'Category B' – of uncertain loyalty – were now included. By early June, all male enemy aliens of appropriate age were interned as were several thousand Italians (including some refugees from Fascism) after Mussolini declared war on Britain. Verbal and written attacks on refugees were not infrequent in May/June 1940, but there were, contrasting to the First World War, few physical assaults on German-origin 'enemy aliens' (although there were some anti-Italian riots). The impact of internment, however, was far from slight.[15]

Some of the refugees, particularly the older ones, were not fit physically or mentally to cope with life behind barbed wire. One such individual was Professor Karl Weissenberg who had worked in Southampton since his University appointment in 1934. Weissenberg was seriously ill and his sponsor, the SPSL, was desperate to obtain his release. Through pressure from the SPSL, the government in late summer 1940 set up a panel reviewing special cases of distinguished scientists and scholars who might, if released, be particularly useful to the war effort. Amongst its first recommendations was the release of Karl Weissenberg, endorsed in the USA by his fellow refugee physicist, Albert Einstein, the only time when he 'made an individual appeal'.[16]

The releases from the Isle of Man, where the majority of the refugees were interned, even for those of immense talent and reputation such as Weissenberg, were slow and haphazard: it was a 'special torture ... one might be released today, tomorrow, in a week or not for years'. The refugees from Nazism managed to make the most of their time in the Isle of Man camps, organising courses, lectures and concerts. Nevertheless, the co-presence of some genuine Nazis – merchant seamen and others – was a source of irritation and unease for the refugees which the authorities were reluctant to address. Fritz Engel was able to persuade the camp authorities to let the interned dentists practise their profession for those in need of urgent attention but his wife 'went through a very hard time. She was so depressed that she could hardly eat and kept on losing weight ... When I returned, I could hardly recognise Anni who looked so very miserable'. The prospects for Desider Furst were bleak: 'I had been away for four months, an eternity to me. I was not allowed to return to Bournemouth, which was still a restricted area for us. Thus, we had lost everything'. Though they were treated decently, they were deprived of freedom and

> separated from our families at a time when we really needed each other. Basically, we were unhappy, disappointed, and frustrated human beings who longed for freedom.[17]

Both Desider Furst and Fritz Engel resisted attempts to send them to the colonies. The sinking of the *Arandora Star*, a ship taking internees to Canada, with enormous loss of life, confirmed their decision not to be separated from family and destroying the roots established in Britain. Others sent to Canada and Australia were robbed and attacked by the British on board.[18]

At a local level few refugees remained in restricted areas such as Hampshire. There were prosecutions of 'enemy aliens' failing to meet the strict terms of aliens regulations in the county as late as 1942.[19] A small number completely avoided internment because of their age or nationality. Slowly, during the latter part of the war and beyond, Hampshire, especially Bournemouth, again became a major centre of settlement for refugees from Nazism. But the rootedness already underway by 1940 was brutally destroyed by the British government's measures. The Engels represented one of the few links between pre and post-war refugees, becoming the 'older sister and brother' of this Bournemouth community.[20]

At the time, Desider Furst felt 'indignant and embittered about our unjustified detention... For me it was not only a financial disaster and separation from my family; I felt I had been let down by a country in which I had faith and trust'.[21] Such concern was not limited to the refugees. In contrast to internment during the First World War, some in the government were concerned about Britain's liberal reputation. After the panic months of spring passed, and fear of invasion subsided, release categories were put into operation and attempts made to justify internment. Nevertheless, parliamentary debate did not occur until July 1940 and unsavoury aspects of internment were suppressed.[22]

In the House of Lords, Henry Page Croft emphasised that 'grounds of military necessity' forced the government to move from a policy of 'individual examination and individual internment' to one of 'the internment of large categories of enemy aliens', adding that, 'every effort is being made to send overseas to the Dominions as many civilian internees as the Dominions are willing to accept and for whom accommodation can be provided'. For Croft and others, internment was the ideal opportunity to rid Britain of refugees – people they never wanted in the first place.[23]

In the Commons, however, a more sustained attack on internment took place. Another Hampshire politician, Viscount Wolmer, Conservative MP for Aldershot, was a major voice calling for a generous and speedy release policy. Wolmer did 'not wish to criticise [the] decision[s of May and June] because we were then in a state of acute emergency' yet was 'profoundly shocked by individual cases which have come to the attention of all of us'. Wolmer wanted a return to a policy in which 'every one of these cases should be properly investigated and dealt with on their merits', otherwise 'we shall do harm to the good name of Great Britain'.[24]

Wolmer called for 'a separate organisation to deal with this problem, with a separate Minister ... and people in charge of it who have the time and the capacity to deal with the cases on their merits'. The government set up two bodies: the Lytton committee pushed for a quick reversal of mass internment but the Asquith committee, which dealt with general policy, was resistant to taking any risks. As a result, releases did not speed up immediately. It was not until late 1940 and early 1941 that most of the non-deported internees gained freedom. By 1942 only a few hundred were still interned.[25] By the end of the war, internment was largely forgotten both locally (except in the Isle of Man where the camps dominated its war experience) and nationally. But for internment to be collectively consigned to oblivion required a process of selective memory.[26]

WAR REFUGEES AND LOCAL MEMORY

Another direct result of the military disaster in spring 1940 was a mass movement of refugees to the south coast from Holland, Belgium, France and the Channel Islands. The Hampshire ports, particularly Southampton, received many of these people. By September 1940 over 6,000 Belgian, Dutch and French refugees had landed in Southampton with a further 2,400 coming from the Channel Islands. It proved easy to incorporate their story into the narrative of the city at war. This inclusive process was similar to that of the Belgians in the earlier conflict: the refugees were innocent victims of the bullying Germans. These sorrowful figures deserved sympathetic and caring treatment. Moreover, their story could be added to one of the great British myths of the Second World War, the 'victory' of Dunkirk and the abandonment of the continent.[27]

In an official history of Southampton at war, it was related how:

> On the evening of 18th May, 1940, a strange-looking and pathetic 'armada' sailed up Southampton Water. It was made up of an extraordinary miscellany of craft ... crammed with the first refugees, from Europe... Within a week, thousands of Belgian, Dutch and French, men women and children had sought sanctuary.[28]

The *Southern Daily Echo* provided a graphic account of how some had escaped: 'Belgian Refugees Reach England, Tell[ing] of Nightmare Trek to Ostend; Gunned on Roads By Nazi Air Criminals':

> The first vessel arrived shortly before 10am, and it was not long before the first of the sad and broken-hearted people started to file down the gangway. All that remained of their belongings they brought with them, some in suitcases [and] baskets... The women generally displayed remarkable fortitude, but some, in deep mourning, wept pitifully. Some children bereft of parents and homes, were found sleeping in the streets of Ostend. They were taken aboard one of the refugee ships, where foster-mothers were found for them.

The evil from which the Belgians had fled was emphasised, linkage to the earlier conflict highlighting how it was a result of *German* rather than Nazi barbarity. One refugee stressed that:

> 'The German airmen have been absolutely ruthless... They have machine-gunned everyone they could find. Refugees making for Ostend from Brussels, Antwerp and Louvain were constantly fired upon as they headed for the coast...' Several of the refugees stated that it was the second time that they had been compelled to leave their homes. 'We were in England in 1914' was a frequent expression accompanied by 'We have again lost everything'.[29]

To further underline their deserving nature, reports were accompanied with heartbreaking photographs of very young and very old refugees. Those helping the refugees inside the local state structure and in the voluntary world were singled out for particular praise for their 'loyal' efforts.[30]

Most of the Channel Islanders were quickly dispatched to Barnsley and Wakefield, although several hundred remained in Hampshire, later forming a Channel Islanders' Association in Southampton. Refugees from the continent were given shelter in public assistance institutions and other buildings in

Southampton before being dispersed across the country. Taunton's School was used for troops fleeing from the continent but no mention was made that it was intimately connected to *other* refugees at this crisis point through its use as an internment camp. The pre-war refugees from Nazism were, especially after the collapse of Holland, seen as a menace to Britain's war effort. Although the contrast was not so severe as during the First World War, the dichotomy of treatment between those of German and those of French-Belgian descent in spring 1940 was immense. Greater ambivalence was shown to Dutch refugees revealing fears that their numbers contained spies relating to the 'Fifth Column' menace which it was believed was responsible for Holland's defeat. The Cabinet in May 1940 highlighted Dutch aliens as being particularly suspect and locally such suspicion also operated. In Portsmouth assistance given to Dutch refugees, who had arrived in the port having survived machine-gun attacks, was criticised by some local councillors; Holland's sudden collapse 'confirmed very thoroughly the[ir] objection'.[31] The internment process of spring 1940 was inconsistent but underneath the chaos were assumptions, frequently prejudicial, working in favour of some groups and against others. Reports on Belgian refugees fleeing Nazi military aggression were unambiguous whereas suspicion and disbelief was attached to the racial and political victims of Hitler's regime. The same ambivalence and antipathy dominated responses during the war to those attempting to escape what was later known as the Holocaust.

THE HOLOCAUST AND LOCAL PLACE

Those studying the Holocaust are paying greater attention to the geography of mass murder, and especially the importance of local sites of destruction whether they be infamous death camps such as Auschwitz or obscure and forgotten killing fields in eastern Europe. Many landscapes that were overflowing with blood and human misery quickly lost all obvious traces of the evil carried out within them, requiring skilled work from geographers and archaeologists to re-establish their importance within the 'Final Solution'.[32] The study of the Western Allies and the Holocaust has grown in sophistication, incorporating the responses of many different governments and international agencies. Nevertheless, obsession with secret intelligence information, available to only a tiny number of people in Western Allied governments during the war, helps obscure that many details of the murder of European Jewry were available in the public domain.[33] As part of this elitist approach and lacuna with regard to the responses of ordinary people, there are no localised studies within the existing literature on the liberal democracies and the Holocaust and none that confront the idea of 'place' in the strands of connection, as well as the total abyss that existed between the killing sites of the European continent and the relatively peaceful 'Home Front' of countries such as the USA and Britain.

Mollie Panter-Downes came to prominence before the war as a journalist after writing about the arrival of Jewish refugee children in London. She became one of the most important British writers for an American audience during the Second World War.[34] In March 1946 she wrote a description of life in a hostel, Wintershill Hall, Durley, near Southampton, for child survivors of the Holocaust. The *New Yorker* article, 'A Quiet Life in Hampshire', stressed the importance of place in differentiating Nazi concentration camps such as Buchenwald in Germany and the death camps of eastern Europe. In contrast to them both, however, was her emphasis on the gentle landscape surrounding Wintershill Hall in 'a tiny hamlet in a part of Hampshire where you see nothing much but quiet, brown fields, an occasional thatched cottage, and a lot of windy sky'. The director of the hostel, Dr Friedmann, told Panter-Downes that 'People say to me, "But in this house, in this lovely country[side] – for the children to come here from Belsen and Terezin and so on must be *heaven!*"'. As we shall see, this was not always the perspective of these children. Nevertheless, as Friedmann added, some of the boys and girls had hidden

> in the ghettos, down in the sewers, and were accustomed to jumping trains, to dodging S.S. guards on the frontier. And the dreadful things all the time in the camps... Here in Hampshire it seems very quiet after that.[35]

In the early nineteenth century, William Cobbett described the rural parish of Durley as 'one of the most obscure villages in this whole kingdom'. By the Second World War it was still essentially rural, consisting of a church, a couple of shops, a school and two pubs, its inhabitants part of 'a close-knit but somewhat isolated community'.[36] Another report stressed the perceived incongruity as the 'Fifty happy, excited children, aged from seven to 16, the first to reach England from the Belsen concentration camp, [were] sleeping tonight in one of England's stately homes'.[37] It was not, however, the quiet landscape that separated Durley from places of mass murder. Simon Srebrnik was one of the two survivors of the first extermination camp to kill Jews, Chelmno, where up to 320,000 people were murdered using mobile gas vans. He returned to the village in the west of Poland 40 years later:

> It's hard to recognise, but it was here. They burned people here ... and the flames reached to the sky... It was always this peaceful here. Always. When they burned two thousand people – Jews – every day, it was just as peaceful. No one shouted. Everyone went about his work. It was silent. Peaceful. Just as it is now.[38]

The children at Wintershill Hall were surprised that rather than the 'golden land, the land of plenty', Britain was in the grip of post-war austerity with rationing of food and clothing. Friedmann 'took them to see the bomb damage in Southampton one day and they could not get over that, either'. It had suffered 51 air raids leaving 631 dead and over 40,000 properties damaged. Yet this trauma generally acted as a barrier rather than a bridge between Holocaust survivors and their British hosts.[39] Points of contact developed with the local community, including twice weekly football games 'between the Durley lads and the lads of Belsen, Buchenwald, and places east'. Yet the 'Belsen children', as they were inaccurately labelled, occupied a different mental and emotional world to those around them. One recalled visiting Durley and being the object of some curiosity because 'we looked different'. More positively, the children were never refused sweets and chocolates at the local shop, showing some awareness of what they had endured even if it fell short of understanding the full enormity of the Nazi crime.[40]

The youngsters' pain was expressed in a song about Treblinka which they knew because it was sung at other camps and in the ghettos. In Treblinka, one of three death camps alongside Sobibor and Belzec established with the major purpose of gassing Polish Jews (the so-called 'Operation Reinhardt'), some 900,000 people (including 2,000 Gypsies and 29,000 non-Polish Jews) perished before it was razed to the ground in 1943. Panter-Downes commented that one of the children, when asked if he was familiar with the song, replied '"Oh, sure, sure", as though he had been asked if he knew the latest swing number'. The world of swing numbers, Vera Lynn, the Home Guard, Dunkirk, the Blitz, evacuation and D-Day were integral to the local experience during the war,[41] but were utterly removed from that of cattle trucks and gas chambers:

> My heart breaks
> When I think of the good friends who there met a violent death.
> My heart breaks
> When I remember that there my brother and sisters perished.
> My heart breaks
> When I remember that there my mother and father were murdered,
> And I join the others at the same shunting site,
> Sobbing bitterly with them and crying,
> 'Don't leave me here alone!'[42]

At the start of the Second World War, however, such sites of mass murder had not been created. It would be two years before the 'Final Solution' was put into operation, though the murderous 'euthanasia' campaign, including the use of gas, was already under preparation.[43] Yet the outbreak of war marked a distinctive break in Nazi policies towards the Jews and liberal democratic responses to their plight.

THE END OF MASS RESCUE

On 3 September 1939 Britain cancelled all visas previously granted to refugees who were now technically regarded as 'enemy nationals'. The Home Secretary, Sir John Anderson, putting the 'objective point of view', defended this action: 'considerations of sympathy with the unfortunate persons cannot be allowed to override considerations of what is best for the security of the country and for the public interest'. Jewish and other refugee organisations, instrumental in opening up admission policies, were now unable or unwilling to influence the government. Their bargaining power was limited as they found themselves near-bankrupt, unable to maintain tens of thousands of refugees whom they hoped would have remigrated. In September 1939 the government reluctantly lent money to the Jewish refugee bodies to avoid public antipathy because 'enemy aliens' were a direct charge on the state. The state also argued that those abroad could no longer be regarded as suitable for entry because 'the practical difficulties of making contact between the refugee in enemy territory and the refugee organizations in the United Kingdom ... [were] likely to be almost insuperable'. Moreover, Home Secretary Anderson told the Czech Refugee Trust in March 1940 that there was

> already considerable uneasiness about the number of aliens in this country, and fresh admissions would add to the public uneasiness and might do much to prejudice the position of refugees already here.[44]

Under his successor, Herbert Morrison, this fear became obsessive, reaching levels not witnessed since the 1920s.

Anderson argued that he 'did not think that it would be in the interests of the refugees themselves who are at present in this country to allow a further influx of refugees from territory under enemy jurisdiction', revealing an astonishingly inept understanding of their day-to-day concerns. Anti-alienism was an irritant, but it was nothing compared to the anguish caused by knowing close relatives with visas to Britain were left behind on the continent. To Alice Sluckin in Southampton the cancellation of visas on 3 September 1939 was agonising: 'if the war hadn't started [my brother in Prague] would have come on 7 September'. At first Alice still received letters from her father, sent through Belgium and Norway. After the military disasters of spring 1940, information about her family was sporadic, coming mainly from Red Cross messages: 'once they were deported I didn't hear any more'. Her parents were sent to Theresienstadt (Terezin) concentration camp in 1942. A 'model camp' used for Czech Jews and 'privileged' Jews from Germany, 33,000 Jews died in Theresienstadt with a further 90,000 deported eastwards mainly to Auschwitz, including Alice's immediate family. It took two and a half years before she received confirmation that her parents and brother had been murdered and all hopes of their survival were quashed.[45]

Age, gender, family responsibilities as well as personality affected how refugees in Britain coped with the strain of leaving close relatives behind in Europe alongside everyday concerns. Hilde Gerrard, working as a domestic and responsible for her young twins, found it progressively intolerable. At the start of the war, 'via America, I got letters from my parents [in Germany]. They were desperately trying to leave, but had no entry visas anywhere'. Communication from Europe became less frequent and more impersonal. By 1941:

We were completely separated from our parents [in Berlin] and our only contacts were Red Cross messages, which we got once a month – at most consisting of twenty five words. These messages told us that our parents ... had to leave their home in Eichendorfstrasse... What could I do? I approached every organisation I knew that [helped] refugees. I approached people. I was so helpless... Through a Red Cross message I knew the date of my parents' deportation. There were still several weeks to go... I was in despair, being unable to help. Heartbroken about it, tears were running down my face almost all the time. I felt rebellious against all the injustice... I looked round and had to be thankful that we saved the children, that we had a roof over our heads and that we were not caught in the European holocaust. After the date on which my parents were to be deported, I felt completely exhausted and ill... I found consolation in living for my family and only recovered slowly over many, many years...[46]

For child refugees isolated in Britain, news or lack of it about their parents could be even more disorientating. The hosts of Vera Schaufeld were at best dutiful to her, refusing to talk about her parents. She received her last letter from her father in late 1941 or early 1942. She was 15 when the war ended and found it almost impossible to come to terms with her loss:

I then started having fantasies that really they were alive, and that they'd started a new life in Shanghai or one of the places that they'd tried to get to, and had another family but just didn't want me... I couldn't accept the reality... I never saw anything written [from the Red Cross confirming the murder of her parents]... [When the letters stopped] that was dreadful... I think that I always thought somehow I hadn't written ... back enough ... [or] that they hadn't wanted to write ... I thought that they could come to me if only they wanted to enough. I never accepted the limitations on their freedom, on their lives.

Her parents were deported to Theresienstadt and transported to Auschwitz, but it was

quite some time after the war before I got this information ... there was never really a time when I can remember one day knowing that my parents, my grandmother, my aunt, Uncle Rudolph, Aunty Elsa, that everybody was actually dead, and that none of them had actually survived. I think this just gradually penetrated.[47]

For the refugees, there was no choice but to get on with their lives. Most found that they could make a living in post-war Britain but suffered the absence of formal mechanisms in an unsympathetic environment to grieve for lost families from a destroyed world.[48] Indeed, immediately after the war there was irritation with Jewish refugees from sections of British society, reaching a local climax in autumn 1945 with the Hampstead petition movement in north-west London which called for their removal from the area. Few in Britain at this stage had the desire to make the refugees feel at home or were aware of the enormity of the damage inflicted upon European Jewry.[49]

After the war, the British government made it hard for Jewish survivors to enter, continuing the restrictionism put into action at the start of the conflict. Some 60,000 (non-military) refugees were accepted into Britain during the Second World War. Only a small percentage were Jewish and these generally came with other movements, such as the Hungarian writer and intellectual, Arthur Koestler, who left France in June 1940 and came to Britain circuitously. He was immediately interned by the British authorities. By this point, it was extremely difficult for Jews to leave countries under Nazi control. The case of Isa Brysh, who settled later in Bournemouth having come from the continent during the war, is remarkable for its lack of typicality.[50]

Isa was born in 1929 in Heilbronn, Germany. The family fled to France where the two children attended the Rothschild school in Paris. Her father joined the French army and was evacuated at Dunkirk, pretending he was of Polish origin. Isa's mother was initially interned along with thousands of other 'enemy aliens' in a sports stadium lacking even basic facilities. In June 1940 the three made their escape by train as the German army occupied Paris, reaching Beaulieu, a village in the free zone of France, where a 'safe house' for children was organised by the Jewish scout movement. Under suspicion they moved further south, eventually reaching Marseilles. Some Jews were turned back after reaching the Swiss border so Isa's mother aimed to find refuge in Spain. Meanwhile her father joined the Aliens Pioneer Corps in Britain and managed to find the whereabouts of his family. Through the Jewish chaplain to the British forces, he fought a two-year campaign to get visas issued for his wife and two daughters. Eventually, her mother received visas from the Spanish consulate in Marseilles and they took a train over the Pyrenees to Madrid. From there they reached Lisbon, obtaining visas to Britain and arriving in Bristol in February 1942 on a diplomatic flight. Her astonishing family story indicates that rescue during the first years of the conflict involved great risk and required good fortune. It was, however, far from impossible and, when it succeeded, did not have the negative effect on the British war effort which so many politicians and civil servants feared.[51]

The decision to ban Jewish emigration from the Reich was not taken formally until the autumn of 1941. Eichmann's role, however, became one of managing deportation to areas of Jewish concentration rather than pursuing 'voluntary' emigration on the lines of Austria, Czechoslovakia and Germany before the war. The first two years of the war for Jews in these countries were marked by expulsions, increased use of concentration camps, reduction of rations, confiscation of remaining wealth and the introduction of forced labour. As all three Jewish communities were impoverished by the outbreak of war, the intensified persecution had a desperate impact. Most energies of the surviving Jewish organisations, aside from relief work, were put into attempts to organise illegal migration to Palestine. In spite of these efforts, only several thousand Jews from the Reich escaped to Palestine during the war, often facing additional hurdles provided by the British authorities.[52]

It was estimated in summer 1941 that within the borders of pre-1938 Germany, some 50,000 Jews were taken for labour service, half in Berlin, many women and youngsters working in the various Siemens enterprises.[53] In the summer of 1942, however, preparations were made for their mass deportation and extermination in the East. One of those at Siemens' electrical works until 1942 was Jack Habel's mother-in-law, who was reunited after the war with her daughter, now helping run a farm near Winchester. Working as a slave labourer, the foreman warned her that the Gestapo were 'coming to collect the Jews'. She hid herself 'until they had gone, [slipping] out through a side door, [going] into hiding ... in an allotment hut somewhere on the outskirts of Berlin.[54]

By the end of 1942 some 33,000 Jews remained in Berlin, declining to fewer than 7,000 six months later. It has been estimated that between 2,000 and 4,000 Jews in Berlin survived the war in hiding, reliant on networks of friends and helpers to provide food, accommodation and security. As far as Jack Habel was able to ascertain, his mother-in-law, having left the factory,

> appeared in Berlin, and said, 'I've come from Dresden, I was bombed out, I've got nothing. All my personal belongings, all my papers were burnt'. So they gave her a ration book ... and she survived... She was [also] fed by somebody.

Those hiding required many ordinary Germans to keep them from the certain death that would have resulted to all concerned on discovery. But the number of survivors needs to be contrasted, as Lenni Yahil points out, with the thriving Jewish population of the German capital in 1933 which stood close to 170,000. The vast majority of Jews still in the Reich after the outbreak of war, including the sister and father of Jack Habel, were deported and murdered in the ghettos, killing fields and extermination camps of eastern Europe.[55]

THE DESTRUCTION OF POLISH JEWRY

With the conquest of Poland in September 1939 3,300,000 Jews were added to those under Nazi control. By the end of that month, Germany and the USSR agreed to the division of Poland with its central and western areas under German control. Parts of Poland, particularly those that had belonged to the German Empire before 1918, were incorporated into the Reich (the Warthegau), the rest becoming a protectorate (the Generalgouvernement). As with the *Anschluss*, Nazi geographical expansion was accompanied by intensification of antisemitism, forced movements and general brutality towards the Jews. Nevertheless, whilst earlier persecutions had been accurately and speedily reported in the liberal democracies, the early measures in Poland received little sustained attention. Many in Britain and elsewhere had great difficulty comprehending that Nazi antisemitism now extended beyond the borders of pre-war Greater Germany and the brutality of the early concentration camps.

On 21 September 1939, Reinhard Heydrich, head of the SS Security Police, sent out orders to commanders of the *Einsatzgruppen*, the units given the special task of murdering and terrorising sections of the enemy alongside the German army. The goals were to clear Jews from the Warthegau and to concentrate them in the larger cities of the occupied territories. Jewish councils were to be established in all areas of Jewish concentration. These orders were accompanied by enormous and brutal movements of people designed to establish the foundations of a new European racial state. Eichmann, working under Heydrich, was given the task of evacuating Poles and Jews to be replaced by 'racially pure' Germans. It has been estimated that some 325,000 people (100,000 of whom were Jewish) had been deported by the end of 1940 who were replaced by 430,000 Germans. One specific scheme, the Lublin reservation, was the first attempt to 'solve' the Jewish question by population transfer: 30,000 Germans were removed with the idea of concentrating all Jews in the area between the San and Bug rivers. The plan was abandoned in spring 1940 as it was unable to deal with the numbers involved and the resultant chaos. Nevertheless, many Jews endured a miserable winter with little food or accommodation and few medical facilities.[56]

The Lublin reservation revealed the growing disparity between what was happening in the East and recorded in the West. The scheme was reported in the British press, but it did not receive widespread publicity nor the detail and comment that was required to bring home the enormity of the racial geo-politics it represented. If featured, it went alongside a British government White Paper on German atrocities the contents of which were confined to the pre-war period. The problems caused by the juxtaposition of the two was illustrated locally in the *Portsmouth Evening News*.[57] A small article covered 'German Plans for Poland' including brief mention of the setting up of a 'Jewish Colony'. In the same issue, however, a lengthy editorial, 'The Evil We Fight', was devoted to the White Paper, failing to mention antisemitism.[58] In many respects, the White Paper of October 1939 brought popular understanding of Nazi atrocities to a limit. The treatment of victims was 'punishment' which took place in the confines of concentration camps in Germany. The nature of these 'punishments' was of 'such a character that they cannot be printed'. Jews, if mentioned, were listed amongst those suffering the universal evil that was Nazism. Persecution of Polish Jewry in the months after September 1939 was not hidden from the outside world but it rarely featured in the dominant war narrative. The 'sadistic savagery' of Nazism was largely confined in popular imagination to the pre-war concentration camps. The implications of the racial reordering of Europe which began so massively in Poland were less well-understood. But for Polish Jewry, this brought to an end 1,000 years of settlement which, for all its moments of poverty and persecution, was home for the largest Jewish community in the world.[59]

By the end of the war over 3 million, or 90 per cent of Polish Jews, had been murdered. Most of the survivors had no family or friends to return to and they had no desire to live in a country whose increasing hostility to Jews was expressed most notoriously in the pogroms and murders of survivors in 1945 and 1946. Either as a temporary place of recuperation, as was the case with Wintershill Hall, or of permanent settlement, Hampshire played host to individuals who were often the sole Jewish survivors of their villages and little towns. Josef Rosensaft, a survivor and post-war Jewish leader in Bergen-Belsen, stressed that some of those helping at the former concentration camp in 1945

> had forgotten that we were not brought up in Belsen, Auschwitz and other concentration camps, but had, once upon a time, a home and a background and motherly love and kindness; that before the calumnity we, too, had our schools and universities and Yeshivot.[60]

Alec Ward, formerly Abram Warszaw, was born in Parysow in the district of Lublin in 1927. His family moved to Laskarzew in the same district and finally Magnuszew, Radom, before the war. He was one of only two Jewish survivors from Magnuszew and all the other Jews of the shtetl of Laskarzew were murdered. He survived a series of concentration and slave labour camps before being liberated at Mauthausen and later sent to Wintershill Hall to recuperate. He recalls the Jewish life in his hometown with great fondness:

> The synagogue in Parysow was very beautiful, with a dome and a stone floor. The cantor's voice reverberated round the Synagogue which is still very vivid in my memory. On Friday afternoon the Jewish town crier proclaimed the coming of the sabbath and announced it was time to go to the Synagogue. On Saturday afternoon the whole Jewish community seemed to walk in the streets...[61]

Though he was also brought up in a small town with a large Jewish population, Richard Stern's testimony has a different emphasis stressing the interaction of the Jewish and non-Jewish worlds. The variations in their perspectives partly reflect age – he was ten years older than Alec Ward – and cultural differences. Richard Stern followed a more assimilated path than Alec, being influenced by secular culture as well as orthodox Judaism, reflecting the dynamic nature of inter-war Polish Jewry. During the war he survived Soviet labour camps in Siberia before joining Polish forces under British command in the Middle East. Afterwards he came to Britain from the Lebanon and continued his training as a chemical engineer, settling and working in the Southampton region before retiring to Bournemouth:

> My little town in Southern Poland, Jedrzejow [had] a population of about 12,000 of whom a third were Jews... There were two Jewish doctors, two lawyers, [and] owners of a brewery, two flour mills and a small nail and shoe-heel protector factory, but the vast majority of Jews were shop keepers, tailors, carpenters and of no fixed occupation. The Civil Service, the Law Courts,

schools and local administration did not employ Jews... Large numbers of Jews lived in poverty and were recipients of help from the Community Office to which the richer members contributed... The majority of the Jewish population was strictly orthodox and ... particularly the older generation, spoke and wrote Yiddish, but younger people, having been to Polish schools, spoke among themselves Polish and with their parents, Yiddish. There were several Jewish organisations, Zionist and non-Zionist, religious and non-religious... There was also a small group of Bund supporters, who were anti-Zionists and proclaimed solidarity with the non-Jewish Socialist Workers Party. With the rise of nationalism and anti-Semitism in the thirties in Poland, Zionist organisations grew in strength.[62]

Antisemitism in Poland at a political, state and popular level intensified in the years immediately before the war, fuelled by intense nationalism and by the localised impact of the global economic depression. Violence and increased discrimination led to a steadily impoverished and brutalised Jewish community. In 1936 five Jews were murdered in the Jedrzejow's neighbouring village, Stawy.[63] Many sought to emigrate but were victims of the racialised restrictionism of the Western world which saw Polish Jews as the least desirable immigrants. Palestine was one place of significant settlement, but its doors were effectively closed in the late 1930s by the British authorities. Nevertheless, Polish Jewish religious and cultural life continued in the face of adversity. As Alec recalled, 'Although there was a certain amount of poverty in Magnuszew, there was also a great amount of laughter and happiness.'[64] Undoubtedly, the growth of native antisemitic fascist movements and their influence in governmental circles, alongside hundreds of assaults and pogroms on a national level, made life for Polish Jewry extremely uncomfortable, undermining those liberals and socialists who believed that full integration into Polish society was possible. But for all this tension, discrimination and violence, it remained that Poles – Jewish and non-Jewish – were part of the same society. On an everyday basis, Jews and non-Jews were in regular contact at school, in the market place and even in the home.[65]

The horrors of the Second World War, however, were to place immense strain on the complex and dynamic nature of relations between Jews and non-Jews in Poland. Although there were important exceptions, the killing of three million non-Jewish Poles (10 per cent of the pre-war population), the fear of persecution, and the poverty of Poland under the Nazi onslaught generally increased antipathy and indifference towards the Jews. Hatred of the Germans was rarely enough to bring together the (unequal) victims of the Third Reich either at the time or in subsequent battles over memory.[66]

In Jedrzejow, thousands of refugees from western Poland filled Richard Stern's 'little town to capacity. These were followed by German armoured units pushing forward, to the remaining, still unoccupied, parts of the country. People were frightened to go out into the street; shops were closed, normal life ceased'. Jews were banned from public places and some individuals were rounded up and shot in the market place.[67] The splitting of Poland between Germany and the Soviet Union later in September 1939, led to further restrictions on the local Jewish community with young men forced into labour camps far away from the town:

> This was a signal for many to make their way to Eastern Poland which by now was under Soviet rule. In our innocence we believed that our Eastern neighbour was a haven of peace and freedom and it was natural to try to run away to that country.

Reaching Cracow, Richard and other young Jews tried to reach Sanok on the new border between Poland and the Soviet Union. After being arrested by the SS, they were released and paid a local farmer to take them across the River San and 'what we thought would be the promised land'. But their joy was shortlived: his group was arrested shortly after entering Soviet territory. It was the beginning of an imprisonment that lasted several years and resulted, for thousands, in death in the Siberian labour camps.[68] Nevertheless, the majority of Polish Jews surviving the war were those who had escaped to the Soviet Union in 1939 or in 1941. Of the 400,000 Jews managing to cross the border, some 250,000 were still alive at the end of the war. The number who survived in Poland was far smaller. Exact figures are uncertain, reflecting the sheer chaos of Poland in 1945, the massive flux of refugee movements and the hidden and marginal nature of the tiny Jewish remnant. Estimates of survivors who were hidden or who survived the concentration camps range from 40,000 to 100,000. The number of Jews hidden by non-Jews in Poland is also unknown.[69]

In Jedrzejow a ghetto was established in spring 1940. Jews of the vicinity were added to it, doubling the numbers, so that by the summer of 1942 some 6,000 people were crammed into its confines. In September 1942 all of the ghetto with the exception of 200 men were deported to Treblinka. The 200 were put into a work camp in the ghetto but were murdered in February 1943. Members of Richard Stern's family – his mother, three sisters, one brother, brother-in-law and two nieces – were part of a transport which reached Treblinka in September 1942. All were murdered. Another brother died in Auschwitz after spending two years in Theresienstadt.[70]

Survival for Jews in Poland depended ultimately on luck. Physical and mental strength and tenacity were important prerequisites, but they were far from sufficient to withstand the Nazis' determination to kill all Jews. The Jews of Poland were, in essence, exposed without any real support from outside sources. They were impoverished, essentially without arms and subject to the full force of Nazi racialism. In such circumstances, surviving five years of brutality was the exception and not the norm as illustrated by the experiences of Alec Ward. His family moved from the ghetto in Magnuszew to the larger one in Kozenice enduring increased poverty and persecution.

Looking after his younger brother, he escaped into the surrounding countryside but they were found by the SS. In the resulting 'selection', the Nazis

> took my little brother and some elderly men whom they considered unfit for slave labour and shot them. This was an extremely painful and unforgettable blow to me and was in a way more tragic to me than leaving my dear family.

Alec was subsequently sent to various slave labour camps in the Radom district. In Werc C camp in Skarzysko Kamienna, Alex spent two 'most unforgettable and brutal years'. Still vivid in his memory were

> the hangings of prisoners, the selections, the dead bodies lying at the barbed wire fences early in the morning of Jewish prisoners who tried desperately to escape during the night and were shot. The painful hunger and malnutrition. The beatings. The man who cried every time he saw me as I reminded him of his young son who perished at the hands of the Nazis.

He also recalls the support offered by fellow prisoners which he believed saved his life.[71]

Surviving Werc C camp, he was transferred to a less horrific one – Rakow in Chestochowa. From there he was moved to Germany and Buchenwald concentration camp where he became a slave labourer in the nearby town of Weimar. A further transfer followed to the concentration camp at Flossberg where he worked in an ammunition factory and again survived against all odds. The final stage in his war of survival was the horrendous 'death march' in which hundreds of thousands of Jewish survivors of the camps perished. Alec was placed on a cattle truck taking him from Flossberg to Mauthausen concentration camp in Austria:

> The journey took 15 days with hardly any food or water. Many prisoners perished on the way... [M]any more prisoners died marching up to the camp which was built in Alpine mountains with the purpose of exposing prisoners to extremes of temperatures... Those of us who reached Mauthausan concentration camp alive went through further torture and degradation. They took our clothes away from us on arrival and we were left naked until we were liberated by the American forces on 5th May 1945.[72]

Alec was taken to recuperate by the Americans to Regensburg in Bavaria and in October 1945 flown to the New Forest and to Wintershill Hall.

Only fragments of the stories involving the hiding of the Jews during the war have subsequently been recovered. Similarly, the full scale of armed Jewish resistance during the Holocaust is only beginning to be recognised, as is the sabotage carried out by many Jews and others in the slave labour camps.[73] The bravery of the men, women and children engaged in such activities, in addition to the ghetto fighters and concentration camp revolts, has to be judged by the enormity of their task. With limited resources and the support of only a few non-Jews, theirs was 'the war of the doomed'. For the ghetto fighters and those in the camps (if less so the Jewish partisans), armed resistance was followed by almost certain death. But for all the efforts of the Jews themselves and those who were sympathetic to their cause, the story of Polish Jewry during the war was one of destruction. As Christopher Browning has so clearly shown, the most vicious period of the genocide was the 11 months between mid-March 1942 and mid-February 1943 when roughly half the Jewish victims were killed, largely in the death camps of Poland (Chelmno, Belzec, Treblinka, Sobibor and later Auschwitz and Majdanek). Browning adds that:

> The center of gravity of mass murder was Poland, where in March 1942, despite two and a half years of terrible hardship, deprivation and persecution, every major Jewish community was still intact; eleven months later, only remnants of Polish Jewry survived in a few rump ghettos and labor camps.[74]

One of the largest surviving concentrations of Jews in Poland was in the industrial city of Lodz, the second ghetto to be created by the Nazi regime in February/March 1940. In the summer of 1940 its population was over 160,000, declining by 12,000 a year later and down to 70,000 by the end of 1942. The Lodz ghetto was the last to survive. The strategy of its controversial leader, Chaim Rumkowski, was to produce goods, particularly clothing, for the Germans and, from 1942, to allow the less productive to be deported. This continued until the approaching Soviet army in summer 1944 pushed the Nazis to liquidate the ghetto, deporting most of the survivors to Auschwitz. Karl Kleiman, who later recuperated at Wintershill Hall, was one of those deported to Auschwitz along with his sister in 1944.[75] Karl, born in 1926, came from an orthodox Jewish family. His father worked in a textile factory and was involved with a small stiebel, or small informal religious community. His parents, two brothers and two sisters lived in a block of flats which they rented in a mixed part of Lodz but their settled life was shattered in the first months of the war. Following the German invasion Jews were forced to wear the yellow star and they were moved from their apartment to the ghetto early in 1940, living in one room in a freezing house.[76]

Perec Zylberberg, born in 1924, was also brought up in Lodz. Like Karl, Perec was brought to Britain in 1945 and recuperated in Hampshire. For him, the start of the war and ghettoisation 'abruptly put an end to childhood, laughter and play':

> To have been a young Jew in pre-war Poland wasn't easy nor very benign [though there] were heights of idealistic and meaningful days... But to find yourself prisoner in your own town was so new and such a degrading experience that it left us all gasping for air.[77]

Karl Kleiman's father was one of the first victims of the poverty of the ghetto, dying in 1940. His mother also became ill, although she lived until 1943. At first, there was, in spite of the immense over-crowding and shortage of goods, a semblance of ordinary life. Some education continued – Karl was part of a Zionist camp in the ghetto where children were looked after – and there were also cultural and religious activities. Plays and concerts took place though these ceased 'when people were starving'. Perec Zylberberg, whose family were prominent members of the Jewish Socialist Party, the Bund, remembers other forms of everyday resistance:

> Although a terrible place of confinement and suffering, the ghetto did not forget the real values of humanity. Amongst the [Bundist] group that I belonged to, we were among the forerunners in the quest for keeping and strengthening our morale and ethical commitments to each other and society at large.

By 1942, however, Perec paints a very different picture of ghetto life: 'With great difficulty did we trudge along the arduous ghetto road ... Sometimes it was an hour-to-hour struggle [yet] somehow the Bund, with its optimistic approach, gave me the *raison d'être* for carrying on'. Two more years of misery in the ghetto was to remove any sense of hope. When in March 1944 Perec was deported to a labour camp, four and a half years of war and ghetto imprisonment had taken their toll: 'I was too numb to take in the significance of the event. I suppose I went into a self-protecting shell of nothingness'.

Such changes in the Lodz ghetto are recalled by Karl Kleiman in relation to the funerals of his mother and father. His father was buried with dignity by fellow members of his stiebel whereas his mother did not even have a proper Jewish funeral. Karl remembers having to give up some of his bread ration to pay someone to bury her. One of Karl's brothers died of TB, the other was taken for forced labour and his elder sister had reached Russia, leaving Karl, aged 15, in charge of his younger sister. He survived by working in the wood factory whilst his sister made straw shoes. In a state of semi-starvation their names were placed on the list for deportation, being told that they were going to a place where their labour was required. They had little choice as they had now lost their right to rations.[78]

The distance from Lodz to Auschwitz was not a long one but it took over a day travelling in a cattle truck without water, food or toilet facilities. Unlike his sister, Karl survived the selection. Shaved and stripped naked, he soon realised that he had entered a world of its own:

> It was so different from the ghetto. [There] things were bad – we were all like walking corpses – but you didn't have that fear that you had in Auschwitz. Every minute of the day fear was all around you. It never left you.

Karl was in Auschwitz for less than two weeks and was then selected to leave the camp by train for a work camp in Germany. In a state of almost total physical collapse, he was liberated by American forces in Dachau at the start of May 1945, the only survivor of his immediate family. By the end of the war, the Nazis had not only destroyed the small town shtetls but also the vibrant pre-war Jewish culture of the large Polish cities such as Lodz, Kracow and Warsaw. The enormity of their crime was hard even for those who had survived and witnessed the worst of Nazi barbarism to take in. As Perec

Zylberberg, liberated from Theresienstadt after surviving work camps, Buchenwald and the death marches, thought to himself:

> Where is my place? What became of the whole world that I knew and felt part of?... Where is my family? What kind of life is there, where we lived before? Where is one to go?[79]

LOCAL KNOWLEDGE OF THE 'FINAL SOLUTION'

By late autumn 1941 *all* Jews encountered by the Germans in Soviet terrorities were killed. At least two million Jews were murdered by 'ordinary' Germans, Lithuanians, Ukrainians and others at the closest of ranges.[80] The archaeologist Richard Wright was employed in 1990 and 1991 by the Australian Special Investigations Unit which had commenced war crimes proceedings against two men who had emigrated from the Ukraine after 1945. In Serniki, one of the sites of mass murder connected to the accused, in a grave 40 metres long and five metres wide, Wright's team uncovered the remains of over 500 bodies:

> An awful scene unfolded. As the eyewitnesses had said, they were mostly women and children. The men were old men. They had been herded down a ramp into the grave. One lot had gone to the left and been shot while lying down within the grave; the others had gone to the right. The majority had entry and exit wounds of bullets in their skulls. Some of them had been clubbed.[81]

Such mass murders were reported in the West late in 1941 although mainly within the minority press such as the *Jewish Chronicle*. Detailed accounts of such killings passed on through Nazi communication lines were also intercepted by the decoders at the British intelligence information centre at Bletchley Park. This information was not relayed to the public but was retained by a small number of people at the top of the British military intelligence world. By the autumn of 1941, these reports were pieced together, revealing a pattern of total murder in areas of the Soviet Union taken over by the Nazis. Code breakers told British intelligence as early as September that:

> Whether all those executed as 'Jews' are indeed such is of course doubtful, but the figures are no less conclusive as evidence of a policy of savage intimidation, if not ultimate extermination.[82]

On a local level, it was not until December 1942 that detailed reports of the mass shootings were published, including special mention of the notorious events at Babi Yar when in two days at the end of September 1941 30,000 Jews were assembled in the Ukrainian city of Kiev and shot in a ravine of the neighbouring forest. According to a Soviet report published in the *Southern Daily Echo*, 'The massacre at Kiev and Dniepropetroysk will never be forgotten. During the first months of the occupation of these towns 60,000

Jews were exterminated'.[83] What, by the end of 1942 was part of collective memory in the areas of mass murder was anything but common knowledge in the democratic world. But from June 1942 a series of detailed accounts became available in the West, outlining the places and techniques of mass murder such as at Chelmno, suggesting that these were part of a *plan* to murder all the Jews of Europe. A group of campaigners, inside and outside the Jewish community, emerged, some of whom had been involved in the refugee movement before the war, highlighting the plight of European Jewry and demanding that action should be taken by the Allied governments to help those still alive. By focusing on local responses to news of the 'Final Solution' in the second half of 1942 and first half of 1943, the difficulties faced by these campaigners is put into sharp focus.[84]

Ronald Hayman grew up in Bournemouth's major Jewish hotel. He had his barmitzvah in the town during 1942, the year when the 'Final Solution' was first reported in Britain. His autobiography, *Secrets*, provides a revealing account of how for British Jews particularly, the fate of European Jewry was recognised but never confronted. His war narrative – with its 'digging for victory' campaign, black-out curtains, Spitfires and Hurricanes, air raids, and pieces of shrapnel – is remarkable only for its ordinariness. There was, however, the additional worry of what would happen if the Nazis crossed the English channel: 'If Hitler was gassing the Jews in Germany, he'd gas us if he invaded England'.[85]

Generally British Jews became remote from the fate of their European brothers and sisters. The end of the war was greeted with celebration and relief rather than mourning as Hayman's *Secrets* neatly encapsulates:

> The summer [of 1945] was full of good news. Hitler's suicide in the bunker. My success in the scholarship exam. Churchill's demands for unconditional surrender...

Fears over invasion and SS troops 'round[ing] up the [Bournemouth] congregation for gassing' were replaced by belief that 'God was on our side'.[86] After the war and a degree at Cambridge, Hayman was determined to move outside the world he was familiar with – Cambridge and Bournemouth – where it would be 'impossible to pretend the war hadn't happened'. Yet rather than full amnesia, it was the *total* nature of the Second World War which remained beyond the grasp of many in British society. Returning to 1942, although there were reports of the gassing of Polish Jewry, it is unlikely that such details would have become part of the everyday consciousness of the Hayman family – a post-war trope has been unconsciously added. Hayman's comments, however, limiting the extermination to *German* Jewry, were not untypical inside and outside the Jewish community.[87]

When the western concentration camps were liberated in spring 1945, the possibility of different types of camps in *eastern* Europe were ignored or discounted. The news that reached the West in the summer of 1942 related to the Jews of Poland rather than Germany. Its reporting was patchy, and the information it conveyed – that the Nazis were intent on murdering all Jews – astonishing. The problems of assimilating this news were intensified, however, by the *pre-war* prism through which atrocity stories relating to Jews had been viewed. Apart from an element of doubt, a specific connection was made between Nazi persecution and the Jews of Greater Germany. Early in the war the *Zionist Review* commented that whilst people might have some idea that the Jews in Poland were suffering, it was questionable 'whether one in a hundred here realises the full nature of the tragedy'. After the brief flurry of reporting linked to the Lublin reservation in late 1939 and early 1940, the fate of east European Jewry in the war was ignored. By 1942, the heart of the Holocaust, few in Britain realised that it was *Polish* Jewry that was now the major focus of Nazi racialism.[88]

In June 1942, the Jewish Labour Bund in Warsaw smuggled out a detailed report of the gassings in mobile vans at Chelmno. The report, publicised by the British section of the World Jewish Congress (WJC), stressed that 700,000 Polish Jews had already been murdered, warning that the Nazis were intent on killing all Eurpean Jews. The MP Sidney Silverman suggested that he 'felt that there had been something like a conspiracy of silence in the Press about this tragic situation'.[89] The Bund report, however, was given prominence, 'the first time that "the greatest pogrom" … has been brought to the notice of the public in this country in such a comprehensive manner'.[90] Locally, reporting was uneven. Newspapers giving it coverage ranged from the *Aberdeen Press and Journal* to the *Sussex Daily News*. In total, 19 papers with a primarily regional circulation gave it prominence. But with the exception of the *Manchester Guardian* – whose importance straddled across the local and national into the international arena – no newspaper outside the Jewish press in Britain gave sustained coverage to the Holocaust during the war.[91] Press coverage of European Jewry's fate was typified by reporting that was marked by brevity, vagueness, lack of comment and infrequency. Many people still relied heavily on the local press for their knowledge of global as well as national and regional news. With the shortage of newsprint, local papers in particular suffered from diminishing space and their overall quality deteriorated during the war. It is not surprising, given the extent and nature of the coverage, that locally only a few came to terms with the scale of the Jewish disaster. In spring 1945 the *Portsmouth Evening News* commented on its reaction to the revelation from the liberated concentration camps. Atrocity stories during the war 'made horrible reading … but too many of us could not dissociate them from propaganda, and all the time we hoped they were not true. Now we know they were'.[92]

At the time the Bund report was publicised, the *Southern Daily Echo* carried the headline 'Southampton Woman's Experience of Nazi Terrorism'. The story related to an individual who had been bombed out of six houses during the air raids which had devastated the city since autumn 1940. Such sensitive reporting of the local domestic situation went alongside less frequent and inaccurate coverage of the Nazis' extermination programme on the continent. For example, both the Southampton and Portsmouth daily papers ran a Soviet news agency report about 'Hitler's "Camp of Death"' relating to work camps for children in Poland, ending with the comment that 'They are part of Hitler's monstrous plan to exterminate the Czech, Polish and Yugoslav peoples'.[93] The Soviet Union's refusal to label victims of Nazism other than through national categories remained unqueried in national and local coverage of atrocities in the British press; one factor amongst many delaying comprehension that a *specific* Jewish tragedy had occurred. Nevertheless, other reports from Poland were published locally in autumn 1942 which did emphasise Jewish suffering if still understating the scale of the losses. In November 1942 the *Portsmouth Evening News* ran a brief front page story:

HORRORS IN POLAND: Mass Killing

More ruthless methods are being used in Poland to give affect to an order by Himmler that half the Jewish population must be exterminated by the end of the year… Victims are dragged out of houses or seized in the streets. Old people and cripples are taken to the cemetery and shot. The remainder are packed into goods trucks at the rate of 150 to a truck normally intended for 40… Half the people arrive dead. Those surviving are sent to special camps and mass-murdered. Children and babies are not spared. By the end of September 250,000 Jews had been eliminated.

By this point, the figure quoted represented only ten per cent of the total Jewish victims. Two weeks later, the *Southern Daily Echo* reproduced a statement from the Soviet Information Bureau indicating that hundreds of thousands of Jews from Poland and other Nazi occupied countries had been sent to concentration camps. It added that 'Nevertheless, there are only 40,000 Jews left alive in the camps in Poland'.[94] Yet the mathematical and geographical implications of this and other reports were rarely grasped. Prominence was also given during the autumn of 1942 to the discriminatory measures taken by the Vichy government in France against the Jews.[95] It led to the murder of some 80,000 Jews, many of them of foreign birth, in Auschwitz, a result not only of the the Nazis' exterminatory antisemitism, but also the Vichy regime's racism which built upon the xenophobia and anti-refugee sentiment of the pre-war years.[96] Yet rather than aiding comprehension of the enormity of the Jewish plight in Europe, reports on the Jews of France added to the general confusion in Britain concerning where the persecution was taking place and whether the Jews' fate was discrimination or extermination.

But in December 1942 some clarification was provided when the Allied governments released a declaration about the extermination of European Jewry. The British government somewhat reluctantly agreed to the statement which was read out in the House of Commons by the Foreign Secretary, Anthony Eden:

The German authorities, not content with denying to persons of Jewish race in all the territories over which their barbarous rule has been extended the most elementary human rights, are now carrying into effect Hitler's oft repeated intention to exterminate the Jewish people of Europe.... The number of victims of these bloody cruelties is reckoned in many hundreds of thousands of entirely innocent men, women and children.[97]

The declaration fell short of campaigners' desires as it refused to mention a *plan* of total extermination and it also understated the scale of murder. Most significant, however, was the refusal to consider any action that could help the victims directly. The Allied governments merely 're-affirm[ed] their solemn resolution to ensure that those responsible for these crimes shall not escape retribution'.[98]

In autumn 1942 the rescue of Jewish children in unoccupied southern France gave a focal point for campaigners in Britain. A Christian-Jewish delegation went to see the Home Secretary, Herbert Morrison, in September 1942 asking him to accept these children before they were deported to Poland. Morrison reported the discussions in detail to the War Cabinet:

There are many foreign persons, both Jews and others ... who are anxious to come to this country, and the general policy has been not to admit during the war additional refugees to the United Kingdom unless in some quite rare and exceptional cases it can be shown that the admission of the refugee will be directly advantageous to our war effort... [W]e already have a very large body of refugees here and not all sections of public opinion are enthusiastic about their presence; pressure on accommodation ... steadily increases and if we get beyond a point in the admission of foreign refugees we may stir up an unpleasant degree of anti-semitism (of which there is a fair amount just below the surface) and that would be bad for the country and the Jewish community.[99]

When, in November 1942, the Germans occupied southern France, the rescue of the children became impossible until liberation had occurred. Nevertheless, the discussions revealed the increasing insecurity in government, and particularly Home Office circles, concerning Jewish refugees. In a policy that was to continue after the war, the government ruled out anything other than a token entry of Jews, and even then only on a temporary basis, because of their fears of provoking anti-alienism. Campaigners were thus anxious to mobilise ordinary people to show their enthusiasm and commitment to measures that could save Jewish lives, thus countering Morrison's analysis of public opinion.[100]

Their greatest problem was to involve people when the government was determined not to commit itself to helping. The sense of despair and hopelessness was highlighted in a day of mourning, fasting and prayer held in Portsmouth and Southsea Synagogue in December 1942 'for the victims of the massacres in Nazi-occupied lands' which saw the solution in divine intervention. Jewry, argued the local rabbi, must take consolation:

that when things appeared blackest for the Jews they seemed to unleash their powers, and by their efforts now they could save the Jewish nation from extinction. 'Our present enemies, the Germans, like the Egyptians, will be swept away from the face of history by the tide of time in consequence of their own wickedness', the Rabbi said. 'We shall live to promote the principles of justice, truth, and liberty among nations that have not yet learned these doctrines in the course of 20 centuries.'[101]

The Allied Declaration stimulated a fresh impulse amongst the campaigners, most famously in the case of Victor Gollancz, the British Jewish publisher, and Eleanor Rathbone. Both wrote pamphlets achieving mass circulation demanding action to save the Jews. Gollancz was particularly aware of the need to connect the fate of Jews in 'remote' places on the continent to the everyday geography of Britain at war: 'Does a little child in Warsaw suffer less and, God forgive us, *fear* less than a child in London, or Leeds, or whatever your town or village may be?' Playing on the concept of home, he concluded by enlisting the British landscape as a further reason why action should be taken:

> Amid the peace, today, of the Berkshire countryside, it is difficult not to feel that there is something about Britain ... that specially fits her to play a most notable part in rebuilding our shattered world.[102]

Rathbone attempted to debunk the statement of the Home Secretary in March 1943 that 'We have already a very fine record and have done more for Refugees than any other Country', instead agreeing with the statement of John Hope Simpson that 'Great Britain has ceased to be a country of asylum'. Rathbone, in the Commons, added that refugees since September 1939 were brought in 'because we or our Allies needed them badly for the war effort. They cannot therefore be claimed as proofs of our generosity'. More positively, however, she concluded that 'the British conscience is not an extinct volcano'.[103]

Another campaigner was the Reverend Dr James Parkes, an independent and radical Church of England minister who had devoted his career since the late 1920s to combating antisemitism and helping Jewish victims of Nazi persecution.[104] In January 1943 Parkes wrote an (unpublished) article outlining in remarkable detail the development of the Nazis' extermination programme emphasising that

> HITLER WAS NOT ONLY THREATENING BUT ACTUALLY CARRYING OUT THE POLICY OF DESTROYING THE WHOLE JEWISH POPULATION WITHIN HIS POWER. Six million human beings, from infants in arms to old men and women, were to be deliberately killed in cold blood.

To Parkes, the Allied Declaration was only the first step. At stake now was not only the literal survival of the Jewish people but also the reputation of the liberal world:

It is said that if we offered unlimited asylum in our own country or the territories we control, it might lead to a dangerous increase of antisemitism. It is even said – as though the idea should terrify instead of rejoicing us – that Hitler might take us at our word, and send us all the Jews still alive in Europe, several million of them.

There was, he believed,

> *only one answer for men who still believe there is any nobility in the cause for which we are fighting*: WE WILL RECEIVE THEM. AND IF THERE REALLY BE THREE MILLION OF THEM WE WILL THANK GOD THAT WE HAVE BEEN ABLE TO SAVE SO MANY FROM HITLER'S CLUTCHES… It is only in the spirit that we desire to save ALL whom we can reach that we can even undertake action that will save any… Men *can* escape from Europe, even if it be only in small numbers.

Finally, Parkes, following the example of other activists, outlined what action should be followed by the British government, including: taking refugees who were in Spain and Portugal so that these countries could be encouraged to take others; looking after Jews reaching Turkish territory and the neutral countries of Sweden and Switzerland; putting pressure on the governments of Nazi satellite countries 'whose certainty of Nazi victory cannot be as strong as once it was'; and making sure that the Vatican and the United Nations take the fate of the Jews seriously. Parkes, like Gollancz and Rathbone, wanted ordinary people in Britain to take responsibility:

> EVERY INDIVIDUAL CAN DO HIS PART IN HELPING TO REALISE THESE PLANS … WRITE TO YOUR MP. IF YOU HAVE A PULPIT, SPEAK FROM IT; IF YOU CAN CALL A MEETING, DO SO. WHEREVER YOU HAVE INFLUENCE USE IT. OUR HONOUR AND SINCERITY ARE AT STAKE AS MUCH AS THE LIVES OF MILLIONS OF THE JEWISH PEOPLE.[105]

Many people did take such action and enough pressure was maintained in the first months of 1943 to persuade the British government to force its even more hesitant American counterparts to call an inter-governmental conference on the refugee crisis.[106] Petitions and protest meetings were held in early 1943 on behalf of European Jewry, but once the initial outcry had died down, the British government took a more relaxed attitude. The conference on refugees, partly because of American procrastination, was delayed until mid-April 1943. It was held on the island of Bermuda, away from activist groups and the world's press.[107] Indeed, public discussion of the Bermuda conference and knowledge of its contents did not occur until 19 May 1943 when the only major debate in the House of Commons on refugees during the war took place. Campaigners were disappointed – they were told that although some limited relaxation of restrictions would be considered and the Intergovernmental Committee on Refugees, created after the earlier Evian conference, revived, nothing would be done to interfere with the war effort.

They responded that:

> The duty of rescuing the Jews from Hitler's Europe ... is that of saving people specifically condemned to murder at the hands of the Nazis who have decreed their annihilation for no reason other than their Jewish race and faith. If nothing is done now, the Jews will no longer be alive to be rescued by the defeat of Hitler.[108]

Thereafter, individuals such as Rathbone and Parkes became very bitter and disappointed in their government. Never again during the war would there be such public interest and knowledge of European Jewry's fate.

Taking Hampshire as a local case study, there was an absence of response to the Jewish catastrophe which rather than being particularly unusual, indicated the limitations of demands for rescue and relief across Britain as a whole. For example, all bar one of the MPs in the Hampshire region approached by the Jewish campaigner Solomon Schonfeld refused to sign his parliamentary motion in February 1943 demanding help and temporary asylum. The exception was William Craven-Ellis, Independent MP for Southampton.[109] All the other MPs represented deeply Conservative constituencies and it is possible that their political affiliation affected their decision refusing to pressurise the government. While there were some Conservative MPs who were sympathetic to the cause of Jewish refugees, the most profound hostility came from the Conservative backbenches.[110] In February 1940, a group of Conservatives wrote to the Prime Minister warning against naturalising refugees because there were already too many Jews in Britain and 'most of us feel that we would rather hand down to posterity a slowly denuding number of people of British stock than provide new material for increasing the stock of Jewish or Jew-British population'. Such anti-alienism was given a fresh impulse with demands for mass internment. In Aldershot, Conservative constituency women greeted with delight demands by their MP to intern all the refugees regardless of their background.[111]

Whether such anti-alienism made people unsympathetic to the fate of European Jewry, as Herbert Morrison was convinced, is far from clear. Yet the negative response of the Hampshire MPs, alongside the lack of activists within the county, and the absence, with the exception of the Portsmouth and Southsea and Bournemouth Synagogues days of mourning, of any public event specifically designed to show solidarity with European Jewry, requires explanation, especially so given the wealth of positive responses to refugees before the war. While the political outlook of the county as a whole cannot be ignored, this had not hindered earlier support. But the rural isolation of much of Hampshire, given the government's lack of encouragement, made it harder for ordinary people to feel they could do anything practical to help those so far away both geographically and experientially. Such powerlessness was in contrast, for example, to the child refugee movement before the war which had the backing of the state and a firm organisational structure enabling the most remote families and individuals to help. Moreover, the cities of

Portsmouth and Southampton had major problems of their own to confront and none of the local newspapers gave particular prominence or sustained coverage to the fate of the Jews.[112]

The case of the Turner family, which had been so involved in helping refugees before the war, provides a microcosm of how the energy of activists could dissipate in spite of the best of attentions. In her memoirs, Peggy Turner wrote of the blitz's impact on Southampton and its surrounding area: 'We could see the flames leaping into the sky, lighting up the destruction'. There were also fears of loved ones away in the forces and the losses throughout the war faced by local people: 'The world was falling apart'. Due to the pressures of the Home Front, and the measures taken against them, the Turners 'lost contact with our friends the refugees'. Peggy recalls seeing the images of the concentration camps in the spring of 1945 and connecting them to the relatives of those they had helped during the 1930s. By the end of the war, she writes: 'The systematic murder of millions had taken place and we did not know'.[113]

Quite simply, the act of imagination demanded by activists such as Rathbone, Gollancz and Parkes to connect ordinary lives in Britain to the extraordinary murder and brutality being carried out against equally ordinary people in Europe was made only rarely. Ultimately, however, the government, by giving so little encouragement to the campaigners, made their task almost impossible. In the last two years of the war, whilst Hitler's 'Final Solution' continued to mean the murder of millions more Jews, local knowledge became almost non-existent when, ironically, the methods of extermination and the general visibility of the genocide became clear for all wanting to be informed. The abyss was most strikingly illustrated in the spring and summer of 1944 when Hungarian Jewry was openly deported and then exterminated.

THE FINAL STAGES OF THE HOLOCAUST

When the Germans invaded Hungary in spring 1944, its Jewish population was roughly 750,000. Ghettoisation, which began in April 1944, and the first Hungarian deportations to Auschwitz the following month, were carried out at enormous speed, organised by Eichmann at his most terrifyingly efficient. In summer 1944, the gas chambers of Auschwitz were working at full capacity. Some 445,000 Hungarian Jews were sent to Auschwitz, three-quarters being gassed on arrival. Of the 1.1 million Jews who perished in Auschwitz, the largest national grouping were the Hungarians, the last major Jewish community to be consumed by the Nazi genocidal machine. Between 500–600,000 Hungarian Jews were murdered in the war, the vast majority between May and September 1944.[114]

In Britain little press attention was given to their fate and public protests were minimal. Concern that was articulated to the government by local campaigners was given short shrift. A resolution following a public meeting in Leicester in April 1944, demanding that the British government do everything in its power to help the Jews, was responded to by one senior Foreign Office official that 'It seems hardly necessary to enter [it]. We get any amount of the same thing'.[115] Even activists in the National Committee for Rescue from Nazi Terror, formed by Eleanor Rathbone, became out of touch with the reality of the Jewish plight. The treasurer of the National Committee, the Liberal MP for North Cumberland, Wilfred Roberts, addressed the Southampton United Christian Council in July 1944 by when the majority of Hungarian Jews had been deported and four to five million Jews had been murdered. His speech provided a misleading and out of date account of the contemporary situation:

> The Nazis had always persecuted the Jews... First they took the children and then they held the able-bodied and made them work for them until some of them even died. Some of the occupied countries ... such as Hungary and Romania, were asylums for the Jews.[116]

Roberts' half-hearted plea that 'He felt that they ought to be quite sure that there was nothing left undone that could be done for them' stands in contrast to the contemporary efforts of the War Refugee Board (WRB) in the USA, formed by Roosevelt in January 1944 to deal explicitly with saving Jewish lives in Europe. As the WRB noted in May-June 1944:

> While assurances of 'warmest support and sympathy' have not been lacking, we have received little active cooperation to date from the British in connection with refugee rescue and relief...

The comments of Herbert Morrison on 1 July 1944 confirmed the WRB's fears. Responding to appeals to save Hungarian Jews, he made it clear that it was 'essential that we should do nothing at all which involves the risk that the further reception of refugees here might be the ultimate outcome'.[117]

It was at this point that the life of Vera Karoly, born in 1931, was transformed. The distance between her devastating year in the Holocaust, which stole her childhood and adolescence and those in her adopted home (she later settled in Hampshire) has never been bridged.[118] Vera was born into an affluent Jewish family of Czech origin in the small Hungarian town of Schahi. Her mother committed suicide shortly afterwards and she was brought up by a stern governess: 'Otherwise my life was uneventful, that is until the German army marched into Hungary in 1944':

> Soon after the Germans entered my hometown, my family, along with all Jewish families, were moved to a ghetto. Life in that ghetto was terrible. Overnight our previous comfortable lifestyle was transformed into a life of scarcity and oppression... Then one day the streets of the ghetto were invaded by what appeared to me thousands of German soldiers. They went in twos and threes to all the homes in the ghetto. They came to our home. I shall never forget their knocking on the door. So menacing, so insistent. They had come for my father... Soon what was left was the sight of the bewildered women and children, fearful at being left abandoned to the nightmarish life of the ghetto.

But not for long. A few days later it was the turn of the women and children. Almost in a state of trance the pathetic remnant of the ghetto were marched off to the railway station. 120 people to a wagon we were packed into trains waiting for us at the station...

Surviving the journey and the initial selection at Auschwitz (a woman told her to claim she was eighteen rather than thirteen):

From the moment I entered the concentration camp, virtually until my liberation, I retreated psychologically into myself. Something deeply buried within me made me distance myself as much as I could from what was happening around me ... I lived from one day to the next in a kind of nightmarish cocoon which surrounded me from all sides. I was lucky because I spoke fluent German, and so I was useful to the camp administration as an interpreter.

Towards the end of the war, Vera was moved to a series of camps and then forced on a death march, surviving freezing conditions with no food or drink: 'The withdrawal from my environment which had helped me survive the torments I was exposed to in the concentration camp, now really helped me pull through'. Many around her died of exhaustion or were shot but 'at long last, we reached Bergen Belsen concentration camp' where:

I spent the remainder of the war, fighting with starvation and disease. From the moment I arrived there to the camp's liberation, I never overcame the mixture of revulsion which I felt for the ever present pile of corpses at the camp. All the inmates were so infeebled and weak that no one had the strength necessary to carry them away.[119]

It was the indescribable sight and smell of Bergen Belsen in April 1945 that provided a revived connection between the European Jewish catastrophe and ordinary people in the democracies as well as a boundless gap of comprehension. For those in Bergen Belsen, the experience of liberation varied immensely. For many, rather than a moment of release, their physical and mental state was such that it had little initial meaning. Magda Bloom was a year younger than Vera Karoly, also coming from a rural Hungarian Jewish background. She came to Britain in the autumn of 1945 as part of the Children from the Concentration Camps scheme, staying initially at Wintershill Hall before eventually settling in Birmingham. Her childhood was happy on the family farm where 'she and her brother lived in idyllic surroundings' but in 1944

Magda's father, who had been serving in the Hungarian army and had in the past been decorated for conspicuous bravery, was sent with his fellow Jewish soldiers to a labour camp. Their rifles were taken away and they were ordered to pick up mines in front of the German army. Before long they heard he was dead. Magda, her mother and brother were driven from their farm, first into a ghetto, and thence by cattle truck to Auschwitz. On her thirteenth birthday, Magda's brother perished in the gas chambers.[120]

In a similar pattern to Vera Karoly, but still with her mother, Magda was forced to Bergen Belsen. On 15 April 1945 the camp was liberated by the British army, but 'Magda hardly cared. The previous night her mother had died, and as the British tanks rolled down the street she had been taken from the barracks'. The idea of liberation providing a neat and satisfactory ending to the Holocaust is rarely matched by the testimony of the survivors. Karl Kleiman, liberated in Dachau by the Americans, remembers soldiers asking the former inmates if they wanted to watch the summary execution of their S.S. tormentors. They did not respond: 'We weren't strong enough to get up'.[121]

What remains unacknowledged is the impact on the liberators themselves. Indeed, many have never recovered from what they experienced. Vera Karoly remembered

> looking at the British soldiers who had come to liberate us. That look of utter horror in their eyes I shall never forget. It was obvious to me that they could hardly tell the difference between the piles of corpses lying there in the camp and the emaciated survivors ...

Nevertheless, bonds of understanding could develop between the liberators and the liberated,[122] including the remarkable marriage between a Southampton shipping company clerk and a young Jewish woman who had survived the Krakow ghetto, Plaszow slave labour camp, Auschwitz, the death marches and Belsen. They had met when he was involved as a British soldier in Belsen's liberation.[123]

The problem of incomprehension and unpreparedness for those who carried out the liberation was subtly communicated by Joy Trindles, then a 23-year-old nursing sister. A veteran of nursing on the Home Front and then France and Belgium, she entered Germany and Belsen. Joy Trindles spent nine weeks in the makeshift hospital created in Belsen after its liberation by the British forces and medical workers. After a career in nursing and teaching, she retired to Chandlers Ford on the outskirts of Eastleigh. Her poem, 'Until Belsen', provides a narrative juxtaposing the 'normal' horrors of life on the Home and western front with the other, secret contemporaneous world of the Holocaust:

We thought we had seen it all.
The London Blitz, bombs, fires, headless corpses,
Screaming children: Yankee Doodle Dandy!
We thought we had seen it all...
Then France.
Day followed night and then another day
Of mangled broken boys.
Irish, Welsh and Scots
Jerries, Poles and French –
They cried in many tongues as needles long and sharp
Advanced

Their blood ran very red and so they died.
We thought we had seen it all…

Until Belsen
There are no words to speak.
We hid within our souls, deep and silent…
We had seen it all.[124]

Gordon Privett, from Portsmouth, was a sergeant with the 113 Light Ack Ack (Anti-Aircraft) Regiment involved in the early stages of Belsen's liberation. Fifty years later he reflected that 'When I came out of the service I couldn't settle, I fell out with my mother and father over the family business, and thinking about it now, Belsen probably had something to do with it'.[125] In Britain itself, the revelations from the concentration camps were met with immense anger and hatred towards the Germans.[126] It is not surprising that the specificity of Nazi crimes would be lost at this particular moment. First, little attention was given to the victims of the Nazis when the western concentration camps were liberated. Utilising a Reuters report, for example, the *Southern Daily Echo* quoted a British major who stated that at Belsen 'Norwegians seemed to be treated best and Dutch worst'. That the majority of those who had recently died in Belsen or who were still alive were Jewish bypassed most observers. Second, differences between the western concentration camps and eastern death camps were obscured. In local Hampshire papers as more generally in the British press, Buchenwald, Belsen and Dachau were all labelled as the worst in the Nazi concentration camp system even though none had functioned as extermination centres.[127] The unique function and history of Belsen was lost as it came to represent, particularly for the British public, *all* Nazi camps.

The director of Wintershill Hall, Dr Friedmann, told Mollie Panter-Downes:

> You know, it's funny, the English press has called all these children who have come over here Belsen children, but many have never been to that camp. Belsen and Buchenwald have taken all the limelight, but there were others far worse, far more horrible, which no one seems to know about.

Similarly, Perec Zylberberg, who had survived the Lodz ghetto, slave labour camps, Buchenwald and a death march to Theresienstadt, recalls reporters visiting the children at Windermere late in 1945: 'At this stage, there were not too many questions about the wartime experiences. The token assertion that we came from the concentration camps sufficed'. He adds that:

> Although we were all called survivors and definitely survivors we were, we were not at all alike in so many ways that one designation was not really embracing for all. We were from big towns, small towns, villages, different countries, different class levels, different cultures and [spoke] different languages.[128]

In such an atmosphere, it is not surprising that the individual needs of the children and other survivors in coming to terms with their specific losses were often forgotten.

SURVIVORS AND THE LOCAL WORLD

The legacy of individuals such as Herbert Morrison who regarded evidence of humanitarianism with contempt and set out to appease those with more unsavoury views on refugees lived well beyond the wartime coalition. Indeed, the post-war government not only did its best to keep out Jewish survivors of the Holocaust, but also considered ways of removing pre-war refugees, the benefactors of a once again forgotten commitment to asylum. Nevertheless, through the tenacity of the refugees themselves, as well as their political supporters, many stayed in Britain, eventually gaining naturalisation. Moreover, a small number succeeded in bringing over relatives who had somehow survived the war.

A Distressed Relatives scheme, aimed at the immediate family members of those coming to Britain during the 1930s, was implemented by the Home Office in 1945 but its restrictions were severe. Leading Home Office civil servants believed that:

> To admit for indefinite periods all 'relatives' *who have had a bad time in a camp* [our emphasis] – brothers, sisters, brothers-in-law, sisters-in-law, uncles, aunts, nephews, nieces, and in some cases their minor children – would involve a substantial addition to our alien population at a time when there is a shortage of housing, food and supplies generally. It is therefore inevitable that many of the applications must be refused.[129]

Those seeking entry had to prove they had no surviving relatives elsewhere and that they could support themselves or be guaranteed. Preference was given to those under 21 years of age so that criticisms that aliens were taking British jobs could be minimised. As a sympathetic Ministry of Labour official put it, criticising the Home Office, the numbers qualifying 'would be in hundreds rather than thousands'. Many of those let in had to lie about their age, their surviving family, and, most famously in the case of Miklos Hammer, even their name and identity. Perec Zylberberg comments that:

> As there were no normally functioning birth registration offices at the time, one could readily become anybody one could think of. I simply registered as PEREC ZYLBERBERG. But my age dropped almost six years.[130]

Once in Britain, Perec was elated to find that his sister, Esther, had survived the war and was now in Sweden. After a year of struggling against the government's regulations, he succeeded in bringing her to join him, but only through a foreign domestic worker's permit. Esther had only just finished recuperating in Sweden and working as a servant in Britain did not appeal. But as Perec stated, 'in a country with very little concern for postwar refugee problems, it [would have been] very difficult [otherwise to have got] any fast results'. Other female Holocaust survivors with relatives in Britain were forced to use this desperate method, continuing the tradition from the 1930s.[131]

In lip service to public pressure, a small scheme which had been proposed by the Jewish Refugee Committee (JRC), to allow up to 1,000 child survivors of the concentration camps to enter temporarily to recuperate, was accepted by the Home Office. As with the proposals put to the Cabinet in 1933 (and those made at Atlantic Park earlier), Jewish refugee organisations promised to cover all costs.[132] Eventually some 732 children, almost all Jewish, were found qualifying for the scheme – an indication of the narrowness of its restraints. Otto Schiff of the JRC visited Sir Alexander Maxwell, Permanent Under-Secretary at the Home Office, on 4 May 1945, putting forward a request from Leonard Montefiore 'for the temporary admission to this country of about 1,000 Jewish orphan children from the camps in Buchenwald and Belsen'. By August 1945, the JRC's secretary wrote to Maxwell limiting the scheme to 800 'for no other reason but that of finance'.[133] The initial restrictions to concentration camps in Germany is indicative of their notoriety in Britain but also the more general ignorance in 1945 of the Holocaust's geographical scope. Eventually the scheme was extended beyond Germany to incorporate other camps, particularly Theriesenstadt.[134]

An even greater problem was the refusal of Zionist leaders in the displaced persons camps to allow the children to go to anywhere but Palestine. Having been liberated from Dachau, Karl Kleiman was determined to go to Palestine: 'I didn't want to go to England'. Fed up of waiting, however, 'I said to myself and a few other boys: "Why not? Let's get away from here at least"'. Perec Zylberberg, as a Bundist, was less difficult to convince about the 'whispered rumour of a British option'.[135]

Schiff and Montefiore advanced arguments designed to convince the Home Office which they knew would be hesitant to accept more Jewish refugees. First, they stressed that a scheme was already in existence, the 'Young People from Occupied Countries', which had been initially designed to offer children from liberated Holland the chance to recuperate in Britain. Later extended to include children from France and Belgium, it brought up to 10,000 children to Britain before it came to an official close in June 1946. Schiff argued that a similar scheme, voluntarily funded, could be used for the children from the camps with an absolute assurance that their stay in Britain would be temporary. Second, according to Maxwell, Montefiore suggested that they

> should be brought to England not because there is no other means of providing for them ... but because he thinks it right that England should do something to show sympathy, and also because he thinks there is no better way of impressing on the British people the horrors of the concentration camps than by bringing some of the actual victims to this country.[136]

Initially, Maxwell suggested it would be better to help the children in Germany itself only to be convinced by Schiff and Anthony de Rothschild that this would be impracticable. It was Schiff's and de Rothschild's argument that France and the USA were helping and 'that it might not help the good reputation of Great Britain if we took no share' that proved decisive. Yielding reluctantly to their moral pressure, Maxwell wrote to the Home Secretary that he 'would like to have avoided any scheme for bringing more refugees into Britain, but obviously this proposal with reference to children will receive [a lot] of public sympathy'. Nevertheless, Maxwell laid down strict criteria: it ought not to be limited to Jewish children; it would depend on careful arrangements with regard to transport and screening the health of the children; and, lastly, finding suitable accommodation in Britain. Maxwell stated that if money to fund the operation was found and all these conditions were met then 'I do not think it would be justifiable for the Home Office to refuse ... on the understanding that it is the responsibility of the refugee organisations to make arrangements for their emigration as soon as emigration becomes practicable'. It was, he added,

> an exceptional arrangement made for dealing with the specially pitiful conditions of children found in concentration camps, and must not be taken as a precedent for requests to bring to this country other children or young persons, or older persons, who are in a distressed condition on the Continent.[137]

The children were flown to Britain in autumn 1945 and the first half of 1946, initially cared for in reception camps/homes set up in Windermere in the Lake District and Wintershill Hall in Durley. From there they were dispersed to 28 hostels across the country.[138] The Lake District and Hampshire countryside locations were not accidental. Those involved in the newly created Committee for the Care of Children from the Concentration Camps (CCCCC) were determined to restore the health of their charges; country air and food were seen as crucial. Other factors included: the availability of suitable accommodation, the closeness to RAF bases (the children were flown on planes returning or taking troops to Prague and then Munich), and their isolation from the wider community (continuing the desire for invisibility which the refugee organisations had followed since 1933). Avoiding urban locations was not for medical reasons alone: it was a response, also, to government concern, especially articulated by Ernest Bevin, that Jewish refugees were congregating in towns, thereby creating a 'Jewish problem'.[139]

The limited historical work devoted to the first place of reception has concentrated on the Lake District at the expense of Wintershill Hall.[140] Though there are many similarities in the experiences in these initial centres, the rebuilding of 'home' was very much linked to the specific locality to which the boys and girls were sent. Michael Perlmutter, who was liberated from Theresienstadt aged just 17, having survived various slave labour camps, writes of

the chains of contact forged by the 'boys of Windermere', and all the other safe
havens, provided by the benefactors of the Jewish community of England...
The connection is profound and permanent... Windermere was born in
1945...[141]

Before coming to Britain, most of the youngsters had been in temporary
recuperation camps. The move to Britain, however, involved a greater wrench
with the past. Perec Zylberberg recalls the impact of arriving in the Lake
District and 'the realisation of the immensity of our personal tragedies ...
Very few of the crowd around me had one or more siblings. Mostly we were
alone'.[142]

The nomenclature surrounding the child survivors in Britain has
developed a significance of its own. The label 'The Boys' has been widely
accepted, although clearly excluding the smaller number of female survivors
who came as part of the CCCCC. The place names associated with specific
groups are also revealing: those who were flown to Stoney Cross airfield in
the New Forest and then settled in Wintershill Hall were collectively referred
to, and remained known to themselves, and to their chronicler, Martin Gilbert,
as the 'Southampton group'. The simplification of local place naming, using
the most well-known and recognised city in the region to provide an identity,
is indicative of the importance of rebuilding a concrete concept of home for
the child survivors. Such naming, however, was far from free of conflict.[143]

The Primrose Club was formed in 1947 by the 'children' and their British
and refugee helpers, providing an important social forum after the hostels
were closed. It formed the basis for the formal survivors' organisation in
Britain – the '45 Aid Society. Meeting in Belsize Park in north-west London,
the founders addressed the question of what the club should be called.
Suggestions such as the 'Churchill Jewish Club' and 'The Freedom Club'
appear to have been motivated by a desire to show gratitude to the Allied war
effort. The Zionists, by way of contrast, wanted it to be called 'The Herzl
Society'. Most controversial, however, was Perec Zylberberg's suggestion of
'The Klepfish Club'.[144]

Perec was a committed Bundist. Michal Klepfish, a leading member of the
Bund during the war, was one of the heroes of the Warsaw ghetto rebellion in
April 1943.[145] The leader of the club, however, a German Jewish refugee, had
not heard of Klepfish and warned that people would make fun of the name
and 'ask "what kind of fish" a klepfish was'. Perec Zylberberg was furious
and his anger continues today: 'You are talking about a kind of fish, while I
am talking about a great Jewish leader'. A different identity, built upon a
different war and a different sense of place was thus rejected. Perec
comments that the club leader's response 'was strange and out of touch with
the Holocaust reality'. Instead, it was agreed to call it 'Primrose' after the
name of the local telephone exchange. On one level, the title tied the
survivors to the area in which they were now settling and meeting. On
another, 'Primrose' was not without ideological associations. Although it

meant nothing to people like Perec, it was tied to notions of Englishness and patriotism, such as the Primrose League founded in memory of Disraeli during the 1880s. Reinventing 'home' was complex, involving various geographical identifications and dissociations.[146]

The sense of displacement and exile is apparent from the song sung by the children on the aeroplane flying them to Stoney Cross: 'We don't know where we're going, but we're going out of the hell of the camps'.[147] The local paper greeted their arrival with more precise local geographical placing but with ignorance of the diversity of the children's wartime experiences: 'From Belsen to New Forest'.[148] The initial welcome from the RAF was commented on by the *Jewish Chronicle*:

> The crews and ground staff were kindness itself to the young visitors, who were given hot, sweetened milk and biscuits on the journey. On their arrival WAAFs went among the children chatting to those who could speak a few words of English... One boy remarked, over a cup of milk, 'Wir sind doch kleine Mutterskinder, wir sin Lagerskinder' [We are not mother's little children, we are children from the camps].[149]

The last comment suggests a greater ambivalence towards the treatment they received than perhaps the reporter was willing to acknowledge. A tension existed in the first months in Britain over control. Many of the youngsters were acutely alive to any attempt to patronise them; although love and kindness were greatly needed, so was the prospect of independence.[150]

Wintershill Hall was the property of James Montefiore, a relative of Leonard. His house was used from October 1945 until the second half of 1946 by the CCCCC and at its peak, some 152 children recuperated there. The Central British Fund provided £100 a week to run the transit camp for a six month period.[151] For most of the former residents, memories of the Hall and the local countryside are affectionate and positive. To Magda Bloom and her friend Marta,

> it was fairyland. It was a mild autumn. The trees were still green and there were roses everywhere. Inside it had all been beautifully fitted up with bunk beds and fresh linen... 'We had some basic English lessons, but for the rest we just revelled in being free'. They took long walks through the gardens and into the woods; pocket money was given to them so that they could go shopping in Winchester. 'Everybody made a fuss of us, there were photographs in the newspapers; I danced a csardas for the newsreels and a young man picked me a rose.'

Alec Ward also stresses the joys of unrestrained living: 'We lived in Southampton for a while where I was intoxicated with the freedom in England. I could walk freely wherever I wanted, I could ride a bicycle and everyone was extremely kind and helpful to me.'[152]

Twenty-eight, or just over one-sixth of those at Wintershill Hall were female. Gender solidarity was evident, with the girls often pairing off in close friendships as was the case with Magda and Marta. Rose Dajch had first met Esther Warszawska in Birkenau:

> In England we arrived in Southampton and subsequently many more hostels – always 'together'. We noticed that the other girls in the hostels did the same thing. Each of us found a 'best friend'… It was more than just friendship. We shared a common past, lived together in the hostels, and dreamed of a bright future, vowing to stay friends for life.[153]

The girls' accommodation was separated from the boys. They slept in the main house at Wintershill Hall which they shared with the teachers. Otherwise, the activities, including the lessons offered to the children, were mixed. The girls, partly through numbers, were somewhat marginalised, beginning a trend that has continued in the '45 Aid Society.[154] Gender differences within the Holocaust experience are being given increasing recognition. It is apparent that these continued after the war for the survivors. Rose and Esther, in spite of the solidarity brought by their friendship were not particularly happy in their first months in England – grieving at their lost world and not at ease in the rather isolated world of Wintershill Hall and subsequent hostels. For the girls, their marginal status in the hostels and beyond added another layer of vulnerability in an uncertain world.[155]

For the boys particularly, however, the rural peace of Wintershill Hall was appreciated for its liberty. Alec Ward was not alone in his passion for cycling round the open countryside. The child survivors were particularly fortunate that under the benign leadership of Dr Oscar Friedmann, Wintershill Hall reintroduced them to the concept of freedom whilst at the same time providing a secure and stimulating home from which to begin the process of rebuilding their shattered and disturbed lives.[156] There were inevitably tensions, frustrations, and uncertainty about the future and recent memories of the war which made life at Wintershill Hall perhaps less idyllic than the survivors have subsequently acknowledged. Mollie Panter-Downes was told by Oscar Friedmann that the children's attitude towards clothing, for example, was highly critical. Those at Wintershill Hall were fortunate that most of the people looking after them were pre-war refugees from Nazism. There was a greater understanding of the losses they had incurred, even if their wartime experiences still set the children apart from their helpers. But outside the world of a few devoted individuals, British society generally had immense difficulty in facing the reality of the Jewish plight since the 1930s. The crudity of responses was represented in the official report of Westmorland County Council on the Windermere children which suggested that 'The tendency to exaggerate their adventures is dying down'.[157]

In the refugee movement as a whole in Britain, however, the policy as ever was to limit the ambitions of their charges in the employment sphere. Leonard Montefiore, when told by the children that they 'would like to spend seven years in this country studying to be a doctor, or a professional pianist'

responded bluntly: 'Think of something else'. The children were allowed in
Britain on two-year visas which permitted the older ones to receive
vocational training. The leaders of the CBF had no intention that the children
would stay in Britain and could not conceive of them other than as, at best,
skilled workers.

Perec Zylberberg recalls that: 'The committee did not encourage anybody
to take up studies. They forever complained of lack of funds. With very few
exceptions everybody was directed to some sort of occupation.' Revealing a
difference of outlook conditioned by class and nationality, Montefiore, a
leading member of the elite West London Reform Synagogue, stated
categorically in 1946 that 'By no stretch of the imagination is it conceivable
that any one of these children will become a member of [this] Synagogue'.[158]
Ironically, three years later, one of the youngsters, Hugo Gryn, whose words
open and close this study, became a theological student based at the West
London Reform Synagogue, later to be its rabbi from the 1970s until his death
in 1996. The determination of the child survivors to make their own way in
the world, resisting attempts to impose a different future on them, runs
through their subsequent lives beyond Windermere and Wintershill Hall.
Nevertheless, the lack of chances to catch up on lost education proved to be
an immense barrier to many in attempts to rebuild their lives.[159]

In theory, the children were allowed choice in the hostels to which they
moved after Windermere and Wintershill Hall. But the experiences in
Overbury Court, three miles from Alton and deep in the Hampshire
countryside, revealed the limitations of this approach. Up to 25 boys were
offered temporary accommodation at Overbury Court, but it proved very
difficult to find wardens who were suited to their needs. Early in 1946, the
boys went on hunger strike in collective resistance to the way the hostel was
run. Perec Zylberberg, the oldest in the hostel, led the strike which he recalls
was over the failure of those running it to give the youngsters pocket money.
The strike was at least temporarily successful, and a small allowance was
given to the hostel residents, allowing them a degree of independence and a
chance of a more interesting life in this quiet part of the Hampshire
countryside.[160]

CONCLUSION

More than half of those brought under the CCCCC made permanent homes
in Britain. With the closure of the hostels in 1946, a concentration of the
youngsters developed in Manchester and north-west London where cohesion
was particularly strong through the formation of organisations such as the
Primrose Club. For those outside these areas, however, isolation for
individual survivors could be intense. This was certainly true of Hampshire
after the closure of Wintershill Hall and Overbury Court for the small number
of survivors who moved there such as Vera Karoly, though Bournemouth

proved a partial exception where a small refugee community, with a growing number of survivors, developed.[161]

Considering the tiny numbers involved, the contribution of Holocaust survivors to British society has been remarkable. Hugo Gryn was deeply mourned across the country because of the warmth of his religious insights and humanism. Also confounding the vision of Leonard Montefiore was Anita Lasker-Wallfisch, born in Breslau and a survivor of Auschwitz and Belsen. An immensely talented cellist, she was a founder member and leading force in the English Chamber Orchestra. On a local level, in Bournemouth, the cultural life of the region was bolstered by the appointment (though not without opposition) of Rudolf Schwartz, formerly with the Berlin Kulturbund Orchestra, and a concentration camp survivor, as head of the Bournemouth Municipal Orchestra in 1947. The paintings of Vera Karoly have found a place in public buildings across Hampshire. Ben Helfgott, born in Piotrkov, and a survivor of many Nazi camps, in addition to a remarkable sporting career, including representing Britain at the Olympics in weightlifting, became a successful business man. Both built upon his days in Southampton, where Ben studied for a degree in Economics during the late 1940s in what was still 'the family atmosphere' of University College, Southampton. It was again a strikingly different path than that intended for the boys and girls, some of them close to the College at Wintershill Hall.[162]

This rich addition to local and national life has largely gone unrecognised, continuing the marginality of the survivors in their first years in Britain. For the few allowed in, the failure to communicate their experiences to those around them in the Jewish and non-Jewish worlds was immensely frustrating. Vera Karoly relates how her

> most painful experiences came after the war was over... The concentration camps ... were horrible. But I felt even worse when I left [Belsen displaced persons camp] and came to Great Britain as a ... refugee. I felt so alone and abandoned... What made me feel so frustrated and sad was that even though I had a burning need to speak about my wartime experiences with the new acquaintances whom I met in London, nobody seemed to want to hear about this. They always changed the subject, saying things like 'We do not want to know about all the suffering you went through in the war.'... Gradually I got the message. I had to keep all the memories of the wartime traumas which I had gone through to myself. As years went by this made me increasingly introspective. Not being in a position of sharing something so pertinent and important to me as my wartime memories with my British contemporaries, I felt quite cut off from them. What did our background and world have in common?[163]

In September 1945 a civil servant in Winchester wrote in her diary that her husband had just received a letter from a Polish Jew with whom he was at college. His friend had spent most of the war in concentration camps and only he and his sister had survived. After reading the letter, her husband remarked:

'We grumble here, but we've none of us been through anything like the things that that man has endured'. Such empathy and understanding was, however, rare.[164]

Rabbi David Soetendorp, when attempting to talk in Bournemouth during the 1970s about his family's war experiences in Holland, felt similar antipathy. The revelations from the concentration camps and the presence of hundreds of survivors in the hostels in Wintershill Hall and Overbury Court had not brought the local world much closer to empathising with victims of the Holocaust. Krystina Livingstone as a very young girl was hidden outside the Warsaw ghetto for most of the war. With her mother she moved from Poland to Australia and then to Southampton in 1970. Although she has now lived in the city for over 28 years, Krystina does not see Southampton as providing more than a comfortable place to live. It is not her 'home'. She has found English culture very closed and, by contrast to Australia and the USA, England a country into which it was impossible to assimilate. She sees herself as regarded, through her accent, 'as a non-English person'. There has been little or no interest in her background in the Holocaust because 'it must distinguish me from the ordinary English experience ... it is too foreign'. As with Vera Karoly and the few other scattered Jewish survivors locally, Krystina continues to feel immense isolation.[165] It remains true that British culture and society, though possessing intimate links to the Jewish catastrophe, has yet to get to grips with the complexity of the background and subsequent lives of survivors who settled in its midst, labelled so crudely when they first arrived as 'children from Belsen'.

Perec Zylberberg reflects that 'when we touched down in the UK we became painfully aware of having gone away from the continent of Europe'. Even so, he believed that 'the quest for a safe haven seemed to have come to a reasonable solution'. But it was far from clear in 1945 in the minds of politicians and civil servants that Britain was to provide a permanent home for *any* of the Jewish survivors. Indeed, Perec Zylberberg was one of many child survivors arriving in 1945 and 1946 who subsequently settled outside Britain. Permanency had never been intended either by government officials or leaders of the refugee organisations.[166] The mood had so changed in Britain by the end of the war that the secretary of the Bournemouth Refugee Committee commented in despair that 'she looked forward to the time when we should all be part of the same community and the hateful words "alien" and "refugee" would be forgotten'. If 'refugee' itself had become such a dirty word, it is easy to understand the additional burden placed on those attempting to re-establish a new sense of place and identity. The Second World War, leaving behind the most horrific evidence of persecution on a scale never witnessed before, rather than reaffirming the right to asylum in Britain had actually left the concept in tatters.[167]

PART 3

Refugees from the Cold War

7
Polish Refugees:
Assistance to Wartime Heroes

Following the Second World War, despite the restrictionism typified by the response to victims of the Holocaust, Britain became home to a heterogeneous mass of people displaced by the war, primarily from eastern Europe, who were unable to return to their place of origin. The government, wishing to avoid moral responsibility, did not classify them as refugees but as 'displaced persons' accepted for economic reasons. The International Refugee Organisation, formed in 1947, defined displaced persons as

> victims ... of the Nazi or fascist ... or ... quisling regimes ... [or] persons who were considered refugees before the outbreak of the second world war, for reasons of race, religion, nationality or political opinion ... who [have] been deported from, or obliged to leave [their] country of nationality or of former habitual residence.

This became the basis for the international benchmark for accepting those fleeing persecution, the 1951 UN Convention on Refugees. But at this stage 'The British and American governments, who found themselves primarily responsible for dealing with the problem, hesitated to use the word "refugee" since that might imply acceptance that the person in question could not return to his home country.'[1]

The acceptance of these 'displaced persons', or 'DPs', was largely based on the need for manpower, as the war had left the British labour force depleted and the economy requiring reconstruction, rather than the emergence of, or the return to, a more generous refugee policy. Those accepted in Britain were from eastern Europe, particularly the Baltic states, but, after the upheaval of the war, they ended up in camps in Germany and Austria. Some had nowhere to return to and others, such as the Poles, found, following political changes affecting eastern Europe, that their homes had become part of Soviet-controlled territory:

> The western authorities slowly became aware of the strength of feeling amongst the refugees against return to the East. There were many deterrents from return: reluctance to submit to the totalitarian regimes established under Soviet

leadership; fear of persecution and the power of the security police at home; the lack of religious freedom; the way in which elections were carried out; the actual or possible presence of Soviet troops in the home country; the extent of nationalisation; the knowledge that boundary changes could affect their nationality.[2]

The Poles had been particularly affected by the territorial changes of the Second World War. The boundaries of their country had first been altered at the start of the war when Poland was divided between the Germans and the Russians, with numerous inhabitants forcibly moved by their captors. At the end of hostilities, Poland's borders were changed again. The country was shifted westwards, gaining former German territory but losing eastern land. With the subsequent establishment of a Soviet satellite state in Poland, thousands of displaced Poles had no desire to return home: 'It wasn't the real Poland after the war. It was not our Poland. It was Communist.'[3]

Rather than accept these people as refugees *per se*, the government established several schemes in which a number were accepted into the country as 'European Volunteer Workers', or EVWs, to help meet labour shortages.[4] An alternative form of immigration could have been encouraged from countries of the newly named Commonwealth whose nationals were entitled to rights of citizenship in Britain under the 1948 British Nationality Act. But east Europeans were favoured over Afro-Caribbeans as the former were regarded as more 'racially' desirable. Among the DPs the Poles received special attention when the Cold War led to the establishment of a communist state in their former homeland. As wartime allies many Poles were already on British soil having fled Poland and come west to fight with the Allied forces. In effect the Poles became refugees from communism, a fate which they shared with the smaller number of Hungarians who arrived in 1956 and Czechs who came to Britain in 1948 and 1968 after uprisings in their countries against communist rule. The British government's Cold War ideology as well as its economic needs meant that these groups were welcomed, if not unambiguously, into the country.

THE POLISH BACKGROUND AND SETTLEMENT IN BRITAIN

In the 1930s there were only a few thousand Poles in Britain, mainly labourers and artisans who settled in London, Manchester and Lanarkshire in Scotland; it was the migration of the Second World War which formed the core of the community.[5] They gave the community a new character as a political 'emigracja', a patriotic, fighting exile community, raising its numbers to 130–135,000.[6] The Poles in Britain consisted of a varied mass of refugees from the Second World War. Significant components of the group were the government and armed forces who had fled their country after the Nazi invasion. These exiles had travelled westwards and arrived in Britain after the fall of France in 1940. Other Poles came to Britain following a traumatic period of imprisonment by forces of the Soviet Union. When Russia invaded Poland, 1.5 million Poles were deported to the Soviet Union, mainly to the harsh conditions of Siberia where they were used to fell trees for road and railway development.[7] In late 1941, however, following the German attack on Russia, an amnesty was called by the Russians, allowing the Polish military leader General Anders to raise an army of 100,000 from among these prisoners to leave the country to fight the Nazis. The Polish Second Corps, also known as Anders' Army, was formed from these refugees and was 'the inflexible backbone of the organised Polish post-war community in Britain'.[8] Most of its members had spent nearly two years as Russian prisoners-of-war and their common experiences of suffering bonded the group:

> The army became a little exile world of its own, first in Palestine and later in Italy, with its own ethos and organisation. When it arrived in Britain in mid-1946 most of its members were unfamiliar with the English language or the British people, politically embittered and facing indefinite exile because their home provinces had been incorporated into the Soviet Union.[9]

In 1945 almost a quarter of a million Polish military servicemen in the West faced an uncertain future. In addition to the Second Corps, Britain's Polish community included over 21,000 Polish prisoners-of-war liberated from German camps, brought to Britain by Polish army units, and over 2,000 political prisoners who had survived German concentration camps. The routes taken by many of the Poles to reach Britain were long and arduous, sometimes following years of exile in the Middle East or African colonies, in addition to time in camps in Germany, Austria, Italy or Russia:

> I was just finishing National Service when Hitler invaded Poland. On 17th September I was taken a prisoner-of-war and imprisoned in Austria. I escaped three times. Twice I was captured. The third time I managed to get to Russia – my home was then under occupation – but they condemned me as a spy. They took me on a train to Siberia. For twenty-two months I laboured in the salt mines. Then General Sikorski managed to get Polish prisoners out – I was one of the lucky ones. First I went to Persia, then through the Middle East and ended in Italy. That is where we finished our war. We stayed as an occupation force for two years and then came to England.[10]

Clearly, many of those who eventually settled in Britain had not expected any such future. One woman recalled that:

> When I left Poland in 1939 it all happened so quickly, there was such a panic, that I hardly brought anything with me, just two suitcases. We were escaping from the Germans and the bombs ... I thought we'd be back in two weeks' time – Britain and France had entered the war, surely they would finish Hitler off?[11]

Another, a resistance worker in Warsaw, who was taken prisoner by the Germans, recalled the trauma of flight, especially

saying goodbye to our houses, our families; it's different when you are leaving
and you are saying as an individual I am emigrating and I am leaving you in
peace ... when it is all in ruins burning all the time you don't know where is
your family, you are alone and you are glad that you are still alive. You are
disappointed because you still want to fight. And when we married very quickly
after the war, this was our family and Warsaw was still occupied by Russia. It
was not exactly the same country and this is why our sorrow is different than
normal people who now emigrate somewhere, it is completely different.[12]

The brutality of life as a Russian prisoner is related in the story of 'Janek',
including a horrific journey to the Pechora district where he was put to work:

At the end of two weeks a column of about 250 prisoners were assembled and
an eleven day supply of food was issued to each prisoner. This consisted of
eleven salt herrings and eleven pieces of dried bread. We were marched in
convoy, with guards stationed every ten yards on each side of the column. They
had dogs on leashes and we were warned that if we attempted to leave the
column we would be shot. The first night we slept in a clearing in the snow...
I remember debating with a group of prisoners whether it was better to take off
our shoes or not. We all decided to keep our shoes on except one man. That was
his last night. Next morning his feet were frozen, his shoes were also frozen so
he couldn't put them on. He had to walk in socks with pieces of cloth tied over
his feet. After a few hours he lagged behind the column, incapable of walking.
One of the guards stayed behind with him. When we lost sight of him we heard
a shot and a few minutes later the guard rejoined the column...[13]

Such descriptions are echoed in a Hampshire resident's testimony whose
town became part of the Ukraine after the war. Her family were taken by
Russian soldiers on a cattle train to Siberia and they were released at the time
of General Sikorski's agreement. On the journey to the west the train stopped
periodically for people to relieve themselves:

The KGB man came and he said, 'We want you men for questioning' ... A few
questions? For what? We just left Siberia... 'Somebody broke the train', they
said, 'We want three men'. And they took my father on the way out from Siberia
and we never saw him since. They said only a few minutes and they'd be back,
in no more than half an hour. The train moved and I was with my brother who
was married and had two children and he said, 'Look at them telling lies. They
said they would bring him back but the train is moving.' He says, 'I'm not
leaving my father', and he jumped off the train and that was it.

Her brother found her father but because he had been locked in a room filled
with ice he died shortly afterwards.[14]

The majority of the Poles in Britain were from a military background and
a further scheme was undertaken to bring them and their dependants to
Britain: some 33,000 people came by this route. In another arrangement at
least 14,000 EVWs of Polish nationality joined the Polish community in
order to assist in national reconstruction. Displaced people from the European
continent were brought to Britain under three schemes: Operation Balt

Cygnet, for women from the Baltic countries brought to work in hospitals; Operation Westward Ho, for men and women of various nationalities, to work in undermanned industries; and a scheme for Ukrainian prisoners of war.[15] These influxes went some way towards restoring the gender balance within the Polish community as more women entered the country. The EVWs had mostly been used in Germany for forced labour and, according to Sword, 'lacked the background of comradeship, group solidarity, moral consensus and military discipline which their ex-combatant colleagues had enjoyed', setting them apart.[16] There was also suspicion, even within the Polish community, that the EVWs included some who had collaborated with the Germans, which led to their exclusion from ex-combatants' clubs. Their conditions of entry prevented them from leaving certain industries without Ministry of Labour consent, which meant that many settled around the north and north-east of Britain. In contrast, by 1950 other Poles had gravitated towards the south-east and London.[17] Not all the Poles arriving in Britain during and after the war wished to stay. Over 33,000 emigrated elsewhere, most preferring to go to the United States, Canada, Australia and Latin America.[18] In 1960, there were an estimated 130–135,000 Polish exiles in Britain, falling to 100–105,000 in 1976 due to the community's age structure and the impact of inter-marriage on the second generation.[19]

The decision to allow the Polish exiles in Britain to stay after the war and to allow their dependants and other displaced Poles to immigrate was a lengthy procedure. Between mid-1945 and early 1947 the government procrastinated about their future, an issue linked to wider debates about Poland itself. Although the Polish forces were under British operational command, their allegiance was to the exiled Polish government in London, but when the war ended there was uncertainty whether it would be reinstated to power. In February 1945, Churchill, as Prime Minister of the wartime National Government, met with Stalin and Roosevelt at Yalta, to discuss the future of post-war Poland. The 'Big Three' agreed that the Polish Provisional Government of National Unity (TRJN), based on the Soviet-sponsored Lublin Committee, would be recognised until free elections could take place. This government, established as the Soviets liberated Poland, was viewed as a sop to Soviet political interests. No Polish representative of the exiled government was present at Yalta. But in the House of Commons, Churchill made an extraordinary statement, apparently supporting the idea of Polish settlement in Britain:

> His Majesty's government will never forget the debt they owe to the Polish troops who have served them so valiantly, and for all those who have fought under our command, I earnestly hope that it may be possible to offer the citizenship and freedom of the British Empire, if they so desire. I am not able to make a statement on that subject today... But as far as we are concerned, we should think it an honour to have such faithful and valiant warriors dwelling among us as if they were men of our own blood.[20]

This speech became known as Churchill's pledge, but when it was made the government still hoped and expected that the majority of the Poles would return home; a leaflet distributed to Polish units abroad advised them to go back although none were to be involuntarily repatriated.[21] Moreover, there was opposition to Churchill's pledge within government circles. The Foreign Office was concerned that Stalin would infer from the offer that Britain was resigned to the loss of Poland to Communism. The Home Secretary, Herbert Morrison, antipathetical to Jewish refugee settlement in Britain during the war, was also opposed to helping the Poles for fear of the effect on 'all those many aliens who desire to stay here and claim they have rendered assistance to the war effort'.[22] With Churchill's strong endorsement, however, the Cabinet agreed to accept the Poles, arguing that they were 'a "special case" and that the concessions extended to them were a question of honour'.[23]

The British General Election of 1945 returned a massive Labour majority, ending the wartime coalition government. Although the new government was initially vague about the practical measures to follow from Churchill's promise to assist the Poles, there was a commitment to the spirit of the pledge. Prime Minister Clement Attlee and Foreign Secretary Ernest Bevin, amongst others, had been members of Churchill's cabinet. On 6 July 1945, the new British government transferred recognition from the London-based Polish government in exile to the Provisional government in Warsaw, assuming direct responsibility for the Polish forces who were still in the country.[24] Nevertheless, Attlee was initially vague about the Poles' future. In reply to a question about fulfilling Churchill's pledge, he stated that:

> This is a matter on which we obviously have to consult with the other Governments of the Commonwealth, but I may say that it was a hope rather than a pledge. It is in the spirit of that, however, that we intend to act. We need to do our utmost for our friends who have been fighting with us so well during the war.[25]

Bevin was anxious to repatriate members of the Polish forces. The problem lay in what future they could expect from the Lublin Committee. On 20 March 1946 the British Foreign Secretary issued a message to all Polish forces under British Command, outlining how

> in execution of the policy announced by Mr Winston Churchill, the British Government will give, in collaboration with other governments, such assistance as is in their power to enable those who fought with us throughout the war to start a new life outside Poland with their families and dependants. But the British Government ... are bound to make it plain that they can promise no more than this.

No guarantee of resettlement was offered and Bevin appealed to the forces to avail themselves of the opportunity to return to Poland.

It became increasingly clear, however, that Poland was falling into the Soviet sphere of influence in eastern Europe. As Foreign Office official,

Robin Hankey, wrote:

> The fact is that conditions in Poland are thoroughly unsatisfactory, a steady drive towards communisation is under way, and there have been many arrests of independent socialists and others who wish this tendency to be resisted ... we really could not accept the responsibility of advising men to go back.[26]

A leading article in *The Times* highlighted the dilemmas:

> It is clear that a Polish army, with units in Britain and Germany as well as in Italy, which disclaims allegiance to the recognised Government in Warsaw, cannot be regarded as a national force or maintained in arms indefinitely. Its demobilisation is a responsibility of the British Government, but so also is the future of the troops affected... Mr Bevin was able to report some success in his efforts to make it possible for these 'magnificent troops' to return home, but was properly downright in his refusal to abandon soldiers who fought side by side with British troops in many a fierce battle from Cassino to Arnhem. It is natural therefore that further reference should have been made to the suggestion thrown out by Mr Churchill nearly a year ago when he informed Parliament of the results of the Yalta Conference... Some permanent settlement must be offered to these Poles who, rightly or wrongly, feel that their own country is closed to them and a clear responsibility rests on the British government, by whom they were armed and equipped. It is on the face of it unlikely that the Dominions, concerned as they now are to attract immigrants, would refuse to cooperate in providing homes for some of these men, whose quality, proved on the battlefield, marks them out as potential citizens of whom any country might be proud.[27]

It was hardly conceivable to force thousands of Poles, many of whom had seen Soviet terror at first hand during their imprisonment, to return home to a Soviet-controlled government in Poland. Repatriation thus became an ever less viable prospect and on 27 March 1947 the Polish Resettlement Act was passed providing entitlement to employment as well as unemployment assistance in Britain. The salient provisions of the Act outlined that the Poles were the responsibility of several government departments covering their employment, health and education. The War Office had been responsible for the Polish Armed Forces, but the Act put the National Assistance Board in charge of the Polish resettlement camps, usually former army or prisoner-of-war camps. It also required the involvement of the Ministries of Labour and National Service and Education in the care of the Poles. This kind of legislation was not used for other refugee groups and reflected the Poles' importance on the national political agenda.

The exceptional nature of this legislation in terms of modern British refugee policy was highlighted with its clauses relating to the entitlement to government support. The Assistance Board:

> may provide accommodation in camps, hostels or other establishments for persons in Great Britain being in any of the categories [of Poles] specified ... or dependants of persons of any of those categories or of members of any of the

Polish resettlement forces serving therewith, or persons formerly dependent on a person who was of any of those categories, or was such a member of any of those forces, at that former time... [Nevertheless, the] Board may make rules for the well-ordering of camps, hostels or other establishments in which accommodation is provided under this section, and any person who contravenes or fails to comply with the rule so made shall be liable on summary conviction to a fine not exceeding twenty-five pounds or to imprisonment for a term not exceeding three months, or to both such fine and imprisonment.

In addition, the Minister of Education

may, for meeting the educational needs of persons being of any description for whom the Assistance Board has power to provide accommodation under section three of this Act or members of any of the Polish resettlement forces, provide any such services and do any such things as a local education authority or the Minister of Education are or is authorised or required to provide or to do, or may be authorised or required to do, by or under the Education Acts, 1944 and 1946 ... The expenses of the Minister of Education under this section shall be defrayed out of moneys provided by Parliament.[28]

THE TRANSITION TO LIFE IN BRITAIN

The Polish troops were demobilised in the autumn of 1946 and subsequently enrolled in the Polish Resettlement Corps which served as a means of maintaining discipline and also smoothing the Poles' transition to life in Britain. Its terms required the Poles to serve as members for two years, entering civilian trades while learning English and to 'undertake work which is helpful to this country'.[29] In practical terms little was on offer for some of the Poles. One woman who had served with the Air Forces in Nottingham recalled that:

At the end of the war we were just chucked out on the street. No money, no home, no families, no help. I went to the headquarters because you were supposed to take all the clothes, coats, uniforms and gas masks, sheets and blankets, back to the store. And when I came with all my things to the store, there was a young lad there and he said, 'Where are you going now?' And I said, 'I don't know. I'm going on the street.' He said, 'Yes, looks like it. What are you going to wear, where're you going to sleep?' I said, 'I don't know what I'm going to do – I'm going to stay with a friend.' He said, 'Keep everything you've got and just give me the gas mask because that's the government's.' He exchanged me a new skirt and I wore that uniform a long, long time. I had that and two blankets, two wool blankets and that's how I started my life. I got eight pounds, sixty coupons, that's all that I got...[30]

The decision to accept the Poles who were already in Britain as permanent settlers and to bring over their relations had several motives. In economic terms, the Labour government recognised that there was a severe labour shortage which threatened the export drive needed to pay off war debts and to finance reconstruction of Britain's shattered infrastructure. The drive for food, energy and housing required workers for agriculture, coal-mining and the building industry. In political terms, there was considerable sympathy for the Poles' plight over their homeland because many believed that Britain had a moral and political responsibility for them. Parliamentary debates showed that the consensus politics of wartime had lasting effects as cross-party support was used to carry through Churchill's pledge of citizenship by the subsequent Labour government. Mr Peake, a Conservative MP, believed the Act went 'a long way to honouring Britain's obligations' towards the Poles. From a different perspective, Mr Titterington, of the Labour Party, considered the bill, 'one of the finest expressions of internationalism made on behalf of His Majesty's Government'.[31]

Although a broad spread of politicians favoured Polish settlement in Britain this was not unanimous. Keith Sword notes that, ironically, the Labour government faced greater opposition to Polish resettlement from its own benches than from the Conservative Opposition.[32] In July 1946, a Labour MP, Arthur Lewis, asked the Secretary of State for Foreign Affairs, 'whether in view of the present food shortage and the introduction of bread rationing, he will reconsider his decision to settle Polish troops in the country?' Mr Noel Barker replied negatively:

> His Majesty's Government do not consider that the reason suggested by my honourable Friend would justify them in changing the decision they have made about the settlement of Polish troops. In any case the Poles under British command who are now abroad have been largely fed from British military supplies, and their removal to this country will simply mean bringing the food to the UK instead of sending it elsewhere.[33]

Robert Miles suggests that in contrast to the insistence that British subjects from the Caribbean and Indian subcontinent integrate,

> In planning for and affecting the resettlement of the Poles, the Labour Government accepted that it constituted a population with a distinct history and culture, and considerable administrative effort and financial resources were devoted to the maintenance of a distinct Polish community.[34]

Miles accepts that there was pressure to learn English, Sword adding that 'the ambition of British policy towards the Poles was gradual assimilation and "depoliticisation"'.[35] It was a process aided by the formation of the Resettlement Corps which was to provide 'a kind of transitional experience to ease former Polish servicemen and women and their families into civilian life'.[36] Clearly, the Corps was also of benefit to Britain's economy as the Poles were channelled to areas of labour shortage. It allowed Poles either to be loaned in groups to employers as 'gang labour' for work of national importance, such as harvesting, or to be released individually to jobs considered suitable by the Ministry of Labour.

Finding employment was not easy for the Polish settlers. Not until July

1950 were all those capable of, and available for, work absorbed into the working population.[37] The majority went into manual labour even though the community was over-represented in the professions compared with pre-war Poland.[38] Occupations of adults in the Polish Resettlement Corps included approximately 6,000 professional officers and non-commissioned officers, 10,000 technicians, craftsmen and qualified engineers, 2,600 civil servants, over 1,000 teachers and lecturers, and many lawyers, writers, artists and doctors. Although there were over 6,300 former farmers and landowners, only 2,500 Poles were agricultural workers of all kinds, disconcerting to the Ministry of Labour which had hoped many would settle as farmworkers.[39]

The majority of Poles, regardless of their background, became unskilled workers in Britain. Many professionals had to requalify to enter their professions in their new homeland. The criteria for settlement was that the Poles should fill labour shortages, or as one remarked, 'do the jobs the British did not want to do'.[40] This meant that most were directed into low paid, insecure jobs or heavy industrial work, especially mining, brick-making, textiles, building, the iron and steel industry, domestic work and the hotel and catering trades. Although this did not mean an end to prospects, as once their English improved and workers' hostility decreased some were able to move into semi-skilled or white collar jobs, few, as is typical of so many refugee movements, regained their former status.

LIFE IN THE CAMPS AND EMPLOYMENT IN BRITAIN

Within Hampshire there were various camps housing the Poles in the resettlement scheme. Many Poles were initially housed in the dependants' camps of the Polish Second Corps at Hiltingbury, near Chandler's Ford, which housed 843 people and Stockbridge, near Andover, with 493 dependants. The Hiltingbury camp was one of the largest camps for Polish dependants, second only in number to that at Doddington, near Nantwich, Cheshire, which housed over 1,000 Poles. It was also one of the longest in existence, closing in 1956.[41] There was also a camp for ex-servicemen and war invalids at Oak Lodge near Emsworth in the Portsmouth area. In addition, the British wife of a Pole recalled the existence of a military camp at Hursley and a displaced persons' camp at Havant where anti-Tito Yugoslavs lived. Further camps nearby at Codford near Warminster and Whitley near Guildford also show how the Poles became a part of rural British life, the gravestones at Codford cemetery acting as a memorial to their presence in the village.[42]

Those in the large camp at Hiltingbury were mainly from the east of Poland. Some had been taken prisoner by the Germans and forced to work on farms in Germany and Austria. There were also Poles who had been deported to Siberia by the Russians, as well as their families, who came later. Many were from Vilnius which had become part of Lithuania making return very difficult. Discussions within Southampton City Council in late 1946 and early 1947 show how the Poles were incorporated into reconstruction efforts, especially as builders. The Borough Engineer reported in December 1946 that:

> These men of whom 150 are at present available, are stationed at Hiltingbury Camp and will be employed as ordinary aliens in a civilian capacity, at the same rates of pay and under the same conditions as British labour. In accordance with agreed working rules, the men will be paid the time actually worked on the site, will travel in their own time and the Contractors will provide free transport. In view of the fact that most of the men have been working during the war under forced labour conditions in Russia and Germany, they will not be employed on sites where German prisoners-of-war are working.

All were employed in various new housing estates for local companies. The project appeared successful: 'the men have proved quite willing and the employing contractors are satisfied with their work', though arrangements had to be made between the Borough Engineer and the contractors because of the high transportation costs involving Polish labour.[43] The importance of such work to regional and national life should not be minimised. Claire Peters, the wife of a Polish man settling in Hampshire, recalled how:

> As well as building new homes, the [Poles] also built the Fawley Oil Refinery and did pile driving in the docks. As they got older and the manual work got a bit hard and the building was done, they went into factories, one or two worked for British Rail and did quite well.[44]

Nevertheless, the Labour government was aware of the sensitivity of British workers regarding job security and the future of the Poles. Plans for Polish employment were drawn up only after consultation with the trade union movement and business leaders. The TUC made clear their provisions for accepting Polish labour: the trade union concerned had to be consulted directly before introducing Polish labour and Poles would not be employed if British labour was available. Even so, there were problems with some of the unions. The National Union of Mineworkers (NUM) was resolutely opposed to the employment of Poles, even if they were experienced miners, which only a small proportion were. There were grounds for such concern as there was economic insecurity in the industry, complicated by the government's plans for nationalisation. Not until January 1947 did the NUM agree to admitting Poles, and then on condition that a five-day week was introduced and that local miners' lodges agreed, which did not always happen. The National Union of Agricultural Workers also showed antipathy, on the basis that conditions should be improved to encourage native workers to join the industry, though Poles were eventually employed on the harvest.[45]

In Portsmouth the case of ten Polish carpenters who were employed in the building trade and then dismissed appeared not only in the *Portsmouth Evening News* but also made national news.[46] The men had come from

Scotland to work as labourers until the Ministry of Labour could supply them with tools to follow their trade. When the tools arrived, however, the Amalgamated Society of Woodworkers forbade them from continuing carpentry work as it did not want them to operate at a skilled grade. Labour opposition to the Poles was not always concerned about their unsuitability. Two Poles working in a southern firm on the production of pins for carburettors were laid off due to their over-zealous production rates, putting their British co-workers to shame. Vivid memories of unemployment during the 'Hungry '30s' and natural fears that introducing large numbers of foreign workers would hold down wage levels, alongside xenophobia, explain such hostile responses.[47] Other trade unions were more welcoming to the Poles. The Transport and General Workers' Union set about active recruitment from the resettlement camps from 1947 and by 1949 had three all-Polish branches with a combined membership of some 6,000.[48] The General and Municipal Workers' Union also acted positively and 'The support of the two largest unions in the country did much to help Poles resettle in civilian employment at a time when the more publicised union reactions were ones of hostility'.[49]

In addition to employment questions, the government was faced with problems over the Poles' accommodation. In a situation of housing shortages, and the return of demobilised soldiers, this was again a sensitive issue. On arrival in Britain during the war, Polish forces were sent to camps and hostels where they were stationed for combat. Their post-war settlement tended to correspond with these areas, with airmen settling in towns like Nottingham, Leicester and Blackpool and naval forces living in Portsmouth, Plymouth and Cardiff, although those returning to Scotland did not fit this pattern.[50] For the Poles who entered Britain after the war, about 40 Polish Resettlement Corps camps and EVW hostels were established across the country where labour was in short supply and accommodation could be found:

> For the Poles, the use of camps and hostels lessened the tension over housing in the immediate post-war period, but it also meant that for several years these Poles remained socially, culturally and linguistically segregated from the receiving society and dependent upon Polish voluntary associations for the satisfaction of most non-economic needs.[51]

It took some years before the Poles left these camps to live in their own homes; in 1959 three hostels were still in operation.

The Foreign Office was certainly sensitive over the question of the formation of Polish ghettoes and, at its request, the Poles were widely dispersed which also had the perceived benefit of breaking up the Polish chain of military command. By October 1946 120,000 Polish troops were quartered in 265 camps, with 161 for the Polish Second Corps and its dependants alone. Many of these were former Allied service camps located in rural areas making them remote from industries where Polish labour was needed. The unwillingness of the government to spend scarce resources in finding more suitable accommodation resulted in financing the transport of Poles from the camps to their places of work as was the case at Hiltingbury.

The use of camps for accommodation was to cause some justifiable complaints from the Poles, especially for those housed in Nissen huts which had been erected as temporary shelters in the war offering little protection against the cold. The Home Office was apparently concerned to keep the Poles in camps to prevent pressure on the already depleted housing stocks and to ensure discipline was maintained. Such policies, however, also acted as an 'immigration "gatekeeper"', to ensure that as few Poles as possible should settle in Britain', on the basis that 'a lengthy period of camp life would do more than any number of politicians' speeches to persuade large numbers of Poles to leave Britain'.[52]

In December 1946, before the Polish Resettlement Act was passed, Marie Woodruff, Vice-Chair of the Catholic Committee for Relief Abroad, visited several Polish camps in Britain. Her stress on the Poles' uncertainty about the future, alongside repeated questions in Parliament, may have prompted Attlee's government to come to a firm decision regarding Polish settlement:

> The living quarters were those formerly occupied by Allied military and Prisoners-of-war... There are, of course, variations from camp to camp; the cooking is not uniformly good, and fuel restrictions come more hardly in some districts than others. In the main, however, there is nothing that effort and goodwill cannot ameliorate... The depression that exists in the camps is something apart from cold and damp and occasional lapses in efficiency. It is a lowness of spirits which is all the more serious because its existence is not perhaps fully appreciated. Many of these people have had weary years of trekking across Asia, Africa and Europe. Others have had years of concentration camps and forced labour. After their release from these, they found temporary harbour in camps in Italy, and waited for news of their fate. When the decision was taken to accept them in England, it was looked upon by them, perhaps foolishly, but no doubt understandably, as a 'coming home' – the last lap of the journey. Now that they are here, in all the uncertainties of a perpetual transit camp, with apparently no future to look forward to, they have lost all courage. This is the real tragedy of the [Polish Dependants'] camps. They are cut off from their own country, they feel misunderstood by their own officials, who have been settled here perhaps for some time, and on account of this misunderstanding they mistrust them.

Sending her notes to the National Assistance Board, Woodruff stressed that whilst matters of policy were being discussed by

> Government Departments and military authorities, a speedy decision of which might be urged, could it not be possible to give some short but definite statement? The knowledge that a camp will exist for six months, that it is to organise itself as a unit with kindergarten, workshops, etc. under permanent officials, frequently in contact with one central authority, would have a better effect on the spirits of the inmates than a perpetual waiting to be transferred elsewhere...

Arguing that morale was bleak, Woodruff provided a 'brief statement of the principal needs common to all camps', covering child welfare, language classes, religious and health needs, libraries, canteens and lastly, and, most extensively, employment, pointing out that women 'have more success than men in obtaining employment, especially those willing to take up domestic service. There are some sad cases of doctors and nurses trying to obtain hospital service, in London and elsewhere. It seems that in spite of the great need for these, everyone is loath to take them'. She concluded on a more hopeful tone:

> It would seem that the big problem of Polish youth in camps is one that should be tackled in its entirety here and now. For the others, since employment and housing are not within our means to settle, we must concentrate on the details. There is the old fighting Polish spirit to be reawakened, faith and hope to be restored and all that we can give to make the life of a camp less dreary and wasteless.[53]

Much of Woodruff's analysis was shared in a Polish account of the Hiltingbury Hostel written two years later which started with a description of the 'general characteristics' of those in the camp:

> Most of them are of peasant origin and profession. They are [mainly] of poor education. Many of them have spent several years as slaves in Germany or Russia. During this period they were deprived of all good influences and care about their moral education. Moreover, the hard conditions of their life in these countries taught them all sorts of wicked things: to deceive, to lie, to swear, to be rude and brutal, in short to be ruthless in fighting for their very existence. Hence their notion of discipline is weakened. They do not appreciate the value of living in a community. A great number of them do not understand fully their political, economic and social position. The last fact is connected with their lack of English. It causes many unfortunate misunderstanding(s) as also the disorientation in the ways and means of life of the British people, their laws and regulations. On the other hand the peasant origin and their deep religious faith determine their decisively good character. They are decent and very honest by nature. That is why the Poles are good and conscientious workers and are praised by many employers. It is known that the Poles are passionately patriotic and they are very sensitive when approached with understanding as regards their national situation...

It then criticised the military administration in its treatment of the Polish refugees for showing 'very little care ... in connection with the moral welfare and education of these bewildered newcomers'. Even as late as February 1949 'This specific confusion continues. The residents show no community discipline nor have they the necessary notion of respect for the authorities.' Particular problems were:

> The lack of knowledge about the British life and about the working of their state and communal institutions... The conditions of the everyday life of the residents do not favour their learning of English. During their work they have

little opportunity to speak to their British workmates. They spend their resting time with their families, again speaking Polish. It is true that the number of Poles learning English increased in the last few months. The conviction that English language is a desirable asset for them is undoubtedly growing amongst them although one has to say that the English language is enormously difficult for them to acquire. It is very doubtful whether the Poles in their middle-forties will be able to learn English in less than two to three years and even then they will speak very bad and poor language… [T]he residents are very shy and feel ashamed of their lack of English … learning English will improve if, besides the English teachers for the advanced, there are more Polish teachers who can be part time employed.

The authorities were also criticised for not encouraging communal representations from the refugees resulting in a lack of independence:

The lack of real and true representation of the residents community … makes the desirable cementing of the community difficult and causes the general feeling of distrust. It is very difficult now to change this attitude … The residents lived for several years in camps free of charge. Hence they were accustomed to think that free lodging and maintenance was 'due' to them and therefore some of them when required to pay even at present feel the 'injustice'. They again feel bitterness that they are required to pay 'so much' in spite of the fact that they have to clothe their wives and children … and are convinced that they could live cheaper if they were allowed to buy the food themselves and cook it in their homes. The further grievances concern the inadequacy of the living quarters. The residents complain that these are too small without the facilities to keep coal, their bicycles, their belongings etc., and again they think that they are paying too much especially when some of them are building new houses and find out that the rent of new houses is so low. One has to admit that the residents, deprived of normal homes for many years are fed up with the huts and are longing, quite naturally, for normal homes.

Its conclusion, aimed at British civil servants, was cautionary:

The residents in Hiltingbury Hostel living on a very small space are forming a Polish *Ghetto*. If we agree that because of the existing housing shortage the Poles must wait at least two–three years for their homes, the best idea seems to be to form a Polish *Village*, living in good and friendly neighbourness with the British and the inhabitants preparing themselves for the future 'dispersal' amongst the British. It means the bettering of the living conditions in the Hostel and serious efforts in the education of the Poles.[54]

The response of the authorities to such pleas was mixed but they did encourage the formation of Residents' Councils in Hiltingbury and elsewhere to allocate accommodation, arbitrate in disputes, provide welfare and organise recreational activities in the camps. Polish schools were also established, the one at Hiltingbury remaining in use until the end of December 1950, later succeeded by a Saturday school.[55] Other complaints remained largely unresolved until the council arranged for the Poles to be accommodated in council houses in the area and the Hiltingbury camp was closed.

As these accounts stressed, the camps were self-contained communities, with their own canteens, clinics and nurseries in addition to schools on the premises. English classes were provided for all those who wished to attend and some attention was paid to training the Poles. Hampshire County Council in May 1948, for example, agreed that an instructor was to be appointed to the Hiltingbury camp to teach a course in Mechanical Engineering draughtsmanship.[56] Gradually the 'ghetto' atmosphere was reduced as adults found work outside the camps and children began to attend local schools, with Polish classes held on Saturdays only. That these classes still continue shows that while the Poles have become integrated into society, they have been reluctant to relinquish totally their national culture and history.

The difficulties of these early years in Britain are described by Zofia Thoroughgood. She was first taken from Poland to Siberia as a Russian prisoner-of-war and after General Sikorski's amnesty lived in Polish refugee camps in Persia and East Africa where she met her future husband who was in the British army. They got married in Tangier in January 1948 and:

> In April we arrived in England. I had no idea where he was going to take me, I couldn't even speak English ... we used to speak Swahili. Coming to England I came to live with my mother-in-law. I think it was six years. We had two children, two daughters.

> It was everything on coupons at that time. And of course not speaking the language. It wasn't very easy. Even if I wanted to go out I was so frightened in case I couldn't find my way back home you see. So it was really terrible. I used to go to bed very early because my mother-in-law was speaking very fast and I was so scared that I can't understand what she is saying so I used to go to bed ... I had a very hard life in England, very. Living with my mother-in-law we couldn't even save because we used to give her the money for food...

> When we moved house I had a baby two weeks old and a daughter five years old. But we moved in there and the place was so black, the walls were black... And my daughter walked in the front room and went out the back and she wouldn't come in. She was scared of it there. We had no furniture, we had nowhere to sit, nowhere to eat... and nothing to eat with. I bought one knife in Woolworths and a fork so he ate with the fork and I ate with the knife...[57]

While the Poles lived in poor conditions for several years after their arrival in Britain, this has to be placed in context. Housing shortages were acute after the bombardments of the war and rationing continued for the British population until the 1950s. At Chandler's Ford there was even a case of a British woman wishing to move into the Polish camp to join her husband, although the government refused to allow this. Nonetheless, as Sword writes, 'While the British community too was experiencing considerable austerity, few started from the low material threshold of the Poles'.[58] The resettlement process was difficult and for several Poles interviewed it was still painful to recall early memories:

The beginning was very difficult. First of all on the British side, there was a problem of communication – the language barrier and the lack of understanding at our disappointment and bitterness over the result of our war sacrifices. While the whole Western world was enjoying the victory and long-awaited peace, our country had only changed from German occupation to Soviet supremacy. No-one who had not experienced life in concentration and labour camps, prisons, deportations and all sorts of deprivation, could understand the feelings and anxieties of refugees. To the British people we were all 'strangers' – strange language, traditions, customs, priorities and reactions – everything was strange. On our side there was a lot of mistrust; mistrust even of the most friendly 'authority' – the policeman or social worker, every 'stranger' knocking at the door. Only the well-known persons were trusted – those who could understand the language and our specific problems. In those first years, self-help within the Polish community was the most important factor...[59]

Discussions about criminal behaviour among the Poles revealed some of the tensions. Petty thieving, though confined to a minority of Poles, nonetheless raised debate within government circles. Some officials believed criminal behaviour should be punished by deportation, a policy that had been used for some Spanish children in the 1930s. The Polish Hiltingbury report sought to explain the hardened behaviour of people who had been forced to beg and steal to survive but concern about the camp was such that Frank Savery of the Foreign Office visited Hiltingbury to investigate. He wrote to his colleague Robin Hankey about the 'delinquents' there in April 1948:

During our first conversation with Mr Graham, the Assistance Board Warden, we asked his opinion on these cases [of burglary]. He was not disposed to attribute very great importance to them or to regard the offenders as 'criminals' – tough guys perhaps but not criminal types... One cannot, he said, regard as criminals lads of seventeen who break into a store, steal a lot of sweets and other attractive looking foodstuffs and then consume their spoils around a bonfire.

It was also reported to Savery that the Poles coming up before the English courts were

at a great disadvantage owing to their ignorance both of our language and also of our judicial procedure. There is, he considers, a real danger of their being treated as more culpable than they really are and of being punished accordingly because they cannot put up their case properly to the magistrates or judge...

Savery concluded by questioning whether it was 'fair to regard a boy of seventeen as being already so hopeless a criminal that the extreme punishment of deportation to a country in as unsatisfactory a state as present-day Poland ought to be applied?' He also wondered whether Polish offenders, 'most of them probably simple people not very well able to express their thoughts even in their native language, are really being given as good a chance of stating their case in court as any accused person is entitled to have?' He was thus convinced that there was a real danger that capital may be made out of cases such as the one mentioned above of the two seventeen-year-old boys in order to spoil our relations with the Polish refugees in this country. Above all, for this, as well as for other reasons the very greatest caution ought, in my opinion, to be taken in applying the punishment of deportation to Poland...[60]

Savery's concern led to correspondence between Hankey of the Foreign Office, Ian Roy of the Home Office and N. Storr of its Aliens Department, and C. Whetmath of the Assistance Board.[61] Hankey believed that 'A firm hand is desirable when dealing with these Poles, providing of course that they are given a proper chance of defending themselves. For this reason I suggest that the sanction of deportation should certainly continue to be held in reserve.'[62] But Whetmath wrote to Roy that Poles must be assured of a fair deal in the courts:

> Justice must not only be done, but must be manifestly done. If through any failure in this respect the Poles, whether rightly or wrongly, acquire the idea that they are being dealt with in a prejudicial manner by one section of British authority it will inevitably be reflected, sooner or later, in their relations with the particular branch of British authority responsible for the administration of the hostels in which they are living.[63]

Storr presented the Aliens Department's view:

> No discrimination, of course, is made between Poles or people of any other nationality, including British, when they appear as accused persons before the court... The problem of the alien accused of an offence and unable to understand English is, as you realise, not one confined to the Poles and it would be impossible to make special arrangements for them... A foreigner in some respects is in a more favourable position than a native in this country. The proceedings are explained to him through the interpreter and the magistrate is most scrupulous to explain what is happening...[64]

Following this lengthy correspondence, officials agreed that there should be a reliable interpreter in court but that this person should not be an advocate to plead the accused's case.[65] The Poles would not receive any further 'special' treatment which generally followed traditional 'aliens' policy', essentially encouraging the Poles to adapt to the British way of life and without any singular policy to deal with their specific needs. Deportation was to remain an option. As Storr wrote to Whetmath, 'We would prefer to encourage such of them as are here to fit into our way of life rather than do anything towards creating a special regime for Poles inside this country.'[66]

LOCAL AND NATIONAL RESPONSES TO THE POLES

While it is harder to assess popular British attitudes towards the Poles than those of the government, Zubrzycki outlines changing relations between the war and its aftermath.[67] Between 1940 and 1941, he argues, the Poles were feted as Britain's sole allies and were welcomed as attractive additions to British social life in areas where they were stationed. After Russia's entry to the war, however, with disputes about responsibility for the Katyn massacre and Poland's frontiers, relations soured, as pro-Soviet feeling was running high in Britain. There was some distinction between the Polish leaders who were considered to be intransigent on the political scene, and ordinary Poles who were seen as decent and reasonable. This ambivalence was recorded by Mass-Observation with the Poles described as 'useful allies', but their government seen as 'an infernal nest of fascists'.[68] After the war problems increased when the Poles were initially decried for being maintained by the taxpayer and were then castigated for taking British jobs. In a Gallup poll of June 1946, 56 per cent disapproved of the government decision to allow Poles to stay in the country.[69] The presence of Poles who had fought in the German army, the Poles' reputation for success with British women, and rumours of profiteering on the black market all counted against them. Communist and left-wing papers such as the *Daily Worker* and *Tribune* tended to be hostile to the Poles viewing them as pro-fascist, while Catholic papers were more sympathetic as were the *Manchester Guardian*, *The Scotsman* and *Yorkshire Post*. The popular press, especially the *Daily Mirror*, tended to stir up opposition, while *The Times* showed greater ambiguity.

Such prejudices were countered in various ways. When personal contacts were established, workers' hostility often decreased, as it was clear that the Poles were prepared to work and join trade unions. The War Office also invited local press correspondents to visit various camps and describe the living conditions and backgrounds of the Poles, in an attempt to diffuse Anglo-Polish tensions. This was evident locally, when the *Hampshire Chronicle*, gave a sympathetic if isolated portrayal of the Poles at Hiltingbury:

> To the passer-by, whether in car or on foot, [the camp simply denotes] a conglomeration of Army huts, a few lines of washing, and occasional glimpses of 'foreigners'. Few perhaps realise the human and often tragic stories which lie behind this seemingly drab appearance, and the tremendous and difficult work of resettlement that is going on there... At Hiltingbury ... more than 800 persons are accommodated – some 400 men, 200 women, and 200 children. All are either former members of the Polish Forces or their dependants. The main object of the Assistance Board is to place them in suitable employment and while they are in residence at the Hostel they pay for their own subsistence and receive the ordinary ration and clothing coupon books which are issued to British citizens. They are all civilians and most of them are looking forward to settling down and making their homes in this country. While at Hiltingbury they learn something of the British way of life and language and generally prepare themselves for the day when they will be absorbed into the British community. But re-settlement cannot be accomplished in a few weeks or even a few months, and there are many difficulties – the housing shortage, and the attitude of certain Trade Unions and professional bodies...

The reporter took particular effort to explain the traumatic background of the residents:

> Although good food and care at the Hostel have worked wonders and generally speaking the people look a happy and healthy crowd, there are still many who bear traces and retain vivid impressions of the cruelty and suffering they endured under the jackboot of the Nazis, which time can never erase. There is a former civil servant who was caught operating a secret wireless station and printing and distributing the BBC Polish news in leaflet form. Three of his friends were shot, and he and another were sent to concentration camps...[70]

Government concern about public opinion continued. Brigadier Watkins, the head of Southern Command, visited the camp at Stockbridge and read a press statement in an attempt to clear up 'misunderstanding about the continued presence of Polish troops in Great Britain and the formation of the Polish Resettlement Corps'. Watkins stressed how the Poles had

> fought side by side with us, their casualties were heavy; they never 'let us down', and this country incurred a great moral obligation to secure their future. This debt had increased because of political developments in Poland under which a large proportion considered they could not return...

He added that their behaviour in Britain had been excellent:

> The British Government have recognised that assistance to these people is a matter of justice to equity and not a matter of charity... One hundred and sixty-eight Poles from the camp have registered for employment, this number being split up into 28 engineering, 31 artisans and craftsmen, 50 agriculture, 14 drivers, 24 clerks and commerce, 11 medical and 10 domestic service.

Turning to accommodation, he explained that the Poles used the camp as a 'sort of hotel, where they would be expected to pay their way'. His statement concluded that 'Both as regards work and accommodation Poles would take second priority to the British', pointing out 'that a steady stream of Poles were applying for repatriation. Up to October 30th 1946, 55,000 had returned, 16,796 were awaiting repatriation, and 3,725 had emigrated to countries other than Poland.' Finally Brigadier Watkins 'referred to criticism of Poles who had served with the German Army being in this country, and pointed out that these Poles had been forced into such service'.[71]

In spite of such reports, however, which aimed to provide Poles with 'the sympathy to which they are entitled', the question of their settlement remained controversial. One woman recollected that fellow Poles complained about the British, but her reply was, 'Do you know any?'. She believed that once friendships were established hostility was broken down.[72] Correspondence in the *Hampshire Chronicle* suggested a concerned minority actively helped the Poles in their resettlement. One correspondent, Monica Stratton, was anxious to help the Poles set up a local club:

> Your readers have doubtless seen the numbers of Polish troops in and around

Winchester, but I wonder if they realise their plight? Many of them have lost their entire family; others have not seen their homes since war broke out, and under present conditions in Poland are not likely to be able to do so. They have no Polish Club and, apart from the cinema, nowhere to go, and their loneliness is great. May I suggest that others may feel inclined to do as we have been doing for the past three years and give hospitality to these forlorn people, whose appreciation of and gratitude for homely surroundings and friendship is immense. We have found them all delightful guests and their behaviour all that could be desired. Nearly all can speak a little English and are anxious to learn more. It is sad to see that in many parts of the country Poles are being ostracised and considered 'beyond the pale'. We were glad enough to welcome them when they came to fight for us, and when by so doing the greater number of them have lost homes, families and health. Surely it is the least we can do to help them now?[73]

Another resident wrote in response to Stratton's letter, outlining the help already given to the Poles but also revealing ambivalence towards singling them out for special attention:

I would refer [Stratton] to the activities of the local YMCA who have during the war and since, done everything possible for the happiness and comfort of all Service personnel, irrespective of nationality or colour, stationed in the vicinity. Any evening she will find large numbers of Polish troops using the canteen and games' rooms in company with the British troops. One Monday ..., over 600 Polish troops were supplied to refreshments. A request to do so was made to the Secretary, giving him one hour's notice. Although the canteen was closed for the time needed, willing helpers were gathered together and everything was done for the comfort of the men who were commencing their journey to Poland. From the expressions of gratitude I heard, it appeared they, at least, appreciated the good work of the local YMCA. The new recruits of the British Army who commence their career in Winchester are no less lonely than our Polish friends but they find in the YMCA a real comfort.[74]

For the Poles themselves, suspicion of authority and communication problems exacerbated difficulties in resettlement. These issues were common to many refugee groups, but the bitterness felt by many due to their wartime sacrifices was unique to the Poles. The British entered the war after the invasion of Poland but over the course of the conflict trust had broken down between the two allies. Most serious were the decisions made under Churchill's National Government during the war, especially the Allied decision to abandon the idea of landing in the Balkans to make a second front in 1943. 'This decision ensured that Poland would be occupied at the end of the war exclusively by Soviet troops, and that Soviet demands about the future of Poland could not be easily opposed or modified by the Anglo-Americans.'[75] Soviet interests were clearly exposed when their forces watched from the sidelines as the Poles attempted to oust the Nazis in the Warsaw Uprising of 1944. Only after many Poles had been killed did the 'liberators' enter the capital, then installing an administration sympathetic to the USSR and its recognition by the Western Allies made the exiled government a spent force. Perhaps the most lasting repercussions from political developments derived from the Yalta Conference when Churchill and Roosevelt were persuaded by Stalin to accept the loss of eastern Poland as the price of what they hoped would be a lasting rapprochement with Russia.[76] This perceived betrayal and the bitter feelings it engendered had lasting effects on the Polish settlers.

THE AFTERMATH OF THE POLISH SETTLEMENT

In terms of adaptation the Poles carried a heavy political baggage. Many had no idea they would have to start a new life abroad when they first fled their homes or were imprisoned by the occupying powers. The Communist takeover of Poland made their exile permanent with a strong sense of loss for those whose families were split up. Some paid visits to Poland years later as the Communists eased travel rules, but found themselves alienated from relations whom they had not seen for years, whilst others were unable to trace their families. In the early years of life in Britain, in addition to adjusting to a period of indefinite exile, many Poles, as former servicemen, had to adapt to life without the ties of comradeship and discipline provided by the military which had replaced family ties during the war. Moving from a rural to an urban lifestyle and from a military to a civilian existence required a new outlook, as much as learning a new language and culture. Different customs also came as a surprise. One Polish woman commented on the insularity of the British compared with her home town where people's doors were always open to visit:

> [The] English – certainly your home is your castle. And if you don't get invited, you can't come, but in Poland if I like to [visit] it's not needed for me to ring. I knock on the door and I am welcome. In England it is your family you must help... In Poland you are together always.[77]

The Poles have come to terms with their exile by establishing strong community links. These have been developed through social clubs and associations and the Polish press, led by the daily *Dziennik Polski*. Forty-two bodies in the Federation of Poles in Great Britain were listed in 1953. Amongst the most important were the Polish Ex-Servicemen's League and the Polish Catholic Mission,[78] later joined by the Polish Scout Movement, the Polish YMCA, the Polish Red Cross, sports clubs, libraries and a plethora of other associations.

Catholicism was another major factor in community cohesion. The majority of Poles were Catholics and religion has remained important in exile, such that the Poles have been granted their own network of priests and parishes in Britain.[79] As a Hampshire Polish parish priest commented, religion became an expression of nationality and the practice of Catholicism itself manifested culture and community, as most Poles attended Polish masses, rather than joining English congregations. Religious faith also reflected past suffering, as for many Poles this was the only means of solace and hope when death seemed imminent. In 1956 Zubrzycki wrote that:

> The Polish Catholic ecclesiastical organisation in Britain today is a factor which operates in the same way as Polish secular organisations and the Press; it assists the Poles to maintain a high degree of social cohesion and ethnic segregation in their national groups and by means of its powerful social and supernatural sanctions acts as a carrier of the Polish language, tradition and institutions.[80]

In terms of adaptation, Sheila Patterson contends that 'The passions and misunderstandings of the early post-war years have long been forgotten by both sides. By 1960 the Poles were no longer conceived of as potential scabs, fascists, or Casanovas. Instead they were seen as good workers, solid citizens and family men.'[81] Patterson, however, measures Polish adaptation by their apparent obscurity even in cities with a large Polish community rather than by general integration. Their invisibility was also due to first generation Poles retreating to the familiar links of the past. In many areas Polish clubs provided a forum for older members of the community to meet for lunch and drinks. In Southampton a Polish club was established in 1966 which continues to hold events to celebrate religious occasions especially at Easter, Christmas and Harvest festival, when there are traditional Polish dances by the community dancing group, 'Karpaty'. Elderly Poles have weekly meetings where they can talk in their mother tongue, take part in exercise classes, celebrate mass, eat together and generally take pride in maintaining cultural traditions. The crisis in Poland in the late 1970s and early 1980s, which brought another influx of Polish refugees to Britain, provoked solidarity movements among the exiles. After the declaration of martial law in 1982 Portsmouth Poles held a street collection to send food and medical supplies 'To Poland with Love'.[82] In Southampton two concerts were held involving Karpaty and younger children, and in 1990 the dancers were invited to go to Poland to perform, which they described as the 'experience of a lifetime'. Complex concepts of 'home' and pride in Polishness, combining local as well as national and international roots, had developed within the community.[83]

Nevertheless, though Polish group meetings and attendance of mass remain important, these links are more valuable to the older generation than their offspring, reflecting the impact of anglicisation. In the future, the need for Polish masses may decline and even die out as English is the mother-tongue for the younger Anglo-Polish community.[84] One of those involved in organising events for the Polish community in Southampton sadly reflected that 'the second generation doesn't seem to get very, or as, involved in the community – a lot of them have dropped out'. One woman explained that after her generation,

> it will be much more difficult. I'm sure the same will happen as in America.

You see a Polish name ... but he can't speak Polish. He knew that his great-grandparents were Polish, but he keeps this tradition. I am sure it will be like this with our generation.[85]

On a governmental level, the Polish influx marked a more positive approach to the needs of the victims of the Second World War than was evident with Jewish survivors of the Holocaust. But as was made clear, the Poles were considered a 'special case' because they had brought Britain into the war and fought alongside her forces. It would have been perceived as morally reprehensible to expect them to return to a country which had changed beyond all recognition. Anti-communism alongside the desperate economic need for fresh manpower, made it possible to offer the Poles the opportunity to resettle in Britain. Yet, even as the United Nations was established and Britain made its historic commitment to refugees by signing up to the UN Convention of 1951, the Poles were rarely called refugees, or offered assistance to come to terms with the ordeals they had suffered before reaching Britain. The Hungarian uprising of 1956 in the deepening Cold War, however, galvanised a more meaningful rediscovery of asylum.

Refugees from Hungary:
Anti-Communist Fervour Takes Hold

In 1956, Britain hosted another major influx of refugees from communism. Their history has not received the same degree of attention as that of the Poles, partly reflecting their lower numbers, but the Hungarian refugee movement has great significance, especially due to the warm welcome the group received. The Hungarians arrived in a period of economic reconstruction when new workers were still in demand and the housing shortage which existed in the immediate aftermath of the war was less acute. Moreover, political conditions were favourable. Internationally, the Cold War was firmly established, with eastern and western Europe in opposing ideological camps aligned with the two superpowers. Hungary had fallen into the communist camp after the war, the Allies abandoning it to the Soviet sphere of influence, contrary to the agreement between Churchill and Stalin in 1944 that Hungary would be equally divided.[1] The Hungarian refugees were seen as brave young freedom fighters with ideals akin to those in western Europe. As one refugee explained, in 1956 they 'treated us as heroes. We were always like refugees. We had a really great reception by the British people.'[2]

THE HUNGARIAN BACKGROUND

At the end of the war, in which Hungary had been a battleground between the Nazis and the Soviets, the Russians were welcomed initially as liberators by the population.[3] But as George Mikes, an earlier Hungarian refugee to Britain, argued, popular discontent was aroused by Communist methods, including indiscriminate shooting and looting in Budapest, excesses which were later denied: 'We could never swallow the Big Lie. It was suffocating and humiliating to see one thing and be compelled to act as if we had seen its very opposite.'[4] Another Hungarian described the methods used by the Communists in Hungary against their opponents as 'the Red Holocaust'.

Gino Csikasz, a Hungarian army officer imprisoned in 1951 for writing propaganda against the USSR, was sentenced to hanging, but his punishment was subsequently changed to 15 years' imprisonment, then reduced to eight years. Later settling in Portsmouth, he recalled the predicament his country faced, caught between two ideological camps:

> So when the war is over, we lose the war again. We getting a bad time but we can't go this side because it was German side, we can't go on the Russian side because it is the wrong side – see how we were in the middle. When 1956 change was taking over – the choice was leave our country... People were escaping our country because of politics. You don't know which way you're going – you go to a military system, you go to a Communist system. So what's in the middle? Nobody could make up their mind.[5]

Slowly, independence was diminished as the Soviets used local Communists to make Hungary a loyal satellite state. In economic terms the people were driven to increase production at all costs, while 'salami tactics' were used to remove political opposition in parliament. Initially the Smallholders Party was squeezed out of power and then the Socialists. Increasing dissent was punished by imprisonment. Even the Prince Primate of the Hungarian Catholic Church, Cardinal Mindszenty, a prominent national figure, was imprisoned. A police state was established, with the dreaded secret police force, known as the AVO, running concentration camps, labour camps and prisons. Wealthy peasants were moved into collectives and in May 1951 thousands of people were deported out of Budapest to the countryside because of their class. As Csikasz explained, 'People were fed up, tired and angry.'[6]

Ferenc Nagy, a Hungarian socialist, who was Prime Minister from 1945 to 1947, and was one of the leaders of the movement for reform, came to symbolise the frustrated aims of the Hungarian Revolution. In 1948 he wrote about the post-war period in *The Struggle Behind the Iron Curtain*. First Hungarians welcomed the Soviets as liberators, taking seriously their pledge of independence. They then

> suffered them as conquerers... The slogans of a year before were exchanged for new ones; the new Soviet terror replaced that of National Socialism ... when the Hungarian people wanted to [exercise their] independence ... the Soviet regarded these acts as aggression .... [and] branded any democratic manifestation as reactionary. It barred the nation from realising its peace aims and diverted the people from its natural and normal stream of life.

Nagy described how the internal terror created by the Communist Party was supplemented at an even cruder level by the open actions of the Soviet government itself, leading to 'the most tragic chapter in Hungarian history, the costly experience in appeasing Soviet Russia':

> Soviet generals ordered the first so-called Parliament convened, according to their own design, and all but appointed the first cabinet... The Soviet Union turned the Allied Control Commission into its own agency, denying a voice to the two great Western powers sharing control. It swallowed blameless leaders,

statesmen and officers in dead of night, never to be heard from again. Its trained agents barnacled the nation as leaders of the Communist Party... It forged the Potsdam agreement into chains for our economic slavery; and forced Hungary, by this stranglehold, into unequal economic collaboration. It coerced the democratic parties, through these economic claims to yield to the Communists... Its armed terror dictated the direction and pace of agrarian reform... It at last perpetrated the putsch which eliminated me from the premiership of my country and forced me into exile.

Hungary, believed Nagy, was a test case of what might occur in the future. In true Cold War rhetoric he warned his readers that:

[E]vents themselves indict the Union of Soviet Socialist Republics; the world must pass judgement. Penetration completed, today there is no breath, no motion, no life, in Hungary without Soviet direction or approval. These appearances have been duplicated in all of Eastern Europe, a part of the world has become dark, impenetrable; where, behind the outward quiescence, a bitter ideological struggle rages against the new tyranny. Were this the end of the black story, there would be no need to spotlight it. But Communist imperialism is an advancing process of penetration, not content with constricting the countries nearest its borders ... I stand on free soil. But unless I voice the warning that weighs on the hearts of people everywhere I shall not regard my obligation to those less fortunate than I, as discharged. By the grace of destiny, democracy shall yet embrace the world.[7]

It was the death of Stalin in 1953 and uncertainty over his successor, with the left and right wings of the Russian leadership vying for power, which offered the Communist states of eastern Europe an opportunity to demand greater freedoms at home. In Hungary, Imre Nagy, a reformist Communist, became Prime Minister, and he and his supporters increased their challenge against Matyas Rakosi, First Secretary of the Party, and the old guard Communists. Nagy was expelled from the party in April 1955, but the struggle behind the scenes continued and was augmented by a more public movement.[8]

In February 1956, President Khruschev's denunciation of Stalin's methods at the Twentieth Congress of the Soviet Communist Party appeared to pave the way for change. Calls for reform in Hungary coincided with movements in Yugoslavia (Tito's 'Socialism in one country') and Poland. Many Hungarians were anxious to throw off the Soviet Communist yoke and regain their political independence. On 23 October a group of intellectuals called for a series of reforms, including the removal of the Stalinist Prime Minister, freedom of the press, free elections, withdrawal of Soviet troops and the establishment of workers' control in the factories. When there was no response, the people of Budapest took to the streets. In the ensuing movement of masses of people, the security forces fired on the crowds and the uprising began in earnest. Symbols of Soviet oppression were targeted – a huge statue of Stalin was smashed and the Hungarian flag was raised with the hammer and sickle emblem removed. One Hungarian boy captured the mood:

> People say we live behind the Iron Curtain. This is not quite true. We lived in a
> tin. As long as a tin is hermetically closed, it's all right. But then during Imre
> Nagy's first Premiership they pierced the tin and let in a little bit of fresh air.
> You know what happens to a tin when a little fresh air gets into it?... Everything
> inside gets rotten.[9]

But the strength of national hopes were dashed in a matter of weeks. Over this
brief period it appeared that the Hungarians might be treated liberally, as
conflicting signals emanated from the Soviet leadership, and Imre Nagy was
temporarily given power. Nagy's demands for more independence went too
far, however, and the Soviets ordered their tanks to crush the dissent.[10] Tens
of thousands of Hungarians were killed and hundreds of thousands more fled
to Austria in the months that followed, some of whom soon came to Britain.

In the West, the uprising in October 1956 was given great publicity and
sympathies lay with the rebels demanding greater freedom. The communist
movement itself was severely discredited with demonstrations in Berlin,
Oslo, Stockholm, Copenhagen, Brussels and Bonn. Parisian crowds burnt
copies of the Communist paper *Humanité* in the streets and ransacked the
Communist Party headquarters, while in Portugal 10,000 students and 50,000
other people marched through Lisbon carrying Hungarian banners and black
flags of mourning. In Britain, dockers in Liverpool refused to handle the
cargo of a Russian ship.[11] Mr Selwyn Lloyd, the British Foreign Secretary,
spoke of a 'deep admiration' for the Hungarians in their struggle for
freedom.[12] Views such as his and that of the European editor of *Newsweek*, Mr
Eldon Griffiths, who was in Hungary at the time of the revolt, were aired,
even in the local press. 'It was a revolt not against the Russians, but against
Communism – the kind of system which had stolen their land and taken their
young men and children and put them into regimented groups where their
whole world has been warped.'[13] A miner's testimony was used to show the
terror experienced by the Hungarians when striking during October against
Soviet actions:

> I went home and stayed there. Then the AVO arrived and told me they'd shoot
> me if I didn't go back to work the next day; my mates said they'd flood the mine
> if anyone went back to work. So I thought I'd run for it. But one of my mates
> got killed by the Russians trying to escape. So you got shot for striking, and shot
> for escaping, and if you went back to work you got drowned. Not much choice.
> Anyway, I decided to make for Austria and here I am.[14]

THE HUNGARIAN REFUGEE MOVEMENT

In the prevailing political situation in Europe, support for Hungary's
dissenters became a rallying cry for anti-communists and an opportunity in
the West to demonise the Soviet Union. In such conditions, it was hardly
surprising that the British Conservative government welcomed a large

number of the Hungarians who were fleeing to Austria. This welcome was partly a sop to an outraged public, as there was a widespread belief that Britain should have done more to help the Hungarians in their struggle against the Soviet oppressor. This echoed British actions in 1938 when the Nazis took over Czechoslovakia and the government set up the Czech Refugee Fund. The Conservative MP for Eastleigh, David Price, was not alone in calling for a tougher stance on Hungary when he said: 'Had force been used to meet force it might have meant a third world war, but I would have been prepared to have risked it a little bit more than we have done'.[15] A few years later, President Eisenhower suggested why the West failed to do more:

> There was no European country, and, indeed, I don't believe ours, ready to say that we should have gone into this thing at once and tried to liberate Hungary from the Communist influence. I don't believe, at this time, that we had the support of the UN to go in and make this a full-out war. The thing started in such a way, you know, that everybody was a little bit fooled, I think, and when suddenly the Soviets came in strength with their tank divisions, and it was a fait accompli, it was a great tragedy and disaster.[16]

Feelings of guilt played a major part in motivating support for the refugees:

> The world threw itself to meet these refugees with almost indecent zest and goodwill... After all, they had witnessed the martyrdom of a small nation with tears in their eyes but without swords in their hands. The Hungarians had fought their battles, too, they had died for their cause as well as the cause of Hungary, and the world at large could not, or would not, do more than say: 'Superb!' and 'What a brave nation!'... Now they had a heaven-sent opportunity to forget the more depressing and sinister aspects of the matter in an [ex]cess of generosity to the refugees.[17]

The initial British government plan to take in only 2,500 refugees was considered insufficient. Conservative MP Peter Kirk of Gravesend stated: 'In this extreme situation we should have said that the gates of Britain are wide open to any Hungarian who wanted to come.'[18] Though R. A. Butler, the Chancellor of the Exchequer, argued that Britain was not an 'immigrant country', his views were out of kilter with popular sentiment and the scope of the project was subsequently widened. The government gave grants totalling £50,000 to the British Red Cross to assist the Hungarians and a further £10,000 was given to the British Council for Aid to Refugees, BCAR (now the Refugee Council), alongside funding from the UN Secretary-General.

The campaign in Britain to aid the Hungarians was part of a much larger effort by the international community coming under the auspices of the United Nations. It was here that various countries, led by the United States (but also including former Russian sympathisers and uncommitted nations like Cuba and Pakistan), deplored Soviet actions. With an overwhelming majority, the UN passed a resolution demanding the withdrawal of Soviet tanks from Hungary and free elections under UN supervision. The British delegation's position was revealed in a telegram to the emergency meeting of the United Nations' General Assembly after Soviet tanks entered Budapest:

> Russian troops are occupying Budapest and the Assembly will have heard … the reports of looting, pillaging and indiscriminate shooting of civilians. We have reports on the mowing down of women in bread queues and shooting down at sight of any Hungarian venturing to tread the pavements of his own city. The civilian casualties run into many thousands… The UN has affirmed the right of the Hungarian people to a government 'responsive to its national aspirations and dedicated to its independence and wellbeing'. The UN has called upon the USSR to desist from all armed attack on the peoples of Hungary and any form of intervention, particularly armed intervention in the internal affairs of Hungary. The Assembly has also called upon the USSR to cease the introduction of additional armed forces into Hungary and to withdraw all its forces without delay from Hungarian territory. The USSR … has ignored all these requests of the UN, and on the contrary is reinforcing its occupation of Hungary… The UN must not relax its attempts to secure to the people of Hungary the right to express themselves in freedom and determine their own affairs as a sovereign state.[19]

Ultimately, appeals to the USSR to 'heed the dictates of the conscience of the world' were futile. Indeed, the failure of the UN to achieve anything more than vocal disapproval of Soviet action in Hungary reflected its vulnerability to the political machinations of the superpowers throughout the Cold War. The fear that conflicts in third countries, where 'Communism' and 'Capitalism' clashed, would become a trigger for a head-on confrontation undermined attempts to solve international crises. At the time of the Hungarian uprising international reactions were further complicated by events in the Middle East. Here, Israeli forces, backed by Britain and France, invaded Egypt in an attempt to prevent President Nasser from nationalising the Suez Canal. Britain and France were forced to retreat from this neo-colonialist venture due to American disapproval, but the focus on events in the Middle East inevitably had repercussions for the Hungarians. George Mikes argued that the attack played a part in persuading Russia to intervene in Hungary, as it seemed to be evidence of Western expansionist aims: 'Had the Anglo-French ultimatum been sent to Egypt a month later, Hungary would be a second Poland today.'[20] Certainly the Hungarians' plight was overshadowed and the fear of 'hot' war heightened by the Middle Eastern crisis, but condemnation of the Soviet Union by the Western powers in the UN proved to be nothing more than a paper tiger.

An estimated 170,000–200,000 Hungarians fled from their country in the mass exodus bringing for the majority permanent exile. While other countries deliberated and procrastinated, Austria took positive action to aid the Hungarians, allowing the refugees to cross its borders unhindered. Such was Austria's generosity that it was forced to appeal to other countries to help take in some 100,000 of the Hungarians who fled there. France, Israel, the United

Home Office Form I.B.23(H)

The Bearer is permitted to land in the United Kingdom on condition that he registers at once with the Police and does not enter any employment paid or unpaid without the consent of the Ministry of Labour and National Service.

1. Surname   RUMI

2. Other Names   Andras - Endre

3. Nationality   Hungarian

4. Date and Place of Birth   21.12.31   Bogojevo

Signature of Bearer   Andras Rumi

IMMIGRATION OFFICER'S STAMP.

IMMIGRATION OFFICER
(16)
20 JAN 1957
DOVER

Home Office entry document (Dover) of Andras-Endre Rumi from Hungary, 20 January 1957. From the private collection of Andy Rumi and with his kind permission.

States, Canada and Yugoslavia all took considerable numbers and the British government agreed to take the initial quota of 2,500. There are no detailed records of the Hungarians who entered Britain, but the Ministry of Labour issued monthly returns, indicating the general situation. The final return of 31 July 1959 shows that Britain accepted 21,692 Hungarians although 5,822 of these were to re-emigrate, almost all to Canada, leaving a total of 14,312 staying in Britain.[21] A further 1,214 had returned to Hungary or other eastern European countries by this date.[22] BCAR, one of the primary movers in the resettlement programme, estimated that by 1959, 2,300 people had returned to Hungary, encompassing 'non-integrated' groups, especially Gypsies and unaccompanied teenagers. In 1965 it estimated that the total eventually settling was about 14,500.

The Hungarians who came to Britain in 1956–57 did not enter a total cultural vacuum. According to the BCAR, there were already 761 Hungarians who had arrived in the country in 1937–38, mainly for domestic service, in a ratio of two men to five women. Most of these were Jews escaping the antisemitism of inter-war Hungary. In 1947–48 a further 2,591 Hungarians were admitted, mainly as European Volunteer Workers. This time the majority were male, with five men entering for every woman.[23] They were scattered across the country and had little social impact. There were only two small community clubs, one in London and the other in Lancashire:

> These Hungarians, unlike many of the Ugandan Asians ... did not find themselves moving into ethnic neighbourhoods populated with relatives or family friends. For most, both their exodus and their final destination were functions of chance and were unrelated to an existing social network.[24]

RESPONSES TO THE HUNGARIAN REFUGEES

In terms of their reception, the Hungarians were not always as popular in Britain as reactions to the 1956 crisis would suggest. An extract from the famous pamphlet of the Hungarians in exile, *Igaszag (Truth)*, provides an indication of British attitudes towards the refugees, but also offers a historical overview of British impressions of both the Hungarian people and nation prior to the 1956 Revolution:

> A great deal has been written about the historic affinities and the links of sympathy and understanding between Hungary and Britain. Certainly there have in the past been a large number of such associations, and it is certainly a fact ... that the men and women of our two nations do easily find one another sympathetic. Nevertheless, it is equally true that for a long time before 1956 serious opinion in this country was not on the whole favourable to Hungary...

The reactionary nature of inter-war Hungary gave it a bad reputation amongst liberals abroad which was not countered by the many tourists who went there bringing back 'memories of agreeable, cheap evenings and charming companions'. 'Today', however, the author argued, 'the position is quite different':

> The Hungarian revolution awoke in Britain a sympathy and an admiration to which I can recall no parallel in my life-time. A Hungarian in our country today starts with an enormous plus of good-will. He has only to disclose his nationality to find himself liked and admired, not primarily for his own sake (although that may come after), but for that of his nation ... he has a duty to show us that the merit exists, and wherein it lies, not only by his personal conduct, but by testifying to his nation. This ... does mean demanding that Hungary should be taken seriously. It is undeniable that for a thousand years Hungary filled a special place in the world and made a special contribution to the history, the thought and the arts of Europe, that it had its own spirit. Now that the soil of Hungary is under foreign occupation, there is most certainly both room and need for her emigration to keep that spirit alive, and also to explain the nature of it to us non-Hungarians so that when the day comes when the plant can flourish again in its native earth, we understand it better.[25]

The lack of preparation in Britain to take in the refugees was shown when, after some 16,000 arrivals, the flow had to be halted temporarily over Christmas because of the pressure on accommodation facilities. The initial limit on the number of entrants and the procedure of screening them were abandoned on 23 November due to the growing pressure of refugees on the Austrian government. The effect of public pressure in Britain is hard to quantify, but marches of support for the revolutionaries by students in Glasgow, all over London and elsewhere in the first two weeks of November suggest that it was considerable. Correspondence in *The Times* confirmed overwhelming support for taking the Hungarians. A. L. Price, of Lincoln's Inn, was concerned about the small number of refugees which the British government had pledged itself to accepting, especially as the figure appeared mean in terms of international comparisons:

> Why only 2,500?... Can there be any convincing answer to it? These refugees are the victims of a tyranny as cruel and as devilish as any in recorded history. Belgium will take in 4,000. This nation of fifty million prosperous people will take no more than 2,500. Surely someone in authority should explain to the nation why we can take only 2,500? Let the reasons be stated quickly, clearly, and without any evasion or concealment. And, Sir, if the reasons are unconvincing, many people will be very angry.[26]

Another contributor, Richard Rhys, of Magdalene College, Cambridge, who, along with fellow undergraduates and 'young English people' had 'just returned from a harrowing few days helping refugees on the Austrian-Hungarian border', made a plea for 'British' justice for the Hungarians extending beyond help for the exiled:

> The pathetic pride and disillusioned hopes of these Hungarians and their stories of Russian brutality have given me greater cause to make this plea. The postwar

policy of the west has been one of peace and justice. Now at this first major trial since Korea, our convictions are found to be rotten and hollow ... We were the first English people that many of the Hungarians had ever met. They were almost all fierce in their anxiety to know why we had not helped them. All I could do was to explain that we were afraid of a third world war, and say that Hungary's magnificent effort had taught the world a great lesson. One refugee retorted that they too had learnt a lesson. How small and ashamed I felt. Every Hungarian has risked his life, and the lives of those he loved to fight for our cause of justice. 100,000 have died. We have shown them no gratitude nor respect other than helping the refugees... Let the Government do something at once to reassure the hopes of those struggling for freedom and the right to live. Many thousands of young people are prepared to fight, rather than just see mankind being so brutally scarred in its tragic nakedness.[27]

No such action was intended by the government but instead attention was focused on assisting the refugees coming to Britain.

The programme to deal with the Hungarians involved state and voluntary sector cooperation. On 6 December, in response to a question in the Commons, the Home Secretary, Major Lloyd George, outlined plans made by the government for the reception and accommodation of the Hungarians. These were to be coordinated by BCAR working with the Home Office and other relevant departments:

On arrival the refugees are taken to barracks which have been placed at the disposal of the Council by the War Office. At these barracks the refugees are registered by the police and provided with any necessary clothing and equipment. They are then moved to hostels in different parts of the country where every endeavour is made to familiarise them with the British way of life and to find employment for them or to place them in accommodation offered by the public. A considerable number of these refugees wish to emigrate to other countries and it is hoped that early arrangements will be made accordingly. Canada, in particular, has offered priority to Hungarian refugees.

In spite of his emphasis on those who would be leaving, the Home Secretary was anxious to point out, ignoring the Austrian contribution, that 'By the 11th instant some 11,000 refugees will have been received in this country and the House will be glad to know that this is a number which has not been equalled by any other country in the world'.[28]

The reception programme was primarily carried out by voluntary agencies, indicated by the response of Mr J. N. Browne, the Secretary of State for Scotland, to a question about the role which would be played by Scottish local authorities in the reception process. 'I am glad to say that voluntary effort seems likely to be fully able to deal with this tragic problem; but I am sure that local authorities will readily consider any requests for assistance which the voluntary bodies may make and which it is within their power to meet.'[29] The cooperation of the state and voluntary agencies was crucial, due to the magnitude of the task, as BCAR stressed. Looking after 17,000 refugees would have been impossible 'but for the generous help of HMG in putting Government buildings and equipment at the disposal of BCAR, and lending civil servants to work with BCAR staff both at Headquarters and in the field'.[30]

Although the government put up considerable money for the transportation and resettlement of the Hungarians, totalling £355,000 by March 1957,[31] the British public raised more through the Lord Mayor of London's appeal which after only a few weeks had raised £895,000. It eventually raised £2,500,000, providing further evidence of the widespread support for the Hungarians.[32] The reception and resettlement process involved many interested parties. The St John Ambulance Brigade and the British Red Cross Society investigated houses offered as hostels and in some cases ran them on behalf of BCAR. They were also involved in ensuring the medical welfare of the refugees. The Women's Voluntary Services carried out similar inspections, and provided information as well as the more basic necessities of clothing, a role they were to repeat with Vietnamese refugees in the 1970s. The YMCA organised educational and recreational activities for the refugees and taught them English in the hostels, while the World University Service helped students undertake courses in Britain and the voluntary organisations helped find jobs for the Hungarians in conjunction with the Ministry of Labour.

The importance of the voluntary organisations in the reception process and the initial interaction between the British helpers and the refugees was related by the wife of one of the volunteers who was the divisional director of the Red Cross at Croydon:

> When it was decided to fly refugees from Hungary to Croydon Airport the Red Cross were asked to stand by to accompany them to their destinations... On the first occasions there were only a small number of refugees and they were taken by coach to somewhere in Surrey... The third lot, however, were a much larger contingent, including children – I remember going out after receiving that information and buying packets of sweets for my husband to take with him... We understood that they did not speak any English ... but sweets speak any language to children! There was a coachful on that occasion, many of them students straight from fighting on the streets, and in a very distressed state. In fact, when they saw the uniforms of the Red Cross personnel some of them tried to run away they were so frightened of anyone in uniform. However, all were got on to the coach and it set off for Tidworth, where a section of the Barracks which was unused at the time had been opened up with staff there to make a hot meal for them when they arrived...[33]

Apart from aiding the Hungarians in their initial reception, voluntary bodies made efforts to help in their permanent resettlement. Interpreters were employed, most of whom had entered Britain following the Communist takeover in 1948. In addition to assisting the Hungarians in their search for housing and job opportunities, English lessons were held in the hostels. The onus, however, was on the Hungarians to deal with the language problem. As

Mr Macleod said in the Commons, 'We are very happy and honoured to have the Hungarian visitors here, but I hope that they will learn English rather than that we shall have to learn Hungarian'.[34] The basic assumption, as ever, was that the refugees must assimilate to British ways. The government made efforts to help them achieve this end. Until December 1957, the Central Office of Information distributed a weekly news-sheet *Heti Hirek* (*This Week*) printed in Hungarian, disseminating information relevant to the refugees, countering hostile rumours and encouraging them to adapt to life in Britain. There were also courses in the 'British way of life' and the Women's Voluntary Service prepared a booklet for the Hungarians, with the help of government departments. The booklet was presented by BCAR for distribution to the refugees to help them in their initial orientation. In a series of 17 chapters it sought to explain the history and law of Britain, language, financial matters, education, social patterns and rights and obligations. The pamphlet provided another example of the pressure faced by refugee groups to conform to a romantically constructed form of Englishness:

The Policeman
The policeman in Britain is kindly, friendly and helpful. He is in the street in order to help the public. You can turn to him with any kind of enquiry (only not to the one on traffic duty who has other things to do).

Autobus
If more than three or four people wait at a stop, you must queue up. This helps everyone. The bus conductor takes care of his passengers, and does not give the starting signal until everybody has boarded the bus, unless it is full...

Shopping
In England there is no bargaining in the shops. In the great stores a tremendous amount of merchandise is often freely displayed without supervision, and the shoppers gaily rummage and choose. It looks as if there could be no control or supervision. Yet there is – a very strict one – only it is very clever and unnoticeable.[35]

LIFE IN BRITAIN

As with the Poles, the Hungarians were housed initially in Army and RAF camps converted into reception centres, before being transferred to hostels. Among the most important of these camps were the barracks at Tidworth and Aldershot in Hampshire.[36] Many of the refugees were flown into Blackbushe airport in the New Forest where they were greeted by volunteers from the British Red Cross and escorted to the camps where they were given food and clothing. The hostels where the Hungarians were subsequently sent, were, like those used for the Spanish children, variable in size and quality. They included YMCA hostels, large country houses (such as that provided by the Ockenden Venture in Surrey), former army camp or industrial training establishments, and even former workhouses. Some of these were used only on a short-term basis for those intending to emigrate, while others became longer-term holding hostels. Of the refugees who re-emigrated from Britain, most went to Canada, but others left for the United States, Australia, New Zealand and South Africa. They were financed by the United States Escapee Programme (USEP) and onward migration was organised by the relevant religious agencies: the Catholic Relief Services, the World Council of Churches, the Lutheran World Federation and the Jewish body, HIAS. The majority were helped by the Catholic agency, since two-thirds of the Hungarians were Catholics, at least nominally. It was not until 1961 that the USEP programme was concluded.

The composition of the group of Hungarians coming to Britain showed a predominance of men, aged between 20 and 30. According to the Minister of Labour, Iain Macleod, in April 1957 there were 11,500 males and 4,000 females aged over 16 in the country.[37] It seems that a significant number of the men were single. In other cases, the men fled first, intending to bring their wives and children out later, but the Communist government in Hungary was not always willing to let them leave. As in other refugee influxes, including the Vietnamese, where large groups of arrivals were allowed entry to the country without individual scrutiny, the group swept up a number of adventurers and there were also several hundred unaccompanied teenagers. According to BCAR, some, as young as 12 or 13, were placed in foster homes. Such arrangements were, however:

> not always satisfactory owing to the independent nature of the young Hungarians, and, in some cases, where they had left their homes and parents more out of a sense of adventure and bravado than because they had taken any active part in the uprising, they succumbed to homesickness and were returned to their families.[38]

The Hungarians' reasons for flight were varied. Some young men left because they had taken an active part in the uprising and feared deportation to the Soviet Union. Those fleeing Hungary included some people who had been in Nazi camps, among them Jews and Gypsies. 'In other cases there is no mention of why they came, but from reading the files it seems that many were running away from their wives and families.'[39] When the uprising occurred, the doors of mental hospitals and prisons were opened and some of the former inmates of these institutions entered Britain as refugees. A small but significant number were to have problems integrating, so that BCAR set up a Hungarian Committee between 1957 and 1962 to locate and visit the mentally ill, estimating that there were between 140 and 170 such cases in the UK in 1979.[40]

The uprising was led in Budapest and other Hungarian cities and therefore the refugees were mainly from an urban background. The first arrivals tended to be students and engineers.[41] A BCAR report, however, noted that apart from

> a very small number of doctors and dentists who were helped to requalify in Britain with the cooperation of the International Medical Advisory Bureau, and

an equally small number of students who succeeded in completing their education at British universities and technical colleges, the Hungarians were mainly industrial workers.[42]

In a sample of one-quarter of the individual files, nearly 300 different occupations were found. Generally the Hungarians came from less skilled occupations, working as leatherworkers, tailors and cooks.[43] The Hungarians, like the Poles, generally had little difficulty in finding work in Britain, even though they possessed limited English, as long as they were prepared to do manual work. Again, they were very much dependent on filling shortages in British industry. Few of the refugees were suited to agriculture and were not able to take advantage of the large numbers of vacancies for farm labourers.[44] A large number of the refugees entered the mining industry. In mid-February 1957, about 3,900 had been taken on as potential coal miners,[45] although initially many worked at the surface and after a short period a number left the industry for other jobs. Some of them were recruited directly by the National Coal Board through advertisements for workers in Austria, others were directed to the industry after their arrival in Britain. One man described how he came to work in the mining industry:

> I was sixteen when I left Hungary. I left on New Year's Eve at the end of 1956 and I came to England on 3 January 1957. I was rather fortunate I suppose because I didn't want to stay in a refugee camp because the longer you stay there the harder it becomes to settle. I came to a place in Austria. The following day I went to Graz, and as I was handing my papers in there was a notice by there – anybody over sixteen to come to England to work for the National Coal Board because you have to have a work permit – and I said to myself I didn't want to stay in the camp because there would be thousands of people waiting to go into different camps and it would be very difficult for me to move along, so I handed my papers in and it came to New Year's Day, and they put us on the train the following day to England. On the third I was in Scotland in Stirling coal mine.[46]

Those Hungarians who were not recruited to agriculture or mining found work through employment exchanges. Of the 15,500 adults in Britain in April 1957, the government reported that over 7,500 had been placed in employment by the Ministry of Labour, 2,000 had found employment through other means, while a further 3,500 were undergoing training.[47] By the end of May it was stated that nearly 12,000 Hungarians had been placed in employment other than coal mining, although this included some placed in temporary positions who had since left for Canada.[48] An estimate from a BCAR survey in 1965 suggests that 80 per cent of the Hungarians were employed in factory work, either skilled or unskilled.[49] The success of the Hungarians in finding work is borne out by their testimony. As one said, 'We'd never had it so good.' [50] Such a high degree of employment among the refugees was not always a feature of later migrations, such as the Vietnamese, who had greater cultural barriers to overcome as well as facing a less welcoming economic climate than the Hungarians. Moreover, the help provided by government agencies was not always so generous for succeeding groups of refugees. The government's positive and exceptional role in comparative terms reflected its political commitment to the Hungarians as well as its need for labour. Grants from the Lord Mayor's Fund were used to set up the BCAR Housing Society to purchase and convert low-cost houses into flats for the refugees. These houses were ones which were not required by local authorities, a proviso 'essential in order that refugees should not appear to be "jumping the housing queue" ahead of the British'.[51] Houses were acquired in the Greater London area at Willesden, Croydon and Luton, and in industrial towns in the Midlands and the North of England, and the hostels were gradually shut down, the last of which, in Manchester, closed in 1959.

Despite all the positive factors in their favour, however, there was still some concern about the Hungarians including opposition voiced in Parliament. First, several MPs expressed concern that the refugees could include Communist agents, indicative of the anti-communist fervour in Britain, responsible for the acceptance of the refugees in the first place.[52] However, as Mr Emrys-Hughes had pointed out in an earlier debate it was 'very difficult to define communists in relation to Hungary'. Some of the strongest opponents of the new regime were different types of communists and it 'would be grossly unfair to regard these as enemy agents'.[53] It was also argued that interpreters with communist leanings were advising refugees not to work in the coal mines because they resembled labour camps. Major Lloyd George was quick to disregard any such rumours:

> The government would not tolerate any attempts at intimidation of, or interference with, refugees who enjoy the protection of this country, and would have no hesitation in taking appropriate action against anyone concerned in such attempts.[54]

The second basis for opposition was that it was believed that many Hungarians were paid during their training for employment in the coal mines but were not always staying to work there. It was asked:

> When does the Paymaster-General expect any substantial number of these refugees will be capable of becoming effective units of production? Can he further inform the House whether it is a fact that they are being paid £8 a week from the day they landed in the country, and whether this expense will be borne by the National Coal Board or shared by the Treasury?[55]

Such antipathy was not common, particularly compared to that voiced against other refugees, though questions about the cost of training the Hungarians as miners were repeated. Such opposition was finally quashed when Iain Macleod of the Ministry of Labour replied that the Coal Board, not the Treasury, was paying the Hungarians while they were undergoing training.[56]

Local press coverage as illustrated in the *Southern Daily Echo*, as well as in national papers like *The Times*, was generally supportive of the Hungarian cause. In the Hampshire press, detailed coverage was given to events in Hungary, followed by British parliamentary statements on the issue, as well as the role played by local people to raise money to help the refugees. Only rarely was any hostility expressed, such as an article entitled 'Council gave five Hungarians a bungalow – now they want to leave'.[57] The group in question had received publicity when they had moved into a house in Ferndown, Hampshire, and hostility arose when they wanted to leave for Canada. The conclusion of the article offered another angle on the issue, noting that some of the Hungarians were paid lower wages in the local building industry which may also have created tension.[58]

The movement of these five Hungarians was part of a wider trend of re-emigration to an apparently brighter future, which gave the Hungarians a bad image in Britain. This was countered to some extent, by a later headline, 'Not stepping stone to US – "We're in Britain to stay" – Hungarians',[59] which went beyond the *Southern Daily Echo's* usual local confines to report that those in Northumberland were sad about rumours that they wished to leave for America. One was reported to have said, 'It's a lie. We have come here not on holiday but to do a useful job and to be, shall I say "re-born".' Favourable comments about the group came from the Coal Board. The refugees were said to be joining local football teams and the local orchestra, generally integrating into the local community.

Danko Joszef, a refugee who later settled in Southampton, described his early experiences working in the mines in Scotland:

> [There was] very good understanding between ourselves plus whoever was with us even just talking the language with your hands and your feet and a little pocket dictionary and looking up odd words. You know that you learn the name of the equipment – what you used every day – and tried to make a conversation of some sort. It was good fun. From time to time you say the wrong thing ... but I managed. You had no fears of somebody watching over your back ... the life was new and things I have never seen in Hungary I have seen here. It's a complete change of lifestyle, even the streets or the housing, public services, just looking around. You think that's nice... For me it worked very well, for others it didn't work so well.[60]

Generally, the British warmly welcomed the Hungarians. This support was not confined to the political right. The Southampton Labour Party was among those groups on the left who empathised with the Hungarian uprising. Its secretary forwarded a resolution to the Foreign Office on behalf of his 17,000 members in the county which had been unanimously supported in November 1956, expressing

> its heartfelt sympathy with the people of Hungary in the suffering they are enduring in their desperate struggle for national freedom. It calls for immediate

withdrawal of all Soviet forces from Hungary so as to make possible the use of a UN Police Force to maintain law and order while free and democratic General Elections are held in the Country under UN auspices.[61]

The Eastleigh MP David Price was voluble in his denunciation of the Conservative government for its failure to help the Hungarians at the stage of Soviet intervention. Speaking at Eastleigh Town Hall he reflected on his unease at what Britain had so far done on behalf of the Hungarian people. He believed the country had

> obligations as members of the UN and as signatories of the Universal Declaration of Human Rights. When you come to look at Hungary, how impotent we have been... The situation is so desperate that any action which has the remotest chance of success is worth trying.

He then praised the help given by the British public to the refugees, emphasising, as many had done in the past, that this was part of a noble British tradition:

> This country had always been proud of the fact that it had been a home and haven for the oppressed, and he believed that had added something to our national life. The Lord Mayor's appeal had passed the £1 million mark and he was delighted to see the excellent response to the Mayor of Eastleigh's fund.[62]

In Winchester, the United Nations Association organised a public meeting for the Hungarian refugee, George Paloczi Horvath, to address local people. Horvath was a prominent Hungarian figure who, in the turmoil of the war, had been a member of the Communist Party but was imprisoned between 1949 and 1954 as a 'bourgeois enemy', having spent some time in the West. In recounting his own personal experience, he wrote that he could now

> understand why all of us had been arrested – from Rajk downwards to such 'inside-the party-fellow-travellers' as myself. Everybody who took the cause seriously had to be eliminated. The aim was to build up a strong war industry and make the largest possible contribution to Stalin's war chest. At that time I still believed that this aim was being achieved. Later, I learnt that, with the hetacombs of innocently murdered people, with all the misery and terrorism unleashed on the people, this system became a fetter on industry, agriculture, commerce, cultural life – on everything. The workers were right. The whole thing stinks as it is.[63]

After his release he joined those writers denouncing the Stalinists within Hungary and pressing for change. He described the time of the uprising as a very rare historical event, when, 'a whole nation rose spontaneously and in the turmoil of fighting found momentary leadership'.[64] As the Russian tanks crushed the Revolution, he made the decision to flee, coming to Britain. Horvath stressed to his Winchester audience that 'intelligent public opinion' in the Hungarian crisis was 'far more important today than ever before'. Describing the fighting in October 1956, he said:

There were some 78 fighting groups in Budapest. In the first two days many people had lost their lives because there was no liaison between these groups, but, he went on – 'We did that because it looked to us that we could prove to the world that a people could throw off the yoke of totalitarian dictatorship.' After speaking next of the need for a keen public opinion, he said the next fight for the coming generation was to establish the rule of law throughout the world, and he concluded – 'Don't drop the pennies, shillings or pounds into collection boxes for us, but please fight for our and your future by doing what has to be done'.[65]

In the growing tensions of the Cold War, such words would not have been lost on his audience.

HAMPSHIRE AND THE REFUGEES

Local interest in the Hungarian issue can be partly attributed to the fact that a large proportion of the refugees were initially accommodated in Hampshire. Several thousand stayed in army barracks at Tidworth, Crookham and, primarily, Aldershot. On 4 December 1956, when a Christmas market was held for them, it was noted that well over a third of the 6,700 Hungarian arrivals were in Hampshire.[66] This meant local voluntary bodies were at the forefront of dealing with the arrivals, especially the Hampshire Red Cross, the Women's Voluntary Service and the St John Ambulance.[67] The Girl Guides' Association even offered their International Training Centre at Foxlease, Lyndhurst, to accommodate a dozen refugee families. The strong local response to fundraising appeals and to helping the refugees generally was part of a broader trend of national support for the Hungarians following the uprising. With over 20,000 offers of help and accommodation received by 24 November by BCAR alone,[68] it is not surprising that some organisations involved were 'almost embarrassed by the warmth of the response'.[69] The Lord Mayor of London's fund was opened up for local authorities across Britain and was supplemented in Hampshire by appeals from local officials. The *Hampshire Chronicle* reported that

> the response has been quite staggering already. From old and young, rich and poor, gifts have been coming in during the week, so much so that in one respect at least – the appeal for clothing – the organisers have been embarrassed by the overwhelming quantity forthcoming. Demonstrative of the public feeling of sympathy for the cause ... was the success of the effort at Winchester ... when members of the local Round Table Club ... arranged a special collection at the City Cross. They started a continuous line of coins around the steps of the Cross and before the day was out the mixture of coins and paper money there realised the extraordinary total ... of over £218.

> All kinds of stories of actions and gestures some of them quite touching are reported. There was the case of a restaurant in Winchester which gave its takings on Monday to the Fund, while a wool shop at Romsey put up a notice

stating that 1d. will be given to the Fund for every ounce of wool sold, and inviting customers to add another penny equally. Many shops have installed collecting boxes on their counters. Children at Sunday schools were quick off the mark with their comparatively small but quite generous gifts on Sunday. Offers of accommodation for refugees have also come in – over 60 of them (for both children and adults) – to the County Headquarters of the Red Cross Society. [O]ffers of 'self contained accommodation' – a cottage, a flat, a house and a caravan – have also been received.[70]

The generosity expressed for these refugees contrasted with the lack of popular response, and indeed the antipathetical press coverage, which subsequent groups, such as the Vietnamese and the Ugandan Asians, received. Public support for the Hungarians was matched by the actions of the local state, including Southampton City Council. In late November 1956, the Mayor of Southampton 'expressed her thanks to the many citizens who had generously responded to her appeal for funds and clothing'. The council responded in similar fashion and a special committee was arranged to help the Hungarians find housing. It provided, in conjunction with the YMCA, free English classes and the Council employed a Hungarian interpreter. In February 1957, responding to a request from the Women's Voluntary Service for accommodation for the refugees, it agreed to buy a suitable property. Finally, goodwill was revealed by the Council's provision of free school meals for Hungarian children at Portswood Infants School.[71]

CONCLUSION

The Hungarians were mainly treated with sympathy, a view confirmed by those who remain in Britain and have, despite their forced displacement, managed to rebuild successful lives. As one of these refugees, Andy Rumi, explained:

When I came here the life was absolutely superb, hard, hard working but I couldn't wish for a better country … I never found anything like discrimination. I describe myself as more British than Hungarian really, as I say I spent twice as much time here … my life is based here. Saying that from time to time you think a lot of your birthplace, your fatherland or motherland, you never forget your place of birth, or your nationality. But I don't feel the odd one out here because I'm as British as any British person can be because my life is started here and based on a British style of life and to change to another one now, I don't think I would like to change.[72]

There were some instances of opposition from workers in industries recruiting the Hungarians, for instance from miners' lodges in South Yorkshire,[73] but BCAR was content with the outcome of the Hungarian resettlement programme, reporting in the late 1960s: 'The great majority of the Hungarians can now be considered as well integrated into their local British communities, and live the lives of normal working-class British citizens in industrial towns'.[74] The report argued that 75–80 per cent of the refugees could be seen as integrated though its criteria was unclear. In terms of finding housing and work, the Hungarians may have been successful, and some of them married or became British citizens. Nevertheless, other indicators are more ambivalent. Several Hungarians interviewed expressed a preference for the company of other refugees in their social life and had links, in particular, with the Polish community. One explained: 'For us in the shops contact with the British was rare. The main contact was always with the Poles – the reason – to me it was easy to make friendship with them. I spoke the language, Russian, Serbo-Croat and German, and I could communicate with them.'[75] Their common east European background and refugee experience makes this understandable, but it suggests a marginal status among the British and a perception that they remained, to some extent, outsiders. It is the children, as is so often the case, that have become more fully integrated into British society. In addition, it was emphasised by BCAR that about 10 per cent were highly unsettled:

> This group consists mainly of the mentally disturbed or mentally retarded most of whom joined the exodus without any clear idea of what was involved or of where they were going. Unable to learn English adequately or to hold down a job, in and out of mental hospitals, they drift around confused and unhappy.[76]

While the Hungarians have been among the most widely accepted groups in Britain, at both a state and a popular level, an ambivalent picture remains. Indeed, locally, the presence of the Hungarians has been obscured by the presence of other more recent refugee groups, and those who are more numerically significant, including the Poles, whose community associations and links are stronger. Poles and Hungarians settled in Britain in different circumstances, but it was viewed on a state level as a moral duty to provide for both. On a popular level, the Hungarians were particularly welcomed, coming after post-war austerity had given way to greater prosperity. Both groups were seen as victims of the Cold War and thus to be assisted in keeping with British notions of liberalism. In the words of Andy Rumi, the acceptance of Poles and Hungarians was strong compared with more recent refugees because:

> For us we never felt that discrimination because we always reached into the category of political refugees, and people will remember the Hungarian uprising and also the cause they [the Poles] were fighting for us in the Second World War... Yes we had a really great reception from the British people, the Red Cross, WRVS, and even financial support – people had an interest in you. For the others, like the Kurdish, if you visit the refugee camps, for them it is very difficult to settle down, [they are] unwanted because there is no employment for them, no housing, they take away from other people.[77]

As Rumi suggests, refugees who came to Britain later received far less assistance. As Part 4 of this study will illustrate, the late 1960s and early

1970s can be seen as a turning point in the evolution of refugee resettlement in Britain, as immigration legislation sought to restrict the entry of foreigners. While several refugee resettlement programmes were undertaken, state generosity was undermined by measures such as the 1971 Immigration Act, laying the trend for the development of a far more restrictive policy and harsher procedures which were to take off in the 1990s.

PART 4

Government Enforced Dispersal during the 1970s and 1980s

9
Ugandan Asian Exiles:
The Colonial Connection

In the 1970s a variety of pressures around the world made people flee their homes in search of a safe haven from persecution. The main groups coming to Britain were Greek Cypriots fleeing from Cyprus following Turkey's invasion, Asians expelled from Uganda by President Idi Amin, exiles from Pinochet's dictatorship in Chile, and later other Latin American refugees and Chinese and Vietnamese refugees escaping Communist Vietnam. British governments of different political persuasions gave significant help to these refugees in a way which was to diminish in later years. Apart from the Cypriots, these groups, unlike earlier influxes, came from countries outside Europe, having little knowledge of the country and even less of the language and way of life in Britain. The refugees therefore required significant government backing to help their reorientation. In the cases of the Ugandan Asians and the Vietnamese the resettlement procedure was directed by agencies specifically set up by the government. Nevertheless, as in the earlier programmes, the government continued to rely on the voluntary sector to implement decisions and deal with the refugees on a daily basis.

This section considers the experiences of those groups coming from outside Europe. Their different cultural backgrounds and the less favourable economic and political climate of the 1970s made their experiences of resettlement harsher than their post-war east European predecessors though problems of adaptation and finding work and accommodation were common to all groups. Legislative changes in the 1960s and 1970s restricted the entry of African and Asian immigrants from the Commonwealth, reflecting the diminishing world view as colonial ties were broken.

THE BACKGROUND TO THE UGANDAN ASIAN CRISIS

The mass migration of Ugandan Asians to Britain was the result of an expulsion order by President Idi Amin on 4 August 1972. The refugees coming to Britain did not enter a cultural vacuum as they followed years of large-scale immigration to the country by Asians from east Africa and from

Asia.[1] At the time of the refugee crisis, South Asians constituted the fourth largest ethnic group in England and Wales after the Irish, West Indians and Jews.[2] Although those who came after the expulsion were termed 'Ugandan Asians', they were also 'British Asians', being citizens of a Commonwealth country, formerly part of the British Empire. As such, they had been granted the status of British Protected Persons, entitling them to British passports and residence in the 'Motherland', laying the basis for their resettlement in the country in 1972–73.[3]

The settlement of Asians in east Africa dated back to the thirteenth century when Indian merchants trading with the Arabs who controlled the coastal regions of Africa, centred around Zanzibar, moved to the region. When Britain gained control of parts of east Africa, Asians from the colonies were introduced as labour for the construction of the East Africa Railway. Economic opportunities also led to the migration of Gujarati clerks, traders, artisans and some professionals. The Asians tended not to take up farming, as the British authorities expected, but, instead, frequently became traders. It has been estimated that 'Before the Second World War Asians controlled over 90 per cent of the total trade of Uganda',[4] fulfilling a 'middleman' role as moneylenders to the Africans, selling soap and textiles in exchange for cotton, coffee or ivory. They established schools, reflecting a concern for education which enabled them to gain access to both the professions and the civil service in Uganda. They occupied an intermediary status and function, encouraged by the British colonial authorities in 'divide and rule' tactics.

It was noted in 1972 that 'The trouble with Uganda's Asians is success'.[5] But 'the supposedly economic roots of anti-Asian feeling in East Africa are more frequently assumed than substantiated';[6] racial tension may have related more to Asian involvement in the colonial bureaucracy than their trading role.[7] Political success was also a major factor in anti-Asian feeling. Vaughan Robinson and Yash Tandon do not dispute the Asians' general economic progress but argue it was not matched with social acceptance. The Asians were accused of standing aloof due to their lack of intermarriage and social mixing:

> Whites either viewed them as a necessary pariah group which had to be tolerated or as direct competitors for political and economic power. Black Africans viewed them as a privileged minority which had access to scarce resources and jobs, and which was exploitative by nature and only a transient part of society.[8]

A racial hierarchy developed, corresponding with the relative power of each group, in which the Europeans were at the top, the Africans at the bottom and the Asians between the two. Mahmood Mamdani, one of those who became a refugee in Britain, argues that 'Race coincided with class and became politicised'.[9]

Ugandan independence in 1962 led to the election of African presidents seeking to overturn the political and economic systems inherited from the

British. To Yash Tandon this meant that 'the ultimate demise of the Asians in Africa was inevitable... The only issue was the manner of the departure'.[10] Such a bleak analysis can be queried, especially as the Asians were initially cultivated by politicians in the post-colonial period. With independence, the Asian minority who were not Ugandan citizens by birth could opt to register for citizenship of the new state within two years. Most preferred to keep their options open. In the newly independent states, Asians all over east Africa appeared to be sceptical of African rule, while also feeling insecure about their own future. As a result, many began transferring their wealth abroad, especially from Kenya. There was a rapid decline in Asian immigration to the region and, in some cases, panic emigration, such as the flight of Goans from Kampala. Many Asians chose not to adopt the citizenship of the newly independent states, preferring to retain the British citizenship which was a legacy of colonial rule.

The specific case of the expulsion of the Ugandan Asians must be seen in the context of changes in east Africa as a whole, and in particular, of questions of nationhood and citizenship. When the Asians became a target for discriminatory policies various underlying issues were at stake. Many remained uncommitted over the crucial question of citizenship in the newly independent states, they had a degree of economic power which was resented and were perceived as socially exclusive. These negative factors combined with the positive African reassertion of a black African national identity after years of colonial rule, made manifest in the policy of 'Africanisation', a movement to establish African control over the organs of political and economic power. Kenya was the first country to practise 'Africanisation', encouraging Africans to gain entry to the civil service at the expense of Asians, and in 1967 removing all non-citizens from public employment. In 1969, President Milton Obote of Uganda took action to stop Asian dominance of commerce in the country by introducing the Immigration and Trade Licensing Acts, favouring Africans in business. The effect of such policies was to encourage a mass exodus of Asians from east Africa. From 1965 to 1967, 23,000 Asians left Kenya for Britain. In Uganda, from 1962 until 1969 one in 25 Asians migrated to Britain.[11] Between 1969 and 1971 over 24,000 of the 74,308 Asians in Uganda left the country,[12] the majority for Britain. Nor did the overthrow of President Obote by the military in Uganda in January 1971 precipitate more favourable treatment of the Asians. His successor, General Idi Amin, held a conference levelling criticisms at the community. On 4 August 1972, Amin announced that any person of Asian origin, extraction or descent who was a subject or citizen of the UK, India, Pakistan or Bangladesh must leave Uganda within 90 days.

Mahmood Mamdani recalled how the broadcasts initially divided the Ugandan Asian community as they differentiated between Ugandan citizens and non-citizens, only the latter to be expelled. Early pronouncements also permitted professional Asians to stay. But then Amin announced that:

'There will be no exemptions.' And finally: 'All Asians, citizens or not, must leave.'... Among the Asian community mass depression set in. It did not matter that, as a result of pressures from within and without, Amin had decided to let citizen Asians stay. All it meant was that he was learning the political importance of legal camouflage. He would now simply change tactics: somehow pronounce these Asians non-citizens and make them leave with the rest... A process of summarily invalidating citizenships began...[13]

Amin achieved several objectives, including diverting attention from economic problems, rewarding his army supporters through auctioning Asian assets and appeasing 'the anti-Asian sentiments of one crucial support group', the urban trader Africans.[14]

The initial response from the Asians indicated a reluctance to leave. Only a small number of the 8,000 who had clearance had entered Britain by 20 September, partly explained by

the treatment received by earlier departees during the bus trip from Kampala to the airport at Entebbe. Many of the Asians were stopped at numerous control points, searched at gunpoint, and had valuables, including jewellery, confiscated. Another, and perhaps more important, motive for delaying departure was the last desperate hope that some business deals could be concluded in order to salvage some measure of financial resource. Also, the unsettled situation of the stateless Asians kept some of their concerned relatives behind to keep tabs on their welfare.[15]

Mamdani suggests that initially 'very few people were taking Amin's announcement seriously. In fact people joked about it.'[16] But the growing anti-Asian movement was clear from the atrocities committed by the authorities against those who did leave:

The first group of Asians to leave Uganda were those that went to India... Letters from them told of being stopped on the way by bands of Ugandan soldiers, of all their belongings taken, of the men made to lie down on the ground while the women were raped.

In the countryside, Asians were reportedly kidnapped and held for ransom money. In the city, business owners were charged with hoarding money, robbed, and in some cases, thrown into the boots of army cars, where they often suffocated to death, before their bodies were cast out into the bush.[17]

The testimony of one Ugandan Asian woman, who later settled in Southampton, shows how the climate of fear took hold among the community. Aged 13, she came to Britain with some of her family ahead of her father and brother who hoped to salvage their business. They left when their shop was targeted:

My dad and my brother used to run the shop. They stayed behind. They sent us away while they could... It's only when they came here we found out what had happened to them... Someone must have come into the shop. We had rolls of textile materials and behind there they planted something, a gun or something...

The [police] 'found' [a gun] and put them in prison. They locked them up; no food, no nothing. I think they kept them for about five days to about a week ... and while they were there they saw torture and things going on... They [officials] just took a stick and they were just hitting innocent people for nothing really ... They were really scared they'd do something to them ... We didn't know what was going on. And we were expecting them ... waiting and waiting.[18]

RESPONSES TO THE UGANDAN ASIAN REFUGEES

The initial international reaction to Amin's expulsion order was one of condemnation. This came from African presidents[19] as well as European leaders but it was clear that the main burden of responsibility for the Ugandan Asians would lie with Britain; over half those leaving held British passports with rights of entry and abode. The Conservative government of Edward Heath was reluctant to take the Ugandan Asians, but agreed to do so in order to fulfil Britain's legal and moral obligation to provide residence for British passport holders. The Ugandan crisis came in a context of increasingly vocal hostility towards non-white immigrants and their descendants and an ongoing political campaign which used the excuse of popular antipathy to tighten immigration laws in Britain. The legal basis for accepting the refugees as 'British Asians' was widely seen as flawed, as it relied on Britain's former colonial heritage. With the establishment of the Commonwealth after the Second World War, Britain retained imperial concepts of citizenship in the British Nationality Act of 1948. This law had defined all citizens of Commonwealth countries as 'British subjects' or 'Commonwealth citizens', with the resultant principle of free entry to Britain. Increasing immigration from Africa, Asia and the Caribbean to fill labour shortages had been viewed with concern both in Parliament and by sections of the public. In 1962, the introduction of the Commonwealth Immigration Act made Commonwealth passport holders subject to immigration control for the first time. With independence at hand in east Africa, an escape clause was adopted to protect British white settlers, enabling them to retain British citizenship, but it was recognised that this right would have to remain available to Asians too.[20] As Asian immigration from east Africa grew in the 1960s, especially from Kenya, more controls were introduced. The Labour government's Commonwealth Immigrants Act of February 1968 introduced entry quotas, allowing entry to only 1,500 British Asians per year, increased to 3,000 in May 1971.[21] Recognising that Asians were still seeking residence in Britain, the Conservative's 1971 Immigration Act restricted rights of abode in Britain to those Commonwealth citizens with a 'patrial' connection, a parent or grandparent born in Britain, discriminating blatantly against those of colour from the former empire.[22]

Amin's expulsion order, however, prompted a more humane reaction from the British Conservative government. Several MPs suggested that Uganda's membership of the Commonwealth should be reconsidered[23] in spite of fears that the arrival of a possible 50–60,000 refugees would engender widespread popular discontent. The acceptance of the Asians by Prime Minister Edward Heath's government flew in the face of considerable public unease and racism fanned by the media. Mamdani recalls that:

> The reports in the British press gave the impression of a public panic. To us it seemed as if the hysteria had been generated, at least in part, by the government itself. They seemed to be getting ready for us as one prepares for a swarm of locusts.[24]

The Conservative Party was divided by the issue. The leading anti-immigrant MPs, Enoch Powell and Norman Tebbit, were not the only opponents of their Prime Minister. Conversely, the inflow was justified in terms of duty, honour and responsibility. Mr Carr, the Home Secretary, stated, 'We have accepted our legal and moral responsibility in this matter, and I believe that as a country we have done it generously.'[25] With the arrival of the Asians imminent, Viscountess Jennifer Enfield of Winchester asked for public support for the influx on the basis that, firstly, the numbers were small, 'not many more than a Saturday afternoon football crowd', secondly, that the people involved had been an 'independent, well educated and responsible community in Uganda for many generations' and spoke English, thirdly, that the Asians were being used as a political pawn and were now 'dispossessed and threatened by an immoral and dangerous man', fourthly that they held British passports which meant 'this country has an obligation to them', and fifthly that the Government had honoured its promises and 'they are coming'.[26]

The government was able to develop support for the Asians by portraying Amin as a despotic leader. In House of Commons debates Amin was frequently referred to as the 'black Hitler', a title which he himself had used.[27] The press, too, vilified him,[28] while extolling the virtues of the Asians as a middle-class group with useful skills to offer. They were depicted as people who could fill labour shortages: the *Evening Standard* carried the headline 'Arriving for the jobs we won't take'. The Labour opposition, in contrast to the Conservative Party, offered overwhelming support for the government's acceptance of the refugees.[29] In 1968, James Callaghan, Home Secretary of the Labour Party, had stated, regarding Asians holding British passports, 'I was asked what we would do about a man who was thrown out of work and ejected from the country. We shall have to take him. We cannot do anything else in the circumstances.'[30] Ugandan Asians were accepted on a grudging sense of political and moral obligation.

Public concerns were voiced by elected representatives. The notorious right-wing MP Enoch Powell articulated popular fears of being swamped by coloured immigrants. On the other side of the debate, references were made to earlier refugee influxes, especially that of the Jews, who had come to symbolise the refugee dilemma in the popular imagination. Mr Douglas-Mann stated, 'I hope that the right hon. Gentleman will recognise that to return Asians to Uganda today is like sending Jews back to Hitler in the 1930s.'[31] The question of increasing British racism, in contrast to Douglas-Mann's use of the past to condemn intolerance, was also raised in the debates. Such hostility, however, was seen to be the work of 'small but very dangerous racialist groups who are using the unfortunate situation of the Uganda Asians to make a general attack on our society and on democratic society generally'. The Home Secretary reacted to allusions to the National Front in a dismissive manner, arguing:

> Of course the disquiet has been fanned by nasty groups, but that is so in any activity... There are always some small numbers of nasty people ready to make mischief out of any situation. What is far more true is the overall response of the British people... That response has been extremely balanced in spite of the disquiet... I think it is remarkable how few demonstrations there have been...[32]

Extremists aside, the popular response to the Ugandan Asians was not altogether positive. After the expulsion order, but prior to the first arrivals, a Gallup sample showed 57 per cent of people were doubtful as to whether the Asians should be admitted to the UK.[33] 'By the end of August, the mood of the British public at its best could be described as sullen, and at its worst, hostile.'[34] Some newspapers attempted to utilise public unease: the *Sunday Telegraph* suggested that 'A further large swift influx of coloured immigrants to Britain is wholly undesirable on social grounds'.[35] Four hundred people demonstrated in London against the 'invasion of Britain' by Ugandan Asians, carrying signs saying, 'Stop Immigration, Enoch is right', and, 'Britain for the British'. A petition with 1,100 signatures stating objections to further Asian immigration was presented to Bolton Town Council.[36] Concern was such that Bolton West's Conservative MP, Robert Redmond, wrote to the Prime Minister asking him to recall Parliament because he had 'never known such alarm in the country'.[37]

Popular antipathy reflected immediate concerns over high unemployment and housing shortages alongside a growing tide of racism against coloured immigrants as well as constricting definitions of Britishness based largely on 'race', evident in the rise of the National Front and 'Paki bashing' in the 1970s. The premise for taking the Ugandan Asians was seen as outdated, a view that Enoch Powell had articulated in 1968, regarding the Kenyan Asians, and again in August 1972. His argument was that Ugandan Asians were only the 'thin end of the wedge' of people around the world for whom Britain should hold no legal obligations.[38]

Concern was such that Mary Dines, Secretary of the Joint Council for the Welfare of Immigrants, a charity assisting in the resettlement of immigrants in Britain, wrote to Earl Mountbatten of Burma, resident in Romsey,

Hampshire, at the end of August, asking for personal intervention from the Royal Family to assist the incoming Asians. Mountbatten, in his capacity as patron of the British Council Ex-Servicemen's League, and as the last Governor-General of India during the empire, may have been seen as a potential friend of the Asian community. Dines wrote that:

> You will have seen from the press and other mass media that the reaction to the eviction of the Asians from Uganda has been incredibly hostile, and that over the last few weeks one politician after another has made statements that have made any sort of welcome for them most unlikely. Mr Carr of course, made it clear that Britain had absolute obligations to them, but local doctors, (and now alas even a bishop) have reacted at once by saying that there is no room for them in their local area. I am most concerned not only by the repercussions of this in this country but also by the effect this is having on the people concerned. It is so sad that having to leave one place they come here to a situation in which everyone is making it clear that they do not want them and that they are nothing but a problem to all concerned. It is quite cruel and the hostility that is being built up locally means that even the children will feel the backlash when they go to school...

Stressing how well the east African Asians had settled in Britain, she pleaded for some sort of gesture from the Royal Family to welcome those fleeing Uganda.[39] In his notes on this request, Mountbatten made clear that he was unwilling to get involved: 'Lord Mountbatten certainly could do nothing about this himself as he never interferes on matters of constitutional advice between the Queen and the Royal Family and Ministers'. He was, however, willing to explore specific cases relating to 'concrete cases of ex-servicemen'.[40]

Other local responses were less ambiguous, revealing strong hostility. None of the main reception camps for the Ugandan Asians were located in Hampshire, but debates on the issue were nonetheless prominent in the local papers, reflecting the racial and political debates raised. One correspondent from Totton wrote in response to 'this invasion' that surely

> the people of our once great country must realise by now that they are the victims of the greatest con trick the world has ever seen. The final insult is that whilst being told how easily they can be sterilised on the National Health because our land will soon be over populated, the biggest air-lift ever of make believe Britons is to be happily accepted, presumably in place of the children they might have had... Have you, our local medium,... been ordered to keep silent?[41]

The editor responded to this racist fantasy that his paper did not accept orders about what to print: 'There have been a few letters about the Ugandan Asians and two were published, one as a lead letter. Most of the others were against the Asians coming. None added anything constructive to the discussion.'[42] He still felt it appropriate to publish an even more hostile letter from a local correspondent entitled 'More Asians':

The British people do not, by any written law, have to adopt the Asians, who hold a so-called British passport... The British people by every opinion poll unanimously disagree with the government. My wife says you wouldn't print this letter on racial grounds. Well, I am not a racialist but am concerned that this country, which has nearly one million unemployed, is to receive more unemployed... I don't worry for myself, but my children. They will be swamped by foreign-speaking Englishmen who don't want to integrate. This has been shown by Derby Road, Southampton, which is totally Asian.[43]

Nevertheless, such hostility was not unrelieved. By September 1972, 2,000 places in private homes in Britain had been offered for the Asians, eventually reaching 5,000.[44] Politicians of all parties and religious leaders of many different faiths were particularly prominent in offering accommodation to the refugees.

In the event, only half the anticipated 50–60,000 Ugandan Asian refugees came to Britain, with Canada taking approximately 6,000 and India 10,000. In addition to these major receiving countries, Pakistan and the United States accepted about 1,000 refugees whilst various other countries, including New Zealand, Kenya and Malawi, took several hundred.[45] Their criteria varied; India took its own passport holders, many of whom were only working on short-term contracts in Uganda, and also agreed to take some British passport holders on a temporary basis if Britain honoured its obligations at a later date.[46] Those refugees who went to India were possibly the wealthier and older Asians whose resources would go further there than in the West.[47] Canada took those who fulfilled the country's general immigration criteria of having reasonable English and a sponsor or job awaiting them, while especially favouring the young. 'Canada was not on a "mission of mercy" so much as on a search for possible contributors to the Canadian economy. They did not ... accept those most likely to become economic burdens.'[48]

The 28,608 refugees[49] who came to Britain differed from those who left for Canada or India, representing a more general cross-section of the Ugandan Asian population. Although joining an Asian community, they were unlike those who had come in earlier migrations from east Africa. Robinson suggests that, before 1967, Asian entrants tended to be young single men sent from Kenya by their families for education, some of whom then settled to work in the UK and brought their relations over. The cost of travel ensured that these pioneer migrants were drawn from wealthier backgrounds. As Africanisation occurred, small shopkeepers and clerks, 'anticipatory refugees' who feared losing their livelihoods, migrated, often bringing their families with them.[50] Some 68,000 Asians had already come over from east Africa before Amin's order but expulsion acted as a social leveller, precipitating a movement of men, women, children and the elderly from various class and social backgrounds. The predominance of large families, with perhaps half a dozen children and several elderly dependants, distinguished the Asians from many other refugee influxes to Britain,[51] although it was also to be a feature of the Vietnamese movement. More than half the heads of household were over 40, which had repercussions for adaptation as these older people had more problems learning English and finding work.[52]

THE DISPERSAL POLICY

In his early response, the Home Secretary announced that the government would create a resettlement board for the arrivals, indicative of the seriousness with which the influx was taken. Sixty welfare, immigrant and charitable bodies formed the Coordinating Committee for the Welfare of Evacuees from Uganda to help in initial reception and promote acceptance of the refugees. Their work was directed by the Uganda Resettlement Board (URB), chaired by Sir Charles Cunningham, Permanent Secretary to the Home Office. Altogether, 28,165 people from Uganda passed through the Board's reception facilities. Its basic aim was to resettle the Asians and limited provisions were offered to help authorities meet the costs involved.[53] In keeping with past traditions of refugee reception, the first holding centres were often military camps. Initially, 16 transit camps were used, taking care of 21,797 refugees who were then dispersed around Britain, some 3,380 remaining in them by March 1973.[54] A relief trust was also set up, with Lord Sainsbury as Chairman, to help the Asians establish themselves. The government donated £50,000 and a further £63,000 was found from other sources.[55]

The URB's interim report laid out the government's agenda which was to minimise friction between host and immigrant communities by directing the Asians in their resettlement. From analysis of statistics relating to early arrivals it was clear to the URB that 'many of the refugees, unless they could be persuaded otherwise, were planning to settle in areas where the housing, educational and social services were already under severe pressure'. It therefore arranged for a senior official to fly to Kampala 'in order to explain the position, and for notices to be inserted in leading Ugandan newspapers advising people affected by President Amin's decree that there were some parts of the United Kingdom in which they would be unwise to settle'.[56]

The URB policy of dispersal denoted red, 'no go' areas and green areas of favourable settlement for the Asians. Such a directed settlement policy was a new concept in dealing with refugees, and although it was argued that this was to ensure they had the best opportunities, it was affected by fears that providing homes for thousands of coloured people would create racism. The Asians were directed to areas where there was an absence of a large ethnic minority presence. Vaughan Robinson points out that Glasgow, a city with an enormous housing problem but without a large ethnic community, was declared green and therefore acceptable for resettlement, whereas Leicester, which suffered only limited housing problems but which had a large pre-existing Asian community, became a red area.[57] While all red areas contained established Asian populations, there were also some green areas with a large Asian presence, such as Barnet, Hounslow, Coventry and Blackburn: 'The Board's job of placating the more vociferous local authorities – the only explanation for the empirically nonsensical "red" and "green" area divisions – gave it a clearly political function which bedevilled the genuine resettlement effort'.[58] Mike Bristow also believes the government's dispersal policy was affected by local authorities' lobbying: 'offensive squawking' had the effect of proscribing certain areas from Ugandan Asian settlement.[59]

Nevertheless, if the URB dispersal policy is evaluated, it proved to be a failure since only 38 per cent of Asians passing through it eventually found homes in green areas.[60] Bristow attributes this failure to the dearth of housing offers, which prompted the Asians to seek accommodation themselves. The URB admitted in its Final Report that, 'Looking back, it is evident that our policy of dispersal would have had greater success had we been able to offer the Ugandan Asians, immediately or very soon after their arrival, housing accommodation outside the areas of stress'.[61] The lack of obligation for local authorities led to only limited offers, due to the existing housing shortage and fears of a white backlash.

Mahmood Mamdani's testimony shows that other factors were at work. The Asians were not simply 'tired of waiting' for houses. Perceptions of racism and paternalistic treatment by the camp authorities also led to a distrust of the URB such that many of the Asians felt they had to take matters into their own hands, however difficult this might be:

> We were the children, and the Board the father… The Board was the unselfish giver, while we were expected to stand at attention and respectfully appreciate the nobility of its sacrifice. It would all have happened according to text, except that we were not refugees. Circumstances had deprived us of our possessions, but not yet our self respect. For that last possession, our humanity, we were willing to fight.[62]

Dispersal could not be enforced, and preference for settling in areas with an established Asian community naturally drew incomers to some red areas and encouraged secondary migration across the country, especially to London and the Midlands. There was some reluctance to go to remoter areas. Scotland was not favoured because of its distance, colder climes and unfamiliarity, a response also noted among Chilean refugees. One woman recalled her family being sent to an isolated part of Wales where there was only one other known Asian family. Subsequently they moved to Southampton through the suggestion of a friend, preferring the atmosphere and its Asian community links. Similarly the family of Urvashi Rajo, who was a child when she came to Britain, initially lived in a camp in Kent for eight months:

> Quite a few families from the camp were offered council houses throughout England. We were actually offered a house in Scotland… My dad knew people

in the camp who said it would be very cold out there – [so] we turned that one down... My dad had a friend in Southampton and he asked my dad if he would like to come with him... And he came and liked it and the next thing we knew, he'd rented a house there. [Through money earned by her sister, aged sixteen, in a factory in Maidstone] we were able to save up a little bit and obviously with the benefits we were entitled to, my dad decided to rent this house in Southampton [shared with another family]. And it was very strange coming to Southampton and walking down Derby Road, with all the Asian shops. There were a lot of Asian shops selling Indian food ... and Indian music playing ... which we hadn't heard in Maidstone shopping area. Walking down, it felt really nice in some way and strange as well. That there were people having businesses of their own and setting up – obviously they must have come here from another country. It felt nice, like home in some ways...[63]

The Community Relations Commission (CRC) evaluation of the resettlement programme in 1976 also suggests that friends and relatives were important factors in the choice of location of settlement.[64] Indeed, some argue that, 'The effects of the resettlement operations on these refugees were minimal.'[65]

The housing issue was crucial to resettlement but local authorities were not obliged to help. Council housing was already in short supply, with high demand, such that allocating scarce resources was liable to prompt popular discontent. Local debate in Hampshire reveals the nature of discussions across the country. A heated council meeting took place during September 1972 after Winchester Rural Council decided to provide housing for Ugandan Asian families. After discussion it was agreed by a large majority to increase the number of families to be helped from four to seven. One decisive speech, which was warmly applauded, came from

Mr Ian Bidgood, who said that the exiling of the Asians reminded him of the Jews in Nazi Germany. They were received into this country. Objecting to calling the people Uganda Asians, which reminded him of such terminology as 'Aberdeen Angus' and 'Rhode Island Red', Mr Bidgood said: 'Let us call them refugees. They are being persecuted by a black Hitler.'... Mr Bidgood said he had heard a government spokesman on the radio say that accommodation could be provided for all the Asians if every housing authority accepted seven families. 'If we take less, then Leicester and Birmingham will have to take more in their ghettoes.'

There was, however, opposition. One councillor said that if accommodation was provided for 'these people' then

it meant that jobs would also have to be found. He would like to see help given in the [rural district council] area, or to neighbouring areas. At Bournemouth ... men had been made redundant by the British Aircraft Corporation. 'If these people cannot be assimilated in Africa, what chance is there that they can be assimilated in this country?' he asked. 'I am worried about the legacy we are leaving our children.'[66]

Subsequently it was clarified that the offer did not imply a commitment to provide council housing,[67] indicating strong public sentiment over the issue, especially the needs of homeless British people and the belief that they should have priority. Such feelings led Droxford district council to refuse help,[68] as did Gosport.[69] Eastleigh offered four houses though these were empty and of a 'low standard', waiting to be demolished.[70] Mark Woodnutt, MP for the Isle of Wight, rejected the possibility of helping. A local resident objected to this mean response, attempting, in the process, to make political capital out of it:

> Lack of employment and housing ... are national problems, and, compared with many other areas the Island must look very favourable – it must be more humane for a proportion of these people to be accommodated in a 'Garden Island' than a city ghetto... While their contribution to the Island's economy is limited to that of consumers, the majority of the Asians are businessmen who have the latent skills to provide employment and perhaps go some way to solve the problem that Mr Woodnutt ... has himself been unable to solve.[71]

Scaremongering over housing was certainly played upon by the press. The *Southern Evening Echo* reported how 'hoax letters purporting to come from the Department of Environment saying that "emergency powers" are being evoked to rehouse Ugandan Asians in private houses' were being sent to locals.[72] In reality, the limited access to council housing meant that most Asians were competing in the private sector, and therefore faced 'all the difficulties of other coloured immigrants, with a restriction of housing options leading to high rents, inadequate accommodation and insecure tenure'.[73]

In Southampton, the City Council's decision to offer accommodation to the Asians came after concerted efforts. A front page article for the *Southern Evening Echo*, entitled 'Southampton "put to shame" over Asians', called for a more positive attitude, emphasising that the city was lagging behind Eastleigh Borough Council, Hampshire County Council and Winchester Rural Council.[74] A local Kenyan Asian recalled that representations were made to the local papers, encouraging a more positive portrayal of the issues surrounding the Ugandans' arrival locally.[75] Central government pressure finally pushed the local council to house 20 families.[76] The Town Clerk was invited to meet Cunningham of the URB in late September 1972. After this meeting, the Town Clerk stated that 'notifications were now being received from the Uganda Resettlement Board of Ugandan Asians apparently destined for the City and that it was known that one or two families had now arrived'. Referring to 'the possible emergency situation which could arise', council officers were authorised to bring in extra staff if necessary to deal with the situation.[77]

Such council deliberations were echoed across the country. Further light is shed on how decisions were made in Hampshire from the testimony of John Arnold, a Southampton Labour Councillor at the time of the Ugandan Asians' arrival, and involved with their resettlement as Chair of the Social Services Committee:

> Beyond housing we didn't do very much. I think we were anticipating a substantial number but in practice there were far fewer... They came and shared houses with people they knew. We had houses which were not normal council stock, purchased for road widening, so they were allocated some of those on a short-term basis... We were very keen to keep it all low profile – it was deliberately kept without any headlines. I remember it because I was subsequently challenged in council because I made a speech welcoming them, saying that they were [part of a tradition] of people being welcomed. I was challenged by a right-wing Conservative. I said a lot of British people who are here had a background as immigrants and he took offence ... There wasn't any conflict between the Labour leadership and the official Conservative opposition but there were factions in the Conservative group who would have liked to make a fuss... We hoped that they would absorb rapidly into the host community and the less fuss there was, the easier it would be. And then housing is always an issue open to misrepresentation and so they were given short-life housing.[78]

Racial abuse and hostility was certainly aroused by the Asian influx. The owner of a camp in the Isle of Wight who had offered temporary homes to 500 Asians received a string of poison pen letters and anonymous phone calls which were not confined to the locality.[79] In Netley, Hampshire, anti-Asian slogans were daubed in public places a week before the intended arrival of two families in the area, although the Chairman of the local Council was quick to denounce the culprits and offer his support for the arrivals.[80]

In parliamentary debates, it was argued that the Asians were receiving help when British people suffering from unemployment and housing shortages were not. Greville Janner demanded extra assistance for the refugees going to Leicester: 'Does the Minister not appreciate that the vast majority of my constituents regard the Government's handling of the situation as utterly deplorable?'[81]

The length of stay in the reception camps was also controversial as the Asians were seen as living in comfort at the taxpayers' expense. Arthur Lewis, Labour MP for West Ham North, a vociferous opponent of the Ugandan Asians, who voiced concern over other refugee movements, alleged that 'Asians are seeking to make the resettlement camps their permanent homes',[82] but he was greeted with some derision for his stance by fellow MPs.[83] After a camp visit, Baroness Eirene White emphasised how impressed she was by the eagerness of the Asians to get out of the camps and make a new start. She described the frustration the Asians felt at waiting for housing and work, concluding that 'the proportion who would really want to go on in that kind of life must be very small indeed'.[84]

The major debate in the House of Commons in December 1972 on the Ugandan Asians revealed how much controversy had been created, reflecting popular concern over housing and employment which were constant features of such discussions. At stake was whether Britain was a country which should accept newcomers and, if so, how they should be treated. Timothy Raison,

Conservative MP for Aylesbury, believed that the state should have minimal involvement in the resettlement of the Ugandan Asians, especially council housing:

> There is no point in denying that there has been considerable opposition in the country to the presence of the Ugandan refugees here or in denying that there are fears that go deeper than mere prejudice. I accept that a heavy concentration of immigrants is a serious problem. I accept that the housing shortage and unemployment are realities. I accept that concern for a way of life is a perfectly legitimate concern.

The answer, he believed, was to 'help people to help themselves' so that 'we can get them absorbed into the community much more rapidly'. Arthur Lewis was far less optimistic about the ability to settle the refugees. His contribution to the debate revealed a deep ambivalence. On the one hand he wanted to show sympathy for the oppressed and to avoid any impression that he was prejudiced. On the other, he hinted that the refugees were receiving favourable treatment compared to his own working-class constituents:

> Unfortunately, we have reached the stage where anyone who tries to deal with the real problems brought about by immigration is dubbed a racialist... It is not being a racialist to try to look at the facts... I accuse the Government of acting deliberately to exacerbate and create problems that they could have avoided... During the war mine was the most bombed borough in London, and we still have not recovered from the damage that was done ... Some of my constituents have been waiting for forty years for a house... By all means let us help the Ugandan Asians in every possible way; let us prepare to help the Kenyan Asians when they come, as they will; but let us also help the people who are already here and have been suffering hardships for years. I do not want them to get any more than the Ugandan Asians; I want them to get the same...

In contrast to Lewis, David Knox, Conservative MP for Leek, strongly supported the government's decision to admit the Ugandan Asians:

> It was a clear-cut matter – on moral grounds because a previous British Government had given their word; on legal grounds because, as passport holders, they had the right to come here, and, above all, on humanitarian grounds because that is in the British humanitarian tradition... The first families have started to arrive in my constituency. They are settling in quickly... What is moving all of us is the amount of good will among people in North Staffordshire who have welcomed the Asians into their new homes. Furnishings have been provided by the local community, and clothing has also been provided.

Knox wanted to portray the Asians as ideal, hard-working citizens, pointing out that locally:

> The head of the household of one of the families and the son in another have started work already. They were the sort of people who want to stand on their own feet and be independent... Many of them have great commercial enterprise

> ... and Uganda will suffer greatly from their departure... We have to remember the advantages that the indigenous population enjoys from having immigrants – hospital doctors and nurses, and the many who work on public transport. These people are not 'scrounging' on our society; they are contributing to it and to the national income and the national wealth, and we all benefit...

Not all Conservatives, however, were so positive about their government's decision to let in the refugees, facing hostility from some of their constituents. Cecil Parkinson, Conservative MP for Enfield West, situated himself between Lewis and Knox but utilised the memory of earlier refugee movements to Britain to back his government's decision:

> I have received a very large number of letters on the subject of the Ugandan Asians. I have not found them easy to answer ... [but it] is not good enough to say, in regard to a person in one's constituency whose business has become bankrupt and who needs help, 'Why do you not give the money to him instead of the man who was deprived of all his assets at very short notice, expelled from the country in which he has always lived and from which he has been shunted abroad?' I never heard those arguments when Hungarians wished to escape from a Communist regime during the uprising. Then it was most noble and honourable to invite them into one's country and look after them. I never heard that argument used in connection with the Jewish refugees from Europe in the 1930s.

This forced a riposte from Lewis who utilised the numbers argument usually associated with the right of the Conservative Party, and especially Enoch Powell: 'There were not 25,000 or 30,000 Hungarian refugees. They did not all go into red areas. By all means have them here, but do not send them into red areas – or better still, do something to encourage them to go to other areas.'

Parkinson relished the discomfort of his Labour opponent but in reality the entry of the Ugandan Asians was at best tolerated by many Conservatives. The memory of the Holocaust, however, continued to be used to dispel criticism and undermine the moral case of those who objected to the government's policy:

> These people do not want to come here and – let us face it – we were not particularly happy about their coming. They were in danger. Their lives were in peril... I do not believe that these people are the parasites, spivs and hangers-on that the hon. Member gave the impression that they were... The basic reason for their expulsion from Uganda was that they were too successful... Sooner or later we, as Members of Parliament, will have to stop thinking about what sounds well and reads well in our constituencies and start to think about what is right and honourable, and what we as a country should be doing to help those in real need... The popularity which we as a Parliament might have lost by doing what we did would have been nothing compared with the unpopularity that we would have earned had people started to die in concentration camps simply because they had a British passport...

It was left to a more independently-minded Conservative MP, Nicholas

Winterton (Macclesfield) to articulate the anti-immigrant feelings felt if not expressed by many in his own party. Winterton supported Lewis and argued that he had:

> reflected very accurately the deep feelings of the great majority of the people in this country... I did not agree with the Government decision to accept the Ugandan Asians... The Government – whether a Labour or Conservative Government – in the interests of the indigenous population and the immigrants already here, should impose a total ban on further immigration from all sources into this country by heads of families for five years. That would allow the indigenous population to get used to coexisting with the many other, perhaps alien, communities that have come here in recent years. It would allow us to catch up with the backlog in education, hospital and welfare facilities. Only if this is done will there be satisfactory coexistence between immigrants and the indigenous population...[85]

LIFE IN BRITAIN

The Asians' resettlement in Britain was clearly coloured by shortages in housing and employment which set the community against the host population. The propitious economic and political climate which the Hungarians had experienced had given way to a far harsher climate, worsened by overt racism. As the Hungarians resident in Hampshire found, employment was often the key to rebuilding a future. At the time of their arrival it was possible to leave a job one week and find a new one the next.[86] Finding work allowed for financial independence and integration with the host community. The Ugandan Asians faced bleaker economic prospects. Their ability to adapt regarding employment requires an assessment of their backgrounds. The URB estimated that of those who had been employed, 11 per cent were professionals; 17 per cent office workers; 6 per cent shop workers; 11 per cent engineers or motor repairers; 7 per cent building craftsmen; and no fewer than 27 per cent had been small traders. The number of people described as unskilled was very small.[87] The Asians were 'neither a small nor an insignificant minority; they were the acknowledged mainstay of commercial Uganda'.[88]

Although the majority of Asians did come from trading, professional or skilled jobs in Uganda, contrary to popular belief, most did not arrive with much wealth. Some had the foresight to send assets abroad prior to Amin's expulsion order, but the rest were forced to leave them in Uganda and start from scratch in Britain. The issue of regaining these assets was to remain a bone of contention in British diplomatic relations with Uganda. Many families who had lived comfortable lives were now forced to accept a drop in status. The high rate of self-employment (a quarter were estimated to run their own businesses)[89] made adaptation difficult as most of the former shopkeepers and traders did not have the resources to start anew.[90]

The lack of attention given to employment prospects in the government resettlement programme did little to assist the Asians' transition to a new life. Sir Charles Cunningham described employment prospects as the URB's third objective after housing and directing people to settle 'outside areas which are known to be already under stress because of the number of people from other parts of the Commonwealth who are living there'.[91] The Asians had to rely on the Department of Employment to find work. No particular provisions were made to prevent any subsequent social and economic problems. Special treatment was ruled out because of the economic stresses being endured by the wider community.[92] And typically, local authority housing offers did not always coincide with job prospects: 'Many local authorities were only able to offer accommodation because the indigenous population had already decided that the local economy offered few opportunities and had therefore left the area.'[93]

The Community Relations Commission (CRC) carried out two studies into Ugandan Asian resettlement. Its first report noted that professionals such as teachers and accountants unable to gain recognition of their qualifications had to take lower skilled jobs like clerical work.[94] Some of the Asians found their skills were not easily transferable to Britain. As the report put it, 'there are no vacancies here for tea-plantation managers'.[95] A survey by Bert Adams and Victor Jesudason suggests that the highest unemployment was found among professionals and skilled workers (who needed retraining) and businessmen (who lacked opportunity).[96] Of those Asians who found employment in Britain, 69 per cent were found to be downwardly mobile, 7 per cent upwardly mobile and 24 per cent stayed at the same level.[97] The plight of the Asians was indicated by the case of Anthony Ferrao reported in the *Southern Evening Echo*: formerly a financial assistant in the quantity surveyor's department of the Kampala post office, he said, 'I have found it is very difficult to get a similar job here. So now I am ready to take any kind of clerical job.'[98] This may have been more typical than the case of Amrit Lal, a former civil servant, whose success in getting a job with a local firm as a purchasing officer also received publicity locally.[99]

The CRC report, a year after the refugees' arrival, suggested that, contrary to public perceptions:

> In their eagerness to avoid 'being a burden on the state', refugees had taken whatever job was initially offered, regardless of whether it made full use of their abilities. After the immediate aim of avoiding unemployment came the search for higher wages, again often regardless of whether the job was appropriate.[100]

A study in 1976 reiterated the point that the Ugandan Asians were flexible because of their desire to rebuild their futures. Many women took on employment, contrary to traditional practice in Uganda, to make ends meet, particularly important as many older men who had been traders and the former family breadwinners had serious problems finding work.[101]

Housing and employment problems were compounded by the propensity for large families. A considerable number of sick or disabled people (an estimated 50–60 per cent of all Ugandan refugee families had one such member) added to financial problems, with residence and National Insurance contribution requirements restricting access to certain benefits. The CRC argued that: 'It is only in education of the children that the ground has been comparatively smooth, with there being few difficulties over school placement, and indications that the children are settling in very well in schools'.[102] The perception that all the Asians were fluent in English did not match reality. Although the younger generation had learnt some English, the older Asians spoke little or none, and they were not always able to overcome these difficulties. Lack of English, health problems and age were the major reasons for non-participation in the labour force in Britain among the Ugandan Asians.[103]

The Asians' own view of their adaptation shows that resettlement was difficult. While varying age and ability to speak English had an impact on the process, the Asians reflect that their background and colour distinguished them from other refugees coming to Britain. In studies of racism in Britain, it has been argued that it is based on differing colour, class and culture. In their resettlement in Britain, the Ugandan Asians fell prey most to the colour barrier. The first impressions the Asians had of Britain reflected their colonial heritage: 'England was regarded with awe. One expected to be dazzled by its beauty, its wealth and its splendour... To the colonial child, England was the rainbow on the horizon'. Nevertheless 'the English were also the colonial masters, the oppressors'.[104]

Mamdani explains how having experienced discrimination in Uganda, he also expected to find it in England. Such impressions were reinforced by articles in papers available to the Ugandans before they left their homeland, such as a report in the *Daily Nation* in October 1972, which described graffiti on tube station walls, posters and buildings stating, 'wogs out'. The *Uganda Argus* also carried advertisements from Leicester saying that there were too many Asians there already and encouraging those leaving Uganda to go elsewhere. Mamdani comments wryly that such warnings backfired:

> Most people had by then heard of England and of London. But now they knew there was some place called Leicester, where there were numerous Asians. All those who had been undecided as to where to go... after reading of the hostile reactions of the British public in general, started making arrangements to go to Leicester.[105]

These discouraging impressions of Britain were soon reinforced on arrival in the country itself. Early experiences were affected by stays in reception camps under the government resettlement programme. Mamdani describes his experiences in the reception centre in Kensington. His first taste of life and contacts with people in the country were generally amiable but, after only a few days, feelings of dependency sunk in:

> Gradually we began to acquire habits that people usually associate with the lower classes; in Uganda with the African domestic servants. Every Friday, we received our £2.10 social security. By Sunday, it was all gone… One's position in the social hierarchy, and its vast influence on the shaping of individual or group life, was gradually becoming clear to us.[106]

The camp in Kensington 'became a nightmare in totally controlled living' with an absence of personal life. The camp administration was particularly oppressive, representing 'the familiarity the master has with the affairs of the servant; not the familiarity a member of a family has of another'. It was highlighted on New Year's Eve when a party was held exclusively

> for the staff of the student centre and the camp administration. Music blared while wine and champagne flowed. Guests came and went in formal attire. In the next room were the camp residents, some watching television, others playing darts, and the rest writing letters. For us it was just another evening…

Mamdani believed that the administration 'had sole control over resources: possible job and accommodation opportunities. These opportunities were never advertised on the camp bulletin boards'. The lack of welcome was emphasised with a board displaying 'a notice in bold letters: HAVE YOU CONSIDERED EMIGRATING?' With a system of patronage and favouritism in operation, 'Gradually a most unhealthy environment developed'.

The contrast between the reality of the camp and outside perceptions of life within it caused immense frustrations for the refugees: 'One morning, splashed across the front pages of the newspapers, we read the headlines: "Asians too Comfortable in Camps". Too comfortable! It seemed a cruel mockery of people who had been uprooted and now disoriented by being thrown in the midst of a different society.' This was particularly the case for those in the reception centre who had

> been rendered stateless in Uganda, and were therefore officially detainees… Being under detention meant that a person was allowed only an hour of freedom daily … The detainees were at the mercy of their host…. The camp administration took every possible advantage of this situation and devised a system whereby all the dirty work … became the duty of the detainees.

In Uganda, the Asians had been situated curiously within the racial hierarchy of the country. Kept below the white British, they nevertheless shared much of the colonial authorities' distrust of their black African neighbours. In Britain they were to face a totally different 'racial' system, now being regarded as simply part of its 'coloured' population. Anti-black racism was another reason why the Ugandan Asians decided to move to areas where there would be safety in numbers. Mamdani reported how a colleague in the camp, Shivji, had 'received a letter from a friend who lived about fifty miles to the north' promising he could find him a job. Shivji visited the friend but was greeted by four white men who shouted at them 'Hey blackie, what are you doing here? Why don't you go home?' A job was offered but Shivji decided that he wanted 'to live in a place where there are a number of our people... I don't care about the Board. I am going to live in a Red Area.'[107]

Within the camps, as the length of stay increased, so a malaise set in. While the young Asians suffered from boredom, many of the elderly lost confidence and retreated into themselves, spending most of their time in their rooms, often sleeping.[108] During their time in the camps, the Asians had to adapt to changes which went beyond the climate and food. The separation of food lines and eating areas for English and Asians led to resentment at Greenham Common camp, near Newbury, leading to threats of a hunger strike.[109] Mamdani portrays a bleak picture of the refugees' first experiences of racism: 'In Uganda we were Asians, and that meant being not-white and not-black. But here in England, we were simply not white.'[110]

Not all memories of the Ugandan Asians are so negative. An Asian woman, Raxa, resident in Southampton recalls the early years of her life in Britain. Her more favourable memories reflect that she was a child when she came to Britain and adaptation was much easier for her than many of the older refugees.

> We came to Gatwick airport. It was really nice actually when we came. There were people there to help us, to greet us. They brought us warm coats and clothing because ... over there you just wear a dress... We hadn't even seen a coat there. Here, it was really freezing all the time... They asked us if we had any relatives or anybody staying here but at that time we didn't know anybody, so we said no. They took us to Greenham camp ... for a couple of days and then they moved us to another one. I think it was somewhere in Wales. After we were there a few days we heard my dad and my brother were coming so we were really happy... I think a couple of days ... after that, they said, 'Right, we've got a house for you in Ellesmere Port'... So they found a council house for us and they put us in there to settle down... And they were really good, they gave us all the help to get started.

Yet even for a young person, problems of adjustment could still be difficult:

> I went to a local school. I was the only Indian there. I felt really out of place, you know. It was quite bad because you see all these white faces – I'm not prejudiced or anything – but they're all staring at you because they've probably never seen an Asian before. So I was really nervous in school to begin with.

Her parents, however, found it even harder, especially being cut off from other Asian friends:

> But then someone came from Southampton and spoke to us because we were in Uganda together... My parents were really happy to see Asian faces – someone they could talk to, you know, properly, in the Indian language. And they said there are a lot of Asians in Southampton, how would you like to move there... So obviously, my dad was all excited and he said, yes please. Although we [children] were quite happy because we could get on, we could get by with our English ... but they found a house for us there and we moved down.[111]

Some Asians were cushioned from prejudice by wealth. Racism, however, often inhibited class solidarity. This was seen in Loughborough where the opposition of British hosiery workers to Asian workers wanting equal treatment in job allocation and promotion led to a six-week strike from the Asians.[112] Such hostility caused some to reject the idea of integration in society at large:

> Integrate where? In England? When I am part of an unwanted minority? No, definitely not. Just one day out of the camp, a couple of nasty experiences, was enough to send us back to our 'kith and kin'... No wonder people started thinking of settling in Balham, in Wembley, in Leicester and in Birmingham ... in a hostile environment you stick together.[113]

The government's refusal to admit the wives of stateless Asian men housed in the camps added to the general sense of alienation. The final straw was when a group of skinheads attacked some of the camp residents and the officials who witnessed it turned a blind eye.[114] The result was a walk-out by the Asians affected, even though this meant they had to find their way alone in their new world.

Adaptation beyond the confines of the camp certainly varied according to the chosen place of settlement and the racism encountered. The CRC's report on Ugandan adaptation a year after arrival stated that two-thirds of families resettled by the government through the Resettlement Board liked their neighbourhoods. Those most satisfied lived in towns like Northampton and Peterborough where they had good housing, work was available and Asian community links existed, or in expanding towns where they were part of a larger group of refugee families. By 1976 the CRC concluded that Asians had adapted more successfully in Leicester, where they had community ties with other east African Asians, and better chances to improve living conditions, than in Ealing which did not have such opportunities.[115] A quarter of the families interviewed in 1974 who were resettled by the Board disliked their neighbourhoods because the areas were tough and isolated and there was hostility from local people. 'This hostility had taken the forms of demonstrations, letters in the press, and, for one family, bricks thrown through their windows on two occasions'.[116] Such incidents were not isolated and continued long after the initial reception of the Asians. In 1985, years after settling in the Conservative middle-class suburb of Bromley, one family reported a tide of racist abuse; their windows were smashed, car tyres slashed, and most of their seven girls were hurt in physical attacks alongside repeated torments of being 'Paki scum'.[117] Another family whom they had met in a reception camp were burnt to death in an arson attack on their home in Ilford in Essex.[118] Eight out of 49 families questioned about the Race Relations Act in the first CRC survey said they would have liked to use it to combat discrimination.[119]

CONCLUSION

The Minister of State for the Home Office, Alexander Lyon, offered his reflections in a debate after the release of the Final Report of the Resettlement Board in July 1974:

> The real question is what this country is doing to ameliorate the position of immigrants who have come here and who have to be absorbed into our society... When one looks around the stress areas of our bigger cities where immigrants have settled one asks oneself whether the inner cities are capable of looking after the people now living within them.... The problems of housing and education, serious problems associated with coloured immigration, are problems that would face us if we had never had coloured immigrants... What kind of work they have obtained is still an open question. But here again the problem they face is a problem faced by any coloured immigrant, and it has to be tackled within the general framework of policies for dealing with discrimination in employment.[120]

The Ugandan or British Asians were rarely considered as 'refugees' in Britain but were termed 'immigrants' for whom Britain had an obligation to provide. The issues which their arrival raised in terms of housing and employment needs were part of wider concerns in the economic downturn of 1970s Britain. At all times, race relations played a part in how the government sought to organise their resettlement. In their own experiences, racism was also a major factor for many. While this has played a negative part in adaptation, many of the Asians achieved considerable success in establishing new lives in Britain. By the end of the century they are now classed as a group of desirable newcomers who have proved their worth, held up as an example of how refugees can adapt. In Leicester, the Ugandan Asians have been described as '"central" to revitalising the city and the rest of the Midlands, where it is estimated that Asian businesses have created at least 30,000 jobs. Throughout Britain, these once impoverished refugees are now one of the wealthiest, most successful and best educated communities.'[121] At the extreme is Manubhai Madhvani, whose family was described as 'a significant force in the Ugandan economy' before being expelled. Manubhai was joint head of the family business before he was imprisoned by Amin, where he saw fellow prisoners being taken away and shot. He was then expelled from the country and came to Britain: 'We had £62 million of property in Uganda when Amin threw us out. We lost it all ... [Asians must] get themselves into the mainstream of British society ...I was born a Ugandan citizen ... I now think of myself as a British Asian'.[122]

Madhvani's London-based business made his family among the wealthiest 500 people in Britain in 1996 along with other Ugandan Asians in pharmaceuticals, financial services, engineering and property.[123] In a Swansea study the number of Ugandan Asian men working in a managerial capacity in

Britain rose from 25 per cent in 1981 to 37 per cent in 1991, while the proportion of Ugandan Asian women in such positions rose from 6 per cent to 24 per cent, reflecting a considerable upward mobility and remarkable progression as newcomers.[124] In March 1997, *The Independent Magazine* carried a feature on the Ugandan Asians entitled 'Who wants to be a millionaire?', answering, 'They do':

> Families like the Kotechas, who were among the 80,000 Asians expelled without a penny from Uganda by Idi Amin in August 1972. Their drive for success has re-made and re-doubled many fortunes and left Britain a far richer place... Twenty-five years after they arrived, Britain is still a nation of shopkeepers, only now they are Asian.[125]

In summing up the reception process, the Under-Secretary for the Home Department, David Lane, believed the Asians' resettlement was a 'success story', quoting the *Daily Mirror*: 'They have been absorbed very quietly and peacefully and usefully. All credit to them. To the Government. And to everyone who helped.'[126] But the reality for this group of reluctant exiles was more complicated. The Ugandan Asians were not welcomed warmly when they first came to Britain and their initial reception was at best ambivalent. Subsequently, like the Jews who escaped Nazi Germany, they have become an idealised group, but the impressive successes of a significant number of the Ugandan Asians have gone alongside more problematic cases of adjustment. While a majority of respondents a few years after arriving felt that they were settling down well or fairly well, 20 per cent felt that they were managing very poorly. Lastly, progress made since the early days of Ugandan Asian settlement should not hide the continued problem of racism. Adaptation remains an issue for the next generation who feel the conflict of living between two cultures; they have struggled in a different, but equally complex, way from their parents to find a place called 'home'.[127]

10
Refugees from Chile:
A Gesture of International Solidarity

In 1973 the Ugandan Asians were joined by a very different movement to Britain. The Chilean refugees attracted much less attention both on a parliamentary and a popular level due to their far lower numbers and also because they were not regarded as so 'racially' different. They had to be more self-sufficient in establishing themselves as their resettlement was not directed by the government, in contrast to the Asian reception programme, instead being largely assisted through working-class and academic solidarity activities. Thus, although the influx had a very low profile, the nature of the links which supported the incomers meant that on a local level there was considerable interest and help from the host community, giving it a particular significance in the history of refugee movements. In many ways there was more 'positive' interest in these refugees who brought Latin American culture to Britain than in the Asians who were more readily dismissed in a racist manner as unwelcome foreigners. Hampshire was particularly important in the history of Chilean refugees in Britain as it was in Southampton that the first arrivals were accommodated.

THE CHILEAN BACKGROUND

Chile became the focus of international concern when the left-wing Unidad Popular (Popular Unity) coalition government of Salvador Allende was overthrown on 11 September 1973 in a violent coup, led by General Pinochet.[1] The coup occurred against a background of political and economic instability and was followed by severe repression, directed against various sections of society. Pinochet undertook an operation to remove people who were seen as sympathisers with the former government from positions of authority, leading, in effect, to a wholesale purge of the civil service, universities and other powerful institutions. The 13,000 non-Chileans resident in the country, many of whom were themselves refugees from other Latin American countries, were also a particular target, as were all left-wing political activists, community workers and trade unionists.

Ester Contreras was an educational psychologist and political activist, working in the northern town of Iquique at the central University of Santiago. She had been involved in attempts to democratise the university, opening it up and 'respond[ing] to the needs of the country':

> We were very political at that time in Chile, no one could be in the middle of the road, everybody was either on the right or the left, we were very polarised, and I sat on the left, so we were the first to be cut off after the coup... When I lost my job ... people were really in a panic, and that was the policy, to create panic... And the military appeared on television every hour, two hours, calling for people to denounce anyone who knew anybody who were criminals, communists, and they had to present themselves. The way they did that was in a very selective way, they start at the top and they work down and they were taking people and making them talk, using all sorts of methods ... all they wanted was names, and more names, so that created a sort of chain... First of all were the heads of the political parties, people in trade unions and people who have any participation in community programmes. Many people were taking personal revenge and accusing someone they didn't like... The way they took you was in the middle of the night ... it was late, everybody was at home and they came with a lot of noise, going round, shooting, and taking people and the rest of the people were thinking when are they coming to me?... I compare the coup to the persecution of the Jews, when they came in the middle of the night, taking the people without anything, without any rights, and many, many disappear forever.[2]

The total number of Chilean refugees is uncertain but liberal estimates suggest that by 1987, some 200,000 Chileans were scattered around the world.[3] The flight from Chile was part of a larger exodus of Latin American refugees, reflecting the repressive methods used by many regimes in South America to deal with dissidents. Military coups in Uruguay in 1973 and Argentina in 1976 contributed to this movement and in 1975 the United Nations High Commissioner for Refugees (UNHCR) was forced to increase its budget for Latin American refugees to $2.9 million out of a total of $12.6 million.[4] Between 11 September 1973 and 31 December 1978, 18,787 people left Chile along with 9,330 from other parts of Latin America to go to some 44 countries under official schemes of the UNHCR and the Intergovernmental Committee for European Migration (ICEM).[5] Unofficially thousands more left Latin America. About 3,000 Latin American refugees were estimated to have come to Britain, by far the majority Chileans, but also including a small number of Brazilians, Urugayans, Argentineans, Paraguayans and Bolivians.

The particular international concern engendered by the Chilean coup, compared to those in Uruguay or Argentina, was, it is argued, because of all Latin American nations, Chile had made so much progress towards democracy.[6] The idea of military intervention in politics was considered an aberration in Chile in contrast to the rest of Latin America. The World University Service (WUS), which was highly involved in resettlement, argues that the movement in Britain of 'Academics for Chile', in support of Chileans in universities targeted by Pinochet, was affected by the immediate and overt brutality during the takeover in Chile: 'Soldiers burning books in the street appeared on television screens – reminiscent of the book burnings in the days of Hitler – a vivid symbol of the anti-intellectual, anti-cultural, anti-democratic values of the new military rulers'.[7] As with other more recent refugee movements, the media provided clear, evocative evidence of the nature of the repression in Chile, encouraging other countries to take note and assist the resultant refugees.

An activist in the reception programme in Britain also believed that the reception of the Chileans differed from that of other groups, arousing more concern because it was more political, being bound up with the Chile Solidarity Movement in Britain, and hence involving the particular interest of the British labour movement.[8] The ideological implications of the overthrow of the first democratically elected Marxist government prompted a widespread reaction from the international labour movement. It was left-wing groups sympathetic to the cause of the Allende government who pioneered much of the support for Chilean dissidents to come to Britain and the election of the Labour government which precipitated a more favourable policy for them. One woman recalls how her family became involved in assisting the first arrivals in Southampton during 1974. Friends told them of the possibility of helping the refugees:

> We said we were Spanish speakers and we had a room to offer and that we had sympathy with the regime of Allende, so there was a political commitment there… We were allocated a couple of refugees, one of whom is still here and they were from completely different backgrounds, but they settled down quite quickly here and lived with us for about six months, until they'd got enough money to establish themselves… In the early stages it was quite easy to get work for them partly because there were jobs around in that time but also because there was … a lot of solidarity from the unions; even the dock workers got them jobs … which is about as good as you can get.[9]

The effects of the coup on life in Chile can be seen in the 1970s Costa-Gavras film 'Missing' which focused on the struggle of an American to find her missing husband. A Chilean exile, herself imprisoned by Pinochet, and now resident in Hampshire, considered it an accurate portrayal of the climate of fear and violence in the aftermath of the coup. Horrific scenes of people who had been brutalised and killed by the military regime and stored in hidden locations matched her memories. She testified that a friend had been to such a place searching for the body of her husband.[10]

After Pinochet's coup, President Allende was assassinated, the Chilean Congress dismissed, a state of siege declared and the military junta began ruling by decree:

> The widespread use of tanks and aircraft against a civilian population, and the initial twenty-four hour curfew, created a climate of fear for thousands of

people which turned into a nightmare as news of many detentions spread by word of mouth while the state-controlled media suppressed all reports of repression.[11]

The Santiago Sports Stadium became one of the most notorious holding centres where people suspected of opposition to the regime were incarcerated, sometimes to disappear, in other cases, to be tortured but later released. Michael Sanders, who was among the detainees in the Santiago Sports Stadium after the coup, reported in 1974 that the number who died fighting, or as a result of torture or execution, was between 5,000 and 15,000.[12] Later assessments suggest some 30,000 people were killed and over 80,000 arrested. Many of the latter were tortured and forced into exile.[13]

Haydee A., from Concepción, was one of those who was held in the stadium, later settling as a refugee in Winchester. She worked in the Economics Department at the university in Concepción but after the coup most people in her faculty were sacked. The university was occupied by the military and in early October they came to Haydee's house and said that they wanted to talk to her:

> So I went with them in this jeep full of soldiers. We were concerned, but I thought, I'm going to go for interrogation and then probably they will release me. [A soldier] said, 'Oh, don't worry. This is like a formality.'... They took me to the police station and I spent all day there [being questioned]. About three o'clock in the morning there was a curfew and they put a lot of people [together] and said, 'We'll take you somewhere else.' And then I was a little bit worried because we didn't know if they were going to take us to the stadium or to an island. For the island you have to cross the sea and a lot of people say you never reach that place, so you were really worried...

> We arrived in the stadium ..., they searched me and a woman who was from the prison service ...took me away and took me into [a] changing room [where] there were a lot of women and they woke up when I arrived... They said, 'Don't worry. It's not so bad.' And they tried to help me. We were tired and ... sad and worried because my family didn't know where I was taken ... And then ... on the day after I arrived ... they start asking for names and weapons. I was so surprised because I haven't any idea of weapons... So they shout – they use all the techniques and ways you can imagine – and then after many times they isolate you. For a week I was in isolation... I remember they use a lot of techniques to try, as a woman, to humiliate you, because they undress you and they said they were going to give me electric shocks. I was lucky. They never did myself but I saw they did that to so many and they did other things...[14]

Over 7,000 people were detained in the National Stadium and thousands of others were held in less conspicuous locations where they were subjected to starvation, torture and violence, leaving psychological traumas which could long outlast any physical scars.[15] Summary executions were used by Pinochet's regime against 'alien parties'. The workforce was terrorised and strikes were outlawed.

Hernan Valdes, who was initially received as a refugee in Britain at the University of Southampton, described the plight of the detainees in his *Diary of a Chilean Concentration Camp*. Written as a novel, it is based on the real experiences of a Chilean who was held in Tejas Verdes military concentration camp near the port of San Antonio. His aim was to make 'known ... the collective experience of the Chilean people ... which, with the hindsight afforded by the loss of all political innocence, one could consider a possibility for any other nation, anywhere in the world, in the event of a fascist-type regression':

> The doors are flying wide open ... Brusquely we're untied from our chairs... They're armed. They force us out of the room, poking their guns in our ribs... At last we reach a space where the air's breathable. They've lined us up, elbow to elbow, facing forward. Maybe it was just a matter of identifying us for their records and now they're going to let us go? Someone from behind forces my head brutally down. My forehead smashes into what seems to be a brick wall... The guards pace up and down behind us, muttering amongst themselves. Then we hear the unmistakeable metallic clink of guns being loaded. So we're going to die, in this stupid fashion. Instances of absurd, gratuitous executions have become commonplace in the last few months and not one of us seems to be shocked or rebel. No one says a word... Behind us, sudden guffaws of laughter. The truth finally dawns. They jostle us with the guns again.[16]

THE SETTLEMENT OF CHILEAN REFUGEES

In this atmosphere of fear and daily violence, on the streets of Santiago as well as behind closed doors, thousands of foreigners and Chilean nationals fled to foreign embassies for protection. Many people also escaped to neighbouring Argentina and Peru, while others sought more permanent refuge beyond. The number of Chilean refugees internationally remains in dispute,[17] and their specific reasons for leaving were also complex:

> About 3,000 went to exile directly from prison, and many others had experienced short periods of detention and been released inside the country. Many fled from detention orders issued against them or because they heard that they were being pursued by the secret police. Others left the country due to fear of persecution or the very real difficulties of subsistence in Chile for people dismissed from their jobs, either for political reasons or because of the drastic changes in economic policy brought about by the new regime.[18]

As this analysis makes clear, it is difficult to separate political and economic intent for flight. It appears that a larger proportion of the exiles were from middle-class and professional than working-class backgrounds, as these were the particular targets of Pinochet's purge. A survey by a Chilean education agency based on interviews with 800 families in six countries of exile (excluding Britain) established that the majority were from political parties that formed the Unidad Popular alliance and the Revolutionary Party, primarily from the Socialist Party. Some 53.6 per cent were university educated and only 22.7 per cent were skilled or unskilled manual workers. Such research has not been conducted in Britain, but it is known from World University Service (WUS) reports that many came from a politically active and academic background.

According to Ann Browne, Coordinator of the Joint Working Group for Refugees from Latin America (JWG), the organisation set up in Britain to meet the needs of the refugees, 'In Britain, the immediate reaction to the coup was more muted than in many other countries'.[19] As one activist recalled, 'The biggest number of refugees went to Spain, France, and Sweden which took tens of thousands. Britain was a bit slow about it all.'[20] The Conservative government of Edward Heath recognised the new Chilean regime and, unlike those elsewhere in Europe, refused to offer protection to non-British asylum seekers who fled to its embassy seeking safe-conduct, a move which led to considerable outrage from the Labour Opposition in Parliament.[21] Moreover, arms continued to be sold to the Pinochet regime. With the Ugandan Asians still occupying the government, there was little inclination to welcome another influx of refugees. Not only had Ugandan Asians encountered severe popular opposition, they had also led to marked divisions within the party. Conservative policy towards the Chileans followed a muted course, as laid out to the United Nations in response to its request for aid to the Chileans on 18 October 1973:

> Her Majesty's Government feel strongly that in principle the problem of refugees in Latin America should be capable of solution within the framework of the conventions on asylum signed by the governments of the Organisation of American States in Caracas in 1954… [It] is in no position to accept refugees from Chile while having to turn away Commonwealth citizens. Nevertheless, in view of the humanitarian terms in which your appeal has been made, the British Government is willing exceptionally to consider some applications on an individual basis from those who express as their first choice their wish to be resettled in the United Kingdom and who have some ties with the United Kingdom.[22]

Lord Windlesham, Lord Privy Seal, added that those assisted by the British would be people with knowledge of the English language, who could 'most easily be assimilated'.[23] However, none were admitted until Harold Wilson's Labour government took over office in February 1974. Seven Chileans arrived in December 1973 only to be detained at Heathrow until some sympathetic politicians intervened. Their requests to stay were still under consideration when the Conservatives lost power.

The election of a Labour government initiated a more generous policy. While the Labour Party had expressed its support for the arrival of the Asians, the case of the Chileans was probably more appealing, since the refugees were predominantly of a left-wing political persuasion, and there had been support for the democratically elected Marxist government of Allende. Foreign Secretary James Callaghan stated on 27 March 1974 that our policy towards the military junta will be governed by our desire to see democracy restored and human rights fully respected there ... the Home Secretary will consider applications from Chilean refugees sympathetically.[24]

The government also suspended aid to the Chilean regime, cancelled a projected naval training exercise and refused to grant any new export licences.[25] A grant of £150,000 was made towards the resettlement programme of the UNHCR for the Chileans.[26] Its role in finding homes for the Chileans all over the world meant an equitable 'responsibility sharing' was possible, contrasting with the Ugandan Asian crisis, where the duty to assist the refugees had fallen primarily on Britain (and to a lesser extent India). In response to criticisms that stopping aid to Chile would adversely affect the country's development, Judith Hart, the Minister for Overseas Development, a prime mover in helping the Chilean refugees reach Britain, argued that

> the three main areas of technical assistance in Chile were in industrial training, where in the whole of industry the trade unions have been suppressed and trade unionists have been imprisoned, persecuted and killed; in agriculture, where the present military regime is totally reversing the programme of land reform to which our aid is directed; and ... in education, where most of the educational institutions are now in the hands of the generals, departments have been closed and there has been suppression and persecution of people engaged in education.[27]

Instead of using these channels to help the Chileans, all technical assistance was transferred to the WUS refugee programme. Labour government policy for resettlement initially echoed the Conservatives' criteria requiring that refugees had ties with Britain, knew some English and were personally acceptable, but, in extreme need, these prerequisites could be ignored. After the coup in Argentina in March 1976, policy was broadened to admit other Latin American nationals who had sought refuge in Argentina. The requirement of ties with Britain was temporarily dropped.[28]

Many of Britain's first Chilean arrivals came via Argentina and Peru. Then in May 1974, Pinochet's regime announced Decree Law 504 allowing all political prisoners who wished to leave the country to do so by commuting their sentences to exile if they could obtain an entry visa from another country. In Britain, however, the time taken to process applications for visas caused serious problems, with backlogs of over six months for some requests. This led to deputations to the Home Secretary, his personal intervention granting entry for 54 out of 63 prisoners in Chile awaiting visas.[29] There were no special arrangements to speed up procedures: Alexander Lyon, the Minister of State at the Home Office, stated in July 1974, 'Applications from Chile are dealt with under the Immigration Rules'.[30]

Labour Home Secretary Roy Jenkins reported on 9 July 1975, that of 6,830 applications received since the coup 1,971 had been granted but that, 'Many of those concerned have not exercised their option to come here and apparently do not intend to do so. Only 893 have arrived in the United Kingdom.' In view of these figures he announced that there would be a change of emphasis in the reception process. While accepting a share in international arrangements, other Chileans would be accepted either if there were marked compassionate circumstances or they had ties with the UK, including family links, or if they were coming to study: 'In all cases acceptance will continue to be dependent upon personal acceptability and reliable sponsorship in this country'.[31] In June 1976 policy was further adapted after members of the JWG visited Chile and Argentina recommending a more effective selection policy to deal with the Chileans. The aim was to give varying priorities to the refugees, first to detainees seeking exile, then people in danger of arrest, followed by individuals with family in Britain and finally those with other ties making it the appropriate country of refuge. The Chileans were treated as a special case in comparison with refugees from other Latin American countries but by mid-1978 the government no longer believed they were worthy of particular attention. The Home Secretary stated that:

> In future, I shall accept for consideration applications from people in Latin America, including those in their own countries, who can show a genuine need for resettlement and who have ties with this country. Cases will be considered on their individual merit and will, as hitherto, be subject to the criterion of individual acceptability.[32]

While the Conservative and Labour governments were slow to respond to the crisis in Chile and followed a policy which was 'clearly modelled on the rules of admission of immigrants',[33] reminiscent of the treatment of Jews fleeing Nazi Germany in the 1930s, there was much grassroots activity to help the beleaguered nation. Chilean Solidarity Committees in Britain adopted political prisoners who were then assisted to enter the country. The first organised resettlement programme for Chilean refugees was prepared in June 1974 by WUS, and was linked with its own international scholarship programme for academics and students. It had earlier undertaken campaigns to help Hungarians in 1956 and over 200 Czech refugees in 1968, but its programme for the Chileans did not anticipate that so many refugees needed help or that the crisis would last so long.

It is estimated that half the Chilean adult refugees in Britain were helped by the WUS scholarship scheme. One recipient was Ester Contreras who came to study in England for two years and later taught at the University of Southampton. She had two other possibilities, Ecuador and Nigeria:

> I really didn't know much about [life in Nigeria which was] so very far from our own experience in Chile. But I was prepared to go – you didn't ask where, you just wait for a ticket to arrive ... but Britain was quick so I received a notice from the Queen. Her Majesty the Queen invites you! So I had a passport ... and when I got here they arranged everything to give me to establish as a political

refugee... A month or two after I left they came [to my friend's house in Chile] for me and they came very, very violently...[34]

Over a ten-year period 900 Chileans were assisted under the WUS programme. It was undertaken as a 'scheme for skills-training and upgrading for qualified personnel from the Third World',[35] combining humanitarian objectives with promoting development. In Britain the campaign was pioneered by academics and overseen by the Ministry of Overseas Development. In material terms the campaigners belonging to the group 'Academics for Chile' helped considerably as they pressured universities to waive fees and carried out fundraising initiatives which helped other Chileans to pay for their courses. There were also efforts to help in the process of integration, with some individuals providing places for the refugees to stay on arrival and becoming involved in the reception process. Jane Freeland, who had housed some of the early Chilean arrivals in Southampton, taught the refugees and then their children at Portsmouth Polytechnic:

> We took a lot of risks ... scholarship money was there and you made room for them in departments when they didn't really have the qualifications ... Some of them actually completed their secondary education at university level ... because they had actually left school early anyway and become workers [aged] 12, 13 or 14. Then they arrived here aged [say] 20 ... got taken on these courses and had to learn English, learn how to write ... The first year we allowed them to write their essays in Spanish and have lessons in English and we allowed them to miss their year abroad and concentrate on their English instead, but they had to do Spanish language work ... and that was actually very complicated... My Spanish was better than theirs, at least when it came to the written forms. We would get into all kinds of jams because if you criticised the way they used their language you were actually making an attack on their identity, since their identities were particularly fragile in the exile situation...[36]

SETTLEMENT IN BRITAIN

The Chilean arrivals were initially reliant on established agencies for their reception, namely the British Council for Aid to Refugees (BCAR) and the Ockenden Venture, a small charity based in Surrey with several homes for refugees. The need for more resources to organise a larger scale response became clear, but the government preferred to let the voluntary organisations tackle this problem. Despite the lack of official support, the Joint Working Group for Refugees from Chile (JWG) was formed,[37] with an initial grant from the voluntary bodies, to carry out the reception and resettlement programme. It included representatives of organisations with knowledge of refugee work: BCAR, Ockenden Venture, WUS, Christian Aid and the Standing Conference on Refugees, and groups specifically concerned with Chile: the Chile Committee for Human Rights and the Chile Solidarity Campaign.

In September 1974 a grant of £10,000 was made through the Voluntary

Services Unit of the Home Office to the JWG, and additional funding was found. Nevertheless, its coordinator argued that 'Up to 1978 it was never certain of its finance for more than six months in advance which has made realistic long term planning impossible ... the JWG's work is not seen as related to any particular government policy'.[38] Such problems continue to plague resettlement project groups, most recently seen with the Bosnia Project set up for Bosnian refugees in the 1990s.[39] The JWG's nature as a temporary *ad hoc* body led to only a minimal service being provided for the refugees.

The JWG's interim report of December 1975 outlined the origins of the resettlement scheme after the Foreign Secretary's announcement in March 1974 that applications from Chilean refugees would be viewed sympathetically. The first programme for the refugees had been prepared in June by WUS who saw that that the 'major needs for academics and non-academics alike were temporary accommodation and intensive courses in English':

> Accordingly, a tentative plan was prepared for a programme based at Southampton University, during the Summer vacation, taking advantage of empty student halls of residence and the language teaching facilities at the University ... The project organised [there] to receive an expected 120 refugees was a test scheme where success provided a model on which we could work thereafter. Eventually only 32 people arrived in time to take part in the scheme but in six weeks the families were housed by the local authority and single persons were accommodated in the homes of local residents. Those Chileans who had suitable academic qualifications were found places at Southampton University and the others were employed in local hospitals and factories. It was not originally intended that the group received at Southampton should necessarily be resettled there, but the response from the trade unions, local authority, academics and numerous individuals was so tremendous that all the refugees who arrived in Southampton were resettled in the area.[40]

The JWG also set up reception centres in London and Birmingham and, later, a series of bed and breakfast lodgings were used. Although these were sometimes in a poor state of repair, the refugees did not stay in them for long. Local committees (often composed of members of local Chile Solidarity or Human Rights Committees) helped in the placement of Chileans around the country. These individuals were the mainstay of the reception process as they organised housing, language courses and helped the refugees find employment. Their local basis was important in securing housing and employment as there were often direct contacts with local councils and the trade union movement. As Ann Browne comments, 'In effect it has been largely due to the efforts of such solidarity organisations that Latin American refugees have been settled in Britain'.[41]

The scheme at Southampton was indicative of the importance of competent helpers as within six weeks the 33 Chileans who had arrived were housed by local authorities and single people with local residents.[42] The role of the city in the Chilean programme was clearly significant but there are few reminders of its role. The local paper carried only two articles referring to the refugees' arrival. One focused on the writer Hernan Valdes, outlining his experiences at the time of the military coup:

> For Hernan Valdes, the morning of September 11 1973, began like any other day. Soon, he would set out for the Catholic University at Santiago where he worked. Then jet planes flew low over the house and there was rifle fire in the streets... Three or four days after the coup the army went to the university.... 'We all lost our jobs. I began to sell some things to buy food', he said ... Before Mr Valdes could leave he was arrested. In February of last year the army took him from his house. He was given no reason for his arrest. 'They never gave anyone a reason... It was like a big conveyor belt. People were constantly being arrested and they were eventually released. Many of my friends were taken to prison'... When Mr Valdes was released from prison he sought asylum in the Swedish embassy and they arranged for him to go to Spain. When in Spain he wrote a book about his experiences... Because of the political nature of the book, pressures were put on him by the Spanish government to leave. From Spain he came to England, and the BCAR found him a place at Southampton. Hernan Valdes has obtained a job as a lecturer in Spanish ... and will continue writing.

Rather naively, the article concluded that Valdes had 'no plans for returning to Chile in the near future'. Not surprisingly, the paper was keen to emphasise the local angle of this refugee movement. It reported that the BCAR was desperately trying to find offers of accommodation for the Chileans from local people, adding that those in Southampton were able to stay at the Glen Eyre University hall of residence 'then they must move elsewhere. High on the list for homes are the four families with young children who are staying at the University'.[43]

The only other report in Southampton's local paper concerned the visit to the town of the former Swedish ambassador to Chile, Harold Edelstam, who was prominent in assisting those fleeing Pinochet's regime. It gave some insight into the more active stance of the Swedish in helping refugees compared with the British, often noted by people involved in the Chileans' reception. His visit, as the guest of the United Nations Association and Amnesty International, marked the first anniversary of Chile's military coup. In the first stop at a speaking tour of Britain, Edelstam addressed an audience of 150 people, including several of the refugees based at the university:

> He explained how he rescued some 8,000 refugees by giving them asylum in his embassy... Writing his own code of diplomatic behaviour, Mr Edelstam decided that humanitarian considerations took precedence over passive neutrality: 'I decided to receive people whom I regarded as in life's danger', he said. More than once he put his own life on the line, as he illegally ferried refugees across Santiago in his diplomatic car to other 'friendly' embassies.

> Every day he would travel to the sports stadium where thousands of supporters of assassinated President Allende were held. The usual method of dealing with these unfortunate people, he said, was to release them on to the streets without papers after curfew, to certain execution by patrols of soldiers... Inevitably Mr Edelstam was expelled from Chile. To a standing ovation he concluded: 'Many have criticised me for rescuing some people whom they call "terrorists". In Sweden we have some thousand refugees and these have all enriched Swedish life also.'[44]

In the absence of more written records, oral testimony helps to throw more light on the part local people played in the Chilean influx largely absent from other sources. Clare Mar-Molinero, a lecturer in the Spanish department at the University of Southampton, who was involved in English language teaching for three groups of Chilean refugees based at Glen Eyre Hall, recalls:

> In Southampton there was only one large group – 30 to 40 people – the first group, then just individuals. People weren't sent here as such except through WUS... It was much more to do with friends and contacts [which brought people] here; equally people went off from Southampton to other places... There were links between Southampton University and Portsmouth Polytechnic which had a strong Latin American department [and thus more refugee] students ... and then ... we had the second generation – the refugees' children.

The group included several Chileans from a Marxist background:

> [One of the Chilean men] who was working on a building site worked all the hours that God gave ... because he wanted to bring his girlfriend over, she was stuck in France ... he was from one of the extreme left parties [and] went off to Swansea in the end to study with his girlfriend... There was an actress [who] went up to London and there was this guy who had been doing photography [who] went off to Bradford. And then there was the group who stayed here. In the end there must have been five or six families maybe that stayed for any length of time and they gradually moved off. Some stayed and then when the regime changed [in Chile] WUS turned its Chile scholarship programme around and made it into a returns programme ... and some of the Southampton group went back.

There were also several academics who came to Hampshire and continue to lived in the county, their history very much hidden due to their isolation. The lack of central direction in the British resettlement procedure for the Chileans meant that there were variations in provisions made for the refugees and these had to be negotiated in every locality. Priority was given to finding accommodation first, employment second, which could cause discrepancies as the two needs did not always coincide, as noted in the experiences of many other refugees.[45] Clare Mar-Molinero believes that of the early Chilean arrivals about 70 per cent were manual labourers or came from relatively low skilled jobs, a profile which was very different from the Chilean refugees as a whole in Britain who tended to be of a professional background. She remembers the group dissipating into the local community as they found work.

> The first one to get a job [did so] in a hospital in Southampton ... the only one
> to get a job straight away... The Council allowed some housing after the first
> period [when the Chileans stayed at Glen Eyre Hall] and we continued some
> further education. That took us up to Christmas and then most of the others
> from the early group began to get jobs, mainly in factories.[46]

Finding housing relied on sympathetic local housing authorities and housing
associations, so that offers often depended on the political leanings of those
in positions of power. In Southampton, the university wrote to the (Labour-
controlled) Council regarding four refugee families and it resolved to spend
£500 'in respect of one of two houses referred to by the Director of Housing
as suitable and available for rehousing the Chilean families'. This gesture
appeared to represent the limit of City Council generosity. In April 1975 a
further request from the Southampton Chile Solidarity Campaign for rehousing was rejected because of the Council's earlier support.[47]

There were total refusals to help, largely because of political biases.
George Tremlett, of the Greater London Council (GLC) Housing Policy
Committee, was approached following a Conservative victory at the local
elections concerning 20 previous housing allocations for the refugees. His
reply was, 'I aim to see that London's own people become number one
priority and because of this Marxist refugees will be given only a low priority,
if any at all.'[48] Funding problems recurred in the resettlement; English
language teaching was denied any Voluntary Services Unit aid in 1977, until
approaches to the Prime Minister, the Home Secretary and a press campaign
made the Home Office agree to give financial help for 1978–79.

BRITISH RECEPTION OF THE CHILEANS

The reception of the Chileans in Britain was not accorded nearly as much
prominence as that devoted to other refugee groups. The eclipse of their
plight was also true in international efforts, although the UNHCR came to
recognise the Chileans as part of a broader movement of Latin American
exiles needing significant assistance.[49] With the Chilean influx to Britain
dwarfed in size by the Asian movement and with the lack of governmental
involvement in the Chileans' resettlement, British responses to the group are
difficult to gauge though they were generally positive. Home Secretary
Alexander Lyon stated that some 80 communications had been received
concerning the Chileans under the Labour administration by 31 July 1974
and, of these, 'only a small proportion indicated opposition to their
admission'.[50] In Parliament, some concern was expressed over whether
entrants might have criminal records abroad or be affiliated with a
Communist Party, and the debates over housing at the GLC also suggested
that there was concern that the Chileans were communist agitators.[51]

The testimony of those working with the refugees provides greater insight
into the impact of the Chileans on British society. Several of those who

worked with reception and teaching in the pilot project at Southampton said that they had found it a challenging experience because of political conflicts within the refugee group. Nonetheless, they also emphasised how rewarding it had been as they had been forced to reassess their own beliefs, and for university lecturers, their methods of teaching, due to the dynamic nature of the Chileans and the cultural differences they raised. The thanks given by a local organiser to the people of Southampton for their 'overwhelming' response to an appeal for clothing for the Chileans suggests that they had a more general popularity.[52] The Chileans were also known for the parties they held where traditional food was available and handicrafts were sold to further aid the cause of their cohorts.

As noted earlier, most of the activity undertaken in Britain to help the Chileans came from Labour councils, trade unions and academics in Hampshire. Solidarity committees were also an important link and Chilean exiles would join these groups themselves. In Portsmouth the committee raised money for a youth group in Iquique and other projects and wrote letters of appeal over the arrest of socialist leaders in Chile. Local campaigning also took place over Britain's abstention in a vote in the United Nations on the human rights situation in Chile. A common practice was for local committees to make contact with individuals who had been imprisoned, 'adopting a political prisoner', and sending money to help their families.[53]

THE CHILEANS' EXPERIENCE OF SETTLEMENT

Due to the dissipated nature of the Chilean arrivals, the recovery of their experiences in Britain is largely dependent on oral history, well-illustrated in Diana Kay's analysis of Chilean exiles in Scotland.[54] She notes that the motives for Chileans to come to Britain, rather than one of the other countries offering refuge, were varied. It was not always a matter of choice. As one individual recounted, 'The truth is I didn't choose Britain. My coming here occurred largely because it was the first opportunity to present itself... I would have preferred some other Latin American country, to be nearer.'[55] Connections through WUS, family, friends, or political connections played a part in the choice of the place of resettlement. The similar outlook of the Chilean Radical Party and the British Labour Party was also important, while some Chileans believed Britain offered positive educational opportunities. Often, it was a case of accepting whatever opportunity was available to escape Chile, including adoption by a British trade union or other organisations which enabled the Chileans to gain safe conduct out of their country.

Images of Britain and Europe generally amongst the politicised Chileans were ambiguous: 'At the same time as being regarded as the "capitalist [and imperialist] monster", Europe was also seen as the centre of culture and learning'.[56] Reconciling themselves to life in Britain could be a difficult process for the Chileans. Well meaning but ignorant actions by British people could have unforeseen consequences, as when arrivals were offered chile con carne to eat, by people assuming it was a Chilean dish, which the exiles had never tasted before. More importantly, questions of work and life differed from home. Many Chilean professionals suffered a loss of status and earning power and were forced to take on manual work, or undertake courses through the WUS programme before they could progress with their lives. Chileans from working-class backgrounds were often surprised by the lack of participation of British workers in the class struggle:

> The difference between Britain and Chile is not just one of nationality. It's a way of looking at politics. There was nobody neutral in Chile. It's the contrast between the situation there where all had an opinion and everyone was politically defined and the situation here, which strikes us most.[57]

The Chileans were not a homogenous group and their sharply differing class and political backgrounds could cause tensions between themselves, as well as between them and the host community. The refugees included members of the Communist Party who were unwilling to admit their political background because their affiliations meant they were expected to stay and fight the regime from within Chile. The feeling that the Unidad Popular government had failed to meet their aspirations could cause bitterness and a search for scapegoats between the different factions. As Diana Kay has shown, gender was also a significant factor affecting experiences of exile for the Chileans. The divergent experiences of male and female refugees in Britain could lead to a total reassessment of gender relations. Kay suggests that Chilean men perceived their exile in political terms, whereas the women, none of whom in her sample had been imprisoned, unlike those in Hampshire, described their experiences primarily in terms of changing family relations. Loss of status both politically and economically could hit men more than women, as they had tended to be both the breadwinners and political activists at home. Those women who had been more politically active also felt a loss of involvement in the political sphere but generally women suffered more from a loss of family support networks, an important factor in Chilean society. The inability to communicate with friends and family they had left behind, exacerbated by the need to stay at home and look after their children which often prevented them from learning English and meeting people in their new social environment, left many suffering from loneliness and depression. The potential for conflict between couples with such changes in the public and private domains in exile led to a reassessment of relationships and several of those interviewed said their marriages had broken down after resettlement in Britain.

While initially rejoicing in their freedom, the reality of building a new life soon hit home. As a former university teacher in Santiago put it:

> You have to learn how to live in a new culture and at [first], I felt so stupid

without the language. I [no longer felt] an intelligent person, and this … was a big humiliation. Th[e] impossibility to express your feeling, your thoughts, to be constricted to basic words. So I studied English quite a lot but sometimes my mind was blocked, I couldn't learn because all the terrible things that happened in my country were living in me as a nightmare. I think during the first three years in England, I suffered each night with nightmares about torture.[58]

Adaptation was further hindered by thoughts of home. Certainly the question of return has been particularly relevant for the Chilean refugees. Although many refugees dream of returning home, this often remains impossible. For the Chileans, however, it became a real possibility when Pinochet issued decrees in the late 1970s formally inviting exiles to come back. While this was always subject to government approval, with lists being drawn up of acceptable and unacceptable entrants, a substantial number of those who had fled did seek to rejoin their families and pick up the pieces of their former lives. Overall returns from 1976 to 1985 are estimated at between 2,640 and 3,017.[59] The WUS and UNHCR put the number of Chileans returning from Britain at 750 by March 1989, when President Aylwim replaced Pinochet as President, perhaps a third of the original number of arrivals attempting to go back at some stage.[60]

The importance of the homeland and the sense of identity it engenders is clearly seen by the fact that so many refugees were prepared to risk going back to Chile, even after over a decade of life in another country. 'England was a very rich experience for me, but I somehow felt incomplete during my nine years there.'[61] But to return was fraught with risks. The son of one family who went back to his country was killed by the military.[62] Clare Mar-Molinero remembers:

It wasn't obvious immediately but it became clear that some of them did not want to integrate too much because it was essential to return home … that they should keep their sense of Chileanness was a quite clear objective. Those who remained politically active here were very politically active in Chile… Some people couldn't, shouldn't and wouldn't go back. One went back because he couldn't get a job at his level here and he never really settled. When he did go back he found it difficult because he was going back to a Chile that was no longer the image he had.[63]

Over ten years after arriving in Britain, Ester Contreras went back to Chile but decided she could not return for good because her former country was so changed. She no longer felt a part of the country she had loved. Another of the Southampton group went to Venezuela but also later returned to Britain. Yet the Chileans who did return home permanently have still left a lasting legacy in Britain. In Oxford, a monument by the famous Chilean artist Roberto Matta pays homage to the Chilean struggle. And those whose resettlement in Britain has taken on a permanent character have introduced a cultural dynamic which has made Latin American culture an integral part of life in Britain.[64] In Hampshire only a handful of Chileans remain, but their hidden history is a remarkable reminder of how international solidarity could play a part in assisting those who dared to oppose a military regime. Such work at a local level enabled the refugees to start rebuilding lives which had been so brutally damaged in their homeland and to find a new home in Britain.

Refugees from Indo-China:
A Media-Driven Resettlement Scheme?

Following the Chileans, a group of refugees whose culture and background was again very different entered Britain. While instability in Latin America continued to bring refugees to the UK in the late 1970s, their significance was overshadowed by a crisis in south-east Asia which led to a new exodus. A United States Department of State report noted that between 1975 and 1990 1,645,867 south-east Asian refugees had resettled outside the region.[1] Many were from Indo-China, where political and economic upheaval, particularly between the late 1970s and early 1980s, caused mass flight. The exodus included nationals of Laos and Cambodia but by far the greatest proportion of the refugees from the region entering Britain were Vietnamese nationals who propelled international relief efforts as they moved in large numbers into Thailand, Malaysia and Hong Kong.[2] In denoting the refugees as 'Vietnamese' it is recognised that this is partly a misnomer since a large proportion of those escaping Vietnam were of Chinese origin. A small contingent of Laotians and Cambodians also reached Britain. The resettlement of the Vietnamese has received particular attention from academics and service providers as this government programme was of a nature and scope unique in the post-war period, dealing with a group of people whose everyday life was far removed from that of much of the British population.

The large-scale exodus began in 1975 when American troops were withdrawn from the country after the Vietnam War. Over 130,000 refugees were admitted to the United States in a matter of only two weeks, while 9,500 were taken in by France and 9,000 already there were allowed to remain. The United Kingdom took only 32 refugees, although a further 300 within the country also stayed. In 1976–77 200 were admitted to Britain.[3] But it was not until 1979 that international attention was fully aroused as hundreds of thousands of Vietnamese took to the seas, risking drowning in shark-infested seas, or attack by pirates from Thailand. The enormity of the crisis was brought home to the world by media images of the 'Boat People'. One refugee reflected the feelings of many when he explained their drastic course of action:

> What have we all got left? An old sailing boat, our only transport to combat the ocean. Our fear for our life was not all that great because we had a great hope of survival: let's go to another part of the world, the world of *freedom* where we will be welcomed with love.[4]

The first refugees fled due to the changing political circumstances following the fall of the Saigon government and the Communist takeover in 1975. The majority of these were members of the south Vietnamese elite and their families. They tended to be fairly wealthy and often came from professional-managerial backgrounds and most went to the United States.[5] In late 1976, a new exodus commenced, subsequently embracing people from north Vietnam, largely of ethnic Chinese origin, known as Hoa, who escaped overland into China or by sea into adjacent countries of south-east Asia.[6] Many Western countries subsequently accepted these refugees on the basis that their flight was from the communist system. Communist indoctrination was used to discourage the practice of religion, intellectualism and capitalist attitudes, and dissidents were detained. However, in a survey of Vietnamese refugees in Britain only 4 per cent gave communism as their reason for flight.[7] Several of those interviewed in Hampshire had family members who had been in the South Vietnamese army sent to new economic zones by the Communist government to redevelop the land, living barely at subsistence level and forced to undergo re-education.[8]

Mai Hoang, who settled in Portsmouth, where she worked as a community development worker supporting the local Vietnamese community, described the events leading to her flight:

> I finished secondary school... After that I applied to attend university but the Communists think my family is very bad because one of my brothers escaped to England [and] my elder brother was a soldier for the Government and he was trained by Americans and after 1975 he had been put in a re-education camp for six years. So at that time the Communists think my family is not very good ... so when I apply to university they fail me twice. After that I work in sewing .... I lived nine years in a Communist government. They are very strict ... We couldn't say anything we want ... like to go somewhere else to visit your friend, your friend had to inform the local authority there...

> The night before [a friend's wedding] about 15 of us young people [wanted] to meet together, to sing a song before the church for the wedding the day after. That night ... all of us [were taken to the authorities] and they said we are not allowed to meet together ... I was very scared ... because I thought maybe they'd keep us for the night but about midnight they let us out. But they said next time you're not allowed to do that... At that time I always [felt] scared... They can arrest you if you have no reason to go out. So it's like you live but you can't speak. You can't say what you want and you're not allowed to do what you want to do.[9]

For other refugees, flight was primarily from economic oppression. Esther Wong, of the World Health Organisation, argues that after 1975 government control of the economy tightened after unification, and the introduction of a single currency and high taxation made business difficult and life unbearable.[10] Most of those interviewed in a British survey had been business or professional people and left because of the loss of property, money and position.[11] A chief engineer at a leading paper mill was prompted to leave when his salary was reduced to a twentieth of its former value after four years of Communism.[12] Another man left when his pay deteriorated so much that he found life impossible. With an allowance of three pounds of rice a week for his family, savings were used up to buy food on the black market.[13] Such problems were exacerbated from July to October 1978 by typhoons and floods sweeping across the lowlands of northern, central and southern Vietnam, leading to great losses in food, livestock and housing. People often left their homes through a combination of political and economic factors: 'I left for my freedom, I could not develop my future in Vietnam'.[14]

Explanations such as these led to criticisms that the refugees from Vietnam did not fit Convention definitions, because they were fleeing economic rather than political conditions. But an evaluation of Vietnamese reception in Britain in 1989 argued that some 80 per cent were ethnic Chinese people from North Vietnam. This was borne out in another survey where 83 per cent of those interviewed were of Chinese origin. This bias towards Chinese-Vietnamese in Britain's intake was because most of those who came were from Hong Kong, where for geographical reasons, the refugees were largely from North Vietnam. The war with America, along with conflict involving China and other neighbouring countries in the 1970s, had increased tensions in Vietnam, creating a climate of instability and terror which prompted some young men to leave to avoid conscription. The Chinese nationals within Vietnam became a particular focus for persecution. Anne Ruffell suggests their clannishness and talent for trade, making them prosperous middlemen, much like the Ugandan Asians, was resented by many Vietnamese. In 1977–78 large numbers began to lose their jobs and businesses, Chinese schools were closed and they were denied the right to hold meetings or travel. China's invasion of Vietnam in February 1979 was a further turning point for the Hoa after which it seemed that there was no possibility of staying:

> Fearing a fifth column, the Vietnamese government stepped up its campaign of oppression to expel the Chinese minority. Deprived of their businesses, hounded from their homes and threatened with conscription or removal to agricultural communes, the Hoa were forced to take to the sea in their thousands.[15]

La Thanh Xuan, a Chinese teacher in north Vietnam, was interrogated by the public security services and given two options: to put out to sea or be sent to a concentration camp in Lam-Dong for the Chinese:

> Reclaiming the land in Lam-Dong means being imprisoned in the deserted

jungle and falling prey to deadly mosquitoes. Putting out to sea means undertaking a perilous journey in which the chance to survive and find freedom due to rescue by a foreign ship was only 10%. I chose the second course, that was 'freedom or death'.[16]

After harassment by the Viet Cong police he fled, leaving his wife and children behind. Like most of the others aboard the ship, Xuan sold his property for a seat, putting his life in the hands of a half-trained captain and engineer who were also refugees. Shipwrecked, his life was saved by a small fishing boat.

Esther Wong suggests there were three means of escape.[17] The first was an illegal movement, consisting of fishermen leaving secretly by boat, with the associated dangers of poorly equipped boats and life imprisonment if caught. A second way was to be 'released after payment' with government approval involving huge amounts of gold. The third was through a semi-official movement of refugees which was unauthorised but where bribery was used to get past coastal officers. Compared to the Chileans, who were given authorised flights out, the Vietnamese journey to freedom was particularly dangerous. On the escape route from the north along the Chinese coast it was possible to stop for supplies just over the Chinese border before heading for Hong Kong. Prospects of survival were greater on this route than for those fleeing from the south who could fall prey to pirates, but all were subject to the perils of ill-equipped boats, the stormy monsoon seasons and guards watching for escapees. Thousands died at sea from shooting, drowning, hunger, thirst and disease: 'They seek asylum but find rape, robbery and a watery death' proclaimed one headline.[18] Lives lost at sea were estimated at 150–250,000, as high as 50 per cent.[19]

OFFERS OF ASYLUM

For those refugees who reached other countries in south-east Asia, particularly Hong Kong, Malaysia and Thailand, shelter was provided in transit camps under the general supervision of the United Nations. On 30 June 1980 there were still 223,339 refugees in such camps and processing centres in south-east Asia.[20] These centres were often overcrowded and provided only the most basic accommodation, such as the Hong Kong camps which included disused factories. British involvement in the Vietnamese crisis began involuntarily when between February 1977 and October 1978 small numbers of refugees were rescued at sea by its ships and brought to Britain as other countries refused them entry. It was not until 1979 that the need arose for a formal policy of reception and resettlement, following a sudden increase in the number of arrivals requiring help. Sea rescues by British ships increased, reflecting the rising scale of movement from Vietnam. Of particular significance was the rescue of 346 refugees in the South China Sea by the British ship *Wellpark*. The ship, heading for Taiwan, was refused permission to land unless the refugees were sent straight to Britain. The Home Office agreed to accept the group and the British Council for Aid to Refugees (BCAR) received them at Kensington Barracks. Another group picked up by the ship *Anco Sceptre* in December 1978 was received with the help of the Ockenden Venture and Save the Children Fund. By January 1979 Indo-Chinese refugees in south-east Asia numbered about 215,000, including 72,000 Vietnamese boat people,[21] prompting considerable alarm and leading to an appeal by the UNHCR and the governments of Hong Kong, Malaysia and Thailand for help from other countries. The Labour government agreed to accept 1,500 people from camps in south-east Asia (1,000 from Hong Kong, 250 from Thailand and 250 from Malaysia) in addition to those rescued by British ships and family reunion cases.

The concern raised by the plight of the Vietnamese was evident in the House of Lords, which debated the issue on 14 February 1979 in the last days of the Labour government. The Lords offered widespread support for accepting more of the boat people, their cause championed by Lord Elton. To him, the persecution of the Chinese was racist, a result of a Communism closely modelled on Nazism. Elton pointed out the generosity of Malaysia, Hong Kong, and especially Thailand in absorbing the refugees. Elton was no supporter of non-white immigration, but believed Britain should respond:

> Imagine over 200,000 refugees pouring into this country in the space of under four years, and only 60,000 of them getting moved on. The outcry that it would cause is unimaginable. However the population of Thailand is smaller than ours and it is infinitely poorer… [T]he Thai people shame us with their generosity… Naturally we are an overcrowded island; and it is vital … not to make the mistake that Governments did in the fifties and sixties of contemptuously ignoring public opinion, as they did over the mass New Commonwealth immigration… [But] if the numbers are kept to reasonable proportions, there will be no difficulty in that respect. Apart from this, the admission of a few thousand people will set an example … to other countries which are less overcrowded than our own.

Not surprisingly, in the Conservative-dominated House of Lords, anti-communism was a recurring theme. Baroness Vickers suggested that the refugees should go to Guyana to which Lord Monson quipped, 'I do not think that these people would like to go from one Marxist frying pan into another Marxist fire'. It became apparent that Baroness Vickers and others were more concerned that the refugees should be kept out of Britain and less bothered about where they could find asylum – contributions reminiscent of the discussion at the Evian conference in July 1938. Other arguments favouring entry to Britain were also less than wholesome. Lord Segal was anxious to allow them in 'because they are a most diligent, honest, hard working people who will more than repay any helping hand that we can hold out to them'. Contrasting them with Filipino domestics in Britain who were 'indifferent workers', he believed the refugees from Indo-China [were] desperate to find work in this country, as in any other country. They will prove themselves a steady, hard-working labour force, especially if recruited to work in our hospitals, where I am sure they would never go on strike. Can we not admit into our population of over fifty million at least 10,000 of these unfortunate people?

As the tone of this debate indicated, internationally, Britain's contribution to the Vietnamese refugee crisis was not to be a major one.[22]

By July 1979, over 195,000 Vietnamese boat people had fled to other parts of south-east Asia, of whom 67,000 were in Hong Kong. The pressure on these countries was intense. In Hong Kong, $10 million had been spent on the refugees with little hope of recovering this from a near bankrupt UNHCR. In Malaysia a desperate announcement was issued that refugee boats would be towed back out to sea. As their Home Minister stated:

> We cannot find the logic of those countries who claim these people to be refugees and yet will categorise when a person cannot speak English, he falls into a different category. When a person has tuberculosis he is not accepted anywhere. If you regard them as refugees it is your privilege. There is no point in calling them refugees and treating them as normal immigrants.[23]

The countries of ASEAN made an agreement that all refugees within their shores would be expelled unless international resettlement efforts were increased significantly. This agreement, combined with intensive media coverage and popular campaigning in Britain, led to an initiative by Margaret Thatcher, Prime Minister of the newly elected Conservative government, to hold an international conference.

The Geneva Conference of 20–21 July 1979, conducted under the auspices of the United Nations, succeeded in focusing the international attention that the crisis demanded. In contrast to Evian, the Geneva Conference led to offers from 65 countries to take a quarter of a million refugees, and more finance to help the UNHCR Indo-China programme.[24] The impact of the Vietnam War in the years prior to the refugee exodus doubtless had an effect on countries which had seen the devastation and destruction on their television screens. One of those involved in the resettlement programme in Hampshire remembered the enormous extent

> to which television had affected public perceptions to Vietnam, the intervention of the West in Vietnam and ... the 'Boat People', as they were [named] ... on our television screens, you could see people on boats in the water and it was pretty obvious that it was horrendous, unbelievably bad and not to be treated lightly... The Vietnamese refugees were obviously perfectly ordinary people ... old people, young people, men and women who were just taking flight from this horror. So there was enormous public sympathy.[25]

Anti-communism also played its part, as did the pressure from the Asian countries bearing the brunt of the crisis. Britain's control of Hong Kong also gave it a vested interest in helping. Thatcher's government agreed to take

10,000 Vietnamese from Hong Kong even before the conference and offered £5 million to the UNHCR relief programme. It then sent officials to interview people in the camps to determine entry selection. Officially, selection was based on 'humanitarian grounds' with no criteria other than 'the refugees being able to successfully resettle in this country'.[26] This last stipulation meant that potential entrants had to answer a multitude of questions,[27] but, according to the BCAR, which was to become the Refugee Council, selection was comparatively lax with 96 per cent of interviewees successful in gaining entry.[28] The result was that those 10,000 accepted were not just the elite of society,[29] although such generosity was affected by wider considerations involving Hong Kong.

The majority of the refugees accepted into Britain came between 1979 and 1981, which 'represented a single gesture of the Thatcher government in the face of the 1979 Geneva conference convened to address the boat refugee crisis'. This 'virtually reduced Indochinese refugee resettlement to a single event – the acceptance of one, extended, largely Chinese-Vietnamese contingent'.[30] Comparatively the British contribution was a minimal one; American figures showed that 18,638 refugees were accepted by the UK between 1975 and 1990, amounting to only 1.1 per cent of all the south-east Asian refugees. The United States accepted the most, taking 54.1 per cent, or 889,974 people. Canada and Australia were also more generous, taking 133,149 and 128,540 refugees respectively, in total 15.9 per cent. In terms of refugees resettled per capita of population the only recipient country to take less than the United Kingdom was Italy, while, measured in these terms, Australia was the most generous.[31] These figures should be treated with caution as they do not distinguish the large number of Chinese-Vietnamese resettled in China. They also conflict with Refugee Council figures which suggest that between 1975 and 1988 22,577 refugees from south-east Asia were accepted for resettlement in Britain possibly because these figures included dependants.

In his comparison of French, British and Dutch responses to the crisis, Haines argues that the United Kingdom showed 'neither the rationalised, humanitarian resettlement of the Dutch, nor the facilitated immigrant adaptation of the French. Rather it was resettlement as off-take from the refugee camps of a country's own colony.'[32] The greater generosity of the French reflected that the boat people were part of an ongoing flow of Indo-Chinese refugees entering France due to its colonial connection. In resettlement policy, Haines argues that the British resembled the French, as both countries relied on the voluntary sector for operational responsibilities: 'The difference between the two is that the English consistency was of a nonpolicy for a nonprogram'.[33]

SETTLEMENT IN BRITAIN

After accepting the refugee quota, the policy of the Conservative government was guided by its commitments to reduce immigration, minimise state intervention, cut government expenditure and encourage individuals to take responsibility for their own welfare and destiny. Government policy towards the Vietnamese took the form of 'front end loading': investing most of the resources into receiving the refugees at the outset.[34] Samantha Hale, in her comparative study of British and Canadian responses, argues that policy was governed by four main principles:

> The refugees were to be prevented from becoming dependent on external assistance and were to be encouraged to enter into mainstream British life. They were to be made job ready as soon as possible in order that they might regain their independence. They were to use existing welfare mechanisms, and they were to be dispersed throughout the country in clusters of four to ten families.

Most of these principles continued policies followed since 1945. Little was done to differentiate refugee incomers from immigrants and resettlement was based on the premise that after initial aid, existing services were sufficient to meet needs. The resettlement process was housing-led rather than employment-led, in contrast to the resettlement of the Poles and Hungarians, when particular attention was paid to finding jobs. Social security provided economic assistance and local government facilities could be used to assist the newcomers with language tuition and finding employment. Reliance on the voluntary services was at the heart of the resettlement process. The main distinction from earlier influxes during the Cold War was that, like the Ugandan Asians, the Vietnamese were to undergo government enforced dispersal into selected areas of settlement, spreading the 'financial and human cost of resettling the refugees', thereby avoiding any serious political backlash.

> The low profile played by the government enabled the Prime Minister to claim that she was not reneging on her election promise to curb immigration, and the lack of positive discrimination ensured that the equal rights principles outlined in the Race Relations Act 1976 were not violated.[35]

The policy of 'front end loading' was not appropriate as it assumed that the Vietnamese could adapt quickly to British life in spite of the vast cultural gulf to be bridged. The skills required for adaptation were neither clearly delineated nor adaquately catered for. The policy of dispersing the Vietnamese for long-term settlement was out of touch with both their needs and new notions of cultural pluralism, which favoured ethnic concentration to provide community support and help the refugees' reorientation. It also suggested that little had been learnt from the experience of dispersing the Ugandan Asians.[36] Robinson suggests that dispersal policy was repeated because there were clear political and economic benefits: taking advantage of voluntary housing offers, defusing local opposition to resettlement (the National Front had just polled 192,000 votes), using existing services and avoiding ghettoisation.[37] The expectation, however, that spatial mixing would automatically reduce prejudice was 'simplistic'.[38]

The need for planning led to the formation of a Co-ordinating Committee by the Home Office. Setting up a central body along the lines of the Uganda Resettlement Board was rejected as it was regarded as too visible. Instead the Joint Committee for Refugees from Vietnam (JCRV) was established in October 1979, chaired by Sir Arthur Peterson, with two representatives each from the Refugee Council, Ockenden Venture, Save the Children Fund and the Home Office. The charitable bodies were to be responsible for the daily operation of resettlement, but a Refugee Council evaluation of resettlement from 1979 to 1988 argued that the government did not formally define or direct Vietnamese resettlement because it 'would have inferred a formal plan, and therefore goals, standards and commitments. The Government avoided making such a categorical acknowledgement of responsibility [declining] to accept any direct responsibility beyond the reception phase'. The JCRV was given powers commensurate with its status of a temporary adjunct to an administrative section within the Home Office.[39]

The JCRV operated for three years as the umbrella organisation responsible for resettling the Vietnamese. Its operation was criticised by the Refugee Council for its ineffectiveness in assessing resettlement initiatives and failing

> at the key moment of reappraisal in 1983, to put forward a strategy for the future... It did not reconsider the ... possible benefits of co-opting civil servants in involved departments, or local authority representatives, or indeed refugee representatives... The JCRV displayed an ethno-centrism common among UK institutions. Its decisions were not informed by an understanding of the social and cultural needs of the Vietnamese... Convened for and committed to a short-term function carrying out the Government-defined goals of reception and resettlement, it had difficulty representing the need three years later for continuing post-settlement support.[40]

Samantha Hale adds that the JCRV and the charities were not given the scope or resources to provide the services required by the refugees, but the dependence on outside bodies led to the government relinquishing 'control of policy implementation'.[41]

The three charities on the committee worked in different areas to carry out the reception and resettlement process, with the costs borne by the government. Broadly, the Refugee Council operated in the south of England and south Wales, Ockenden Venture in north Wales, the north-west and from the Midlands northwards, and Save the Children Fund in Scotland, Northern Ireland, the east and the north-east. Over 40 centres with an average of 100 places were used. Each agency had its own approach and its own reception centres, resulting in different experiences for the refugees and conflict in procedures. Problems arose when the refugee aid agencies established networks of member groups in other agencies' zones and over housing if local authorities bypassed the agency in their area.[42]

The reception process required the Vietnamese to spend a transitional time in camps but this often extended, encouraging dependency and malaise. The Refugee Council suggested the length of stay in the camps should be three months, but it often proved longer, as the refugees waited for accommodation and struggled to adjust to the new language, environment, climate and culture in Britain. Five months was the average stay during 1979.[43] Recreation and education were encouraged, with football matches and cricket seen as good introductions to the 'British' way of life. Yet this did not disguise the problem that many Vietnamese found even basic communication difficult. At Thorney Island the problem of prolonged stay was described: 'They get camp conditioned and the less-motivated people can lose the enthusiasm to think on their own'.[44]

The Refugee Council, which had taken the first Vietnamese refugees, and had been involved in refugee resettlement since the Second World War, had a conventional centralised approach to reception. Its centres varied, the smaller ones taking 60–80 people while the largest took 700 or more. The major reception centres for the Vietnamese were Sopley, on the border of Dorset and Hampshire, and Thorney Island at Emsworth in Hampshire, both of which were run by the organisation.[45] The common feature between these and their smaller centres was that they were tightly regulated. The larger centres had the advantage of more organised services such as language tuition but they could also become 'ethnic enclaves', discouraging interaction with the host community. In its own evaluation, the Refugee Council believed that staff structures were confused and anxiety over the camp's futures caused motivation problems.[46] Lack of qualified personnel and training was also criticised.[47]

In July 1979 the Chief Executive of Hampshire County Council provided an account to his Policy and Resources Committee of the provisions made for the 600 Vietnamese at RAF Sopley, part of a group of 900 refugees rescued at sea by the *S.S. Sibonga*. Its success had much in common with the treatment of the Ukrainian transmigrants at Atlantic Park over 50 years earlier. Indeed, the local state has often shown flexibility and imagination when dealing with the presence of refugees, especially when, as in this case, 'a careful record is being kept of all County Council expenditure on this project and Central Government w[as] asked to meet these costs'. Initially, the 'County Chief Executive immediately called a conference of officers representing all local government interests to clarify the problems which might arise and to set up coordination machinery'. The County Council's Education Service provided teaching facilities

> for some 200 children and more than 300 adults in the camp. Schoolrooms have been equipped and appointments have been made of a headteacher, nine

teachers, three nursery staff and an adult education organiser. In addition sufficient part-time adult education tutors have been appointed to enable groups of ten to fifteen adults to receive daily lessons from the same tutor... The school opened on 3rd July and the primary task of the staff is to impart an understanding of the English language to both children and adults [as well as] instruction ... in health and hygiene... [T]here should be considerable social training in preparation for the assimilation of the refugees into the community... [R]ecreational facilities are being provided in conjunction with the County Recreation Officer, the County Librarian and the New Forest District Council.

As the camp was only temporary, local authorities throughout Britain were asked 'to consider providing accommodation for refugee families where there are employment opportunities'. Hampshire took this seriously, liaising with the Social Services Departments and recognising that there would 'inevitably be problems of social isolation for the refugees after they are dispersed from the camp'. It anticipated 'a residual problem for the County Council in helping to look after those who are not easily settled'. Reflecting on the experience, the Chief Executive stressed that the response of the public and local voluntary services to the refugees at Sopley was 'overwhelming' and 'a tribute to the people of Hampshire and the adjoining areas of Dorset that, with minor exceptions, an enthusiastic welcome has been given to these unfortunate people who have been driven from their homeland as a result of persecution'.[48]

The Ockenden Venture had a completely different approach in running its reception facilities. Since 1971 the organisation had involvement with the Vietnamese when orphanages had been created for handicapped children in Saigon. From 1977, it expanded its facilities to provide help to refugee arrivals. The emphasis was on small reception centres with a family approach and volunteer staff, settling small refugee groups together and encouraging interaction with the local community. The approach was based on the philosophy that refugees were not problem people, but rather resourceful and capable, temporarily needing help to re-establish themselves in a new environment. The Refugee Council argued that, 'despite avowed commitment to avoiding refugee dependency, Ockenden gained a reputation as paternalist, inflexible and even authoritarian in its attitude towards refugees'.[49] Such criticism reflected the different philosophies of each charity, leading to competition in the resettlement process; others suggest that the supportive smaller centres enabled stronger relationships between staff and residents facilitating the transition to life outside.

Paul Rushton ran the Ockenden Venture centre in Gosport, known as Sunshine House, and helped set up other reception centres in Portsmouth. His aim was to foster links with local councils and housing associations so that refugees could settle locally. Rushton turned down an opportunity to run the reception centre at Thorney Island because 'being in charge of 2,000 people in a remote location with nothing of any significance in their lives didn't appeal to me'. In contrast, Sunshine House, an old nursery, initially housing 30 people, was in the community: 'there was a huge upsurge of public concern and interest and we were able to put it together in three days using the Lions and the Rotary and [the Women's Royal Voluntary Service]'. Normally, the organisers met the refugees at Heathrow airport:

> You never quite knew what you were getting, Chinese or Vietnamese, north or south, male or female, quite difficult to plan, but it didn't matter because most of these people ... have quite pronounced social skills and were able to overcome all our inadequacies. When we brought people here we always tried to put them in rooms together, because they needed to be close to each other, and their family, [they had a] very strong head of family, had an idea of themselves and that's specific to their culture ... and I remember taking them all over Hampshire, we went camping and ... all that sort of thing. What we did in Hampshire ... was to make people feel comfortable in the community in which they found themselves... [The] Vietnamese here did a lot of very good work with the local community ... It's a two way thing ... We set up another facility in Portsmouth ...we re-built this place with the refugees, because I thought it would be good to get them involved... They couldn't get over there fast enough.[50]

Ockenden Venture was supported by Southampton City Council. In February 1979 its Policy and Resources Committee was informed by the Association of District Councils that the government had decided to permit another 1,500 Vietnamese refugees to enter and it was 'requesting authorities to assist, where possible with housing'. Two months later Ockenden Venture requested that six Vietnamese families be rehoused locally. Detailed information was provided and a representative of the Social Services Department 'indicated that his Department could give support to the Vietnamese families should housing be made available to them'. It was also noted that 'other voluntary bodies had offered to assist, and that the Education Department did not envisage problems in settling the children in schools'. Agreement was made to house the six families but that 'the Ockenden Venture be informed that, while acceding to their request, this authority consider this to be the extent of their commitment in the foreseeable future'. Revealing the tendency towards secondary migration, of the six families accepted, four moved to Birmingham. Although the Council was willing for four replacement families to be housed, it decided that an appeal from Ockenden Venture for further accommodation, 'in view of this Authority's shortage of Council housing', should be passed on to other local housing authorities 'in anticipation of an equitable allocation of housing accommodation, for these refugees, throughout Hampshire'. But the campaigners were persistent and brought in clergy from the Southampton Council of Churches to inform the Council members 'of the plight of the refugees and their resettlement needs'. A compromise was reached: housing associations in the city were encouraged to provide assistance and four properties awaiting improvement were made available.[51]

Save the Children Fund (SCF) was also greatly involved in the Vietnamese refugee movement. Its centres tended to be small and control decentralised, with under 90 refugees, but the volume of work was such that a new organisation, Refugee Action, was created specifically for the SCF's Vietnamese programme. The reception centres were a part of the community in which the refugees settled. Staff lived in and were expected to get to know the refugees. Regarded as the 'most "open", flexible leadership among agencies, with many decisions delegated to centres', with a 'professional ethic ... and a collective spirit inculcated in reception centre staff',[52] its weakness was that the SCF lacked experience and resources to provide welfare support once the centres closed.[53]

Beyond reception, the resettlement procedure followed a policy of establishing clusters of refugees, accommodating between four and ten families within the area of each housing authority. As with the Ugandan Asians, the plan was to spread the refugees evenly over the country to avoid creating ghettoes, but to allow for some community support.[54] The Home Office sent out appeals to local authorities for help in housing in January and June 1979. Housing associations were also approached. The initial response was good but offers dropped off by January 1980, partly because 'local authorities us[ed] the Vietnamese programme as a political football in their defence against the introduction of Government restrictions on their autonomy and expenditure'.[55] As with the Ugandan Asians, the dispersal policy failed, as the geography of resettlement was dependent on the pattern of housing offers. The preponderance of large families also made allocation difficult. As one refugee recalled, waiting for council housing could take many months and could be problematic:

> At first they say we got very big family we want to live all together and they say in England they don't have any houses for nine people. You got to split into two families, you cannot live together. You know most Vietnamese families, were nine, or ten, and they say you wait one year, two years, better for you to split. But in the end they offer us a house with three bedrooms and we accept it. The house is damp and they move us to another house, kept moving again and again.[56]

The refugees themselves proved unwilling to settle in remote areas. Richard Barnett, reporting for the City of Southampton Housing Department on Vietnamese resettlement in 1986, concluded that the dispersal policy had been far from successful and, in future, 'Most essential would seem to be that the refugees themselves should be consulted before producing a carefully planned scheme.'[57]

Only when housing offers dropped was dispersal reviewed and it found necessary to accept accommodation regardless of quality or location so that many Vietnamese eventually settled in metropolitan centres with high ethnic concentrations.[58] Over a third of refugees reported problems with their first house, such as severe damp.[59] The south-east, the north-west and the West Midlands (especially Birmingham) all attracted refugees while areas such as East Anglia, West Wales and Cumbria had relatively few. By 1986 8,000, almost half of the Vietnamese refugees, had moved to London because of the attractions of the metropolis and its large Chinese community.[60]

In 1985 the House of Commons Home Affairs Select Committee report on the Vietnamese recognised that:

> It is hard to think of any problem facing the Vietnamese which would not have been less severe or difficult to resolve if the disastrous policy of dispersal had not been adopted. In the long term it might well have been cheaper for the government to subsidise housing so that the Vietnamese were housed in larger groups than to try to deal with the problems of scattered populations.[61]

Truc Long Pham, Regional Officer for the Vietnamese Settlement Programme in the south-west of Britain, concurred, looking back six years after dispersal was implemented:

> The South of England is still an example of this, with many Vietnamese in small places. The idea by central government was that if you settled people in small amounts in different areas they would be less of a draw on services. Also that if there were less people of their own culture, then the Vietnamese would have to settle more quickly into British culture. The mistaken thinking behind this is that you can take people and shape them into any culture you want, as if they were made of clay.

Dispersal made it difficult to assess the overall needs of the refugees so that 'the Vietnamese Programme has become an attempt to cope with the problems of dispersal [and] assist the Vietnamese community towards their own community development'. Moreover, the tendency towards refugee concentration was, he argued, a sign of integration:

> The Vietnamese are coming together not to escape from the realities of British Society – in fact just the opposite. Like any community the Vietnamese feel that they can take a part in the mainstream of society with strength and effectiveness if they have the security of their traditions and family values as a base.

Local authorities, he concluded, should recognise this and provide the 'support we need to become active Members of British Society'.[62]

THE LIVES OF VIETNAMESE REFUGEES IN BRITAIN

The Vietnamese, unlike the Ugandan Asians, had no large established community or kinship networks to rely on. There were some 60,000 Chinese people in London and larger cities like Manchester and Liverpool,[63] but their reaction to the refugees was

> cautious; there has been some resentment of the privileged treatment they have

received, particularly in terms of housing and furnishings... Slowly, [they have become] more positive but ... tensions [still exist] between the Chinese from Hong Kong and the Vietnamese.[64]

In their own accounts of resettlement the Vietnamese noted the difference of lifestyles between British cities and the countryside. Those who came from the hustle and bustle of life in Saigon disliked rural Britain, finding it isolated. One Vietnamese teenager said, 'My parents are lonely. They just stay at home and learn English from the TV programme. My family are not happy to live there. We like [to] live in noisy crowded city. We sat and cried when we came here. There was nothing'.[65] 'The intensity of social interaction in Vietnam was so much greater and so fundamental to all social relations that even [British] urban life ... was regarded by the refugees as quiet.'[66]

City life offered the advantage that provisions were better, such as teaching English as a second language. City social services normally had some understanding of the needs and problems of ethnic minorities and refugees were less conspicuous. By contrast, in small towns and suburbs there could be fewer problems of poverty and housing shortages, improving community spirit. Housing also tended to be well-furnished and material support better. Where there were groups of ten to 12 families in a small town, those interviewed by the Commission for Racial Equality said they felt happy and secure and did not want to move. In this respect, Vietnamese settlements in Hampshire offered reasonable support from the local populace and the development of an active Vietnamese community. The heart of the community in the Southampton and Portsmouth areas reflected Vietnamese preferences for living in cities and links with Ockenden Venture reception centres. By August 1982, 209 refugees were settled in Hampshire by the Refugee Council and 117 by Ockenden Venture with the county divided by the zoning process. Of those settled by Ockenden Venture, 21 Vietnamese went to Eastleigh, 18 to Gosport, 22 to Portsmouth and 56 to Southampton.[67] Those settled by the Refugee Council also went to other regions of the county such as the New Forest, some having been resident at Sopley.

In 1991, the Regional Development Worker for Refugee Action, Hildegard Dumper, assessed the settlement of Vietnamese refugees in Hampshire, pointing out the continuing need for community development work to assist those who had settled there:

> It is ten years since the first boat people arrived in the UK. Now there are around 22,000 refugees from Vietnam living here and the British government recently agreed to accept 2,000 more from the camps in Hong Kong to be settled over the next three years. Whilst Hampshire is not formally a resettlement area for these 2,000, it will undoubtedly be affected, albeit in small numbers, through family reunion applications and secondary resettlement.

Because the refugees were spread across the county, the extent of their poverty was hidden. They were reticent, for cultural reasons, to seek state support. Normally, they would look to other members of the extended family but these were 'either still in Vietnam or scattered around the globe in countries like Australia or the USA':

> Their reticence to ask for help from governmental agencies is further compounded by the difficulties many still have in communicating adequately in the English language, and the limited expertise many of the welfare services in parts of Hampshire have in accommodating the needs of people whose mother-tongue is not English.

When in 1986, Southampton City Council hosted a seminar on meeting the needs of the Vietnamese in South England the

> degree of goodwill in the county towards refugees from Vietnam was demonstrated by the attendance of representatives from a vast range of organisations and included sixteen councillors. Up until 1987, there was an active and supportive community association assisted by three … part-time community workers.

The withdrawal of funding made it difficult to offer the same level of support later in the period of resettlement. Dumper concluded that the main difficulty facing the

> Vietnamese speaking community in Hampshire [wa]s the lack of a bi-lingual, Vietnamese speaking professional worker … available both to the community for advice and support, and to service providers to advise and assist them in improving access to their services.[68]

The creation of a Vietnamese Community Development Worker for south-east Hampshire was as a step forward in community relations, even if it was not permanent; there was, however, no nationwide policy maintaining such positions meeting the needs of refugees.

THE RECEPTION CAMPS AND BEYOND

Many of the Vietnamese came to Britain simply because it was the first country to accept them enabling them to leave the camps in south-east Asia. Often they had very little knowledge about the country though it was seen as peaceful, where a good education was available.[69] Tang Trinh My and ten members of her family left Vietnam because of their Chinese origin, paying for each passage the equivalent of three years of an average salary. In Britain they hoped to get life saving treatment for her father who was suffering from cancer. The family were scared at

> the thought of coming to Britain, because we didn't really know anything about it. We looked at the English businessmen in Hong Kong in their bowler hats and pin-striped suits, and thought all English people dressed like that. We threw away all our clothes because we thought they would be too scruffy. We thought we would get jobs immediately and soon replace them. It was a big shock to find no chance of jobs and no pin-striped suits when we arrived.

At Thorney Island camp life boredom soon resulted because of their isolation and the lack of money to go anywhere or do anything.[70]

Nguyen Thanh Phuong provides a more favourable, mythical, first impression of Thorney Island, showing the personal nature of being a refugee with the competing emotions of loss and gratitude:

> The sky was blue and serene. The golden sunshine of late Autmun covered the whole region of Southern England... Wild geese with snow-white plumage were playing on the river, and white flowers embellished English gardens... As I was rambling and gazing at the landscape of England, conflicting feelings arose in me. I was both happy and sad. You wild birds of England!... How lucky you are! Because you are free... No one can hurt you... But... in many areas of the world there are humans who have lost their freedom, where human rights are being trampled underfoot, where thousands of people have put out to sea at the risk of their lives while others have been herded into deserted jungle areas and compelled to live on roots of trees. I was fortunate enough to come here. I am free to gaze at the beautiful scenery of Southern England. But while I enjoy help and care given us by the British government and people ... I feel a deep sorrow over the plight of the millions of my compatriots who still suffer. Poverty, starvation, war, separation, when will these things come to an end? When will families be reunited?

Phuong was effusive about his hosts but gently expressed the gulf separating their different worlds:

> Here, in the pretty houses of a peaceful and happy England, you can hear people say, 'Vietnamese friends! Don't worry! Cheer up! Remember that we are always here beside you. We will help you study English, find jobs for you, take you out for a visit to London... We will organise recreational activities to give you opportunities to practise English and forget your homesickness. Our country is not very rich ... but we will help you secure a good life.' Are those mere expressions of my own feeling and wishes? No. They are realities in Thorney Island... On the streets of Emsworth, I came across people with smiling faces who were ready to give me any information and advice I needed. 'You speak English very well', they said, trying to encourage me, although I knew I could speak only a few words... Who created the myth that English people are always ill-tempered, cold and disdainful of coloured people?... I don't think I need to argue with them. England, with its richness and beauty, and the humane spirit of its people, can answer for itself.[71]

Similarly, La Thanh Xuan paints a romantic picture of the first sight of Britain and the early stages of settlement:

> Viewed from the air, London looked splendid in the bright sunshine. It is majestic with its Gothic buildings and high steeples. It is fresh and shady with its woods of lofty trees, its parks, its flower gardens, its botanical gardens. It is animated with unending lines of traffic on straight and level roads... One cannot be tired of looking at this big and beautiful city of England... Upon arrival at the entrance to the camp, we were greeted with a smile by an English

gentleman rather advanced in age, with grey hair and a mild face. Around the director of the camp were English young men with shining faces and our fellow refugees who came a few days ago. They rushed towards us, carried our suitcases, held out their arms to welcome the children, helped the elderly and asked all sorts of questions... After that first contact with these extremely warmhearted people, we were very happy and felt quite confident about our future.[72]

But such descriptions hid the trauma of persecution and flight. Positive first emotions could give way to despondency and depression; in June 1980, a refugee who had left her parents in Vietnam committed suicide at Sopley.[73]

The change of culture the Vietnamese faced was significantly greater than for many previous refugee groups coming to Britain, reflected by the prolonged stays in the reception camps. Cultural change was regarded by Nhung Tuyet Bui, coordinator of the Tower Hamlets Community of Refugees, as the hardest part of the transition to life in Britain. One family commented that 'In Vietnam we live in one room, no gas, no electricity'. Coming to Britain, 'they found the houses, the pavements, the buses, everything extraordinary',[74] everyday matters such as food being sold in shops and not on the streets.[75]

> Yet the surprise is ... how quickly people seem to be adapting to the endless practical details of daily life. Cultural shocks hit at all sorts of levels. One family learned pretty fast that the local buses don't appreciate a cargo of live and squawking chickens... Mothers have learned that outside doors and windows have to be kept shut in the coldest weather England has known for years.[76]

The Vietnamese, like the Poles, found that the British liked to keep themselves to themselves, in contrast to Vietnamese customs: 'In Vietnam everyone visits; in England people shut their doors'.[77] To counter feelings of isolation, they attempted to foster community links, forming groups such as the Vietnamese Community Association in Portsmouth which organised cultural activities and education to maintain traditions. A further step was the publication of a monthly magazine in London.

POPULAR RESPONSES TO THE VIETNAMESE

Public reaction to the Vietnamese was not dissimilar to that to the Ugandan Asians. In Hampshire, as elsewhere, the same concerns over housing and employment were raised.[78] One correspondent to the Portsmouth *News* wrote congratulating Havant council for rejecting requests to accommodate Vietnamese families:

> It is about time councils said 'no' to any Tom, Dick, or Harry that is dumped on them, and cared, like Havant, about their own people first. [H]ow can you help other people if you can't help your own... Let the vicarages take them, they have more than enough room to spare.[79]

The housing debate raged as it had with the Ugandan Asians.[80] When the first 77 refugees arrived at Sopley, four people stood outside the gates of the former RAF camp and demanded jobs for British citizens, shouting, 'This country is being given over to the foreigners'.[81] But some lessons had been learnt on a local level at least. Members of the Chichester Council of Churches were asked to help the Vietnamese. Two houses were offered within the city 'near to services, and next door to one another so that the families could give each other support', contrasting to when one Ugandan Asian family was housed locally leaving it 'rather isolated'.[82] Protest from a county councillor ensued when she visited Sopley camp, taking some clothes with her. A security guard allegedly remarked, 'Why should these people have all this stuff? ... We should not be taking them. If it was our children we would not be getting it.'[83]

Instances of hostility were counterbalanced by welcoming activities undertaken by local people. Regional support groups, including members of welfare groups and churches, helped meet the refugees' needs. Dominated by middle-class women, who were not always familiar with government bureaucracy, their role ranged from providing furniture and equipping houses, to helping the Vietnamese in their search for work, registering with local doctors, dentists, accessing social services and employment offices, and offering friendship and communal activities. The District Organiser of the Women's Royal Voluntary Service in Gosport remembered the arrival of about 30 Vietnamese, mainly women and children brought under the auspices of the Ockenden Venture in December 1978:

> Beds had to be made up and quarters arranged in the National Children's Home... Bedding etc was collected from other centres and also as a result of appeals in the local papers, we clothed them the next day. We had snow and they had not seen any before, and wandered about wondering what this stuff was... One Mother had eight children with her. They stayed quite a few months... My impression is that these particular refugees were not the ordinary people, and that they had bought their way out of their own Country. Our local Sub-Postmaster was most incensed at the way the Social Security was collected in one hand and most of it sent back to Vietnam immediately. Further people arrived at intervals over perhaps a year and eventually some families were provided with Council Houses in Gosport, Portsmouth and Southampton... Unfortunately contact was lost as they were settled in.[84]

Local support of the refugees was critical. The expanding activities of a support group in Portsmouth, which started after an article in the Portsmouth *News*, were related somewhat optimistically a year after its foundation:

> Letters to *The News* and to MPs brought growing support and practical offers of help – money, clothes, hospitality. In July we took a party of the Boat People to Ockenden celebrations at Haslemere ... and gave a welcoming party for the Vietnamese, attended by more than a hundred people... September saw the first [m]eeting of 'The Portsmouth Refugee Support Group'. The title had been

generalised to enable us possibly in the future to concern ourselves with refugees other than the Boat People ... 200 copies of our monthly newsletter were distributed... In October, we held a second party ... and were particularly pleased to welcome back Vietnamese friends from Gosport who were now settled in Southampton. 300 newsletters went out this month, and a steady flow of offers of help was established... By November there had been much local involvement in the preparation of Avenue House, Hilsea, including help from schools, the Royal Navy and the Gosport Vietnamese...

In January, the Support Group, with the excellent co-operation of the WRVS and the local church of St Francis, helped with the settlement in Leigh Park, Havant, of Sunshine's family. 'Sunshine' had been the first Vietnamese baby to be born in Gosport... In February and March we [prepared] for the next family resettlements in Portsmouth ... encouraged by continued local support, including the donation of a considerable number of cooking pots, and the benefit of the experience of kind counterparts in Eastleigh, where four Vietnamese families had been settled... April-August saw the completion of resettlement in Paulsgrove, with five families now living within very easy reach of each other. Employment opportunities were being pursued, with some success. Children were settling in at school, with daily attendance, too, at the English Language Centre in Southsea. Adults attending regular classes were developing their command of English, and with help from neighbours, community workers and Support Group members, were getting to grips with the practical realities of living in an English city. Visits were made to Hilsea families resettled in London and elsewhere...

The 'Friends of the Vietnamese' stressed that the reception centres still required support, 'chiefly friendship, conversation' and

hospitality, to give our new neighbours as much experience as possible of English life – and language – before they have to cope on their own, wherever it may be in the United Kingdom; and we believe it is also important to maintain contact with our 'own' local people as they gradually adjust and begin to rebuild their shattered lives within the free society for which we ourselves should be so thankful.[85]

In other parts of the region, help was provided for ten Vietnamese teenagers to join a group of youngsters on a holiday in the Isle of Wight. It was the first time they had been out of the camp at Sopley for more than a day, giving them a chance to see the island and mix with local people.[86] Such was the degree of support that some of the volunteers at the camps gave up their jobs to help.[87]

REFUGEE INTEGRATION

A report on the backgrounds of the refugees at Sopley described the variety of their former occupations as 'astonishing'. Among the 580 refugees there were potters, carpenters, boat builders, truck drivers, farmers, tailors, doctors and a Buddhist monk. Most followed Confucian or Buddhist religions but there were also some Christians, mainly Catholics.[88] Reverend Partridge at the camp maintained that 'People here have slightly the wrong idea about [the] refugees. Most of them are middle class or upper class. They are the upper crust of Hanoi and not the riff raff. This is not the dregs of society',[89] but this was untypical. The Refugee Council argued that most of Britain's ethnic Chinese-Vietnamese were from subsistence fishing communities. It highlighted that their education was limited with many illiterate: 'Two-thirds of the pool of refugees available for resettlement in late 1980 had previously submitted applications to north America. Many of them had failed north American selections, whose criteria assessed ability to integrate in Western society'.[90] Furthermore, 'the original notion that the Vietnamese would bring with them entrepreneurial talents only needing modification to UK business methods' was never substantiated.[91]

Samantha Hale's overview of the Vietnamese concluded that the entrants were divided fairly evenly in terms of sex.[92] There was a high proportion of young people, 24 per cent aged 21–30, but the majority of refugees came in family groups, 49 per cent with six or more members. One noticeable feature was the high number of unaccompanied children, mainly those picked up at sea, who were to cause particular problems for the resettlement agencies as relatives could not always be traced.[93] Almost half the Vietnamese were skilled manual workers with another quarter semi-skilled. According to a Somerset study, 75 per cent received education below secondary level. The refugees had few capital assets or belongings on arrival. The JCRV concluded that

> the Vietnamese [were] one of the most disadvantaged groups ever to come to [Britain]. Many lack marketable skills or even skills which can be easily adapted to our society. Many lack education and literacy even in their own language. Most, having come from North Vietnam, have had little contact with Western civilisation. For many, Britain was a last resort as a settlement country following refusals from the USA and other countries. Unlike other refugee and immigrant groups they had no established community in this country to receive them.[94]

Given also that they arrived at a time of acute housing shortages, rising unemployment and local government cuts, the conclusion of the Refugee Council that 'the task of bringing in refugees and resettling them into our society has not been easy'[95] is easy to understand.

Many of the refugees had to accept a fall in status. Chay, a government official in Saigon, worked in a pewter factory in Sheffield, followed by a job with a double glazing company. When his family joined him from Vietnam they lived in one room in Stoke Newington while Chay worked 13 hours a day as a West End chef.[96] Mr Quan, a highly qualified mechanical engineer who had worked his way up from nothing, recalled how he had a beautiful villa in Saigon with servants and acres of gardens. 'Now all I desire is to live in my council home and provide a safe future for my wife and children, nice furniture and a smart car. I'm not important any more.'[97]

Vietnamese language difficulties and the absence of vacancies (over three million were without work) created employment problems for some if not all. There were individual success stories such as Minh To, who set up his own clothing business, later supplying leading stores in Britain, another man who became director of a leather factory in Manchester, and a 16-year-old was signed up with Manchester United.[98] The Refugee Council reported in 1980 that in some areas, mostly where smaller groups were resettled,

> 100% employment has been achieved. In a Hampshire [town] all those able to work are employed – three men in a high quality pine furniture factory and nine women and men in a prosperous turkey farm. Both firms have stated that the refugees are excellent workers... In Worthing ... with a larger refugee population, 100% employment has been maintained for some time.[99]

Efforts were made to help teachers and other professionals requalify, and schemes such as the 'New Homeland Crafts' project provided employment for refugees in Hampshire and West Sussex. But these were local initiatives, not forming part of a national programme. The report also failed to point out that 21 per cent of refugees were resettled in the north-west which had very high male unemployment.[100]

By 1980, the JCRV found that only a third of adult wage earners had jobs, slightly higher than a Home Office study which found as little as 16 per cent of all Vietnamese refugees employed, 20.4 per cent men and 10.2 per cent women.[101] Regional variations were distinct with the Vietnamese having more success in the south than the north.[102] Both reports suggested that most of those gaining employment did so not through job centres but by direct negotiation between agency staff/support group members and employers or through their own initiative. The work was largely of an unskilled nature, even for former skilled white-collar workers. Esther Wong suggests that some 20 per cent of breadwinners were able to establish private businesses like restaurants, market stalls and tailoring industries and about 40 per cent found satisfactory employment as mechanics, carpenters, or in catering, transport, tailoring, brick-making, forestry and the building trades. Some jobs were found through the Chinese community.[103]

A Refugee Council evaluation in 1989 was less optimistic than Wong and contradicted its own initial positive assessment almost a decade earlier: unemployment had reached 85–95 per cent in 1983 and

> it was thought that a considerable proportion of the refugees were undergoing serious personal problems like isolation, family breakdown and mental illness. The incidence of serious health problems – hepatitis, lactose intolerance, worms, glaucoma and cataracts, tooth decay – was unusually high, as was physical handicap. There were reports of neglect of children ... there were problems with management of DHSS claims, debts and rent arrears. School attendance was low, and many refugee children were failing to achieve their potential in class.[104]

Adaptation had clearly been difficult. In terms of education, it is instructive to compare the experiences of the Vietnamese with that of the Chileans. The latter were constrained by the British style of learning, preventing them from challenging ideas as they were used to. By contrast, teacher Lien Mai-Duval stated 'the Vietnamese child may find it difficult to take the initiative and will perhaps passively wait for the teacher to decide what s/he should do'.[105] The Vietnamese had their high fliers, but according to some community members, they have not all reached their potential in Britain.

Further testimony of the refugees gives a pessimistic account of their resettlement. Tang Trinh My, a community social worker for the Vietnamese in Greenwich, said very few of the Vietnamese had found jobs, 'either because they had no skills to offer, or because their skills were unsuitable'.[106] They suffered the same problems faced by the Ugandan Asians that their skills were not easily transferable, exacerbated by language difficulties:

> The need to learn the language was, in many ways, greater for the Vietnamese than for many other ethnic minorities, partly because of the 'scatter' policy and partly because there was no already well-established community with its own know-how and solidarity.[107]

The importance of language in the Vietnamese group's orientation is shown by the fact that 69 per cent of those who found jobs possessed a native or bilingual proficiency in English.[108] Learning English was a particular problem for the Vietnamese, as many had little formal education and had to learn a new and unfamiliar script. The government made available some funding for teaching English as a second language in the reception centres and sometimes student awards were given to refugees without the usual residence requirements. But beyond these measures, the Vietnamese were reliant on existing services which varied according to the area of settlement. Typically, many local authorities did not offer language teaching provisions because of the small number of refugees living under their jurisdiction. Central funding was not available to reimburse their spending.

My Tang, a social worker, argues that, 'One of the key issues underlying the needs of refugees from Vietnam in the UK is the break-up of the traditional family structure and thus the traditional means of support'. Not all families left Vietnam together and, with the different criteria for their acceptance abroad, many were scattered. In Britain, the dispersal policy further eroded family links. The effect was that where three generations had lived together in their homeland, life in exile brought a tendency to follow British patterns of the nuclear family. Roles also altered within families. Contrary to the situation of many Ugandan Asian women, those from North Vietnam moved from a position of working to coping with unemployment. In her report on their occupational backgrounds in Britain, Dalglish states that, since only one per cent of women were categorised as housewives in the

Hong Kong camps and only six per cent categorised themselves as unemployed, 'The assumption can be made that the refugees are used to a family situation in which all adults work, and this includes the elderly'.[109] With the war in Vietnam, women worked at home, in factories or in the fields. In Britain their opportunities outside the home were limited as were those of Vietnamese men who were often no longer able to find work, losing respect within the family.[110]

A further manifestation of the role of gender relations concerned learning English. Ann Shearer, writing early in the resettlement process, suggested that the men needed no persuading to go on courses: 'They would like volunteers to come in every day to practise with them [but only] a couple of the women go to the college, and it has been less easy to persuade all the husbands that their wives should go to a mother and baby group'.[111] This caused tensions, leading to women giving up learning English to avoid embarrassing their husbands. Moving from a patriarchal society, where age and male gender engendered respect, to one where such values were open to question created dilemmas in family and gender relationships, exacerbated by elders' and fathers' dependence on their children and wives for information. It was noted that wife battering increased.

The elderly Vietnamese faced particular problems, like the Ugandan Asians, in adjusting to the British environment. As a report for Refugee Action suggests, the change of environment led to premature ageing, as language difficulties resulted in a loss of confidence, and an inability to find work and downward mobility. Many in their fifties who would have been active in their homeland became housebound and isolated.[112] It also led to 'a debilitating reversal of roles. In Vietnamese society they are regarded as people of wisdom, well respected for their life experience and are expected to advise and educate younger generations ... Now they have become a burden to their children and a nuisance'.[113] The elderly came as respected, self-assured individuals who had contributed to family survival through the war and escape, but in the new society their authority was challenged and their judgement disputed:

> Life in England is very hard at first when the language problem is huge – you cannot listen to the radio, cannot read the newspapers, cannot watch television, cannot talk to your neighbour and worst of all, there is no temple to go to, to soothe your soul. I was as good as deaf and dumb, or dead.[114]

Another refugee commented that, 'Gone is the time that people seek me out for advice and guidance... Since birth, this is the first time that I witness such [a] humiliating reverse of order'.[115] For the elderly, cultural habits were ingrained, so that traditional festivities and ancestor worship were more likely to be missed. The elderly became 'scapegoats for the shame, frustration and inferiority the young feel in facing British society with its cultural contradictions ... personification and representation of the frustrations of the young'.[116]

Teenagers confronted different adaptation problems, dominated by generational and cultural conflicts. They faced expectations to speak their mother-tongue, maintain their culture *and* to achieve at school, developing prospects for the future. Threats of racism added further pressure. Parents trying to organise their children's marriages could also lead to conflict within the family if such attempts were rejected.[117] Young, single people who left their families in Vietnam, or moved away from them in Britain, had problems with isolation, unemployment, language and a disrupted education, exacerbated by lack of family support. Chris Mougne suggests that there was 'widespread disillusionment and apathy among many young Vietnamese who see no way out of their predicament ... in most parts of Britain [they] are both unemployed and inactive'.[118]

A further differential in adaptation was because 80 per cent of the refugees were ethnic Chinese. In interviews it was noted that, 'Almost none of the Chinese Vietnamese wanted to go back and a similar percentage said they missed nothing. "My family is gone. What is there to miss?"'[119] This group of refugees were used to being an immigrant and minority group. That a large number were from a peasant background meant that living in Britain did not always lead to a fall in material status. In contrast, all the Vietnamese families said they wanted to go back. Those from the south wanted to instruct their children in the culture of their ancestors.[120] Local interviews ten years later suggest a change of emphasis. The desire to return has dissipated now the Vietnamese have settled and have jobs and families here, but cultural bonds remain. In Hampshire, as elsewhere, Vietnamese community associations organise events to celebrate traditional festivals such as the Moon festival. Lessons in the mother-tongue are organised for the children in a similar vein to the Polish Saturday schools which remain in use 50 years after the initial settlement. One of those involved with the refugees described their aspirations as 'jobs and homes, perhaps specialised clothing, but most of all, the chance for the father of each family to restore his self-respect by supporting the family group'.[121] If all this is used as criteria for success, the Vietnamese still have some way to go.

CONCLUSION

In the late 1990s, Home Office asylum statistics continue to denote south-east Asian arrivals coming to the UK under family reunion schemes following the earlier Vietnamese influx. By 1989 over 22,500 people had come to Britain. Only in the mid-1990s were the last reception camps in south-east Asia being closed and individuals forcibly returned to their homelands. In Britain, the Vietnamese refugee movement remains a benchmark in refugee policy development as the resettlement of large numbers of people from a distinctly different cultural, political and economic background was undertaken with considerable government support. Analysis by the government, service providers and academics has shown that the Vietnamese programme amplified many inherent weaknesses in refugee policy. Resettlement failed to appreciate the backgrounds and needs of the refugees, took little account of the state of the British economic and social scene and followed traditional patterns, namely that refugees should become rapidly self-sustaining, use existing welfare mechanisms and be settled in dispersed clusters to avoid any serious political backlash. Employment may be seen as the key to refugee resettlement and there were few attempts to assist the Vietnamese to utilise and develop their skills enabling them to find work and adapt to their new environment. Paul Rushton, whose work in reception in Portsmouth was impressive, believed that helping the refugees find jobs was not a priority because it seemed:

> that it was a choice very often between employment and housing, and I think some of the secondary movements have shown the refugees themselves place a different priority than ourselves on it. There was an ulterior motive for us because once they were moved on from reception centres they were no longer ... being cared for and looked after by specific agencies, they were just out there somewhere ... it just seemed like a fatal move really to try to take it on as a priority because there's so many people unemployed anyway and most of the employment initiatives were around the idea of training and that's served up in the local community...[122]

Like other refugee groups coming to the UK in the 1970s, the Vietnamese found resettlement was housing-led and once accommodation had been found, there was little assistance for them to adapt and settle. The benefits of welfare provision which refugees of the 1970s enjoyed were no consolation for the stifling of opportunities to rebuild their futures in a country loath to recognise their potential. The Vietnamese, although they have received significant support at the local level, were forced to stumble along in the dark in their transition to a new life. But the refugee search for a place called home is never an easy one, caught between places that have persecuted them and places of asylum that accept their presence grudgingly. Ving Huynh was trained in computing but was unable to find work in Britain. Now running a successful shop in Portsmouth, he visited Vietnam 15 years after leaving his homeland at the age of 17. Permanent return, however, was inconceivable because

> I get used to living here and ... I like it ... the life [there] has changed, nearly everything ... the way we speak ... [It's] different when you go back ... they say, excuse me, you foreign... If you go you feel strange, lot of people say there's improvements over there, but friends they care nothing, just angry at us, they change, everything change.[123]

PART 5

World Asylum Seekers at the End of the Century: Closing the Doors

The Kurds: A Moment of Humanity in an Era of Restriction?

Since the 1980s refugees have caused increasing concern, but there has been a growing unwillingness to provide shelter for them especially within the countries of western Europe which have sought to tighten their laws against people they argue are 'economic migrants'. Although it is clearly difficult to distinguish between the political and economic motivations for movement, agencies monitoring human rights violations have repeatedly argued that genuine refugees are suffering from the effects of such restrictionism. In Britain, the Asylum and Immigration (Appeals) Act 1993 and the Asylum and Immigration Act 1996 were manifestations of the changing climate in dealing with refugees.[1] Economic circumstances have not been propitious for refugee resettlement in Britain, but it is the political climate which has significantly changed. Refugee policy is now affected by European harmonisation policies and a 'Fortress Europe' mentality. Migrants of any sort, including refugees, are regarded as problematic and unwanted. The Conservative government from 1979 to 1997 adopted a 'hands-off' approach after its efforts to help the Vietnamese refugees. Subsequently, there have been no refugee assistance programmes on such a large scale with the only exception being the Bosnians affected by the outbreak of war in the former Yugoslavia. Even then, the number assisted, in the form of temporary protection, was small in comparison with the influxes of the 1970s. All other involuntary migrants arriving in Britain now have to make individual applications for asylum and may be granted either refugee status, in keeping with the UN Convention of 1951, exceptional leave to remain, a temporary humanitarian status allowing them to stay in the country, or may face refusal and be subject to deportation.[2]

The development of travel and communications have made borders easier to traverse, but governments have put up barriers to the entry of foreign nationals. Individual asylum applications stood at only 13,000 for the whole of Europe in 1972 (as far as they were measured). In 1980, 158,500 applications were recorded. By 1991, over half a million asylum claims were received on the continent.[3] In the UK there were only 4,000 applications for asylum in 1986 but over 27,000 by 1996. Yet in proportion to the world refugee crisis these numbers are paltry. The UNHCR recorded over 27 million people of concern in the world in 1996, including asylum seekers, refugees, internally displaced people, returning refugees and others on the move. By far the majority of those in flight are received by neighbouring countries far from Europe.[4] Of those who have reached the UK, the rise and fall of different groups reflect the changing human rights abuses around the world with some refugee arrivals sparking greater concern than others. Of particular significance were the Kurds whose persecution in Iran, Iraq and Turkey and elsewhere, led to a massive refugee movement in and from the region. The Kurdish crisis has sparked international condemnation at various points since the mid-1980s and the refugees have received significant coverage and sympathy in Britain. There have also been numerous other refugee movements to Britain, including Colombians fleeing Latin America, Iraqis and Iranians fleeing the Middle East and Sri Lankan Tamils, Indians and Pakistanis coming from Asia. Those from African countries, which, in the late 1990s, produced the majority of asylum applications in the UK, especially those fleeing Nigeria, Somalia and Zaire, have been less welcomed. To consider British asylum policy during the 1990s Kurds, former Yugoslavs and Zaireans will be analysed. The experiences of these refugees, though different, have all been coloured by the closing doors of western Europe, and especially Britain, in granting a safe haven to refugees.[5]

THE KURDISH BACKGROUND

Since 1989, considerable human rights violations against the Kurds in Turkey and in Iraq, followed by a substantial refugee influx, have led to their persecution reaching the national agenda in Britain. The persecution of Kurdish people in Turkey, Iraq and to a lesser extent Iran, has a long history gaining only sporadic recognition in the West. These particular moments of concern require explanation.[6] Gerard Chaliand suggests that, 'The Kurds have the twofold distinction of having been, for the past sixty-five years, one of the most heavily repressed minorities and one of the most numerous, with a population of some twenty to twenty-five million individuals spread unevenly [largely] between Turkey, Iran and Iraq'.[7] Estimates are uncertain due to the unwillingness of the states concerned to recognise their Kurdish minorities; official statistics suggest only about 12 million Kurds live in the region while Kurdish sources report an exaggerated 40 million.[8] Most of the Kurds live in Turkey, about a third live in Iran and a quarter in Iraq. A further million Kurds are estimated to live in Syria with smaller numbers in parts of the former Soviet Union, in addition to over half a million who have migrated to western Europe.

Many of the Kurds' difficulties stem from problems caused when those in the Ottoman Empire and Persia were divided into four different countries in the peace settlement following the First World War. The Treaty of Sevres of

10 August 1920 anticipated the creation of a Kurdish state in the south-east of present-day Turkey, but the Kurds fell victim to the emerging nationalism of both the Turks and the Iranians. British and Soviet support for these powers further retarded Kurdish nationalism. The Treaty of Lausanne in 1923 and the establishment of a Turkish republic led to the idea of a sovereign Kurdistan being dropped and the territory was divided. The treaty recognised the rights of certain minorities, but the Kurds were not among them, emphasising their political marginalisation in international politics. Subsequently, in both Iran and Turkey laws were passed forbidding the public use of Kurdish. Only Iraq failed to suppress the Kurds in the inter-war period.[9] Not until the 1940s did Kurdish political organisations develop sufficiently across the region to press for greater rights, but they remained divided by rival leaders and ideologies which, alongside severe repression, hindered their impact.

The closest the Kurds have come to self-government is in Iran, following the Iranians' loss of control of northern areas at the end of the Second World War. The Kurds benefited from Soviet bids for influence which led to their support for the creation of the Kurdish republic of Mahabad in Iran in 1945. The Mahabad republic proved very shortlived, however, as the Shah, with British support, re-established control and the leaders of the republic were hanged. Indeed, Kurdish nationalism has been used repeatedly as a bargaining counter in diplomacy in the Middle East. In Iraq, since British control ended with the coup of July 1958,[10] intermittent warfare between the Kurds and the Iraqi government has been the norm. Chaliand argues that for the past three decades only when the Iraqi administrations are in a weak position will they negotiate with the Kurds and offer them increased rights, most notably in a March 1970 agreement in which autonomous status for Iraqi Kurdistan was promised. Typically, however, once the state regained sufficient power, negotiations stalled and the agreement was violated:

> To the impatient, proud, regional powers that already enjoy statehood, the Kurds are in the way. In the way of Saddam's dream of a greater Babylon, glory of the Arabs. In the way of Turkey's plan to earn international respect by modernising and assimilating the Kurdish provinces. In the way of Iran's scheme for a republic based on Shi'ite Islam. In the way of Syria's wish to make a militarised nation out of a patchwork of religious and ethnic minorities. The Kurdish national motto, with origins older than anyone can remember, is simply: 'The Kurds have no friends'.[11]

Ibrahim Ahmed's poem, 'It is March Again', expresses both the Kurds' anguish and determination:

> It is March again;
> it is spring and the time of flowers,
> but for the Kurds
> it is a time of sorrow and pain.

> The buds on the trees
> are wounds; the mother whose son is killed
> is the violet,
> the garden a field of death...
>
> Yet even if March brings pain
> a thousand times worse...
> even so, we know
> we must make the sacrifice.
>
> Our spring will come –
> one without sorrow...
> Our nation long ago
> decided to be free.
>
> Oh, you who seek to destroy us, hear:
> freedom will grow from our grief.

In the three countries where the majority of Kurds live their needs have been marginalised. Moreover, there has been little state investment in developing the infrastructure of Kurdish regions. The Kurds' geographical isolation and landlocked position has led to a search for external allies to support their cause but they have fallen victim to wider concerns. In the Iran–Iraq war of 1980–88 the Kurds in each state were aided by their nation's opponent for purposes of destabilisation but at the end of the war the outcome was simply increased repression at home. In Iraq the government used up to 70,000 troops and chemical weapons against the Kurds. The massacre at Halabjah in Iraq on 16 March 1988 was immortalised by the presence of Western television crews whose pictures made international headlines. As Christopher Hitchens commented, Halabjah has 'the same resonance for the Kurds as does the Warsaw Ghetto for the Jews or Guernica for the Basques',[12] a view echoed by Labour MP Jeremy Corbyn in the House of Commons.[13] Out of 70,000, 6,000 died there and 40,000 fled to Turkey. The survivors still suffer the effects of burns from the toxic agents dropped on the town. Forcible resettlements and military actions are estimated to have brought the deaths of 100,000 Kurds in Iraq during the 1980s.[14]

These atrocities in Iraq, together with ongoing repression in Turkey, brought the Kurds to international prominence in 1989. The forced cultural assimilation of the Kurds was 'most systematic' in Turkey,[15] despite the group comprising almost 20 per cent of the population. The Turkish ban on Kurdish has criminalised publishing books or papers in the language as well as teaching it at school. Imprisonment of Kurdish dissidents has been well documented; the International Index on Censorship estimated that in 1990 there were 3,000 people held in Turkish prison for expressing their views, most connected to the Kurdish question. In 1993 the Refugee Council suggested that 100,000 Kurds have been imprisoned since 1980 for a number of offences.[16] These include Mazhar Kara of Dicle University in Diyarbakir, who was sentenced to four and a half years' imprisonment in June 1989 following a speech he made allegedly demanding 'freedom for Kurdistan and an education in Kurdish'.[17] For those imprisoned in Turkey, torture has been used systematically. The use of mass deportations and population resettlements to assert state control has also been evident over the century as a means of suppressing Kurdish rebellions.[18] It has been argued that from 1983 until Iraq's invasion of Kuwait in 1990, Turkey and Iraq cooperated closely to contain their respective Kurdish populations, and that Turkish incursions into Iraq to hunt out Turkish Kurdish militants occurred 'with the consent and sometimes in coordination with Baghdad'.[19] In 1997, Turkey continued to attack Kurdish settlements in Iraq with international impunity.

One of the Kurdish arrivals who arrived in Britain in the late 1980s and settled in Hampshire explained how as a left-wing Kurdish political activist he became a target for the government. Working with the Dev-Geng in Istanbul and trying to build up a union in the chemical factories, he began to encourage political opposition activism 'against the fascist government'. After a Kurdish massacre in Maras, 'six students and myself staged a demonstration at school' and were thrown out. His political involvement intensified but:

> In 1979 one of my friends was arrested whilst we were putting up posters against the government. [M]y home was raided and I was also arrested. I was taken to the police station where he identified me… I was detained for ten days. During my detention I was blindfolded, electric shocks were applied to me through my earlobes and I was also hit with a stick on the soles of my feet… I refused to admit anything and I was eventually released… [and] continued to work with Dev-Geng… After the coup in September 1980 many Dev-Geng members and sympathisers were arrested. I fled to Kurdistan [and joined] the Kurdish separatists… The leader of my group was killed in a clash with the authorities. One other activist was killed and five were arrested at the same time … four were sentenced to death…

In 1981 he was arrested by the army in Kurdistan and forced into military service. After its completion he renewed his political work 'organising and taking part in hunger strikes, supporting families of political prisoners and holding meetings' in Istanbul. Intimidated by the police he moved back to Kurdistan 'but there were heavy police operations there as well. Many political activists were questioned and arrested. I was advised by the village headmen where I was staying to leave.' Returning to Istanbul, he hid with his eldest brother but the police 'continued to look for me and my house was raided on four occasions'. His parents were arrested and questioned:

> I became frightened that the police would eventually find and arrest me. My family also became increasingly intimidated by the police… I decided to leave the country. I paid one and a half million Turkish lira for a passage on a ship from Turkey to the UK… As I was too frightened to go back to Turkey, my brother and I decided I should apply for asylum…[20]

The question remains why the exodus of Kurds from their homelands reached the international agenda in the late 1980s and early 1990s. As the above testimony shows, the Kurds had suffered persecution for many years. In Turkey, the 1980s had seen a crisis developing as Kurdish protests against the government increased. While Turkish dissidents as a whole were subject to imprisonment and torture, the Kurds joined forces resorting to armed struggle for the recognition of their rights. The most notorious grouping was the Marxist Kurdish Workers' Party, or PKK, formed by Abdullah Ocalan in 1974 and banned in 1980. After 1984 it became the largest organisation to use paramilitary tactics against the Turkish government. Its destabilising guerrilla activities (a 1993 report estimated that there were 10,000 members),[21] resulted in the Turkish military increasingly bombing villages on the pretext of destroying the PKK. Subsequently, eastern Turkey has been described as a 'sort of concentration camp'.[22]

David Jessel has contended that the mass flight of Kurds from Turkey in summer 1989 was due to the imposition of effective martial law in the Alevi Kurdish area of eastern Turkey. This is substantiated by David McDowell who has shown that many of the Kurds in Britain are Alevi Shi'ite Muslims, in contrast to most Turkish Kurds who are Sunni Muslims. In the 1970s, the Alevis were targeted by rightist groups, most notoriously at the Maras massacre organised by the Fascist 'Grey Wolves' in 1978. The official death toll was 117; Alevis claim 800 or more died. In March 1989 Kurdish fears were rekindled when an instigator of this incident, Okkes Kengar, who had served a prison sentence for political violence, obtained a substantial number of votes in elections in Maras province. To many Kurdish Alevis this was 'the last straw in a situation of mounting danger'.[23]

In addition to fears of renewed Turkish persecution was concern over the activities of local Sunni Muslims. This group, including some Kurdish as well as Turkish landlords, was authorised to raise militia to retain control of their areas on behalf of the government. They were, however, reported to be abusing their power by taking Alevi land for personal benefit. Sunni Muslim teachers assigned to Kurdish Alevi primary schools were alleged to have indoctrinated the children and informed on villagers. Some Alevi farmers also complained that they could only obtain half the price for cotton given to other Muslims. McDowell suggests it 'is neither purely Turkish persecution of Kurds, nor Sunni persecution of Alevis which is going on, but rather a combination of the two, whereby Kurdish Alevis have good reason to claim they are persecuted', concluding that those who returned faced 'a catalogue of risks, ranging from daily harassment, through economic dispossession and cultural or religious harassment through to torture and killing'.[24]

In 1991 another exodus of Kurds from the Middle East began, this time from Iraq. Following the Gulf War in the spring, Iraqi Kurds joined Shi'ite Muslims in an anti-government uprising, but failed to oust President Saddam Hussein. The Kurds' fear of reprisals was made abundantly clear by the mass exodus of people from their villages to the mountainous border regions. Between 700,000 and a million Kurds were thought to have fled to Iran and 300–400,000 to Turkey.[25] It was the ensuing publicity which was responsible largely for sparking a Western response. As Iraqi troops pushed the Kurds back to the 36th parallel, Allied coalition forces from the war intervened to create a 'safe haven' for the Kurds around Dohuk and Zakhu, and subsequently a 'no fly zone' for Iraqi forces above the 36th parallel. 'The creation of such a zone to be protected by largely European and American UN forces, was the first time in history that an international force had been deployed to protect the Kurds.'[26]

International reaction to events in Iraq seemed to offer the Kurds new hope. In the United Nations, Resolution 688 condemned 'the repression of the Iraqi civilian population in many parts of Iraq, including most recently in Kurdish populated areas'.[27] In the European Parliament, a resolution was adopted, strongly condemning 'the attempted genocide against the Kurds by Saddam Hussein's regime', which was regarded as falling within the 1948 Convention definition. The motion supported the movement of American, British and French governments to send troops to guarantee safe zones for the 'Kurds and other displaced persons in Iraq' and called on Iran and Turkey to 'facilitate the supply of aid to the Kurdish populations and to open their national frontiers to refugees'. The European resolution even called for the Kurdish problem to be placed on the agenda of a Middle East peace conference, 'to secure recognition of the Kurds' right to existence and autonomy in all countries in which they are to be found'. This was the strongest indication of international support for the Kurds, proving, however, to be more an expression of hope than of intent.[28]

RESPONSES IN BRITAIN

The Conservative government, in contrast to its help for the Vietnamese, did not undertake a large-scale resettlement scheme for the Kurds. The anti-communist impetus of the Thatcher regime, which was to the benefit of the Vietnamese, worked against the Kurdish refugees, many of whom came from left-wing backgrounds. Anti-Islamic tendencies in the West may also have hindered the Kurds, due to their tendency to come from Muslim backgrounds. In the first two weeks of May 1989, Britain received 456 applications for asylum from Turkish nationals. Home Office asylum statistics do not record the ethnicity of asylum seekers and Kurds were not recorded in a separate category from Turks as a whole. It was clear, however, that the majority of the ensuing Turkish incomers were of Kurdish origin. The government made no special provisions to reimburse local authorities for accommodating the refugees, even in overburdened areas, such as Hackney in London, where many of the Kurds sought accommodation and maintenance.[29] When London boroughs asked for an extra £500,000 to help house the Kurds, they were refused. By June 1989 the number of Turkish arrivals had risen to 2,838, evidence of the growing exodus from the country: 132 of these, however, returned to Turkey voluntarily by mid-July, a statistic used by hostile voices to portray them as 'bogus refugees'.[30]

Despite opposition, the influx was such that Home Office Minister Timothy Renton was asked in July 1989 what further measures would be provided for Kurdish asylum seekers. He replied that though central and local government services provided for their basic needs, he had

> agreed to reimburse some of the exceptional expenses incurred by churches, community and voluntary organisations in helping Kurdish asylum seekers who have recently arrived from Turkey. We are considering whether any further assistance is required.[31]

Concern was voiced in Parliament that more should be done. In May 1989, Labour MP, Brian Sedgemore, argued that Home Office pronouncements that Kurdish asylum seekers were economic migrants led to officials rejecting refugee applications so that their contention became self-fulfilling. Contrasting the 'cynicism and meanness on the part of the Home Office', he suggested that on a public level there was 'a deep undercurrent of sympathy for the Kurdish workers'.[32]

The motives of Kurds entering Britain were subject to considerable debate in the government and press, reflecting the propensity to question the genuine nature of refugees. Timothy Renton gave the Home Office view when accounting for the surge of applicants:

> It is clear that for a substantial number their real objective is to find work in the United Kingdom. Some have said so explicitly. There is evidence that middle-men selling air tickets have been exploiting the economic situation in Turkey, with stories of job opportunities in London, and briefing on how to claim asylum.[33]

The rise of agents seeking to profit from trafficking in asylum seekers, as people desperate enough to flee paid large sums of money in the hope of escaping to safety abroad, was a developing phenomena in refugee movements around the world. But additional statements by Renton that 'In every case where asylum was claimed, they have been admitted while we examined their claims' was disproved in the media.[34] Moreover, government antipathy towards the Kurds was evident later in Renton's speech on the same day. There was an unwillingness to distinguish the Kurds as the primary emigrants from Turkey, despite the conflict in the Kurdish areas of the country:

> Those people have come here without any notice or invitation. In many cases they do not appear to be political refugees by any stretch of the definition. They are in an entirely different situation from the Ugandan Asians or the Vietnamese boat people where reception centres were set up in this country in advance. The Turks are here on a temporary basis until such time as decisions are reached on

their applications. The Government have no special responsibility for those people who are not refugees coming here as part of a Government programme.[35]

Denial of responsibility was aided by sensationalist reports in national newspapers especially the consistently anti-refugee *Daily Mail*:

An international gang smuggling hundreds of Kurdish refugees into Britain each year has been smashed in Bulgaria. Documents seized during the police operation indicate that more than 1,000 – men, women and children – may have slipped in during the last 12 months. Many have claimed political asylum. But others have simply disappeared into the population. Investigators were stunned by the scale of the racket. Immigration authorities believe that for every person caught, there are up to three more who are not. The story of the operation emerged yesterday when the police in the Bulgarian Black Sea resort of Burgas disclosed they had intercepted 170 Kurds with forged British visas bound for Stansted Airport, Essex... They had sold everything in a desperate attempt to swap poverty and suppression in Turkey and Iraq for a new future in England, paying more than £2,600 each to a middle man in some cases.[36]

The reporter was indignant that 'Home Office immigration officials have no choice while examining their cases but to grant [Kurds] temporary permission to stay and provide accommodation', during which time those concerned could claim income support. It was forced to admit, however, that, 'The exodus coincides with increased Turkish military action against supporters of the Kurdish Workers' Party, the militant movement seeking an independent Kurdistan', and that, 'Recently, Kurdish claims have been among the most successful compared with those from other nationalities because of the problems they face in their homelands'.[37]

In spite of the expression of such hostile sentiment, the Kurds did have significant support in Parliament, including Labour MPs Bernie Grant and Jeremy Corbyn who repeatedly raised questions about them. After the suicide of the Kurdish asylum seeker Siho Iyiguven, Corbyn gave a long speech asking that plans to deport Kurds who had not been granted asylum should be suspended due to fears in the Kurdish community raised by the tragedy. He criticised government policy, stating that what had been happening since May 1989

is a disgrace to the British government and this country. It is a sordid tale of people who have fled oppression and torture. People who have a well-founded fear of persecution have had their asylum applications refused. The British Government refuse to give financial support to the local authorities and voluntary organisations that have done wonderful work in supporting these people, who are threatened with removal from this country.[38]

In 1991, by which time John Major had replaced Margaret Thatcher as Prime Minister, debates about the Kurds were rekindled due to the crisis with Iraq. Several MPs referred to the actions against the Kurds as constituting genocide.[39] Douglas Hurd stated the government's position on the question of Kurdish autonomy:

The countries of the area disagree about most things, but they are all clear about
one thing – the need not to meddle with frontiers. But within frontiers it is
entirely reasonable and right that the Kurds should enjoy autonomy and decent
respect for their way of life. That is our view and that must be the long term
aim.[40]

John Major made clear his support for the safe haven scheme for Kurds in
Iraq. Conservative MP Jeffrey Archer, in response to media images of the
Kurdish refugees displaced *en masse* in the mountainous border areas of Iraq,
organised a worldwide pop concert in May 1991 for their benefit. Held in
conjunction with the British Red Cross and following in the footsteps of Live
Aid, it was attributed to have raised even more money. The sum of £57
million was collected for the Kurds and a massive relief effort was undertaken
through the UNHCR and the Red Cross. It became apparent, however, as the
winter of 1991 set in, that those displaced from their homes were not reaping
all the benefits of the funds raised. Most of those Kurds who had left Iraq and
could therefore be defined as refugees under the UN Convention, were
received in Turkey where they continued to live in tents months after the
relief campaigns were initiated.

In spite of professed support for the Kurds in Britain, even at a high level,
and the obvious fears of the displaced Kurds that they would be persecuted if
they returned home, Major's government confined its help to relief efforts
under these international programmes with no undertaking to resettle the
Kurds in Britain. Government efforts centred on containing the people within
the Middle East. Home Secretary Peter Lloyd stated on 22 April 1991, 'We
do not consider that the large-scale resettlement of Iraqi Kurds in Western
countries is an answer to the current problem'.[41] The reluctance of the
government to raise the issue further diplomatically was affected by the
political context, particularly Turkey's application for membership of the
customs union of the European Community. Granting membership was seen
as the best way to help it out of economic problems and to deter radicalism,
particularly from Islamic groups. A British official was reported to have said,
'There is no doubt that Turkey has acquired greater weight in the region as a
result of the end of the Cold War and that must be taken account of'.
Nevertheless, in the 1990s EU members continued to prevent Turkey from
entering because of the human rights abuses the state carried out.[42]

Refugee Council records show that a trickle of Kurdish asylum seekers
reached Britain, of whom only a minority have been granted refugee status.
The Home Office records, which exclude dependants, give a total of 6,115
applications for asylum in the UK by people from Turkey from 1989 to
1991.[43] Danièle Joly notes 2,360 asylum applications by Kurds in 1989, by far
the largest number of asylum applications recorded as emanating from
Europe and the Americas, totalling 2,655.[44] Home Office figures reveal that
over the longer time span of ten years, between 1986 and 1996, there have
been over 15,000 applications for asylum by Turkish nationals. In 1993, the

Refugee Council estimated that the majority of Turkish applications were from Kurds and that, since 1980, an estimated 12,500 Turkish Kurds, including dependants, had come to Britain.[45] In 1997 the total Kurdish community in Britain was estimated to number over 20,000.

The Kurds reaching Britain have, unlike many preceding refugee groups, come solely under their own initiative, involving covert and dangerous journeys. Indeed, the Conservative government positively discouraged them.[46] In June 1989, it became mandatory for travellers from Turkey to the United Kingdom to hold visas, making it extremely difficult for asylum seekers who had to enter the country under false pretences to gain a visa and laying them open to suspicions from the authorising agencies. The visa is just one manifestation of the new political agenda in Britain, and western Europe as a whole, undermining the concept of international protection for asylum seekers. As primary immigration has been all but curtailed in Britain, asylum seekers have been targeted. The Kurds have had particular problems in gaining refugee status and many entrants to Britain have only been granted the provisional status known as exceptional leave to remain (ELR). Of a total of 8,090 decisions reached between 1988 and June 1993 on Turkish nationals (not all of whom were Kurdish), 6,065 were refused asylum, and only 995 were considered to fulfil the 1951 UN Convention definition enabling them to be granted refugee status. The remaining 2,500 were granted ELR.[47] ELR has various ramifications, most importantly that an applicant has to reapply regularly to be able to stay. It is also an uncertain status, preventing individuals from being able to send for their families until after four years, except in exceptional circumstances such as 'pressing compassionate reasons'. Parents who left their children behind because they could not afford a passage for all the family may not be reunited with them for years. In August 1990 several Kurds went on a hunger strike outside the Home Office to protest over their separation from their families.

A television documentary 'Taking Liberties' broadcast in January 1990 provided considerable evidence that measures were being used to keep the Kurds out. It alleged that immigration officials sent back Kurdish asylum seekers within hours of their arrival after only a cursory interview, and, contrary to government statements, with no proper investigation of their claims. The Immigration Department argued that those removed had entered the country seeking employment and were deported back to Turkey because they did not have work permits. Two Kurds interviewed, however, said that they told officials they were seeking asylum but intimidating tactics were used to prevent their entry into Britain. Officials boarded the plane and took the men to a large hall, where they were questioned. The first man interviewed related how he 'spoke to an officer through a translator. The questioning lasted three or four minutes at most before being told to move on. I'm absolutely sure I told them I was seeking asylum'. Another Kurd was asked why he came: 'To seek asylum', I told them. Again he asked, 'Why did

you come?' 'For asylum', I repeated. 'I've got documents as proof.' They
said, 'No need for them, sit down.' The first man added that the interpreter
had said angrily 'We know why you come here. You want to get work –
you're here for economic reasons. You're spoiling the image of Turkey.'

The confused asylum seekers were told to follow a Turkish-speaking
woman, at which point one of them realised they were being taken back to the
plane. He tried to run ahead and shouted, 'Stop, my friends. They want to take
us back'. In the ensuing panic, an Immigration Officer cut himself, police
were called and the group were finally bundled on to the plane and sent back
to Turkey.

Of these two Kurdish men deported back to Turkey, one was arrested by
the Turkish authorities but with the help of a friend on the airport staff
managed to escape. His companion was said to be in hiding. Another returnee
was put in jail for a month and was tortured again. He was described as a
broken man, under surveillance in Turkey and open to questioning at night,
so that any further escape would be impossible.[48] These reports suggest that
Kurdish individuals with genuine fears of persecution were being denied
asylum without a hearing. It raised serious doubt as to whether Britain was
meeting its obligations to provide international protection to asylum seekers
while claims were examined. In July 1989, the Turkish embassy admitted that
some Kurds seeking asylum may have been tortured. Yet the British
government continued its hostility to the Kurds, even sending Immigration
Officers to Turkey to prevent them from leaving. The Home Office was
forced to admit illegally preventing entry in 19 cases during February 1991,
settling out of court for £120,000, presumably to reduce embarrassing
publicity.[49] Kurdish anger at the situation was such that in July a group
attempted to storm the Turkish embassy, resulting in shots being fired by
embassy officials and 31 Kurdish arrests.

In keeping with the questioning of their refugee status, Kurdish asylum
seekers, like others entering Britain without the correct documentation, have
been held in detention. In another television documentary, broadcast in
December 1989, it was noted that while 3,000 Kurds had fled Turkey over the
summer, over 100 were being held in prisons in southern England.[50] It was a
harsh way of dealing with those viewed as 'potential absconders' also evident
in the treatment of African asylum seekers.[51] The Kurds also complained
about the use of hostile Turkish interpreters in their immigration interviews.
In late 1989, Peter Lloyd was forced to report that 13 formal written
complaints had been issued by asylum seekers against Turkish interpreters.
The government investigated just three cases and only two of the interpreters
were removed from its lists.[52] While 84 Turkish interpreters were employed
on a casual basis by the immigration service in 1989 a mere seven Kurds held
such jobs.[53] These problems are not unique to the Kurds but offer a glimpse
of the concerns faced by asylum seekers as a whole in determination
procedures in Britain during the 1990s.[54]

The deportation of Kurds failing to be granted refugee status has been a further cause for concern, especially following the death of asylum seeker Siho Iyiguven, who set himself on fire, apparently in fear of being deported back to Turkey. His death prompted Kurdish solidarity movements, for instance at Haslar Detention Centre, near Gosport, where one of the detainees, who had been on hunger strike in protest over detention, threatened suicide if he was not given fair treatment. Subsequently, all of the Haslar Kurds were released by immigration officials except for eight who were returned to Winchester Prison and held under high security conditions. Local visitors recalled the genuine fear of these Kurds of deportation. One who was returned was seen screaming and shouting in fright.[55]

RESPONDING TO THE KURDISH REFUGEES AT A LOCAL LEVEL

The publicity over the death of Siho Iyiguven triggered considerable anger among British people as government methods of dealing with asylum seekers came under the media spotlight. Some 2,000 people protested outside Whitehall at Iyiguven's death. Around the country support groups sprang up based around detention centres where asylum seekers were held, well-exemplified by responses in Hampshire. While in the 1990s the county is no longer a main place of arrival for refugees, the majority of whom enter the country at airports in London, it is one of the primary areas for detention of asylum seekers at both Winchester and Haslar Prisons. Developments at Winchester show how local contacts with refugees have now largely become confined to dialogue with detainees, and campaigns against their incarceration, in contrast to the constructive assistance with their integration which was possible in the past.

In the largely prosperous town of Winchester, a core of local people in 1989 were sufficiently horrified to discover that Kurds were being detained at their own local prison to form a support group to visit the asylum seekers. The Winchester Action Group for Asylum Seekers (WAGAS) was led by the reverend of a local church, Sir John Alleyne, with the support of Reverend David Haslam of the British Council of Churches, but gained support from a motley group of local residents. The complexion of the group showed that diversity did not prevent action for a common cause, as those involved included lifelong Conservative supporters, as well as Liberals, working-class and middle-class people, men and women. As their links developed they campaigned to raise local awareness about the situation and sought to free the Kurds. Tamils and others had been detained in Winchester Prison before and other groups would follow, but it was the treatment of the Kurds that sparked local interest.

WAGAS was initially formed to offer support to 15 Kurds in Winchester but it 'discovered to its astonishment that the Home Office habitually treats genuine refugees in this manner', that asylum seekers had little legal protection and were 'often not informed of the reasons for their imprisonment or for how long'. A sensitivity to the needs of the refugees emerged, its members recognising that 'on arrival they are often too traumatised to present their cases clearly' suppressing 'particularly distressing episodes such as torture because these are too painful or degrading to admit until they feel more secure and can find an understanding listener'. In response, WAGAS's tasks were to arrange

> regular visiting, to search for interpreters, find the best solicitors, invite people to stand bail for them, appeal for clothing, continue its support when they leave prison, campaign through public demonstrations, letter writing, Parliamentary lobbies, using the press and television, and to keep lawyers well informed in a constant watch against the not infrequent risk of Home Office maladministration. WAGAS also works with comparable groups such as Charter 87 and the Churches Support Group in Hackney, and has helped create further groups at Pentonville and Haslar.[56]

In addition to local work, WAGAS campaigned to end the detention of asylum seekers in British prisons where no crime was suspected, to bring in a right of appeal in the country against deportation, to allow asylum seekers to earn a living if they were granted Temporary Admission and for their families to be allowed to join them if they were granted ELR. When asked what motivated him to join WAGAS, a Romsey resident commented that:

> Some people say ... 'why should we be bothered about the Kurds?' The Kurds are in a country far away from here, it's nothing whatever to do with us. And to them I say, the world is small and getting smaller, and what happens in one country today affects what happens in many other countries, including our own. And if we turn our back on these issues we are not progressing as a society, we are getting smaller and tighter and more intolerant, and so I think our reaction to this basic question of refugees and asylum seekers tells us a lot about ourselves, whether we're the caring part of society or whether we're the closed-in 'I'm alright Jack' part of society.[57]

Much of the outrage over the plight of asylum seekers came from the middle-classes. One female member of the group was willing to stand surety of £1,000 for any Kurd in Winchester Prison who was granted bail, and to take the asylum seeker into her home if necessary. It was, to her, 'an act of faith'. The Kurds had endured suffering and had 'no rights as a community'. To objections that they were economic migrants she responded, 'There is a danger of thinking that because a person might come over here and says he would like to work, he is coming as an economic immigrant. It means he is not prepared to sit back and be dependent on other people'.[58]

Several members of the group believed Britain was implementing asylum laws in a racist way: 'If these people had come from somewhere behind the Iron Curtain, one wonders whether the attitude would be rather different'.[59] In November 1989 the group organised a Winter Aid campaign to collect clothes for the freed asylum seekers unable to support themselves. One member, David Thomas, explained, 'It's a catch-22 situation – they have been given permission to stay but can't support themselves while they are here ... With winter coming how are they to cope?'[60] Government restrictions preventing asylum seekers from working for the first six months in the country certainly hampered their ability to survive economically.

The links made between the local campaigners and Kurds were remarkable. A son of a WAGAS member relates attending a wedding reception with 600 people in north London where 'Dancing, at once stylised and abandoned, dominated the room, while the bride and her groom sat looking nervous. Men jumped up onto the tables and gave it all they had. My head spun.' He was one of

> 20 English people there: we were white, middle-class, I was the youngest, and we were all from Winchester... We were guests of honour. Why? Because a curious, even miraculous thing had happened over the previous six months. Relationships of love and dependence had grown between two different worlds, circles had been squared, lives had been changed...

Recalling that a document describing the intimidation and torture of Kurds in Turkey 'remains one of the most horrific things I have ever read', he provided a laconic description of British refugee policy:

> The Kurds are frequently forced to escape because of their political activities, and many, convinced that this country is one of equity and friendliness, seek asylum here. The Home Office, naturally enough and true to form, welcomes them with open prison doors. After a spell of illegal imprisonment, notices are served that the Government is minded to refuse applications for asylum, whereupon the Kurds are sent back home. Their screaming and crying on the plane quite often disturbs their fellow passengers.

After several Kurds were detained at Winchester, 'the miracle began':

> Local people, life-long Tory voters for the most part, began to do something about this paradigmatic example of the British Government's xenophobia. These Kurds were visited, befriended, despite the language barriers. Their cases were backed, demonstrations took place, petitions were presented, and, eventually, they were released on bail, granted 'temporary' or 'exceptional' leave. It was not an easy process. On 5th October last year, one tried to burn himself to death, and died two days later. There were also many hunger strikes. By the end of October, however, the English people at that wedding had helped to ensure that there were no longer any Kurds being held illegally in Winchester prison. Now they are living at Halkevi Community Centre in Stoke Newington, safe for a while. The wedding must have occasioned a brief moment of relaxation.

He wondered, however, if they ever 'truly stop thinking about the families and homes they have left behind': several carried 'scars of torture that will make sure they are never able to forget Turkey'.[61]

Such support for the Kurds in Winchester was not indicative of all of Britain and was frequently countered. The *Winchester Extra,* for example, became a ground for airing hostile views. One correspondent wrote suggesting the Kurds 'should return to wherever they came from. They were obviously supporting themselves ... and what with winter coming on they would probably be warmer ... I say to them find some work and don't beg'. He also made reference to the need of the homeless in Winchester. Predictably, it was argued that British people's needs precluded helping these 'foreigners'.[62] David Thomas responded that several members of WAGAS had for some time been working for local homeless people.[63]

Activities in Winchester were significant enough to gain attention nationally. *The Guardian* in 1989 revealed how local pressure was a decisive force in the battle for individual detainees, also articulating the disappointment and concern of campaigners when one man, Selahattin Ozberk, who was held for a time in Winchester Prison, was deported. It was not 'a typical Home Counties scene':

> Some eighty Kurds, singing, dancing and making merry with a group of local residents on a blustery November day in the hallowed precincts of Winchester Cathedral. A couple of hundred red helium balloons float into the sky. They have been released by some of the seventeen Kurdish men who spent this Summer in Winchester prison and have now been freed. It is a celebration, but one or two balloons become entangled in a nearby tree, symbolising the two men who are not there to celebrate... [Through WAGAS] these Winchester folk had become familiar with men who had sold their land and left wives and young families to escape the racial, political and cultural persecution perpetrated by the Turkish Government on the Kurdish people, to come to Britain where they hoped to find freedom and protection. It was a time of intense education for the Winchester group. They became amateurs in the peculiar Home Office Alice in Wonderland language by which a person can 'arrive' in this country, but not 'land', and therefore has no access to the law of appeal...

Selahattin Ozberk came from a Kurdish family in south-east Turkey. His father was an Alevi Kurd and they had been harassed since 1965. Selahattin was arrested and tortured but escaped in 1989 only to be taken in by immigration officers at Heathrow leading to detention at Haslar and Winchester. A group of demoralised Kurds at Winchester, including Selahattin, had been on hunger strike, but this did not stop the Home Office from ordering his deportation. Eventually he was able to go to Italy but on an invalid passport: 'At last he became a free man, for the first time in the five months since his escape from persecution. And how did the Winchester group feel? Pretty sick. Relieved of course, but pretty sick. Difficult to feel good about your country at a time like this'.[64]

Such British solidarity with the Kurds was evident elsewhere in Britain, especially among more radical groups and left-wing political activists, including trade unionists and human rights campaigners. At a meeting at

Cardiff University in November 1994 a Friends of Kurdistan-Wales organisation was formed. Sinn Fein Councillors Mary Nelis and Robin Percival speaking at the Halkevi Community Centre, allied themselves with the Kurds, drawing parallels between the situation in Northern Ireland and Kurdistan.[65] Kirklees UNISON affiliated to the Kurdistan Solidarity Committee and adopted a model resolution which it sought to pass on to the regional council. It called for 12 measures, including recognition of the Kurdish people's right to self-determination, an end to Turkey's genocidal actions and to all military and economic aid to Turkey and for the British government to argue that Turkey's admission to the European Union remain conditional upon respect for human and trade union rights.[66]

Demonstrations and support activities took place in 20 European cities in June 1993 concerning Kurdish human rights. In Britain ten Kurds were arrested when 100 demonstrators attempted to halt traffic in Piccadilly Circus. Articles in the highly political *Kurdistan Report* suggested that the British government was seeking to criminalise the Kurdish Community.[67] When PKK activist Kani Yilmaz came to London to address a meeting of MPs and the public at Westminster, as 'the European Spokesperson of the PKK', in October 1994, he was arrested on the orders of the Home Secretary and held pending deportation. A final appeal failed and he was reported to be subject to extradition to Germany for alleged criminal activity.[68]

The Kurds also had support in the House of Lords. Lord Eric Avebury, Chair of the Parliamentary Human Rights Group, wrote to the Foreign Office in November 1994 that:

> To dismiss the PKK as 'terrorists', while excusing a government which commits heinous crimes against the whole people, is to see the conflict through the wrong end of a telescope. The fact that Kurds have rebelled against Turkish rule in 1880, 1925, 1938 and 1984 indicates that the PKK are the latest manifestation of a Kurdish will to self-rule, though not necessarily in a separate state. History shows that for peace and stability in the region, constitutional change is necessary, and this can only come about through a process of negotiation. Britain, whose withdrawal of support for an independent Kurdish state after the Cairo Conference of 1921 left the Kurds without a voice of their own in the councils of the world, has a special responsibility to promote a dialogue.[69]

KURDISH REFUGEE LIFE

Those Kurds finding sanctuary in Britain have had problems adapting. Many have become reliant on the support of Kurdish community organisations, such as the Kurdish Workers' Association, formed in 1985, or on friends and relatives. Very few arrive with proficient English. The Kurdish Workers' Association suggest only 7 per cent have either good or fair knowledge of the language, 90 per cent have very little, and 2 per cent none at all. As most

Kurds come from an agrarian background they have difficulty adjusting to urban Britain. 'Even educated, skilled Kurds often find jobs very difficult to come by; many end up doing menial tasks.'[70] Some find casual work through the Turkish-Kurdish community in London, often in textiles or fast food catering. They tend to be housed by local authorities, friends and relatives or voluntary organisations, but, like many asylum seekers arriving since the late 1980s, 'Many are housed in bed-and-breakfast hotels, where the management can be hostile. Accommodation tends to be dirty and overcrowded, often with a lack of furnishings. Delays in getting housed or rehoused can be long'.[71] Kurds, like other refugees, suffer particular health problems. While older Kurds are known to have problems with tuberculosis, the wider community also has a high rate of sight and hearing difficulties. This may be an after-effect of torture which many Kurdish refugees have clearly suffered, as leading British doctors and members of the Medical Foundation for the Victims of Torture have testified. The methods commonly used in Turkey, including falaka (tying a victim up and beating the soles of the feet), cigarette burns, high pressure cold water hosing, beating, electric shock treatment and rape inevitably leave lasting damage.

Kurds seeking refuge abroad have also proved to be vulnerable to attack. In Germany, one of their main destinations, tensions between Kurds and Turks caused clashes. Some 1.8 million Turks live in Germany, about a third of whom are Kurds. Violence erupted when the Turks invaded northern Iraq in March 1995[72] and the Kurds were targeted repeatedly by neo-nazi groups. In Berlin alone, 5,000 Kurds were reported to have formed gangs for self-defence.[73] One young Kurd explained the dilemma he and others faced as exiles: 'We are watched by the Turkish embassy, which hates Kurdish nationalism. We are watched by Turkish extremists, who believe all Kurds are dogs [and] we are attacked by German fascists who shout "Auslander raus – Foreigners out!" and paint it on their walls'.[74] Such antipathy is not confined to mainland Europe. In Britain, at the end of 1994, a prominent Turkish leader in London who campaigned for the Kurds and for trade union rights in Turkey was the target of an assassination attempt.[75] Violence in the 20,000-strong Turkish-Kurdish community in London, including a series of shootings, firebombings and beatings was also reported, with allegations that the PKK and the revolutionary Dev Sol had extorted money from the community for their struggle, and counter claims that far-right nationalist Turks or members of the Turkish secret service caused the violence. The issue was further confused by the involvement of a small number of criminals in the drugs trade and the professional importation of illegal immigrants.[76]

While focusing on the experiences of Turkish Kurds, it must be remembered that the Kurdish exile community is not homogenous, including, in particular, a substantial number of Kurds from Iraq and Iran. In Britain, however, those from Turkey represent the large majority. As a whole, the community in Britain tends to be dominated by young men, typical of the asylum seekers arriving in Britain in the 1990s.[77] In consideration of the Turkish-Kurdish community, the Refugee Council reported, 'The identity of Kurds is ethnic and national, rather than religious; 99 per cent of Turkish Kurds are Moslem, and the vast majority of these are Sunni'.[78] There are also a number of Alevi Muslims. Turkish-Kurdish refugees retain their own political divisions in the UK. Nevertheless, they face common problems of adaptation. One commented that, 'The only bad thing in Turkey is the oppression by the police and the authorities. But here every aspect of life is unbearable'.[79] His negative outlook was because he had no job, no home, was unable to speak English and faced prejudice: 'I'd love to live back in my own country; here I'm nothing.' As an educated chemical engineer, this man found his lack of prospects in Britain deeply demoralising.[80]

For Musa Kuneker, the reality of life in Britain was a run-down, dirty council flat, encouraging marital tensions: 'I don't want to settle down in this country. As soon as things get better I will go back, but ... I had to come out of Turkey to save my life'.[81] His position echoes the experience of other Kurds. As legislation has become more draconian, so the prospects for asylum seekers have become bleaker. A Kurdish man who fell prey to the change in government regulations in 1996, denying many asylum seekers access to benefits, attempted to commit suicide:

> Although I grew up not speaking the Kurdish language, I felt Kurdish in my blood. It was in 1986 ... that I started to have trouble with the police. I was arrested and held in a police cell for ten days. I was given hot and cold water baths and then electric shocks. They shone bright lights in my face and beat me. I arrived in Bristol in early February having come from Spain on a ship. I came to London to my sister's place. She let me stay until my money ran out. Then she told me I had to go and sleep on the streets. I was out on the streets for 39 days... On 6 April I jumped off Tower Bridge. I wanted to die. I had nothing. I had been to the Home Office, to the police, to my sisters. No one would help me.[82]

More positively, there is still a powerful sense of cultural identity among Kurds in Britain, evident in their celebration of various festivals, especially Newroz, the Kurdish New Year. In London, Turkish Kurds have established the Halkevi Community Centre and other associations where the community gather. A glimpse of Kurdish culture in Hampshire was provided in November 1989 when several Kurds released from Winchester Prison dressed up in national costumes and performed a traditional dance outside Winchester Cathedral in appreciation of those who had campaigned for their release.[83]

In the late 1990s, Kurdish asylum seekers continue to come to the UK in significant numbers, though hampered by the visa requirement and the continuing restrictions placed on asylum seekers by successive governments. A large influx of Kurds coming by ship to Italy in late 1997 and the beginning of 1998 prompted anxiety from EU states fearing the refugees would move north. It led to hasty international diplomacy attempting to curtail further influxes.[84] While Western protection of the Kurdish area of northern Iraq may have helped in the establishment of Kurdish self-rule there in June 1992, as the century comes to a close, reluctance to do more remains the predominant characteristic of Western diplomacy on the issue. In addition:

> The US remains, for the moment, a most reluctant 'protector' of this experiment in Kurdish self-rule, forced by Turkey's need to stem the refugee crisis that would come with Iraq's reconquest … little has changed: Western complicity and silence in the face of Baghdad's war of extermination in 1987–8 is reprised … in the studious inattention to the latest Turkish 'final offensive' to crush political militancy within its borders.[85]

Turkey continues to be regarded by the West as a bulwark against the spread of Islam in the Middle East and has been a major recipient of Western aid for years in spite of ongoing human rights abuses against the Kurds and other dissidents.[86] Kurdish refugees coming to Britain from Turkey thus faced a policy of no special provisions, but official responses to them reflect more general changes in asylum laws which were increasingly draconian in effect. It has been left to local activists, such as those in WAGAS, to form a bond of understanding with the Kurds: 'a strange coming together of cultures; campaigners drawn from one of the most affluent areas of England with one of the most persecuted peoples in the world'.[87] Restrictionism at a state level was such that even refugees from former Yugoslavia, whose plight became so famous, were to find entry extraordinarily limited.

13
Refugees from Former Yugoslavia: The Last 'Programme' Refugees?

THE COLLAPSE OF YUGOSLAVIA

Refugees from former Yugoslavia have fled from a crisis whose history is still being written and the outcome of which is far from settled. The causes of the war, following the collapse of the Yugoslav federation and calls for independence by the republics of Croatia, Slovenia and Bosnia-Herzegovina, are still open to fierce debate. The conflict has been described as a 'civil war' ensuing from the breakdown of order after the collapse of communism in eastern Europe and attributed to ethnic strife where 'Nationalism has come to fill the political and ideological void left by the erosion of communism'.[1] While the countries of western Europe were quick to celebrate the collapse of the Berlin Wall and the crumbling former Soviet Empire in the eastern bloc, the status quo was shattered, giving way to a 'new world order' full of hope and promise but also of fear and instability. The crisis has led to the emergence of new nation-states in a war demonstrating that 'ethnic cleansing' and methods of brutality witnessed during the Second World War were capable of re-emerging.[2] Within the conflict almost two million people were displaced out of a total of some 20 million inhabitants, hundreds of thousands within Yugoslavia and many more forced to cross the country's former borders. Some fled under their own initiative, while others left with the assistance of the UNHCR which attempted to coordinate international 'burden sharing' in Europe's new and massive refugee crisis.

As the dispute spread from Croatia to Bosnia, with both republics claiming independence, new borders were established between the former regions of the Yugoslav state. Slavenka Drakulic, a Croatian, explained her feelings when entering Slovenia:

> 'What would happen if I started to run now', I thought, suddenly remembering the Berlin Wall. 'Would he shoot me?' For the first time, I experienced the border physically – it felt like a wall. In that moment, I knew that all that is said about walls in Europe coming down [was] lies. Walls are going up all over Europe, new invisible walls that are much harder to demolish, and this is one of them.[3]

Historical rivalries also played a part in the outbreak of conflict.[4] Yugoslavia only emerged as a state after the First World War, when it was founded as a Slavic kingdom for Serbs, Croats and Slovenes in the peace settlement in which European boundaries were redrawn. The state also incorporated other groups, including Hungarians and Albanians. The rivalry between the Serbs, who dominated the new kingdom, and the Croats, who had been subjects under the preceding Austro-Hungarian Empire, was 'one of the causes for the collaboration of the Croats with Germany' during the Second World War.[5] Memories of atrocities carried out during the war by the Croatian Ustasha regime and the Serb Chetniks were close enough to be revived by unscrupulous politicians on all sides 50 years later. After 1945, a socialist republican state was created, headed by Marshal Tito, who credited himself with leading the Yugoslav people to freedom by liberating the country from the Nazis and their collaborators. Subsequently a federation of six republics (Slovenia, Bosnia-Herzegovina, Croatia, Serbia, Montenegro and Macedonia) and two autonomous regions (Kosovo and Vojevodina) was formed, held together by a Serb-dominated totalitarian communist regime. The outbreak of fighting in the 1990s was closely related to the different ethnic minorities and their rights within the former federation controlled by 'an authoritarian, corrupt and nationalist administration in Belgrade'.[6]

Ethnic rivalry within Yugoslavia was ignited after the death of President Tito. Problems emerged as economic inequalities were exacerbated by political rivalries with Serbia dominating the republic. Slovenia was the first republic to seek independence, followed by Croatia. In Croatia, where fighting erupted in 1991, tensions between the ruling Croats and minority Serbs were

> fuelled by the activities of President Franjo Tudjman: Once in power, he quickly began to restore many of the symbols and trappings of Croatian sovereignty, eliminating all references to the Serb minority in Croatia, which constituted 12% of the population; these Serbs also feared that they would be subjected to political and economic discrimination. This contributed to the rise of Serb nationalism among the Serb minority in Croatia.[7]

In Bosnia-Herzegovina, the 'powder keg republic' where the First World War began, the situation was further complicated due to the existence of three significant groups: Muslims, Serbs and Croats.[8] Although these groups were mainly Slavic and Serbo-Croat speaking, they used different scripts and followed different religions. While the majority of the Bosnians were Muslims, there were many Serbs of Eastern Orthodox faith, and Croats, the majority of whom were Catholic. Ethnic divisions were exacerbated by religious identity. Petya Nitzova also argues that:

> Each of these groups has a distinct subculture unrelated to religious beliefs and practices. It is obvious in expressive elements of culture such as costume, home interior, folk music and dance, cuisine and dialect. However minor such

differences seem to outsiders, they are highly significant socially, both in terms of group identity and out-group self-distinction.[9]

Nitzova suggests that religion also became a political, social and cultural phenomenon defining the community and creating divisions between people who had lived together peacefully for many years, adding that the conflict in Bosnia had 'significant class underpinnings' with the wealthier Muslims fighting for their right to political self-expression.[10]

> In seeking to identify the causes of the war, conventional wisdom has either stressed hatreds dating back over the past millennium or the immediate decision by Croatia to seek independence in May 1991, as a result of which the Serbian minority, fearing for its fate and wishing to remain part of Yugoslavia, rebelled.

Such an analysis fails to acknowledge that Muslims, Serbs and Croats had lived peacefully together for years. Indeed, Norman Cigar believes that the key catalyst for the war was to be found

> in the decision taken in the mid-1980s to seek the establishment of a Greater Serbia (that is claiming for Serbia any lands where the Serbs have settled, even if only constituting a minority of the population) and in the subsequent attempts to implement that goal.[11]

Stressing that ethnic tensions have not been constant, he believes that political accommodation of the Serb minority in Croatia would have been possible.

Vedat Spahovic, who fled from Bosnia to Britain in 1994, offers a similar view on the conflict from a personal perspective, highlighting the retreat from multi-culturalism to nationalist aggression:

> I grew up as a Yugoslav with a multicultural, multireligious way of life. I became a Bosniak only at the very end of my life there. Yet when the war broke out in 1992, Yugoslavia became associated only with the idea known as Greater Serbia. When the former Yugoslavian Army (the JNA) allied itself with a bunch of rigid Serb nationalists, together they embarked on a vicious campaign for Greater Serbia, first in Croatia and later in Bosnia. Anyone who was not with them was against them. I had to become a Bosniak because to be a Yugoslav took on a new meaning – Serb and Orthodox. My Muslim and Bosnian cultural background did not fit into the project of Greater Serbia. Indeed, those who called themselves Bosniak or Muslims were destined to disappear, and the long enjoyed cosmopolitanism of Yugoslavia had to be abandoned... Bosnia had been truly multicultural ... This was destroyed, not by the mix of people, but by the desire of the nationalists to conquer a territory and purify a nation, leading to exterminations, killings, expulsions and uncertainty.[12]

In April 1992 Misha Glenny, the central European correspondent of the BBC World Service, described the complex and disastrous situation in Bosnia:

> The central struggle, but not as yet the bloodiest, is being fought by Serbs who are opposed to the independence of Bosnia-Herzegovina. They are determined

to keep 68% of the republic's territory within either Yugoslavia or Serbia by force. In this struggle, they are fighting largely against Muslims in central, southern and eastern Bosnia. A separate struggle has broken out, which remains confined within Herzogovina, between Croats in the west of the region and Serbs in the east... The Croats here are not fighting on behalf of Bosnian independence. Indeed, Croats from western Herzegovina are insulted if you call them Bosnian... These people do not want to remain in Bosnia-Herzegovina, they wish to join Croatia, a dream they share with the Croat President Franjo Tudjman... There is a third struggle under way – the battle for the army. The federal army and its bloated officer class cannot exist without Bosnia-Herzegovina, where more than 100,000 soldiers are stationed, and 65% of Yugoslavia's remaining military industries are there. Of those, some 60% are in Muslim or Croat territorities.[13]

The spreading conflict was at least partially due to the deteriorating economic situation in Yugoslavia which undermined the federation. It has been suggested that the federation was founded on an erroneous economic basis and that the republics within the federation were allowed to develop independent economies without links to one-another:

Political relations within the country were influenced by the disintegration of the economy, expensive and unproductive production processes, and the autarkic and polycentric etatism on the part of the republics – all of which stimulated nationalism... [T]he Yugoslav example supports the proposition that nationalism is engendered wherever weakly developed productive forces are confined to a provincial market.[14]

Some go even further towards a Marxist analysis, explaining the conflict as part of 'the growing world disorder of capitalism' in which 'Yugoslavia's aspiring capitalists have draped themselves in different national flags, as they fight among themselves to maximise the territory and resources under their control'.[15]

Economic tensions within the federation undoubtedly existed. The different republics were given considerable economic independence under Tito and national wealth was redistributed. The more developed regions, particularly Slovenia and Croatia, and to a lesser extent Serbia, were more productive than Montenegro and Macedonia, and even Bosnia. Disagreements about the administration and amount of aid channelled from the more developed to the less developed regions were causes of dissent, exacerbated in the late 1980s by growing foreign debt, spiralling inflation and a continuous fall in real wages. Yet even taking account of these severe economic problems, it is simplistic to conclude that 'what is taking place is not national, religious, ethnic or tribal struggle. It is the modern class struggle'.[16]

It is hardly surprising, given the complexity of the background, that the debate over the primary causes of the conflict is ongoing.[17] But the impact of this disaster is not in doubt. A multitude of people became victims of the war and thousands more were displaced. It was no 'modern' war with clearly defined fronts and large-scale movements. A town will be surrounded, attacked by mortars, taken, and then the armed bands move on. Undamaged villages lie next to ones that have been totally destroyed. The tactics of the war do not centre on the defeat of one's military opponents but rather on the terrorising and expulsion of civilians.[18]

Attempts at 'ethnic cleansing' and the mass movement of civilians created a refugee crisis where an estimated one to three million people were displaced, though most remained within the borders of the former Yugoslavia.[19] Refugees, forced to flee abroad leaving their bombshelled homes and communities in search of safety, found sanctuary mainly in neighbouring Hungary and Austria. In 1996 the UN noted that 650,000 people had fled to the former republic of Yugoslavia from Bosnia-Herzegovina and Croatia, while altogether 1.33 million had fled from Bosnia-Herzegovina. They were the third largest national group of refugees in the world after Afghans and Rwandans.[20]

The Yugoslav crisis forced western Europe to reassess the political status quo as communism collapsed in the east. International responses to the crisis and the ensuing displacement of people were largely channelled through organisations seeking to restore peace, including the United Nations, the European Community and NATO. British participation in these peace efforts was significant, with Lord Carrington acting as chairman of the first peace conference in The Hague in autumn 1991. But such responses were hampered by inter-governmental divisions over whether to support the continuation of the confederation or the right of the Yugoslav republics to self-determination. European Community (EC) responses centred on providing humanitarian aid to areas of need, with the United Nations sending forces to ensure it reached its destination. A combination of diplomatic presssure and economic sanctions against Serbia were the favoured means for reaching a solution. Nevertheless, UN soldiers became embroiled in the conflict with some taken hostage and used as human shields on the ground. UN Secretary-General Boutros Boutros-Ghali was reluctant to expend massive resources in what he perceived as a 'rich man's' conflict, in the face of severe problems elsewhere such as Somalia and the Great Lakes region of Africa. Seeking to contain intervention, he argued that otherwise 'it would be a kind of Vietnam for the United Nations'.[21]

At the crux of the debate was attributing responsibility for the conflict. Sympathy in Britain, led by the government, was towards the breakaway republics. In the press, reports of Serbian atrocities, particularly against the Bosnian Muslim community and 'ethnic cleansing', dominated coverage. Government policy sought to punish Serbia, with the imposition of an arms embargo and later the deployment of NATO forces to carry out air strikes against Serb positions – action which aimed to control the future shape of Bosnia. Although NATO action paved the way for a ceasefire in Bosnia, followed by the Dayton Peace Accords in November 1995, tensions remained in many parts of the newly established states, with Bosnia divided into two regions, the Republika Srpska and Bosnia-Herzegovina.

BRITISH RESPONSES TO THE CRISIS

The tone of the British political debate was well illustrated in the House of Commons at the end of 1991, described as 'the first real airing of the tragedy in Croatia'. The Conservative MP for Staffordshire South, Patrick Cormack, urged the government to take action because of the enormity of Serbian actions. He was aware of Croatian atrocities during the Second World War and

> that even during these last months of the conflict, acts of unjustified violence have been committed by Croats against Serbs... [But] we must also recognise the reality, and the enormity, of what has happened in Croatia – and recognise that the great majority of acts of wanton wickedness have been perpetrated by the forces of a state that has ... forfeited its right to be recognised as a sovereign independent nation... [P]erhaps the time has come to stop acting as the honest broker between victim and aggressor. The evidence of responsibility for the carnage and destruction is too overwhelming to be ignored...

A different, but equally strident contribution was made by the Labour MP for Hamilton, George Robertson, who revealed the astonishment and inherent sense of superiority of many, that Europe, of all places, should again be experiencing such horrors. Robertson believed that the Yugoslav conflict was a portent of what was to come following the collapse of the Communist states of the former eastern bloc but warned that intervention could make matters worse:

> [O]n our continent, on the doorstep of the most civilised part of the world, we are watching human beings killing each other for no other reason than the fact that they live next door to each other... The point at issue is that what is happening today is not only a tragedy of today but a portent of tomorrow. We are witnessing in Yugoslavia what happens when the cap of communism is lifted to reveal the suppressed anger that is contained. That may happen in other countries where the same situation applies... There are some who say that we should involve peacekeeping forces right away. However, we in this country know more than most that, unless there is a peace to keep, putting in forces simply places troops in danger.

The government's position in the debate was outlined by Douglas Hogg, the Minister of State at the Foreign and Commonwealth Office. He showed that government favour lay with the breakaway republics but argued cautiously that a collective European approach was needed before taking any further action:

> The fault lies with those who are guilty of the violence. It is not our fault that we cannot persuade them to stop... [I]f we are to express a view about where

the fault lies, I share the view … that it is with the JNA and Serbian forces…
[W]e accept the principle of recognition of the republics of Yugoslavia which
wish it. The essential problem is that of timing and pace…[22]

Within Britain, public outrage was subsequently aroused by reports of 'ethnic
cleansing' of Muslims as the conflict spread to Bosnia. The popular belief
that the Bosnians should be allowed to buy arms to protect themselves against
Serb aggression was expressed in local and national marches, but others took
a different view. Comparing her experiences in Hungary with the situation in
Yugoslavia, Niki Kortvelyessy argued that military intervention would not
help the people in the war zone:

> The Hungarian uprising lasted less than a month… In all, 50,000 people died.
> A quarter of a million people fled… Then, as now, the 'freedom fighters' called
> for Western military intervention, but more detached analysts saw that only
> escalation, not solutions, would result. I believe the same applies to Bosnia's
> call today and plead with politicians to resist the pressures from all sides.
> Foreign troops can only increase the carnage of civilians in a guerilla war,
> where the enemy is indistinguishable from the victim, and make martyrs of the
> aggressors, leading to further grievances for the next generation.

To her the most important support the West could offer was to revive its
tradition of asylum as it had in 1956:

> Britain still bore the marks of the Second World War and rationing had recently
> ended, yet the first wave of refugees from behind the iron curtain were met with
> humanity and compassion from the British people. Lives could be begun again,
> the heat of hatred given a chance to cool, and children such as myself offered a
> future with choices. But it also has to be recognised that the Western Cold War
> effort was well served by offering asylum to the Soviet bloc's dissidents.
> Today's response is that the Maastricht treaty will bring about a very restrictive
> immigration and asylum policy throughout Western Europe, dramatically
> restricting the number of future victims of turmoil in Eastern Europe and
> elsewhere from finding the safety net that we were offered.[23]

British action to help those Yugoslav citizens who had fled their homes,
reported to number almost two million as early as April 1993,[24] was confined
largely to efforts through the EC and UN. Within the country the prevailing
context of tightening immigration laws in Europe, which closed the doors on
immigrants and asylum seekers, permeated government decision-making,
already lacking a clearly defined refugee policy. The Asylum and Immigration
(Appeals) Act, introduced as a bill to Parliament in 1991, was enacted in 1993.
It limited asylum seekers' access to housing, increased the carriers' liability
fine to £2,000 for transporters who brought illegal entrants into the UK, and
introduced measures to return asylum seekers to 'safe third countries' if they
had passed through another European Union state in transit to the UK.[25]

Britain's response to a refugee crisis, the scale of which had not been seen
in Europe since the Second World War, was extremely limited. Charles

Wardle, the Under-Secretary of State for the Home Department, denied the existence of a 'fortress Europe' mentality, but then argued that 'firm but fair controls were needed'.[26] Following the introduction of the 1993 Act, increasing numbers of asylum seekers faced refusal of their applications. In 1994, only 825 asylum seekers were granted full refugee status, with 12,655 applications refused.[27] Inevitably, those from the former Yugoslavia were affected by the tightening procedures and unwelcoming political climate faced by all asylum seekers. Many came to Britain as spontaneous arrivals, entering on visitor's visas or as students. One such arrival, a Bosnian Serb, was forced to move away from her home town on the Croatian-Bosnian border when fighting began there in the summer of 1991. She had been convinced that Bosnia would not be affected with the Yugoslav army over the river: 'We used to say, stupid, not Croatians, but stupid people in Croatia, look what they let happen there, we're not that stupid in Bosnia and this is not going to happen here', but then:

> The first troubles in Bosnia started in my town... Even before I came to England we were refugees first in Yugoslavia. I had the opportunity to come because I knew some friends living here in Southampton and originally I just came for six months... We didn't know what was going to happen to us ... you didn't know where you were going to go and what is going to happen, so that is why I decided to come... My older sister's husband is Croatian, living on the other side [of the river] ... he saw that everything is burned over there, my house and everything.[28]

The Inter-Governmental Consultations on Asylum, Refugee and Migration Policies in Europe, North America and Australia estimated that between 1985 and 1992 about 15 million people migrated to western Europe, including growing numbers of asylum seekers. At the end of 1992, well over half a million Yugoslavs were recorded to have entered western Europe but only about 50 per cent had applied for asylum.[29] In the summer of 1992 the UNHCR called on western European governments to take more responsibility for those who had been displaced. More than a third of the Yugoslav refugees coming to western Europe went to Germany, revealing their inequitable distribution and reflecting the varied responses from governments to the crisis. Within Britain, 44,000 arrivals of nationals from Yugoslavia were recorded in 1992 but only 5,635 were noted to have applied for asylum. In the same year only one former Yugoslav asylum application was granted refugee status, showing the government's initial unwillingness to make any special provisions.[30]

In the early years of the conflict, Britain's response was limited to offering aid to the area through donations to the EC. By October 1991, one million 'ecu' was provided in emergency assistance to Yugoslavia for the purchase of transport and distribution of medical supplies and essential services.[31] Initially the Croatian declaration of independence was not recognised, but at the same time Douglas Hogg stated, 'The republics which wish to receive independence will have it'.[32] By November 1991, 35,000 Yugoslav refugees were registered in Hungary, between 5,000 and 8,000 in Austria, and an unknown number in Italy.[33] As the crisis escalated, aid increased, but British contributions for refugees were still confined to donations from the EC budget. In reply to a question in February 1992 about the extent of British help to the refugees of the former Yugoslavia in Hungary, Linda Chalker, the Minister for Overseas Development, stated: 'The EC has so far contributed some two million ecu to the refugee problem in neighbouring countries of the former Yugoslavia, mainly via the UNHCR and the ICRC [to which we are the] major contributors'.[34]

As the fighting escalated in Bosnia, more questions were raised in Parliament over government action to help the numerous displaced Yugoslavs. But the existence of over 40,000 people from the former Yugoslavia already in Britain coloured government reactions. The Home Secretary, Kenneth Clarke, indicated his reluctance to accept any further substantial numbers of people from the war zone, even for temporary shelter. That those in Britain clearly could not return seemed to be sufficient ground for Clarke to feel that Britain was doing enough in 'making a humanitarian contribution to the most needy'. Those in Britain included students and others who had entered the country on visitor's visas. Among them were Serbs, Croats and Bosnians. Only a small minority applied for asylum because of the long-term ramifications of such a move. As one of those in Hampshire explained: 'I didn't think I am going to be a refugee'. She was forced to apply after being told her house had been destroyed in the war and her town had become a battleground in the conflict:

> You don't know what is going to happen tomorrow … my passport was not valid anymore so I [asked] my embassy if I can prolong it … and they say no, only if you have a visa valid for two years, and I couldn't have another visa because I didn't have a valid passport. I [couldn't] go home, there's nowhere to go [so] I applied for refugee status and I went to the Home Office.[35]

As 'ethnic cleansing' of Bosnian Muslims and the use of concentration camps in parts of Bosnia were exposed in the media, public outrage demanded a further response from the British government. Reports of 'genocide' evoked the treatment of the Jews in popular memory. In August 1992, systematic rape was reported by Muslim women in Tuzla, Bosnia, some becoming pregnant as a result. As one of 40 women who were raped in a small town, Brezovo Polje, stated, 'I wouldn't want anyone else to have the same experience. It is worse than any other punishment in the world.' In separate interviews, four women at Tuzla said that they had been raped by three or four men every night for ten nights. Some suggested that rape was used as an instrument of war, with men operating under orders.[36]

Pressure for international action was further intensified when reports such as that by Roy Gutman, foreign correspondent for *Newsday*, from Omarska, Bosnia-Herzegovina, were given widespread media attention:

> The vast mining complex here ... looks like anything but a concentration camp. The nondescript buildings ... have been cleaned up, and there is no trace of the blood reputedly shed here. But during the last month dozens of eye witnesses have provided compelling new evidence of murder and torture on a wide scale at this complex, where the Serbs who conquered Bosnia brought several thousand Muslims and Croats to die. According to former detainees, the killing went on almost everywhere. Inside the huge hangar-like building that houses earth-moving equipment, armed guards ordered excruciating tortures ... The tarmac outside was an open-air prison where 500 to 1,000 men had to lie on their bellies from dawn to dusk. Thousands more packed the offices, workshops and storage rooms... All were on starvation diets. The two most feared locations were small outbuildings some distance from the main facilities: the 'Red House', from which no prisoner returned alive, and the 'White House', which contained a torture chamber where guards beat prisoners until they succumbed. Unlike Nazi concentration camps, Omarska kept no records, making it extremely difficult to determine exactly how many died.

Newsday first reported mass murders at Omarska and other camps at the beginning of August 1992. Within days, as television pictures of emaciated prisoners were broadcast worldwide, Serb authorities closed the camp and dispersed the prisoners. But not until some of the former detainees reached the West, aided by the International Red Cross, was it possible to draw a detailed account of what had happened. Amongst the testimonies recorded by Gutman was that of Redzep Tahirovac, aged 52 who

> was brought to Omarska with hundreds of others on May 26 after Serbs destroyed and 'cleansed' the nearby Muslim town of Kozarac. In a sworn statement given to the Bosnian State Commission on War Crimes, he said guards called out a dozen people a day for five days and decapitated them with chain saws near one of the five main pits.[37]

These reports left no room for equivocation, but it was not until 17 November 1992 that Kenneth Clarke announced British government plans to help some of the former detainees in Bosnia from camps such as Omarska:

> We have informed the UNHCR that we are ready to receive in the first instance 150 former detainees and their dependants, probably making 600 in all. At the same time, I announced the imposition of visas on certain nationals of the former Yugoslavia, making it clear that such action was needed to enable us to target our humanitarian assistance where it was most needed.[38]

This action can only be described as a token gesture, the use of visas ensuring that the government kept extremely tight control of the scale as well as the type of refugee entry to Britain. Those assisted were to be offered 'temporary protection', a new phenomenon in the treatment of refugees in Europe. As evaluators of the Bosnia Project, established to assist those arriving under the government programme, noted in 1996:

> The implied promise to European countries was that they need not consider

long term integration measures. In the UK and elsewhere in Europe the sense of tentativeness in committing the full range of reception and resettlement measures continues to raise serious problems for those offered temporary protection and for those providing services.[39]

The lucky 600 would join 68 wounded people who had been taken at the request of the Red Cross as medical evacuees. Later this quota was increased to 1,000 former detainees and their dependants, an anticipated 4,000 people in all, which Labour MP, Tony Blair, attributed to the 'strength of feeling in the country about the need for Britain to do more'.[40] Nevertheless, the concurrent imposition of visas did little to add credibility to government claims to be helping the needy. Concern was raised by the actions of the Leeds European Refugees Trust, ALERT, who attempted to evacuate several coach loads of Bosnians to Britain, having arranged for their accommodation. One of their convoys was caught in transit as the new visa regulations were imposed. Kenneth Clarke's reaction was that 'visas may be authorised for six members of the group who have existing family close ties with the United Kingdom ... I also decided that another 180 members of the group should be refused visas because they have insubstantial or no links to the United Kingdom'.[41] The reason for this decision was clear; fear of setting a precedent in the war zone. As Clarke added: 'Their cases are indistinguishable from the plight of about two million people in the former Yugoslavia.'[42]

On behalf of the Labour Party, Tony Blair responded:

> Although everyone accepts that there must be proper regulation of the flow of refugees, in this case of clear suffering – involving mothers and children, where accommodation in Britain has been agreed and where the Red Cross on the ground has recommended help – would not the Minister command more support in the country if, instead of every day placing new barriers in the way of help, the Government were to show the same spark of humanitarian concern as has been shown by the British people?[43]

There was more vociferous outrage from Robert Maclennan, MP for Caithness and Sutherland, who, with only lip service to historical accuracy, asked whether

> the Home Secretary [was] aware that his voice sounds like that of his predecessor, Sir Samuel Hoare, who bundled Jewish refugees back on planes to Germany in 1939? When he speaks of allowing 150 people in desperate straits into the country on the one hand and of two million refugees on the other, he does less than justice to our international role as a humanitarian country and simply deposits the problem in the lap of the German people.[44]

The popularization of the Holocaust in popular imagination was such that it had entered British political discourse, becoming a benchmark for all problems relating to racial persecution and refugees. Kenneth Clarke's response matched Maclennan for distorting the chronology of the persecution of the Jews:

I am sure that the hon. Gentleman will not find any comparison between the returning of Jews to a regime which was systematically killing them in gas chambers and my refusal to allow people into this country from hotels and hospitals on the peaceful mountainsides of Slovenia where they are far removed from the fighting, having escaped from it, and where I trust that no one will attempt to pursue or kill them.[45]

The overriding concern of the government was to keep those displaced close to their homes so that they could return when peace came. Towards this end, Kenneth Clarke stated that some £70 million had been provided in humanitarian aid by mid-November 1992 with 2,300 troops employed ensuring the aid reached its destinations. Moreover, 200 mercy flights had taken aid to provide winter shelter for 20,000 people in the worst affected areas.[46] To Clarke, this contribution was 'one of the most formidable from western Europe',[47] a rather distorted interpretation given that Germany was sheltering a quarter of a million displaced former Yugoslavs.

THE FORMER YUGOSLAVS IN BRITAIN

For those people coming under the 1,000 quota programme to be given temporary shelter in Britain, government funds were dispensed to the Refugee Council and the British Red Cross Society for transport and reception. These two organisations set up a reception programme in conjunction with the Scottish Refugee Council and Refugee Action. The first refugees were housed in three locations (a former mental hospital in Surrey, an existing Refugee Council hostel in London, and a former residential care home owned by the British Red Cross in Cambridge), before more permanent housing was found in the community. The number of reception centres later increased to 12, most based in London, but with additional support in the Midlands, East Anglia, north-east England and Scotland. The Refugee Council, with the agreement of the Home Office, believed that stay in the centres should be brief to avoid the refugees becoming dependent. As of November 1994, 803 principal refugees had arrived under the government programme, some with their families, making a total of 1,907 Bosnians, including 76 medical evacuees.[48] The main areas of settlement were the Midlands, West Yorkshire, north-east England, Edinburgh and London. Applications for asylum had risen to 7,685 from inhabitants of the former Yugoslavia, including Croatians and Muslims, but the Refugee Council reported that only 455 decisions on former Yugoslav applications had been made by the end of February 1994.

In August 1993, the case of Irma Hadzimuratovic, a child who was in need of considerable medical help, received prominent media coverage, increasing public sympathy. In response, the government agreed to take more medical evacuees through 'Operation Irma'. This help was limited and medical evacuees arrived at very short notice. With reports in early 1994 of the bombing of Sarajevo, the main city of Bosnia where Muslims, Croats, Serbs and others had long lived peacefully in a multi-cultural society, more medical evacuees were taken. But no larger scale provisions were made to assist former Yugoslavs until the summer of 1995, when an upsurge in fighting dispelled hopes for an imminent solution to the discord in the region. UNHCR called for further resettlement provisions to be made. Three weeks after the closure of the Refugee Council reception centre at Batley, when such facilities were being wound down and with efforts concentrating on mid-term support for residents in Britain, plans had to be made to reopen it. On 5 August 1995 the Home Secretary announced a new programme for 500 individuals and 20 further medical evacuees who were to be assisted under the auspices of the International Organisation for Migration.

By February 1996, 2,342 arrivals under the two quota schemes had been recorded by the Refugee Council. Fewer than 150 people had come in total under the medical evacuees' scheme and the number of former Yugoslav nationals in the UK claiming asylum had risen substantially. Between 1992 and 1996, 11,445 asylum applications had been submitted. Among these were a substantial number of ethnic Albanians from the region of Kosovo in the former Yugoslavia. They had also suffered ethnic conflict, though their situation was overshadowed by reports of the situation in Bosnia. It was not until 1996, however, that significant numbers of asylum applicants from former Yugoslavia began to be granted refugee status. In 1994, 1,265 former Yugoslav asylum applicants were granted exceptional leave to remain (ELR) but numbers given refugee status increased dramatically, rising from 25 in 1994 to 1,155 in 1996. The expansion in these figures suggest changes in the decision-making process at the Home Office, in keeping with political developments in the region and strategic concerns in Britain. In 1994 former Yugoslavs benefited from the policy to provide considerable numbers of asylum seekers with ELR, a common feature of claimants' treatment in Britain who though not strictly falling under the protection of the UN Convention could not, on humanitarian grounds, be sent home. By 1996, with continued outbreaks of fighting in parts of the region, it became clear that most former Yugoslavs could not be returned for the foreseeable future. Within the UK asylum determination procedure, use of ELR as a provisional status had fallen out of favour. In other European countries temporary protection had given way to providing more settled status to former Yugoslav nationals. In Britain, too, increasing numbers obtained refugee status.

Over this period, the difficulties of resettlement for former Yugoslavs have been acute as painful memories retained their power. For Edin Elkaz, one of those resettled outside London, who had been held at Omarska, nightmares recurred: 'his head filled with screams of the men being tortured in the room next door at the "White House"'.[49] Another couple came as medical evacuees after suffering injuries in Sarajevo, haunted since their arrival in Britain with thoughts of a camp run by Chetniks:

> People were taken there and were not able to leave. They were raped. It was terrible what people were doing. Often snipers killed the children if a mother was out with a child, or they might kill both mother and child.[50]

With the conflict in the region still raw and unresolved, and with many refugees coming to Britain having suffered in camps where torture was regularly practised, it is not surprising that mental health has been a serious problem. Those arriving were highly traumatised from their experiences of war and loss as well as through cultural dislocation. The uncertainty of the status offered to those given 'temporary protection', and the lengthy determination procedure common to all asylum seekers submitting applications in the UK during the early 1990s, increased stress. The ever-present threat of being returned to a disrupted homeland did little to help adjustment. The criteria for family reunion also proved to be very restrictive, further exacerbating anxieties. Procedures were eased but delays led to great unrest; in early 1994, hunger strikes were held in a reception centre in Newcastle over the issue. In December 1993, Lejla Ibrahim, a Bosnian asylum seeker, killed herself after losing a year-long battle with the Home Office for her husband to enter Britain. Two days later her husband was given a temporary visa allowing entry into the country, on compassionate grounds, because the couple's children had now become 'unaccompanied minors'.[51]

Tragedies such as this revealed the inadequacies of Britain's resettlement procedure. The existence of families with members of mixed ethnicity added to the problems. The trauma for such individuals caused by procedural red tape and lack of appreciation of the desperate and isolating circumstances people faced was evident locally. An asylum seeker recalled the problems for a woman seeking entry who was refused because of the failure to comprehend the ethnic issues at stake:

> She had troubles because she was a Croatian from Croatia so there is no problem for her to live in Croatia... You know it's hard to understand that she can have her problems just because she had a Serbian boyfriend and she's from a small village and everybody knew that she lived with him for five years... [Now] he's a Serbian soldier in the army. He's from Bosnia but he lived in Croatia at the time.[52]

For those who came under the government programme, which comprised only a small proportion of those seeking asylum in Britain from former Yugoslavia, some lessons had been learnt from earlier resettlement schemes. In terms of relocation, the Bosnia Project ensured that the Bosnians were settled in 'clusters' of perhaps 20 families in order to facilitate community support. Areas of housing were located in urban areas to minimise secondary migration. These were mostly found within four months but the Bosnia Project's inability to plan effectively due to constantly changing demands and its lack of funding for anything other than short-term arrangements led to serious problems. After moving out of the reception centres, Bosnians were offered six months' support from caseworkers. Though this help was appreciated, concerns of 'favouritism' for certain clients and difficulties over the ethnicity of workers and clients emerged.[53]

Hampshire was not one of the chosen resettlement areas for the 'programme' Bosnians but other former Yugoslav nationals came to the county for their own reasons. One, a student at the University of Southampton, knew at least ten people from former Yugoslavia from various ethnic backgrounds, including Croatians, Serbs and Muslims from different regions of the country, living in the city. They were all young, mostly in their 20s and 30s. Several were students and another worked at a local restaurant: 'We live completely all right here, no problems, but I think if we were back home [it] would be difficult'. For her, people in Britain had been friendly, but, echoing the responses of the refugees from Nazism over half a century earlier, she commented on the frustration of being unable to communicate the horrors left behind:

> Everybody was helping financially, I was supported, I had income support, housing benefit [but] I wanted to talk about things in Yugoslavia a lot because I was angry, extremely angry… [The British] are quite distant… People ask, 'So what's happening over there?' and I would just start: 'It was a shame, shame, it was awful' and then they would change the subject completely. I couldn't speak to anybody because nobody was ready to listen. That I find is really hard because I needed to talk about it, not now, but then… Maybe people were just too embarrassed to talk about these things.[54]

She also found it almost impossible to find work, 'especially when you are foreign and especially from Yugoslavia, people are suspicious of me, because I'm not English'.[55]

Language barriers exacerbated the sense of isolation. One Bosnian woman, evacuated after losing her right arm in a mortar attack, and already worried about her family in Bosnia, was concerned about her future in Britain: 'I don't speak any English. I don't know why, I can't learn it – it's hard. I'm afraid if I go into a flat in Shepherd's Bush there won't be any Bosnians and there will be no one for me to talk to.'[56] Perhaps the most significant issue for those coming under the temporary protection programme has been their insecure status in Britain. In March 1995, Louise Garner, who ran the Goldhawk Road reception centre in London, argued that it was very difficult

> for people to settle here when they are constantly reminded that they could be sent home at any time. We should be taking more refugees here. The war is still going on and there are many people who are trying to be reunited with their families.[57]

The Refugee Council believed that the temporary status granted to the Bosnians under the temporary protection programme was unjust and that they should be given full refugee status. In 1995 Lord Alf Dubs, Chief Executive of the organisation, wrote to *The Guardian* outlining two concerns:

> The first is the tragedy of the 150 families who have yet to arrive under the quota who are still trapped in some of the most dangerous parts of Bosnia. The

other is the ambiguous 'temporary refugee' status given to the Bosnians which must be renewed on an annual basis. The Refugee Council believes this status, which leaves many refugees vulnerable and unsure about their future, should be made more secure.[58]

While temporary protection gave little security to the programme arrivals, asylum applications submitted by other nationals of the former Yugoslavia outside the Bosnia Project also met an ambivalent response, revealed in a letter from the Immigration and Nationality Department to a Bosnian Serb resident in Hampshire who had applied for asylum on grounds of 'a well-founded fear of persecution in Bosnia-Herzegovina for reasons of race, religion, nationality, membership of a particular social group or political opinion'.

The Secretary of State notes that prior to your arrival in the United Kingdom on 8 April 1992 you lived in the Bosnian town of ***. You have stated that when the war started, Serbs in your town ... were exposed to ethnic and religious harassment and that the majority of Serbs living in the Croatian part of the town lost their jobs. You have stated that you left the town after some of the neighbouring houses were burnt down and travelled to Serbia. However, persons compelled to leave their country of origin on account of national or international armed conflicts are not normally considered refugees under the terms of the 1951 United Nations' Convention relating to the Status of Refugees.

You have stated that the situation in Serbia got worse when sanctions were imposed and that people were running out of food and medical supplies. The Secretary of State understands the difficulties faced by individuals in such circumstances but economic reasons do not satisfy the criteria for granting refugee status under the terms of the 1951 UN Convention. [He] fully appreciates the reasons why you feel unable to return to Bosnia at present, but notes that nearly 70% of Bosnia is controlled by Bosnians of Serb ethnicity. He therefore considers that as a Bosnian Serb there are areas of Bosnia Herzegovina where you would not have a fear of persecution for any of the reasons within the 1951 [Convention] and where you could avail yourself of the protection of the authorities if so required...

The letter ended that 'in light of the evidence provided and for the reasons given above, the Secretary of State has concluded you do not qualify for asylum'. The woman concerned was granted ELR but was reminded that it did not mean entitlement to permanent settlement:

You should [also] understand that if during your stay in the United Kingdom you take part in activities involving, for example, the support or encouragement of violence, or conspiracy to cause violence, whether in the United Kingdom or abroad, the Secretary of State may curtail your stay or deport you.[59]

LOCAL RESPONSES

The paltry offers of sanctuary by the government contrast with the more positive initiatives undertaken by individuals and charitable organisations in

Britain to relieve the plight of people in the war zones. John Pilger argued in 1993 that public opinion was acting as a potent force in the Yugoslav conflict:

> The semantics of Douglas Hurd are now unacceptable to people watching the Balkan horrors on television. Public opinion has become more than a fleeting force. Having been made witnesses to genocide, perhaps for the first time, people want it stopped.[60]

The Refugee Council reported that some 2,000 Bosnians had come to Britain separately from the government programme through 'convoy groups' involving local support teams.[61] The actions of ALERT were just one example of many spontaneous efforts. Lorries of medical supplies and educational equipment were sent out by other local support groups. In the Southampton district a national organisation, 'Women's Aid to Former Yugoslavia', was formed in 1992 'to provide humanitarian aid for women refugees; to provide support to women's groups and women working with refugee and displaced women; and to support anti-war and human rights groups in former Yugoslavia', which subsequently delivered tonnes of supplies in lorry convoys.[62]

In 1993, the Ockenden Venture undertook an emergency shelter programme in Krajina where thousands of Serbs were displaced from their homes. Their aims were to upgrade accommodation and provide sanitation, water supplies, heating and cooking facilities for some 500 people. In addition, a home for displaced elderly people was set up through voluntary donations.[63] Popular support at an institutional level in Hampshire was articulated at the University of Southampton which funded four undergraduate studentships as well as collecting equipment for students in Bosnia at the universities in Tuzla and Sarajevo. It was noted in May 1995 that 'After last term's appeal for stationery for Bosnia ... the University Rag Office was overwhelmed by the generosity of both staff and students'.[64]

In Eastleigh, an initiative was undertaken to bring 60 orphans aged between six and 11 from Bosnia for a two-week holiday, during which time the children would stay with local families. Local activists, who had delivered aid to Bosnian orphanages, wanted to provide the children with a respite from their miserable surrounds. The organiser stated that the children had 'been taken out from Bosnia from various villages which have been torn apart by the war. We're bringing them out of hell to give them a bit of heaven. These kids' feelings have gone wild, so we're bringing them into a home-like atmosphere for love and affection'.[65]

One hundred and fifty local families responded to the appeal – another indication of ordinary British people's desire to help. It was not clear, however, whether this scheme succeeded, fraught as it was with logistic and practical problems, especially the dilemma of returning highly traumatised children to a war zone. Nevertheless, the goodwill behind the move was genuine, begging the question whether such enthusiasm could have been exploited by a national appeal used to more practical effect helping those already in the country. The willingness to help children, perceived as the innocent and vulnerable victims of war, echoed responses to the Spanish Civil War, where popular energy was channelled locally to assist thousands of youngsters. In contrast to the Basques' experience, however, initiatives in Eastleigh for the Bosnians were ultimately limited by the British government's desire to restrict entry of refugees to a bare minimum. It insisted that if the scheme was to go ahead the children chosen should be very young, fearing older ones might abscond. The ease with which the Basques were brought to Eastleigh contrasted starkly with the insurmountable red tape required half a century later to give the young Bosnians a short holiday.

Elsewhere in Britain initiatives to assist the refugees were more successful. In autumn 1992, the School of Slavonic and East European Studies of the University of London set up a committee to develop and implement a nationwide scholarship programme for Bosnian refugees. It followed precedents set after the crises in Hungary in 1956, Czechoslovakia in 1968 and Poland during the 1980s, also echoing World University Service efforts for the Chileans in the 1970s and, much earlier, the Academic Assistance Council's efforts for scholars displaced by the Nazi regime. All British universities were asked to make one free place available for a Bosnian refugee by offering fee waivers and raising additional funds to cover living expenses. Seventy fee waivers were offered and many institutions were successful in raising enough money to cover maintenance costs for the students. In the academic year 1992–93, 45 Bosnian students were placed in universities at Belfast, Birmingham, Central Lancashire, Dundee, Nottingham, Sheffield, Southampton, Staffordshire, Sunderland, Sussex and York with 50 part-time and 38 full-time studentships available the year after.[66]

CONCLUSION

Although these local efforts were important, the response overall to the displaced people of the former Yugoslavia was fragmentary, helping only a fortunate few. Those who came outside the government programme had all the problems faced by contemporary asylum seekers in the UK, but without the support mechanisms offered to the quota refugees. There were clearly logistical difficulties as some individuals granted entry visas to Britain were trapped in areas of fighting, but in 1994 it was apparent from Refugee Council reports that the Bosnia programme was unlikely to meet its anticipated target of helping 4,000 people.[67] In February 1995, Mr Nicholas Baker explained on behalf of the government that:

> Due to the declining number of evacuees from the former Yugoslavia in recent months, it has been decided, following discussions between the Home Office, UNHCR and the voluntary agencies running the centres, that two of the present nine centres should close at the end of March 1995 and a further five … by the

end of April. Of the.two remaining centres, one will close at the end of June, and we will review in April the timing of the closure of the last centre against the background of developments in Bosnia.[68]

Following the Dayton Peace Accords in November 1995, which suggested that a resolution to the conflict was possible, Home Secretary Michael Howard announced that Bosnian nationals who came under the government programme, and, uniquely, those seeking asylum individually in the UK, would be allowed to make a visit of up to three months to Bosnia and return to Britain without endangering their asylum status. This concession, which Howard described as a 'window of opportunity' enabling the refugees to assess the prospects of return, was unprecedented. Its impact, however, was very limited, as many of the areas of the region remained unstable and reports reached the media of ethnic attacks in various places, ruling out for many a safe return to their former homes. The changing map of the region also raised serious problems. Some returnees found their homes destroyed but were prepared to start rebuilding their communities even in the face of huge problems such as the lack of basic amenities. For the majority, however, more time was needed before the prospect of returning home for good could be judged a viable prospect.

At the end of 1996 all the Bosnia Project reception centres in Britain had closed though some caseworkers believed that the most vulnerable refugees would be unable to cope outside. The reception centres had provided interpreters, hospital transportation, general assistance for the refugees and contact with others in their situation as well as shelter. Nevertheless, 30 staff were still available in 1996 for development work, the area in which some believed government funds should have been concentrated earlier. The reduction of government funding from £6 million to £1 million from 1994–95 to 1995–96 and the subsequent closure of the Bosnia Project, in addition to the ending of most funding for community development workers, has again left those still requiring help to rely on existing services.

In 1997, with the election of a Labour government for the first time since 1979, an additional concession was made for those who had come under the previous administration's quota programmes. At last the Bosnians' 'temporary status' was to be reassessed. All those with this status were to be confirmed as refugees, allowing them full rights to family reunion and removing the insecurity of their uncertain status. Other former Yugoslav nationals, however, had to wait for their applications to be processed through the system, along with other asylum seekers. But asylum statistics show that before the Conservatives left office most were granted either refugee status or ELR. Out of 2,145 decisions in 1996, only 560 cases were refused after full consideration, a much smaller proportion compared to refusal rates for almost all other nationalities. High recognition rates continued in the early days of the new Labour government.

In his evaluation of the Bosnia programme,[69] Philip Rudge, General

Secretary of the European Council for Refugees and Exiles, noted that the handling of the refugee crisis showed both all that was good and bad about existing European refugee policy:

> On the territory itself, despite intolerable pressures and the daily confrontation with the appalling realities of ethnic discrimination, torture and murder, a massive humanitarian effort was mounted and saved many lives. Such a demonstration of personal commitment and institutional mobilisation indicates that the spirit of granting asylum to those in danger is still very much alive, despite the economic and social problems that currently preoccupy European governments and the lack of support for, even in many high political circles open hostility to, the work of the United Nations and international bodies. On the negative side we have witnessed the failure of the concept of safe haven in the region of conflict, the imposition by many European states of visas at a time of maximum human need, and the failure of what is officially known as 'burden sharing' ... among European states.

He concluded that there was 'still no mechanism in place which guarantees that refugees can be sure of protection ... and which assures public opinion that solidarity and responsibility is shared'.[70]

The government's unwillingness to grant refugee status to former Yugoslavs until 1996–97 reflected the hope that they would not become permanent residents and that the refugees, like the crisis itself, could be contained away from British soil or without the country's direct involvement. Yet the change of policy, leading to the majority of asylum seekers from former Yugoslavia being granted refugee status and enabling them to stay indefinitely in Britain, reflected that temporary protection is an ineffective solution to refugee problems. It was a policy which left those concerned in an ambiguous situation, always with the prospect of being returned to their former countries, making it difficult to adjust to life in Britain and to find work. Such status was also very hard for the government to revoke, with the future of the region concerned still uncertain and safety far from guaranteed for returnees. The repatriation of Bosnians from Germany has shown the worst failures of the provision of temporary protection, and raised the attendant danger of breaking international conventions which forbid the refoulement of refugees. As the century draws to a close, international solutions to the refugee crisis even within Europe have proved elusive. Comparisons were repeatedly made during the crisis in former Yugoslavia to the experiences of Jews in the Nazi era, but the responses shown exposed that little had been learnt about dealing with a refugee problem of similar scale to provide sanctuary for those in need.

Refugees from the Former Zaire:
The Context of Colour

In January 1989, Paul Weller of the European Churches Working Group on Refugees and Asylum, suggested that:

> The differential treatment accorded to white asylum seekers from European countries with Communist-led governments as compared with that meted out to black refugees from the Two-Thirds' World reveals the racism and political prejudice that pervades so much of our legal and administrative system.[1]

Asylum seekers have come to Britain from many African countries in the 1980s and 1990s, including Algeria, Angola, Ghana, Somalia, Nigeria and Zaire, but governmental responses to them have been laid open to charges of racism. These groups have not received anything approaching the publicity accorded to past refugee arrivals, or even contemporary groups, like the Kurds, indicating the marginal status accorded those from the African continent. As the century draws to a close, asylum seekers as a whole, but Africans in particular, have been regarded with suspicion and labelled as economic migrants seeking a better life rather than people fleeing persecution. As increasing numbers of asylum seekers come to Britain in the 1990s they have been scapegoated and denoted as 'bogus refugees'. On average between 1992 and 1996, only 5 per cent of asylum applicants were given refugee status, and in the case of some nationalities, including most Africans, refusal rates have been almost total.[2] While each arriving group has its own dynamics and history, the reception and response to and experience of the Zaireans reveals many of the issues raised by the recent arrival of many African asylum seekers.

THE ZAIREAN BACKGROUND

During President Mobutu's rule, beginning in 1965, oppression was considerable in Zaire. Following independence from Belgium on 30 June 1960, only a fragile nationhood was achieved, superimposing

> a parliamentary model on a people with no tradition of political organisation in the Western sense. Colonialism had crystallised ethnicity but controlled overt

confrontation. Ethnic loyalties were strengthened when political parties were hastily formed in the few months before independence.[3]

Even after the end of Belgium's nominal rule, the colonial legacy remained. The existence of some 200 ethnic groups within the country, with their own regional interests and social and economic divisions, ensured that political unity did not follow independence. Instead a conflict ensued in which the Belgians who remained in Zaire and their African sympathisers became a target of radicals who favoured African control. Tensions were exacerbated by ethnic competition and the rivalry between different political leaders, primarily, Joseph Kasavubu and Patrice Lumumba. The ensuing unrest led to a conflict which saw the intervention of both Belgian troops and UN peacekeeping forces. Continuing unrest paved the way for the military coup of General Mobutu in November 1965.

Mobutu's presidency, whilst initially promising the creation of a multi-party democracy, led to the consolidation of power by the president, through the Mouvement Populaire de la Revolution (MPR), and the creation of coercive apparatus to support his authoritarian regime which lasted over 30 years. Opposition was co-opted, eliminated or repressed. The leader established a personality cult, Mobutuism, to 'exalt the authoritarian state and the president as the agencies of national renovation, national independence and peace',[4] and suppressed popular dissent, partly through the use of force. Atrocities by the army against opposition activists and civilians, including arbitrary killings, looting and robbery, became a feature of the regime. In 1989 there were reports of rapes of schoolgirls in various regions and assaults against women who demonstrated in protest against deteriorating economic conditions in the capital, Kinshasa.[5] The secret police, the Agence national de documentation (AND) became an additional instrument of oppression.

In the 1990s low living standards and prolonged oppression brought increasing unrest:

> The situation changed radically in 1989 in response to the fall of the Berlin Wall in November and the subsequent prodemocracy movement in Eastern Europe and elsewhere. Resistance to the regime [became] more sustained, open, confrontational and violent. The MPR ... lost its legitimacy. To the man in the street, the party's acronym mean[t] mourir pour rien (to die for nothing), an indication of the blame placed on the regime for the socio-economic deprivation.[6]

Mobutu was forced to begin a 'dialogue with the people' in which Zaireans were allowed to express their views on national institutions. Criticism followed, but demands for change led to reprisals by the security forces. Uprisings by students, trade unions and the church brought open confrontation, including the killing of 100–150 students at Lubumbashi university campus on 9 May 1990. In April 1990 Mobutu announced that the one-party state would be abolished and a multi-party democracy established, but although outwardly

Mobutu's power decreased, he remained in control. Members of the opposition groups in Zaire were harassed by the military, using violent methods including sexual abuse. One Zairean refugee testified that:

> A group of soldiers would come to the house and some of these soldiers would search for UDPS material which, if they found it, they would destroy. Some soldiers would beat me up, question me and try to force me to say that I would leave the opposition. Other soldiers would concentrate on my wife and sister. They would often force me to watch what they were doing to [them].[7]

Another described the situation in late 1993:

> You have different factions of military accountable to nobody... You are not certain when you go to bed tonight, whether you are going to wake up alive tomorrow morning. In that climate, I think sending someone back to Zaire is signing a death warrant.[8]

It has been suggested that 'the international system has been a crucial source of support for the Mobutuist state'.[9] Western powers favoured the stability Mobutu offered because Zaire was seen as strategically important and a useful ally in central Africa. Belgian and French intervention in the riots of autumn 1991 was seen as further evidence of Western attempts to support and protect a repressive government. In 1992 a Sovereign National Conference (CNS) formulated a new constitution and enacted legislation establishing a transitional government, directly challenging Mobutu. Subsequently, the US State Department noted that there was a 'turbulent contest for political leadership between the governments of Etienne Tshisekedi and Faustin Birindwa'.[10] Belgium, France and the United States 'evacuated their citizens, virtually eliminated their diplomatic presence in the country, and suspended aid in view of escalating political and economic instability and Mobutu's failure to appoint a credible and legitimate transition government'.[11] Western attitudes varied over Mobutu, and the question of his removal, but it was not until 1997 that the President was forced to give up power after conflict in the Great Lakes region of east Africa embroiled Zaire. The presence of Rwandan refugees exacerbated ethnic tensions in the east of the country and prompted a revolt by Banyamulenge ethnic Tutsis and other groups which observers believed was supported by Rwanda and Uganda. Opposition movements in the country were given a boost and one of their leaders, Laurent Kabila, was able to take advantage of the situation to seize power and declare himself ruler of the renamed country – the Democratic Republic of Congo. The change in power prompted an exodus of refugees. Mobutu, now an aged dictator, living in Europe and undergoing medical treatment, was both unwilling and unable to prevent the demise of his regime. He died soon after the challenge to his power. In 1998 the Democratic Republic of Congo's highly volatile and unstable situation continued to leave its people subject to violence and prey to further mass uprooting with different groups vying for control of the nation.

THE ZAIREAN REFUGEE MOVEMENT

It was in this context that at the start of the 1990s the number of asylum seekers coming to western Europe from Zaire increased. According to the UNHCR in 1995:

> The most important cause of flight of Zairean refugees during the past decade has been ethnic conflict and political and inter-communal violence. There has also been internal displacement due to ethnic conflict in the Shaba province and in the Kasai Provinces, aggravating an already serious humanitarian crisis in these regions. In March 1993, the ethnic conflict spread to North Kivu Province resulting in further internal mass displacement. Over 775,000 Zaireans were uprooted from their homes by the end of 1994 (and) some 600,000 persons, mainly Kasaians from Shaba Province and persons from the Kivu province were internally displaced.[12]

The total of 74,000 Zaireans applying for asylum between 1990 and 1994 constituted some 3 per cent of all asylum seekers in Europe. In 1991 the number of asylum applications from Zaireans was 21,000, falling to 9,300 in 1994. But the UNHCR suggested that 'Convention status as well as humanitarian recognitions of Zairean asylum seekers remained relatively low compared to other nationalities'.[13] Britain, which received almost a quarter of the Zairean asylum applications in western Europe, saw applications increase from 525 in 1989 to 2,590 in 1990 and 7,010 in 1991.[14] In 1991, Zairean nationals comprised over a quarter of the applications for asylum from Africa recorded by the Home Office and were the largest national group seeking asylum in the UK, comprising some 17 per cent of the total. British arrivals were, however, tiny in comparison with the number of Zaireans reaching Swaziland and Angola, each estimated to have received about 20,000 or more people between 1990 and 1992.[15] As western Europe sought to curtail asylum movements, the vast majority of refugees continued to be sheltered in neighbouring countries with fewer resources, making a mockery of the economic arguments used by Western commentators to refuse refugees entry.

The Zaireans arriving in Britain were not supported by the British government partly because their homeland was not a priority on the international political agenda, in contrast to the Middle East and countries in the former Soviet Union.[16] As the number of asylum seekers from Zaire increased, conversely the Conservative government of Margaret Thatcher showed growing signs of hostility. A visa was imposed on Zairean nationals seeking entry into Britain, a well-known measure of deterrence making it harder for asylum seekers to come. Those fleeing persecution were unlikely to be able to wait for visas to be processed as it involved risking the danger of alerting their presence to the very authorities they were seeking to flee. No resettlement initiatives were undertaken to assist Zairean nationals, or, later to provide effective international protection to nationals of Rwanda and Burundi who, in the mid-1990s, faced a crisis of even greater proportions as conflict between ethnic Hutus and Tutsis led to the flight of hundreds of thousands of people to neighbouring countries, including Zaire.[17] In 1994–96, increasing ethnic tensions prompted further conflict in which tens of thousands of Zaireans fled to Rwanda and Uganda.[18]

In spite of this serious crisis, the UNHCR noted that Britain was far less generous than other states in its recognition of Zairean applications. While 330 Zaireans (9 per cent of all decisions taken) were granted refugee status or humanitarian leave to remain in the Netherlands from 1990–94, only 170 were given such status in the UK (1 per cent of all decisions).[19] The restricted level of British assistance to refugees in the region contrasted with the (albeit limited) initiatives taken to assist former Yugoslav refugees through temporary resettlement, and the international efforts to establish a safe haven in Iraq for the protection of the Kurds. Zaireans, along with other African groups of asylum seekers, have, according to many, encountered racism in British asylum determination procedures, becoming more sharply evident as the 1990s have progressed, with by far the majority of Africans refused refugee status. Between 1992 and 1997, the only African nationals gaining exceptional leave to remain in large numbers were Somali and Sudanese applicants, and, in 1992–93, Ugandan and Ethiopian asylum seekers. Between 1992 and 1996, of 9,250 decisions made on Zairean cases, only 55 were granted refugee status, 75 exceptional leave to remain and the remainder, over 9,000, were rejected, a refusal rate of 99 per cent.[20]

The particular antipathy faced by the Zaireans was manifested in the practice of detention.[21] Under immigration rules those seeking asylum in Britain could be detained at the behest of immigration officials. This arbitrary practice was usually used in asylum cases to hold people seeking entry to Britain without the required travel documents. This was in conflict with international guidelines from the UNHCR that asylum seekers might have to seek entry in this way due to the desperate nature of their plight.[22] The power of detention resulted in the confinement of hundreds of asylum seekers (up to 800 at any one time), sometimes alongside convicted criminals, with no automatic right to an independent judicial review of the decision to detain them, no requirement for written reasons to be given to them to explain why they were being held and no maximum time limit on their detention. While not even convicted criminals were subject to such practices in Britain, individuals seeking refuge, in some cases having fled imprisonment and torture in their own country, could be confined in prisons at vast cost both in economic and humanitarian terms for periods of up to a year.[23] One Algerian asylum seeker, detained in Campsfield Detention Centre near Oxford, wrote to Amnesty International that 'Today is my birthday and I'm in such a hopeless situation that I wish I was never born ... I did nothing to deserve it, I only wanted peace and to be free. This prison without hope and faith to survive, is hell. Please help me.'[24]

It was alleged that 'The Home Office plays it down, but a higher proportion of Zaireans are detained than most other nationalities'.[25] Members of a group against the detention of asylum seekers further argued that since 1990,

> Zairean asylum seekers arriving in the UK have received some of the harshest treatment of all nationalities. Many have been detained on arrival, often for months. Even those with competent solicitors and those with physical evidence of torture have been refused refugee status. Some have been returned to Kinshasa under guard. Most of these have never been heard of again and are presumed dead. The majority are ... liable to detention at any time.[26]

As one Zairean commented, getting temporary admission to Britain had become extremely difficult: 'There are cases of people applying for asylum that will have to wait for seven or eight months before they can actually be accepted as asylum seekers, and in the meantime they are liable to be detained and even deported'.[27]

The Zaireans' reception came at a time of increasing hostility towards asylum seekers. At the height of the Zairean exodus in 1991, the British government was in the process of introducing legislation to crack down on asylum seekers. In November it was reported that its Asylum Bill 'was far tougher than expected and imposed formidable hurdles in the way of people trying to find sanctuary in Britain'. Though Ministers accepted that their plans were 'bound to have an effect on some genuine asylum seekers', Kenneth Baker, the Home Secretary, stated that 'the refugee issue had to be tackled', dismissing 'Labour accusations that he was playing the race card in the run-up to the general election'. The growth in asylum claims from 5,000 in 1988 to 30,000 in 1990 which were expected to reach 46,000 in 1991 meant that it 'would be highly irresponsible for any government not to react to this influx'. Baker added that there was evidence 'of racketeers helping bogus refugees claim asylum'. The Bill proposed to 'severely tighten the tests fugitives have to pass before they are accepted as genuine'. The increase in fines for airlines carrying passengers to the UK without the proper documents encouraged them to make 'stringent checks' before letting a refugee on board. Peter Lloyd, the Immigration Minister, accepted that a man in fear of his life would be unlikely to queue for the correct documents at a British embassy before he fled. He added that a refugee denied a seat on a flight could still leave a despotic country by crossing land borders into a neighbouring state but 'If that country is designated as "safe" by the Home Office, then the refugee would be automatically disqualified from moving on to claim asylum in Britain'.[28]

The Asylum Bill of 1991, which became law as the Asylum and Immigration (Appeals) Act in 1993, introduced various new procedures. As well as the positive measure allowing asylum seekers to appeal against refusal of their applications, several draconian changes were made, limiting asylum seekers' access to housing, introducing fingerprinting of asylum seekers, increasing the fine for carriers bringing illegal entrants to Britain to £2,000 and introducing the practice of returning asylum seekers to third countries if they had passed through a 'safe third country' in transit to the UK.[29] The Act marked the continued process of closing the doors on asylum seekers. Home Secretary Kenneth Baker explicitly outlined that its purpose was to 'restrain the number of people who come to this country as asylum seekers'.[30]

In June 1994, Alfred Banya, representative of the National Union of Refugee Organisations (NURO), reported that since the Act, his organisation had been inundated with calls for help. This was not only for asylum seekers detained at ports of entry or in prisons and detention centres, but also those

> who are legitimately in the UK who are increasingly being picked up off the streets by police officers, questioned, harassed, abused and detained. Simple incidents such as domestic quarrels in black families have instead increasingly led to detention of people on suspicion of being illegal immigrants... If we reflect on the criteria of people being detained in the UK for asylum or immigration matters we will find that it is mainly people of colour, black people. In terms of nationalities, NURO comes across mainly non-English speaking people from Algeria, Zaire and Angola. Apart from nationality and colour, the criteria for detention remains baffling.[31]

THE USE OF DETENTION AND THE ASSAULT ON ASYLUM

At a conference calling for the release of asylum seeking detainees, Margaret Finnegan of the Stop the Detentions Action Group, suggested that the new legislation was racially discriminatory. Referring to many Zaireans visited in detention centres, she described how several who had claimed asylum as soon as they arrived in the country had been imprisoned, being held for as long as eight to nine months. In particular, she made reference to a young couple who were in a state of great fear. The man was detained at Harmondsworth in London, then transferred to Haslar and Winchester prisons in Hampshire, while the woman was given temporary admission and sent to London:

> Neither could speak any English. She did not even know how to find the place where her husband was detained and ... had no money for fares as she was only receiving less than £30 per week income support because of her age. The first time I met him in Harmondsworth he was extremely distressed and did not know where his wife was. Eventually he was sent back to Zaire but she disappeared in London.[32]

Most asylum seekers now enter Britain at airports in London or come via the Channel Tunnel or on ferries arriving on the Kent coast. Hampshire's significance for refugees now rests, as was noted with the Kurds, as a major centre of detention. Haslar Prison near Gosport, Harmondsworth Detention Centre near Heathrow Airport, and the purpose-built Campsfield Detention Centre near Oxford, are the three main centres used to accommodate immigration detainees, including asylum seekers. The testimony of a Zairean shows how the county has been touched by current government policy. Arriving in Britain in October 1989:

> As soon as I entered the airport and before I could utter a word of my mission I was dragged into a small room, where I was stripped naked by two customs officers. They claimed it was an airport formality carried out on any passenger suspected of carrying drugs...

The next day he was interviewed 'by an immigration officer who appeared to be putting words into my mouth. The interview was brief, which did not allow me to express myself fully. Questions demanded quick answers. Oh my, it was a complete intimidation.' Five days later he was transferred to Harmondsworth detention centre where 'You made friends today and tomorrow they were gone. People came and went as day and night, and it was like sitting on a time bomb wondering when yours would go off'. He was then transferred to Haslar, '80 miles from London. My dreams and hopes were shattered as contact with relations and my solicitor were no longer easy and communication on the telephone was more costly':

> During my stay in Haslar I found the situation like being jailed for life. Nobody informed me about the progress of my case; no court recommended me to be detained; I was only told I was not entitled to bail rights. All I could do was sit and wait. Some of us chose hunger strikes as a means to draw attention to our plight; others saw suicide as a way out of their predicament. As a political activist I got involved in various environmental issues. Dynamism was my motto... On 22 February 1990 the good news finally reached me that I had been granted exceptional leave to remain in the UK. I was not very impressed as my bones were near to breaking point and I felt rather bitter. The ordeal of my detention has not been easy to recover from. After being released I can say the compensation is not enough even to release me from nightmares about what I had undergone...[33]

Such experiences were not isolated: another Zairean, also held at Haslar, found it 'shocking to come from a country like my own, where democratic norms are constantly being upset and where illegal detention almost cost me my life only to find myself in prison again after all the efforts made to save my life'.[34] The criminality associated with detention has caused many asylum seekers to feel humiliated and misunderstood. The power to detain asylum seekers exists in other countries. But nowhere is it used as in Britain to detain entrants at the *beginning* of the asylum process before any accurate assessment can be made of the nature of a claim, suggesting that detention is intended as a deterrent to entry. One Zairean described detention as feeling like a 'caged animal':

> Is it a crime to be an asylum seeker in the UK? I am saddened and powerless in the face of this situation in a civilised country where human rights are respected. I have suffered and I continue to suffer psychologically and mentally

since, as an asylum seeker, I am given this unsound treatment... God alone knows how many tears I have shed and how much suffering I have endured every night.[35]

Kenneth Osei-Afriyie, a Ghanaian asylum seeker who was detained in Pentonville Prison, referred to the Zaireans he had known there at a conference on detention. He made special mention of the 50 Zaireans there because 'perhaps due to the cultural shock or the language problem, they looked more disoriented than anybody else'.[36] As a fellow African, he tried to

> raise their morale, but when I began by saying, 'Are you all right?' their response would be 'Oh, oh not all right ... prison no good ... British no good ... at all'. It sounded amusing when they said this, but the desperation behind these words was amply manifested at night... Then the Zaireans, unable to cope any longer, start banging their doors and shouting at the same time, 'Liberté! Liberté! Liberté!' ... [reaching] a crescendo which bec[ame] really deafening.

Adding that such distress was not unique to the Zaireans, he concluded that 'it demands a great degree of resilience and fortitude to survive in such regimental conditions. One is constantly haunted at night and feels haggard in the day'.[37]

In addition to detention, Zaireans were subject to further legislative measures designed to reduce immigrant inflows, threatening their right to seek international protection. As well as the 1987 Immigration Carriers Liability Act, whereby airlines have become subject to fines for bringing illegal immigrants to Britain,[38] the government also increasingly used the 'safe third country rule' to deport asylum seekers to other European countries, on the basis that applicants should claim asylum in the first safe country they reached. This rule, part of European attempts to harmonise asylum procedures, has been used to return people to countries where they may have only been in transit. In one instance it was reported that a Zairean asylum seeker arriving in Britain during December 1992 was refused entry and returned to France having stopped there for just a few hours. The danger of this practice is that other countries may refuse the asylum seeker entry, as occurred in this case when the man was returned to Britain on the same day. It has encouraged a situation of 'refugees in orbit', risking undermining the international principle of 'non-refoulement' with people being shuttled as 'human cargo' from one country to another and returning them to the country of origin without proper assessment of their claim.[39]

The Zaireans, like many present-day refugees, face growing suspicion whether their fears of persecution are genuine. The case of Adrien Kabongo, a Zairean national, shows how it is not always possible to separate economic and political persecution as British law requires. Kabongo's plans to leave Zaire were based on his belief that he was persecuted because he had been

> denied the right to make a living and feed his family... After his company's offices were wrecked and the owners fled the country, Adrien was put on

technical leave. He is paid a third of his former salary, but with inflation out of control, a month's pay buys food for just ten days.[40]

Economic and political motives for flight have become increasingly blurred in a world where transport to far-off places is now easily accessible. The Zaireans, one immigration official believed, were one of the most difficult national groups on which to make decisions.[41]

RESPONSES TO ZAIREANS IN BRITAIN

Zaireans have fled to many countries, including neighbouring Congo, but after the Congolese authorities started forcibly removing people, they had to look elsewhere for sanctuary. Ironically, Britain has been chosen as a destination partly because of its image as a just society welcoming the oppressed. Adrien Kabongo explained that he knew

> from friends living in France and Belgium that most of them would like to leave and go to England. A lot of Zaireans preferred to go to France or Belgium because there they could speak French. But according to what they are saying, England is better if you are black. In France and Belgium, it is very difficult to be black, very difficult to get work. People do not like us.[42]

Such impressions of more favourable treatment in Britain reflect the publicity given on Zairean television to the anti-immigrant stance of France's National Front leader Jean Marie Le Pen. In Britain, too, however, Zaireans have met considerable hostility. According to Kukwikila Muzemba of the Association of Zairean refugees in London:

> It is a very sad situation that Zairean people, despite all the political problems going on in Zaire at the moment, have been marginalised in this country, being called economic migrants. There are no such people as economic migrants. People are fleeing the political situation. I myself don't know whether my brother-in-law will be alive tomorrow, because he turned down a ministerial post.[43]

As another commentator has suggested:

> The ideology of 'bogus refugees' reflects the double vision of the West on the issue. Refugees who stay where they are, dying in the mountains of Iraq or starving in refugee camps in Africa, are 'real' and victims to be pitied; those who attempt to get to the West are 'bogus', adventurers in search of a better life, and are to be deterred, detected and removed.[44]

Abusers of the system undoubtedly exist. But detention even before any investigation of an asylum application has begun, which for some applicants has meant waiting over five years for a decision and subsequent deportation if refugee status is not granted, may encourage people to evade the system.

Government practice of returning Zaireans has, indeed, led to life-threatening situations. One Zairean seeking asylum in Britain was deported in a case later found to be unlawful in a 'landmark ruling'.[45] Home Secretary Kenneth Baker was held to be in contempt of court when he ignored a judge's instructions regarding a Zairean teacher from Kinshasa. The man was deported despite last minute requests for a judicial review by his lawyers. A High Court Order was obtained for the man to be brought back to Britain but this was ignored by the Home Secretary. David Burgess, the solicitor involved, stated that the Home Office had treated the case 'as a matter of no consequence. They just wanted to get rid of the man'.[46] The ramifications of this judgement were seen as far-reaching, particularly for immigration and asylum cases. Judges could make significant interventions ordering the Home Office not to deport asylum seekers until their case had been heard. Nevertheless, following a judgement of the House of Lords, Baker was not punished. Lord Woolf argued that the contempt of court ruling was 'sufficient to "vindicate the requirements of justice". It was for Parliament to "determine what should be the consequences of that finding"'.[47]

In debate in the House of Commons in December 1991 about the case, Baker received considerable support from fellow party members, but there was criticism from the Opposition. Jeremy Corbyn, Labour MP for Islington North, asked whether

> the Home Secretary [was] aware that his decision ... put that Zairean teacher in an extremely dangerous and vulnerable position and that it is not the first time that his Department has deported people in the face of a court decision that they should remain in this country?

Not surprisingly, Corbyn's plea that Baker should 'withdraw the Asylum Bill under consideration and instead institute a proper system of legal appeal that gives automatic rights of appeal to asylum seekers and does not leave them at the mercy of his erroneous decisions' was ignored.[48]

Despite the importance of this action by the Home Secretary, the government was not held to account for his actions. Human rights activists were appalled. *The Guardian* was one of the few papers to devote significant coverage to the situation of Zairean refugees in Britain. On the same day as reporting the judgement against Baker, it carried an article about the death of the Zairean asylum seeker, Omasase Lumumba. This man was the nephew of the murdered Zairean President Patrice Lumumba. He had survived torture in his own country only to die in a British prison following his arrest in south London, in September 1991, over the alleged theft of a bicycle, a charge which was never pursued. Held under the Immigration Act 1971, he was reported to have become depressed and angry. Unable to comprehend his imprisonment, he refused an order to return to his cell and was taken to the punishment block by six officers. When a doctor was called to sedate him he was found dead. Although the cause of death was uncertain, the pathologist stated that 'there was a "strong possibility" he had suffered an acute cardiac arrest following a prolonged struggle against restraint'.[49] It was reported that a fellow prisoner had testified to seeing officers standing on Lumumba and kicking him. The officers said they had only applied approved control and restraint techniques. By an eight to one majority jurors decided Lumumba had died 'as the result of the use of improper methods and excessive force in the process of control and restraint'.[50]

The death of Omasase Lumumba and the lack of punishment for the perpetrators exacerbated concern about the treatment of asylum seekers. Firstly, it raised alarm about restraint methods used in prisons. Police and security officials' brutality had aroused deep unease in several immigration cases, the most famous being that of the illegal immigrant Joy Gardner, who died during attempted deportation proceedings. Secondly, Lumumba's case suggested the presence of racial prejudice and a disturbing and damaging level of ignorance among immigration officials dealing with asylum seekers. In court it transpired that the immigration officer who questioned Mr Lumumba knew little of Zaire and had never heard of his uncle.[51] If immigration officers were not informed about political conditions abroad, it is questionable whether asylum seekers could receive a fair hearing in Britain.

The dubious treatment of Zaireans at the hands of the Home Office, immigration officials and prison officers in the 1990s, has been reinforced by much of the British press which has done little to promote their cause. The tabloids have been quick to portray Zaireans as fraudulent 'crooks', especially following the discovery of several individuals making false claims for social security, a recurrent theme in coverage of asylum issues. On 12 December 1991, *The Sun* carried an article entitled, 'The Bogus Refugee on £1,250 a week'.[52] The *Daily Mail* carried a story in which 'One man was using fifty names to rake in £8,000 a week' in a huge 'benefits racket' whilst the *News of the World* commented 'This man has 15 names and gets benefit on them all'.[53] Such negative imagery of asylum seekers fails to reflect how benefits fraud was the practice of only a small number of people, the majority of whom were in fact British, but hostile coverage even extended to the broadsheets. In October 1994, for example, *The Daily Telegraph* reported on 'Immigrants in benefit fraud trial'.[54]

The general tone can be explored further with a detailed examination of *The Sun* article. The Zairean individual was described as a man who 'looked like a wealthy businessman, lived in a smart house and travelled to Paris to buy designer clothes', but was a 'smooth-talking African', one of 'an estimated 70,000 bogus asylum-seekers living illegally in Britain'.[55] The man was said to have first left Zaire for Belgium but then came to Britain, 'where it is easier to obtain social security handouts'. The blatantly hostile report considered the arrest of 'Albert' and his wife along with seven other men as only 'the tip of the iceberg', stating that in north London alone 56 houses were under surveillance. It concluded by giving details of a further six cases of social security fraud by asylum seekers, of which two were stated to involve Zaireans.[56]

Organisations working for asylum seekers have been forced on to the defensive by such overtly negative media coverage. Lord Alf Dubs, then Chief Executive of the Refugee Council, countered such inflammatory reports, deploring the Home Secretary's attempts:

> to inflame the British public with statements about huge numbers of 'bogus' asylum seekers flooding our country when the numbers are not huge and the vast majority come from countries where there is a total breakdown of law and order and where human rights abuses are the norm. Raising the spectre of the bogus refugee is a cheap trick at the expense of asylum seekers for the purpose of political gain.[57]

LOCAL RESPONSES AND ZAIREAN REFUGEES IN HAMPSHIRE

Responses in Winchester to Zaireans serve as a microcosm of national debates and reveal the conflicting attitudes asylum issues arouse in Britain during the 1990s. In Hampshire contact with asylum seekers was largely confined to those who had been detained. By the 1990s some 80–90 per cent of refugees were estimated to live in London, and most of the remainder in other large cities. The county was not a major area of settlement but local newspapers reflected national debates about 'bogus' entrants applying for asylum in Britain, provoking fears of an unmanageable alien mass of people coming to the region to take jobs and housing.[58] Local activists campaigning against detention were given coverage when several Zairean asylum seekers, on hunger-strike to publicise their cause, were transferred from Haslar to Winchester Prison. Sir John Alleyne of the Winchester Action Group for Asylum Seekers (WAGAS), stated that the Zaireans were protesting that

> they came to this country applying for asylum under the Geneva Convention, not accused of crime. They came from Zaire in distress and the Government recognises that it is a nasty place. Everyone should be amazed that innocent people are put in prison.[59]

But publicity about 'bogus refugees' had permeated public consciousness and given Zaireans, among other groups, a bad name. It was intensified when a Zairean, whose bail had been put up by WAGAS, absconded, fearing that he would be deported by the Home Secretary. Members of WAGAS defended their support of the Zaireans, pointing out that 'the Home Office don't seem to be acknowledging that Zaire has exploded and is on the verge of civil war. They shouldn't return anyone to Zaire regardless of whether their case is genuine or not.' Sir John Alleyne added that WAGAS believed that detention was unlawful:

> These are innocent people and they should not be put in prison. We are concerned about their general health. We urge the Government to act justly and to keep to the Geneva Convention. It should put a priority on getting them out of prison.

The *Hampshire Chronicle* elicited the views of an immigration spokesman at the Home Office to comment on this local controversy. In spite of the hunger strike and the obvious distress of the people concerned he said that there was 'nothing unusual about their cases. There is a massive backlog of asylum seekers, around 50,000. Only a minority are kept in detention for fear they will abscond'.[60]

The context of the disappearance of the individual was thus given some perspective. Nevertheless, it prompted considerable acrimony in the local press including a letter from a Winchester resident asking:

> Why are the action group still supporting these particular detainees who have now quickly reverted to attempting blackmail to support their cause? What a way to treat a host country, first they enter illegally, then quickly complain their accommodation is unacceptable, followed by a hunger strike which indicates them using threats and blackmail by saying: 'we're here now, let us stay or we will starve ourselves to death and it will be your fault!!'[61]

Sir John Alleyne was quick to reply, reaffirming support for the asylum seekers,[62] and later expressing his deep concern over a Zairean held at Winchester Prison who was refused leave to remain and then deported.[63] In his initial asylum application this Zairean tried to convince immigration officers that he was genuinely at risk. He believed he was a wanted man because as secretary of a club in Kinshasa he had refused to let it be transformed into a youth party supporting Mobutu, despite the offer of bribes in the form of 'presents, transport and other gifts':

> I was arrested in the street and taken to a military camp. It was night. I don't know which camp – there were many. The club president and vice president were also arrested and taken to the same camp. We were ill-treated. We were put in dark cells, no light, hardly any food. We were there for three and a half months ... the Club President died. He was found dead. The soldiers told us. We were afraid we would be next. We didn't know what had happened to him. My family didn't know I was there. There was an officer who asked me my name. I was crying. I spoke to him in Swahili, my maternal language, and told him of my origins. He was also of the same origins and took pity on me. He helped me escape... He gave me a military uniform as a disguise. He took me to his house. I spent the night there and the next day he did the necessary to help me escape. He took my parents' address. He bought me my clothes. He took me to Ndjili airport, to a depot where he put me on the plane...[64]

After landing at Heathrow he immediately claimed asylum and was briefly held at Harmondsworth detention centre, before transfer to Pentonville Prison where he remained for over six months. He was then moved to Haslar where he learnt that there would be further delays in dealing with his case, provoking him to go on hunger strike. Consequently he was removed to Winchester Prison. After almost a year of detention in British prisons he was deported back to Zaire on the basis that his situation failed to convince the Home Secretary that he had a 'well-founded fear of persecution'. In informing the individual that asylum was being refused, the Immigration and Nationality Department of the Home Office reviewed the testimony he had given. Revealing their general antipathy to such cases, they noted that:

> you have not provided any evidence to substantiate your claim. Moreover it is considered unlikely, in view of the current political situation, that you would incur harassment or persecution simply because you refused to join the youth party supporting Mobutu and even if you had incurred some discrimination [the Home Secretary] considers the account of how you escaped detention and fled Zaire to be implausible. There is no suggestion that your family experienced any difficulty with the 'authorities' or that you incurred problems in reaching the airport. The Secretary of State further considers that the fact that you did not approach the Nigerian authorities for assistance also casts doubt on your claim to be in need of international protection.

His chances were also undermined because he failed to apply for asylum coming out of Nigeria, despite the endemic human rights abuses in that country, which in itself prompted the flight of over 15,000 asylum seekers to Britain from 1986 to 1996. His refusal letter continued that Nigeria was a signatory to the 1951 United Nations Convention Relating to the Status of Refugees:

> The Secretary of State is satisfied, on the basis of his knowledge of the policies and practices of the Nigerian authorities that they would have considered any such application in accordance with their obligations as a signatory to the 1951 ... Convention.[65]

It should be added that the US State Department has described prison conditions in Zaire as 'life threatening' and the authorities are known to have killed individuals in similar circumstances.[66]

In exile, the Zaireans have attempted to help themselves and highlight their cause. But as detainees, many have little bargaining power and the only way they know to gain attention is to go on hunger strike. Such activities have not been confined to Haslar Prison or to Zaireans alone. According to the Detention Advisory Group, there is at least one hunger strike likely to be going on at any point in time at some detention centre in Britain.[67] The hunger strike at Haslar in March 1993, however, was dealt with particularly harshly. On 19 April 1993, the Zaireans there, some of whom had been detained for months, decided to send a letter to the Home Secretary. They were depressed, and also concerned about one of their group who was in constant pain, talking of suicide and allegedly denied medical attention for a tropical illness. Their 'request for temporary admission' was signed by ten Zaireans:

> [Y]ou are not unaware of the state of political crisis prevailing in our country at the moment, nor the traumatic state of mind we are suffering. That is why we are now asking you to deal favourably with our cases within the brief period of one week, beginning on April 19th, granting us Temporary Admission until the situation at home returns to normal. At the end of this period, you will be responsible for any consequences that follow.[68]

The Stop the Detentions Action Group stated that these refugees awaited their reply calmly – there were no boycotts, hunger strikes or 'acts of indiscipline' as later alleged by an immigration officer. The reaction to the letter was to remove the Zaireans the next day from Haslar, hand-cuffed together in pairs, and to disperse them to prisons at Winchester, Dorchester, Lewes and Sutton. A solicitor interviewing another client on 20 April was told to leave the building as her 'life was in danger'. Apparently, prison authorities wanted no one to witness the removals, especially if the Zaireans resisted. A regular prison visitor arriving that day was simply told that 'All the Zaireans have gone.' Other detainees did not know what had happened to the Zaireans and were very concerned. Two of the 'Haslar Ten' were able to telephone solicitors and a friend the next morning to inform them of the events. They requested that their letter and story be communicated widely. However, a copy of the letter was said to be attached to all the men's files, and some reported being told in writing it would 'cost them dearly' in relation to their applications for asylum. Two of the ten were pressurised into signing papers revoking their claims for asylum until friends and solicitors intervened.

As of August 1993 two of the 'Haslar Ten' had been released with Temporary Admission, one had been sent back to Zaire, with no news of his whereabouts, two others had their claim to asylum refused and were awaiting deportation. One of those that the Home Office tried to deport was Meya Mangete who, because of his fear of being killed upon arrival in Kinshasa, resisted and was severely beaten. He was returned to prison with 'facial injuries inflicted by police'. His solicitor pursued the assault matter and tried to lodge an appeal but Mangete was deported in November. Amnesty International confirm that he was initially arrested by the authorities, but was then released and subsequently fled to Luanda, Angola.[69] Meya Mangete gave a statement to the Zairean Community Association articulating his feelings before being deported:

> I don't know what crime I have committed to … serve a prison sentence as I am only an asylum seeker. I don't want to spend all of my life in this country either, but I need assurance of democratic freely conducted elections under international supervision before I return to my country. Why are we treated like illegal immigrants or enemies? Immigration and the Home Office are simply not aware of the problems in my country Zaire.[70]

CONCLUSION: THE FUTURE OF ASYLUM

In 1995, the UNHCR reported that 'security forces loyal to President Mobutu have repeatedly harassed political opponents who have returned to the country'. It added that 'Some opponents who found refuge in neighbouring countries (Congo, Burundi and Uganda) have been kidnapped by Zairean security forces and imprisoned in Zaire.' In 1998 violence continued to be a feature of the new regime in the Democratic Republic of Congo, as reported by Amnesty International and other human rights groups.

When in 1994 the United Nations Committee against Torture examined a case of a Zairean whose refugee status in Switzerland was rejected, they ruled that 'he could not be returned to his country because there was a real risk that he would be in danger of being detained and subjected to torture on account of his ethnic origin and alleged political connections'. In spite of such reports and rulings many European countries, including Britain, have deported Zaireans to an unknown fate in their homeland.[71]

In order to combat the general prejudice, distrust and disbelief that they encountered in Britain and elsewhere, a group of Zairean asylum seekers formed a Community Association in 1991 called Lisanga. One member, Bob Ilunga, highlighted their aims and the problems faced:

> Firstly we have to educate our own people about British society and their legal rights. And then we need to inform the British about the Zairean situation ... of course there are problems with some people coming to this country. But ... the administration is corrupt, and obtaining Zairean papers is very easy, whether you are Angolan, Ugandan or from many other parts of Africa. So there are some people from Africa who will obtain Zairean papers which are bogus, come to the UK and make false claims for social benefits. Of course there are cheats, as there are cheats from this country... It also happened in France and Belgium, where everybody assumed that every African in the street was Zairean... We have had a bad experience in Belgium and France, which explains, since 1989, the increase in the UK of Zairean refugees.[72]

The Zaireans clearly feel they face a tide of hostility. Until the crisis in 1997, when Kabila seized power, there were few reports on the political situation in Zaire in the British press. At a popular level, the Zaireans have certainly not received the same concern with which the Kurds were greeted in 1989. They have been forced on to the defensive by negative perceptions of them. Bob Ilunga explains that it is important to understand

> the type of society that Zairean refugees come from. Most of us fled in our twenties. We have known no other government than cruel dictatorship. Refugees have never had votes, experience of free speech or any human rights. We find it difficult to understand the benefits of a democratic society. We now have to educate them into understanding what democracy is. We also have to re-learn many human responses which are common for British people but not for us. We are often seen as an unfriendly people. This is not true, but our culture has suffered during the years of dictatorship. We no longer have the words for 'sorry' or 'please' in our country...[73]

Reports of police and government antipathy towards asylum seekers add to their unease. One Nigerian died when an immigration official and two police officers burst into his house in a raid and he 'fell to his death' from a window.[74] Widespread belief that the police carry out physical abuse of black people has inspired little confidence in its treatment of black asylum seekers.[75]

As the 1990s progressed, activities by the Conservative Home Secretary Michael Howard also fuelled refugees' fears about their status in Britain. In 1995, a crisis over Home Office funding left the Refugee Legal Centre doubting its ability to deal with increasing numbers of appeals by asylum seekers.[76] Other agencies working with refugees were also threatened with massive cuts in 1996. In 1995, Howard outlined plans to give employers a legal duty, backed by heavy penalties, to crack down on illegal immigrants in the workforce, one of the clauses of the subsequent Asylum and Immigration Act, enacted in July 1996. Anti-racist organisations feared the impact this would have on black people in the job market. Narendra Makanji, chair of the Anti-Racist Alliance, commented that 'Illegal immigrant has become a euphemism for black, and black people will become the objects of suspicion. They will be required to produce passports and documents, while white people will be assumed to be legal'.[77]

On 5 February 1996 the Social Security Secretary, Peter Lilley, announced new regulations restricting asylum seekers' access to benefits. Already denied the right to work for the first six months in Britain, and able to claim only 90 per cent of income support levels received by UK nationals, many asylum seekers were now denied even the right to basic housing and food for subsistence. The changes removed entitlement to a range of benefits from those asylum seekers submitting their applications in-country and those who had been refused asylum but were appealing against this decision. The only evident logic was that it was considered that 'genuine' refugees would apply as soon as they arrived in the country and thus remain eligible for benefits. But the government's own statistics revealed that the majority of people granted refugee status were in-country applicants.[78] The changes also overlooked the many valid reasons individuals would have for applying once they were safely in the country – not only the fear they may be undergoing after fleeing their homeland, or not being able to speak English, but also that they may not know anything about asylum procedures in Britain. In addition, it is only a change in circumstances after coming to Britain which may require some individuals to claim asylum having entered first as visitors or students. The effect of these draconian measures was to leave many asylum seekers homeless and destitute in Britain.[79] A Zairean woman affected by the changes, who was staying with the Ockenden Venture in Surrey, was described as 'very isolated' in a tracking project carried out by the Refugee Council. Speaking only Swahili, which was not spoken by any Ockenden Venture staff, and living away from friends in London, she survived on £10 a week. Her anxiety was reinforced by concern about her husband and children who were still in Zaire.[80]

Opposition to the government measures came from all quarters, including human rights activists, lawyers, religious groups, members of the judiciary, the House of Lords and perhaps most significantly, the government's own advisory committee on social security. Opposition was such that a legal challenge succeeded in overturning the regulations, requiring primary legislation to enable them to become effective. The passage of the Asylum and Immigration Bill, however, provided an immediate opportunity for the government to reintroduce the changes. A House of Lords' amendment seeking to allow asylum seekers three days' grace, during which time they could apply for asylum after arrival in the UK and still be entitled to benefits, was narrowly defeated.

But opposition continued, with thousands of people attending demonstrations against the Asylum and Immigration Bill in Trafalgar Square. Although the Act was passed later in 1996, legal challenges led to a ruling by the High Court which restored some statutory assistance to those asylum seekers affected by the new rules, allowing provisions of food and shelter to be made by local authorities under the National Assistance Act of 1948 and the Children Act 1989. In effect the burden of provisions was passed from central government to local government, so that certain areas bore a disproportionate burden. The majority of the cost fell on selected London boroughs. The experience of a Zairean woman displaced by the conflict in her country in the late 1990s offers insight into the problems faced by asylum seekers due to this legislation which adds to the mental anxiety induced by fleeing abroad. After returning to her country from abroad to see if her family was safe following reports of conflict in her home town, she was arrested by the authorities who told her that her father, who had worked for Mobutu's government, had been killed. She was held in detention where she was repeatedly raped and her passport was confiscated. With financial help she managed to escape to Britain, but having arrived on a false passport, she fell prey to the new regulations after failing to apply for asylum at the port of entry where she arrived with an agent.

> I was very afraid that people would look at my passport and see that the passport didn't have my photo. But the man told me not to worry... There were two queues – one with many black people, one with many whites. We joined the one with the whites because I had a European passport. I was afraid but we passed through. We took the train from the airport. We went to an underground station and the man told me to claim asylum. He changed some money for me and gave me ten pounds – I didn't know it wasn't much. He said good luck and went, having ... given me the address of Lunar House to claim asylum... When I came here I found out I was pregnant following the rape. I had counselling and I didn't know what to do. I am Catholic and I prayed to God and thought a lot about my situation... After some time I decided I had to keep the baby because the child is innocent... I also thought after all that had happened to me that I did not want to kill this child.

Alone and also denied benefits under the 1996 Act, this woman was given local authority assistance under the National Assistance Act:

> I am living in a hotel but I feel like a prisoner. The local council pays for my food, £43 a week, but I have to go with a shopper to buy the food. I am not a

> teenager and I don't understand why they treat us in this way. It would be better
> to have less but to be able to buy the food myself and to save any other money
> for other needs like travel. I have no money for travel but I have to go and see
> the Home Office every month to sign that I am here and I have to see my
> solicitor.

As her testimony shows, she, like many people, became a refugee not because
of her own politics but through her family background, compounding her
isolation in Britain:

> I am not interested in politics but it is difficult for me here because other
> Zaireans here who are the victims of the war will not see that. They will see that
> I am the daughter of a man who worked for Mobutu and they will not see that
> I am in the same situation as they are… My baby is due soon and every night I
> go to sleep I think about what will happen.[81]

In addition to the benefits changes which threatened the well-being of those
reaching Britain, the Asylum and Immigration Act 1996 also introduced other
measures undermining the protection of asylum seekers. Those from a
government designated list of 'safe' countries, namely Poland, Romania,
Bulgaria, India, Pakistan, Ghana and Cyprus, all known to suffer from human
rights abuses and nationals of which had been granted refugee status in
Britain, were made subject to a fast-tracked procedure. Individuals from
almost all countries also became subject to a shortened determination
procedure which provoked fears that they would be unable to obtain vital
information in support of their claim within the time limits.[82]

European harmonisation has further raised concern for asylum seekers.[83]
Alfred Banya of NURO has noted Immigration Service plans for 'shackle
points' on Channel Tunnel trains where suspect asylum seekers or
immigrants could be handcuffed if an immigration officer on board was
dissatisfied with the person's documents or believed the person would evade
the authorities at the final destination. Train officials would, like airline
officials, become responsible for policing entry. He concluded:

> While we hear politicians singing about free movement of people and goods in
> Europe we are shocked at the double standards when we unearth such
> horrendous hidden agenda for refugees and black people in Europe. The colour
> of our skin will no doubt serve as good reason for us to be shackled up on these
> Channel Tunnel trains just like in the old days of slavery. 'Let the chain take the
> strain' is probably an appropriate advert for black people intending to use the
> Channel Tunnel train link.

In this context Zairean asylum seekers are not the only group to have reason
to question their welcome and ability to find sanctuary in Britain. The
possibility of detention in the UK, restricted access to housing and the denial
of basic social welfare provisions have reduced assistance to those reaching
Britain. Changes to the determination process, including faster decision-
making and appeals procedures may hinder the ability of individuals to gather

evidence for their cases. The climate of disbelief, with the designation of so-called safe countries and attempts to control numbers leave over three-quarters of applicants facing refusals of their claims, with some nationalities, including the Zaireans, facing even higher rates.[84] Policy developments have also made it more difficult for asylum seekers to even reach Britain, with European harmonisation at work, carriers liable to fines for people without correct entry documents, and visas required for over 100 nationalities of entrants. It has encouraged people to seek recourse to dangerous and fraudulent methods to enter the country, including false passports and exploitative agents acting as middlemen in the process. It is not surprising in the light of such treatment of refugees that, as the 1990s draw to a close, one commentator has suggested that the concept of asylum as we know it may not outlive the century.[85] In this context it is vital to remember the contributions refugees have made to their adopted homes in Britain and elsewhere over the twentieth century and the lessons of history, that today's refugees may be tomorrow's leaders. This will be impossible if refugees, such as the Zaireans, are treated essentially as criminals who should be discouraged, detained and deported. The international community has a legal obligation and a moral duty to offer sanctuary to people in need of protection. Ultimately, it is ordinary people who become refugees; no one is immune from becoming an exile from their country. To deny asylum seekers protection may endanger our own future.[86]

Conclusion:
Asylum, Refugees and 'Home'

In May 1938, two months after the antisemitic violence of the *Anschluss*, Sir Cosmo Parkinson, Permanent Under-Secretary at the Colonial Office, wrote that

> everyone here will have sympathy with the wretched Jews in Austria, and everyone would like to help them. But, while doubtless there will be a good deal of pressure, it is not specially for [His] Majesty's Government to find homes for Jewish refugees.[1]

From the perspective of 1900, Parkinson's sentiments would have been incomprehensible. The right of refugees to asylum in Britain was 'writ in characters of fire on the tablets of our Constitution'. To remove that right, as a Hampshire MP stated in the debate on the Aliens Bill in 1904, was to 'abandon one of the highest principles on which the State has been built up'.[2] But in spite of the clauses inserted into the 1905 Aliens Act exempting some victims of persecution, asylum thereafter in Britain became a privilege granted by the state and not an automatic right. In the early years of the Act prior to the First World War, exceptional reasons had to be found to refuse entry or expel unwanted 'aliens'. But as the twentieth century draws to a close, it is only the lucky few that are allowed permanent entry. Internationally, Britain has become one of the least important places of refuge; after its asylum legislation and procedures of the 1990s, the path to full refugee status is often tortuously complex and protracted. Why have the right to asylum and the status of the refugee diminished so dramatically? Is it legitimate to conclude, as the former General Secretary of the European Council for Refugees and Exiles suggested in 1997, that the concept of asylum will not last into the next century?[3]

This study provides grounds for both optimism and pessimism. On the negative side, the potential for anti-alien sentiment in Britain, on both a state and a popular level, has been realised at specific moments in the destruction of established refugee communities and the denial of entry or the right of settlement to those desperately in need of asylum. The internment measures of both world wars and the racist restrictionism of the 1920s or the last decades of the twentieth century are reminders that reliance on notions of essential British decency and tolerance to protect refugee interests is misplaced.[4]

More positively, there have been times of greater generosity such as the late 1930s for those escaping Nazism and the early 1970s with the arrival of refugees from East Africa. Nevertheless, in both cases many more could have been allowed entry and the lives of those who reached Britain could have been easier had the government and its state apparatus not been so concerned about racism at home. Even more ambivalent has been the simultaneous existence of hostility and openness towards different groups of refugees. The First World War witnessed perhaps the largest refugee movement in British history – some 250,000 Belgians – but also the most open and devastating outbreak of anti-alienism which ultimately affected all those of 'foreign' origin, including, ironically, those received initially as helpless victims of the murderous 'Hun'.

Immediately after the Second World War, the second largest influx of refugees occurred – over 100,000 east European refugees from communism. But their entry into Britain was, despite the huge numbers involved, selective: Jewish survivors of the Holocaust, some of the most traumatised victims of the twentieth century, were largely and deliberately excluded by the British authorities. More recently, racialised selections of the 'right type of refugees' have meant that those of colour are far less likely to gain asylum and more likely to be mistreated if they reach Britain than their white counterparts.

Returning to Sir Cosmo Parkinson, one logical conclusion to be drawn from his statement was that the principle of asylum might well have been abandoned before the Second World War, rather than surviving this murderous century. It might therefore be more appropriate to rephrase the question posed earlier: why, after the abandonment of the right to asylum in 1905 and the rise of anti-alienism thereafter, has there continued to be any state refugee policy and refugee presence in Britain?

One does not need to be cynical to accept that the twentieth-century state structure, even in a relatively prosperous and stable liberal democracy, rarely acts out of altruism. Nevertheless, especially in a country such as Britain which prides itself on its humane image (particularly in relation to others), the *possibility* of appearing uncaring and mean-spirited has often been a moderating factor, acting as an obstacle to the total removal of the right of asylum. In the late 1990s, when Britain has been criticised by human rights organisations for its treatment of refugees, and comes near the bottom of league tables in the granting of asylum, politicians of various political hues have defended policies as being 'firm but fair'. The 'firm' is self-evident in terms of the limited number allowed refugee status, but the claim to fairness rests circularly on the assumption of natural British impartiality. As one

Home Office minister stated, in the face of evidence relating to the exclusion and mistreatment of asylum seekers: 'This country has a proud and consistent record in its treatment of refugees. Our humanitarian record is second to none'.[5] But that many refugee groups across the century have chosen Britain as a last resort and have left for other countries at the first opportunity questions such glib complacency.

Such retreats into rhetoric can hide the reality of unpleasant home truths – that, for example, humanitarian gestures towards child refugees are often made at the expense of adults, as in the cases of the Basques and the victims of Nazism during the 1930s and the child survivors of the concentration camps in 1945. At other times, however, the concept of asylum as an integral part of British political and cultural identity has been important *in itself* in stimulating liberalised refugee policy. This has been especially evident since the Second World War when the anti-Nazi credentials of Britain and its role in destroying the Third Reich have been evoked by those protesting against later dictatorships and attempting to support its victims, such as the Ugandan Asians in the early 1970s, perceived as deserving victims of the 'black Hitler', Idi Amin. Nevertheless, belief in the fundamental justice of granting asylum to the oppressed has rarely been enough on its own to change restrictionism. The reality is that since 1905 the most 'generous' moments of British refugee policy have been as much the result of guilt, economic self-interest and international power politics (including, to a lesser extent, international law) than of notions of 'natural justice' *per se*.

Several of the largest refugee movements fit neatly into the guilt category. The failure of Britain or its allies to intervene militarily on behalf of oppressed nations or peoples with whom it has identified (often through a common enemy) has been the most obvious cause of positive responses. This was certainly the case with the Belgian refugees in the First World War and was even more transparently true after the Munich agreement and the British state-sponsored Czech Refugee Trust. Similarly, the failure to protest diplomatically after 'Kristallnacht' (as well as Britain's closing of the doors to Palestine) helped to encourage the government to ease immigration procedures for Jews attempting to escape Greater Germany in the last year before war. The positive reception given to those fleeing the European continent after the British army had abandoned the continent in 1940 had parallels with the Belgian movement in the earlier conflict.

State support of the Hungarians in 1956 mirrored that given to the Czechs at another point of British failure to intervene against the military and political expansionism of a dictatorship. Lastly, the slightly more generous response from Conservative ministers to refugees from former Yugoslavia compared to other asylum seekers owes much to unease at non-intervention in a bloody European civil war. In this last case, however, the anti-refugee rhetoric of the government and sections of the media ensured that the numbers granted refugee status was still pitifully small.

In the aliens debate of the early 1900s, opponents of free entry succeeded in transforming the language in which discussion was conducted, referring to the east European newcomers as undesirable 'aliens' causing economic and social problems rather than as deserving refugees fleeing persecution. The current debate about whether asylum seekers are 'genuine' or economic migrants, the basis of the draconian Asylum and Immigration (Appeals) Act of 1993 and the Asylum and Immigration Act of 1996, has a long pedigree. It is not surprising that the second most important factor enabling freer entry of refugees has been the perceived needs of the British economy. In essence, the east European refugees of the Cold War era were treated as foreign workers at a time of dire shortage of labour. This process was eased by defining them through the euphemism 'displaced persons' rather than as refugees.[6] Other factors were at work in ensuring the desirability of the east Europeans, including their anti-communism and perceived 'racial' suitability (they were deemed to have possessed the necessary attributes to assimilate into Britain, in contrast to Jews and new Commonwealth immigrants). Restrictive refugee policy has corresponded to periods of high unemployment such as the 1920s and early 1930s or the last decades of the century. Yet it has been assumed in these years of depression that refugees *create* economic problems, taking away resources rather than contributing positively.

In the periods of most repressive anti-asylum policies, such as the 1920s and the last two decades of the century, racist and xenophobic arguments have lurked very close to the surface beneath more ethically 'acceptable' economic arguments. As the Conservative Home Secretary, William Joynson-Hicks, said of the Jewish refugees in Atlantic Park in 1925: 'They are the class of people who come from the east of Europe that we do not want, and America does not want them either'.[7] Opposition to world asylum seekers nearly three-quarters of a century later is still clearly informed by racialism hiding behind 'rational' economic arguments. The difference is that skin colour, as with the Zaireans and Slovak Roma, now plays a major role stimulating and directing the scope of restrictionism.

As the twentieth century has progressed, class, although by no means disappearing, has played a proportionately less important role than racism in informing anti-refugee sentiment. In the aliens debate of the 1900s, middle-class refugees were not the major focus; those with some means were largely exempt from the clauses of the Aliens Act of 1905. It was the poverty stricken aliens who were of greatest concern for those worried about the threat to the 'health of the nation'. In the First World War, the treatment of the Belgians was explicitly related to class and status with the poorer Belgians facing the greatest animosity, extending at times to violence. During the 1920s, the Ukrainians in Atlantic Park were seen as doubly undesirable because of their race and lowly background compared to the 'aristocratic' white Russians who were, by contrast, allowed to settle in Britain. But, by the following decade, the bourgeois status of many German, Austrian and Czechoslovakian Jews was not enough to overcome the problematic nature of their origins. These refugees were perceived as a 'racial' problem, and not only by their declared opponents. By the early 1970s, the impeccably respectable entrepreneur credentials of the Ugandan Asians were forgotten as they were automatically attacked in Britain with unreconstructed racist abuse. Although the anti-black content of contemporary reactions and responses may be blatant, it has been built on an increasing tradition of anti-refugee *racism* directed towards 'white' groups since the inter-war period.

The undermining of economic arguments in favour of refugees by the growth of racism and xenophobia has made the last factor ensuring the continuation of some meaningful tradition of asylum – the role of international politics – increasingly important. Most directly, the development of international agreements on the treatment of refugees, particularly the 1951 United Nations Convention, has theoretically placed responsibility on countries not to turn away those who are genuine refugees. In practice, increasingly complex procedures in countries such as Britain have enabled at best a tokenistic refugee policy to emerge at a time when the number of refugees globally – now estimated in the tens of millions – continues to escalate. Nevertheless, political considerations have sometimes helped modify refugee restrictionism, if in a selective and racialised manner. After 1918, 15,000 White Russian anti-Bolshevik refugees were allowed into Britain when the less 'racially desirable' Armenians and Jews were excluded. International moral pressure after the Evian conference started the process of easing control procedures for refugees from Nazism. Much more impressive, in this respect, was the 1979 Geneva conference which led to offers from 65 countries to help 250,000 refugees from Indo-China.

The anti-Stalinism of the Labour government undoubtedly facilitated the arrival of large numbers of east Europeans after 1945 just as the even stronger anti-communism of the Thatcher government in the 1980s allowed the entry of Vietnamese refugees. The latter movement was small in comparison to other European countries following the Geneva conference but was one of the few exceptions to a general hostile policy towards asylum seekers pursued by the Conservative government. A decade earlier, positive responses to Chilean refugees corresponded to the opposition within the British labour movement to the right-wing military dictatorship of General Pinochet. No Chilean refugees were allowed entry until the Labour Party took office in February 1974. More negatively, the desire not to upset or embarrass trading or diplomatic partners has been present in the failure to respond to specific refugee movements in the last years of the twentieth century, including the Zaireans. This was also true of the Thatcher government's response to the Kurdish refugees escaping from Turkey, a country valued and supported by the western world for strategic reasons. That the Kurds, contrasting to the Vietnamese, were generally on the left-wing did not help elicit favourable responses from the Conservatives.

Lastly, in terms of international influences, the restrictionism of one country or region may encourage similar responses elsewhere. During the inter-war period the USA indirectly increased pressure on other countries and provided a negative example through its immigration quotas of 1921 and 1924. Similar racialised legislation was followed by South Africa in the late 1920s and early 1930s. European Union policies from the 1980s onwards are setting a similar restrictive role model in the western world. Overall, however, international political considerations, treaties and conventions, as well as less formal pressures have more frequently opened up (if within distinct limits) than closed the gates of entry.

Identifying baser motives such as compensatory guilt, economic self-interest and international political manoeuvring should not minimise the positive contributions to refugee crises by many sincere and dedicated individuals inside and outside the British government. It is these people who have helped the concept of asylum to survive and become meaningful in practical terms. One of the major themes of this study has been the vital role played by ordinary people in not only caring for refugees locally but also in campaigning for their well-being at the level of national and international politics. Grassroots responses at critical moments, such as the late 1930s and 1942 during the Nazi era, or with support more recently for groups working with the Chileans, Kurds and Zaireans, have stopped governments from being merely negative. On a very practical level, humanitarianism was evident in such small, spontaneous gestures as the hundreds in Eastleigh who prepared fields for the arrival of the Basque refugees or the efforts of thousands who organised clothes and offered homes for the Ugandan Asians. This is not to deny the existence of other traditions of popular anti-alienism. At a local level, the case of Henry Page Croft, who campaigned on his own and in various organisations against east European, Basque and German Jewish refugees from the 1910s through to the 1940s, provides a classic example. Yet governments and their state apparatus have often been too eager to satisfy negative sentiment and too willing to dismiss alternative voices calling for more generous refugee policies. As the French Socialist leader Laurent Fabius warned in 1997 to those who wanted to pre-empt the quasi-Fascist National Front by instituting their own racist immigration policies: 'Beware! The apple rarely eats the worm'.[8] Rather than discourage anti-alienism, anti-asylum and anti-immigration laws have only legitimised and increased hostile sentiment.

It is all the more remarkable, and one cause for qualified optimism, that popular attachment to the concept of asylum has in the last years of the century remained strong *in spite of* the atmosphere created by successive governments and the popular press. Evidence supporting this more positive reading comes from one of the most prominent offenders amongst those attempting to criminalise and problematise refugees: the right-wing populist tabloid newspaper, *The Sun*. In a survey of its readers carried out in 1991, half of the sample stated that they did not want the government 'to turn its back on our tradition of giving haven to refugees'.[9] In a more detailed survey carried out in 1997 by the Institute for Public Policy Research (IPPR), three-quarters agreed that 'most refugees in Britain are in need of our help and support', suggesting that most still believe in the *concept* of the right to asylum. Outside the fringe world of neo-nazis, few politicians or sections of the media would not at least pay lip service to maintain British traditions of providing refuge.[10]

Nevertheless, it is significant that the IPPR's figure is almost halved to roughly 40 per cent when the sample was asked if they disagreed with the statement that 'most people claiming to be refugees are not real refugees'. A century questioning the legitimacy of refugees has not been without a profound and cumulative impact. Even so, only 12 per cent of the IPPR sample *definitely* agreed with the statement.[11] This study provides qualitative evidence to back up such statistics. Why is it, however, that British governments of past and present continue to pay greater attention to the hostile 12 per cent than the sympathetic 75 per cent of the population?

A curious ambivalence towards racism and racist movements exists in Britain. It is assumed that Britain is 'different' and immune to the 'foreign' diseases of hatred and political extremism, making it hard for racism to be politicised but difficult for less extreme manifestations of hostility to be acknowledged and confronted. The presence of racism and intolerance in Britain causes unease but also fascination with a problem that should not logically exist, leading to a detailed literature on groups that have been hostile to ethnic minority groups in Britain and a media tendency to highlight manifestations of violent racist behaviour.[12] In contrast, the literature and attention given to those who have supported refugees and others is miniscule – even though their positive responses fit much more comfortably within the deeply held myth of British decency and tolerance. The case of Dover in Kent and the Roma refugees in 1997 shows this process at work. Much attention has been devoted to local animosity towards these refugees (and also to the attempt of neo-nazi groups to exploit the situation). Yet the generous and long-lasting efforts within the town, particularly through local churches, on behalf of the Roma, has been ignored, as has the success of the local state in helping the refugees. For example, the work of Father John Weatherall, a local priest, in welcoming the Czech Roma into his church, providing them with spiritual and practical support, has been bypassed by a media looking out for sensation. Similarly, hearsay about the alleged criminality and problematic nature of the Roma has been reproduced without question, contrasting to the testimony of a local guest house owner who expressed a preference for the refugees because they 'were clean, tidy and polite'.[13]

This study has emphasised the importance of local initiatives made on behalf of and in conjunction with refugees. It is a distinctly neglected tradition. Yvonne Kapp, a British-born Jew, and Margaret Mynatt, an

Austrian exile, were devoted members of the Czech Refugee Trust. They wrote in 1940 that

> little has ever been said or written about the relief committees which were spontaneously formed, financed and voluntarily staffed by artists, architects, journalists, lawyers and youth organisations for their refugee opposite numbers... Nor has any tribute ever been paid to the countless voluntary committees formed in towns, villages and country districts throughout the United Kingdom. The remarkable thing about the local committees is ... that these bodies, for years on end and, in most cases without official recognition, subsidy or so much as a say in the affairs of the central refugee organisations or their policy, carried the entire burden of looking after the refugees who had been drafted into their neighbourhood.[14]

It is telling that Kapp and Mynatt's account of the refugee movement remained unpublished for over 50 years; a further indication that grassroots refugee work, whilst involving literally thousands of local committees (over 2,000 were created to deal with the Belgians in the First World War alone) and millions of people across the century, has yet to achieve widespread recognition and approbation. It is surely not irrelevant, returning to the IPPR survey, to stress that it is women and the young who are particularly sympathetic to refugees – groups that have been marginalised in the British political system. Refugee organisations at a local level have largely been set up and organised by women, often linked to religious groups. In contrast, the overt male aggression of neo-nazi groups has received disproportionate attention, the violent extremists indirectly influencing asylum and immigration policies well beyond what their numbers would merit.[15]

It is on a local level, hostile groups and individuals notwithstanding, that popular support for refugees has been able to assert its greatest influence. Yet the very possibility of local responses to global refugee movements is under threat. The railway town of Eastleigh illustrates the changes that have taken place this century. During the 1920s, Eastleigh was the close neighbour of the Atlantic Park Hostel with its stranded and stateless Jewish refugees from eastern Europe. Joynson-Hicks assured the House of Commons that 'They are kept quite carefully where they cannot intermix with the British population at all'.[16] In fact, those at Atlantic Park had contact with the local population through schools, sporting events and individual friendships. The refugees were not free to settle in Britain but nor were they precluded from becoming part of the local scene. The children were educated at schools in the area and football was just one activity bringing people together. This was even more true of the Basque refugees in the North Stoneham camp adjoining Eastleigh. Close bonds developed with the children from the Spanish Civil War. Subsequent reunions have been joyous, emotional occasions. As with the refugees from Nazism, ordinary people had the chance of offering their homes to those fleeing misery and persecution. But the case of Bosnian children from the civil war in former Yugoslavia in the 1990s provides a very different story. The attempt to bring Bosnian orphans to Eastleigh for a short holiday met with local support but faced enormous bureacratic obstacles and restrictions designed partly to ensure that permanent refuge in Britain would not be sought.[17] Today, in localities outside London, contact with asylum seekers is largely confined to those willing to visit refugee detention centres. Hampshire has a proud if hidden history of refugee settlement and support. Its connection to refugee movements is now limited to the detaining of refugees at HM Prisons at Winchester and Haslar or to the tiny number settling in the area.

The role of local pro-refugee campaigners has thus been circumscribed, but their determination to provide support has remained undiminished. Indeed, the Winchester Action Group for Asylum Seekers (WAGAS), has a special place in history as 'the first organised group to start visiting immigration detainees'. Formed during 1989 in response to the plight of Kurdish asylum seekers on hunger strike in Winchester Prison, Shirley Firth, a founder member, relates its early days:

> I had seen details in the paper and I thought, well, I live right by the prison and this is terrible... We talked to about ten of [the Kurds] altogether. They had been on hunger strike for some time and they seemed a bit washed out and weak. We got really het up about it, so we decided we'd ring round everybody we could think of who we thought would be concerned ... gradually the network spread... Once we got ourselves established and things moving, we became aware of what was happening at Haslar.

This diverse group has had major triumphs in getting detainees released, becoming a local focus for those campaigning against recent asylum legislation. It has acted as a barrier between the refugees and the British state, providing friendship and support for those not only suffering the results of persecution but also dislocated and lonely in detention camps and prison cells.[18]

Such help is far removed from that possible in earlier times when local people could provide hospitality to refugees in their own homes, and meet them at work and at leisure. But the trend towards increasingly fast track decision-making procedures now severely limits the possibility of local interventions. Asylum seekers still have the right to appeal against refusal (a right introduced in 1993) but speeding up the system through shortened determination procedures and fast track appeals reduces asylum seekers' access to services. Under safe third country rules, people can be returned to other European Union countries which they passed through in transit. Moreover, as the century draws to a close, the possibility of enforced return for refugees has increased, becoming a threat for former Yugoslavs given temporary protection in Britain and a reality for those in countries such as Germany whose compassion has run its course, in spite of continuing unrest and instability in the Balkans.[19]

In 1992 Women's Aid to former Yugoslavia (WATFY) was formed in

Southampton. Asking 'Where were we when it mattered?', WATFY has organised and delivered conveys of humanitarian aid to former Yugoslavia:

> We must not continue to sit back and watch it happen. When we let the Nazis systematically kill millions of Jews, people could say they didn't know. But we did not act when we watched the people of Srebrenice being massacred in an act of genocide, live and uncut, on TV across the world. We don't have the excuse of ignorance, this war has been broadcast into our homes every night for five years.

It has also campaigned for Bosnians attempting to gain refugee status in Britain: 'We have a responsibility towards these people'.[20] But British politicians and civil servants increasingly follow a 'culture of disbelief' to asylum seekers. If this process is extended the story of refugee organisations working at a local level could be limited to the twentieth century. The many involved locally in refugee work may be replaced by the remarkable few, such as those involved in WATFY, willing to risk their lives in helping refugees and the displaced *outside* the relative security of Britain.

REFUGEES

The conclusion has so far concentrated on the right of asylum, over which refugees have had little or no control. The emphasis throughout this study, however, has been to avoid portraying refugees as merely victims or people to whom things are done, though this is how they are often treated. As Mahmood Mamdani, a Ugandan Asian refugee, states with bitter irony:

> Contrary to what I believed in Uganda, a refugee is not just a person who has been displaced and has lost all or most of his possessions. A refugee is in fact more akin to a child: helpless, devoid of initiative, somebody on whom any kind of charity can be practised; in short, a totally malleable creature.[21]

Instead, an effort has been made to relate their lives before, during and after their flight, emphasising their resistance to poor treatment such as the tradition of hunger strikes starting with Atlantic Park refugees in 1924 and running through to the Kurds and Zaireans in Haslar and Winchester prisons. But has there been a common refugee experience in the twentieth century?

The horrors of war, genocide and 'ethnic cleansing' unite many of the individual and collective stories of those suffering persecution and forced movement. This is not to minimise the differences in the scale and type of oppression but merely to emphasise the dangers of romanticising what it is to be a refugee. Indeed, some 'positive' responses to refugees have been based on their becoming symbolic of wider struggles, making it harder to deal with their mundane everyday problems as happened with some idealistic supporters of the Basque children. It is salutary to remember that all refugees escape various forms of misery, leaving behind them relatives, friends, possessions: fundamental to their history must be the central theme of loss. As one Ethiopian states:

> Being a refugee is the worst thing that can happen to a person. You are missing your country – it is like being in a desert and seeing water you can't drink... But you can't go back. The more you know and understand, the more lonely you become.

Most recovered from their ordeals enough to rebuild shattered lives, creating a new sense of home. But those who were unable to do so should not be forgotten. The comments of a social worker involved with the welfare of Hungarians coming to Britain after the events of 1956 provides amplification of this point, especially as the percentage of successful adaptations amongst some other refugee groups (particularly those who suffered the unimaginable horrors of the Holocaust and the Vietnamese 'boat people') has been far lower:

> For a few years during the 1970s we tended to believe, with the best intentions, that a refugee 20 years after immigration is no longer a refugee. We were quite right in 99% of these cases [but] the remainder refuse to go away and will be with us until the end of their natural lives. What we have learned is that an unattached and unintegrated refugee living in isolation, with or without the added handicaps of mental disorder, instability, depression or [old] age and infirmity, will remain a refugee even after decades of residence and will need specialised attention to live anything like a life that we integrated ones might consider human. They are the lost sheep of migrations.[22]

Yet, if only a small minority remain traumatised, even those who have adjusted successfully retain scars of forced migration. Many refugees left behind successful careers, having to start from the bottom of the ladder in rebuilding their lives in their place of asylum and frequently never recovering their previous status in society as a whole or within their own families. As one Vietnamese refugee, previously a professional, stated of his new life in Britain: 'I'm not important any more'. Gender and age played a significant role in readjustment. Young people have a greater opportunity to integrate, although many start with the burden of separation from their parents, other close relatives and friends. The possibilities of 'getting on' have sometimes been outweighed by the loss of cultural identity for young refugees. Paradoxically, the status of some women improved through the refugee experience. Out of economic necessity, female refugees from Nazism and Amin's Uganda were far more likely to work and exert control over their lives in Britain than in the place of flight (though Vietnamese women, many from an agrarian background, went from a pattern of high employment to the other extreme). Such activities further undermined the status of male refugees coming from highly structured patriarchal communities.[23]

It is highly significant that almost all the groups covered have, in their later lives in Britain, collectively abandoned the epitaph 'refugee'. There is one major exception to this trend – those that fled Nazism during the 1930s. The Association of Jewish Refugees was formed in 1941 and continues under this title to this day. Membership strength has been maintained, partly because the second generation have been willing to join it.[24] It is clear, however, why other former refugees want to escape from the term. A Ukrainian woman, an artist, who fled KGB oppression in the last days of communism, explains why she doesn't 'like the label refugee':

> I don't like the question why I came. I get irritated and can be rude... Somehow the word refugee is a swear word. I have a friend, a new refugee and she has the same attitude. Nobody ... like[s] to inform everyone else of their personal circumstances. My friend was similar – she thought [people] would not like her if she said she was a refugee. Our present circumstances, running away from our country, is very painful... People like us don't feel good, it doesn't feel right that we had to run away. We're trying to put it behind us. It feels like something to be ashamed of saying you are a refugee.[25]

In May 1945, Miss Clement Brown, secretary of the Bournemouth Refugee Committee, stated that she looked forward to the time when 'the hateful words "alien" and "refugee" would be forgotten'. Earlier, the Jewish Refugee Committee had temporarily removed the word 'refugee' from its title because of its negative contemporary connotations.[26] It seems all the more remarkable that those who fled Nazism before the war, who were subject in their early days in Britain to anti-alienism in their everyday life (including internment in 1940), should want to retain the concept 'refugee' in their collective identity. One right-wing commentator in the moral panic of 1997 concerning the arrival of Roma in Dover indirectly provided the answer to why almost all refugees, except those from Nazism, try to distance themselves from the category:

> What I object to about the present influx of middle-European gipsies [*sic*], all claiming to have suffered political persecution, is that they are deliberately blurring the distinction between political asylum and economic migration...

He stressed, however, his 'sensitivity to the plight of *genuine* [our emphasis] refugees', a category never defined.[27]

Of all groups in the twentieth century, refugees from Nazism are now widely and popularly perceived as 'genuine', but *at the time*, German, Austrian and Czechoslovakian Jews were treated with ambivalence and outright hostility as well as sympathy. Slowly, after the war, as understanding of the Holocaust emerged into general consciousness, questions about why these refugees fled became increasingly illegitimate. This contrasts responses to Roma and Sinti groups whose mass murder by the Nazis has barely been recognised and whose continued persecution in post-war Europe hardly registers disapproval. The ease with which the Roma refugees at Dover have been dismissed as economic migrants, the so-called 'Giro Czechs', reflects unwillingness in Britain to accept the murderous and brutal anti-Gypsy racism of eastern Europe. Anti-Gypsy prejudice still retains social acceptability whereas the refugees from Nazism have become, in memory, the new Huguenots, true victims of persecution who found a haven from oppression and a humane welcome in Britain.[28]

Refugees from Nazism, however, like almost all refugees, by nature 'blurred the distinction between political asylum and economic migration'. The vast majority of adult refugees from the 1930s were allowed into Britain to fill gaps in the labour market. Those women who came under Ministry of Labour permits as domestic servants, for example, were simply treated as foreign workers. But in popular memory and in recent political debates, the Jewish refugees from Nazism are now, ironically, alongside the Protestants who escaped persecution several centuries before, perceived as classic 'refugees'.

Just as there are still Huguenot societies in Britain that bring great satisfaction to the descendants (no matter how watered-down their genealogical connection), the children and grandchildren of Hitler's pre-war victims, as well as the sadly fast-disappearing first generation, take pride in being associated with the identity 'refugee'.[29] It is possible that this may also happen to later generations of other groups. But, for those stigmatised by a term increasingly linked to dishonesty, selfishness, and even criminality, it is hardly surprising that escape from 'refugee' status has been the dominant strategy.

In a well-meaning manner, a Hampshire campaigner in the 1970s stated that he would prefer not to call the victims of Idi Amin 'Ugandan Asians. Let us call them refugees'. These victims of Africanisation refused generally to accept the refugee label which to them was far from positive. As Yasmin Alibhai-Brown, now a journalist and broadcaster, remarked over 20 years later:

> We saw, and threw away with fury, huge newspaper adverts telling people not to go to Leicester because it was too full of Asians already. We listened to the educated voice of Enoch Powell talking about us as if we were vermin. And worst of all was the way people were expected to show enormous gratitude to Britain for being allowed into their own country. We were not refugees. We were British. This is something that no British politician has properly acknowledged.

The problem of adopting the identity of 'refugee' has been further problematised by its shifting meaning at different times and in different places. A Chilean woman, Sylvia Velasquez, eloquently describes the dilemma created for those desperately attempting to recreate a sense of belonging in their lives:

> The word refugee has an interesting ring to it, but it's part of a compulsory C.V. that we refugees have to present every time we meet someone new in the English world. The different meanings and implications of the word are still not clear to me since they have changed with the circumstances in which I have had to use it. Sometimes the word has sounded proud and self-sufficient, a shield with which to face the world. At other times it is shameful and sad like a penance for someone else's crime laid against my soul. It is always present. For so many years in this foreign land where I have had to find an identity, fight for

my survival, the idea 'refugee' has served to justify my emotions and actions, to justify myself to others around me. But after so much time, justification is no longer enough. I am tired of the longing for a land lost forever, for cultures remembered in dreams and raised to unattainable heights of perfection. I am sick of failure and rejections from a changing world, and of people wrapped in their own lives, incapable of seeing the way history repeats itself in different parts of the world.[30]

The danger is that British complacency and the tendency towards self-congratulation will be strengthened, at the cost of future refugees, if attention is only focused on the now idealised groups *of the past* such as Huguenots and Jews. Distortions have also occurred in official and popular memory in relation to these groups by collectively losing sight of the complex contemporary reactions to them in the impetus towards celebratory history. Huguenots and Jews also faced many of the acute uncertainties expressed by Sylvia Velasquez. But by excluding other groups, and rewriting the experiences of Huguenots and Jews as an uncomplicated story with a happy ending, more probing questions are avoided. It is disturbing that the only public monument linked to refugees in Hampshire (and one that is rare taking Britain as a whole) is a garden created in 1985 in Southampton's historical heritage area, commemorating the arrival and

> *integration* [our emphasis] of French Huguenot Refugees to the City 300 years earlier to escape the persecution which followed the revocation of the Edict of Nantes by Louis XIV.

The presence of far less integrated and 'desirable' refugees in the area, such as those in Atlantic Park, has not been acknowledged: the making and remaking of official memory involves the process of forgetting as well as remembering, distorting the reality of the past. It is such marginalisation that refugees have difficulty in coming to terms with. As one Ethiopian states: 'The biggest problem we have is the difficulty in being accepted in the mainstream. We are kept on the periphery'.[31]

The majority of the refugees from Nazism during the 1930s (with the exception of the political opponents of the regime), and much more so the tiny number of Holocaust survivors who came after the war, were also less ambivalent about their 'homeland' than many other groups. 'Home' was something that had been destroyed or that was tainted by the murder of whole communities. This was very different to the Chilean refugees of whom it was said that 'To adapt too fully is to reject one's past and in rejecting one's past one is also denying the possibilities of progressive change in, and a return to Chile'.[32] Here, the political refugees from Chile had much in common with what was otherwise a very dissimilar movement to Britain – the First World War refugees from Belgium. The instructions given by the Belgian authorities in Britain in 1915, which had official approval, stressed that 'nothing is more delightful than to find the characteristic life of Belgium reproduced in Great

Britain'.[33] The Belgians, like the Chileans, saw themselves fundamentally not as refugees but as exiles. Almost without exception, they went home or were repatriated after 1918. Return for most exiled groups, however, has not been possible and increasingly enters the realm of the mythical. The final section analyses the concept of 'home' in relation to the place of exile or refuge.

'HOME'

It has been suggested that:

> The situation of the refugee has been described as a person with Janus' two faces: One that looks back on past experiences who sees the flight, the loss, the separation, the nostalgia, and the other who sees the present, the future, in which one sees the unfamiliar, the unpredictable, full of fears, real or unreal.[34]

The need to establish a sense of belonging is crucial for the forcibly displaced and dispossessed. One strategy is to forge identities rooted in the new environment but attempting a degree of continuity with past places. Providing such a bridge is not easy, especially if the refugee group is small in number and geographically dispersed. Amongst those retaining the strongest group identity are Jewish refugees from the turn of the century and the Nazi era and Poles after the Second World War. In these cases, religion, combined with ethnicity and common geographical origins, helped maintain organisational structures such as synagogues, churches and educational-cultural societies well after the original settlement. A problem remains even with these groups to keep later generations' interest in their cultural and religious heritage, particularly so in an increasingly secular British society, that has been, in contrast to the United States, until recently, hostile to the concept of pluralism.

Other movements into the county of Hampshire were essentially temporary, such as those at Atlantic Park in the 1920s and the Basques a decade later. More recent world asylum seekers, especially those in detention centres, have even less chance to forge local identities owing to their isolation. But their stay in the county has been deeply disturbing. To revisit the testimony of a Zairean detainee in Haslar Prison:

> My dreams and hopes were shattered as contact with relations and my solicitor were no longer easy... During my stay in Haslar I found the situation like being jailed for life... All I could do was sit and wait.

It is clear that such detention centres are designed to put off other asylum seekers. Previous refugee camps in Britain, such as Hiltingbury for the post-war Poles, were basic and kept that way partly to encourage resettlement elsewhere. Nevertheless, the brutality and cynicism of using prisons such as Haslar to act as deterrents remains in an inhumane category of its own in modern British responses to refugees.[35]

For the isolated refugees, the dilemma of maintaining self-worth and pride in origins once they have left the original reception centres has been acute. It has been even more difficult for those who are part of very small refugee movements lacking the presence of a significant settled grouping in Britain of the same nationality/ethnicity/religion. The Chileans and Hungarians have had particular problems in this respect. Nevertheless, the presence of a previously established community can create its own tensions. The responses of the settled British Jewish community to refugee co-religionists both at the turn of the century and in the Nazi era were ambivalent, especially in the complex organisational structures they set up to 'help' the newcomers. Like many of the organisations set up to deal with refugees, these Jewish organisations had a major objective of encouraging anglicisation. Not surprisingly, given their vulnerability, many of the refugees internalised such pressure to conform. The testimony of John Grenville, who came to Britain during the 1930s as a child, provides a classic example of this process at work:

> There was the reaction to be more English than the English, wanting to change one's name from the German ... to wipe out all traces ... and taking up English sports like playing cricket.[36]

One of the more surreal details of this study is that refugees ranging from Ukrainian Jews to Vietnamese 'boat people' have been forced to confront 'English' culture through learning the obscure pleasures of cricket.

It should not be assumed that refugees have always been hostile to attempts to acculturate them. Frequently refugees have been keen to learn English and to adjust to their new surroundings. Nevertheless, other aspects of anglicisation, and especially the pressure to forget the culture of the 'homeland', have been unhelpful in developing positive identities amongst the refugees. Although progress, through the concept of multi-culturalism, has been made in helping newcomers to maintain elements of the culture of their homeland, the dominant response in Britain has been to expect assimilation – a policy leading to explicit policies of dispersal as with the refugees from Nazism in the 1930s, the Ugandan Asians and Vietnamese in the 1970s, and, more humanely, with Bosnian refugee programmes in the 1990s. Instructions given in the First World War to Belgian refugees to keep alive a sense of Belgianness were exceptional. Almost all refugee groups have been given formal guidelines on how they should 'behave' in Britain. In such literature the dominant themes have been the dangers of appearing foreign or congregating together. Despite these formal and informal measures and instructions, the tendency amongst the refugee groups has been to concentrate in the same locality, enabling solidarity and the preservation of past culture. One unfortunate result has been the near-total isolation of those who, for various reasons, have been unable to move to larger refugee settlements. Recognising that refugees' needs extend beyond those of housing and jobs has taken far too long. Loneliness and the inability to share experiences of the past and the frustrations of the present are recurring problems for refugees separated from others of similar background.

In the 1970s the journal of the Association of Jewish Refugees reflected on the success of its American counterpart, the *Aufbau*, which, from the start, was published in German:

> It could only have happened in America, a country of immigrants where it was considered natural that new citizens should continue to speak their native language, at least among themselves, and retain many of their social and cultural peculiarities. It could certainly not have happened over here. This country has a long tradition of granting asylum to the persecuted, but it has always expected them either to conform or *to go back where they came from* when persecution ended. (Refugees over here have all heard this phrase at one time or another, most of the time prompted by a total lack of understanding rather than by unkindness or antagonism.) We all knew from the start that we should have to come to terms with the English language, and it would not have occurred to anyone to publish an independent German-language newspaper or to hold public meetings where German was the main language.[37]

There has been more understanding in the post-war period with information and advice for refugees in their 'native' language. In the case of the Hungarians, a special introductory booklet was produced by aid agencies. Nevertheless, its emphasis was to introduce the group to *British* customs though refugees have used their own initiative to produce 'native' language publications, the Poles particularly prominent for their literary activity.

The option of total assimilation, however, has rarely been available because of subtle (and often not so subtle) forces of exclusion, particularly for non-white refugees. Even those who were less readily identifiable as different, such as the child refugees from Nazism, found it extremely difficult to submerge into the British population, and therefore a frustrating exercise. As John Grenville remembers: 'one did play a sort of role and felt a little bit false and artificial'. Nevertheless, many felt they made a successful compromise, like the Hungarian reflecting on his identity 40 years after his initial arrival:

> I describe myself as more British than Hungarian really, as [I've] spent twice as much time here… [But] from time to time you think a lot about your birthplace … you never forget your place of birth or nationality.[38]

Yet, for many, it is fair to conclude that Britain and its localities have never fully become 'home'. As a result of their complex relationship to their place of origin, flight and place of settlement (further complicated by ethnicity, gender, class and age), refugees have frequently adopted multi-layered identities incorporating a sense of local, national and global affinities. An intriguing example was provided in an exhibition at Southampton City Art Gallery in 1997. The items for display were chosen by a local Asian women's group, some of them of refugee origin. The paintings and sculpture exhibited, which represented landscapes, buildings and images from Britain and Europe, evoked memories of other places and other times. The beach scene,

'Collioure', of south-west France, by the Welsh landscape painter, James Dickson Innes (1887–1914), reminded one woman 'of childhood holidays in Kenya'. Another was struck by John Bellamy's powerful painting Bethel: 'Strong images ... on the one hand [of the] life of fishermen, on the other ... stark images of Auschwitz'. Experiences of belonging and exclusion in the homeland; the interplay of local and global identities and the relationship between past and present were apparent in the choice of art and their responses to it. National boundaries at the level of the imagination collapsed, becoming an irrelevance, and a dream close to that offered by the novelist, Jeanette Winterson: 'All times can be inhabited, all places visited. In a single day the mind can make a millpond of the oceans.'[39]

The implementation, however, of ever-increasing controls against asylum seekers in the twentieth century has made the creation of stable refugee communities difficult to sustain and such visions harder to realise. Refugees have been people on the move, not just in the place of their persecution and flight but also in countries of supposed asylum. The Vietnamese, for instance, made clear their desire for community support by secondary migration from areas of dispersal to cities such as London and Birmingham. This fundamental fluidity and temporariness should not disguise the lasting and important impact refugees have made on national society. As this study has emphasised, the contribution made at a local level, culturally and economically, has been of great significance. Yet because Britain in the twentieth century has still to come to terms with the presence of refugees, this endowment has hardly been recognised.

It is helpful to return to a point made in the introduction concerning the marginality of refugee studies in the academic world. This is the first detailed history of modern refugee movements in Britain. At best general historians have yet to move beyond token recognition of this subject. Refugees are also absent in work on ethnic minorities – including the 1996 PSI survey, the most detailed of its type yet undertaken in Britain.[40] Perhaps refugees' lack of fixity and the searching questions that emerge from their existence are too troubling for them to receive the attention they deserve. Yet the failure to confront both the plight and the presence of refugees has led to a denial of the reality of the global, national and local experience. As this study has shown, even those refugees who passed through Hampshire for the briefest of moments made an impact on those experiencing or witnessing their passage.[41]

Refugees force governments as well as ordinary people to think beyond national boundaries. As the twentieth century comes to an end, the ability to think globally through modern means of communication and transport has run alongside the counter forces of national and regional exclusivity. In terms of the latter, 'Fortress Europe' has become one of the crudest and most blatantly self-interested manifestations of such developments, helping to increase the likelihood that refugee asylum in Britain could end. Throughout this study, ships have been a recurring motif. They have brought refugees to

Britain or on to other places of asylum but have also been used off the English south coast to keep the 'menace' of refugees from British soil. Despite the increasing use of air travel, ships still play an important and often tragic role in the life of refugees. On Christmas Day 1996, a boat carrying 'illegal immigrants' from the Indian sub-continent to Europe sunk, drowning up to 300 men. Little international attention was given to this disaster. As the journalist breaking the story commented:

> Fortress Europe does not want to know what's happening on its shores; it doesn't want to accept people are dying, daily, because of co-ordinated draconian immigration laws, many drawn up in a spirit of populism rather than humanity. The dead were acting illegally and they were black. And no one cared.

Ultimately, such inward-looking tendencies will be at the cost of countries such as Britain which once boasted an open-door policy for the oppressed. It is not only the economy and culture of Britain which could lose out, but the ability to come to terms with world developments which it must eventually confront.[42]

Miss Clement Brown of the Bournemouth Refugee Committee spoke in 1945 about the need to look ahead beyond words such as 'alien' or 'refugee' to a time 'when we should all be part of the same community'.[43] The diverse refugee groups and individuals of the twentieth century fit into no neat categories of national boundaries. Some have only been able to define their identities by reference to a world transcending passports and visas. Returning to the refugee artist, she writes:

> My father is Ukrainian and my mother is Russian. I don't speak Ukrainian and I grew up in Georgia. I don't feel like any nationality – just a human being. I remember as a student we opposed nationality being placed on any paper. We came here and there is the same emphasis on nationality. I don't think it really matters.

Similarly, Yasmin Alibhai-Brown concludes her autobiography, *No Place Like Home*, by recalling conversations with Hugh Blaschko, a former Jewish refugee from Nazism and later a world-renowned scientist at Oxford University. Adjusting to her new life in Oxford having left Uganda with almost nothing,

> Hugh taught me about how dispossessed people lose much less than they gain, that not having a nation, a country, a flag, is a liberation which enables you to see, feel and taste the whole world as an insider.[44]

For many governments and people nationality *does* matter and the ideal of global citizenship is so vague and remote as to be almost meaningless. But by starting with local knowledge, and with local identities, through an incorporation and acknowledgment of the needs and presence of refugees, the possibilities, as well as the responsibilies, of thinking and acting globally become far less remote and idealistic. As Yvonne Kapp and Margaret Mynatt wrote in the difficult days of the Second World War, 'In championing the cause of the refugees, we take a stand for our own democratic rights; in fighting for these, we vindicate the refugees'. In similar vein over 50 years later, Auschwitz survivor Rabbi Hugo Gryn implored that:

> There are so many scars that need mending and healing it seems to me that it is imperative that we proclaim that asylum issues are an index of our spiritual and moral civilisation. How you are with the one to whom you owe nothing, that is a grave test and not only as an index of our tragic past. I always think that the real offenders at the half way point of the century were the bystanders, all those people who let things happen because it didn't affect them directly. I believe that the line our society will take in this matter on how you are to people to whom you owe nothing is a signal.[45]

More self-interestedly, the twentieth century experience shows that no one is safe from becoming a refugee. Many places of asylum have later created their own refugee movements.

This study argues that local people and local governments are not only able to cope with refugees but can also gain in a host of different ways from the experience. The impact of refugee movements across the twentieth century has tended to be felt with particular force at a local level. In the case of the largest group, the Belgians in the First World War:

> Some idea of the extent of the work at [the Kent port of] Folkestone may be gained from the fact upwards of 120,000 refugees passed through the town, and that the number of meals provided there for refugees and Belgian soldiers from September, 1914, to February, 1919, approximated to half a million.

There are examples of local government structures opposing settlement of refugees, such as Havant council refusing to accept Vietnamese families in 1979. But the most famous case of such opposition – that of Leicester and the Ugandan Asians in 1973 – proved that the fears of the local city council were misplaced. Leicester has profited enormously from the presence of the Ugandan Asians who are now well-integrated into local society. Leicester City Council had much to learn, but it subsequently played a valuable part in helping a thriving community to develop. Returning to Hampshire, from the Ukrainians during the 1920s through to the Vietnamese in the 1970s/1980s, its county and city councils have generally coped well and shown commitment and ingenuity when dealing with the specific problems of refugees, helped by the involvement of local organisations – religious and secular – as well as committed individuals. With support and encouragement nationally, local government in partnership with refugee organisations can help ensure that integration is achieved.[46]

The many success stories on a local level are proof that refugees have not been and need not be 'a problem'. On the contrary, refugees should be treated as a positive challenge. Some of the gains from their presence are measurable, including the creation of jobs and new enterprises as well the development of intellectual and cultural life. Bringing energy and innovations, all refugee groups, when given the freedom to do so, have revitalised British society at a national and local level. In the light of Britain's twentieth-century experience, the removal of asylum can only be detrimental in terms of its future well-being. But a word of caution is in order: the spectacular endowment provided by groups such as east European Jews, refugees from Nazism and the Ugandan Asians should not overshadow those made by other refugee movements. There is a danger of elitism leading to refugees only being vindicated by the material contribution which they make.

Indeed, perhaps the most important, but unquantifiable, benefit bestowed by the presence of refugees is that the process of local involvement challenges the divisions created by geographical distance. As Peggy Turner, who grew up in the inter-war period experiencing a constant flow of refugees in her family home, recalls: 'What I was receiving was a rich, vital [education] which stayed with me all my life. I didn't go to university but I didn't need to'. For her, international responsibilities were part of the everyday world even in the isolation of semi-rural Hampshire. The words of the editor of the *Aufbau* during the 1970s, exploring the relationship between the local, national and global, have resonance here:

> *Aufbau* is an American paper, and yet it is written in German and deals in great detail with German topics. *Aufbau* is a New York local paper, and yet it has faithful readers in 45 countries all over the world. *Aufbau* is a Jewish paper, and yet it is read by countless non-Jews and has a great many non-Jewish staff-members and contributors. *Aufbau* is the voice of a group which was torn by force from its German cultural background, and yet it remains faithful to German language, literature, culture and traditions.[47]

The decline in provision of asylum and the ending of the refugee presence would end such achievements which have, in a hidden and subtle way, also occurred in Britain during the twentieth century. Total restrictionism would mark the end of a millennium and the beginning of a new one by a retreat into the fiction of the immutability of national boundaries. Ultimately, it would herald the closing and demise of local cultures, signalling the triumph of parochialism. There is now a very grave danger of Britain swallowing whole its own mythologies to the point of hypocrisy: of it becoming a country committed to asylum without the possibility of entry; of a haven for the oppressed without the presence of refugees. We will conclude on a note of cautious optimism and a call for action. By facing our global responsibilities towards the displaced, we begin the process of changing for the better a world which creates the misery of growing refugee movements. It is, in the words of Hugo Gryn, 'the critical signal that we give to our young, and I hope and pray that it is a test we shall not fail'.[48]

Notes

INTRODUCTION

1. Rabbi Hugo Gryn, speech made in autumn 1996 quoted by Nick Hardwick, Chief Executive of the Refugee Council at its AGM, 18 November 1997; Roger Zetter, 'Refugees and Refugee Studies – A Label and an Agenda', *Journal of Refugee Studies*, Vol.1, No.1 (1988), p.1; John Berger, *Keeping a Rendezvous* (London: Granta Books, 1992), p.12.
2. Charles Phythian-Adams, 'Hoskins's England: A Local Historian of Genius and the Realisation of his Theme', *The Local Historian* (November 1992), p.170; W. G. Hoskins, *Local History in England* (London: Longman, 1972, 2nd edition, orig. 1959), p.7.
3. Alan Everitt, *New Avenues in English Local History: An Inaugural Lecture* (Leicester: Leicester University Press, 1970); H. Arthur Doubleday, *The Victoria History of the Counties of England: Hampshire and the Isle of Wight* (London: Archibald Constable & Co., 1900), p.1; Christopher Ellington, 'The Victoria County History', *The Local Historian* (August 1992), pp.128–37.
4. H. Finberg, 'Local History', in H. Finberg and V. H. T. Skipp, *Local History: Objective and Pursuit* (Newton Abbot, Devon: David & Charles, 1967), p.37; Hoskins, *Local History in England*, p.15.
5. Charles Phythian-Adams, 'Local History and National History: The Quest for the Peoples of England', *Rural History*, Vol.2, No.1 (1991), p.6. See also idem, *Re-thinking English Local History* (Leicester: Leicester University Press, 1987); Hoskins, *Local History in England*, p.179.
6. Pythian-Adams, 'Local History and National History', pp.3–4; idem, *Re-thinking*, chapter 1.
7. Michael Marrus, *The Unwanted: European Refugees in the Twentieth Century* (New York: Oxford University Press, 1985), p.3.
8. Hannah Arendt, *The Origins of Totalitarianism* (London: George Allen & Unwin, 1958, 2nd edition), p.284. UNHCR figures for 1996 suggest 27 million people are of concern including internally displaced people, asylum seekers, refugees and returnees of whom 14 million were classified as refugees. *The Guardian* and Amnesty International (UK) in *No Refuge* (1997) gives figures of 23 million refugees forced to live outside their countries with a further 27 million displaced within the borders of their own country.
9. Zetter, 'Refugees and Refugee Studies', p.2; abstract description of *Journal of Refugee Studies* (Oxford University Press, 1988).
10. Bernard Porter, *The Refugee Question in Mid-Victorian Politics* (Cambridge: Cambridge University Press, 1979), p.23.

11. Michael Marrus, 'Introduction', in Anna Bramwell (ed.), *Refugees in the Age of Total War* (London: Unwin Hyman, 1988); idem, *The Unwanted*, p.13.

12. Alan Travis and Ian Traynor, 'Britain's little refugee problem', *The Guardian*, 22 October 1997. For further discussion of the Roma asylum seekers in Dover, see the Conclusion.

13. Gordon Horwitz, *In the Shadow of Death: Living Outside the Gates of Mauthausen* (London: I. B. Tauris, 1991), pp.2, 4; Robert Jan van Pelt and Deborah Dwork, *Auschwitz: 1270 to the Present* (New Haven: Yale University Press, 1996), pp.10–11; Arendt quoted by Marrus, 'Introduction', p.6.

14. John Hope Simpson, *The Refugee Problem: Report of a Survey* (London: Oxford University Press, 1939), p.339.

15. *Census of England and Wales, 1901: County of Hampshire* (London: HMSO, 1902), pp.96–7; *Census of England and Wales, 1901: General Report* (London: HMSO, 1904), pp.196–7, 282–4; *1991 Census: County Report: Hampshire*, Vol.1 (London: HMSO, 1993), pp.16, 104–17.

16. Tony Kushner, 'The Memory of Refugees in Hampshire' (unpublished typescript).

17. Nick Merriman (ed.), *The Peopling of London: Fifteen Thousand Years of Settlement from Overseas* (London: Museum of London, 1993); *Destination Bradford: A Century of Immigration: Photographs and History* (Bradford: Bradford Libraries and Information Services, 1987); Sylvia Collicot, *Connections: Haringey Local-National-World Links* (London: Haringey Community Information Service, 1986), p.112.

18. E. G. Bennett, *In Search of Freedom: The Story of Some Refugees and Exiles who Found a Haven in Bournemouth and District* (Bournemouth: Bournemouth Local Studies Publications, 1985), Foreword; Steve Cohen, *From the Jews to the Tamils: Britain's Mistreatment of Refugees* (Manchester: South Manchester Law Centre, 1988).

19. Valerie Marett, 'Resettlement of Ugandan Asians in Leicester', *Journal of Refugee Studies*, Vol.6, No.3 (1993), pp.248–59.

20. A. Sayer, 'Behind the Locality Debate: Deconstructing Geography's Dualisms', *Environment and Planning A*, Vol.23 (1991), pp.306–7; Doreen Massey, 'Places and Their Pasts', *History Workshop Journal*, No.39 (Spring 1995), p.183; idem, 'Double Articulation: A Place in the World', in A. Bammer (ed.), *Displacements: Cultural Identities in Question* (Bloomington, IN: Indiana University Press, 1994), p.120; Doreen Massey and Pat Jess, 'Introduction', in idem (eds), *A Place in the World? Places, Cultures and Globalization* (Oxford: Oxford University Press and Open University, 1995), pp.2, 4; *The Times*, 13 August 1996.

21. Elizabeth G. Ferris, *Beyond Borders: Refugees, Migrants and Human Rights in the post-Cold War Era* (Geneva: World Council of Churches Publications, 1993).

22. Two Slovak Roma families, asylum seekers, interviewed by Katharine Knox in Dover, 14 November 1997.

23. John Hope Simpson, *Refugees: Preliminary Report of a Survey* (London: Royal Institute of International Affairs, 1938), pp.2–3.

24. *Convention and Protocol Relating to the Status of Refugees* (1951 Geneva Convention article 1A).

25. Danièle Joly and Robin Cohen (eds), *Reluctant Hosts: Europe and Its Refugees* (Aldershot: Avebury, 1989), p.6.

26. Danièle Joly, *Refugees: Asylum in Europe?* (London: Minority Rights Publications, 1992), pp.5–16.

27. Hope Simpson, *Refugees*, p.1.

28. Claudena Skran, 'The International Refugee Regime: The Historical and Contemporary Context of International Responses to Asylum Problems', *Journal of Policy History*, Vol.4, No.1 (1992), p.19.

29. Joly, *Refugees: Asylum in Europe?*, p.13.

30. Ibid., p.14: 41 African states are signatory to the OAU Convention.
31. Ibid.
32. E. F. Kunz, 'The Refugee in Flight', *International Migration Review*, Vol.7 (Summer 1973), pp.130–36.
33. Joly and Cohen, *Reluctant Hosts*, p.7.
34. Ferris, *Beyond Borders*, p.18.
35. Ibid.
36. Barry Stein, unpublished paper on refugees in Gosport Local Studies library. See also his 'Indochinese Refugees: The New Boat People', *Migration Today*, Vol.6, No.5 (December 1978).
37. 'Return to Chile: International Humanitarian Law in the Contemporary World', 6–9 June 1990 (a document submitted to a conference in Berlin), Refugee Council archives, WC/Q46.
38. See note 36 above.
39. 'Return to Chile'.
40. Some refugees, such as the White Russians in the 1920s, the Italians in the inter-war period, Czechs in 1968, the Greek Cypriots during the 1970s and many nationalities in the 1990s, will be covered briefly because of the confines of space and the desire to address key developments in trends, giving full justice to the groups covered by reporting in depth their experiences in global, national and local context.
41. Clifford Geertz, *Local Knowledge* (London: Fontana, 1993), p.233.

CHAPTER 1

1. Mark Wischintzer, *To Dwell in Safety: The Story of Jewish Migration Since 1800* (Philadelphia: Jewish Publication Society of America, 1948), chapters 2–4; John Klier, 'Russian Jewry on the Eve of the Pogroms', in idem and Shlomo Lambroza (eds), *Pogroms: Anti-Jewish Violence in Modern Russian History* (Cambridge: Cambridge University Press, 1992), pp.5–7; Lloyd Gartner, *The Jewish Immigrant in England: 1870–1914* (London: George Allen & Unwin, 1960); idem, 'North Atlantic Jewry', in Aubrey Newman (ed.), *Migration and Settlement: Proceedings of the Anglo-American Jewish Historical Conference* (London: Jewish Historical Society of England, 1971), p.121 and 'Notes on the Statistics of Jewish Immigration to England, 1870–1914', *Jewish Social Studies*, Vol.22, No.2 (1960), pp.97–102. For a general overview, see Michael Marrus, *The Unwanted: European Refugees in the Twentieth Century* (New York: Oxford, 1985), chapter 1.
2. On earlier east European Jewish immigration, see Bill Williams, *The Making of Manchester Jewry: 1740–1875* (Manchester: Manchester University Press, 1975), chapter 11.
3. David Cesarani, 'The Myth of Origins: Ethnic Memory and the Experience of Migration', in Aubrey Newman and Stephen Massil (eds), *Patterns of Migration, 1850–1914* (London: Jewish Historical Society of England and Institute of Jewish Studies, 1996), pp.247–54; Klier and Lambroza (eds), *Pogroms*; Hans Rogger, *Jewish Policies and Right-Wing Politics in Imperial Russia* (Basingstoke, Hants: Macmillan, 1986); Salo Baron, *The Russian Jews under Tsars and Soviets* (New York: Macmillan, 1964), chapters 4–9.
4. John Klier, 'Russian Jewry on the Eve of the Pogroms', pp.3–12, esp.5–6; on the Russo-Jewish committee see Eugene Black, *The Social Politics of Anglo-Jewry 1880–1920* (Oxford: Blackwell, 1988), pp.254–67.
5. Records of Jewish Board of Guardians, 173/1/5/3, University of Southampton archive (SUA).
6. Rogger, *Jewish Policies*; Shlomo Lambroza, 'The Pogroms of 1903–1906', in Klier

and Lambroza, *Pogroms*, pp.195–212.

7. Israel Efros (ed.), *Complete Poetic Works of Hayyim Nahman Bialik*, Vol.1 (New York: Histadruth Ivrith of America, 1948), pp.129–43, esp. 129; David Roskies, *Against the Apocalypse: Responses to Catastrophe in Modern Jewish Culture* (Cambridge, MA: Harvard University Press, 1984), pp.88–92.

8. Klier and Lambroza, *Pogroms*, Part IV 'The Pogroms of 1903–1906'.

9. Lambroza, 'The Pogroms of 1903–1906', in Klier and Lambroza, *Pogroms*, p.227 provides a month-by-month graph of pogrom frequency; David Feldman, *Englishmen and Jews: Social Relations and Political Culture 1840–1914* (New Haven: Yale University Press, 1994), pp.127–32, chapter 12.

10. Diary of Jack Myers, papers of Carl Stettauer, MS 128 File 1, SUA.

11. Joseph Kissman, 'The Immigration of Rumanian Jews up to 1914', *YIVO Annual of Jewish Social Science*, Vols2–3 (1947/1948), pp.160–79; *Correspondence with His Majesty's Government Relating to the Treaty Rights of the Jews of Roumania* (London: Joint Foreign Committee of the Deputies of the British Jews and Anglo-Jewish Association, 1919); Raphael Mahler, 'The Economic Background of Jewish Emigration from Galicia to the United States', *YIVO Annual of Jewish Social Science*, Vol.7 (1952), pp.255–67.

12. John Higham, *Strangers in the Land: Patterns of American Nativism 1860–1925* (New York: Atheneum, 1978), chapter 4.

13. Bernard Gainer, *The Alien Invasion* (London: Heinemann Educational Books, 1972), chapter 4; John Garrard, *The English and Immigration: A Comparative Study of the Jewish Influx 1880–1910* (London: Oxford University Press, 1971), pp.51–65.

14. C. Gershaler, 'From Lithuania to South Africa' and Gustav Saron, 'Jewish Immigration, 1880–1913', in Gustav Saron and Louis Hotz (eds), *The Jews in South Africa: A History* (Cape Town: Oxford University Press, 1955), pp.59–78 and 88–91; Milton Shain, *The Roots of Antisemitism in South Africa* (Charlotsville: University Press of Virginia, 1994), chapters 2 and 3.

15. Jonathan Sarna, 'The Myth of No Return: Jewish Return Migration to Eastern Europe, 1881–1914', *American Jewish History*, Vol.71 (1981), pp.256–68.

16. On the importance of the Boer War to Southampton's development, see Gordon Sewell, 'Southampton in the Twentieth Century', in J. B. Morgan and Philip Peberdy (eds), *Collected Essays on Southampton* (Southampton: Southampton City Council, 1958), pp.99–100. Some 419 transports left the port and 476 arrived 'carrying between them some 25,000 officers, over half a million men and 27,900 horses, besides munitions and equipment for the campaign'; Colin Holmes, *Anti-Semitism in British Society, 1876–1939* (London: Arnold, 1979), pp.66–70. On South African antisemitism in the Boer War, see the papers of Joseph Hertz, MS 175/37/1, SUA.

17. For the Milner telegram, see *The Times*, 22 January 1900 and Mr Soulsby of the Transvaal Refugees Fund to Mr Stephany, Secretary of the Jewish Board of Guardians, 15 February 1900 in MS 173/1/11/2, SUA.

18. *Jewish Chronicle*, 26 January 1900.

19. 'So-Called Refugees', *Daily Mail*, 3 February 1900.

20. 'The "Cheshire" Refugees', *Jewish Chronicle*, 9 February 1900.

21. 'Jewish Refugees from South Africa', *Jewish Chronicle*, 9 February 1900 which includes drawings of the immigrants.

22. Holdensky to Stephany, 29 January 1900 in MS 173/1/11/2, SUA.

23. 'Refugees from the Cape', *Southampton Times*, 3 February 1900.

24. Nathan Levy to the Mayor of Southampton, 4 February 1900 in MS 173/1/11/2, SUA. See also minutes of the Jewish Board of Guardians, 12 February 1900 in MS 173/1/1/2.

25. 'Letter from Refugees', *Jewish Chronicle*, 9 February 1900.

26. See V. D. Lipman, *A Century of Social Service 1859–1959: The Jewish Board of*

Guardians (London: Routledge & Kegan Paul, 1959), pp.94–102, esp. 94–7; S. Hochberg, 'The Repatriation of East European Jews from Great Britain 1881–1914', *Jewish Social Studies*, Vol.50, Nos1–2 (Winter-Spring 1988–92), pp.49–62; minutes of the Jewish Board of Guardians, 11 December 1905 in MS 173/1/1/3.

27. Feldman, *Englishmen and Jews*, pp.303–4; on the aliens issue from 1900, see Garrard, *The English and Immigration*, pp.36–41.

28. Royal Commission on Alien Immigration, *Report of the Royal Commission on Alien Immigration* (London: HMSO, 1903 Cmd 1741); Bernard Porter, *The Refugee Question in Mid-Victorian Politics* (Cambridge: Cambridge University Press, 1979), p.2; Feldman, *Englishmen and Jews*, p.305; Gainer, *The Alien Invasion*, p.187.

29. London Committee of Deputies of British Jews, *Objections to the Aliens Bill* (London: London Committee of Deputies of British Jews, 1904), pp.11–12. See Geoffrey Alderman, *Modern British Jewry* (Oxford: Oxford University Press, 1992) p.137 for a critical perspective on the Board and the aliens agitation.

30. *Hansard* (HL), Vol.CXLI Cols8–9 (14 February 1905).

31. On the Liberals, see Gainer, *The Alien Invasion*, chapters 7 and 8; Garrard, *The English and Immigration*, chapter 6.

32. J. E. B. Seely, *Adventure* (London: William Heinemann, 1930), p.100.

33. *Hansard* (HC), Vol.145 Cols755–9 (2 May 1905).

34. 'Free Trade for Southampton', *Southampton Times*, 29 April 1905.

35. 'Freemantle Liberals Talk About Aliens', *Southampton Times*, 22 April 1905.

36. Garrard, *The English and Immigration*, chapter 7.

37. *Aliens Act, 1905* (11 August 1905), 5 EDW.7.

38. 'The Immigration Question in the United States', *Jewish Chronicle*, 1 January 1904.

39. Higham, *Strangers in the Land*, p.159.

40. London Committee of the Deputies of the British Jews, *A Defence of the Alien Immigrant* (London: London Committee of the Deputies of the British Jews, 1904), p.9.

41. United States Diplomatic Records, Despatches from US Consuls in Southampton, 1790–1906 (T239) Roll 9, Vol.9, No.55, 9 August 1904.

42. 'Colonel Albert W. Swalm', *The Syren and Shipping*, 15 March 1905.

43. See the figures in the records of the US Consuls, Roll 9, Vol.9, 1900–1911.

44. Testimony of Albert Gibbs in Southampton Oral History Unit, Southampton City Heritage; Donald Hyslop and Sheila Jemima, 'The "Titanic" and Southampton: The Oral Evidence', *Oral History*, Vol.19, No.1 (Spring 1991), pp.41–2; for more detail on the hostel and a photograph, see Alan Leonard and Rodney Baker, *A Maritime History of Southampton in Picture Postcards* (Southampton: Ensign Publications, 1989), p.38 and *Stevens Directory of Southampton and Neighbourhood, 1895* (London: Stevens, 1895), p.360.

45. 'Sam Smith: "Southampton Water" and other objects made by Sam' (Southampton City Art Gallery, no date); Accession, No. MO 112, 'Seafarers Project', interviewed by Sheila Jemima, 7 July 1997, Southampton City Heritage.

46. Oral testimony of Jack Farber, Manchester Jewish Museum tapes, J82 and Sadie Raphael J201; Hyslop and Jemima, 'The "Titanic"', pp.41–2; Donald Hyslop, Alastair Forsyth and Sheila Jemima, *Titanic Voices: The Story of the White Star Line, Titanic and Southampton* (Southampton: Southampton City Council, 1994).

47. Geoffrey Green, *The Royal Navy and Anglo-Jewry: 1740–1820* (London: Geoffrey Green, 1989), *passim*; Aubrey Weinberg, *Portsmouth Jewry* Portsmouth Papers, No.41 (Portsmouth: City of Portsmouth, 1985), p.15. For the Moss sisters, see the manuscript of their *Romance of Jewish History* (1840) and other materials in MS 160, SUA; and for Katie Magnus, Ruth Sebag-Montefiore, *A Family Patchwork: Five Generations of an Anglo-Jewish Family* (London: Weidenfeld & Nicolson, 1987), pp.64–8.

48. Harold Pollins, *Economic History of the Jews in England* (Rutherford: Fairleigh

Dickinson University Press, 1982), pp.243–4, table 3.

49. Weinberg, *Portsmouth Jewry*, pp.6–11; *The Jewish Year Book, 1907* (London: Greenberg & Co., 1907), p.194.

50. 'Zionist Meeting at Portsmouth', *Jewish Chronicle*, 5 February 1904.

51. Ian Mikardo, *Back-Bencher* (London: Weidenfeld & Nicolson, 1988), pp.6–8.

52. Ibid., p.17; Michael Gold, *Jews Without Money* (London: Noel Douglas, 1930), p.41.

53. Mikardo, *Back-Bencher*, pp.21–5, 28.

54. *Jewish Year Book, 1907*, pp.149 (Basingstoke), 155 (Bournemouth). See also Anne Ruffell, 'Bournemouth's Hebrew Heritage', *Hampshire Magazine* (November 1980), pp.42–5. For Aldershot see *The Jewish Year Book, 1896* (London: Greenberg & Co., 1896), p.64 and Malcolm Slowe, 'The Foundation of Aldershot Synagogue', in Aubrey Newman (ed.), *Provincial Jewry in Victorian Britain* (London: Jewish Historical Society of England, 1975), pp.1–13.

55. Cecil Roth, *The Rise of Provincial Jewry* (London: Jewish Monthly, 1950), p.100; V. D. Lipman, *Social History of the Jews in England: 1850–1950* (London: Watts, 1954), pp.21, 39, 66; the earliest minute book of the Southampton Hebrew Congregation has disappeared so details of the early schism are unknown. For its richer members, see accounts of the community in Executive minutes, 28 November 1914, records of the Southampton Hebrew Congregation and S. Fyne to Dr Hirsch of the Chovrei Zion, 31 January 1895, Central Zionist Archives, Jerusalem (CZA), A2/78.

56. Ivor Montagu, *The Youngest Son: Autobiographical Chapters* (London: Laurence & Wishart, 1970), pp.48, 62. On Townhill Park see *Country Life*, 14 and 21 April 1923; *Southern Daily Echo*, 11 February 1946; *Southern Evening Echo*, 13 May 1976 and *Hampshire Chronicle*, 11 December 1987.

57. Geoffrey Alderman, *The Federation of Synagogues: 1887–1987* (London: Federation of Synagogues, 1987); Daniel Gutwein, *The Divided Elite: Economics, Politics and Anglo-Jewry 1882–1917* (Leiden: E. J. Brill, 1992), pp.219–306; Lily Montagu, *Samuel Montagu: First Baron Swaythling* (London: Truslove & Hanson, 1913), pp.13, 51.

58. Lady Battersea, *Reminsicences* (London: Macmillan, 1922), pp.164–5; 418–23.

59. Edward Kessler (ed.), *An English Jew: The Life and Writing of Claude Montefiore* (London: Vallentine Mitchell, 1989), pp.12, 14; Lucy Cohen, *Some Recollections of Claude Goldsmid Montefiore* (London: Faber & Faber, 1940), pp.86–9.

60. Cohen, *Some Recollections*, pp.89–90; Leonard Stein and C. C. Aronsfeld (eds), *Leonard G. Montefiore 1889–1961: In Memorium* (London: Vallentine, Mitchell, 1964), pp.108–9.

61. *Jewish Guardian*, 17 June 1927 for the obituary of the second Lord Swaythling; *Southampton Times*, 11 April 1914.

62. Bill White, Sheila Jemima and Donald Hyslop (eds), *Dream Palaces: Going to the Pictures in Southampton* (Southampton: Southampton City Council, 1996), p.46; *Southampton 1921 Street Directory*; Southampton City Archives, Town Clerk's records, Box 127 for details on the Ehrenbergs.

63. *Jewish Year Book, 1907*, p.196; Executive minutes, 27 January 1901 with accounts, and 19 May 1908, resignation of Holdinsky. There is correspondence concerning Holdinsky in the records of the community which suggest that his American life was difficult. His son was brought up in an orphanage in New Orleans after Holdinsky's wife died.

64. Executive Minutes of Southampton Hebrew Congregation, July 1908.

65. Executive Minutes of Southampton Hebrew Congregation, 27 January 1901.

66. Executive Minutes of Southampton Hebrew Congregation, 10 December 1905, 5 March 1911; index cards on the history of the Jewish community of Southampton prepared by Sidney Weintroub in the records of the Hebrew Congregation; Fyne to

Hirsch, 31 January 1895, CZA A2/78.

67. Edward Bristow, *Prostitution and Prejudice: The Jewish Fight Against White Slavery, 1870–1939* (Oxford: Oxford University Press, 1982); Lloyd Gartner, 'Anglo-Jewry and the Jewish International Traffic in Prostitution 1885–1914', *American Jewish Studies Review*, Vol.7/8 (1982/3), pp.129–78.

68. Gentlemen's Committee minutes, 21 June 1896, MS 173/2/2/1.

69. Gentlemen's Committee minutes, 15 October 1899, MS 173/2/2/5; Lara Marks, 'Jewish Women and Prostitution in the East End of London', *The Jewish Quarterly*, Vol.34, No.2 (1987), pp.6–10.

70. Gentlemen's Committee minutes, 19 November 1899, MS 173/2/2/5.

71. Gentlemen's Committee minutes, 4 October 1900, MS 173/2/2/5.

72. Executive minutes of Southampton Hebrew Congregation, 6 November 1912.

73. Executive minutes of Southampton Hebrew Congregation, 1 January 1914; Montagu, *The Youngest Son*, pp.18, 43.

CHAPTER 2

1. Daniel Pick, *War Machine: The Rationalisation of Slaughter in the Modern Age* (New Haven: Yale University Press, 1993), chapters 11–15; Michael Marrus, *The Unwanted: European Refugees in the Twentieth Century* (New York: Oxford University Press, 1985), pp.51–2.

2. Marrus, *The Unwanted*, chapter 2; John Hope Simpson, *The Refugee Problem: Report of a Survey* (London: Oxford University Press, 1939), chapters 9 and 10; Gary Cross, *Immigrant Workers in Industrial France: The Making of a New Laboring Class* (Philadelphia: Temple University Press, 1983).

3. David Cesarani, 'Anti-Alienism in England after the First World War', *Immigrants and Minorities*, Vol.6 (March 1987), pp.5–29.

4. Byles and McKenna in *Hansard* (HC), Vol.65 Cols1989–90 (5 August 1914).

5. *Aliens Restriction Act, 1915* (5 August 1914), 4 & 5 GEO.5.

6. 'Germans in Southampton', *Southern Daily Echo*, 5 August 1914.

7. 'Aliens in Portsmouth', *Hampshire Telegraph and Post*, 21 August 1914.

8. *Hansard* (HC), Vol.65 Col.1989 (5 August 1914).

9. 'The Aliens Order: Prosecution at Portsmouth', *Hampshire Telegraph and Post*, 16 October 1914.

10. Panikos Panayi, *The Enemy in Our Midst: Germans in Britain During the First World War* (Oxford: Berg, 1991), chapter 8; idem, 'Anti-German Riots in London During the First World War', *German History*, Vol.7, No.2 (1989), pp.184–203; 'Anti-German Riots in Britain During the First World War', in idem (ed.), *Racial Violence in Britain in the Nineteenth and Twentieth Centuries* (London: Leicester University Press, 1996), pp.65–91 and 'The Lancashire Anti-German Riots of May 1915', *Manchester Region History Review*, Vol.2 (1988), pp.3–11.

11. 'German Spy Scare: Portsmouth Shopkeepers' Window Smashed', *Hampshire Telegraph and Post*, 21 August 1914.

12. J. C. Bird, 'Control of Enemy Alien Civilians in Great Britain 1914–1918' (unpublished PhD thesis, University of London, 1981), pp.8, 9, 12–13, 127 (for the balance within the Commons), 134 (for the Southampton Ice Rink); for the effect of such measures, see Stella Yarrow, 'The Impact of Hostility on Germans in Britain, 1914–1918', in Tony Kushner and Kenneth Lunn, *The Politics of Marginality: Race, the Radical Right and Minorities in Twentieth Century Britain* (London: Frank Cass, 1990), pp.97–112.

13. William Rubinstein, 'Henry Page Croft and the National Party 1917–22', *Journal of Contemporary History*, Vol.9, No.1 (January 1974), pp.129–48; Panayi, *The Enemy*

in Our Midst, chapter 7.

14. Beresford in *Hansard* (HC), Vol.68 Cols1381, 1386–7 (26 November 1914).

15. Bottomley in *John Bull*, 15 May 1915. See Panayi, *The Enemy in Our Midst*, pp.233–4 for comment and other parts of this editorial which the left-wing *New Statesman* described as 'the most disgraceful passage we have ever read in an English paper'; Beresford in *Hansard* (HC), Vol.68 Cols115–16 (12 November 1914); Cols1386–7 (26 November 1914); Vol.71 Cols1611–12 (11 May 1915).

16. Yarrow, 'The Impact of Hostility', pp.109–10; Panayi, *The Enemy in Our Midst*, p.283; *Census of England and Wales, 1911: County of Hampshire* (London: HMSO, 1914), table 31 and *Census of England and Wales, 1921: Hampshire and the Isle of Wight* (London: HMSO, 1923), table 22 and p.xxxix.

17. *Census of England and Wales, 1921*, table 22 and p.xxxix; Colin Holmes in *Immigrants and Minorities*, Vol.6, No.2 (July 1987), pp.265–6. The Belgian exodus is not covered in Marrus, *The Unwanted* nor Simpson, *The Refugee Problem*, p.1. For a detailed account of the relevant statistics, see T. T. S. de Jastrzebski, 'The Register of Belgian Refugees', *Journal of the Royal Statistical Society*, Vol.79 (March 1916), pp.133–53.

18. Peter Cahalan, *Belgian Refugee Relief in England During the Great War* (New York: Garland, 1982), p.18; 'Belgian or German?', *Hampshire Telegraph*, 18 September 1914; Belgian Relief Fund Crumpsall Depot, leaflet in Manchester Central Reference Library.

19. Ivor Montagu, *The Youngest Son: Autobiographical Chapters* (London: Laurence & Wishart, 1970), pp.93–4; more generally, see R. Johansson, *Small State in Boundary Conflict: Belgium and the Belgian-German Border, 1914–1919* (Lund: Lund University Press, 1988); John Horne and Alan Kramer, 'German "Atrocities" and Franco-German Opinion, 1914: The Evidence of German Soldiers' Diaries', *The Journal of Modern History*, Vol.66, No.1 (March 1994), pp.1–33 and esp. p.22; Trevor Wilson, 'Lord Bryce's Investigation into Alleged German Atrocities in Belgium, 1914–15', *Journal of Contemporary History*, Vol.14 (1979), pp.369–83, esp. 380. See also Ruth Harris, 'The "Child of the Barbarian": Rape, Race and Nationalism in France During the First World War', *Past & Present*, No.141 (November 1993), pp.170–206; on Belgian refugee movements at the start of the war see *First Report of the Departmental Committee Appointed by the President of the Local Government Board To Consider and Report on Questions Arising in Connection with the Reception and Employment of the Belgian Refugees in this Country* (London: HMSO, 1914 Cmd.7750), p.4; Herbert Samuel letter to the press, 7 January 1915 in Ministry of Health, *Report on the Work Undertaken by the British Government in the Reception and Care of the Belgian Refugees* (London: HMSO, 1920), pp.98–9. See this report, pp.60, 72–3 for population figures and geographical and occupational details; Samuel in *Hansard* (HC), Vol.66 Col.558 (9 September 1914).

20. Samuel in *Hansard* (HC), Vol.66 Col.558 (9 September 1914); Cahalan, *Belgian Refugee Relief*, pp.1, 3–4 and chapter 3; Simpson, *The Refugee Problem*, p.1. On a more popular level, Francesca Wilson, *They Came as Strangers: The Story of Refugees to Great Britain* (London: Hamish Hamilton, 1959), pp.216–17 whilst ending in 1914, does include the Belgians in her epilogue though comments that these refugees 'were a passing episode'; *First Report of the Departmental Committee*, p.4; *Report on the Work Undertaken*, pp.3–6 for the origins of the War Refugees Committee and its connection to Belgian relief. Robert Waley Cohen, a prominent Anglo-Jewish refugee worker during the 1930s, 'reminded his colleagues [in a November 1939 memorandum] that when, in 1914, Belgians had fled to Britain to escape German persecution, government resources had been harnessed to assist them. It was [his] conviction that the government should now provide similar aid for

the refugees who had fled from the Nazis'. Quoted by A. Gottlieb, *Men of Vision: Anglo-Jewry's Aid to Victims of the Nazi Regime 1933–1945* (London: Weidenfeld & Nicolson, 1998), p.154. Francesca Wilson, cited above, was another individual whose involvement in the refugee movement started by helping the Belgians. See also note 46 below for further examples of such refugee work connections.

21. Montagu, *The Youngest Son*, pp.88–9; Cahalan, *Belgian Refugee Relief*, pp.169, 200; *First Report of the Departmental Committee*, p.36 and *Report on the Work Undertaken*, p.9 for the number of local committees and p.73 for a county by county analysis of settlement; Holmes in *Immigrants and Minorities*, Vol.6, No.2 (July 1987), p.265.

22. *Report on the Work Undertaken*, p.73 for local distribution of refugees; 'The Belgian Refugees: Winchester's Hospitality', *Hampshire Chronicle*, 24 October 1914.

23. 'Alresford: Belgian Refugees Invited', *Hampshire Chronicle*, 7 November 1914.

24. 'Belgian's Tribute to England', *Hampshire Chronicle*, 7 November 1914.

25. 'Homes from Home: Refugees at Gosport', *Hampshire Telegraph and Post*, 18 September 1914.

26. Cahalan, *Belgian Refugee Relief*, pp.11, 58–9 for McKenna; Lucy Cohen, *Lady de Rothschild and Her Daughters 1821–1931* (London: John Murray, 1935), p.307 for Lady Battersea.

27. Correspondence in PRO HO 45/10737/261921/1.

28. Cahalan, *Belgian Refugee Relief*, p.59.

29. Biographical details of Ruth Dent from her daughter, Dionis McNair, September 1996; Eleanor Ruth Dent, 'The Chronicles of the Belgians (unpublished diary in possession of Miss McNair). I am extremely grateful to Miss McNair for the loan of this diary. Brief extracts are included in James O'Donald Mays (ed.), *The New Forest Book: An Illustrated Anthology* (Burley, New Forest: New Forest Leaves, 1989), pp.186–7. For her post-war work see Ian and Ruth McNair, *The Adventures of Wong Wing Wu* (Oxford: Basil Blackwell, 1933).

30. Information from Miss McNair. Copies of *The Pierrot* are deposited at the Museum of Childhood in Edinburgh.

31. Eleanor Ruth Dent, 'The Chronicles of the Belgians'.

32. Ibid.

33. Colin Holmes, *John Bull's Island: Immigration & British Society, 1871–1971* (Basingstoke, Hants: Macmillan, 1988), p.102; Cahalan, *Belgian Refugee Relief*, p.259 for the Fulham disturbance; *Report of the Work Undertaken*, p.27 has details of the specific hostels 'providing hospitality for better class refugees, members of the aristocracy and those who had occupied superior positions in Belgium'.

34. C. W. Hawkins, *The Story of Alton* (Alton, Hants: Alton District Council, 1973), pp.64–5; Dent, 'The Chronicles of the Belgians'.

35. Translation of letter from Mr and Mrs Stroobants to Mrs Dent, 24 October 1915 in the possession of Miss McNair.

36. Monument to the Belgian soldiers in Southampton Cemetery: 23 soldiers are listed alongside the inscription 'In Memorium Militum Belgic orum Qui Mortem Pro Patria oppetierunt'; 'Honouring the Brave: Belgian Minister Unveils Local Memorial', *Southampton Times*, 27 May 1916.

37. 'Homes from Home', *Hampshire Telegraph and Post*, 18 September 1914.

38. Information about Devon from Dr Mark Stoyle, interview with Tony Kushner, 5 December 1996; Montagu, *The Youngest Son*, p.204. For a typical account of the leaving of Belgian refugees, see the *Souvenir of The Farewell Gathering of the Belgian Refugees who have been Befriended by the Belgian Protestant Relief Committee 1914 to 1918* (London: Protestant Alliance, 1918).

39. 'Belgians in Britain: Why the Clogs Have Gone: Successful Battle With Adversity', *Hampshire Telegraph*, 26 May 1916.

40. Holmes, *John Bull's Island*, p.91; A. J. P. Taylor, *English History 1914–1945* (Oxford: Clarendon Press, 1965), pp.19–20, note 5; *First Report of the Departmental Committee*, pp.43–4; *Report on the Work Undertaken*, p.8 for the Earl's Court Camp.
41. Cahalan, *Belgian Refugee Relief*, pp.8, 42, 58, 67.
42. Hawkins, *The Story of Alton*, p.65.
43. Holmes, *John Bull's Island*, p.101 and *Report on the Work Undertaken*, pp.36–7, 48 on the decision to repatriate taken in 1916; *Census of England and Wales, 1921*, p.xxxix.
44. *Hampshire Telegraph*, 26 May 1916; *Hansard* (HC), Vol.110 Col.3176 (18 November 1918), questions by Denman and Butcher and (HC), Vol.122 Cols421–2 (3 December 1919), question by Stanier; Norman Gardiner, *The University of Southampton as a War Hospital* (Southampton: Kingfisher, 1983), pp.6–7; *First Report of the Departmental Committee*, p.44; *Report on the Work Undertaken*, pp.47–8 for the Liverpool Committee and p.80 for the high percentage of Flemish refugees amongst those remaining in Britain after the war.
45. Lloyd George letter of May 1919 in *Report on the Work Undertaken*, p.113.
46. Jastrzebski, 'The Register of Belgian Refugees', p.158; *Jewish Chronicle*, 29 August 1997, letter from Joan Stiebel on the work of Oscar Schiff with Belgian refugees in the First World War. As will be seen, Schiff played a controversial role in the 1920s and during the Nazi era with regard to Jewish refugees from eastern and central Europe.

CHAPTER 3

1. J. M. Rich to Robert Gower, 1 June 1927 in records of the Board of Deputies of British Jews (BD), E3/79, Greater London Record Office (GLRO).
2. For the renewal of the aliens orders and the implementation of the Act see David Cesarani, 'Anti-Alienism in England After the First World War', *Immigrants & Minorities*, Vol.6, No.1 (March 1987), pp.5–29; J. R. Clynes to D'Avigdor Goldsmid, 26 February 1930, following a Jewish delegation on 5 November 1929 in BD, E3/80, GLRO.
3. Minutes of proceedings, Arthur Henderson and members of the Board of Deputies, 8 May 1924 in BD, E3/77; Board of Deputies delegation to the Home Office, 6 February 1925, BD, E3/78, GLRO.
4. Sir John Hope Simpson, *Refugees: Preliminary Report of a Survey* (London: Royal Institute of International Affairs, 1938), p.99.
5. Sibley and Elias quoted by M. J. Landa, *The Alien Problem and its Remedy* (London: P. S. King and Son, 1911), p.261; 'The Aliens Bill', *Manchester Guardian*, 12 July 1927, circulated as a leaflet by the Board of Deputies.
6. Cesarani, 'Anti-Alienism'.
7. A. H. Lane, *The Alien Menace: A Statement of the Case*, 3rd edition (London: Boswell Printing and Publishing Co., 1932), pp.67–9.
8. On the cross-over between Fascist and non-Fascist antisemitism in Britain, see Tony Kushner, 'The Impact of British Anti-semitism, 1918–1945', in David Cesarani (ed.), *The Making of Modern Anglo-Jewry* (Oxford: Blackwell, 1990), pp.191–208; David Cesarani, 'Joynson-Hicks and the Radical Right in England after the First World War', in Tony Kushner and Kenneth Lunn (eds), *Traditions of Intolerance: Historical Perspectives on Fascism and Race Discourse in Britain* (Manchester: Manchester University Press, 1989), pp.118–39; Donald Bloxham, 'On the Memory of the Armenian Genocide and the Holocaust', *The Journal of Holocaust Education*, Vol.4, No.1 (Summer 1995), pp.74–86.
9. Donald Miller and Lorna Miller, *Survivors: An Oral History of the Armenian*

Genocide (Berkeley: University of California Press, 1993), part 1; D. M. Lang, *Armenia: Cradle of Civilization* (London: George Allen & Unwin, 1970) and idem, *The Armenians: A People in Exile* (London: George Allen & Unwin, 1981).

10. Richard Hovannisian, 'The Historical Dimensions of the Armenian Question, 1878–1923', in idem (ed.), *The Armenian Genocide in Perspective* (New Brunswick, NJ: Transaction Press, 1986), pp.19–40, esp. p.26.

11. Vahakn Dadrian, *The History of the Armenian Genocide: Ethnic Conflict from the Balkans to Anatolia to the Caucasus* (Oxford: Berg, 1995); Robert Melson, *Revolution and Genocide: On the Origins of the Armenian Genocide and the Holocaust* (Chicago: University of Chicago Press, 1992); Richard Hovannisian, *The Armenian Genocide: History, Politics, Ethics* (London: Macmillan, 1992).

12. *The Treatment of Armenians in the Ottoman Empire: Documents Presented to Viscount Grey of Fallodon* (London: Hodder & Stoughton, 1916), pp.20–1.

13. *Hansard* (HC), Vol.75 Col.75 (16 November 1915).

14. *Hansard* (HL), Vol.19 Col.1003 (6 October 1915).

15. Akaby Nassibian, *Britain and the Armenian Question: 1915–1923* (London: Croom Helm, 1984), pp.259–60.

16. Williams and O'Connor in *Hansard* (HC), Vol.75 Cols1759–73 (16 November 1915).

17. Robert Cecil and Major Lane-Fox in *Hansard* (HC), Vol.75 Cols1776, 1777–8 (16 November 1915); Nassibian, *Britain and the Armenian Question*, chapters 2 and 3.

18. B. Jenazian, 'The Armenian Merchants and the Armenian Community in Manchester' (unpublished typescript, 1965) in Manchester Central Reference Library, Local Studies F301 45 Je1.

19. Nassibian, *Britain and the Armenian Question*, p.260.

20. Generally, the pro-Armenians were, at best, ambivalent about mass campaigning. See Nassibian, *Britain and the Armenian Question*, chapter 2.

21. Manoug Somakian, *Empires in Conflict: Armenia and the Great Powers, 1895–1920* (London: I. B. Tauris, 1995); Nassibian, *Britain and the Armenian Question*, chapters 5 and 6; Salahi Ramsdan Sonyel, *The Ottoman Armenians: Victims of Great Power Diplomacy* (London: K. Rustem & Brother, 1987).

22. Nassibian, *Britain and the Armenian Question*, pp.64, 253.

23. Hope Simpson, *Refugees: Preliminary Report*, pp.26–7; idem, *The Refugee Problem: Report of a Survey* (London: Oxford University Press, 1939), chapter 3 (p.42 for Cyprus) and p.340; Robin Oakley, 'The Control of Cypriot Migration to Britain Between the Wars', *Immigrants & Minorities*, Vol.6, No.1 (March 1987), pp.30–43.

24. For an earlier period, see T. S. R. Boase (ed.), *The Cilician Kingdom of Armenia* (New York: St Martin's Press, 1978); Dr Larry Day, interview with Tony Kushner, 22 November 1995.

25. Hitler quoted by Miller and Miller, *Survivors*, p.5. The *Sheffield Telegraph*, 6 August 1938, asked 'must the Jews of Germany perish in the wilderness as a million Armenians did when deported by the Turks?' Quoted in Andrew Sharf, *The British Press and Jews Under Nazi Rule* (London: Oxford University Press, 1964), pp.96–7.

26. *Census of England and Wales, 1921: Hampshire and the Isle of Wight* (London: HMSO, 1923), p.86 table 22; Simpson, *The Refugee Problem*, p.340.

27. Bloxham, 'On the Memory of the Armenian Genocide'.

28. Dr Mark Stoyle, interview with Tony Kushner, 5 December 1996 for the memory of the Armenian genocide within one family. Dr Stoyle's grandmother retained a strong and troubling memory of the genocide which she did not, however, communicate to her son.

29. *Hansard* (HC), Vol.114 Col.2759 (15 April 1919).

30. *Hansard* (HC), Vol.114 Col.2790 (15 April 1919).

31. *Hansard* (HC), Vol.114 Cols2762–3 (15 April 1919).

32. *Hansard* (HC), Vol.114 Cols2775, 2778 (15 April 1919). See, in the same debate, the comments of Mr Stanton (Col.2798) and Pemberton Billing in *Hansard* (HC), Vol.120 Col.86 (22 October 1919).

33. *Hansard* (HC), Vol.120 Cols86–7 (22 October 1919).

34. Wedgwood in *Hansard* (HC), Vol.120 Col.84 (22 October 1919). See also John Jones (Col.90) and T. Griffiths in *Hansard* (HC), Vol.120 Col.1414 (4 November 1919).

35. *Aliens Restriction (Amendment) Act, 1919* (23 December 1919), 9 & 10 GEO. 5.

36. Haldane Porter of the Home Office reported in minutes of the Gentlemen's Committee of the Jewish Association for the Protection of Women and Children, 24 June 1919, MS 173/2/2/6, University of Southampton archive (SUA).

37. *Hansard* (HC), Vol.120 Cols209–10 (23 October 1919).

38. William Rubinstein, 'Henry Page Croft and the National Party 1917–22', *Journal of Contemporary History*, Vol.9, No.1 (January 1974), pp.143–4.

39. Paul Rich, *Race and Empire in British Politics* (Cambridge: Cambridge University Press, 1986), chapter 7.

40. *Statutory Rules and Orders 1920*, Vol.1 (London: HMSO, 1921), pp.138–64 S.R. & O., No.448.

41. Colin Holmes, *John Bull's Island: Immigration & British Society, 1871–1971* (Basingstoke, Hants: Macmillan, 1988), p.114; Cesarani, 'Joynson-Hicks'.

42. Sylvain Levy to the President of the Council of the League of Nations, 8 December 1920, in Lucien Wolf, *Russo-Jewish Refugees in Eastern Europe* (London: Joint Foreign Committee, 1921), p.15 Appendix 1.

43. Wolf, *Russo-Jewish Refugees*, p.7.

44. Ibid., p.15.

45. Hope Simpson, *The Refugee Problem*, chapter 10; Michael Marrus, *The Unwanted: European Refugees in the Twentieth Century* (New York: Oxford University Press, 1985), chapter 2, esp. p.90.

46. Hope Simpson, *The Refugee Problem*, p.192.

47. Ibid., pp.203–7.

48. Paul Weindling, 'A Virulent Strain: Typhus, Bacteriology and Scientific Racism' (unpublished paper, Social History of Medicine Conference, University of Southampton, 18 September 1996), pp.6–7.

49. Jews' Temporary Shelter, *Thirty-Second Report For the Three Years Ending October 31st, 1921* (London: Jews' Temporary Shelter, 1923), pp.7–8, 12–13.

50. See the minutes of the Cunard Company in C1/251, University of Liverpool archives (ULA), for its ambitions with regard to Southampton in the post-war period; Alan Leonard and Rodney Baker, *A Maritime History of Southampton in Picture Postcards* (Southampton: Ensign Publications, 1989), p.38 for Atlantic Hotel.

51. For the accounts of the Atlantic Park Hostel Company see D42/AC/14/517, ULA.

52. Minutes of the Gentlemen's Committee, Jewish Association for the Protection of Women and Children, 14 April 1920, 12 April 1921, MS 173/2/2/6, SUA.

53. John Higham, *Strangers in the Land: Patterns of American Nativism 1860–1925* (New York: Atheneum, 1978), pp.308–11.

54. Jews' Temporary Shelter, *Thirty-Third Report*, p.8.

55. Jewish Association for the Protection of Women and Children, 'Report on the Protection of Migrants to the Permanent Advisory Committee of the League of Nations on the Traffic in Women and Children', February 1924, MS 173/2/4/2, SUA.

56. Savage reports in 841.56/15 (27 January 1922) and 841.56/24 (February 1924), Department of State, National Archives, Washington, DC (NA); Sir Arthur Geddes, *Despatch from H.M. Ambassador at Ellis Island Immigration Station* (London: HMSO, 1923 Cmd. 1940).

57. Cyril Orolowitz, interview with Tony Kushner, 1 June 1994; Southampton City Council Minutes, Health Committee, 7 October 1931; John M. Savage report, 27

January, 841.56/15, Department of State, NA.

58. Savage report, 27 January 1922, 841.56/15, Department of State, NA.
59. Higham, *Strangers in the Land*, pp.316–24.
60. Minutes of the General Committee of the Jews' Temporary Shelter, 6 March 1923, Jews' Temporary Shelter archive.
61. *Hansard* (HC), Vol.180 Cols313–14 (11 February 1925).
62. 'Stranded Russian Jews', *Southern Daily Echo*, 14 June 1924; Southampton City Heritage, 'Seafarer Project', Accession, No.MO 112, interviewed by Sheila Jemima, 7 July 1997.
63. Savage to the Secretary of State, 16 June 1924, 811.111/42697, Department of State, NA.
64. Correspondence in the case file of the Kachura family in 811.11 Kachura (1924), Department of State, NA.
65. Report, 'Atlantic Park, the Immigrants' Hostel at Eastleigh, From the Immigrants' Standpoint', pp.9–10, 6 February 1924 in 841.56/24, Department of State, NA.
66. Jews' Temporary Shelter, *Thirty-Fifth Report for the Year Ending October 31st, 1925* (London: Jews' Temporary Shelter, 1926), p.12.
67. Cyril Orolowitz, interview with Tony Kushner, I June 1994; 'Russia in Reality: A Terrible Tale of Actual Experience', *The Friend* (no date, 1929) in Orolowitz papers, MS 250, SUA.
68. Orolowitz papers, MS 250, SUA; Cyril Orolowitz, interview with Tony Kushner, 1 June 1994.
69. For Davis, see Higham, *Strangers in the Land*, pp.318–19; letter in Orolowitz papers, MS 250, SUA.
70. Jacob Solomon to Coolidge, 14 January 1924 in Orolowitz papers, MS 250, SUA.
71. Higham, *Strangers in the Land*, p.23 for Lazarus; 'Russia in Reality', *The Friend*.
72. Edna Bradlow quoted by Milton Shain, *The Roots of Antisemitism in South Africa* (Charlottesville: University Press of Virginia, 1994), pp.137–41.
73. Cyril Orolowitz, 'The Family Shleimowitz – Later Known as Solomon', in Orolowitz papers, MS 250, SUA.
74. Minutes of the Gentlemen's Committee, 4 March 1925, MS 173/2/2/6, SUA.
75. Wilbur Carr to Albert Johnson, Chairman of the House of Representatives' Committee on Immigration and Naturalization, 6 February 1926, 150.006/6, Department of State, NA.
76. Geoffrey Alderman, *Modern British Jewry* (Oxford: Oxford University Press, 1992), pp.115–17 for the Poor Jews' Temporary Shelter before 1914. See David Cesarani, 'The Transformation of Communal Authority in Anglo-Jewry, 1914–1940', in idem, *The Making of Anglo-Jewry*, pp.115–40 for the slow change in power structure after the First World War.
77. Schiff in meeting at New Court, March 1924 in Jews' Temporary Shelter archives.
78. Jochelman quoted in *Jewish Guardian*, 4 July 1924.
79. 'Action by Ukrainian Federation', *Jewish Guardian*, 13 June 1924: Jochelman at Board of Deputies of British Jews meeting, 15 June 1924 reported in *Jewish Chronicle*, 20 June 1924.
80. Minutes of General Committee of Jews' Temporary Shelter, 15 January, 24 June and 10 July 1924, Jews' Temporary Shelter archive; Jochelman in Executive Committee of the Federation of Ukrainian Jews, *Jewish Guardian*, 4 July 1924. See also *Jewish Chronicle*, 20 June, 4, 11 July 1924 and 23, 30 January, 6 February 1925 for the dispute.
81. Minutes of Gentlemen's Committee of Jewish Association, 4 March 1925, MS 173/2/2/6; Aharon Weiss, 'Jewish-Ukrainian Relations in Western Ukraine During the Holocaust', in Peter Potichnyj and Howard Aster (eds), *Ukrainian-Jewish Relations in Historical Perspective* (Edmonton, Alberta: Canadian Institute of

Ukrainian Studies, 1990), pp.409–20. See also chapter 6 of this study.

82. Minutes of the Executive Committee of the Union of Jewish Women, 14 September 1926, MS 129/B/6.
83. Joynson-Hicks to Hudson, 15 October 1926 in PRO HO 45/12776.
84. See delegations of the Board of Deputies in PRO HO 45/24765 and in Board of Deputies records, E3/77, 78 79 and 80 and Aliens Committee minutes (1919–30), C2/1/3 and C2/1/4, GLRO.
85. 'The Eastleigh Migrants', *Jewish Chronicle*, 6 February 1925.
86. Prag to Rich, 1 June 1927, E3/79, GRLO.
87. For Prag's pre-war activities, see Alderman, *Modern British Jewry*, pp.249–50.
88. 'Six Years of Waiting Without Hope', *Daily Express*, 29 November 1929.
89. Jews' Temporary Shelter, *Fortieth Report for the Year Ending October 31st, 1930* (London: Jews' Temporary Shelter, 1931), p.12.
90. Death certificate of Ita Furman in Southampton Registry Office. There are at least six Jews from Atlantic Park buried in the Jewish cemetery, most having had photographs within the headstones; Jews' Temporary Shelter, *Fortieth Report*, p.12.
91. 'Protecting the Emigrant', *Southern Daily Echo*, 4 June 1924.
92. Cyril Orolowitz, interview with Tony Kushner, 1 June 1994; 'The Atlantic Park Hostel: Story of a Recent Visit', *Eastleigh Weekly News*, 1 October 1926.
93. For the hunger strike see *Daily Herald*, 7 and 8 January 1925; *Daily News*, 7 and 8 January 1925; *Jewish Chronicle*, 9 January 1925; 'The Transmigrants at Eastleigh: Interview with Col. R. D. Barbor', *Jewish Chronicle*, 6 February 1925.
94. *Jewish Chronicle*, 6 February 1925; Morris Myer, 'Transmigrants at Eastleigh: An Independent Inquiry', *Jewish Guardian*, 23 January 1925.
95. *Jewish Chronicle*, 6 February 1925; *Jewish Guardian*, 23 January 1925.
96. For Barbor, see 'New Manager at Atlantic Park', *Eastleigh Weekly News*, 21 September 1923; for Johnson, *Eastleigh Weekly News*, 25 May and 20 July 1923.
97. *Jewish Guardian*, 23 January 1925; *Jewish Chronicle*, 6 February 1925.
98. Letter to Barbor, 27 June 1930 in Cunard papers, D42/AC 14/517, ULA.
99. Jews' Temporary Shelter, *Thirty-Third Report, For the Year Ending October 31st, 1922* (London: Jews' Temporary Shelter, 1923), pp.8–9; Jews' Temporary Shelter, *Thirty-Fourth Report*, pp.10–11.
100. 'Atlantic Park, The Immigrants' Hostel at Eastleigh, From the Immigrants' Standpoint', p.9, 6 February 1924, 841.56/24, Department of State, NA; *Morning Post*, 1 October 1926; Peter New, 'Atlantic Park', *Hampshire Magazine* (April 1971), p.26.
101. *Morning Post*, 28 September 1926.
102. "Mentor", 'Eastleigh', *Jewish Chronicle*, 27 January 1925; Kevin Robertson, *Eastleigh: A Railway Town* (Crediton, Devon: Hampshire Books, 1992).
103. Minutes of the Executive Committee of Union of Jewish Women, 28 April 1925, MS 129/B/6; Jews' Temporary Shelter, *Thirty-Fourth Report*, p.10.
104. 'Atlantic Park, the Immigrants' Hostel', p.8.
105. Minutes of the Executive Committee of the Union of Jewish Women, 21, 24 April, 8 September 1925, 19 January 1926 MS 129/B/6; Cyril Orolowitz, interview with Tony Kushner, 1 June 1994.
106. Minutes of the Executive Committee of the Union of Jewish Women, 5, 12, 26 May, 23 June, 29 September 1925 MS 129/B/6; 'Atlantic Park, the Immigrants' Hostel', p.9; Liza Schlomovitz, school notebook, 1924, in possession of Cyril Orolowitz.
107. *Eastleigh Weekly News*, 28 November 1924; *Jewish Chronicle*, 28 November 1924.
108. *Hampshire Magazine* (June 1971), p.24.
109. Allen Robinson, 'Refugees at Atlantic Park, 1920, and North Stoneham, 1937', *Eastleigh and District Local History Society Special Paper*, No.20 (1991) and letter to Katharine Knox, 1 May 1995.

110. *Eastleigh Weekly News*, 25 May 1923; Jews Temporary Shelter, *Thirty-Fourth Report*, p.10; *Jewish Guardian*, 1 August 1924.
111. For Lady Swaythling's role see *Jewish Chronicle*, 13 February 1925 and *Eastleigh Weekly News*, 13 February 1925. On the YMCA conference see *Southampton Times*, 7 June 1924.
112. *Eastleigh Weekly News*, 2 October 1931.
113. Report of N. Gunger in Executive Committee of Union of Jewish Women, 8 December 1925 MS 129/B/6.
114. Jochelman in *Jewish Chronicle*, 23 January 1925.
115. Delegate D. Davies in the YMCA conference, *Southampton Times*, 7 June 1924; Cyril Orolowitz, interview with Tony Kushner, 1 June 1994; Peter New, 'Atlantic Park', *Hampshire Magazine* (April 1971), pp.26, 28.
116. Hope Simpson, *The Refugee Problem*, pp.41–6, 339–40; W. Chapin Huntington, *The Homesick Million: Russia out of Russia* (Boston: The Stratford Company, 1933), *passim*.

CHAPTER 4

1. Dorothy Legarreta, *The Guernica Generation: Basque Refugee Children of the Spanish Civil War* (Nevada, USA: University of Nevada Press, 1984), p.10. Legarreta's book offers a comprehensive account of the flight and resettlement of the Basque children, not only in Britain, but also in other countries.
2. Ibid., p.22.
3. Jesus Urbina Santamaria, 'My Life in Exile: May 1937/August 1940' (unpublished manuscript, Eastleigh Local History Society papers). These recollections are of his last three months in Euzkadi before coming to England. After only two days in the Eastleigh camp, Jesus was sent to the Salvation Army hostel at Clapton and later to Brixton and Camberley. In 1940, after staying with an English lady in London, he and his sister, Anita, who had stayed with a family in Farnborough, were sent to France. In August 1940 they returned to Spain.
4. Dorothy Legarreta, *The Guernica Generation*, pp.40–1.
5. Ibid., p.50.
6. Ibid., pp.32–3.
7. Ibid., p.99.
8. As quoted in Sheila Hetherington, *Katharine Atholl 1874–1960, Against the Tide* (Aberdeen: Aberdeen University Press, 1989), p.186. Hetherington's biography of Katharine Atholl offers some information on the British parliamentary reaction to events in Spain as well as the Duchess' personal involvement with the Basque refugees.
9. Ibid., p.188.
10. Jim Fyrth, *The Signal was Spain: The Aid Spain Movement in Britain 1936–9* (London: Lawrence & Wishart, 1986), p.21. Fyrth's account of the Aid Spain Movement devotes a chapter to the assistance given to the Basque children in Britain, charting the involvement of a wide range of people and organisations.
11. Ibid., p.203.
12. Legarreta, *The Guernica Generation*, p.101.
13. Ibid.
14. *Southampton Echo*, 18 May 1937.
15. *Eastleigh Weekly News*, 21 May 1937.
16. *Daily Herald*, 19 May 1937.
17. PRO HO 213/287.
18. Information on the Basque children of E. N. Cooper, 4 May 1937, HO 213/287. Government documents on the Basque children are fragmentary. This set of papers

consists of letters concerning the entry of the children. HO 213/995 includes papers about the children from 1943 to 1944.

19. Legarreta, *The Guernica Generation*, p.106.
20. Tom Buchanan, 'The Role of the British Labour Movement in the Origins and Work of the Basque Children's Committee, 1937–9', *European History Quarterly*, Vol.18 (April 1988), p.155.
21. Paper of the Spanish Ministry of Labour and Social Welfare, *Caring for Refugee Children*, 27 February 1938, archive of Duchess Katharine Atholl, ref 45/2.
22. Buchanan, 'The Role of the British Labour Movement', p.162.
23. Ibid., p.164.
24. *Eastleigh Weekly News*, 21 May 1937.
25. Minutes of Southampton Trades Council, Southampton City Record Office, ref D/TU1/2, 23 June 1937.
26. Buchanan, 'The Role of the British Labour Movement', p.171.
27. Legarreta, *The Guernica Generation*, p.104 argues that 20,000 children signed up for the evacuation to Britain; Fyrth, *The Signal Was Spain*, p.221 suggests a more moderate 10,000.
28. A former exile remarked on the Basque–British ties at a reunion in Hampshire in 1991. A paper reporting his speech is held by the Eastleigh Local History Society.
29. Former Defence Secretary, Michael Portillo is the son of one of the teachers who came with the Basques.
30. Video coverage of the arrival of the children recorded by the BBC, entitled *Los Ninos*, and footage of life in the camp at Eastleigh are available from the Eastleigh Local History Society.
31. Oliver Marshall, *Ship of Hope – The Basque Children* (London: Ethnic Communities Oral History Project/North Kensington Archive at Notting Dale Urban Studies Centre, 1991), p.6.
32. 'British Duchess talk on Spanish Refugee Children and work of the Joint National Committee for Spanish Relief', 13 May 1937, Imperial War Museum, Department of Sound Records, 3777/F/B, access code B, reel 1.
33. Gregorio Arrien, *Ninos Vascos Evacuados a Gran Bretagna 1937–40* (Bilbao, Spain: Asociacion de Ninos Evacuados el 37, 1991), p.58. In addition to this book describing the reception of the Basques in Britain, the Association for the Refugee Children of 1937 has produced a pictorial history of the refugees: *Ninos Vascos Evacuados en 1937: album historico* (Bilbao, Spain: Asociacion de Ninos Evacuados el 37, 1988).
34. Legarreta, *The Guernica Generation*, p.109.
35. 'Basque children cheerfully taking to camp life', *Southern Daily Echo*, 24 May 1937.
36. Oliver Marshall, *Ship of Hope*, p.8.
37. Amador Diaz, *Recollections of the Basque Children's Camp at North Stoneham, Eastleigh* (Eastleigh and District Local History Society, extended paper, No.3, July 1987).
38. Yvonne Cloud and Richard Ellis, *The Basque Children in England: An Account of Their Life at North Stoneham Camp*, (London: Victor Gollancz, 1937), extracts taken from chapter three, 'Camp Life'.
39. Arrien, *Ninos Vascos Evacuados a Gran Bretagna 1937–40*, p.59.
40. Extract from log book of Marjorie White, a record of events in the Eastleigh camp from 1937, held by Eastleigh Local History Society.
41. Letter from Freda Sibley, Southampton, to Katharine Knox, 3 January 1995.
42. Cloud and Ellis, *The Basque Children in England*, pp.54–5.
43. Legarreta, *The Guernica Generation*, p.115; Diaz, 'Recollections of the Basque Children's Camp'.
44. 'Basque Children in Stampede from Camp: Hysteria when told of Bilbao's fall', *Daily Dispatch*, 21 June 1937.

45. Cloud and Ellis, *The Basque Children in England*, p.53.
46. Arrien, *Ninos Vascos Evacuados a Gran Bretagna 1937–40*, p.60.
47. Legarreta, *The Guernica Generation*, p.111.
48. Cloud and Ellis, *The Basque Children in England*, p.52.
49. Arrien, *Ninos Vascos Evacuados a Gran Bretagna 1937–40*, p.60.
50. *Southampton Advertiser*, 29 May 1937.
51. Cloud and Ellis, *The Basque Children in England*, p.36.
52. Ibid.
53. By-mid 1938 this number had fallen to 40 and by 1940 only five remained open. See Legarreta, *The Guernica Generation*, p.116.
54. Ibid., p.119.
55. For details of life in Nazareth House, Southampton and Weston Manor on the Isle of Wight see Arrien, *Ninos Vascos Evacuados a Gran Bretagna 1937–40*, pp.81–8.
56. 'Basque children: Happy at their Moorhill home', *Southern Daily Echo*, 28 October 1937.
57. *Daily Herald*, 16 June 1937.
58. Legarreta, *The Guernica Generation*, p.118.
59. Ibid., p.125.
60. Fyrth, *The Signal was Spain*, pp.227–8.
61. *Eastleigh Weekly News*, 27 August 1937.
62. Buchanan, 'The Role of the British Labour Movement', p.165.
63. Legarreta, *The Guernica Generation*, p.115.
64. *Sunday Dispatch*, 25 July 1937.
65. *Daily Mail*, 26 July 1937.
66. Fyrth, *The Signal was Spain*, p.231.
67. *Daily Telegraph*, 25 September 1937.
68. *Daily Herald*, 26 July 1937.
69. 'Basque children: The stark truth', *John Bull*, 21 August 1937.
70. S. Richards, 'Basque refugee children', *New Statesman and Nation*, 21 August 1937.
71. Fyrth, *The Signal was Spain*, p.231.
72. Mark Phillimore, 'Basques at Stoneham', *Hampshire Magazine*, December 1978, p.50.
73. Legarreta, *The Guernica Generation*, p.130.
74. Ibid., p.134.
75. HO 213/995.
76. Legarreta, *The Guernica Generation*, p.253.
77. Ibid., p.255.
78. Ibid., p.258.
79. Testimony of Mrs Diana Molina, concerning her husband Rodolfo, from correspondence with Katharine Knox, 3 January 1995.
80. Fyrth, *The Signal was Spain,* pp.241–2.
81. Ibid.
82. Seraphim Martinez, interview with Katharine Knox, 14 February 1995.
83. 'Basques back to remember', *Southern Evening Echo*, 20 June 1987.
84. Mark Phillimore, 'Basques at Stoneham', pp.49–50.
85. Walter Greenaway, 'Visitors from Spain, fifty years ago', *Hampshire Magazine* (January 1987), p.17. 'Strange Cargo' was written by Brendan Murray, the action taking place in Spain and in Eastleigh, between May and September 1937.

CHAPTER 5

1. The best overview of Jewish refugee movements from Greater Germany is provided in Herbert Strauss, 'Jewish Emigrants from Germany: Nazi Policies and Jewish

Responses (1)', *Leo Baeck Institute Yearbook*, Vol.XXV (1980), pp.313–61, and Vol.XXVI (1981), pp.343–409.

2. A. J. Sherman, *Island Refuge: Britain and Refugees from the Third Reich 1933–1939* (Berkeley: University of California Press, 1973), chapters 7 and 8; Louise London, 'British Immigration Control Procedures and Jewish Refugees, 1933–1939', in Werner Mosse *et al* (eds), *Second Chance: Two Centuries of German-Speaking Jews in the United Kingdom* (Tubingen: J. C. B. Mohr, 1991), pp.506–12.

3. See, for example, Richard Breitman and Alan Kraut, *American Refugee Policy and European Jewry, 1933–1945* (Bloomington, IN: Indiana University Press, 1987); Irving Abella and Harold Troper, *None is Too Many: Canada and the Jews of Europe, 1933–1948* (New York: Random House, 1983); and Louise London, 'British Immigration Control Procedures and Jewish Refugees, 1933–1942' (unpublished PhD thesis, University of London, 1992).

4. David Wyman (ed.), *The World Reacts to the Holocaust* (Baltimore: Johns Hopkins Press, 1996).

5. McDonald in *Report of the Fourth Meeting of the Governing Body of the High Commission for Refugees (Jewish and Other) Coming From Germany, July 17th 1935* (London: High Commission for Refugees, 1935), pp.5–6.

6. James McDonald, 'Letter of Resignation', idem, *The German Refugees and the League of Nations* (London: Friends of Europe Publications, 1936), p.6.

7. Viscount Cecil, Foreword in Norman Bentwich, *The Refugees from Germany: April 1933 to December 1935* (London: Allen & Unwin, 1936), pp.13–14.

8. For the change of title of the Jewish Refugee Committee, see German Jewish Aid Committee, Executive Committee minutes, 5 January 1938, records of the Central British Fund, Reel 32 File 174/263.

9. Louise London, 'Jewish Refugees, Anglo-Jewry and British Government Policy, 1930–1940', in David Cesarani (ed.), *The Making of Modern Anglo-Jewry* (Oxford: Blackwell, 1990), p.164; Wolfe minute, 5 March 1935 in PRO LAB 8/78; 'The Refugees', *Daily Herald*, 25 August 1938.

10. See the memorandum, 6 April 1933 in CAB 24/239; London, 'Jewish Refugees', p.170.

11. Bentwich, *Refugees From Germany*, pp.121–2.

12. Ibid., pp.39, 107.

13. Vicki Caron, 'Prelude to Vichy: France and the Jewish Refugees in the Era of Appeasement', *Journal of Contemporary History*, Vol.20 (1985), pp.157–76; Timothy Maga, 'Closing the Door: The French Government and Refugee Policy, 1933–1939', *French Historical Studies*, Vol.12 (Spring 1982), pp.424–42; Breitman and Kraut, *American Refugee Policy*.

14. McDonald in *Report of the Second Meeting of the Governing Body of The High Commission for Refugees, May 2,3, and 4 1934* (London: High Commission for Refugees, 1934), pp.23, 32. Latin American countries taken together became, by the mid-1930s, the other most common route of escape. See Strauss, 'Jewish Emigration from Germany' (II), pp.363–82. For the later period see Allan Metz, 'Latin American Immigration Policy and the Jews, 1938–43: The Discrepancy Between Word and Deed', *Immigrants & Minorities*, Vol.11 (July 1992), pp.130–55.

15. On Palestine from a contemporary refugee worker perspective, see Bentwich, *Refugees From Germany*, pp.144–56; Bernard Wasserstein, *The British in Palestine: the Mandatory Government and the Arab-Jewish Conflict 1917–1929* (London: Royal Historical Society, 1978); Michael Cohen, *Palestine to Israel: from Mandate to Independence* (London: Frank Cass, 1988) and idem, *Palestine: Retreat from the Mandate: The Making of British policy, 1936–45* (London: Elek, 1978).

16. In the early discussions with the Cabinet, Otto Schiff had predicted that only 3,000 to 4,000 German Jews would come to Britain. See note 13 above and London,

'Immigration Control Procedures', p.487 for comment about numbers.

17. See, for example, 'How Many Went Overseas? Refugee Migration from Great Britain', *AJR Information*, June 1946.

18. Saul Friedlander, *Nazi Germany & The Jews: The Years of Persecution 1933–39* (London: Weidenfeld & Nicolson, 1997), pp.1–2.

19. Fred Uhlman, *The Making of an Englishman* (London: Gollancz, 1960), pp.134, 136, 140–1.

20. Jacob Boas, 'Germany or Diaspora? German Jewry's Shifting Perceptions in the Nazi Era 1933–1938', *Leo Baeck Institute Yearbook*, Vol.27 (1982), pp.109–26; John Dippel, *Bound Upon a Wheel of Fire: Why So Many German Jews Made the Tragic Decision to Remain in Germany* (New York: BasicBooks, 1996); Abraham Margalioth, 'The Problem of the Rescue of German Jewry During the Years 1933–1939: The Reasons for the Delay in their Emigration from the Third Reich' in Yisrael Gutman and Efraim Zuroff (eds), *Rescue Attempts During the Holocaust* (Jerusalem, Yad Vashem, 1977), pp.247–65.

21. Yitkah Arad, Yisrael Gutman and Abraham Margaliot (eds), *Documents on the Holocaust* (Jerusalem: Yad Vashem, 1981), pp.15–18 – Programme of the National Socialist German Workers' Party; Donald Niewyk, *The Jews in Weimar Germany* (Manchester: Manchester University Press, 1980); Friedlander, *Nazi Germany & The Jews*, chapters 3–5; Karl Schleunes, *The Twisted Road to Auschwitz: Nazi Policy Toward German Jews 1933–1939* (Urbana, IL: Illinois University Press, 1970).

22. For the April 1933 measures, see Arad, *Documents on the Holocaust*, pp.32–44.

23. Avraham Barkai, *From Boycott to Annihilation: The Economic Struggle of German Jews 1933–1943* (Hanover, NH: University Press of New England, 1989).

24. Hilde Gerrard, 'We Were Lucky' (unpublished typescript, London Museum of Jewish Life, 1984/34), pp.1–2.

25. Ibid., pp.2–3.

26. On the Jews of Munich, see Hans Lamm, *Von Juden in Munchen* (Munich: Ner-Tamid-Verlag, 1958); Baruch Ophir and Falk Wieseman, *Die judischen Gemeinden in Bayern 1918–1945* (Munich: R. Oldenbourg, 1979); Strauss, 'Jewish Emigration from Germany' (I), p.321; Edgar Feuchtwanger, 'I Was Hitler's Jewish Neighbour', *The Independent on Sunday*, 7 May 1995; Edgar Feuchtwanger, interview with Katharine Knox, 11 January 1995; Lothar Kahn, *Insight and Action: The Life and Work of Lion Feuchtwanger* (Rutherford: Fairleigh Dickinson University Press, 1975). On the strength and limitations of Nazism in Bavaria, see Ian Kershaw, *Popular Opinion and Political Dissent in the Third Reich: Bavaria 1933–1945* (Oxford: Clarendon Press, 1983).

27. Leonard Baker, *Days of Sorrow and Pain: Leo Baeck and the Berlin Jews* (New York: Macmillan, 1978); on the ostjuden, see Steven Ascheim, *Brothers and Strangers: the East European Jew in German and German Jewish Consciousness, 1800–1920* (Madison, WI: University of Wisconsin, 1982) and Jack Wertheimer, *Unwelcome Strangers: East European Jews in Imperial Germany* (New York: Oxford University Press, 1987); Bessel, *Polital Violence, passim* on SA antisemitism in Berlin; testimony of Jack Habel, 'Living Memory of the Jewish Community', NSA, C410/033.

28. Testimony of Jack Habel, 'Living Memory of the Jewish Community', NSA, C410/033.

29. Ibid.

30. Arad, *Documents on the Holocaust*, pp.72–88; Abraham Margalioth, 'The Reaction of the Jewish Public in Germany to the Nuremberg Laws', *Yad Vashem Studies*, Vol.12 (1977), pp.75–107.

31. Strauss, 'Jewish Emigration from Germany (1)', p.326; testimony of Jack Habel, 'Living Memory of the Jewish Community', NSA C410/033; Friedlander, *Nazi*

Germany & The Jews, chapter 8 'An Austrian Model?'.

32. Joseph Fraenkel (ed.), *The Jews of Austria: Essays on their Life, History and Destruction* (London: Vallentine, Mitchell, 1967); Steven Beller, *Vienna and the Jews 1867–1938: A Cultural History* (Cambridge; Cambridge University Press, 1989); Bruce Pauley, *From Prejudice to Persecution: A History of Austrian Anti-Semitism* (Chapel Hill: University of North Carolina Press, 1992); testimony of Liese Richards, 'Living Memory of the Jewish Community', NSA C410/003.

33. Desider Furst and Lilian Furst, *Home Is Somewhere Else: Autobiography in Two Voices* (New York: State University of New York Press, 1994), p.13; Desider Furst, 'Sopron', in Furst papers, University of Southampton archives (SUA), 116/68.

34. Raphael Patai, *The Jews of Hungary: History, Culture, Psychology* (Detroit: Wayne State University Press, 1996), chapters 38 and 39; Nathaniel Katzburg, 'Hungarian Jewry in Modern Times: Political and Social Aspects', in Randolph Braham (ed.), *Hungarian-Jewish Studies* (New York: World Federation of Hungarian Jews, 1966), pp.137–70; Furst, 'Sopron', SUA, 116/68; Furst and Furst, *Home Is Somewhere Else*, pp.181–202, esp. 190–1.

35. Furst and Furst, *Home Is Somewhere Else*, pp.15–17, 21.

36. Desider Furst, 'The Superfluous Man: Reminiscences of a Dental Surgeon', p.20, SUA, 116/68; Furst and Furst, *Home Is Somewhere Else*, p.30.

37. Fritz Engel, 'A Chain of Events' (unpublished memoir), chapter 1 *passim*, pp.89, 95–6. See also Engel's obituary in *Jewish Chronicle*, 21 February 1997.

38. For Eichmann's role and the Central Office for Jewish Emigration, see Arad, *Documents on the Holocaust*, pp.93–5, 99–102; Jochen von Lang (ed.), *Eichmann Interrogated: Transcripts from the Archives of the Israeli Police* (New York: Bodley Head, 1983), pp.49–57; Hannah Arendt, *Eichmann in Jerusalem: A Report on the Banality of Evil* (New York: Viking Press, 1965); Furst and Furst, *Home Is Somewhere Else*, p.22.

39. Furst and Furst, *Home Is Somewhere Else*, p.22.

40. S. Adler-Rudel, 'The Evian Conference on the Refugee Question', *Leo Baeck Institute Yearbook*, Vol.XIII (1968), pp.235–73; Shlomo Katz, 'Public Opinion in Western Europe and the Evian Conference', *Yad Vashem Studies*, Vol.9 (1973), pp.105–32; Tommie Sjoberg, *The Powers and the Persecuted: The Refugee Problem and the Intergovernmental Committee on Refugees* (Lund: Lund University Press, 1991).

41. Resignation speech reproduced in James McDonald, *The German Refugees and the League of Nations* (London: Friends of Europe, 1936), p.12; Friedlander, *Nazi Germany & The Jews*, p.248; Arad, *Documents on the Holocaust*, pp.95–8.

42. Fritz Engel, 'A Chain of Events', pp.96–101.

43. Furst and Furst, *Home Is Somewhere Else*, pp.34–5, 46–7.

44. Desider Furst, 'The Superfluous Man', pp.20–24.

45. Furst and Furst, *Home Is Somewhere Else*, pp.69, 72, 75.

46. Ibid., pp.50, 53–4.

47. Tony Kushner, 'An Alien Occupation: Jewish Refugees and Domestic Service in Britain, 1933–1948', in Mosse, *Second Chance*, pp.553–78; testimony of Liese Richards, 'Living Memory of the Jewish Community', NSA, C410/003.

48. Norman Bentwich, 'Report on a visit to Vienna', 17 August 1939 in archives of the Central British Fund, reel 25, file 1; Norman Bentwich, *Wanderer Between Two Worlds* (London: Kegan, Paul, Trench, Trubner and Co, 1941), chapters 10–12 and idem, *My 77 Years: An Account of My Life and Times, 1883–1960* (Philadelphia: Jewish Publication Society of America, 1961), chapter 5.

49. Fraenkel, *The Jews of Austria*; Furst and Furst, p.41; Desider Furst to M. Schwab, 5 November 1975 in SUA, 116/68; testimony of Liese Richards, 'Living Memory of the Jewish Community', NSA, C41/003; Engel, 'A Chain of Events', p.3.

50. Edgar Feuchtwanger, 'I Was Hitler's Jewish Neighbour'; Society for the History of Czechoslovak Jews (ed.), *The Jews of Czechoslovakia: Historical Studies and Survey*, Vol.II *The Inter War Years* (Philadelphia: The Jewish Publication Society of America, 1971).

51. On the expulsion of Polish Jews and the Zbaszyn camp, see Sybil Milton, 'The Expulsion of Polish Jews from Germany, October 1938 to July 1939: A Documentation', *Leo Baeck Institute Yearbook*, Vol.XXIX (1984), pp.169–99 and Arad, *Documents on the Holocaust*, pp.121–4.

52. Anne Mayer, 'Kristallnacht Memorial', unpublished report, 1980, author's possession; Friedlander, *Nazi Germany & The Jews*, chapter 9.

53. Rita Thalmann, *Crystal Night: 9–10 November 1938* (New York: Holocaust Library, 1973); Walter Pehle (ed.), *November 1938: from 'Reichskristallnacht' to genocide* (Berg: Oxford, 1991).

54. Ernest [Ernst] Guter, 'Kristallnacht seen as rehearsal for Final Solution', *Canadian Jewish News*, 10 November 1988; Dogmar Schmieder, 'Die Familie Guggenheim-Heilbronn', *Allmende*, No.45 (1995), p.150.

55. Edgar Feuchtwanger, 'I Was Hitler's Jewish Neighbour'.

56. Testimony of Jack Habel, 'Living Memory of the Jewish People', NSA C410/033.

57. Anne Mayer, 'Kristallnacht Memorial'.

58. Winterton's contribution reproduced in Norbert Kampe (ed.), *Jewish Immigrants of the Nazi Period in the USA*, Vol.4 Part 2 *Jewish Emigration from Germany 1933–1942* (Munich: K. G. Saur, 1992), p.338.

59. Ibid., pp.338–9, 366–7.

60. Mr Butcher, MP, in *Hansard* (HC), Vol.341 Col.1453 (21 November 1938).

61. Sir Samuel Hoare in *Hansard* (HC), Vol.341 Col.1468 and Cols1473–5 (21 November 1938) for the announcement concerning the child refugees; British Union of Fascists, 'Jewish Immigration Stopped By British Union', leaflet in Communist Party archive, National Labour Museum. See later in chapter 5 on the opening up of immigration procedures and Louise London, 'Immigration Control Procedures', pp.506–12.

62. Noel Baker in *Hansard* (HC), Vol.341 Col.1440; Cols1435, 1439 and 1463 for Noel Baker and Hoare on post-war immigrants and Cols1473–4 (21 November 1938) for the refugee children and the parallel to the Belgian refugees.

63. Wilma Iggers (ed.), *The Jews of Bohemia and Moravia: A Historical Reader* (Detroit: Wayne State University Press, 1992), part V; *Aldershot News*, 7 and 14 October 1938; von Lang, *Eichmann Interrogated*, pp.57–9; Sherman, *Island Refuge*, chapter 6 on the British government and the Czech refugees; Yvonne Kapp and Margaret Mynatt, *British Policy and the Refugees, 1933–1941* (London: Frank Cass, 1997) for a history of the Czech Refugee Trust; testimony of Vera Schaufeld, 'Living Memory of the Jewish Community', NSA, C410/008.

64. 'Klatovy' in *Encyclopedia Judaica*, Vol.10 (Jerusalem: Keter, 1971), pp.1087–8; testimony of Vera Schaufeld, 'Living Memory of the Jewish Community', NSA, C410/008.

65. Testimony of Vera Schaufeld, 'Living Memory of the Jewish Community', NSA, C410/008.

66. Alice Sluckin, interview with Tony Kushner, 5 November 1995.

67. Peake in *Hansard* (HC), Vol.348 Cols1111–12 (13 June 1939); *Zionist Review*, 22 June 1939; Josiah Wedgwood in *Manchester Guardian*, 26 May 1939 on the types of potential refugees excluded.

68. Furst, 'The Superfluous Man', pp.1, 85–6, SUA, 116/68; testimony of Vera Schaufeld, 'Living Memory of the Jewish Community', NSA, C410/008; Noel Baker in *Hansard* (HC), Vol.341 Col.1434 (21 November 1938).

69. 'Persecution of the Jews', *Southern Daily Echo*, 10 April 1933. See the comments in

the same issue's 'Topics of the House' on his speech. On Perlzweig, see *Zionist Review*, 22 June 1939.

70. *Southern Daily Echo*, 10 April 1933; Tony Kushner, *The Holocaust and the Liberal Imagination: A Social and Cultural History* (Oxford: Blackwell, 1994), chapter 1: 'Liberal Culture and the Nazi Persecution of the Jews, 1933 to 1939'; Andrew Sharf, *The British Press & Jews under Nazi Rule* (London: Oxford University Press, 1964), chapters 1–3.

71. Records of the Southampton Hebrew Congregation, minutes of the Executive Committee, 13 April 1933; *Southern Daily Echo*, 10 April 1933; *Southampton Times*, 1 July 1939 for numbers coming into the port.

72. Lord Marley in World Committee for the Victims of German Fascism, *The Brown Book of the Hitler Terror and the Burning of the Reichstag* (London: Gollancz: 1933), pp.9–10.

73. Morley at a public meeting of 500 people in Fratton, Portsmouth reported in 'Victims of German Fascism', *Hampshire Telegraph and Post*, 24 November 1933.

74. Records of the Southampton Hebrew Congregation, minutes of the Executive Committee, 29 January 1933 and General Meeting, 9 May 1933.

75. Records of the Southampton Hebrew Congregation, minutes of the General Meeting, 9 May 1933.

76. Aubrey Weinberg, *Portsmouth Jewry* (The Portsmouth Papers, No.41; Portsmouth: Portsmouth City Council, 1985), pp.11, 15–18; 'What Portsmouth Jews Think', *Portsmouth Evening News*, 28 March 1933.

77. Sharon Gewertz, 'Anglo-Jewish Responses to Nazi Germany 1933–39: The Anti-nazi Boycott and the Board of Deputies of British Jews', *Journal of Contemporary History*, Vol.26 (1991), pp.255–76; David Cesarani, 'The Transformation of Communal Authority in Anglo-Jewry, 1914–1940', idem, *The Making of Modern Anglo-Jewry* (Oxford: Blackwell, 1990), pp.126–8; *Portsmouth Evening News*, 28 March 1933 and 24 April 1933.

78. Records of the Southampton Hebrew Congregation, Executive Committee, 25 January 1939. See the records of the Jewish Association for the Protection of Women and Children, University of Southampton archive (SUA), 117/2/5/2 for Reverend Gordon's dock work which the organisation subsidised.

79. 'Strangers in a Strange Land', *Southampton Times*, 19 August 1939. For other material on the Southampton Refugee Committee see *Southampton Times*, 1, 8 July and 5 August 1939.

80. See Ronald Stent, *A Bespattered Page? The Internment of His Majesty's Most Loyal Enemy Aliens* (London: Deutsch, 1980), p.201 for Croft's role.

81. Lymington in *Hansard* (HC), Vol.277 Cols1031, 1033 (4 May 1933). For the response to similar, hostile questions see Sherman, *Island Refuge*, p.28.

82. Earl of Portsmouth, *A Knot of Roots: An Autobiography* (London: Geoffrey Bles, London, 1965), pp.127, 149, 160.

83. *New Pioneer*, Vol.1, No.1 (December 1938); Vol.1, No.5 (April 1939); Vol.1, No.9 (August 1939).

84. *New Pioneer*, Vol.2, No.14 (January 1940); Earl of Portsmouth, *A Knot of Roots*, pp.197, 201. For his continuing antisemitism in the war, see Earl of Portsmouth, *Alternative to Death: the Relationship Between Soil, Family and Community* (London: Faber & Faber; 1943). On members of the English Array who were interned, see the Ivan Greenberg papers, SUA 110/5; Richard Griffiths, *Fellow Travellers of the Right: British Enthusiasts for Nazi Germany 1933–39* (Oxford: Oxford University Press, 1983), p.318 for another prominent Hampshire member, the MP, Reginald Dorman-Smith.

85. British Union of Fascists, 'Boycott This Show', leaflet in Communist Party archives, National Museum of Labour History, Manchester; G. Webber, 'Patterns of

Membership and Support for the British Union of Fascists', *Journal of Contemporary History*, Vol.19 (1984), pp.575–606.

86. *Blackshirt*, 14, 28 August 1937, October 1938; *Southern Daily Echo*, 1, 2 November 1937. See also Richard Thurlow, *Fascism in Britain: A History, 1918–1985* (Oxford: Blackwell, 1987), p.116; David Cairns, *Southampton Working People: A Wee History Book* (Southampton: Southampton City Museums, 1991), pp.42–3 for a hostile response to Oswald Mosley in the city in 1937.

87. On Mount Temple, see Griffiths, *Fellow Travellers*, pp.185–7 and his papers in SUA, MS 62.

88. Barry Domville, *From Admiral to Cabin Boy* (London: Boswell Publishing Co., 1947); Griffiths, *Fellow Travellers*, pp.179–82; on local membership and activities, see *Hampshire Telegraph and Post*, 8 July 1938, 11 August 1939 and J. S. Wiggins, 'The Link' (unpublished MA dissertation, University of St Andrews, 1985), p.54.

89. For Mount Temple's resignation, see *The Times*, 19 November 1938; Tennant to von Ribbentrop, 7 September 1935 in Ashley papers, SUA, BR 81; Griffiths, *Fellow Travellers*, pp.339–40.

90. *Portsmouth Evening News*, 14 November 1938; Neville Henderson to Mount Temple, 27 November 1938 in Ashley papers, SUA, BR 76.

91. 'Hitler's Great Achievement', *Hampshire Telegraph and Post*, 10 January 1936.

92. 'Jewry in Arms', *Southern Daily Echo*, 25 March 1933.

93. *Portsmouth Evening News*, 1 April 1933; *Southern Daily Echo*, 16 September 1935; *Southern Daily Echo*, 10 November 1938.

94. *Portsmouth Evening News*, 27 March 1933, 13 April 1933, 16 September 1935.

95. 'Scholar' in *Portsmouth Evening News*, 12 November 1938; 'The Barbarians', *Portsmouth Evening News*, 14 November 1938.

96. Letter of B. Fairfax in *Portsmouth Evening News*, 15 November 1938 and J. Robinson in idem, 16 November 1938.

97. 'Hitler's Hell Camps', *Portsmouth Evening News*, 21 April 1945; Foley quoted in *Sunday Times*, 26 February 1995.

98. Charles Madge and Tom Harrisson, *Mass-Observation* (London: Frederick Muller, 1937); Nicholas Stanley, '"The Extra Dimension": A study and assessment of the methods employed by Mass-Observation in its First Period 1937–40' (unpublished PhD, Birmingham Polytechnic, 1981). On the self-assessment of the antisemitism survey as a success, see Charles Madge, memorandum, 18 January 1940 'Mass-Observation Panel and Its Function in Mass-Observation Archive (M-O A): Organisation and History, Box 1, University of Sussex. For Bitterne, see Bitterne Local History Society, *Bitterne: A Village Remembered* (Southampton: Bitterne Local History Society, 1983).

99. M-O A: Topic Collection: Antisemitism: Box I Files C and D.

100. Ibid.

101. Ibid.

102. Bertrand Russell, 'The Persecution of the Jews: What Can We Do To Help Them?', *Portsmouth Evening News*, 6 July 1938.

103. Raymond Burns, 'East Africa Haven for Refugees?', *Portsmouth Evening News*, 16 July 1938.

104. 'Jewish Immigrants', *Bournemouth Daily Echo*, 11 July 1938.

105. British government officials were interested in such schemes as a way of deflecting criticism for their exclusionary policies with regard to the United Kingdom and Palestine. See Sherman, *Island Rescue*, pp.117–19 and Lord Winterton's contributions to the Evian conference, 15 July 1938 reproduced in Norbert Kampe (ed.), *Jewish Immigrants of the Nazi Period in the USA*, Vol.4/2 *Restrictions on Emigration and Deportation to Eastern Europe* (Munich: K. G. Saur, 1992), pp.365–6. On refugee numbers in Kenya see Paul Bartrop, 'The British Colonial

Empire and Jewish Refugees during the Holocaust Period: An Overview', idem (ed.), *False Havens: The British Empire and the Holocaust* (Lanham, MD: University Press of America, 1995), p.4; Sherman, loc.cit., p.192 on responses from the colonial authorities in Kenya; for Sigmund Heilbronn see Ruth Goodman, interview with Tony Kushner, 4 October 1997; *Die Gailinger Juden* (Arbeitskreis fur Regionalgeschichte: Konstanz: 1981); Dagmar Schmieder, 'Die Familie Guggenheim-Heilbronn', *Allmende* No.45 (1995), pp.132–51; information provided to Ruth Goodman by Grete Roesler-Heilbronn, November 1997; Grete Roesler-Heilbronn, 'Old country doctor meets the jungle', *Jerusalem Post*, September 1995 (?).

106. 'Hitler's Loss, Our Gain' and 'The Alien Specialist', *Portsmouth Evening News*, 19 July 1938.
107. 'Nazis Strongly Denounced', *Bournemouth Daily Echo*, 14 November 1938; Mount Temple, 'Persecution of the Jews in Germany', in Ashley papers, SUA, BR 81.
108. John Presland [Gladys Bendit], *A Great Adventure: The Story of the Refugee Children's Movement* (London: Refugee Children's Movement, 1944), pp.1–2; Movement for the Care of Children from Germany, *First Annual Report November 1938 – December 1939* (London: Bloomsbury House, 1940), pp.3–4; *The Times*, 9 December 1938 for the Baldwin appeal and broadcast. For responses to the broadcast, see *The Times*, December 1938 – February 1939. The broadcast was published as a pamphlet: Earl Baldwin, *The Plight of the Refugees* (Ottowa: Canadian National Committee on Refugees and Victims of Political Persecution, 1939) and also on a gramophone record: *The Times*, 15 December 1938. A stamp scheme 'for those with moderate means who wish to help the Lord Baldwin Fund for Refugees' was instituted. See *The Times*, 12 January 1939. Baldwin's prestige, alongside the backing of *The Times* made this one of the best marketed and national of all appeals made on behalf of refugees in Britain during the twentieth century. Some £220,000 of the money was set aside for the child refugee movement. For later histories of the child refugee movement, see Mary Ford, 'The Arrival of Jewish Refugee Children in England, 1938–1939', *Immigrants & Minorities*, Vol.2, No.2 (July 1983), pp.135–51; Barry Turner, *...And the Policeman Smiled: 10,000 Children Escape from Nazi Europe* (London: Bloomsbury, 1990).
109. Bendit, *A Great Adventure*, p.4; Movement for the Care of Children, *First Annual Report*, pp.4, 10.
110. Movement for the Care of Children, *First Annual Report*, pp.10–11, county distribution map between pp.16–17; Movement for the Care of Children from Germany, *Instructions for the Guidance of Regional and Local Committees* (London: Bloomsbury House, no date).
111. Movement for the Care of Children from Germany, *First Annual Report*, pp.4–7.
112. Turner, *...And the Policeman Smiled, passim* for the variation in experience. See also K. Gershon (ed.), *We Came as Children* (London: Gollancz, 1966) and B. Leverton and S. Lowensohn (eds), *I Came Alone: The Stories of the Kindertransporte* (Lewes, Sussex: Book Guild, 1990); Bendit, *A Great Adventure*, p.16; Movement for the Care of Children from Germany, *First Annual Report*, p.8.
113. Movement for the Care of Children from Germany, *First Annual Report*, pp.7–8.
114. Lilian Levy, letter to Tony Kushner, 10 February 1997 on the breakdown of figures from the records of the Central British Fund. I am extremely grateful for this analysis of the confidential personal files. See *The Times*, 12 January 1939 on the impending arrival in Southampton of 95 children on a transport on board the liner *Manhattan* from Hamburg and the photograph of refugee children arriving in Southampton, 24 March 1939 on the same ship reproduced in Turner, *...And the Policeman Smiled*, between pp.150–1.
115. Ruth Freiman, letter to Tony Kushner, 14 February 1997; Bray testimony, pp.43–4 in

Leverton and Lowensohn, *I Came Alone*.

116. John Grenville, interviewed by Zoe Josephs, no date, transcript in author's possession. See also Zoe Josephs, *Survivors: Jewish Refugees in Birmingham 1933–1945* (Warley, West Midlands: Meridian Books, 1988), pp.57–60, 68–9.

117. Amongst John Grenville's many books are *Europe Reshaped, 1848–1878* (London: Fontana, 1976) and *A World History of the Twentieth Century* (Brighton: Harvester Press, 1980); testimony of Vera Schaufeld, 'Living Memory of the Jewish Community', NSA, C410/008.

118. Grenville, interview with Zoe Josephs.

119. The cover of Josephs' *Survivors* reproduces a typical section of 'Refugee Advertisements' from the *Manchester Guardian*: 'Guarantor asked for my Mother, aged 67, still in Vienna: speaks also English and French: able to household: contribute for maintenance already provided'; 'In Great Despair – Married Couple, with girl (11) and with affidavit to USA, implore benevolent persons to help by guarantee until visas will be given in October: woman (31), origin Catholic, very good in all housework, good dressmaker, man (40), Jew, clever, accept any kind of work: both adaptable, laborious; John Grenville, interviewed by Zoe Josephs, no date (Birmingham Jewish History Research Group), transcript in author's possession.

120. Kushner, 'An Alien Occupation', pp.553–78; idem, 'Asylum or Servitude? Refugee Domestics in Britain, 1933–1945', *Bulletin of the Society for the Study of Labour History*, Vol.LIII (Winter 1988), pp.19–26. More generally, see Pam Taylor, 'Daughters and mothers – maids and mistresses; domestic service between the wars' in John Clarke, Chas Critcher and Richard Johnson (eds), *Working Class Culture: Studies in History and Theory* (London: Hutchinson, 1980), pp.121–39.

121. Central Office for Refugees (Domestic Bureau), *Domestic Service: Some Suggestions for Employers and Employees* (London: Bloomsbury House, 1938–9).

122. German Jewish Aid Committee minutes, 22 November 1938 in Barash papers, M533 Box 1, Manchester Central Reference Library Local Studies Unit.

123. Conference of representatives of local domestic committees, Bloomsbury House, 1938/1939 in Barash papers, M102. For the setting up of the domestic hostel in Bournemouth see 'Plight of Refugees from Germany: Bournemouth to offer help and sympathy: Ways and means discussed at Public Meeting', *Bournemouth Daily Echo*, 24 November 1938.

124. Hilde Gerrard, 'We Were Lucky' (unpublished memoir, London Museum of Jewish Life, 34–1984), pp.13–22, 29 and *passim*.

125. Sheila Lewenhak, *Women and Trade Unions* (London: Ernest Benn, 1977), pp.230–1 on the nature of inter-war nursing.

126. Alice Sluckin, interview with Tony Kushner, 5 November 1995; see also David Williamson, *Ninety Years of Service: A History of Southampton Children's Hospital 1884–1974* (Southampton: Southampton General Hospital, 1990).

127. Alice Sluckin, interview with Tony Kushner, 5 November 1995; personal documents in the possession of Alice Sluckin. The police records in Southampton include details of the confiscation of her property in May 1940 – Southampton City archives, SC/P/32/2.

128. A. Gotthelf, letter to Tony Kushner, 14 February 1988.

129. Tony Kushner, *The Holocaust and the Liberal Imagination: A Social and Cultural History* (Oxford: Blackwell, 1994), chapter 2; 'Their First Day in England', *Picture Post*, 17 December 1938.

130. On the agricultural schemes, see Sir Samuel Hoare in *Hansard* (HC), Vol.341 Col.1972 (24 November 1938); Norman Bentwich, *They Found Refuge* (London: Cresset Press, 1956), pp.86–114; *The Land Worker*, February and August 1939; *Jewish Chronicle*, 6 January 1939.

131. Viscount Lymington, 'Refugee Labour?', *New Pioneer*, July 1939; oral testimony of

Jack Habel, 'Living Memory of the Jewish Community', NSA, C410/033.

132. Oral testimony of Jack Habel, 'Living Memory of the Jewish Community', NSA, C410/033.

133. Doron Niederland, 'The Emigration of Jewish Academics and Professionals in Germany in the First Years of Nazi Rule', *Leo Baeck Institute Year Book*, Vol.XXXIII (1988), pp.285–300; Society for the Protection of Science and Learning, *Fourth Report, November 1938* (London: SPCL, 1938), p.3 and more generally Norman Bentwich, *The Rescue and Achievement of Refugee Scholars: The Story of Displaced Scholars and Scientists 1933–1952* (The Hague: Nijhoff, 1953); R. M. Cooper, *Refugee Scholars: Conversations With Tess Simpson* (Leeds: Moorland Books, 1992) and idem, *Retrospective Sympathetic Affection: A Tribute to the Academic Community* (Leeds: Moorland Books, 1996).

134. SPCL, *Fourth Report*, pp.12–13; Paul Hoch, 'Some Contributions to Physics by German-Jewish Emigres in Britain and Elsewhere', in Mosse, *Second Chance*, pp.237, 241.

135. A. Temple Patterson, *The University of Southampton: A Centenary History of the Evolution and Development of the University of Southampton, 1862–1962* (Southampton: University of Southampton, 1962). Menzies was appointed to the chair in Physics in May 1933. See the University of Southampton archives (SUA), MBK 7/2; for his correspondence with the SPCL see its records, 129/1, Bodleian Library, Oxford University; University College of Southampton, Senate minutes, 7 February 1934 in SUA, MBK 2/5; University College, Southampton, *Proceedings of the College, 1933–34* (Southampton: University College, Southampton, 1934), p.6; idem, *Proceedings of the College, 1937–1938* (Southampton: University College, Southampton, 1938), p.19.

136. Esther Simpson of the SPCL to Stephany of the Central Council for Jewish Refugees, November 1939, in records of the Central British Fund for Jewish Relief, reel 6; Hoch, 'Some Contributions to Physics', pp.234–41 and idem, 'The Reception of Central European Refugee Physicists of the 1930s: USSR, UK, USA', *Annals of Science*, Vol.40 (1983), pp.217–46, p.226 for brief mention of Weissenberg.

137. On the MPU, see Kushner, *The Holocaust and the Liberal Imagination*, pp.83–4 and Frank Honigsbaum, *The Divisions in British Medicine: A History of the Separation of General Practice from Hospital Care 1911–1968* (London: Kogan Page, 1979), pp.275–83; Samuel Hoare, *Nine Troubled Years* (London: Collins, 1954), p.240.

138. Engel, 'A Chain of Events', pp.105–9, 114–16.

139. Ibid., pp.115, 118, *passim*; profile in *AJR Information*, December 1996 and obituary in *Jewish Chronicle*, 21 February 1997.

140. Desider Furst and Lilian Furst, *Home Is Somewhere Else*, pp.92, 95–7, 98, 100–1.

141. John Rae, former headmaster of Westminster College, letter to Tony Kushner, 17 March 1986; James Sabben-Clare, *Winchester College after 600 Years, 1382–1982* (Southampton: Paul Cave, 1981); Edgar Feuchtwanger, interview with Katharine Knox, 11 January 1995.

142. Edgar Feuchtwanger, anonymous contribution to Karen Gershon, *We Came as Children*, p.73; interview with Katharine Knox, 11 January 1995; Edgar Feuchtwanger, *Democracy and Empire: Britain 1865–1914* (London: Arnold, 1985); idem, *From Weimar to Hitler: Germany, 1918–33* (Basingstoke, Hants: Macmillan, 1993).

143. Obituary in *The Times*, 29 November 1993; Dick Richardson and Glyn Stone (eds), *Decisions and Diplomacy: Essays in Twentieth Century International History in Memory of George Grun and Esmonde Robertson* (London: Routledge, 1995).

144. Edgar Feuchtwanger, interview with Katharine Knox, 11 January 1995.

145. Alan Toogood, *Exbury Gardens* (Exbury: Exbury Gardens, 1988), pp.12–13; C. Lucas Phillips and Peter Barber, *The Rothschild Rhododendrons: A Record of the*

Gardens at Exbury (London: Cassell, 1967); Derek Wilson, *Rothschild: A Story of Wealth and Power* (London: Andre Deutsch, 1988), pp.357–8, 362–4.

146. Rothschild archives, 315c 'Refugees and Foreign Affairs, 1938–45'.
147. Ernest Guter, 'Kristallnacht seen as rehearsal for Final Solution', *Canadian Jewish News*, 10 November 1988; idem, letter to the University of Southampton, 5 July 1988, Parkes Library; Anne Lewin, 'Reflections of dark days of war', *Hartley News*, No.11 (Summer 1989), p.14 and Louise London, 'Refugee Agencies and Their Work', *Journal of Holocaust Education*, Vol.4, No.1 (Summer 1995), p.4.
148. See *Who's Who in Hampshire* (Worcester: Ebenezer Baylis & Son, 1935), p.282 and *Who's Who 1939* (London: Adam and Charles Black, 1939); Guter to University of Southampton, 5 July 1988, Parkes Library.
149. Anni Engel, interview with Tony Kushner, 13 March 1997; Fritz Engel, 'A Chain of Events', pp.103, 106; *Milford-on-Sea Record Society*, Vol.2, No.6 (September 1921), p.67 for Rose Cottage.
150. Anni Engel, interview with Tony Kushner, 13 March 1997.
151. For the suicide, see Fritz Engel, 'A Chain of Events', p.104; Anni Engel, interview with Tony Kushner, 13 March 1997 and *Bournemouth Daily Echo*, 1, 2 November 1938 which includes details of the inquest.
152. Annie Engel, interview with Tony Kushner, 13 March 1997.
153. Peggy Rayburn, 'Blythe Street' (unpublished autobiography), pp.1, 11.
154. Peggy Rayburn, 'Pigs, Poetry and Politics' (unpublished autobiography), pp.7, 104–5; idem, 'Blythe Street', pp.4–6.
155. Peggy Rayburn, interview with Tony Kushner, 21 May 1997; Gerhard Furstenheim, unpublished report, July 1997, author's possession and letter to Tony Kushner, 30 May 1997.
156. Peggy Rayburn, interview with Tony Kushner, 21 May 1997.
157. Herbert Strauss, 'Jewish Emigration from Germany: Nazi Policies and Jewish Responses (II)', *Leo Baeck Institute Year Book*, Vol.XXVI (1981), pp.363–83; Allan Metz, 'Latin American Immigration Policy and the Jews, 1938–43: The Discrepancy Between Word and Deed', *Immigrants and Minorities*, Vol.11 (July 1992), pp.130–55.
158. Strauss, 'Jewish Emigration', pp.363, 364, 375, 378 (note 36); for the later period and the intensification of Bolivian antisemitism/anti-refugee sentiment, see Jerry Knudson, 'The Bolivian Immigration Bill of 1942: A Case Study in Latin American Anti-Semitism', *American Jewish Archives*, Vol.XXII, No.2 (November 1970), pp.138–58. More generally see Herbert Klein, *Bolivia: The Evolution of a Multi-Ethnic Society* (Oxford: Oxford University Press, 1982).
159. Letter of Albrecht Hammerschlag to the Turners, 14 April 1939 in possession of Peggy Rayburn.
160. Peggy Rayburn, interview with Tony Kushner, 21 May 1997 and idem, 'Pigs, Poetry and Politics', *passim*.
161. Uhlman, *The Making of an Englishman*, p.249.
162. Furst and Furst, *Home Is Somewhere Else*, p.229; Edgar Feuchtwanger, interview with Katharine Knox, 11 January 1995.
163. Furst and Furst, *Home Is Somewhere Else*, p.217; Hilde Gerrard, 'We Were Lucky' (unpublished memoir, London Museum of Jewish Life, 34–1984), pp.30, 35; Anni Engel, interview with Tony Kushner, 13 March 1997; oral testimony of Liese Richards, 'Living Memory of the Jewish Community', National Sound Archive, C410/003.
164. John Grenville, interview with Zoe Josephs, transcript in possession of author.
165. British Union of Fascists, 'Boycott this Show!', Communist Party leaflet collection, National Museum of Labour History; 'An Englishman's Home', *New Pioneer*, August 1939; for discrimination, see Marion Berghahn, *Continental Britons:*

German-Jewish Refugees from Nazi Germany (Oxford: Berg, 1988), pp.139, 141; Peggy Rayburn, interview with Tony Kushner, 21 May 1997.

166. Bournemouth Hebrew Congregation, 5 November 1939 to Chief Rabbi, 5 November 1939 in Rothschild archive, 315c.

167. *Bournemouth Daily Echo*, 24 November 1938; Keith Hamilton, *60 Glorious Years: The Queen Mary* (Southampton: *The Daily Echo*, 1994), p.3. See the Maritime Museum in Southampton and local Burger King chains for the *Queen Mary*; Louis Macniece, *The Strings are False: An Unfinished Autobiography* (London: Faber, 1965), p.199. The refugees from Nazism feature prominently in Macniece's poetry including his 'British Museum Reading Room' (July 1939) and 'Refugees' (September 1940).

168. 'United Garden Party', *Southampton Times*, 8 July 1939.

169. Peggy Rayburn, interview with Tony Kushner, 21 May 1997; Lord Morley in *Hampshire Telegraph and Post*, 24 November 1933.

CHAPTER 6

1. Michael Marrus, *The Unwanted: European Refugees in the Twentieth Century* (New York: Oxford University Press, 1985), p.297.

2. Tony Kushner, 'Clubland, Cricket Tests and Alien Internment, 1939–40', in David Cesarani and Tony Kushner (eds), *The Internment of Aliens in Twentieth Century Britain* (London: Frank Cass, 1993), pp.79–101.

3. Anderson in *Hansard* (HC), Vol.354 Col.367 (4 September 1939); Kushner, 'Clubland', pp.80–6 for early measures and PRO HO 144/21258 for pre-war discussion in the Home Office.

4. H. Spooner, *A History of Taunton's School 1760–1967* (Southampton: Taunton's School, 1968), p.272.

5. *Taunton's School Journal*, No.286 (4 April 1939), p.4; for the experiences of one of the first alien internees in Britain, see Eugene Spier, *The Protecting Power* (London: Skeffington & Sons, 1951); 'The Enemies at Home', *New Pioneer*, January 1940; on Croft see Maurice Cowling, *The Impact of Hitler: British Politics and British Policy 1933–1940* (Chicago: University of Chicago Press, 1975), pp.371, 386 for his relationship with Churchill and his promotion as a Minister; for his early career see Larry Witherell, *Rebel on the Right: Henry Page Croft and the Crisis of British Conservatism, 1903–1914* (Cranbury, NJ: Associated University Presses, 1997) and for his contributions to the debate see *Hansard* (HC), Vol.359 Cols221–2 (5 March 1940). For the secondary literature on internment see Peter and Leni Gillman, *'Collar the Lot': How Britain Interned and Expelled Its Wartime Refugees* (London: Quartet Books, 1990); Ronald Stent, *A Bespattered Page? The Internment of 'His Majesty's Most Loyal Enemy Aliens'* (London: Andre Deutsch, 1990); Cesarani and Kushner, *The Internment of Aliens*.

6. Kushner, 'Clubland', pp.79–101.

7. *Statutory Rules and Orders 1940*, No.468 *Alien Protected Areas* (London: HMSO, 29 March 1940).

8. Southampton Police Records, 'Aliens property book 1939 and Aliens Leaving Southampton', SC/P/32/2, Southampton City record office; Alice Sluckin, interview with Tony Kushner, 5 November 1995.

9. Dill quoted by Gillman and Gillman, *Collar the Lot*, p.94; for Anderson see PRO CAB 65/7 WM (40) 123, 15 May 1940.

10. Memorandum by the Home Secretary, 22 May 1940 in PRO FO 371/25189; Gillman and Gillman, *Collar the Lot*, pp.95–7. On the temporary camps, see Gillman and Gillman, loc. cit., p.99 for Lingfield; for Warth Mills, see Imperial War Museum

collection, 'Britain and the Refugee Crisis, 1933–47', tape Nos.4300, 4343, 3771, 4483 and 3941; PRO HO 214/8; and *Bury Times*, 15 June 1940; on Belle Vue Zoo, see PRO HO 215/503.

11. Fritz Engel, 'A Chain of Events', pp.118–19; Desider Furst, 'The Isle of Man', 116/68, SUA and Furst and Furst, *Home Is Somewhere Else*, p.100.

12. The list of internment camps envisaged before the war was very limited – see PRO HO 144/21258. See files in PRO HO 215 series for the range of temporary camps. Gerhard Furstenheim and his brother were held in Andover for one or two days. Letter to Tony Kushner, 20 August 1997.

13. Carroll memorandum, 11 May 1940 in PRO FO 371/25244 W7848; for the Bland report, see PRO 371/25189.

14. Southampton City Council minutes, Parliamentary and General Purposes Committee, 17 May 1940.

15. Churchill in PRO CAB 65/7 WM (40) 123, 15 May 1940 and WM (40) 137, 24 May 1940 for the extension of the measures. For the Italians, see Lucio Sponza, 'The British Government and the Internment of Italians' and Terri Colpi, 'The Impact of the Second World War on the British Italian Community', in Cesarani and Kushner, *The Internment of Aliens*, pp.125–44 and 167–87.

16. R. M. Cooper, *Refugee Scholars* (Leeds: Moorland Books, 1992), pp.159–60.

17. F. Uhlman, *The Making of an Englishman* (London: Gollancz, 1960), chapter 16 and esp. pp.227–9. See also his internment sketches, idem, *Captivity: Twenty-four drawings* (London: Jonathan Cape, 1946).

18. Engel, 'A Chain of Events', pp.127–8; Furst and Furst, *Home Is Somewhere Else*, pp.123, 128; on the deportations, see Louise Burletson, 'The State, Internment and Public Criticism in the Second World War', in Cesarani and Kushner, *The Internment of Aliens*, pp.102–24; Gerhard Furstenheim, unpublished memoirs, author's possession; Peggy Rayburn, 'Poetry, Pigs and Politics', p.108.

19. See, for example, 'Isle of Wight Alien Doctor Summoned', *Southern Daily Echo*, 14 October 1942.

20. Edgar Feuchtwanger, interview with Katharine Knox, 11 January 1995; testimony of Jack Habel, 'Living Memory of the Jewish Community', NSA, C410/033; on the Engels, David Soetendorp, conversation with Tony Kushner, 13 March 1997.

21. Furst and Furst, *Home Is Somewhere Else*, p.121; Uhlman, *The Making of an Englishman*, p.227.

22. See *Hansard* (HC), Vol.362 Cols 1208–1302 (10 July 1940).

23. Croft in *Hansard* (HL), Vol.116 Col.877 (10 July 1940).

24. Wolmer in *Hansard* (HC), Vol.362 Cols1224–5 (10 July 1940). See, however, his rather less nuanced views expressed earlier in *Aldershot News*, 31 May 1940.

25. Wolmer in *Hansard* (HC), Vol.362 Cols1225–6 (10 July 1940); Gillman and Gillman, *Collar the Lot*, chapter 20 for the committees and release policy.

26. On the memory of internment, see Tony Kushner and David Cesarani, 'Alien Internment in Britain During the Twentieth Century: An Introduction', in Cesarani and Kushner, *The Internment of Aliens*, pp.1–11.

27. See *Southern Daily Echo*, 18, 20, 24 May 1940; *Hampshire Telegraph and Post*, 24 May 1940; *Bournemouth Daily Echo*, 17, 18, 21 May and 6, 12, 21 June 1940.

28. H. C. Maurice Williams, *The Years of War in Southampton* (Southampton: no publisher, 1947), p.6 based on *Annual Report of the Health of the County Borough and the Port of Southampton For the Year 1945* (Southampton: Southampton City Council, 1947), pp.158–9. This short section on refugees arriving in May/June 1940 was then incorporated into Bernard Knowles, *Southampton: The English Gateway* (London: Hutchinson, 1951), p.117.

29. 'Belgian Refugees Reach England', *Southern Daily Echo*, 18 May 1940.

30. For photographs, see *Southern Daily Echo*, 20 May 1940; Southampton City Council

minutes, Health Committee, 5 June 1940 and Public Assistance Committee, 6 June 1940.

31. Maurice Williams, *The Years of War in Southampton*, p.6 and *Southern Daily Echo*, 9 October 1942 for the Channel Islanders; Spooner, *A History of Taunton's School*, pp.252, 272–3; Carroll memorandum, 11 May 1940 in PRO 371/25244 W7848 on Dutch refugees; 'Dutch Refugees Landed at Portsmouth', *Hampshire Telegraph and Post*, 24 May 1940. For further evidence of ambivalence towards the continental refugees at the time of Dunkirk, see Mass-Observation Archive: Topic Collection Politics, Box 1 File D.

32. Claude Lanzmann, *Shoah: An Oral History of the Holocaust* (New York: Pantheon Books, 1985); Gordon Horwitz, *In the Shadow of Death: Living Outside the Gates of Mauthausen* (London: I. B. Taurus, 1991); Robert Jan van Pelt and Deborah Dwork, *Auschwitz: 1270 to the Present* (New Haven: Yale University Press, 1996); Richard Wright, 'Uncovering Genocide. War Crimes: The Archaeological Evidence', *International Network on Holocaust and Genocide*, Vol.11, No.3 (1996), pp.8–11.

33. For a more detailed historiography, see the introductory chapter in Tony Kushner, *The Holocaust and the Liberal Imagination: A Social and Cultural History* (Oxford: Blackwell, 1994); for releases in 1993 see David Cesarani, 'Secret Churchill Papers Released', *Journal of Holocaust Education*, Vol.4, No.2 (1995), pp.225–8; *The Times*, 27 November 1993 and *The Guardian*, 26 November 1993. See also PRO HW1/929 for one of the most significant Holocaust-linked files. For the most recent releases linked to the de-coding team at Bletchley Park, see PRO HW16/6 and 10 and for continuing media interest reports in national press, 20 May 1997.

34. See Caroline Moorehead, 'Letter to America ... from the blitz', *The Times*, 11 November 1985 and her obituary in *The Guardian*, 31 January 1997; William Shaun (ed.), *Mollie Panter-Downes: London War Notes 1939–1945* (London: Longman, 1972), p.41.

35. Mollie Panter-Downes, 'A Quiet Life in Hampshire', *The New Yorker*, 2 March 1946, pp.54–64.

36. G. D. H. and Margaret Cole (eds) *William Cobbett: Rural Rides* , Vol.1 (London: Peter Davies, 1930), p.175, entry for 6 August 1823; John Bosworth, *Durley in Old Pictures* (Southampton: John Bosworth Publications, 1989); George Molesworth, *Sancta Cruce de Durle: An Analysis of the Vestry Records of Holy Cross, Durley* (Durley: Parochial Church Council of Durley, 1961), pp.2–3.

37. On the history of the specific site, see Hilda Stowell, *Wintershill Hall Hampshire from the Period of Roman Occupation to 1972* (Chichester: Chichester Press, 1972); *News Chronicle*, 31 October 1945 and similarly Mollie Panter-Downes, 'In An English Country Mansion Live The Children Who Don't Trust Anybody', *Sunday Dispatch*, 7 April 1946.

38. Lanzmann, *Shoah*, pp.5–6. The camp has received little attention from Holocaust historians, but see the entry by Shmuel Krakowski in Israel Gutman (ed.), *Encyclopedia of the Holocaust*, Vol.1 (New York: Macmillan, 1990), pp.283–7 and Aharan Weiss, 'Categories of Camps', in Yisrael Gutman and Avital Saf (eds), *The Nazi Concentration Camps* (Jerusalem: Yad Vashem, 1984), pp.126, 131–2.

39. Friedmann quoted in Panter-Downes, 'A Quiet Life', pp.56–7. On the impact of the blitz in Southampton and Portsmouth see Tom Harrisson, *Living Through the Blitz* (Harmondsworth: Penguin, 1978), chapter 7 and Claire Frankland, Donald Hyslop and Sheila Jemima (eds), *Southampton Blitz: The Unofficial Story* (Southampton: Southampton Local Studies Section, 1990).

40. Panter-Downes, 'A Quiet Life', pp.54, 55 and 61. For the emphasis on Belsen, see, for example, the editorial in *The People*, 7 October 1945, 'The Mockery of Belsen'. Testimony of Karl Kleiman, National Sound Archives (NSA), 'Living Memory of

the Jewish Community' collection, C410/097.

41. Yitzhak Arad, *Belzec, Sobibor, Treblinka: The Operation Reinhard Death Camps* (Bloomington, IN: Indiana University Press, 1987); Panter-Downes, 'A Quiet Life', p.57; Martin Doughty (ed.), *Hampshire and D-Day* (Crediton, Devon: Hampshire Books, 1994); Bosworth, *Durley in Old Pictures*, No. 103 for the local Home Guard.

42. Song reproduced in full in Panter-Downes, 'A Quiet Life', p.57.

43. Srebrnik in Lanzmann, *Shoah*, p.6; Michael Burleigh, *Death and Deliverance: 'Euthanasia' in Germany 1900–1945* (Cambridge: Cambridge University Press, 1994).

44. For the decision to cancel pre-war visas see Cooper of the Home Office to Randall of the Foreign Office, 18 September 1939 in PRO FO 371/24100 W13792; Anderson to Eleanor Rathbone, 6 March 1940 in Rathbone papers, XIV/2/17, University of Liverpool archives (LUA). On the government providing financial support for the refugee organisations, see PRO HO 213/298.

45. Rathbone to Anderson, 3 February 1940 and Anderson to Rathbone, 6 March 1940; Alice Sluckin, interviewed by Tony Kushner, 5 October 1995; Callum MacDonald and Jan Kaplan, *Prague In the Shadow of the Swastika* (London: Quartet Books, 1995), p.131; H. G. Adler, *Theresienstadt, 1941–1945* (Tubingen: J. C. B. Mohr, 1960) and Zdenek Lederer, 'Terezin', in Avigdor Dagan (ed.), *The Jews of Czechoslovakia: Historical Studies and Survey*, Vol.3 (Philadelphia: Jewish Publication Society of America, 1984), pp.104–64.

46. Hilde Gerrard, 'We Were Lucky', pp.27–9, unpublished typescript, London Museum of Jewish Life, 34/84.

47. Testimony of Vera Schaufeld in 'Living Memory of the Jewish Community', NSA C410/008.

48. Ibid. More generally, see Karen Gershon (ed.), *We Came as Children: A Collective Autobiography of Refugees* (London: Gollancz, 1966), chapters 'Facing the Future' and 'Facing the Past'.

49. For the Hampstead petition movement, see *Hampstead and Highgate Express*, 12 October 1945 and Rathbone speech notes, 22 October 1945 in Rathbone papers, XIV/3/80, LUA.

50. On war refugees see Bernard Wasserstein, *Britain and the Jews of Europe 1939–1945* (Oxford: Oxford University Press, 1979), pp.81–2 and 'Survey of Recent Activities of His Majesty's Government on Behalf of Refugees, JR (44) 16, 29 June 1944 in PRO CAB 95/15; Arthur Koestler, *Scum of the Earth* (London: Jonathan Cape, 1941) which deals also with his experiences in a brutal internment camp in France at the start of the war.

51. Isa Brysh, interview with Katharine Knox, 26 March 1995 and letter to Katharine Knox, 6 February 1995. More generally, see Robert Paxton and Michael Marrus, *Vichy France and the Jews* (New York: Schocken Books, 1983), and Lucien Lazare, *Rescue as Resistance: How Jewish Organizations Fought the Holocaust in France* (New York: Columbia University Press, 1996).

52. On the banning of emigration and Jewish life in Greater Germany see Leni Yahil, *The Holocaust: The Fate of European Jewry, 1932–1945* (New York: Oxford University Press, 1990), pp.253–4, 288–301; Christopher Browning, *The Final Solution and the German Foreign Office* (New York: Holmes and Meier, 1978); idem, *The Path to Genocide: Essays on Launching the Final Solution* (New York: Cambridge University Press, 1992), part 1 and Philip Friedman, *Roads to Extinction: Essays on the Holocaust* (New York: Jewish Publication Society of America, 1980), chapter 2. Wasserstein, *Britain and the Jews of Europe, passim*, on Palestinian policy.

53. Report of Robert Prochnik, 18 August 1941 reproduced in Yitzhak Arad, Yisrael Gutman and Abraham Margaliot (eds), *Documents on the Holocaust* (Jerusalem: Yad Vashem, 1981), pp.150–3.

54. Testimony of Jack Habel in 'Living Memory of the Jewish Community', NSA C410/033.
55. Yahil, *The Holocaust*, p.408; Leonard Gross, *The Last Jews in Berlin* (London: Sidgwick & Jackson, 1983); testimony of Jack Habel in 'Living Memory of the Jewish Community', NSA C410/033.
56. Heydrich orders reproduced in Arad, *Documents on the Holocaust*, pp.173–8; Yahil, *The Holocaust*, pp.138, 160 and Philip Friedman, *Roads to Extermination*, chapter 2.
57. Andrew Sharf, *The British Press & Jews under Nazi Rule* (Oxford: Oxford University Press, 1964), pp.85–7, 89–90.
58. *Portsmouth Evening News*, 31 October 1939.
59. 'A Terrible Indictment', *Southern Daily Echo*, 31 October 1939; for disbelief, see *Bristol Evening World*, 30 November 1939 quoted by Sharf, *The British Press*, p.87. On popular debate on the White Paper, see Kushner, *The Holocaust and the Liberal Imagination*, pp.123–5; Israel Gutman and Shmuel Krakowski, *Unequal Victims: Poles and Jews During World War II* (Washington: United States Holocaust Memorial Museum, 1987).
60. Josef Rosensaft in *Belsen* (Tel Aviv: Irgun Sheerit Hapleita Me'Haezor Habriti, 1957), pp.25–6.
61. Alec Ward, 'My Story', p.1 unpublished memoir in author's possession.
62. For his obituary, see *Jewish Chronicle*, 25 March 1994; Richard Stern, *Via Cracow and Beirut: A Survivor's Saga* (London: Minerva Press, 1994), pp.9–15.
63. Joseph Marcus, *Social and Political History of the Jews in Poland 1919–1939* (Berlin: Mouton Publishers, 1983); Antony Polonsky, Ezra Mendelsohn and Jerzy Tomaszewski (eds), *Polin*, Vol.8 *Jews in Independent Poland 1918–1939* (London: Littman Library, 1994); Stern, *Via Cracow*, p.207.
64. Ward, 'My Story', p.3.
65. Yisrael Gutman *et al.* (eds), *The Jews of Poland Between Two World Wars* (Hanover, NH: University Press of New England, 1989).
66. Gutman and Krakowski, *Unequal Victims*. For an alternative perspective, see Richard Lukas, *Forgotten Holocaust: The Poles Under German Occupation 1939–1944* (Lexington, Kentucky: University Press of Kentucky, 1986) and idem, (ed.), *Out of the Inferno: Poles Remember the Holocaust* (Lexington, KY: University Press of Kentucky, 1989). On Polish-Jewish relations in the war, see Antony Polonsky (ed.), *My Brother's Keeper? Recent Polish Debates on the Holocaust* (London: Routledge, 1990).
67. Stern, *Via Cracow*, pp.16–18.
68. Ibid., pp.19–25. More generally, see Norman Davies and Antony Polonsky (eds), *Jews in Eastern Poland and the USSR, 1939–1946* (Basingstoke, Hants: Macmillan, 1991).
69. Davies and Polonsky, *Jews in Eastern Poland*; Nechema Tec, *When Light Pierced the Darkness: Christian Rescue of Jews in Nazi-Occupied Poland* (New York: Oxford University Press, 1986).
70. Stern, *Via Cracow*, pp.207–10.
71. Ward, 'My Story', pp.2–6.
72. Ibid., pp.6–8; Daniel Goldhagen, *Hitler's Willing Executioners: Ordinary Germans and the Holocaust* (New York: Little, Brown and Company, 1996), Part V.
73. Jane Marks, *The Hidden Children: The Secret Survivors of the Holocaust* (Toronto: Bantam Books, 1995); Yisrael Gutman, *The Jews of Warsaw 1939–1943: Ghetto, Underground and Revolt* (Brighton: Harvester Press, 1982); Wladyslaw Bartoszewski and Antony Polonsky (eds), *The Jews in Warsaw* (Oxford: Blackwell, 1991); Shmuel Krakowski, *The War of the Doomed: Jewish Armed Resistance in Poland, 1942–1944* (New York: Holmes & Meier, 1984).
74. Browning, *The Path to Genocide*, p.169.

75. Alan Adelson and Robert Lapides (eds), *Lodz Ghetto: Inside a Community Under Siege* (New York: Viking, 1989).
76. Testimony of Karl Kleiman, 'Living Memory of the Jewish Community', NSA C410/097.
77. Perec Zylberberg, 'Recollections', diary entries, 28 June and 28 July 1993, possession of the author.
78. Testimony of Karl Kleiman, 'Living Memory of the Jewish Community', NSA C410/097; Perec Zylberberg, 'Recollections', diary entries 12, 19 August, 12 September 1993.
79. Testimony of Karl Kleiman, 'Living Memory of the Jewish Community', NSA C410/097; Yisrael Gutman and Michael Berenbaum (eds), *Anatomy of the Auschwitz Death Camp* (Bloomington, IN: Indiana University Press, 1994). For an early post-war appreciation of what was lost, see James Parkes, 'Life is with people: the story of the little-town Jews of Eastern Europe', *Common Ground*, Vol.6, No.5 (August–October 1952), pp.16–21; Perec Zylberberg, 'Recollections', diary entry 30 September 1993.
80. Ronald Headland, *Messages of Murder: A Study of the Einsatzgruppen of the Security Police and the Security Service, 1941–1943* (Rutherford, NJ: Fairleigh Dickenson University Press, 1992); Yitzhak Arad *et al.* (eds), *The Einsatzgruppen Reports* (New York: Holocaust Library, 1989); on the debate about the timing of orders, see Christopher Browning, *Fateful Months: Essays on the Emergence of the Final Solution* (2nd edition, New York: Holmes & Meier, 1991), chapter 1; Ernst Klee *et al.* (eds), *'Those Were the Days': The Holocaust Through the Eyes of the Perpetrators and Bystanders* (London: Hamish Hamilton, 1991).
81. Wright, 'Uncovering Genocide', p.9.
82. David Cesarani, *The Jewish Chronicle and Anglo-Jewry 1841–1991* (Cambridge: Cambridge University Press, 1994), pp.174–6 on its reporting of the Einsatzgruppen murders; Andrew Sharf, *The British Press & Jews Under Nazi Rule*, p.91 suggests that the general British press did not cover reports of the mass shootings until the summer of 1942. Bletchley Park report, 12 September 1941 in PRO HW 16/6. For comment, see *The Times*, 19 and 20 May 1997; *The Guardian*, 20 May 1997 and correspondence, 22 and 24 May 1997; *Jewish Chronicle*, 23 May 1997 and *The Independent*, 20 May 1997.
83. Lev Ozerov, 'Kiev, Babi Yar' and 'Letters from Dnepropretrosk' in Ilya Ehrenberg and Vasily Grossman (eds), *The Black Book* (New York: Holocaust Library, 1981), pp. 3–12 and 59–68 and Yahil, *The Holocaust: The Fate of European Jewry*, pp.256–7; *Southern Daily Echo*, 19 December 1942. For a variation on this report, see 'Millions More Jews to Suffer', *Bournemouth Daily Echo*, 19 December 1942.
84. See generally, Tony Kushner, *The Holocaust and the Liberal Imagination: A Social and Cultural History* (Oxford: Blackwell, 1994), chapter 4.
85. Ronald Hayman, *Secrets: Boyhood in a Jewish Hotel: 1932–1954* (London: Peter Owen, 1985), pp.61, 64–6, 76, 86; Angus Calder, *The Myth of the Blitz* (London: Jonathan Cape, 1991) and Patrick Wright, *On Living in an Old Country: The National Past in Contemporary Britain* (London: Verso, 1985) on the importance of war mythology in British national identity.
86. Richard Bolchover, *British Jewry and the Holocaust* (Cambridge: Cambridge University Press, 1993); Kushner, *The Holocaust and the Liberal Imagination*, pp.129–31 and Cesarani, *The Jewish Chronicle*, pp.165–83 on British Jews and the Holocaust; Hayman, *Secrets*, p.96.
87. Hayman, *Secrets*, pp.210–11; Kushner, *The Holocaust and the Liberal Imagination*, chapter 4; James Young, *Writing and Re-Writing the Holocaust: Narrative and the Consequences of Interpretation* (Bloomington, IN: Indiana University Press, 1990), chapter 6 'The Holocaust Becomes an Archetype'.

88. 'Misery of Polish Jewry', *Zionist Review*, 21 September 1939; 'Do We Realise?', *Zionist Review*, 4 January 1940; Sharf, *The British Press*, pp.89–90 on reporting of the Lublin reservation.

89. Yehuda Bauer, 'When Did They Know?', *Midstream*, Vol.14 (April 1968), pp.51–8 reproduces the report; Silverman, 29 June 1942, in World Jewish Congress, British section (WJCB) papers, Central Zionist Archives, Jerusalem (CZA), C2/409.

90. *Zionist Review*, 3 July 1942; *Daily Telegraph*, 27 June 1942.

91. On the local press, see the list provided in WJCB papers, CZA, C2/409. On the *Manchester Guardian* see *Zionist Review*, 4 September 1942 which commented on how, in exception to all other newspapers, it provided daily news on the Jews of Europe. For its contacts with pro-Jewish campaigners, see *Manchester Guardian* archive, 223/5 and B/N8A in University of Manchester archive.

92. On the significance of the local press in the 1930s and 1940s, see Mass-Observation, *The Press and Its Readers* (London: Arts & Technics, 1949), chapters XIII and XIV; Ian Jackson, *The Provincial Press and the Community* (Totowa, NJ: Manchester University Press, 1971); Royal Commission on the Press 1947–1949, *Report* (London: HMSO Cmd 7700, 1949), pp.9–13, 88–9; PEP, *Report on the British Press* (London: PEP, 1938), pp.28–9; *Portsmouth Evening News*, 21 April 1945.

93. *Southern Daily Echo*, 27 June 1942; *Southern Daily Echo*, 25 September 1942; *Portsmouth Evening News*, 25 September 1942.

94. *Portsmouth Evening News*, 24 November 1942; *Southern Daily Echo*, 11 December 1942. See also *Bournemouth Daily Echo*, 19 December 1942.

95. On the local press and the Jews in France see *Bournemouth Daily Echo*, 19 December 1942; *Southern Daily Echo*, 18 July 1942; 3 August 1942; 7 September 1942; 11 December 1942; *Portsmouth Evening News*, 7 September 1942.

96. Robert Paxton and Michael Marrus, *Vichy France and the Jews* (New York: Schocken Books, 1983).

97. For the campaign for a declaration, see Kushner, *The Holocaust and the Liberal Imagination*, pp.169–72; Eden in *Hansard* (HC), Vol.385 Cols2082–7. For local reporting of the Allied declaration, see *Bournemouth Daily Echo*, 17 December 1942 and *Portsmouth Evening News*, 17 December 1942.

98. On the refusal to accept the idea of a 'plan of extermination', see David Allen comments, 27 November 1942 in PRO FO 371/30923 C11923; *Hansard* (HC), Vol.385 Cols2083–4 (17 December 1942).

99. See PRO FO 371/32683 for the early discussion of the Vichy children and HO 213/615 for the negative British government response to the surviving children after the war. Morrison's memorandum to the Cabinet is in PRO CAB 66/29 WP (42) 427, 23 September 1942 and follow up memorandum WP (42) 444, 2 October 1942.

100. See, for example, the evidence presented to the Foreign Office by Eleanor Rathbone, February 1943 in PRO FO 371/36653 W332.

101. 'City Jews' Day of Mourning', *Portsmouth Evening News*, 15 December 1942 and *Bournemouth Daily Echo*, 17 December 1942; *Jewish Chronicle*, 11–25 December 1942.

102. Victor Gollancz, *Let My People Go* (London: Gollancz, 1943), pp.8, 32; Ruth Dudley Edwards, *Victor Gollancz: A Biography* (London: Gollancz, 1987), p.375.

103. Morrison in *Hansard* (HC), Vol.387 Cols1319–20 (18 March 1943); Eleanor Rathbone, *Rescue the Perishing* (London: National Committee for Rescue from Nazi Terror, 1943), pp.9, 25; Sir John Hope Simpson, *The Refugee Problem: Report of a Survey* (London: Oxford University Press, 1939), pp.344–5.

104. James Parkes, *Voyage of Discoveries* (London: Gollancz, 1969); Robert Everett, *Christianity Without Antisemitism: James Parkes and the Jewish-Christian Encounter* (Oxford: Pergamon Press: 1993).

105. Parkes papers, 60/9/5/1, University of Southampton archive.

106. For the National Committee for Rescue from Nazi Terror, formed after the Declaration, see its records in Parkes papers, 16/15/057, University of Southampton archive.

107. On the protest meetings and the Bermuda conference, see Kushner, *The Holocaust and the Liberal Imagination*, pp.176–84. Some coverage of the Bermuda conference was given in the local Hampshire press. See *Southern Daily Echo*, 14 April 1943; *Portsmouth Evening News*, 20 April 1943 and most intensively, *Bournemouth Daily Echo*, 19 and 24 April 1943.

108. Reports of the World Jewish Congress (British Section), *A Note on Bermuda – And After* (London: British Section of the World Jewish Congress, 1943), p.10.

109. Schonfeld papers, 153/1, SUA.

110. Ibid.

111. Charles Ponsonby MP to Neville Chamberlain, 21 February 1940 in PRO HO 213/44 E409; *Aldershot News*, 31 May 1940; Gerhard Furstenheim, unpublished memoirs, in author's possession.

112. A list of the National Committee postholders can be found in Rathbone, *Rescue the Perishing*. See *Portsmouth Evening News*, 15 December 1942 and *Bournemouth Daily Echo*, 17 December 1942 for the day of mourning. Taking the period from June to December 1942, each of the three Hampshire daily papers had between five and ten reports relating to the fate of European Jewry, relying largely on reports from the Reuters news agency. There was, however, no editorial comment on these rather random accounts which might have pulled them together.

113. Peggy Rayburn (née Turner), 'Pigs, Poetry and Politics' (unpublished memoir), pp.104–5, 107–8; interview with Tony Kushner, 21 May 1997.

114. Randolph Braham, *The Politics of Genocide: The Holocaust in Hungary*, 2 Vols (New York: Columbia University Press, 1981); David Cesarani (ed.), *Genocide and Rescue in Hungary, 1944* (Oxford: Berg, 1997).

115. Tony Kushner, 'The Meaning of Auschwitz: Anglo-American Responses to the Hungarian Jewish Tragedy', in Cesarani, *Genocide and Rescue*, pp.159–78; Cheetham minute, 4 May 1944 and Randall minute, 4 May 1944 in PRO FO 371/42751 W6988.

116. National Committee for Rescue from Nazi Terror, *Continuing Terror* (London: National Committee, 1944); *Southern Daily Echo*, 5 July 1944.

117. For a positive assessment of the War Refugee Board, see Richard Breitman and Alan Kraut, *American Refugee Policy and European Jewry, 1933–1945* (Bloomington, IN: Indiana University Press, 1987), chapters 9 and 10; 'War Refugee Board Weekly Reports, 29 May–3 June 1944: Relations With Great Britain' in David Wyman (ed.), *America and the Holocaust*, Vol.11 (New York: Garland, 1989), p.165; Morrison, 1 July 1944 in PRO FO 371/42807 WR 170 quoted in Yehuda Bauer, *Jews for Sale? Nazi-Jewish Negotiations, 1933–1945* (New Haven: Yale University Press, 1994), p.188.

118. Interview with Vera Karoly in David Soetendorp, 'On the Way to the Past' (unpublished memoir), pp.139–61.

119. Ibid.

120. Zoe Josephs, *Survivors: Jewish Refugees in Birmingham 1933–1945* (Warley, West Midlands: Meridian Books, 1988), pp.177–9.

121. Ibid., p.178; testimony of Karl Kleiman, National Sound Archives (NSA), 'Living Memory of the Jewish Community' collection, C410/097.

122. Karoly in Soetendorp, 'On the Way to the Past', pp.148–9.

123. Mina W, interview with Helen McGiveron, 11 November 1996.

124. Joy Trindles 'Until Belsen' in Victor Selwyn *et al.* (eds), *The Oasis Selection: More Poems of the Second World War* (London: J. M. Dent, 1989), pp.265–6.

125. 'Horrors of War', in Portsmouth News, *VE Day: It's All Over!* (Portsmouth:

Portsmouth News and Hampshire County Council, 1995), p.11.

126. 'Hitler's Hell Camps' *Portsmouth Evening News*, 21 April 1945 and subsequent correspondence; Portsmouth News, *VE Day*, p.11; M-O A: D M5380, 24 April 1944.

127. 'Horror of Belsen Compound', *Southern Daily Echo*, 21 April 1945; 'SS Women Most Vicious in Horror Camp: Experiments on Jewish Girls', *Portsmouth Evening News*, 21 April 1945; 'Dachau – Worst of All Torture Camps Taken', *Portsmouth Evening News*, 30 April 1945; 'MPs to see Death Camps', *Portsmouth Evening News*, 19 April 1945; Tony Kushner, 'The Memory of Belsen' in Joanne Reilly *et al.* (eds), *Belsen in History and Memory* (London: Frank Cass, 1997), pp.187–92; Eberhard Kolb, *Bergen-Belsen: From 'Detention Camp' to Concentration Camp, 1943–1945* (Gottingen: Vandenhoeck & Ruprecht, 1985).

128. Mollie Panter-Downes, 'A Quiet Life in Hampshire', *The New Yorker*, 2 March 1946, p.57; Perec Zylberberg, 'Recollections', diary entries 8, 13 October 1993.

129. Prestige memorandum, 21 September 1945, PRO HO 213/618 E409. See also PRO LAB 8/99 and FO 1071/2 for the administration and inter-departmental discussion of this scheme.

130. Gee to Dennys, 16 October 1945 and Dennys to Ince, 18 October 1945 in PRO LAB 8/99; on Hammer, see Gerald Jacobs, *Sacred Games* (London: Hamish Hamilton, 1995); Zylberberg, 'Recollections', diary entry 7 October 1993.

131. Marian Shapiro and Esther Brunstein (née Zylberberg), 'Stranger in a Strange Land', *Jewish Socialist*, No.24 (October–December 1991), pp.23–4; Perec Zylberberg and Esther Brunstein, conversation with Tony Kushner, 10 July 1997 and Perec Zylberberg, 'Recollections', diary entry 7 October 1993. The sister of the cartoonist, Vicky, also came to Britain after the war on a domestic permit. See Russell Davies and Liz Ottoway, *Vicky* (London: Secker & Warburg, 1987), p.79; PRO LAB 8/99 for Ministry of Labour perspectives. The file also contains the views of Chuter Ede (Home Secretary) and Bevin. See also Cabinet minutes of 6 November 1945 in PRO CAB 128/2.

132. The administrative history of the scheme is contained in PRO HO 213/1797.

133. Maxwell to Prestige, 10 January 1946 following a meeting with the Jewish Refugee Committee representatives, PRO HO 213/1793. For the limitations of numbers to 800, see Fellner to Maxwell, 20 August 1945 in PRO HO 213/1797.

134. Schiff to Maxwell, 4 May 1945 in PRO HO 213/1793. For its extension see minutes of Maxwell, 22 January 1946, idem.

135. Testimony of Karl Kleiman, 'Living Memory of the Jewish Community', NSA C410/097 and in contrast Zylberberg, 'Recollections', diary entries 3, 4 and 6 October 1993.

136. On the wider children's transports scheme, see HO 213/781 and 782; Schiff to Maxwell, 4 May 1945 and Maxwell, memorandum 22 May 1945 in HO 213/1793.

137. Maxwell to the Home Secretary, 4 May 1945; memorandum, 22 May 1945 and letter to Schiff, 1 June 1945 in PRO HO 213/781; Wellstead to Fellner, 27 September 1945 in PRO HO 213/781. A home in Essex for those requiring intensive medical care was created. See Eva Kahn-Minden, *The Road Back: Quare Mead* (London: Grafton Books, 1988).

138. The details of the flights are covered in PRO HO 213/781. On the administration of the hostels, see records of the Central British Fund, Reel 37 File 198; Martin Gilbert, *The Boys: Triumph Over Adversity* (London: Weidenfeld & Nicolson, 1996), chapters 13–16. See also Joan Stiebel, 'Children from the Camps', *Journal of the '45 Aid Society*, No.19 (December 1995), p.3.

139. Bevin to Isaacs, 21 February 1946 in PRO LAB 8/99; Maxwell to Carew-Robinson, 6 June 1945 concerning the request of the Refugee Children's Movement organisers. Rabbi Schonfeld went to the Home Office on 3 May 1945 attempting to take over the proposed scheme of Montefiore and Schiff. He suggested that the children 'might be

obstreperous'. Prestige memorandum, 11 May 1945 in PRO HO 213/1797.

140. Norman Bentwich, *They Found Refuge* (London: Cresset Press, 1956), pp.74–7 and Sarah Moskovitz, *Love Despite Hate: Child Survivors and Their Adult Lives* (New York: Schocken Books, 1983), chapter 1 limit their attention to the Lake District; and Anton Gill, *The Journey Back from Hell: Conversations With Concentration Camp Survivors* (London: Grafton Books, 1988), p.179 has a passing reference to Windermere alone; Gilbert, *The Boys*, chapter 14 provides a more balanced approach.

141. Michael Perlmutter, 'The Bonds of Windermere', *Journal of the '45 Aid Society*, No.18 (December 1994), pp.8–9.

142. Alec Ward, 'My Story', p.8; Josephs, *Survivors*, p.178; Perec Zylberberg, 'Recollections', diary entry 13 October 1993.

143. On the 'Southampton group', see Jack Hecht, 'Where There is Life There is Hope', *Journal of the '45 Aid Society*, No.18 (December 1994), pp.7–8. On Stoney Cross airfield, see Ken Davies, *New Forest Airfields* (no place of publication: Niche Publications, 1992) and Robin Brooks, *Hampshire Airfields in the Second World War* (Newbury, Berks: Countryside Books, 1996). More generally on the politics of naming, see the special issue of *Patterns of Prejudice*, Vol.31, No.2 (1997).

144. Perec Zylberberg, 'Recollections', diary entry for 21 October 1993; Gilbert, *The Boys*, chapter 18 and pp.377–8 for a less conflictual account; Perec Zylberberg, conversation with Tony Kushner, 10 July 1997.

145. On Klepfish's role in the ghetto revolt, see Marek Edelman, *The Ghetto Fights* (London: Bookmarks, 1990), pp.73, 78 and 94 and generally Yisrael Gutman, *Resistance: the Warsaw Ghetto Uprising* (Boston: Houghton-Mifflin, 1994).

146. Zylberberg, conversation with Tony Kushner, 10 July 1997; Perec Zylberberg, 'Recollections', diary entry for 21 October 1993 and Gilbert, *The Boys*, p.378; Paul Smith, *Disraeli* (Cambridge: Cambridge University Press, 1996), pp.211–22.

147. Song quoted in Josephs, *Survivors*, p.178.

148. *Southern Daily Echo*, 31 October 1945. See also 1 November 1945 for this paper's coverage of later flights to Stoney Cross.

149. 'Belsen Orphans in England', *Jewish Chronicle*, 2 November 1945.

150. Testimony of Karl Kleiman, 'Living Memory of the Jewish Community', NSA, C410/097; Alec Ward, 'My Story', p.8. For the perspective of the man in charge of the children with regard to their independence, see Leonard Montefiore, 'Our Children', *Jewish Monthly,*, No.1 (April 1947), pp.19–23.

151. Hilda Stowell, *Wintershill Hall Hampshire*, p.12; Leonard Montefiore, report on the accounts of the Committee for the Care of Children from the Camps, 15 August 1945–30 June 1946 in Rothschild archives, 000/315c.

152. Josephs, *Survivors*, p.179; Alec Ward, 'My Life', pp.8, 12.

153. Josephs, *Survivors*, pp.178–9; Gilbert, *The Boys*, p.314.

154. Panter-Downes, 'A Quiet Life in Hampshire', p.52 and *passim*; Gilbert, *The Boys*, chapter 23.

155. Joan Ringelheim, 'The Holocaust: taking women into account', *The Jewish Quarterly*, Vol.39 (Autumn 1992), pp.19–23; for Rose Dajch and Esther Warszawska, see Gilbert, *The Boys*, pp.337–8; Josephs, *Survivors*, p.179; on other young female survivors who came to Britain see Kitty Hart, *Return to Auschwitz* (London: Sidgwick & Jackson, 1981); Anita Lasker-Wallfisch, *Inherit the Truth 1939–1945* (London: Giles de la Mere, 1996).

156. For Friedmann, see the obituary in the *Journal of the Psychoanalytical Society* reproduced in *Journal of the '45 Aid Society*, No.20 (December 1996), pp.25–6 and Panter-Downes, 'A Quiet Life in Hampshire', *passim*.

157. Panter-Downes, 'A Quiet Life in Hampshire', pp.52–3; J. Dow and M. Brown, *Evacuation to Westmorland, from Home and Europe 1939–1945* (Kendal:

Westmorland Gazette, 1946), pp.50–9 quoted by Gilbert, *The Boys*, p.292.

158. The Home Office became very cross with Friedmann when he was quoted in an article distorting the restraints on the children's employment rights. See Mollie Panter-Downes, 'In an English Country Mansion', *Sunday Dispatch*, 7 April 1946 and Wellsteed to Fellner, 9 April 1946 in PRO HO 213/1797; Montefiore, 'Address Given to the Cambridge University Jewish Society', p.17; Zylberberg, 'Recollections', 21 October 1993 and for an alternative perspective on Montefiore from Jerzy Herzberg, who subsequently became an academic, see Leonard Stein and C. C. Aronsfeld (ed.), *Leonard G. Montefiore 1889–1961* (London: Vallentine, Mitchell, 1964), pp.33–4: 'To him I owe the opportunity I had of being a full-time University student'.

159. For Gryn see Gilbert, *The Boys*, p.391 and his obituaries in *The Times*, *Daily Telegraph*, *The Independent* and *The Guardian*, 20 August 1996 and *Jewish Chronicle*, 23 August 1996; Lasker-Wallfisch, *Inherit the Truth*.

160. C. W. Hawkins, *The Story of Alton* (Basingstoke, Hants: Alton Urban District Council, 1973); the tensions at Overbury Court can be followed in Central British Fund records, Reel 37 File 198; Perec Zylberberg, conversation with Tony Kushner, 10 July 1997 and unpublished memoirs, Vol.10, diary entry 16 October 1993; Gilbert, *The Boys*, chapter 16 provides a more harmonious picture of life in the hostels.

161. For the importance of the clubs for the male survivors in Manchester, see the testimony of Karl Kleiman, 'Living Memory of the Jewish Community', NSA C410/097; on Bournemouth, see advertisements in *AJR Information*, 1958 for hotels and guest houses catering for refugees; 'Refugees in Bournemouth: A Christmas Party', *Bournemouth Daily Echo*, 23 December 1942.

162. Lasker-Wallfisch, *Inherit the Truth*; Perec Zylberberg, 'Recollections', diary entry 15 October 1993; Gilbert, *The Boys*, pp.337–9, 382; *AJR Information*, July 1949 on Schwartz which comments that 'His appointment to Bournemouth aroused some controversy in the British press, but it is gratifying to find him so obviously well loved by his players as well as his public'; Helen McGiveron, 'Art helps ease Nazi camp agony', *Southern Daily Echo*, 12 November 1996. Vera Karoly's art is exhibited in Southampton General Hospital. Her 'After Auschwitz' is on permanent display at the Sternberg Centre, London; Ben Helfgott, 'The Past Confirmed: Poland 1993', *Journal of the '45 Aid Society*, No.17 (1994), pp.13–16; talk to Southampton University History Students, 5 March 1996; Gilbert, *The Boys, passim* and Gill, *The Journey Back from Hell*, pp.168–87.

163. Soetendorp, 'On the Way to the Past', pp.150–1; Tony Kushner, 'Holocaust Survivors in Britain', *Journal of Holocaust Education*, Vol.4, No.2 (Winter 1995), pp.157–63 on responses to survivors and enforced silence.

164. M-O A: D AC5239 17 September 1945.

165. Soetendorp, 'On the Way to the Past', *passim* and conversation with Tony Kushner, 13 March 1997; Krystina Livingstone, interview with Tony Kushner, 29 June 1997.

166. Zylberberg, 'Recollections', 13 October 1993.

167. Miss Clement Brown, secretary of the Bournemouth Refugee Committee quoted in 'Refugees and Re-Settlement', *Bournemouth Daily Echo*, 17 May 1945.

CHAPTER 7

1. Bernard Wasserstein, *Vanishing Diaspora: The Jews in Europe since 1945* (London: Hamish Hamilton, 1996), p.8.

2. J. A. Tannahill, *European Volunteer Workers in Britain* (Manchester: Manchester University Press, 1958), p.8. Tannahill notes that there was an increase of about

200,000 aliens in Britain between 1939 and 1950 and that this consisted of 130,000 Poles and 85,000 displaced people from the European continent brought under three schemes: Balt Cygnet, for women from the Baltic countries brought to work in hospitals; Westward Ho, for men and women of various nationalities, to work in undermanned industries; and the scheme for Ukrainian prisoners of war. A further 10,000 single German women and widows, 2,000 single Austrian women and widows and 5,000 Italian men and women came under temporary schemes, usually on two-year work contracts to help fill labour shortages but they tended to return home (see pp.5–6).

3. Stephanie P., interviewed by Katharine Knox, Eastleigh, 21 March 1995.
4. For information on the European Volunteer Worker scheme see J. A. Tannahill, *European Volunteer Workers*, and Diana Kay and Robert Miles, 'Refugees or migrant workers? The case of the European Volunteer Workers in Britain (1946–1951)', *Journal of Refugee Studies*, Vol.1, No.3/4 (1988), pp.214–36.
5. Jerzy Zubrzycki, *Polish Immigrants in Britain: A Study of Adjustment* (The Hague: Martinus Nijhoff, 1956); Keith Sword, Norman Davies and Jan Ciechanowski, *The Formation of the Polish Community in Britain, 1939–50* (London: School of Slavonic and East European Studies, University of London, 1989) and Sheila Patterson, 'The Poles: an exile community in Britain', in James Watson (ed.), *Between Two Cultures: Migrants and Minorities in Britain* (Oxford: Basil Blackwell, 1977), pp.214–41.
6. Patterson, 'The Poles', p.214.
7. For an account of the Polish forced exodus to Siberia, see Alick Dowling, *Janek: A Story of Survival* (Lydney, Gloucestershire: Ringpress Books, 1989).
8. Patterson, 'The Poles', p.215.
9. Ibid.
10. Anne Ruffell, 'A matter of Polish pride', *Hampshire Magazine,* (December 1981), p.69.
11. Pam Schweitzer (ed.) *A Place to Stay: Memories of Pensioners from Many Lands* (London: Age Exchange Theatre Company, 1984).
12. Krisha B., interviewed by Katharine Knox, Southampton, 6 February 1995.
13. Dowling, *Janek: A Story of Survival*, p.68.
14. Marciniak R., interviewed by Katharine Knox, Hampshire, 8 January 1995.
15. See Tannahill, *European Volunteer Workers, passim.*
16. Sword *et al.*, *The Formation of the Polish Community*, p.339.
17. Ibid.
18. Sword *et al.*, *The Formation of the Polish Community*, p.314.
19. Patterson, 'The Poles', pp.217–18.
20. *Hansard* (HC) Vol.408 Col.1284 (12 February 1945). This pledge followed a meeting between Churchill and General Anders who made clear that he felt his country had been betrayed at Yalta.
21. Sword *et al.*, *The Formation of the Polish Community*, p.241.
22. PRO CAB 66/62 quoted in Sword *et al.*, *The Formation of the Polish Community*, p.233.
23. Sword *et al.*, *The Formation of the Polish Community*, p.233.
24. Keith Sword, 'The Absorption of Poles into Civilian Employment in Britain, 1945–50', in A. C. Bramwell (ed.), *Refugees in the Age of Total War* (London: Unwin Hyman, 1988), p.233.
25. *Hansard* (HC) Vol.414 Cols23–5 (9 October 1945).
26. PRO FO 371/66161 N7087, Letter from Robin Hankey of the Foreign Office to C. J. Whetmath of the National Assistance Board, 2 July 1947.
27. 'An army in exile', *The Times*, 22 February 1946.
28. *Polish Resettlement Act, 1947* (Acts 1947, chapter 19).

29. PRO FO 371/56627 N4191, Memorandum by Home Secretary for Cabinet Polish Forces Committee, 27 March 1946.
30. Marciniak R., interviewed by Katharine Knox, Hampshire, 6 January 1995.
31. Sword *et al.*, *The Formation of the Polish Community*, p.328.
32. Ibid., pp.327, 346.
33. *Hansard* (HC) Vol.424 Col.292 (written answers, 3 July 1946).
34. Robert Miles, review of Keith Sword *et al.*, *The Formation of the Polish Community in Britain 1939–50*, in *Journal of Refugee Studies*, Vol.2, No 4 (1989).
35. Sword *et al.*, *The Formation of the Polish Community*, p.207.
36. Ibid., p.208.
37. Sword, 'The Absorption of Poles into Civilian Employment', p.247.
38. Patterson, 'The Poles', p.220.
39. Ibid., p.219.
40. Stephanie P., interviewed by Katharine Knox, Eastleigh, 21 March 1995.
41. PRO AST 18/1.
42. Claire Peters, interviewed by Katharine Knox, Winchester, 27 January 1995.
43. Extracts from *County Borough of Southampton Minutes of Proceedings of Councils and Committees* concerning Polish refugees, 6 December 1946 and 7 February 1947 in Vol.1946–53, p.155 and p.428.
44. Ibid.
45. Sword *et al.*, *The Formation of the Polish Community*, p.258.
46. Ibid., p.381.
47. Ibid., p.383.
48. Ibid., p.259.
49. Ibid.
50. Patterson, 'The Poles', p.222.
51. Ibid., p.226.
52. Sword *et al.*, *The Formation of the Polish Community*, p.270.
53. PRO AST 18/99, notes of a visit to a Polish Dependants' Camp, sent by Marie Woodruff Vice-Chair of the Catholic Committee for Relief Abroad to Miss Hope Wallace of the National Assistance Board, 18 December 1946.
54. PRO AST 18/5, Report by I. Banach about the Hiltingbury Polish Dependants' Camp near Chandlers Ford, Hampshire, 15 February 1949.
55. Hampshire County Council, Education Committee, 'School at Polish hostel, Hiltingbury to close', *County Council Reports and Proceedings 1948–9*, minute 5240, 4 October 1950, p.134.
56. Hampshire County Council, 'Education of DPs: Hiltingbury Camp classes', *County Council Reports and Proceedings 1948–9*, minute 2490, 4 May 1948.
57. Zofia Thoroughgood, interviewed by Katharine Knox, Southampton, 9 March 1995.
58. Sword *et al.*, *The Formation of the Polish Community*, p.388.
59. Extracts from a talk given by Mrs I. Horbaczewska, Welfare Officer of the Polish Ex-Combatants' Association in Britain, at a joint meeting of The British Council for Aid to Refugees and exiled national groups, 21 January 1981. From Refugee Council records, ref RP/QU56.
60. PRO HO 213/1199, letter from Frank Savery, Foreign Office adviser, to Robin Hankey at the Foreign Office re Polish delinquents at Hiltingbury, 5 April 1948.
61. PRO HO 213/1199.
62. PRO N4133/725/55, 23 April 1948.
63. PRO, PR 80/2, 8 June 1948.
64. PRO, N4133/725/55, 23 August 1948.
65. PRO PR 80/2, 18 September 1948.
66. Ibid.
67. See Zubrzycki, *Polish Immigrants in Britain*, pp.80–6, and also Sword, *The*

Formation of the Polish Community, pp.342–54.

68. Sword *et al.*, *The Formation of the Polish Community*, p.345.
69. Ibid., appendix 10, pp. 476–7.
70. 'A Polish Community in Hampshire: The work of resettlement', *Hampshire Chronicle*, 27 December 1947.
71. 'The Polish Resettlement Corps, Visit to Stockbridge Camp: Help – Justice not Charity', *Hampshire Observer*, 7 December 1946.
72. Marciniak Roberts, interviewed by Katharine Knox, Cowplain, Hampshire, 5 June 1995.
73. Letter from Monica M. Stratton of Winchester to the *Hampshire Chronicle*, 4 January 1947.
74. Letter from Major R. G. Boucher to the *Hampshire Chronicle*, 11 January 1947.
75. Sword *et al.*, *The Formation of the Polish Community*, p.33.
76. Ibid., pp.154–5.
77. Krisha B., interviewed by Katharine Knox, Southampton, 6 March 1995.
78. Zubrzycki, *Polish Immigrants*, p.107.
79. Patterson, 'The Poles', pp.314–15 notes that there were 86% Roman Catholic, 4% Greek Catholic, 4% Orthodox, 4% Protestant, 2% Jewish among those registered in the Polish religious community in 1948.
80. Zubrzycki, *Polish Immigrants*, p.123.
81. Patterson, 'The Poles', p.240.
82. Forty years pamphlet, available from Polish parish priest, Father Zuziak, Southampton.
83. History of Karpaty leaflet, available from Jan Kosniowski, Southampton.
84. Father Zuziak, interviewed by Katharine Knox, Southampton, 17 February 1995.
85. Krisha B., interviewed by Katharine Knox, 6 March 1995.

CHAPTER 8

1. David Pryce-Jones, *The Hungarian Revolution* (London: Ernest Benn, 1969), p.13. On 9 October 1944 a meeting was held in Moscow in which spheres of influence post-war were discussed.
2. Andy Rumi, interviewed by Katharine Knox, Winchester, 28 February 1995.
3. For general background to the Hungarian situation see Jorg Hoensch, *A History of Modern Hungary 1867–1986* (London: Longman, 1987) and Bill Lomax, *Hungary* (London: Alison & Busby, 1976). For personal accounts see George Mikes, *The Hungarian Revolution* (London: Andre Deutsch, 1957) and George Paloczi-Horvath, *The Undefeated* (London: Martin Secker & Warburg, 1959).
4. Mikes, *The Hungarian Revolution*, p.32.
5. Gino Csikasz, interviewed by Katharine Knox, Portsmouth, 27 March 1995.
6. Ibid.
7. Ferenc Nagy, *The Struggle Behind the Iron Curtain* (New York: MacMillan, 1948), preface.
8. See Ferenc Feher and Agnes Heller, *Hungary Revisited: The Message of a Revolution a Quarter of a Century After* (London: George Allen & Unwin, 1983); see also Imre Nagy, *On Communism: In Defence of the New Course* (London: Thames & Hudson, 1957).
9. Mikes, *The Hungarian Revolution*, p.131.
10. For details of the political questions of this time see Hoensch, *A History of Modern Hungary 1867–1986*, pp.208–20 and for debates over Soviet intention see Feher and Heller, *Hungary Revisited*, *passim*.
11. For this and other incidents see Mikes, *The Hungarian Revolution*, pp.176–8.

12. *Southern Daily Echo*, 2 November 1956.
13. *Southern Daily Echo*, 1 December 1956.
14. Mikes, *The Hungarian Revolution*, p.164.
15. *Southern Daily Echo*, 1 December 1956.
16. Pryce-Jones, *The Hungarian Revolution*, p.117.
17. Mikes, *The Hungarian Revolution*, p.173.
18. *Southern Daily Echo*, 20 November 1956.
19. Telegram No. 1151 from New York to Foreign Office from Sir P. Dixon of the United Kingdom delegation to the United Nations on 9 November 1956. Re Hungary: Emergency Special Session of General Assembly in PRO FO 371/122387/10110/478.
20. Mikes, *The Hungarian Revolution*, p.141. This point makes reference to Poland being allowed to pursue a course of 'Socialism with a human face' under Gomulka's leadership.
21. Refugee Council (BCAR) report, 'Hungarian Refugees in Britain', p.4, ref RH/QU 59.2.
22. Ibid.
23. Refugee Council paper, ref RH/QU 61.
24. W. G. Kuepper, G. L. Lackey, E. N. Sinerton, *Ugandan Asians in Britain: Forced Migration and Social Absorption* (London: Croom Helm, 1975), pp.10–11.
25. Extract from A. C. Macartney, 'Hungary and Truth', *Igazsag*, (*Truth*), London, July 1958.
26. *The Times*, 17 November 1956, 'Hungary'.
27. *The Times*, 20 November 1956, 'Hungary'.
28. Description of the government programme for the reception of Hungarian refugees in Britain by the Secretary of State for the Home Department, Major Lloyd George, in response to a question in the House of Commons by Mr Langford-Holt, MP in *Hansard* (HC) Vol.561 Cols159–60, written answers (6 December 1956).
29. *Hansard* (HC) Vol.560, 24 written answers (14 November 1956).
30. 'Hungarian Refugees in Britain', September 1957, Refugee Council, ref RH/QU 59.2.
31. *Hansard* (HC) Vol.566 Cols342–3 (6 March 1957).
32. *Hansard* (HC) Vol.561, 1–2 written answers (26 November 1956).
33. Extract from a letter from Mrs P. M. Reynolds to Katharine Knox (5 December 1994).
34. *Hansard* (HC) Vol.560 Col.1925 (22 November 1956).
35. Extract from *The Hungarian in Britain*, later translated into Hungarian by the British-Hungarian Cultural Fellowship and entitled *Magyarok Angliaban*, available in records of the Refugee Council, ref RH/QU.
36. David J. Croman, *A History of Tidworth and Tedworth House* (Sussex: Phillimore & Co. Ltd, 1991), p.55.
37. *Hansard* (HC) Vol.568 Cols1287–8 (11 April 1957).
38. 'Hungarian Refugees in Britain', p.2, Refugee Council, ref RH/QU 59.2.
39. Ruth Smith, 'Report on findings in Hungarian files', p.1, 21 October 1983, Refugee Council, ref RH/QU 56.
40. C. S. de Kisshazy, 'The needs of former refugees in specialised social work', p.1, Refugee Council, ref RH/QU 61, March 1979.
41. *Hansard* (HC) Vol.561 Col.1442 (6 December 1956).
42. 'Hungarians in Britain', p.2, Refugee Council, ref RH/QU 59.2.
43. Smith, 'Report on findings in Hungarian files', p.2, 21 October 1983, Refugee Council, ref RH/QU 56.
44. See parliamentary debates in *Hansard* (HC) Vol.561 Col.1442 (6 December 1956).
45. *Hansard* (HC) Vol.565 Cols585–7 (21 February 1957).

46. Danko Joszef, interviewed by Katharine Knox, Southampton, 23 February 1995.
47. *Hansard* (HC) Vol.568 Cols1287–8 (11 April 1957).
48. *Hansard* (HC) Vol.571 Col.6000 (30 May 1957).
49. 'Hungarian refugees in Britain', p.4, Refugee Council, ref RH/QU 59.2.
50. Andy Rumi, interviewed by Katharine Knox, Winchester, 28 February 1995.
51. 'Hungarian Refugees in Britain', p.3, Refugee Council, ref RH/QU 59.2.
52. *Hansard* (HC) Vol.562 Col. 238, written answers (21 December 1956).
53. *Hansard* (HC) Vol.562 Cols 610–14, oral answers (13 December 1956).
54. *Hansard* (HC) Vol.562 Col. 238, written answers (21 December 1956).
55. *Hansard* (HC) Vol.566 Cols 16–17, oral answers (4 March 1957).
56. *Hansard* (HC) Vol.569 Cols1172–3, oral answers (9 May 1957).
57. *The Southern Daily Echo*, 21 January 1957.
58. Ibid.
59. *The Southern Daily Echo*, 22 February 1957.
60. Danko Joszef, interviewed by Katharine Knox, Southampton, 23 February 1995.
61. Resolution of Southampton Labour Party expressing sympathy for Hungarians, forwarded to Foreign Office by H. T. Willcock, Secretary of the Labour Party, Southampton, 8 November 1956 in PRO FO 371/122387/10110/495.
62. 'Eastleigh MP on Hungary: Any action with chance of success worth trying', *Southern Daily Echo*, 1 December 1956.
63. Paloczi-Horvath, *The Undefeated*, p.210.
64. Ibid., p.279.
65. 'The Hungarian Revolution: Refugee speaks to Winchester UNA', *Hampshire Chronicle*, 16 March 1957.
66. *Southern Daily Echo*, 4 December 1956.
67. *Hampshire Chronicle*, 1 December 1956.
68. *Southern Daily Echo*, 24 November 1956.
69. *The Times*, 9 November 1956, 'Growing response to appeal for Hungarian refugees' and additional articles about Volunteers seeking to fight in Hungary and protest marches.
70. 'Lord Mayor's Hungarian Relief Fund: Remarkable Response in Towns and Countryside', *Hampshire Chronicle*, 17 November 1956.
71. Minutes of Southampton City Council, November 1956 to February 1957.
72. Andy Rumi, interviewed by Katharine Knox, Winchester, 28 February 1995.
73. *Hansard* (HC) Vol.565 Cols 585–7 (21 February 1957).
74. 'Hungarian Refugees in Britain', p.3, Refugee Council, ref RH/QU 59.2.
75. Andy Rumi, interviewed by Katharine Knox, Winchester, 28 February 1995.
76. 'Hungarian Refugees in Britain', p.3, Refugee Council, ref RH/QU 59.2.
77. Andy Rumi, interviewed by Katharine Knox, Winchester, 28 February 1995.

CHAPTER 9

1. Kenya, Uganda and Tanzania formed British East Africa. Tanzania, formerly Tanganyika, was part of German East Africa before the First World War.
2. Ernest Krausz, *Ethnic Minorities in Britain* quoted in W.G.Kuepper, G.L.Lackey and E.N.Swinerton, *Ugandan Asians in Britain: Forced Migration and Social Absorption* (London: Croom Helm, London, 1975), p.12.
3. For details of rights of citizenship see James Read in M.Twaddle (ed.), *Expulsion of a Minority: Essays on Ugandan Asians* (London: University of London Institute of Commonwealth Studies and Athlone Press, 1975), pp.193–209. See also Yash Tandon and Arnold Raphael, *The New Position of East Africa's Asians: Problems of a Displaced Minority* (London: Minority Rights Group Report no 16, 1978) p.6. for

Ugandan Asians status as a dual minority.

4. Vaughan Robinson, *Transients, settlers and refugees: Asians in Britain* (Oxford: Clarendon Press, 1986), p.40.
5. Kuepper et al, *Ugandan Asians in Britain*, p.29, quoting E.Huxley, 'England faces the great migration', *National Review*, 13 October 1972.
6. Twaddle, *Expulsion of a minority*, p.5.
7. Ibid., p.6.
8. Robinson, *Transients, Settlers and Refugees*, p.41.
9. Mahmood Mamdani, *From Citizen to Refugee: Ugandan Asians come to Britain* (London: Francis Pinter, 1973), p.15.
10. Tandon and Raphael, *The New Position of East Africa's Asians*, p.17.
11. Robinson, *Transients, Settlers and Refugees*, p.42.
12. J.S.Read notes that in 1969 there were 74,308 Ugandan Asians of whom 26,657 were recorded as citizens, and 36,593 as British Asians. See M.Twaddle, *Expulsion of a Minority*, p.193.
13. Mamdani, *From Citizen to Refugee*, pp.19–20.
14. These crucial supporters were the urban trader Africans, the Nubians, whose advancement was obstructed by the Asians. See M.Twaddle, *Expulsion of a Minority*, p.10.
15. Kuepper et al, *Ugandan Asians in Britain*, p.39.
16. Mamdani, *From Citizen to Refugee*, p.18.
17. Ibid., p.25.
18. Raxa, interviewed by Katharine Knox, Southampton, 23 January 1995.
19. President Nyerere of Tanzania said 'Every racialist in the world is an animal of some kind or another, and all are kinds which have no future.' President Kaunda of Zambia condemned Amin's action as 'terrible, horrible, abominable and shameful'. President Kenyatta of Kenya remained silent but Vice-President Moi warned 'Kenya is not a dumping ground for citizens of other countries'. See Kuepper et al, *Ugandan Asians in Britain*, pp.7–8. But President Sekou Touré of Guinea, formerly an opponent of the regime reportedly became a supporter – see J.Read in M.Twaddle, *Expulsion of a Minority*, p.209.
20) See Kuepper et al, *Ugandan Asians in Britain*, p.48, and Tandon and Raphael, *The New Position of East Africa's Asians*, p.13.
21. Tandon and Raphael, *The New Position of East Africa's Asians*, p.13 state that 13,600 Asians came to Britain in 1967, almost double the intake for 1966 and p.14 for consequences of the 1968 Act and p.15 for Asian methods of entering Britain. See also J.Read in M.Twaddle, *Expulsion of a Minority*, passim.
22. The net effect of this legislation was that large numbers of Australians, Canadians and New Zealanders held rights of abode in Britain but few Afro-Caribbeans or Asians.
23. *Hansard* (HC) Vol.843, Cols770–3, oral answers (23 October 1972).
24. Mamdani, *From Citizen to Refugee*, p.64.
25. *Hansard* (HC) Vol.846 Cols35–8, oral answers (13 November 1972).
26. *Hampshire Chronicle*, 15 September 1972.
27. *Hansard* (HC) Vol.848 Cols1125–34, oral answers (19 December 1972). See also Kuepper *et al.*, *Ugandan Asians in Britain*, p.55.
28. See *The Times*, 25 September 1972, 'God help the people'.
29. Derek Humphry and Michael Ward, *Passports and Politics* (Harmondsworth, Middlesex: Penguin, 1974), pp.16–95, and *Hansard* (HC) Vol.843 Cols261–75, oral answers (18 October 1972).
30. *Hansard* (HC) Vol.759 Col .1501 (28 February 1968).
31. *Hansard* (HC) Vol.846 Cols35–8, oral answers (13 November 1972).
32. *Hansard* (HC) Vol.843 Cols261–75, oral answers (18 October 1972), Home

Secretary Mr Carr responding to Mr Torney MP.

33. Vaughan Robinson, *Transients, Settlers and Refugees*, p.45.
34. Kuepper *et al.*, *Ugandan Asians in Britain*, p.43.
35. Ibid., p.43.
36. Ibid., p.55.
37. *The Times*, 2 September 1972.
38. *The Guardian*, 17 August 1972, in Mike Bristow, 'Britain's Response to the Ugandan Asian Crisis: Government Myths Versus Political and Resettlement Realities', *New Community*, Vol.5, No 3 (Autumn 1976), pp.267.
39. Letter to Earl Mountbatten of Burma from Mrs Mary Dines, Hon. Secretary of JCWI, 28 August 1972, MB9/23 BCEL – British Council Ex-Servicemen's League file in Mountbatten papers, University of Southampton archive.
40. Barratt letter to Secretary-General of BCEL, 5 September 1972. MB9/23 BCEL – British Council Ex-Servicemen's League file, Mountbatten papers, University of Southampton.
41. *Southern Evening Echo*, 2 September 1972.
42. Ibid.
43. *Southern Evening Echo*, 11 September 1972.
44. Kuepper *et al. Ugandan Asians in Britain*, pp.78–9.
45. The UK, India and Canada took 80–90 per cent of the Ugandan Asians who left in August–November 1973. See Bert N.Adams and Victor Jesudason, 'The Employment of Ugandan Asians in Britain, Canada and India', *Ethnic and Racial Studies*, Vol.7, No.4 (October 1984), p.463.
46. Kuepper *et al.*, *Ugandan Asians in Britain*, p.40.
47. See for instance, Adams and Jesudason, 'The Employment of Ugandan Asians', pp.464–5 and Mamdani, *From Citizen to Refugee*, p.81.
48. Adams and Jesudason, 'The Employment of Ugandan Asians', p.464.
49. For details see Home Office, *Ugandan Resettlement Board Final Report* (London: HMSO, 1974 Cmd 5594), p.7.
50. Robinson, *Transients, Settlers and Refugees*, p.43.
51. Refugee influxes, particularly to the West, are usually noted for the predominance of young, single men.
52. *Refuge or Home? A Policy Statement on the Resettlement of Refugees* (Community Relations Commission, London, 1976), p.43.
53. Bristow, 'Britain's Response to the Uganda Asian Crisis', p.271.
54. For a list of bases see *Ugandan Resettlement Board Final Report*.
55. *Hansard* (HC) Vol.855, Cols1745–56, oral answers (4 May 1973).
56. Extracts from Charles Cunningham, *Interim Report of the Uganda Resettlement Board*, (London: HMSO, 1973, Cmd 5296).
57. Robinson, *Transients, Settlers and Refugees*, p.45.
58. David Stephens, 'Uganda Asians', *New Society*, 10 May 1973.
59. Bristow, 'Britain's Response to the Uganda Asian Crisis', p.271.
60. Ibid., pp.272–3.
61. *Uganda Resettlement Board Final Report*, p.19.
62. Mamdani, *From Citizen to Refugee*, pp.126–7.
63. Urvashi R., interviewed by Katharine Knox, Southampton, 10 January 1995.
64. *Refuge or Home*, p.8.
65. Kuepper *et al.*, *Ugandan Asians in Britain*, p.75.
66. 'District Council Homes for Seven Asian Families', *Hampshire Chronicle*, 29 September 1972.
67. *Hampshire Chronicle*, 6 October 1972.
68. *Hampshire Chronicle*, 20 October 1972.
69. *Southern Evening Echo*, 20 October 1972.

70. *Southern Evening Echo*, 3 November 1972.
71. Letter from A. Curtis, Bitterne: 'Asians for the Isle of Wight?', *Southern Evening Echo*, 14 September 1972.
72. *Southern Evening Echo*, 27 October 1972. The issue arose when a woman living in Portswood, Southampton, went to the police, genuinely upset because she did not know how she was going to cope with the expected arrival of two Asians to take up lodgings.
73. *One Year On: a Report on the Resettlement of Refugees from Uganda in Britain* (London: Community Relations Commission, 1974), pp.42–3.
74. These calls were led by the Community Relations Commission and pointed out that the URB had appealed for help to disperse the Asians evenly throughout the country, which would mean Southampton taking 21 families.
75. Anver Jeevanjee, interviewed by Katharine Knox, Southampton, 19 December 1994.
76. *Southern Evening Echo*, 9 November 1972.
77. Minutes of City of Southampton Proceedings of Councils and Committees, 2790, 25 September 1972, 3022, 22 October 1972, 13 November 1972, Southampton City Record Office.
78. John Arnold, Labour councillor and presently (1998), leader of Southampton City Council, interviewed by Katharine Knox, Southampton, 6 March 1995. Mr Arnold was formerly a university teacher of Third World Studies.
79. *Southern Evening Echo*, 18 September 1972.
80. 'Anti-Asian slogans denounced', *Southern Evening Echo*, 2 November 1972.
81. *Hansard* (HC) Vol.847 Cols 1657–60, oral answers (7 December 1972).
82. *Hansard* (HC) Vol.845 Cols 206–10, written answers (9 November 1972), Vol.846, Col.75, written answers (14 November 1972), and Vol.846 Cols 195–8, written answers (16 November 1972).
83. See, for instance, the debate of 13 November 1972.
84. Kuepper *et al.*, *Ugandan Asians in Britain*, p.66.
85. *Hansard* (HC) Vol.847 Cols 1441–84, oral answers (6 December 1972).
86. Danko Joszef, interviewed by Katharine Knox, Southampton, 23 February 1995.
87. See *Ugandan Resettlement Board Interim Report*.
88. Kuepper *et al.*, *Ugandan Asians in Britain*, p.3.
89. See *Refuge or Home?*, pp.22–30 on employment.
90. Adams and Jesudason, 'The Employment of Ugandan Asians', p.468. Their survey of three countries shows almost 50 per cent of uneducated small traders and shopkeepers were unemployed.
91. Bristow, 'Britain's Response to the Uganda Asian Crisis', p.265.
92. *Ugandan Resettlement Board Final Report*, p.19.
93. Robinson, *Transients, Settlers and Refugees*, p.46.
94. *One Year On*, p.15.
95. Ibid.
96. Adams and Jesudason, 'The Employment of Ugandan Asians', p.468.
97. Ibid., p.472.
98. *Southern Evening Echo*, 10 October 1972.
99. *Southern Evening Echo*, 17 November 1972.
100. Ibid.
101. Ugandan Asian women interviewed by Katharine Knox, Southampton, 10 and 23 January 1995.
102. *One Year On*, p.22.
103. Adams and Jesudason, 'The Employment of Ugandan Asians', p.467, compares the reasons for employment problems among the refugees. In India wealth, retirement and temporary residence were the prime reasons for non-participation in the workforce. In Canada, language and training were factors but only 3 per cent of the

sample were not in work there which Adams and Jesudason attribute to the biased entry procedures.

104. Mamdani, *From Citizen to Refugee*, pp.79–80.
105. Ibid., pp.64–5.
106. Ibid., pp.83–5.
107. Mamdani, *From Citizen to Refugee*, pp.92–108.
108. See Mamdani, *From Citizen to Refugee*, *passim*, and Richard Bourne, 'The Last Asians', *New Society*, 31 May 1973. The latter article describes how different camps had different atmospheres; Hemswell residents were suffering malaise, while West Malling's Asians showed optimism and purpose.
109. See *Southern Evening Echo*, 11 November 1972, '"We won't eat" threat: Asian camp uproar', and comments on press coverage in a letter on 24 November 1972, 'Deep sense of gratitude to British people'.
110. Mamdani, *From Citizen to Refugee*, p.108.
111. Raxa, interviewed by Katharine Knox, Southampton, 23 January 1995.
112. Mamdani, *From Citizen to Refugee*, p.110.
113. Ibid., pp.111–12.
114. Ibid., p.127.
115. *Refuge or Home?*, pp.20–1.
116. *One Year On*, p.28.
117. *The Times*, 21 October 1985.
118. Ibid.
119. *One Year On*, p.37.
120. Speech by the Minister of State for the Home Office, Alexander Lyon from *Hansard (HC)* Vol.878 Cols439–50, oral answers (29 July 1974).
121. 'Who wants to be a millionaire?', *The Independent Magazine*, 1 March 1997.
122. Ibid., p.16.
123. *The Sunday Times*, 14 April 1996. See also the Refugee Council, *Credit to the Nation* (London: The Refugee Council, 1997) for details of famous exiles in Britain and the wealthiest entrepreneurs of refugee backgrounds.
124. Over this period, the proportion of white men in managerial positions rose from 23 per cent to 28 per cent. Findings are quoted in the Commission for Racial Equality Report, *Roots of the Future* (London: Commission for Racial Equality, 1996).
125. 'Who wants to be a millionaire?', *The Independent Magazine*, 1 March 1997.
126. *Hansard* (HC) Vol.855 Cols1745–56, oral answers (4 May 1973).
127. Yasmin Alibhai-Brown, *No Place Like Home* (London: Virago, 1997).

CHAPTER 10

1. For an outline of the history of Chile see Leslie Bethell (ed.), *Chile Since Independence* (Cambridge: Cambridge University Press, 1993), esp. chap.4 for the coup and its aftermath.
2. Ester Contreras, interviewed by Katharine Knox, Southampton, 9 February 1995.
3. Alan Angell and Susan Carstairs, 'The Exile Question in Chilean Politics', *Third World Quarterly*, Vol.9, No.1 (January 1987), p.159.
4. UNHCR, *El Refugio: Refugees from Chile* (Geneva: UNHCR, 1975), p.38.
5. Ann Browne, 'Latin American refugees: British government policy and practice', in *Britain and Latin America: An Annual Review of British Latin American Relations* (London: Latin American Bureau, 1979), p.45. For an overview of international action to help Chilean refugees see UNHCR, *El Refugio*.
6. Harold Blakemore, 'Back to the Barracks: the Chilean Case', *Third World Quarterly*, Vol.7, No.1 (1985), pp.44–62.

7. *World University News*, February 1987.
8. Jane Freeland, interviewed by Katharine Knox, Southampton, 30 January 1995.
9. Ibid.
10. Haydee A., interviewed by Katharine Knox, Winchester, 28 February 1995.
11. Angell and Carstairs, 'The Exile Question in Chilean Politics', p.151.
12. Michael Sanders, 'Book Burning and Brutality', *Index on Censorship*, Vol.3, No.1 (1974), pp.7–13.
13. Angell and Carstairs, 'The Exile Question in Chilean Politics', p.149.
14. Haydee A., interviewed by Katharine Knox, Winchester, 17 February 1995.
15. See Hernan Valdes, *Diary of a Chilean Concentration Camp* (London: Victor Gollancz, 1975). Valdes' account is also backed up by the testimony of another Chilean living in Southampton, Abelardo Piga, who was also detained in horrific circumstances (interview by Katharine Knox, 21 February 1995).
16. Valdes, *Diary of a Chilean Concentration Camp*, p.40.
17. See Angell and Carstairs, 'The Exile Question in Chilean Politics', pp.152–3.
18. Ibid., p.153.
19. Browne, 'Latin American refugees: British government policy and practice', p.28.
20. Susan Carstairs, telephone interview by Katharine Knox, January 1995.
21. *Hansard* (HC) Vol.863, Cols965–67, oral answers (7 November 1973).
22. *Hansard* (HC) Vol.864 Col.518, written answers (22 November 1973).
23. Browne, 'Latin American refugees: British government policy and practice', p.29.
24. *Hansard* (HC) Vol.871 Cols423–7, oral answers (27 March 1974).
25. Ibid.
26. *Hansard* (HC) Vol.880 Cols267–8, written answers (8 November 1974).
27. Ibid.
28. For a full description of changing government policy, see Ann Browne, 'Latin American refugees: British government policy and practice', pp.28–56.
29. Ibid., p.33.
30. *Hansard* (HC) Vol.876 Col.361, written answers (8 July 1974).
31. *Hansard* (HC) Vol.895 Col.173–4, written answers (9 July 1975).
32. See Browne, 'Latin American refugees: British government policy and practice', p.35.
33. Ibid., p.35.
34. Ester Contreras, interviewed by Katharine Knox, Southampton, 9 February 1995.
35. See World University Service, *A Study in Exile: A Report on the WUS (UK) Chilean Refugee Scholarship Programme* (London: WUS, 1986) p.15.
36. Jane Freeland, interviewed by Katharine Knox, Southampton, 30 January 1995.
37. The Joint Working Group for Chilean refugees, formed in 1974, later became the Joint Working Group for Latin American refugees and wound up in 1980–81 after the Conservative government decided a special body was not needed. Latin American refugees were then dealt with by the British Refugee Council.
38. Browne, 'Latin American refugees: British government policy and practice', p.41.
39. See Chapter 13, this volume, on former Yugoslavs in the UK.
40. Extract from: 'Refugees from Chile: Interim Report of the Joint Working Group for Refugees from Chile', December 1975, Refugee Council, ref WC/QU 56. Ann Browne, 'Latin American refugees', notes that the ICEM, the Intergovernmental Committee for European Migration, was originally set up to take qualified specialists from Europe to developing countries and to provide facilities for people to travel to Europe for specialist training. The ICEM signed an agreement with the Chilean authorities in 1974 allowing them to negotiate with foreign embassies to obtain visas for prisoners seeking to commute their sentences to exile and thus served as the main coordinator for the prisoner release scheme.
41. Browne, 'Latin American refugees: British government policy and practice', p.41.

42. 'Refugees from Chile: Interim Report', p.9 gives details of regional variations, for instance the north-east offered limited support, while Manchester was one of the best areas. Jobs were easier to find in some places such as the south-west and Wales compared to the north-east and Scotland, but there was less housing in those areas.
43. 'Refuge for victims of Chile coup', *Southern Evening Echo*, 7 September 1974.
44. 'Southampton visit by Chile's ex-envoy', *Southern Evening Echo*, 17 September 1974.
45. Clare Mar-Molinero, interviewed by Katharine Knox, Southampton, 25 January 1995; 'Refugees from Chile: Interim Report', p.19.
46. Clare Mar-Molinero, interviewed by Katharine Knox, Southampton, 25 January 1995.
47. Minute 1290, 13 September 1974 and Minute 906, 11 April 1975, City of Southampton Minutes of Proceedings of Councils and Committees, 1974–75.
48. Quoted in Browne, 'Latin American refugees: British government policy and practice', p.44.
49. See UNHCR, *El Refugio*, p.13, and the UN High Commissioner Khan's speech.
50. *Hansard* (HC) Vol.878 Cols 209–10, written answers (31 July 1974).
51. *Hansard* (HC) Vol.882 Col.60, written answers (25 November 1974).
52. For example, Clare Mar-Molinero, interviewed by Katharine Knox, Southampton, 25 January 1995; *Southern Evening Echo*, 7 September 1974.
53. See Chile Committee for human rights report on solidarity activities with the people of Chile, Refugee Council, ref WC/QU 59.6.
54. See in particular Diana Kay's important history of Chileans based on the collection of testimonies of Chilean men and women in Scotland, *Chileans in Exile: Private Struggles, Public Lives* (Basingstoke, Hants: Macmillan, 1987).
55. Ibid., p.52.
56. Ibid., p.53.
57. Ibid., p.75.
58. From a radio transcribing unit transcript recording of 'Haven of Refuge', 28 September 1982, Radio 4, Refugee Council, ref WC/QU 56.
59. Angell and Carstairs, 'The Exile Question in Chilean Politics', p.156, from CIDE figures.
60. Chile Democratico: Committee for the Return to Chile, *Report of a survey of the Chilean exile community in Britain* (London: Chile Democratico, 1989).
61. *The Observer*, 27 September 1987, 'Broke but unbroken: Chile's exiles return'.
62. Pauline Jones, interviewed by Katharine Knox, Southampton, 5 March 1995.
63. Clare Mar-Molinero, interviewed by Katharine Knox, Southampton, 25 January 1995.
64. See Maria Eugenia Bravo Calderara, *Prayer in the National Stadium* (London: KATABASIS, 1992), for a series of poems on life as a Chilean in exile.

CHAPTER 11

1. David Haines, 'Southeast Asian Refugees in Western Europe: American Reflections on French, British and Dutch Experiences', *Migration World*, Vol.19, Part 4 (1991), p.16.
2. Throughout 1978–79 a steady trickle of Laotians entered Britain, though no special programmes were set up for them. Hostel premises were provided in Brighton and by 1982 small communities had become established in Worthing and Portsmouth as well as London. The Cambodians were more widely dispersed, though with a larger number in Greater London. For details see The Refugee Council, *Refugee Council Annual Report 1980–82* (London: Refugee Council, 1982).

3. See Peter Jones, *Vietnamese Refugees* (London: HMSO, Home Office Research and Planning Unit Paper 13, 1982), p.2.

4. *Thorney Island Newsletter*, May 1980.

5. See Jones, *Vietnamese Refugees*, pp.3–4.

6. Joint Council for Refugees from Vietnam, 'JCRV information sheet 1', p.2, kindly made available by Paul Rushton.

7. Felicity Edholm, Helen Roberts and Judith Sayer, *Vietnamese Refugees in Britain* (London: Commission for Racial Equality, 1983) p.36.

8. *Southern Evening Echo*, 20 August 1979.

9. Mai Hoang (presently working for Portsmouth Social Services as a community development worker specifically looking after the interests of the South Hampshire Vietnamese community), interviewed by Katharine Knox, Portsmouth, 16 January 1995.

10. Esther Wong, 'The exodus', 1982, unpublished paper made available by Ockenden Venture.

11. Edholm *et al.*, *Vietnamese Refugees in Britain*, p.37.

12. Ibid.

13. Anne Ruffell, 'New Homeland for the Boat People', *Hampshire Magazine* (October 1980), p.41.

14. *The News*, 13 June 1979.

15. Ruffell, 'New Homeland', pp.38–9.

16. *Thorney Island Newsletter* (May 1980).

17. Esther Wong, 'The exodus'.

18. *Sunday Times*, 10 August 1980.

19. Esther Wong, 'The exodus', p.11; Joint Council for Refugees from Vietnam, 'JCRV information sheet 2', p.1.

20. JCRV, 'JCRV information sheet 2', p.1.

21. British Council for Aid to Refugees, *BCAR Annual Report 1978–79*, p.5.

22. Extracts from *Hansard* (HL) Vol.398 Cols1352–87 (14 February 1979).

23. See Lesleyanne Hawthorne, *Refugee: The Vietnamese Experience* (Melbourne: Oxford University Press, 1982), pp.228–9.

24. Ibid., p.229.

25. Paul Rushton, interviewed by Katharine Knox, Gosport, 19 March 1995.

26. JCRV, 'JCRV information sheet 2', pp.1–2.

27. Hanh Van Hoang, interviewed by Katharine Knox, Portsmouth, 13 February 1995.

28. The Refugee Council (formerly BCAR) *Vietnamese Refugee Reception and Resettlement 1979–88* (London: Refugee Council, no date), p.11.

29. Margaret Dixon, interviewed by Katharine Knox, Guildford, 1995.

30. Haines, 'Southeast Asian Refugees in Western Europe', p.16.

31. In terms of refugees resettled per capita of population the only recipient country to take less than the United Kingdom was Italy, with 0.1 per thousand taken compared to the UK's 0.3 per thousand. Measured in these terms it was Australia which was the most generous nation, accepting 8.0 per thousand, with the Americans managing only 3.6 per thousand. See David Haines, 'Southeast Asian Refugees in Western Europe', *passim*.

32. Ibid., p.17.

33. Ibid.

34. Samantha Hale, 'The Reception and Resettlement of Vietnamese Refugees in Britain', in Vaughan Robinson (ed.), *The International Refugee Crisis: British and Canadian Responses* (Basingstoke, Hants: Macmillan, 1993), pp.273–92. See pp.279–280 for an assessment of government policy.

35. Ibid., p.280.

36. See Vaughan Robinson, 'British Policy Towards the Settlement Patterns of Ethnic

Groups: An Empirical Evaluation of the Vietnamese Programme, 1979–88', in idem, *The International Refugee Crisis*, pp.319–53.

37. Ibid., pp.326–7.
38. Ibid., p.323.
39. The Refugee Council, *Vietnamese Refugee Reception and Resettlement 1979–88*, p.2.
40. Ibid., p.4.
41. Hale, 'The Reception and Resettlement of Vietnamese Refugees in Britain', p.282.
42. This led to a JCRV ruling that all new housing offers be chanelled through its secretariat first.
43. The Refugee Council, *Vietnamese Refugee Reception and Resettlement, 1979–88*, p.15.
44. *The News*, 28 September 1981.
45. Thorney Island was a former RAF base.
46. For the organisation's evaluation see Refugee Council, *Vietnamese Refugee Reception and Resettlement 1979–88*, p.7.
47. See Michael Levin, *What Welcome? Reception and Resettlement of Refugees in Britain* (London: Acton Society Trust, 1981).
48. Hampshire Policy and Resources Committt Minutes, 14 May 1979–31 March 1980, Nos. 391–406, Hampshire County Record Office, Ref H/CZ4/11/8.
49. The Refugee Council, *Vietnamese Refugee Reception and Resettlement 1979–88*, p.8.
50. Paul Rushton interviewed by Katharine Knox, Gosport, 19 March 1995.
51. Minutes 570 (26 February 1979); 1121 (18 April 1979); 1654 (18 July 1979); 1938 (17 September 1980); and 173 (17 December 1980) from City of Southampton, Minutes of Proceedings of Councils and Committees, 1979–81.
52. The Refugee Council, *Vietnamese Refugee Reception and Resettlement 1979–88*, p.8.
53. S. Hale, 'The Reception and Resettlement of Vietnamese Refugees in Britain', p.283; P. Jones, *Vietnamese Refugees*, p.10.
54. *Hansard* (HL) Vol.398 Cols1353–87, oral answers (14 February 1979).
55. The Refugee Council, *Vietnamese Refugee Reception and Resettlement 1979–88*, p.18.
56. Ving Huynh, interviewed by Katharine Knox, Portsmouth, 1 February 1995.
57. Uncatalogued record of seminar from Southampton City archives, 10 June 1986.
58. See Vaughan Robinson quoted in S. Hale, 'The Reception and Resettlement of Vietnamese Refugees in Britain', p.286.
59. Ibid.
60. Adriana Caudrey in *New Society*, 3 January 1986.
61. See Robinson, 'British Policy Towards the Settlement Patterns of Ethnic Groups', p.329.
62. Speech by Truc Long Pham at Southampton, from the record of the Seminar held between Vietnamese settlers and local authorities in the South of England, 5 June 1986, uncatalogued, Southampton City Record Office.
63. See Edholm *et al.*, *Vietnamese Refugees in Britain*, p.35.
64. Ibid., p.35.
65. Ibid., p.16.
66. Ibid., pp.16–17.
67. See the record in appendix B of the *Report of the Joint Committee for Refugees from Vietnam* (London: Home Office, 1982).
68. Hildegard Dumper (Regional Development Worker, Refugee Action) 'A Background to Refugees from Vietnam in Hampshire', unpublished report of a seminar on Vietnamese refugee issues in Britain presented by the Hampshire Council

of Community Service, in conjunction with Refugee Action and the British Refugee Council, June 1991.

69. Edholm *et al.*, *Vietnamese Refugees in Britain*, p.38.
70. *The News*, 16 May 1985.
71. Extract from the first edition of *New Homeland* (a newspaper written by the Vietnamese at the Refugee Council Reception Centre at Thorney Island in West Sussex), May 1980.
72. *Thorney Island Newsletter*, May 1980.
73. *The News*, 'Heartbroken Refugee took overdose', June 1980.
74. Edholm *et al.*, *Vietnamese Refugees in Britain*, p.26.
75. Mai Hoang, interviewed by Katharine Knox, Portsmouth, 13 January 1995.
76. *New Society*, 7 June 1979.
77. Edholm *et al.*, *Vietnamese Refugees in Britain*, p.40.
78. See for instance, correspondence in *The News*, 10 April 1979.
79. *The News*, 18 September 1979.
80. See *The News*, 23 July 1979. Portsmouth originally refused help but as the anticipated number of arrivals rose to 10,000 changed its policy. The debates were also evident in Arun and Gosport; see *The News*, 25 July 1979 and 13 September 1979.
81. *The News*, 13 June 1979.
82. *The News*, 14 June 1979.
83. *The News*, 14 June 1979.
84. Testimony of Mrs Joyce White, District Organiser of the Women's Royal Voluntary Service in Gosport, from correspondence, 3 February 1995.
85. 'Vietnam: Our Contribution, The Portsmouth Refugee Support Group – The First Year', *Portsmouth Refugee Support Group Newsletter*, No.10 August–September 1980.
86. *The News*, 23 July 1979.
87. *The News*, 28 September 1981.
88. Anne Ruffell, 'New Homeland for the Boat People', p.40.
89. *The News*, 17 September 1979.
90. The Refugee Council, *Vietnamese Refugee Reception and Resettlement 1979–88*, p.11.
91. Ibid., p.10.
92. P. Jones, *Vietnamese Refugees*; Carol Dalglish, 'Occupational Background of the Refugees from Vietnam in Britain', *New Community* Vol.8, No.3 (Winter 1980), pp.344–6; S. Hale, 'The Reception and Resettlement of Vietnamese Refugees in Britain', p.279.
93. See *Report of the JCRV*, p.8.
94. Ibid., p.12.
95. See Refugee Council report 1979–80, p.7; and for a further evaluation see Edholm *et al.*, *Vietnamese Refugees in Britain*, passim.
96. A. Caudrey in *New Society*, 3 January 1986.
97. *Southern Evening Echo*, 20 August 1979, 'The end of a new beginning'.
98. A. Caudrey, *New Society*, 3 January 1986.
99. The Refugee Council, *Refugee Council Annual Report 1979–80*, p.10.
100. S. Hale, 'The Reception and Resettlement of Vietnamese Refugees in Britain', p.287.
101. P. Jones, *Vietnamese Refugees*, pp.27–8.
102. According to the JCRV in the north-east the Vietnamese employment level was 9 per cent compared with 40 per cent in the south.
103. Esther Wong, 'The Exodus', p.18.
104. The Refugee Council, *Vietnamese Refugee Reception and Resettlement 1979–88*, p.21.

105. Hampshire Council of Community Service, *Meeting the needs of the Vietnamese* (Winchester: Hampshire Council of Community Service, 1991), p.13.
106. *The News*, 16 May 1985.
107. Edholm *et al.*, *Vietnamese Refugees in Britain*, p.22.
108. See S. Hale's analysis in 'The Reception and Resettlement of Vietnamese Refugees in Britain', p.288 using Jones' *Vietnamese Refugees*, pp.20–25. The Home Office survey shows how age and gender affected the Vietnamese's English ability, with younger men doing better. Length of stay does not seem to lead to much improvement in English ability because English as a Second Language teaching, while available in the reception camps, might not be afterwards, which for some individuals meant that they received no formal tuition after initial resettlement, a real handicap to progressing in Britain.
109. Carol Dalglish, 'Occupational Background of the Refugees from Vietnam in Britain', p.345.
110. See Diana Kay's study on gender differences among the Chileans in the previous chapter.
111. *New Society*, 7 June 1979. The article gives some insight into the early adaptation of a group of Vietnamese arrivals in Swindon.
112. Dalglish, 'Occupational Background of the Refugees from Vietnam in Britain', p.345 states of 70,868 refugees analysed in the camps in Hong Kong, only 29 claimed to be retired, though 865 were aged over 70, suggesting retirement was a new concept.
113. Hampshire Council of Community Service, *Meeting the needs of the Vietnamese*, p.15.
114. See Refugee Action, *Last Refuge: Elderly People from Vietnam in the UK* (London: Refugee Action, 1987), p.1 which estimated that there were 995 elderly in the community in the UK: taken to include women over 60 and men over 65. The study states that to consider those aged over 55 as elderly would be more appropriate because of the premature ageing suffered in exile. In this case there would be 1,400 elderly Vietnamese in Britain at the time of the study. This is notable because exiles in the UK tend to be dominated by young single men whose needs amd experiences are clearly different.
115. Ibid., p.11.
116. Ibid., p.15.
117. *The News*, 16 May 1985.
118. See Chris Mougne, *Study of Young, Single Vietnamese in Britain* (London: Refugee Action, 1986) pp.12 and 15. Mougne notes that the Home Office estimated that 22.7 per cent of the Vietnamese refugees were aged 15–24, approximately 4,500 people in a population of 20,000 in 1985; his study shows 3,169 in Britain. Of these the Home Office found 600–700 were young single people. According to agencies this figure was 400–500. The male-to-female ratio was approximately 4 or 3 to 1 in the young single age group because more young men were initially likely to have left Vietnam and they were also more likely to move away from home in Britain than females. Mougne argues that approximately 30 per cent of young single Vietnamese people were in employment. Only 40 per cent of those in London had work despite the belief that it is easier to find work there. The type of work undertaken was almost entirely unskilled.
119. Edholm *et al.*, *Vietnamese Refugees in Britain*, p.25.
120. Ibid., p.41.
121. *The News*, 12 June 1979.
122. Paul Rushton, interviewed by Katharine Knox, Gosport, 19 March 1995.
123. Ving Huynh, interviewed by Katharine Knox, Portsmouth, 1 February 1995.

CHAPTER 12

1. Details of the legislation will be provided later in this section, in Chapter 14 on Zaireans.
2. Recognition rates for asylum seekers are very low. In 1986 82 per cent of applicants were given leave to remain in the UK, either with refugee status or ELR. In 1996 only 20 per cent of applicants were given such leave, while 80 per cent of applicants were refused. As many analysts argue, it is not simply the nature of the claims which has changed but the Volume, as increasing numbers of asylum seekers now reach our shores, due to improved travel and communications opportunities.
3. Danièle Joly, *Haven or Hell? Asylum Policies and Refugees in Europe* (Basingstoke, Hants: Macmillan, 1996), p.48.
4. The Refugee Council, *Asylum Statistics, 1986–1996* (London: The Refugee Council, 1997). In 1996, the main countries of asylum noted by the UNHCR were: Iran, Zaire, Pakistan, Tanzania and the former republic of Yugoslavia. The main countries of origin were: Afghanistan, Rwanda, Bosnia and Herzegovina, Liberia and Iraq. (See international comparisons section, p.29.) Within Europe, Germany has received by far the greatest proportion of asylum seekers, with almost 1.5 million applications for asylum from 1990–1995. (See asylum applications in Europe section, p.15.)
5. See The Refugee Council, *The State of Asylum* (London: The Refugee Council, 1996) for an overview of restrictionist tendencies in asylum policy in the UK in the 1980s and 1990s.
6. Gerard Chaliand, *The Kurdish Tragedy* (London: Zed Books, 1994) and David McDowell, *A Modern History of the Kurds* (London: I. B. Tauris, 1995) provide an important historical overview of the Kurdish crisis. For a more personal account of the Kurds' suffering see Sheri Laizer, *Martyrs, Traitors and Patriots: Kurdistan after the Gulf War* (London: Zed Books, 1996). A brief history can be found in Amir Hassanpour, 'The Kurdish Experience', *Middle East Report*, Vol.24, No.4 (July–August 1994). Political developments are recorded in the magazine, *Kurdistan Report*.
7. Chaliand, *The Kurdish Tragedy*, p.3.
8. International Association for Human Rights in Kurdistan, *Annual Report 1993: On the Situation of Human Rights in Northern Kurdistan and the Kurds in Turkey* (Bremen: International Association for Human Rights in Kurdistan, 1993) p.2.
9. Robert Olson, 'The Kurdish Question in the Aftermath of the Gulf War: Geopolitical and Geostrategic Changes in the Middle East', *Third World Quarterly*, Vol.13, No.3 (1992), pp.475–99, esp. p.476.
10. The British held the territory as a mandate until 1932, but the area remained very much under British control until 1958.
11. Christopher Hitchens, 'Struggle of the Kurds', *National Geographic*, August 1992.
12. Ibid.; For the poem see Refugee Council, Kurdish records, ref GTK.
13. *Hansard* (HC) Vol.153 Cols1257–66, oral answers (26 May 1989).
14. Olson, 'The Kurdish Question', p.477.
15. Chaliand, *The Kurdish Tragedy*, p.5.
16. The Refugee Council, *Kurds: Turkish Kurdish Refugees in the UK/ Kurds in Turkey* (London: The Refugee Council, 1993), p.4.
17. See Amnesty International report of 13 September 1989. For details of human rights abuses see reports by Human Rights Watch, Amnesty International, the Refugee Council and other human rights agencies, and annual reports of the International Association for Human Rights in Kurdistan.
18. International Association for Human Rights in Kurdistan, *Annual Report 1993*, p.22.
19. Olson, 'The Kurdish Question', p.478.
20. Extracts from the official statement of a Kurdish refugee who now lives in

Hampshire.
21. See Refugee Council, *Kurds*.
22. See paper by David McDowell held by the Winchester Action Group for Asylum Seekers providing background on Kurdish Alevis seeking asylum in the UK.
23. Ibid.
24. Ibid.
25. Olson, 'The Kurdish Question', p.486.
26. Ibid.
27. Chaliand, *The Kurdish Tragedy*, appendix 1, p.94.
28. Ibid., appendix 2, pp.96–7.
29. *Hansard* (HC) Vol.153 Col.97, written answers (15 May 1989).
30. *Hansard* (HC) Vol.157 Cols72–3, written answers (17 July 1989).
31. *Hansard* (HC) Vol.157 Col.301, written answers, 20 July 1989).
32. *Hansard* (HC) Vol.153 Cols1257–66, oral answers (26 May 1989).
33. *Hansard* (HC) Vol.153 Cols1257–66, oral answers (26 May 1989); see also The Refugee Council; *The Cost of Survival* (London: The Refugee Council, 1998) [a study of the trafficking in refugees].
34. 'Taking Liberties', BBC2, 23 January 1990.
35. *Hansard* (HC) Cols1264–5 (26 May 1989). Consideration was given to establishing a short-term hostel in Tower Hamlets but the government preferred to rely on existing agencies, like the Refugee Council and refugee community organisations, to offer assistance to the Kurdish arrivals.
36. 'Phoney visa ploy lets in 1,000 Kurds', *Daily Mail*, 13 January 1995.
37. Ibid.
38. *Hansard* (HC) Vol.158 Col.25, oral answers (17 October 1989).
39. *Hansard* (HC) Vol.189 Cols157–60, oral answers (16 April 1991).
40. *Hansard* (HC) Vol.189 Cols21–39, oral answers (15 April 1991).
41. *Hansard* (HC) Vol.189 Cols297–8, written answers (22 April 1991).
42. *The Independent*, 3 February 1995, 'EU abandons Kurds to gain a stable Turkey'.
43. *Home Office Statistical Bulletin 1995* (London: Home Office, 1996).
44. Joly, *Haven or Hell?*, p.29.
45. Refugee Council report, Refugee Council archives, ref GTK/QU 44.2523.
46. See comments concerning the reported poisoning of Kurdish refugees in Turkey in 1990 in *Hansard* (HC) Vol.167 Cols235–6, written answers (14 February 1990) for evidence of government self-interest.
47. *Home Office Statistical Bulletin 1996*. It is important to note that of those refused asylum, 740 were refused on grounds that they had come through a safe third country and 730 were refused for failure to submit evidence within the time limits. It should be noted that from 1991–93 larger numbers of Turkish asylum seekers were being granted refugee status and ELR. In spite of the continuing Kurdish crisis, since 1995, refusals have increased.
48. 'Taking Liberties', BBC2, 23 January 1990.
49. See information from Refugee Council, *Kurds*, p.2.
50. 'Facing South', TVS, 14 December 1989.
51. See Chapter 14 on refugees from former Zaire.
52. *Hansard* (HC) Vol.160 Col.203, written answers (14 November 1989).
53. *Hansard* (HC) Vol.157 Col.73, written answers (17 July 1989).
54. Other asylum seekers have also complained about inaccurate interpretation at interviews. The Home Office continue not to use tape recorders, preventing any chance of checking or any redress for the applicant.
55. 'Facing South', TVS, 14 December 1989.
56. Winchester Action Group for Asylum Seekers, information bulletin, written by Reverend Sir John Alleyne, 11 July 1991. The information bulletin was subsequently

circulated to all Winchester churches.

57. 'Facing South', TVS, 14 December 1989.
58. Ibid.
59. *Southern Evening Echo*, 15 July 1989.
60. *Winchester Extra*, 19 October 1989.
61. 'Turkish Kurds and Winchester Tories', a paper written by James Harris, the son of a member of the Winchester Action Group for Asylum Seekers, kindly provided by a member of the group, undated (?1989).
62. *Winchester Extra*, 2 November 1989.
63. *Winchester Extra*, 9 November 1989.
64. 'Makes you sick to be British', *The Guardian*, 22 November 1989.
65. *Kurdistan report* No.20 (January/February 1995), p.43.
66. Ibid., p.41.
67. Ibid., pp.4–9.
68. Ibid.
69. Extract from a letter of Lord Avebury to the Foreign Office, 1994, printed in ibid, p.21.
70. Refugee Council, *Kurds*, p.2.
71. Ibid., p.2.
72. See for instance reports in *The Guardian*, 4 April 1995.
73. *National Geographic*, August 1992.
74. Ibid.
75. *The Guardian*, 31 December 1994.
76. *The Guardian*, 31 December 1995.
77. The Kurdish Workers' Association estimated that 70 per cent of Kurds were single, and only 10 per cent of them were female.
78. Refugee Council, *Kurds*.
79. *The Independent*, 30 October 1989.
80. Ibid.
81. Ibid.
82. A Turkish Kurdish asylum seeker interviewed by Katharine Knox, London, 23 April 1996. His name is witheld to protect his identity.
83. See *The Guardian*, 31 December 1995 and 'Facing South', TVS, 14 December 1989.
84. See *The Financial Times*, *The Guardian* and other newspapers 5–7 January 1998.
85. Amir Hassanpour, 'The Kurdish Experience', *Middle East Report*, Vol.24, No.4 (July–August 1994), p.24.
86. Ibid., p.24. President Clinton, in a meeting with Prime Minister Tansu Ciller on 15 October 1993, said, 'It's not fair for us … to urge Turkey to not only be a democratic country but to recognise human rights and then not to help the government of Turkey deal with the terrorism within its borders'.
87. See 'Turkish Kurds and Winchester Tories', Winchester Action Group for Asylum Seekers.

CHAPTER 13

1. F. Stephen Larrabee, 'Instability and Change in the Balkans', *Survival* (Summer 1992), p.36.
2. Slovenia and Croatia seceded in 1992. Macedonia's claim for international recognition was not so well received but it has also ceased to be part of the new Federal Republic of Yugoslavia (composed of Serbia and Montenegro). Bosnia-Herzegovina achieved independence in April 1992.
3. *New Statesman and Society*, 7 February 1992.
4. For a full political history of the breakdown of the former Yugoslavia see the account

by journalist Misha Glenny, *The Fall of Yugoslavia: The Third Balkan War* (Harmondsworth, Middlesex: Penguin Books, 1992). See also L. Cohen, *Broken Bonds: The Disintegration of Yugoslavia* (Boulder: Westview Books, 1993).

5. See Petya Nitzova, 'The Bosnian Crisis: Anatomy of the Conflict', *New Community*, Vol.19, No.3 (April 1993), pp.507–12.
6. *New Statesman and Society*, 17 April 1992.
7. Larrabee, 'Instability and Change', p.36.
8. Roy Gutman in his journalistic account of events in Bosnia notes that in Bosnia 44 per cent of the population were Muslim, 31 per cent Serbian and 14 per cent Croatian. See R. Gutman, *A Witness to Genocide* (Dorchester, Dorset: Element Books, 1993), p.7.
9. Petya Nitzova, 'The Bosnian Crisis', p.508.
10. Ibid., pp.509–10.
11. Norman Cigar, 'The Serbo-Croatian War, 1991: Political and Military Dimensions', *Journal of Strategic Studies*, Vol.16, No.3 (September 1993), pp.297–338.
12. Vedat Spahovic, 'Death of a Multicultural Society', *Connections* (Winter 1997), pp.4–5.
13. Glenny, *The Fall of Yugoslavia*.
14. Bogomil Ferfila, 'Yugoslavia: Confederation or disintegration?', *Problems of Communism* (July–August 1991), p.20.
15. George Fyson, Argiris Malapanis and Jonathan Silberman, *The Truth About Yugoslavia: Why Working People Should Oppose Intervention* (New York: Pathfinder, 1993), pp.13–14.
16. Ibid., p.30.
17. Nitzova, 'The Bosnian Crisis', p.511. For a detailed account of the history of Yugoslavia and an indication of its inherent instability see Stephan Pavlowitch, *The Improbable Survivor: Yugoslavia and Its Problems, 1918–1988* (London: Hurst, 1988).
18. Patrick Moore, 'A New Stage in the Bosnian Conflict', *RFE/RL Research Report*, Vol.3, No.9 (4 March 1994), p.36.
19. Danièle Joly and Clive Nettleton, *Refugees: Asylum in Europe?* (London: Minority Rights Publications, 1992), p.83.
20. See UNHCR asylum statistics, 1996, reprinted in The Refugee Council, *Asylum Statistics, 1986–96* (London: Refugee Council, 1997).
21. Cohen, *Broken Bonds*, p.242.
22. Extracts from *Hansard* (HC) Vol.200 Cols1160–7, oral answers (12 December 1991). Although this was the 'first real airing of the tragedy in Croatia', the EC had already deployed monitors and was brokering a peace conference, developments which had taken place in November 1991.
23. Letter from Niki Kortvelyessy, 'Refugees to the UK: Hungary 1956, Bosnia 1992', *The Independent*, 17 August 1992.
24. Nitzova, 'The Bosnian Crisis', p.511.
25. For information on the Act see the Refugee Council factfile, *The Asylum and Immigration (Appeals) Act 1993* (London: Refugee Council, 1993). For details of the problems resulting from the return of asylum seekers to 'safe third countries', see Amnesty International, *Playing Human Pinball* (London: Amnesty International, 1996).
26. *Hansard* (HC) Vol.214 Cols352–3, written answers (19 November 1992).
27. See Home Office statistics for 1994. Refusals exclude those refused on safe third country grounds (865) or refused under paragraph 340 of the Immigration Rules for refusals without substantive consideration of the asylum claim (2,985). For a statistical analysis of asylum applications and decisions see The Refugee Council, *Asylum Statistics 1986–96*.

28. Serbian asylum seeker from Bosnia, interviewed by Katharine Knox, Southampton, 14 February 1995.
29. *The Economist*, 5 December 1992, pp.47–8.
30. Ibid. It noted the following number of Yugoslavs in Europe in 1992: Austria: total arrivals 57,500; asylum applicants 12,600. Britain: total arrivals 44,000; asylum applicants 4,400. France: total arrivals 52,000; asylum applicants 2,400. Germany: total arrivals 260,000; asylum applicants 171,000. Sweden: total arrivals 75,000; asylum applicants 75,000. Switzerland: total arrivals 70,500; asylum applicants 20,000. Between 1992 and 1996, 11,445 asylum applications were submitted by former Yugoslav nationals in Britain. This figure masks a large number of asylum seekers as it excludes dependants and those who came under the Bosnia quota programme.
31. *Hansard* (HC) Vol.196 Cols349–50, written answers (21 October 1991).
32. Ibid.
33. *Hansard* (HC) Vol.199 Cols105–6, written answers (19 November 1991).
34. *Hansard* (HC) Vol.203 Col.649, written answers (14 February 1992).
35. Serbian asylum seeker from Bosnia interviewed by Katharine Knox, Southampton, 14 February 1995.
36. Gutman, *A Witness to Genocide*, p.69.
37. Ibid., pp.90–101. As Gutman reports, well over 1,000 people were killed at Omarska, and as many as a thousand disappeared without trace when the camp was closed after international intervention. The majority of the detainees were civilians, mostly draft-age Muslim and Croat men, but there were also many men under 18 or over 60, and a small number of women.
38. *Hansard* (HC) Vol.214 Cols141–9 (17 November 1992).
39. Lois Graessle and George Gawlinski, *Responding to a Humanitarian Emergency: An evaluation of the UK's Bosnia Project to Offer 'Temporary Protection' to People from Former Yugoslavia 1992–5* (London: Planning Together Associates, 1996), p.1.
40. *Hansard* (HC) Vol.215 Cols30–8 (30 November 1992).
41. *Hansard* (HC) Vol.214 Col.141–9 (17 November 1992).
42. Ibid.
43. Ibid.
44. Ibid.
45. Ibid.
46. Ibid.
47. Ibid.
48. Information from the Bosnia Project of the Refugee Council. See Refugee Council records, QY/QU 59.2.
49. Ibid.; Gutman, *A Witness to Genocide*, p.92.
50. A Bosnian couple interviewed by Katharine Knox, 1996; The Refugee Council, *Credit to the Nation* (London: Refugee Council, 1997).
51. *The Last Resort* (London: Human Rights Convention Report, No.9, no date), p.8.
52. Serbian asylum seeker from Bosnia interviewed by Katharine Knox, Southampton, 14 February 1995.
53. The Bosnia Project made clear its concern to implement equal opportunities in its own recruitment of caseworkers who could interpret for the refugees, and not mirror the ethnic divisions in Yugoslavia. For some clients, however, there was still suspicion and a lack of trust in interpreting. See Graessle and Gawlinski, *Responding to a Humanitarian Emergency, passim*.
54. Serbian asylum seeker from Bosnia interviewed by Katharine Knox, Southampton, 14 February 1995.
55. Ibid.
56. *The Guardian*, 31 March 1995.

57. Ibid.
58. *The Guardian*, 3 April 1995.
59. Information provided by an asylum seeker in Hampshire. For critical consideration of current Home Office refusal letters for asylum seekers and the 'climate of disbelief' see The Refugee Council, *The State of Asylum* (London: Refugee Council, 1996).
60. *New Statesman and Society*, 7 May 1993, pp.14–15 and John Pilger, *Distant Voices* (London: Vintage, 1994), p.213.
61. Information from the Bosnia Project, Refugee Council records, QY/QU 59.2.
62. *Hansard* (HC) Vol.215 Cols30–8 (30 November 1992). For the activities of the Women's Aid to Former Yugoslavia, see their reports from 1992 onwards.
63. *Ockenden Venture Annual Report 1994* (London: Ockenden Venture, 1995), p.10.
64. *New Reporter*, 20 February, 9 May and 18 December 1995 for accounts of the University of Southampton's assistance to the refugees.
65. 'Heaven for 60 Bosnian Orphans', *Southampton Advertiser*, 24 August 1995.
66. Information from Refugee Council records, QY/QU 53.
67. Ibid.
68. *Hansard* (HC) Vol.254 Col.113, written answers (6 February 1995).
69. Graessle and Gawlinski, *Responding to a Humanitarian Emergency, passim*.
70. Ibid., Foreword, p.iii.

CHAPTER 14

1. See handouts for documentary, Channel 4, January 1989, 'Exceptional leave to remain', document 3.
2. These statistics will be explored further later in this chapter.
3. Winsome J. Leslie, *Zaire: Continuity and Political Change in an Oppressive State* (Boulder, San Francisco and Oxford: Westview Press, 1993), p.21.
4. Ibid., p.35.
5. Ibid., p.45.
6. Ibid., p.49.
7. The Medical Foundation for the Care of Victims of Torture, *A Betrayal of Hope and Trust* (London: Medical Foundation, 1994), p.8. This Zairean left his country for the UK after his wife disappeared without trace. After being detained for 16 months and making more than 20 applications for his release he was finally granted temporary admission into the country after which time his asylum application could be fully considered. The UDPS stands for the Union for Democracy and Social Progress, the major opposition movement led by Etienne Tshisekedi, founded in 1980. Thirteen of its leaders who called for an end to Mobutu's arbitrary rule were sentenced to 15 years in prison in 1982 after making allegations about corrupt financial dealings by the Mobutu family: UNHCR, *Background Paper on Zairean Refugees and Asylum Seekers* (Geneva: UNHCR, Centre for Documentation and Research, 1995), p.8.
8. Charles Kukwikila, a Zairean national testifying at 'The people's tribunal on immigration and asylum', held in London on 25 November 1993, to discuss asylum issues in the UK.
9. Leslie, *Zaire*, p.170.
10. US State Department, *Country Reports on Human Rights Practices for 1996* (Washington, DC: US State Department, 1997), pp.307–15.
11. Ibid., p.170.
12. UNHCR, *Background Paper on Zairean Refugees*, p.4.
13. Ibid.
14. See the Refugee Council, *Asylum Statistics 1986–96* (London: The Refugee Council,

1997), pp.94–5.

15. Charles Kukwikila of the Association of Zairean refugees speaking at 'The people's tribunal on immigration and asylum', 25 November 1993. See UNHCR statistics.

16. Leslie, *Zaire*, p.176.

17. In 1997 Zaire itself fell prey to charges of attacking refugees from Rwanda. Forces of the Alliance des forces democratiques pour la liberation du Congo-Zaire (AFDL), apparently assisted by Rwandese government forces and militias responsible for the 1994 genocide in Rwanda, attacked Hutu refugees seeking protection in camps in the east of Zaire. According to Amnesty International, 'Virtually all refugee camps emptied and more than one million refugees and displaced Zaireans were deprived of all humanitarian aid by the fighting. In November, the UN Security Council called for a ceasefire and authorised the deployment of an international force to aid the refugees. In mid-November, some 500,000 refugees trekked back to Rwanda. Following the mass return of refugees, the multinational intervention force was not deployed, although hundreds of thousands of refugees and displaced Zaireans remained dispersed inside Zaire.' See *Amnesty International Report 1997* (London: Amnesty International, 1997), pp.342–5.

18. See *Human Rights Watch World Report* (London: Human Rights Watch, 1997), pp.60–6. According to this report, more than 18,000 Zairean Tutsis fled to neighbouring countries in the first half of 1996.

19. UNHCR, *Background Paper on Zairean Refugees and Asylum Seekers*, p.3.

20. See Home Office statistics in the Refugee Council, *Asylum Statistics 1986–96*. In 1998 recognition rates for asylum seekers from the former Zaire did improve radically, recognising the chaos ensuing from the change of regime to the Democratic Republic of Congo.

21. Many reports have been written on the injustice of detaining asylum seekers. See Amnesty International, *Prisoners Without a Voice* (London: Amnesty International, 1994); Refugee Council, *The Detention of Asylum Seekers*, factsheet number 3, February 1995, and subsequent briefings (Refugee Council, London, 1995–97); Mark Ashford, *Detained Without Trial: A Survey of Immigration Act Detention* (London: Joint Council for the Welfare of Immigrants, 1993) and Christina Pourgourides, *A Second Exile: Mental Health and Detention* (London: no publisher, 1997).

22. Immigration officials do not have to give written reasons for detaining individuals, but it is usually assumed that this is due to the fear that an asylum seeker might abscond from a given address. However, according to the Refugee Council, 'There is no evidence showing levels of absconding by asylum seekers after release from detention, nor of their failure to comply with other conditions of Temporary Admission. From 1989–93 about 3.6 per cent of passengers granted TA absconded – yet there is no evidence to suggest that they are all asylum seekers.' From Refugee Council, *The Detention of Asylum Seekers*.

23. For details of these practices see the June 1997 briefing from the Refugee Council on the detention of asylum seekers. The organisation noted here that: in an Amnesty International survey of 150 detainees, 86 per cent had not had an independent review of the decision to detain them, despite having been detained for an average of five months; 82 per cent of the detainees had been detained from the first day they had applied for asylum, with no indication of the illegitimacy of their claim; the cost of detention was some £20 million in 1996, but the majority of asylum detainees were released prior to a decision showing that detention was not being used as a last resort. In the survey by Dr Christina Pourgourides, a research psychiatrist, *A Second Exile*, 5 of the 15 detainees interviewed had made serious attempts at self-harm and 6 of the 15 were eventually given refugee status or exceptional leave to remain.

24. Ibid. This man was subsequently released and after 297 days in detention (241 in

prison) was granted asylum. The Medical Foundation for the Care of Victims of Torture found evidence that he had been tortured.

25. *The Independent on Sunday*, 8 December 1991.
26. *Refugee Participation Network*, 15 September 1993, letter from information from the Stop the Detentions Action Group.
27. Charles Kukwikila at 'The people's tribunal'.
28. *The Independent*, 'Refugee sanctuary to be slashed', 5 November 1991.
29. See the Refugee Council, *Asylum and Immigration (Appeals) Act, 1993* (London, Refugee Council, 1993).
30. *Hansard* (HC) Vol.205 Cols22–73, oral answers (2 March 1992).
31. 'Release for the Captives', report of a conference held in London in September 1993 about the detention of immigrants and asylum seekers in Britain, June 1994.
32. Ibid., p.9.
33. Extract from Mark Ashford, *Detained Without Trial*, pp.58–61.
34. Testimony of a Zairean national sent to the Refugee Council, May 1997.
35. Ibid.
36. Testimony of Kenneth Osei-Afriyie, from the report of a conference in London on the detention of immigrants and asylum seekers in Britain, 'Release for the Captives', June 1994.
37. Ibid.
38. This has forced airline officials to police immigration and threatens to prevent the entry of asylum seekers, as carriers are now faced with a fine of £2,000 for each person they bring to Britain without the right entry documents. The Immigration Service is also increasingly using officials at airports in other countries to police immigration, again reducing the likelihood of asylum seekers being able to receive sanctuary in Britain, as they may even be prevented from escaping their country.
39. See Amnesty International, *Passing the Buck* (London: Amnesty International British Section, 1993). The Zairean case is one of many outlined. See esp. p.5.
40. *Independent on Sunday*, 8 December 1991.
41. Comments expressed by an attendant at the Liberal Party conference fringe meeting in October 1996.
42. *The Independent*, 8 December 1991. Such testimony has been confirmed by other Zaireans in Britain who believe that racism is more overt in Belgium and France.
43. Ibid.
44. *Race and Class*, UK commentary p.80 undated cutting in Refugee Council press archive.
45. *The Guardian*, 28 July 1993.
46. Ibid.
47. Ibid.
48. *Hansard* (HC) Vol.200 Cols30–35, oral answers (2 December 1991).
49. *The Guardian*, 28 July 1993.
50. Ibid.
51. Ibid.
52. *The Sun*, 12 December 1991. In 1992, it had similar articles, one entitled, 'Bogus refugee fiddled £2,500 a week'.
53. *News of the World*, 12 January 1992. Undated articles come from cuttings collected by the Winchester Action group for asylum seekers.
54. *The Daily Telegraph*, 27 October 1994.
55. The '70,000' may be seen as an erroneous and misleading reference to the number of asylum seekers awaiting decisions on their cases – not illegal or bogus – with their claims still being processed in slow and laborious determination procedures.
56. *The Sun*, 12 December 1991.
57. *The Guardian*, 10 March 1995.

58. In many ways the tone of debates had not progressed since the beginning of the century, with reference to foreigners threatening provisions for local people, in a climate where job insecurity was especially resonant. The additional factor now was that the legitimacy of the individual asylum seeker's need for help was now also immediately under question.

59. *Hampshire Chronicle*, 27 December 1991.

60. *Hampshire Chronicle*, 10 January 1992, 'Winchester man forfeits bail cash as Zairean absconds'.

61. *Winchester Extra*, 9 January 1992.

62. *Winchester Extra*, 30 January 1992.

63. Sir John Alleyne, interviewed by Katharine Knox, Autumn 1994.

64. Details of dates and names are withheld to protect the individual's anonymity.

65. Letter from Immigration and Nationality Department (date withheld to protect anonymity).

66. See US Committee for Refugees, *Country Reports on Human Rights Practices* (Washington, DC: US State Department, 1991–97).

67. A member of the Detention Advisory group, interviewed by Katharine Knox, April 1996.

68. *Refugee Participation Network* 15 September 1993.

69. Amnesty International, 'UK: Cruel, inhuman treatment', reference, AI EUR 45/05/94.

70. Charles Kukwikila at 'The peoples tribunal'.

71. UNHCR, *Background Paper on Zairean Refugees and Asylum Seekers*, p.15.

72. The Refugee Council, *Exile* (London: The Refugee Council, no date).

73. Ibid.

74. *The Guardian*, 4 April 1995.

75. *The Guardian*, 2 March 1995.

76. *The Guardian*, 5 April 1995.

77. A briefing paper by the Refugee Council and the Commission for Racial Equality on the effects of the legislation also suggests discrimination since these employment regulations came into force. See their 'A Culture of Suspicion: the Impact of Internal Regulations' (1998).

78. See statistical analyses available from the Refugee Council, 1997.

79. For details, see reports of the Refugee Council which show how the measures affected individuals including *Poverty and Prejudice, Welcome to the UK* and *Just Existence* (London: The Refugee Council, 1996–97).

80. See the Refugee Council, *Welcome to the UK* (London: The Refugee Council, 1996) for this and other individual's experiences.

81. A Zairean asylum seeker interviewed by Katharine Knox, London, October 1997.

82. The Refugee Council, *The Asylum and Immigration Act 1996*.

83. International diplomacy in Europe seeking to reduce asylum movements within Europe has been marked in 1997–98 as asylum seekers have fled from certain areas, namely Roma people from the Czech Republic, Romania and Slovakia, and Kurds from Turkey and Iraq. The flight of some 1,200 asylum seekers to Italy, over December 1997–January 1998, the majority of whom were Kurds from Turkey, led to fears from the German and French governments that the Schengen Agreement allowing freedom of movement within signatory European countries would enable asylum seekers to enter through 'weak' border points and migrate north. Following this diplomacy, Turkey was reported to have rounded up and arrested over 1,000 citizens, including would-be migrants, raising even more concern over the situation for dissidents within the country and further undermining international protection.

84. In 1996 38 per cent of asylum seekers coming to Britain were from African countries. The majority were refused. Zaireans and Nigerians faced a refusal rate of

99 per cent. The only nationalities with significant numbers of individuals being granted refugee status were former Yugoslavs, Iraqis and Iranians.

85. Philip Rudge, former General Secretary of the European Council for Refugees and Exiles, London, 1997.
86. See the Refugee Council, *Credit to the Nation: A study of refugees in the United Kingdom* (London: Refugee Council, 1997).

CONCLUSION

1. Parkinson to Lord Dufferin, 16 May 1938 in PRO CO 323/1605/2. Thanks to Joanna Westphal Newman for this reference linked to her doctoral thesis on refugee movements to the British West Indies, 1933–1948.
2. N. Sibley and A. Elias, 'The Aliens Act and the Right of Asylum' quoted by M. J. Landa, *The Alien Problem and Its Remedy* (London: P. S. King, 1911), p.261; J. E. B. Seely in *Hansard* (HC) Vol.145 Cols755–9 (2 May 1905).
3. Comments made by Philip Rudge, former General Secretary of the European Council for Refugees and Exiles based in London.
4. On such myths see Colin Holmes, *A Tolerant Country? Immigrants, Refugees and Minorities in Britain* (London: Faber & Faber, 1991).
5. Charles Wardle quoted in 'Desperately Seeking Asylum', Network First documentary series, Yorkshire Television, February 1995.
6. For discussion of terminology in relation to displaced persons, see Bernard Wasserstein, *Vanishing Diaspora: The Jews in Europe Since 1945* (London: Hamish Hamilton, 1996), pp.8–9.
7. Joynson-Hicks in *Hansard* (HC) Vol.180 Cols313–14 (11 February 1925).
8. Fabius quoted in 'France's sound of silence: Opposition politicians are found wanting on migrant rights', *The Guardian*, 27 February 1997.
9. *The Sun* survey quoted by John Pilger, *Distant Voices* (London: Vintage, 1992), p.36.
10. *IPPR attitudes to race surveys: Summary of Surveys*, press release, 5 February 1997, question 7.
11. Ibid.
12. For further discussion of this point see Tony Kushner, 'The Fascist as "Other"? Racism and Neo-Nazism in Contemporary Britain', *Patterns of Prejudice*, Vol.28, No.1 (1994), pp.27–45.
13. For hostile press coverage see *Daily Express*, 21 October 1997; *Evening Standard*, 13, 14 November 1997; *Daily Mail*, 14 November 1997; *The Times*, 14 November 1997. For a critique of this response see Heather Mills, 'No Gypsies Please, we're British', *The Observer*, 26 October 1997; Alan Travis and Ian Traynor, 'Britain's little refugee crisis', *The Guardian*, 22 October 1997; Edie Frieman, 'Asylum madness', *Jewish Chronicle*, 28 November 1997 and Vitali Vitaliev, 'Gypsy rights go down the tube', *The Guardian*, 1 December 1997. For the exclusive stress on local resentment see *The Times*, 20 and 21 October 1997; *Daily Telegraph*, 20 October 1997 and *The Independent*, 21 October 1997. Information on positive Dover responses from research carried out by Katharine Knox on behalf of the Refugee Council. On local anti-Nazi initiatives see *Searchlight*, No.270 (December 1997).
14. Yvonne Kapp and Margaret Mynatt, *British Policy and the Refugees, 1933–1941* (London: Frank Cass, 1997), pp.38–9.
15. *IPPR attitudes to race surveys*, p.2. There is also a clear involvement of liberal-minded elderly activists who provide financial and other support for organisations such as the Refugee Council.
16. Joynson-Hicks in *Hansard* (HC) Vol.180 Col.314 (11 February 1925).
17. '"Heaven" for 60 Bosnia Orphans', *Southampton Advertiser*, 24 August 1995.

18. Interview with Shirley Firth in *AVID Newsletter*, No.1 (July 1997).

19. Refugee Council briefing, 30 October 1997, outlines how the Labour Party Home Secretary, Jack Straw, announced new measures on 27 October 1997, in response to the Roma refugee panic, cutting the asylum determination procedure to five working days from 28 days with regard to further representations to be made after initial interviews (i.e. submitting evidence from home countries or medical evidence may become virtually impossible in this short time, but asylum seekers can still appeal against refusal). For Straw's later input see Home Office, *Fairer, Faster and Firmer – A Modern Approach to Immigration and Asylum* (London: HMSO, Cmd 4018, 1998).

20. *Women's Aid to Former Yugoslavia* Report, No.10 (March 1996).

21. Mahmood Mamdani, *From Citizen to Refugee: Ugandan Asians Come to Britain* (London: Francis Pinter, 1973).

22. Ethiopian refugee, interviewed by Katharine Knox, London, summer 1996; C. S. de Kisshazy, 'Hungarian Welfare', March 1979, Refugee Council archives, RH/QU61.

23. Mr Quan quoted by *Southern Evening Echo*, 20 August 1979.

24. For its origins, see Tony Kushner, *The Holocaust and the Liberal Imagination: A Social and Cultural History* (Oxford: Blackwell, 1994), pp.163–4. Its journal, *AJR Information*, was started in 1945.

25. Refugee Council, *Changing Lives: Stories of Exile* (London: Refugee Council, 1997).

26. Miss Clement Brown, quoted by *Bournemouth Daily Echo*, 17 May 1945. Miss Brown was described as a 'very kind woman totally devoted to the refugees' – comment made at a talk by Tony Kushner at B'nai B'rith Leo Baeck Lodge, 3 December 1997 by a member of the audience whose parents were helped by her; 'Change of Name of the Committee', 5 January 1938, German Jewish Aid Committee Executive Committee minutes, Central British Fund archives, 174/263.

27. John Torode, 'Must Britain be Europe's soft touch?', *Daily Mail*, 21 October 1997.

28. The *Evening Standard* coined this phrase. On the persecution of Roma people in the Czech and Slovak Republics see Refugee Council 'News Briefing', October 1997 and *Searchlight*, No.270 (December 1997), especially for the involvement of neo-fascist skinheads in murderous attacks.

29. The *Proceedings of the Huguenot Society of Great Britain and Ireland* were first published in 1887; Robin Gwynne, *Huguenot Heritage: The History and Contribution of Huguenots in Britain* (London: Routledge, 1988); Iren Scouloudi (ed.), *Huguenots in Britain and their French Background, 1550–1800: Contributions to the Historical Conference of the Huguenot Society of London, 24–25 September 1985* (Basingstoke, Hants: Macmillan, 1987). On the second generation of refugees from Nazism, see Marion Berghahn, *Continental Britons: German-Jewish Refugees from Nazi Germany* (Oxford: Berg, 1988), *passim*, esp. chapter 7.

30. *Hampshire Chronicle*, 29 September 1972; Yasmin Alibhai-Brown, *No Place Like Home: An Autobiography* (London: Virago, 1995), p.185 and similar comments on 'Newsnight', BBC 2, 27 November 1997 reporting the thanksgiving service at Westminster Abbey 25 years after the first arrival of Ugandan Asians in Britain; 'Refugee Women: A Chilean Refugee Woman in Britain: A Personal Account by Sylvia Velasquez', *Refugee Participation Newsletter* (4 March 1989).

31. The 'Huguenot Garden' is next to bottom of High Street, Southampton. The full text of its plaque reads:

> This small garden of French species of plants was created in 1985 by Southampton City Council. It commemorates the arrival and *integration* [our emphasis] of French Huguenot Refugees to the City 300 years earlier to escape the persecution which followed the revocation of the Edict of Nantes by Louis XIV. The white mulberry tree was a gift to the City from the Huguenot Society of London.

On the contrasting failure to remember those at Atlantic Park, see Tony Kushner and Ken Lunn, 'Memory, Forgetting and Absence: The Politics of Naming on the English South Coast', *Patterns of Prejudice*, Vol.31, No.2 (1997), pp.31–50; Ethiopian refugee, interviewed by Katharine Knox, London, Summer 1996.

32. 'Return to Chile: International Humanitarian Law in the Contemporary World: 6–9 June 1990', a document submitted to a conference in Berlin, Refugee Council archives, WC/Q46.

33. Government Belgian Refugees Committee, *First Report of the Departmental Committee* (London: HMSO, 1914, Cmd 7750), pp.43–4.

34. 'Return to Chile', Refugee Council archives, WC/Q46.

35. Quoted in Mark Ashford, *Detained Without Trial: A Survey of Immigration Act Detention* (London: Joint Council for the Welfare of Immigrants, 1993), pp.58–61. For the reviewing of detention by the Labour government in 1998, which views it as a necessary if unfortunate practice, see Home Office, *Fairer, Faster and Firmer*.

36. Oral testimony of John Grenville interviewed by Zoe Josephs, Birmingham Jewish History Research Group records.

37. Margot Pottlitzer, 'Civilisation in Exile: The Story of the "Aufbau"', *AJR Information*, Vol.27, No.10 (October 1972).

38. John Grenville, interviewed by Zoe Joseph; oral testimony of Andy Rumi interviewed by Katharine Knox, 28 February 1995.

39. The items were chosen by Clovelly and Shirley Asian Women's Group which provides 'the women with an informal and supportive setting to meet and learn new skills'; Jeanette Winterson, *Sexing the Cherry* (London: Verso, 1989), p.80.

40. Tariq Modood *et al.*, *Ethnic Minorities in Britain: Diversity and Disadvantage* [The Fourth National Survey of Ethnic Minorities] (London: Policy Studies Institute, 1997).

41. Katharine Knox, *Credit to the Nation: A Study of Refugees in the United Kingdom* (London: Refugee Council, 1997); Mayerlene Frow, *Roots of the Future: Ethnic Diversity in the Making of Britain* (London: Commission for Racial Equality, 1996).

42. Euan Ferguson, 'Voyage to Hell', *Observer*, January 1997 reprinted 28 December 1997.

43. *Bournemouth Daily Echo*, 17 May 1945.

44. Refugee Council, *Changing Lives*; Alibhai-Brown, *No Place Like Home*, p.194.

45. Kapp and Mynatt, *British Policy and the Refugees*, p.150; Hugo Gryn, autumn 1996, quoted by Nick Hardwick, Chief Executive of the Refugee Council, AGM, 18 November 1997.

46. *Report on the Work Undertaken by the British Government in the Reception and Care of the Belgian Refugees* (London: HMSO, 1920), p.7.

47. Oral testimony of Peggy Rayburn (née Turner), interviewed by Tony Kushner, 21 May 1997; *Aufbau* editor quoted in Pottlitzer, 'Civilisation in Exile'.

48. There is some cause for cautious optimism in the increased recognition rates of refugee status under the first months of the Labour government as measured by Home Office asylum statistics for October and November 1997 and Home Office, *Fairer, Faster and Firmer*. See note 45 for Hugo Gryn's speech.

Bibliography

PRIMARY: MANUSCRIPT COLLECTIONS

PUBLIC COLLECTIONS

Bodleian Library
Society for the Protection of Science and Learning papers

Central Zionist Archives, Jerusalem
Chovrei Zion papers
World Jewish Congress papers

Hampshire Record Office
Hampshire Education Committee minutes
Hampshire Policy and Resources Committee Minutes

London Jewish Museum
Hilde Gerrard papers

London Metropolitan Archives
Board of Deputies of British Jews records

Manchester Central Reference Library
Pamphlets relating to Belgian refugees
Jenazian papers on Armenians in Manchester
Barash papers

Manchester Jewish Museum
Harris House diary

National Archives, Washington, DC
United States Diplomatic Records, Despatches from US Consuls in Southampton, 1790–1906
Department of State papers, 841.56, 811.111

National Labour Museum, Manchester
Communist Party archive: Fascist leaflet collection

Public Record Office, Kew
AST series: 18
HO series: 45; 144; 213; 214; 215
CAB series: 24; 65; 66; 95; 128
FO series: 371; 1071

HW series: 1; 16
LAB series: 8
N series: 413
PR series: 80

Southampton City Archives
Papers relating to Vietnamese refugees in Southampton
Police records
Southampton Trades Council minutes
Town Clerk's records

Southampton Register Office
Birth and death certificates

University of Liverpool archive
Cunard papers
Eleanor Rathbone papers

University of Manchester archive
Manchester Guardian papers

University of Southampton archive
Ashley papers
Central British Fund archive
Desider Furst papers
Ivor Greenberg papers
Joseph Hertz papers
Jewish Association for the Protection of Women and Children papers
Jewish Board of Guardians papers
Moss sister papers
Mountbatten papers
Cyril Orolowitz papers
James Parkes papers
Solomon Schonfeld papers
Carl Stettauer papers
Union of Jewish Women papers
University of Southampton papers

University of Southampton Cope Collection
Southampton City Council Minutes

University of Sussex
Mass-Observation archive:
Organisation and history files
Topic Collection Antisemitism
Diaries, 1939–1945

PRIVATE COLLECTIONS

Atholl Family Archive
Papers of Duchess Katharine Atholl

Eastleigh Local History Society
Jesus Urbina Santamaria, 'My Life in Exile: May 1937/August 1940', unpublished
    memoir

'Los Ninos', BBC film on Spanish refugees, 1937
Log Book of Marjorie White, 1937
Press cuttings

Anni Engel
Unpublished memoir of her husband, Fritz Engel, 'A Chain of Events' and related papers

Ruth Goodman
Papers relating to her father

Jews' Temporary Shelter
Minutes and correspondence

Joint Council for Refugees from Vietnam
Papers and unpublished reports

Dionis McNair
Diary, papers and letters relating to her mother and grandparents

Ockenden Venture
Papers relating to Vietnamese refugees

Cyril Orolowitz
Correspondence, photographs and school books relating to his mother and family; unpublished family history

Peggy Rayburn
Unpublished memoirs: 'Pigs, Poetry and Politics'; 'Blythe Street' and family correspondence

Refugee Council
Bosnia Project records, QY/QU 59.2
Chilean refugees, WC/QU 46, 56
Hungarian refugees, RH/QU 56, 59 and 61
Kurdish refugees, GTK/QU 44.2523
Polish refugees, RP/QU 56
Vietnamese refugees, EU/QU 40
Zairean refugees, NZ/QU 40

Rothschild archive
Papers of Anthony de Rothschild

Alice Sluckin
Personal papers; letters from her parents; photographs

Southampton Hebrew Congregation
Minutes, papers and correspondence, 1880–1945

Southampton Polish Club
Papers relating to the history of the club and its members

Alec Ward
Unpublished memoir 'My Story'

Winchester Action Group for Asylum Seekers
Papers relating to Kurdish and other asylum seekers
WAGAS Information Bulletin

Perec Zylberberg
Unpublished memoir 'Recollections'

ORAL TESTIMONY

PUBLIC COLLECTIONS

British Library National Sound Archive
'Living Memory of the Jewish Community'
C410/03; 008; 033; 097

Imperial War Museum
'Britain and the Refugee Crisis, 1933–47', tapes 3771, 3941, 4300, 4343 and 4483
Duchess of Atholl recording, 1937

Manchester Jewish Museum
Jack Farber
Sadie Raphael

Southampton City Heritage Oral History Unit
Albert Gibbs
Seafarers Project, interview no. MO 112

PRIVATE COLLECTIONS
Birmingham Jewish History Group
John Grenville, interview with Zoe Joseph

Helen McGiveron
Interviews with refugees from Nazism and Holocaust survivors in the Southampton region

INTERVIEWS CARRIED OUT BY THE AUTHORS
Sir John Alleyne, interview with Katharine Knox, Winchester, Autumn 1994
Haydee A., interview with Katharine Knox, Winchester, 28 February 1995
John Arnold, interview with Katharine Knox, Southampton, 19 December 1994
Krisha B., interview with Katharine Knox, Southampton, 6 February 1995
Isa Brysh, interview with Katharine Knox, Bournemouth, 26 March 1995
Susan Carstairs, telephone interview with Katharine Knox, January 1995
Ester Contreras, interview with Katharine Knox, Southampton, 9 February 1995
Gino Csikasz, interview with Katharine Knox, Portsmouth, 27 March 1995
Larry Day, interview with Tony Kushner, Southampton, 22 November 1995
Detention Advisory Group Member, interview with Katharine Knox, London, April 1996
Margaret Dixon, interview with Katharine Knox, Guildford, spring 1995
Anni Engel, interview with Tony Kushner, Bournemouth, 13 March 1997
Edgar Feuchtwanger, interview with Katharine Knox, Southampton, 11 January 1995
Jane Freeland, interview with Katharine Knox, Southampton, 30 January 1995
Ruth Goodman, interview with Tony Kushner, Winchester, 4 October 1997
Nina Harper, interview with Tony Kushner, Southampton, 15 August 1996
Han Van Hoang, interview with Katharine Knox, Portsmouth, 13 February 1995
Mai Hoang, interview with Katharine Knox, Portsmouth, 16 January 1995
Ving Huynh, interview with Katharine Knox, Portsmouth, 1 February 1995
Lili Jahn, interview with Tony Kushner, Southampton, 10 April 1997
Anver Jeevanjee, interview with Katharine Knox, Southampton, 19 December 1994
Pauline Jones, interview with Katharine Knox, Southampton, 5 March 1995
Danko Joszef, interview with Katharine Knox, Southampton, 23 February 1995
Krystina Livingstone, interview with Tony Kushner, 29 June 1997
Clare Mar-Molinero, interview with Katharine Knox, Southampton, 25 January 1995
Cyril Orolowitz, interview with Tony Kushner, Southampton, 1 June 1994

Stephanie P., interview with Katharine Knox, Eastleigh, 21 March 1995
Claire Peters, interview with Katharine Knox, Winchester, 27 January 1995
Aberlardo P., interview with Katharine Knox, Southampton, 21 February 1995
Urvashi R., interview with Katharine Knox, Southampton, 10 January 1995
Raxa, interview with Katharine Knox, Southampton, 23 January 1995
Peggy Rayburn, interview with Tony Kushner, Southampton, 21 May 1997
Marciniak R., interview with Katharine Knox, Cowplain, 8 January 1995
Andy Rumi, interview with Katharine Knox, Southampton, 28 February 1995
Paul Rushton, interview with Katharine Knox, Gosport, 19 March 1995
Serbian asylum seeker, interview with Katharine Knox, Southampton, 14 February 1995
Alice Sluckin, interview with Tony Kushner, Southampton, 5 November 1995
Mark Stoyle, interview with Tony Kushner, Southampton, 5 December 1996
Slovak Roma families, interview with Katharine Knox, Dover, 14 November 1997
David Soetendorp, interview with Tony Kushner, Bournemouth, 13 March 1997
Zofia Thoroughgood, interview with Katharine Knox, Southampton, 9 March 1995
Zairean asylum seeker, interview with Katharine Knox, London, October 1997
Father Zuziak, interview with Katharine Knox, Southampton, 17 February 1995

PRINTED SOURCES

OFFICIAL
Aliens Act, 1905 (11 August 1905, 5 EDW.7)
Aliens Order 1920 (S.R. & O, No.448).
Alien Protected Areas (Statutory Rules and Orders 1940, No.468, 29 March 1940)
Aliens Restriction Act, 1914 (5 August 1914, 4 & 5 GEO.5)
Aliens Restriction (Amendment) Act, 1919 (23 December 1919, 9 & 10 GEO.5)
Asylum and Immigration (Appeals) Act, 1993
Asylum and Immigration Act, 1996
Census of England and Wales (1901–1991)
Convention and Protocol relating to the status of refugees (1951 Geneva Convention article 1A)
First Report of the Departmental Committee Appointed By the President of the Local Government Board to Consider and Report on Questions Arising in Connection with the Reception and Employment of the Belgian Refugees in this Country (London: HMSO, 1914 Cmd.7750)
Sir Arthur Geddes, *Despatch from H.M. Ambassador at Ellis Island Immigration Station* (London: HMSO, 1923, Cmd.1940)
Hansard (House of Commons and House of Lords Debates, 1900–1997)
Home Office, *Fairer, Faster and Firmer – A Modern Approach to Immigration and Asylum* (London: HMSO, 1998, Cmd.4018)
Home Office, *Interim Report of the Uganda Resettlement Board* (London: HMSO, 1973, Cmd.5296)
Home Office, *Report of the Joint Committee for Refugees from Vietnam* (London: Home Office, 1982)
Home Office, *Ugandan Resettlement Board Final Report* (London: HMSO, 1974 Cmd.5594)
Peter Jones, *Vietnamese Refugees* (London: HMSO, 1982, Home Office Research and Planning Unit Paper 13)
Ministry of Health, *Report on the Work Undertaken by the British Government in the Reception and Care of the Belgian Refugees* (London: HMSO, 1920)
Royal Commission on Alien Immigration, *Report of the Royal Commission on Alien Immigration* (London: HMSO, 1903, Cmd.1741)

Polish Resettlement Act, 1947 (Acts 1947, chapter 19)
United States State Department, *Country Reports on Human Rights Practices for 1996*
    (Washington, DC: US State Department, 1997)

NEWSPAPERS AND JOURNALS
National
AJR Information
Daily Dispatch
Daily Express
Daily Herald
Daily Mail
Daily News
Daily Telegraph
The Economist
The Guardian
The Illustrated London News
The Independent
Independent on Sunday
Jewish Chronicle
Jewish Guardian
John Bull
Manchester Guardian
Morning Post
News of the World
New Society
New Statesman and Society
Observer
Picture Post
The Sun
Sunday Times
The Times
World University Service News
Zionist Review

Local
Aldershot News
Bournemouth Daily News
Eastleigh Weekly News
Hampshire Chronicle
Hampshire Magazine
Hampshire Observer
Hampshire Telegraph and Post
Portsmouth Evening News (later *The News*)
Southampton Advertiser
Southampton Times
Southern Daily Echo
Southern Evening Echo
Winchester Extra

Other
Action
Blackshirt
New Homeland
New Pioneer

Portsmouth Refugee Support Group Newsletter
Kurdistan Report
Thorney Island Newsletter

ANNUAL REPORTS AND YEAR BOOKS
Jewish Year Book, 1900–1997
Jews' Temporary Shelter Annual Reports, 1918–1934
Journal of the '45 Aid Society, 1978–1997
Ockenden Venture Annual Report, 1994
Refugee Council Annual Reports (formerly British Council for Aid to Refugees), 1978–1997
Stevens Directory of Southampton, 1880–1939
Taunton's School Journal, 1938–1950
University of Southampton Annual Reports, 1933–1997
Women's Aid to Former Yugoslavia Reports, 1994–1997

DOCUMENT COLLECTIONS, BOOKS, PAMPHLETS AND ARTICLES
Amnesty International, *Passing the Buck* (London: Amnesty International, 1993)
Idem, *Playing Human Pinball* (London: Amnesty International, 1996)
Idem, *Prisoners Without a Voice* (London: Amnesty International, 1994)
Yitzhak Arad *et al.* (eds), *Documents on the Holocaust* (Jerusalem: Yad Vashem, 1981)
Idem *et al.* (eds), *The Einsatzgruppen Reports* (New York: Holocaust Library, 1989)
Mark Ashford, *Detained Without Trial: A Survey of Immigration Act Detention* (London: Joint Council for the Welfare of Immigrants, 1993)
Earl Baldwin, *The Plight of the Refugees* (Ottowa: Canadian National Committee on Refugees and Victims of Political Persecution, 1939)
Norman Bentwich, *The Refugees from Germany April 1933 to December 1935* (London: Allen & Unwin, 1936)
Ann Browne, 'Latin American Refugees: British Government Policy and Practice', in, *Britain and Latin America: An Annual Review of British Latin American Relations* (London: Latin American Bureau, 1979)
Central Office for Refugees (Domestic Bureau), *Domestic Service: Some Suggestions for Employers and Employees* (London: Bloomsbury House, 1938–39)
Chile Democratico, *Report of a Survey of the Chilean Exile Community in Britain* (London: Committee for the return to Chile, 1989)
Yvonne Cloud and Richard Ellis, *The Basque Children in England: An Account of Their Life at North Stoneham Camp* (London: Gollancz, 1937)
Community Relations Commission, *One Year On: A Report on the Resettlement of Refugees from Uganda in Britain* (London: Community Relations Commission, 1974)
Idem, *Refuge or Home? A Policy Statement on the Resettlement of Refugees* (London: Community Relations Commission, 1976)
H. Arthur Doubleday, *The Victoria History of the Counties of England: Hampshire and the Isle of Wight* (London: Archibald Constable & Co., 1900)
Ilya Ehrenberg and Vasily Grossman (eds), *The Black Book* (New York: Holocaust Library, 1981)
George Fyson, Argiris Malapanis and Jonathan Silberman, *The Truth About Yugoslavia: Why Working People Should Oppose Intervention* (New York: Pathfinder, 1993)
Victor Gollancz, *Let My People Go* (London: Gollancz, 1943)
Lois Graessle and George Gawlinski, *Responding to a Humanitarian Emergency: An Evaluation of the UK's Bosnia Project* (London: Planning Together Associates, 1996)
Roy Gutman, *A Witness to Genocide* (Dorchester, Dorset: Element Books, 1993)
Hampshire Council of Community Service, *Meeting the Needs of the Vietnamese* (Winchester: Hampshire Council of Community Service, 1991)

High Commission for Refugees, *Report of the Fourth Meeting of the Governing Body of the High Commission for Refugees (Jewish and Other) Coming From Germany, July 17th 1935* (London: High Commission for Refugees, 1935)

W. H. Hudson, *Afoot in England* (London: J. M. Dent, 1924 edition)

Idem, *Hampshire Days* (London: J. M. Dent, 1935 edition)

Human Rights Watch World Report (London: Human Rights Watch, 1997)

Derek Humphry and Michael Ward, *Passports and Politics* (Harmondsworth, Middlesex: Penguin, 1974)

International Association for Human Rights in Kurdistan, *Annual Report 1993: On the Situation of Human Rights in Northern Kurdistan and the Kurds in Turkey* (Bremen: International Association for Human Rights in Kurdistan, 1993)

T. T. S. de Jastrebski, 'The Register of Belgian Refugees', *Journal of the Royal Statistical Society*, Vol.79 (March 1916), pp.133–53

Joint Working Group for Refugees from Chile, *Refugees from Chile: Interim Report* (London: Joint Working Group, 1975)

Danièle Joly, *Refugees: Asylum in Europe?* (London: Minority Rights Publications, 1992)

Yvonne Kapp and Margaret Mynatt, *British Policy and the Refugees, 1933–1941* (London: Frank Cass, 1997)

M. J. Landa, *The Alien Problem and its Remedy* (London: P. S. King & Son, 1911)

A. H. Lane, *The Alien Menace: A Statement of the Case* (London: Boswell Printing and Publishing Co., 1932 edition)

Sheri Laizer, *Martyrs, Traitors and Patriots: Kurdistan after the Gulf War* (London: Zed Books, 1996)

Jochen von Lang (ed.), *Eichmann Interrogated: Transcripts from the Archives of the Israeli Police* (New York: Bodley Head, 1983)

Michael Levin, *What Welcome? Reception and Resettlement of Refugees in Britain* (London: Acton Society Trust, 1981)

London Committee of the Deputies of the British Jews, *A Defence of the Alien Immigrant* (London: London Committee of the Deputies of the British Jews, 1904)

Idem, *Objections to the Aliens Bill* (London: London Committee of the Deputies of the British Jews, 1904)

James McDonald, *The German Refugees and the League of Nations* (London: Friends of Europe Publications, 1936)

Peter Mason, *Hampshire: A Sense of Place* (Crediton, Devon: Hampshire Books, 1994)

Mahmood Mamdani, *From Citizen to Refugee: Ugandan Asians Come to Britain* (London: Francis Pinter, 1973)

Medical Foundation for the Care of Victims of Torture, *A Betrayal of Hope and Trust* (London: Medical Foundation, 1994)

Arthur Mee, *The King's England: Hampshire with the Isle of Wight* (London: Hodder & Stoughton, 1939)

George Mikes, *The Hungarian Revolution* (London: Andre Deutsch, 1957)

H. V. Morton, *In Search of England* (London: Methuen and Co., 1933 edition)

Chris Mougne, *Study of Young, Single Vietnamese in Britain* (London: Refugee Action, 1986)

Movement for the Care of Children from Germany, *First Annual Report November 1938–December 1939* (London: Bloomsbury House, 1940)

Mollie Panter-Downes, 'A Quiet Life in Hampshire', *The New Yorker*, 2 March 1946

William Portal, *Some Account of the Settlement of Refugees (L'Eglisse Wallonne) at Southampton* (Winchester: Jacob & Johnson, 1982 edition)

Earl of Portsmouth, *Alternative to Death: the Relationship Between Soil, Family and Community* (London: Faber & Faber, 1943)

Christina Pourgourides, *A Second Exile: Mental Health and Detention* (London: no publisher, 1997)

John Presland [Gladys Bendit], *A Great Adventure: The Story of the Refugee Children's*

Movement (London: Refugee Children's Movement, 1944)

J. B. Priestley, *English Journey* (London: William Heinemann, 1934)

Eleanor Rathbone, *Rescue the Perishing* (London: National Committee for Rescue from Nazi Terror, 1943)

Refugee Action, *Last Refuge: Elderly People from Vietnam in the UK* (London: Refugee Action, 1987)

Refugee Council, *Asylum Statistics 1986–1996* (London: Refugee Council, 1997)

Idem, *Changing Lives: Stories of Exile* (London: Refugee Council, 1997)

Idem, *Kurds: Turkish Kurdish Refugees in the UK/Kurds in Turkey* (London: Refugee Council, 1997)

Idem, *The State of Asylum* (London: Refugee Council, 1996)

Idem, *Welcome to the UK* (London: Refugee Council, 1996)

W. H. Shears, *This England: A Book of the Shires and Counties* (London: The Right Book Club, 1938)

T. W. Shore, *A History of Hampshire including the Isle of Wight* (London: Elliot Stock, 1892)

John Hope Simpson, *Refugees: Preliminary Report of a Survey* (London: Royal Institute of International Affairs, 1938)

Idem, *The Refugee Problem: Report of a Survey* (London: Oxford University Press, 1939)

Society for the Protection of Science and Learning, *Fourth Report, November 1938* (London: SPSL, 1938)

F. E. Stevens, *Hampshire Ways: Forest, Sea and Downland* (London: Heath Granton, 1934)

The Treatment of Armenians in the Ottoman Empire: Documents Presented to Viscount Grey of Fallodon (London: Hodder & Stoughton, 1916)

UNHCR, *Background Paper on Zairean Refugees and Asylum Seekers* (Geneva: UNHCR, 1995)

Idem, *El Refugio: Refugees from Chile* (Geneva: UNHCR, 1975)

Brian Vesey-Fitzgerald, *Hampshire Scene* (London: Methuen & Co., 1940)

Lucien Wolf, *Russo-Jewish Refugees in Eastern Europe* (London: Joint Foreign Committee, 1921)

World Committee for the Victims of German Fascism, *The Brown Book of the Hitler Terror and the Burning of the Reichstag* (London: Gollancz, 1933)

World Jewish Congress (British Section), *A Note on Bermuda – And After* (London: World Jewish Congress, 1943)

David Wyman (ed.), *America and the Holocaust* 13 volumes (New York: Garland, 1989)

AUTOBIOGRAPHIES AND BIOGRAPHIES

Yasmin Alibhai-Brown, *No Place Like Home: An Autobiography* (London: Virago, 1995)

Lady Battersea, *Reminiscences* (London: Macmillan, 1922)

Norman Bentwich, *My 77 Years: An Account of My Life and Times, 1883–1960* (Philadelphia: Jewish Publication Society of America, 1961)

Idem, *Wanderer Between Two Worlds* (London: Kegan, Paul, Trench, Trubner & Co., 1941)

Lucy Cohen, *Lady de Rothschild and Her Daughters 1821–1931* (London: John Murray, 1935)

Idem, *Some Recollections of Claude Goldsmid Montefiore* (London: Faber & Faber, 1940)

R. M. Cooper, *Refugee Scholars: Conversations with Tess Simpson* (Leeds: Moorland Books, 1996)

Lord Croft, *My Life of Strife* (London: Hutchinson, 1948)

Russell Davies and Liz Ottoway, *Vicky* (London: Secker & Warburg, 1987)

Barry Domvile, *From Admiral to Cabin Boy* (London: Boswell Publishing Co., 1947)

Alick Dowling, *Janek: A Story of Survival* (Lydney, Gloucestershire: Ringpress Books,

1989)

Marek Edelman, *The Ghetto Fights* (London: Bookmarks, 1990 edition)

Ruth Dudley Edwards, *Victor Gollancz: A Biography* (London: Gollancz, 1987)

Robert Everett, *Christianity Without Antisemitism: James Parkes and the Jewish-Christian Encounter* (Oxford: Pergamon Press, 1993)

Desider and Lilian Furst, *Home Is Somewhere Else: Autobiography in Two Voices* (New York: State University of New York Press, 1994)

Karen Gershon (ed.), *We Came as Children: A Collective Autobiography of Refugees* (London: Gollancz, 1966)

Robert Hamilton, *W. H. Hudson: The Vision of Earth* (London: J. M. Dent, 1946)

Kitty Hart, *Return to Auschwitz* (London: Sidgwick & Jackson, 1981)

Ronald Hayman, *Secrets: Boyhood in a Jewish Hotel: 1932–1954* (London: Peter Owen, 1985)

Sheila Hetherington, *Katharine Atholl 1874–1960: Against the Tide* (Aberdeen: Aberdeen University Press, 1989)

Samuel Hoare, *Nine Troubled Years* (London: Collins, 1954)

Gerald Jacobs, *Sacred Games* (London: Hamish Hamilton, 1995)

Lothar Kahn, *Insight and Action: The Life and Work of Lion Feuchtwanger* (Rutherford: Farleigh Dickinson Press, 1975)

Edward Kessler (ed.), *An English Jew: The Life and Writings of Claude Montefiore* (London: Vallentine Mitchell, 1989)

Arthur Koestler, *Scum of the Earth* (London: Jonathan Cape, 1941)

Claude Lanzmann, *Shoah: an Oral History of the Holocaust* (New York: Pantheon Books, 1985)

Anita Lasker-Wallfisch, *Inherit the Truth 1939–1945* (London: Giles de la Mere, 1996)

B. Leverton and S. Lowensohn (eds), *I Came Alone: The Stories of the Kindertransports* (Lewes: Book Guild, 1990)

Louis Macniece, *The Strings are False: An Unfinished Autobiography* (London: Faber, 1965)

Ian Mikardo, *Back-bencher* (London: Weidenfeld & Nicolson, 1988)

Ivor Montagu, *The Youngest Son: Autobiographical Chapters* (London: Laurence & Wishart, 1970)

Lily Montagu, *Samuel Montagu: First Baron Swaythling* (London: Truslove & Hanson, 1913)

Katharine Moore, *A Family Life: 1939–45* (London: W. H. Allen, 1989)

Ferenc Nagy, *The Struggle Behind the Iron Curtain* (New York: Macmillan, 1948)

George Paloczi-Horvath, *The Undefeated* (London: Martin Secker & Warburg, 1959)

James Parkes, *Voyage of Discoveries* (London: Gollancz, 1969)

John Pilger, *Distant Voices* (London: Vintage, 1994)

Earl of Portsmouth, *A Knot of Roots: An Autobiography* (London: Geoffrey Bles, London, 1965)

Morley Roberts, *W. H. Hudson: A Portrait* (London: Eveleigh, Nash & Greyson, 1924)

Pam Schweitzer (ed.), *A Place to Stay: Memories of Pensioners from Many Lands* (London: Age Exchange Theatre Company, 1984)

N. Rose (ed.), *Baffy: the Diaries of Blanche Dugdale 1936–1947* (London: Vallentine Mitchell, 1973)

J. E. B. Seely, *Adventure* (London: William Heinemann, 1930)

William Shaun (ed.), *Mollie Panter-Downes: London War Notes 1939–1945* (London: Longman, 1972)

Eugene Spier, *The Protecting Power* (London: Skeffington & Sons, 1951)

Leonard Stein and C. C. Aronsfeld (eds), *Leonard G. Montefiore 1889–1961: In Memorium* (London: Vallentine Mitchell, 1964)

Richard Stern, *Via Cracow and Beirut: A Survivor's Saga* (London: Minerva Press, 1994)

Fred Uhlman, *The Making of an Englishman* (London: Gollancz, 1960)

Hernan Valdes, *Diary of a Chilean Concentration Camp* (London: Gollancz, 1975)

Bill White, Sheila Jemima and Donald Hyslop (eds), *Dream Palaces: Going to the Pictures in Southampton* (Southampton: Southampton City Council, 1996)

NOVELS, POETRY, PLAYS AND FILMS

Maria Eugena Bravo Calderara, *Prayer in the National Stadium* (London: Katabasis, 1992)

Israel Efros (ed.), *Complete Poetic Works of Hayyim Nahman Bialik*, Vol.1 (New York: Histadruth Ivrith of America, 1948)

Michael Gold, *Jews Without Money* (London: Noel Douglas, 1930)

Brendan Murray, 'Strange Cargo', Solent People's Theatre, March–April 1991

Joy Trindles, 'Until Belsen' in Victor Selwyn *et al.* (eds), *The Oasis Selection: More Poems of the Second World War* (London: J. M. Dent, 1989)

Jeanette Winterson, *Sexing the Cherry* (London: Verso, 1989)

FILM, TELEVISION AND RADIO

Maziar Bahari, 'The Voyage of the St Louis' (1996)

'Desperately Seeking Asylum', Network First, Yorkshire Television, February 1995

'Exceptional Leave to Remain', Channel 4, January 1989

'Facing South', TVS, 14 December 1989

'Haven of Refuge', BBC Radio 4, 28 September 1982

'Los Ninos', BBC Film, 1937

'Taking Liberties', BBC 2, 23 January 1990

MISCELLANEOUS

UNPUBLISHED THESES AND PAPERS

J. C. Bird, 'Control of Enemy Alien Civilians in Great Britain 1914–1918' (PhD thesis, University of London, 1981)

Ben Helfgott, Lecture to University of Southampton History Department, 5 March 1996

Louise London, 'British Immigration Control Procedures and Jewish Refugees, 1933–1942' (PhD thesis, University of London, 1992)

David Soetendorp, 'On the Way to the Past' (unpublished typescript)

Andrew Spicer, 'The French-speaking Reformed Community and their Church in Southampton, 1567–1620' (PhD thesis, University of Southampton, 1994)

Nicholas Stanley, '"The Extra Dimension": A Study and Assessment of the Methods Employed by Mass-Observation in its First Period 1937–40' (PhD thesis, Birmingham Polytechnic, 1981)

Paul Weindling, 'A Virulent Strain: Typhus, Bacteriology and Scientific Racism' (Paper given at Social History of Medicine conference, University of Southampton, 18 September 1996)

J. S. Wiggins, 'The Link' (MA thesis, University of St Andrews, 1985)

EXHIBITIONS

Southampton International Airport, Visitors' Gallery

Sam Smith, 'Southampton Water', Southampton City Art Gallery

PERSONAL COMMUNICATIONS

Isa Brysh, letter to Katharine Knox, 6 February 1995

Ruth Freiman, letter to Tony Kushner, 14 February 1997

Gerhart Furstenheim, unpublished account of his life as a refugee, July 1997 and letters to

Tony Kushner, 30 May and 20 August 1997
Ernest Guter, letter to the University of Southampton, 5 July 1988
Betty Irvine, letter to Tony Kushner, September 1995
Norman Kitchen, letter to Katharine Knox, December 1994
Lilian Levy, letter to Tony Kushner, 10 February 1997
Anne Mayer, 'Kristallnacht Memorial', unpublished report, 1980
Diana Molina, unpublished memoir relating to her husband and letter sent to Katharine Knox, 3 January 1995
John Rae, letter to Tony Kushner, 17 March 1986
P. M. Reynolds, letter to Katharine Knox, 5 December 1994
Allen Robinson, letter to Katharine Knox, 1 May 1995
Grete Roesler-Heilbronn, information provided through Ruth Goodman, November 1997
Freda Sibley, letter to Katharine Knox, 3 January 1995
Joyce White, letter to Katharine Knox, 3 February 1995

SELECT LIST OF SECONDARY LITERATURE

General on refugees

Anna Bramwell (ed.), *Refugees in the Age of Total War* (London: Unwin Hyman, 1988)
Steve Cohen, *From the Jews to the Tamils: Britain's Mistreatment of Refugees* (Manchester: South Manchester Law Centre, 1988)
Elizabeth Ferris, *Beyond Borders: Refugees, Migrants and Human Rights in the Post-Cold War Era* (Geneva: World Council of Churches Publications, 1993)
Robin Gwynne, *Huguenot Heritage: The History and Contribution of Huguenots in Britain* (London: Routledge, 1988)
Colin Holmes, *A Tolerant Country? Immigrants, Refugees and Minorities in Britain* (London: Faber & Faber, 1991)
Danièle Joly, *Haven or Hell? Asylum Policies and Refugees in Europe* (Basingstoke, Hants: Macmillan, 1996)
Danièle Joly and Robin Cohen (eds), *Reluctant Hosts: Europe and Its Refugees* (Aldershot: Avebury, 1989)
Journal of Refugee Studies, 1988 onwards
Katharine Knox, *Credit to the Nation: A Study of Refugees in the United Kingdom* (London: Refugee Council, 1997)
Michael Marrus, *The Unwanted: European Refugees in the Twentieth Century* (New York: Oxford University Press, 1985)
Bernard Porter, *The Refugee Question in Mid-Victorian Politics* (Cambridge: Cambridge University Press, 1979)
John Hope Simpson, *The Refugee Problem: Report of a Survey* (London: Oxford University Press, 1939)

Chapter 1

Geoffrey Alderman, *Modern British Jewry* (Oxford: Oxford University Press, 1992)
David Feldman, *Englishmen and Jews: Social Relations and Political Culture 1840–1914* (New Haven: Yale University Press, 1994)
Bernard Gainer, *The Alien Invasion* (London: Heinemann, 1972)
Lloyd Gartner, *The Jewish Immigrant in England: 1870–1914* (London: George Allen & Unwin, 1960)
Colin Holmes, *Anti-Semitism in British Society, 1876–1939* (London: Arnold, 1979)
John Klier and Shlomo Lambroza (eds), *Pogroms: Anti-Jewish Violence in Modern Russian History* (Cambridge: Cambridge University Press, 1992)
Mark Wischintzer, *To Dwell in Safety: The Story of Jewish Migration Since 1800* (Philadelphia: Jewish Publication Society of America, 1948)

Chapter 2
Peter Cahalan, *Belgian Refugee Relief in England During the Great War* (New York: Garland, 1982)
Colin Holmes, *John Bull's Island: Immigration & British Society, 1871–1971* (Basingstoke, Hants: Macmillan, 1988)
Panikos Panayi, *The Enemy in Our Midst: Germans in Britain During the First World War* (Oxford: Berg, 1991)
William Rubinstein, 'Henry Page Croft and the National Party 1917–22', *Journal of Contemporary History*, Vol.9, No.1 (January 1974), pp.129–48

Chapter 3
David Cesarani, 'Anti-Alienism in England After the First World War', *Immigrants & Minorities*, Vol.6, No.1 (March 1987), pp.5–29
Idem (ed.), *The Making of Modern Anglo-Jewry* (Oxford: Blackwell, 1990)
John Higham, *Strangers in the Land: Patterns of American Nativism 1860–1925* (New York: Atheneum, 1978)
Richard Hovannasian (ed.), *The Armenian Genocide in Perspective* (New Brunswick, NJ: Transaction Press, 1986)
Tony Kushner and Ken Lunn, 'Memory, Forgetting and Absence: The Politics of Naming on the English South Coast', *Patterns of Prejudice*, Vol.31, No.2 (1997), pp.31–50
Tony Kushner and Ken Lunn (eds), *Traditions of Intolerance: Historical Perspectives on Fascism and Race Discourse in Britain* (Manchester: Manchester University Press, 1989)
Akaby Nassibian, *Britain and the Armenian Question: 1915–1923* (London: Croom Helm, 1984)
Milton Shain, *The Roots of Antisemitism in South Africa* (Charlottesville: University Press of Virginia, 1994)

Chapter 4
Gregorio Arrien, *Ninos Vascos Evacuados a Gran Bretagna 1937–40* (Bilbao: Association de ninos evacuados el 37, 1991)
Tom Buchanan, 'The Role of the British Labour Movement in the Origins and Work of the Basque Children's Committee, 1937–9', *European History Quarterly*, Vol.18 (April 1988), pp.155–74
Amador Diaz, *Recollections of the Basque Children's Camp at North Stoneham, Eastleigh* (Eastleigh: Eastleigh and District Local History Society, 1987)
Jim Fyrth, *The Signal Was Spain: The Aid Spain Movement in Britain, 1936–39* (London: Lawrence & Wishart, 1986)
Dorothy Legarreta, *The Guernica Generation: Basque Refugee Children of the Spanish Civil War* (Nevada: University Press of Neveda, 1984)
Oliver Marshall, *Ship of Hope: The Basque Children* (London: Ethnic Communities Oral History Project/North Kensington Archive, 1991)

Chapter 5
S. Adler-Rudel, 'The Evian Conference on the Refugee Question', *Leo Baeck Institute Yearbook*, Vol.XIII (1968), pp.235–73
Paul Bartrop (ed.), *False Havens: The British Empire and the Holocaust* (Lanham, MD: University Press of America, 1995)
Steven Beller, *Vienna and the Jews 1867–1938: A Cultural History* (Cambridge: Cambridge University Press, 1989)
Marion Berghahn, *Continental Britons: German-Jewish Refugees from Nazi Germany* (Oxford: Berg, 1988)
Vicki Caron, 'Prelude to Vichy: France and the Jewish Refugees in the Era of Appeasement', *Journal of Contemporary History*, Vol.20 (1985), pp.157–76

David Cesarani and Tony Kushner (eds), *The Internment of Aliens in Twentieth Century Britain* (London: Frank Cass, 1993)

Mary Ford, 'The Arrival of Jewish Refugee Children in England, 1938–1939', *Immigrants & Minorities*, Vol.2, No.2 (July 1983), pp.135–51

Saul Friedlander, *Nazi Germany & The Jews: The Years of Persecution 1933–39* (London: Weidenfeld & Nicolson, 1997)

Peter and Leni Gillman, *'Collar the Lot': How Britain Interned and Expelled Its Wartime Refugees* (London: Quartet Books, 1990)

Richard Griffiths, *Fellow Travellers of the Right: British Enthusiasts for Nazi Germany 1933–39* (Oxford: Oxford University Press, 1983)

Ivo Herzer (ed.), *The Italian Refuge: Rescue of Jews During the Holocaust* (Washington DC: The Catholic University of America, 1989)

Zoe Josephs, *Survivors: Jewish Refugees in Birmingham 1933–1945* (Warley, West Midlands: Meridian Books, 1988)

Norbert Kampe (ed.), *Jewish Immigrants of the Nazi Period in the USA*, Vol.4, Part 2 (Munich: K. G. Saur, 1992)

Tony Kushner, *The Holocaust and the Liberal Imagination: A Cultural and Social History* (Oxford: Blackwell, 1994)

Louise London, 'Jewish Refugees, Anglo-Jewry and British Government Policy, 1930–1940', in David Cesarani (ed.), *The Making of Modern Anglo-Jewry*, pp.163–90

Allan Metz, 'Latin American Immigration Policy and the Jews, 1938–43: The Discrepancy Between Word and Deed', *Immigrants & Minorities*, Vol.11 (July 1992), pp.130–55

Werner Mosse *et al.* (eds), *Second Chance: Two Centuries of German-Speaking Jews in the United Kingdom* (Tubingen: J. C. B. Mohr, 1991)

Andrew Sharf, *The British Press & Jews under Nazi Rule* (London: Oxford University Press, 1964)

A. J. Sherman, *Island Refuge: Britain and Refugees from the Third Reich 1933–1939* (Berkeley: University of California Press, 1973)

Tommie Sjoberg, *The Powers and the Persecuted: The Refugee Problem and the Intergovernmental Committee on Refugees* (Lund: Lund University Press, 1991)

Herbert Strauss, 'Jewish Emigrants from Germany: Nazi Policies and Jewish Responses', *Leo Baeck Institute Yearbook*, Vol.XXV (1980), pp.313–61 and Vol.XXVI (1981), pp.343–409

Barry Turner, ... *And the Policeman Smiled: 10,000 Children Escape from Nazi Europe* (London: Bloomsbury, 1990)

Chapter 6

Alan Adelson and Robert Lapides (eds), *Lodz Ghetto: Inside a Community Under Siege* (New York: Viking, 1989)

Richard Bolchover, *British Jewry and the Holocaust* (Cambridge: Cambridge University Press, 1993)

Randolph Braham, *The Politics of Genocide: The Holocaust in Hungary*, 2 vols (New York: Columbia University Press, 1981)

Richard Breitman and Alan Kraut, *American Refugee Policy and European Jewry, 1933–1945* (Bloomington, IN: Indiana University Press, 1987)

Christopher Browning, *Ordinary Men: Reserve Police Battalion 101 and the Final Solution in Poland* (New York: HarperCollins, 1992)

Idem, *The Path to Genocide: Essays on Launching the Final Solution* (New York: Cambridge University Press, 1992)

David Cesarani (ed.), *Genocide and Rescue in Hungary, 1944* (Oxford: Berg, 1997)

Avigdor Dagan (ed.), *The Jews of Czechoslovakia: Historical Studies and Survey*, Vol.3 (Philadelphia: Jewish Publication Society of America, 1984)

Martin Gilbert, *The Boys: Triumph over Adversity* (London: Weidenfeld & Nicolson, 1996)

Idem, *The Dent Atlas of the Holocaust* (London: Dent, 1993 edition)

Anton Gill, *The Journey Back from Hell: Conversations with Concentration Camp Survivors* (London: Grafton Books, 1988)

Yisrael Gutman, *The Jews of Warsaw 1939–1943: Ghetto, Underground and Revolt* (Brighton: Harvester Press, 1982)

Yisrael Gutman and Michael Berenbaum (eds), *Anatomy of the Auschwitz Death Camp* (Bloomington, IN: Indiana University Press, 1994)

Shmuel Krakowski, *The War of the Doomed: Jewish Armed Resistance in Poland, 1942–1944* (New York: Holmes & Meier, 1984)

Tony Kushner, *The Holocaust and the Liberal Imagination* (Oxford: Blackwell, 1994)

Robert Paxton and Michael Marrus, *Vichy France and the Jews* (New York: Schocken Books, 1983)

Joanne Reilly *et al.* (eds), *Belsen in History and Memory* (London: Frank Cass, 1997)

Bernard Wasserstein, *Britain and the Jews of Europe 1939–1945* (Oxford: Oxford University Press, 1979)

David Wyman (ed.), *The World Reacts to the Holocaust* (Baltimore: Johns Hopkins Press, 1996)

Leni Yahil, *The Holocaust: The Fate of European Jewry, 1932–1945* (New York: Oxford University Press, 1990)

Chapter 7

Diana Kay and Robert Miles, 'Refugees or Migrant Workers? The Case of the European Volunteer Workers in Britain (1946–1951)', *Journal of Refugee Studies*, Vol.1, No 3/4 (1988), pp.214–36

Sheila Patterson, 'The Poles: an Exile Community in Britain', in James Watson (ed.), *Between Two Cultures: Migrants and Minorities in Britain* (Oxford: Basil Blackwell, 1977)

Keith Sword, Norman Davies and Jan Ciechanowski, *The Formation of the Polish Community in Britain, 1939–50* (London: School of Slavonic and East European Studies, University of London, 1989)

J. A. Tannahill, *European Volunteer Workers in Britain* (Manchester: Manchester University Press, 1958)

Jerzy Zubrzycki, *Polish Immigrants in Britain: A Study of Adjustment* (The Hague: Martinus Nijhoff, 1956)

Chapter 8

Ferenc Feher and Agnes Heller, *Hungary Revisited: The Message of a Revolution a Quarter of a Century After* (London: George Allen & Unwin, 1983)

Jorg Hoensch, *A History of Modern Hungary 1867–1986* (London: Longman, 1987)

Bill Lomax, *Hungary* (London: Alison & Busby, 1976)

David Pryce-Jones, *The Hungarian Revolution* (London: Ernest Benn, 1969)

Chapter 9

Bert Adams and Victor Jesudason, 'The Employment of Ugandan Asians in Britain, Canada and India', *Ethnic and Racial Studies*, Vol.7, No.4 (October 1984), pp.462–77

Mike Bristow, 'Britain's Response to the Ugandan Asian Crisis: Government Myths versus Political and Resettlement Realities', *New Community*, Vol.5, No.3 (Autumn 1976), pp.265–79

W. Kuepper, G. Lackey and E. Swinerton, *Ugandan Asians in Britain: Forced Migration and Social Absorption* (London: Croom Helm, 1975)

Vaughan Robinson, *Transients, Settlers and Refugees: Asians in Britain* (Oxford: Clarendon Press, 1986)

Yash Tandon and Arnold Raphael, *The New Position of East Africa's Asians: Problems of a Displaced Minority* (London: Minority Rights Group, 1978)

M.Twaddle (ed.), *Expulsion of a Minority: Essays on Ugandan Asians* (London: Athlone Press, 1975)

Chapter 10
Leslie Bethell (ed.), *Chile Since Independence* (Cambridge: Cambridge University Press, 1993)
Diana Kay, *Chileans in Exile: Private Struggles, Public Lives* (London: Macmillan, 1987)
Michael Sanders, 'Book Burning and Brutality', *Index on Censorship*, Vol.3, No.1 (1974), pp.7–13
World University Service, *A Study in Exile: A Report on the WUS (UK) Chilean Refugee Scholarship Programme* (London: World University Service, 1986)

Chapter 11
Carol Dalglish, 'Occupational Background of the Refugees from Vietnam in Britain', *New Community*, Vol.8, No.3 (Winter 1980), pp.344–6
Felicity Edholm, Helen Roberts and Judith Sayer, *Vietnamese Refugees in Britain* (London: Commission for Racial Equality, 1983)
Samantha Hale, 'The Reception and Resettlement of Vietnamese Refugees in Britain', in Vaughan Robinson (ed.), *The International Refugee Crisis: British and Canadian Responses* (Basingstoke, Hants: Macmillan, 1993), pp.273–92
David Haines, 'Southeast Asian Refugees in Western Europe: American Reflections on British, French and Dutch Experiences', *Migration World*, Vol.19, Part 4 (1991), pp.15–18
Lesleyanne Hawthorne, *Refugee: The Vietnamese Experience* (Melbourne: Oxford University Press, 1982)
The Refugee Council, *Vietnamese Refugee Reception and Resettlement 1979–88* (London: Refugee Council, 1989)
Vaughan Robinson, 'British Policy towards the Settlement Patterns of Ethnic Groups: An Empirical Evaluation of the Vietnamese Programme, 1979–88, in Robinson, *The International Refugee Crisis*, pp.319–53

Chapters 12 to 14
Gerald Chaliand, *The Kurdish Tragedy* (London: Zed Books, 1994)
Norman Cigar, 'The Serbo-Croatian War, 1991: Political and Military Dimensions', *Journal of Strategic Studies*, Vol.16, No.3 (September 1993), pp.297–338
L. Cohen, *Broken Bonds: The Disintegration of Yugoslavia* (Boulder: Westview Books, 1993)
Misha Glenny, *The Fall of Yugoslavia: The Third Balkan War* (Harmondsworth, Middlesex: Penguin Books, 1992)
Danièle Joly, *Haven or Hell? Asylum Policies and Refugees in Europe* (Basingstoke, Hants: Macmillan, 1996)
Winsome J. Leslie, *Zaire: Continuity and Political Change in an Oppressive State* (Boulder, San Franscisco and Oxford: Westview Press, 1993)
David McDowell, *A Modern History of the Kurds* (London: I. B. Tauris, 1995)
Robert Olson, 'The Kurdish Question in the Aftermath of the Gulf War: Geopolitical and Geostrategic Changes in the Middle East', *Third World Quarterly*, Vol.13, No.3 (1992), pp.475–99
Stephan Pavlowitch, *The Improbable Survivor: Yugoslavia and Its Problems, 1918–1988* (London: Hurst, 1988)
Refugee Council, *Asylum Statistics, 1986–1996* (London: Refugee Council, 1997)

Index

liberal state - pluralty individuals

BA0566 Flight London.

multi cultural - no Heathrow

rascism : 10.00 am DM.
nationalism -

assimilation -

inside changes when outside comes in.

ethnicity = americans out of a group A
dif people

how a group constructs itself being dif from another group scadenain American

But can't absorb ethic groups.

colonial setches change - Brit.

USA - slavery.

1930's bits ex-colonies Lit Brit.

identity - what is British?

Milly: 0171 602 7535